Essentials of Consumer Behavior / Concepts and Applications

Essentials of
Consumer Behavior

**Concepts and
Applications**

**Second
Edition**

Carl E. Block
University of Missouri

Kenneth J. Roering
University of Missouri

dp **The Dryden Press**
Hinsdale, Illinois

Copyright © 1979 by The Dryden Press
A Division of Holt, Rinehart and Winston
All rights reserved
Library of Congress Catalog Card Number: 78-56212
ISBN: 0-03-041961-1
Printed in the United States of America
9 039 98765432

To Joyanne, Kim, and Dan
To Betsy, Tess, and Josh

The Dryden Press
Series in Marketing

Blackwell, Engel, and Talarzyk
Contemporary Cases in Consumer Behavior

Block and Roering
Essentials of Consumer Behavior, second edition

Boone and Kurtz
Contemporary Marketing, second edition

Boone and Kurtz
Foundations of Marketing

Churchill
Marketing Research: Methodological Foundations, second edition

Dunn and Barban
Advertising: Its Role in Modern Marketing, fourth edition

Engel, Blackwell, and Kollat
Consumer Behavior, third edition

Engel, Kollat, and Blackwell
Cases in Consumer Behavior

Green
Analyzing Multivariate Data

Green and Rao
**Applied Multidimensional Scaling:
A Comparison of Approaches and Algorithms**

Green and Wind
Multiattribute Decisions in Marketing: A Measurement Approach

Johnson, House, and McDaniel
Readings in Contemporary Marketing, second edition

Kollat, Blackwell, and Robeson
Strategic Marketing

Kotler
Marketing Decision Making: A Model Building Approach

Marquardt, Makens, and Roe
**Retail Management: Satisfaction of Consumer Needs,
second edition**

Nicosia and Wind
**Behavioral Models for Market Analysis:
Foundations for Marketing Action**

Rosenbloom
Marketing Channels: A Management View

Scheuing
New Product Management

Schultz, Zaltman, and Burger
Cases in Marketing Research

Talarzyk
Cases for Analysis in Marketing

Talarzyk
Contemporary Cases in Marketing, second edition

Terpstra
International Marketing, second edition

Young and Mondy
Personal Selling: Function, Theory and Practice

Zaltman and Burger
Marketing Research: Fundamentals and Dynamics

Zaltman, Pinson, and Angelmar
Metatheory and Consumer Research

Preface

The purpose of this book has remained essentially unchanged from that stated in the 1976 edition—to provide the beginning student with a clear, interesting and systematic treatment of what is known about consumer behavior. Consistent with this purpose, we have included the major trends, their theoretical origins, the principles they sustain, and a sufficient (but not exhaustive) review of the literature. Moreover, we have endeavored to demonstrate the practical implications of the subject matter throughout the text. As a result, this book can be used by those who have no opportunity to pursue further formal study of consumer behavior as well as by those who plan to take additional courses in this or a closely related area.

Once again, we have concentrated on the fundamental areas within consumer behavior and have deliberately omitted extensive summaries of empirical studies, theoretical refinements, and methodological issues. We believe that the latter areas are more properly suited to an advanced course. While the systematic evaluation of complex theoretical and methodological issues is necessary for the development of an understanding of consumer behavior, too heavy reliance on such issues is inappropriate for the student preparing for a professional career in the business world. We have attempted to relate the results of scientific research to the real and immediate problems of the marketing decision maker. Moreover, in recognition of the relevance of consumer behavior analysis to nonbusiness organizations, we have given numerous nonbusiness examples throughout the book.

We have again chosen to use the comprehensive model developed by Engel, Blackwell, and Kollat as an integrating framework and have, with their encouragement, creatively modified the rich synthesis of theoretical and empirical research included in the third edition of their *Consumer Behavior*. Our resulting essentials book eliminates some topics and simplifies others, adds new topics, provides numerous real world examples, draws more managerial implications out of the various topics, and brings to life consumer behavior from the perspective of the marketing decision maker and other interested individuals.

The book has been organized into five major sections. Part 1 provides an introduction and orientation to the study of consumer behavior. Particular attention is given to the development of a conceptual basis for its systematic study. This part introduces the Engel, Blackwell, and Kollat model of the consumer decision-making process, which serves as the framework for studying the subject matter presented throughout the remainder of the text. It also includes a discussion of aggregate market characteristics and their relevance to the development of effective marketing strategies.

Part 2 explains and illustrates how the major environmental influences—culture, social class, groups, and family—affect consumer behavior. It presents some of the most important and most interesting (yet often neglected and misunderstood) aspects of the study of consumer behavior.

Part 3 focuses on the internal factors that influence and shape an individual's buying behavior. Some of the variables treated—personality, life-style, learning, evaluative criteria, and attitudes—have direct operational meaning in terms of day-to-day consumer buying patterns. Each of these variables offers insights into the buying process that are fundamentally important. Without such insights, any analysis of consumer behavior would be purely speculative and superficial.

Part 4 deals with how individual consumers, given their social settings and internal state variables, make decisions. It addresses problem recognition, information processing, information search, immediate choice situation, choice and its outcomes, and choice patterns.

Part 5 includes two quite different subjects. It focuses on some of the ways in which limits have been imposed on marketing strategies developed to influence consumers. It also provides a means for taking account of the progress that has been made in the formal study of consumer behavior.

Three aids to furthering the understanding of the material have been provided at the end of each chapter. First is the summary, which highlights the important chapter concepts. Next is the series of ten questions and topics for discussion. None of these questions can be dealt with by simply going back to a page in the chapter and noting the answer. Rather, each is designed to stimulate thinking and discussion about the material. Finally, two cases that offer a unique opportunity to apply the material presented in the chapter in a realistic setting are provided.

This edition of *Essentials of Consumer Behavior* reflects many suggestions provided by the users of the first edition. For example, we have added topics, treated some topics more thoroughly, incorporated a somewhat more analytical focus, included many more illustrations and applications, and developed longer cases.

We gratefully acknowledge our debt to the authors of *Consumer Behavior*—Jim Engel, Roger Blackwell, and Dave Kollat. We are also grateful to the users of the first edition of *Essentials of Consumer Behavior* for their helpful comments and suggestions. We appreciate too the suggestions offered by the reviewers of this edition: Robert L. Anderson, University of South Florida; Fredrick Kraft, Wichita State University; Anthony McGann, University of Georgia; George Prough, University of Akron; Thomas J. Stanley, Georgia State University; Orville C. Walker, Jr., University of Minnesota; Robert B. Woodruff, University of Tennessee; and William K. Zikmund, Oklahoma State University.

The Dryden staff, of course, contributed immeasurably to the final product. We are particularly grateful for the assistance of Jo-Anne Naples and Nedah Abbott.

Finally, we want to give special recognition to our wives and children. Their understanding, patience, and encouragement throughout this project are greatly appreciated.

Carl Block
Kenneth Roering
February 1979

Contents

Part 1 / Introduction to Consumer Behavior   1

**1 Consumer Behavior:
Scope and Contributions to Management Decisions**   2

The Field of Consumer Behavior   6

Problems Common to the Study of Consumer Behavior   8

The Practical Importance of Studying Consumer Behavior   12

Developing a Conceptual Basis for Study   16

The Orderly Study of Human Behavior   18

Economic Perspectives of the Consumer   19

Consumer Analysis in Marketing   22

Case 1. Beetleboards   30

Case 2. Craigman Company   31

2 Consumer Decision Processes   36

Approaches to the Study of Consumer Behavior   38

Integrative-Comprehensive Models of Consumer Behavior   41

Using the Model to Explain Consumer Behavior   58

Case 1. Natural Light Beer   67

Case 2. The Electric Car   70

3 Macro Perspectives of Consumer Behavior   74

Demographics: Aging of the Population   77

Social Patterns: Changes in Women's Roles   81

Major Market Composition: The Young Single Adult   85

Attitudes and Public Opinion: A Longitudinal Study of Public
Opinion and Attitudes toward Advertising   88

Case 1. Cal Design Construction 92

Case 2. Interpreting Consumer Views
and Regulatory Actions toward Advertising 93

Part 2 / Environmental Influences on Consumer Behavior

97

4 Cultural Influences 98

The Nature of Culture 100

Basic Characteristics of Culture 102

Characteristics of Culture in the United States 105

Cross-Cultural Analysis of Consumer Behavior 111

The Nature of Subculture 119

Case 1. Electronic International 132

Case 2. The Ideal Auto 134

5 Social Class and Group Influences 142

Social Class Defined 144

Measurement of Social Class 147

Social Class Distribution in the United States 149

Effect of Social Class on Consumer Behavior 152

Social Groups 154

Types of Social Groups 155

Functions of Groups 156

Reference Groups 161

Case 1. Johnson Stores Incorporated 168

Case 2. The Tennis Shoe Market 170

6 The Family in Consumer Behavior 176

Family Forms 179

Family Influences on Individual Members 181

The Family as a Buying and Consuming Entity 188

Case 1. Vantage Machines, Incorporated 205

Case 2. The Eldercare Corporation 207

Part 3 / Intrapersonal and Interpersonal Determinants of Consumer Behavior 211

7 Personality and Life-styles 212

Personality Theories in Consumer Behavior 213
Personality and Product Choice 222
Implications for Marketing Strategy 223
Marketing Applications of Personality Research 224
Life-style Concept 229
Forces Shaping American Life-styles 232
Application of the Life-style Concept 248
Case 1. Warner Communications, Inc. 257
Case 2. Homestead Bros. 259

8 The Role of Learning 264

The Study of Learning 267
Learning in Consumer Behavior 267
The Learning Process 272
The Components of the Learning Process 276
Further Notions from Learning Theory as Applied to Consumer Behavior 282
Case 1. The United States Department of the Treasury 289
Case 2. Subliminal Systems, Inc. 290

9 Evaluative Criteria 294

Variability in Evaluative Criteria 298
How Evaluative Criteria Are Formed 302
Evaluative Criteria Are Not Always What They "Ought" to Be 309
How Evaluative Criteria Can Be Identified 310
Other Practical Considerations in Focusing on Evaluative Criteria 312
Case 1. A Shift in Eating Habits 316
Case 2. The Medi-Diagno Clinic 318

10 Attitudes — 322

The Meaning of Attitudes — 324
Attitudes toward Alternatives: Expectancy-Value Models — 329
Extending the Expectancy-Value Model — 334
Implication for Marketing Strategy — 337
Attitude Change Strategies — 338
Foundations for Managing Attitude Change — 340
Managing Attitude Change — 345
Case 1. Budson Yogurt — 355
Case 2. Great Midwestern Trade Bank — 357

Part 4 / Consumer Decision Process: Analysis and Applications — 363

11 Problem Recognition — 366

The Nature of Problem-Recognition Processes — 368
Types of Problem-Recognition Processes — 372
Unique Aspects of Problem-Recognition Processes — 374
Marketing Implications of Problem Recognition — 384
Measurement of Problem-Recognition Processes — 385
Using Information on Problem-Recognition Processes: An Illustration — 386
Attempts to Trigger Problem Recognition — 388
Case 1. Albany Incorporated — 391
Case 2. Stoko Company — 394

12 Information Processing — 400

The Foundation of Information Processing — 403
The Dynamics of Information Processing — 404
Exposure — 405
Attention — 406
Reception — 413
Response — 416
Controlling Information Processing — 417

Case 1. Flame & Fume Watchman   426
Case 2. Metro Mobile Home Sales   429

13 Information Search   434
Search Defined   438
Search in the Decision Process   438
Internal Search   442
External Search   446
Case 1. Mutualco Life Insurance   466
Case 2. Midwest Advertising Agency Assembly   468

14 Immediate Choice Situation   472
Store Selection as a Purchasing Process   474
In-Store Purchasing Processes   483
Case 1. Booneville Mailback, Inc.   498
Case 2. Skatesite Parks   499

15 Choice and Its Outcomes   502
The Nature of Consumer Choice   504
The Effect of Unanticipated Circumstances on
Consumer Choice   504
Understanding Unplanned Consumer Choice   508
Nonretail Store Consumer Choice   509
The Outcomes of Consumer Choice   510
Managerial Implications of the Outcomes of
Consumer Choice   520
Case 1. Avon Products, Inc.   525
Case 2. Steady Mark, Incorporated   527

16 Choice Patterns   532
The Meaning of Brand Loyalty   535
Explaining Brand Loyalty   537
Understanding Brand Loyalty   538
Managerial Implications of Brand Loyalty   540
Importance of Understanding the Diffusion of Innovations   541

Elements of the Diffusion Process   545
Diffusion of Innovations and the Adoption Process   547
Identifying Innovativeness   554
Case 1. General Mills, Incorporated   560
Case 2. Imaginetics International, Inc.   563

Part 5 / Consumer Behavior in Perspective   567

17 **Evaluating the Use of**
Consumer Behavior Knowledge   568
Approaches to Regulation   570
Consumer Protection at the Federal Level   571
Consumer Protection at the State Level   578
Evaluating Consumer Protection Laws and Agency Actions   581
Voluntary Self-regulation   584
Personal Conviction and Ethics in the Marketplace   588
An Evaluation of Business Practices   589
Case 1. Darcolor Paints   595
Case 2. Consumers' Need for Information   597

18 **Future Directions of Consumer Behavior**   600
Consumer Behavior as a Field of Study   602
Examples of Emerging Applications   610
Sources of New Insight into Consumer Behavior   621
Case 1. The Changing Nature of Shopping Center
Management   627
Case 2. The New Product Adventure   629

Glossary   633

Index   641

Part 1 Introduction to Consumer Behavior

This section of the text contains three chapters that provide an introduction and orientation to the study of consumer behavior. Chapter 1 is the broadest in scope in that it defines consumer behavior, identifies some of the most bothersome problems in studying the subject, and discusses as well as illustrates the growing importance of such knowledge in management decision making in both the private and public sectors. Chapter 2 introduces the Engel, Blackwell, and Kollat model of the consumer decision-making process, which serves as the framework for studying the subject matter presented throughout the remainder of the text. Chapter 3 gives specific attention to aggregate market characteristics and their relevance to business managers who are responsible for contributing to the development of marketing strategy.

Although this section is meant to be read first, it contains material that will be helpful as a reference as you read further in the text. This kind of review can be useful in keeping the proper perspective toward the subject and in avoiding problems in studying consumer behavior.

Chapter 1

Consumer Behavior: Scope and Contributions to Management Decisions

Outline

The Field of Consumer Behavior
Defining Consumer Behavior
An Applied Discipline with
    Interdisciplinary Roots

**Problems Common to the Study of
    Consumer Behavior**
Myopic View of Behavior
Oversimplification
The Logic Trap

**The Practical Importance of
    Studying Consumer Behavior**
Evaluating New Market
    Opportunities
Public Policy Formation

**Developing a Conceptual Basis
    for Study**

**The Orderly Study of Human
    Behavior**

**Economic Perspectives of the
    Consumer**
A Microeconomic Perspective
A Macroeconomic Perspective

Consumer Analysis in Marketing
Early Attempts to Understand
    Buyer Behavior
Recent Contributions to the Study
    of Consumer Behavior

Summary

**Questions and Issues for
    Discussion**

Cases

Key Terms

consumer behavior
ultimate consumer
purchase decisions
applied discipline
myopic view
representativeness
oversimplification
logic trap
macromarketing
micromarketing
psychological field
market opportunities
marketing concept
public policy
life space
behavioral cues
motivational determinants
model
theory
microeconomic perspective
macroeconomic perspective
conflict models
machine models
open-system models

The topic of consumer behavior has drawn substantial attention in recent years as a field for serious study, and it is fair to say that much has been learned. But because it is a dynamic field, many discoveries are still to be made. As you read this text, you will have the opportunity to become aware of what has been learned and to bring your personal experiences and perceptions to bear upon each subject as you reach new levels of understanding. This chapter serves as a basis for defining the boundaries of the topic of consumer behavior, illustrating its usefulness, and presenting a brief historical overview of its development.

Because marketing professionals have generally been the group most involved in organizing the study of consumer behavior, one might assume that all businesses with marketing programs would be actively pursuing an understanding of the implications of such findings in their markets. However, this is not the case. Even though companies such as General Mills, Ford Motor Company, and Procter and Gamble have been among the most progressive in attempting to gain insight into consumer market behavior, other firms—large as well as small—have been willing to rely solely on intuitive judgment and traditional business practices in dealing with consumers. Some industries have recently recognized the value of actively seeking an understanding of the consumer market. For instance, only within the last several years have many banks and savings and loan associations begun serious study of consumer behavior in relation to their markets. This is certainly consistent with the marketing concept which recognizes that the greatest long-term success comes from well-planned and executed strategies that are responsive to consumer preferences.

The growing sophistication of consumers combined with such factors as changing social mores and increasingly aggressive competition dictate that an ongoing effort at "knowing the consumer" is no longer a casual matter. Even a local independent retailer often cannot adequately characterize its key competitor as the regional chain store down the street. There are an increasing number of instances where new mass merchandising organizations are tapping the potential of previously ignored locales with direct mail, modern catalog stores, and computer-assisted nationwide telephone campaigns where the prospective customer hears only a recorded message and is given the opportunity to respond immediately. Consequently, even many moderate-sized, regional companies are beginning to seek answers to some fundamental questions that arise in serving their customers. Often, the initial questions asked are "Who are our customers?" and "How can they best be described?"

The importance of gaining a fundamental understanding of consumers' interests and a sensitivity to their likely market behavior is illustrated in each of the following three situations.

● Eyeglasses are now being successfully marketed through drugstore chains such as Revco. The results of the aggressive efforts of these outlets and those of the specialty eyeglass chains have provided these retailers with a growing share of the $3-billion-a-year market. One consequence of this success, however, has been that the dominant market position of independent opticians has declined from 86 to 60 percent in just five years. Many claim that the drugstore environment is a "natural" for adding this product and its accompanying service. Nevertheless, any such success requires responsive consumers, and certainly this product has been no exception. When recent court decisions permitted price advertising of eyeglasses, consumers were ready to receive the promotional messages offering lower prices and written guarantees available to them through the new outlets.[1]

● The acceptance of American-made fine china has become a reality through a keen understanding of the "femme fatale," according to John Chamberlain, the president of Lenox, Inc. The "aim was to convey the idea that Lenox is the sign of a hostess with excellent taste." This strategy has been well received by consumers and, therefore, has contributed substantially to Lenox's move from a 10 percent share of the U.S.-made fine china market in 1949 to slightly over 50 percent of the $80 million market in 1978. Such fine names as Wedgwood and Royal Doulton hold about a 40 percent share together.[2]

● *Sales and Marketing Management* magazine gave Vlasic Foods a Grand Award for outstanding marketing achievements in 1977. Vlasic, the leading domestic pickle marketer, expanded its distribution and increased its share of the market despite competition from several companies many times its size. Its success in 1977 primarily resulted from tailoring the elements of its marketing plan to its newest market venture, the West Coast. In 1977 Vlasic's market share grew 25 percent and its sales were over $100 million—ten times greater than they had been just a decade earlier.

In the fall of 1975, Vlasic used consumer taste tests in various shopping malls to determine which products it should offer West

Coast consumers. For instance, the results showed that people on the West Coast generally like a sweeter pickle than persons living elsewhere. West Coast residents also like less garlic in their Kosher dills than do those living on the East Coast.[3]

The Field of Consumer Behavior

History shows that every human community develops some means by which it produces and exchanges goods and services to meet its members' needs. In the most primitive societies, this process is simple and often involves a barter system. However, in industrially advanced areas, such as those of North America, Japan, Australia, and Europe, the production and distribution system is complex, and the available range of goods and services is wide. Consequently, a full understanding of consumption decisions in these geographical areas would require the study of every aspect of a person's entire lifetime of experiences. Also, in the broadest sense, consumer behavior and human behavior would be nearly identical fields of study because the consumption of economic goods pervades almost every activity in which humans are involved. For practical reasons the field must be limited to include only a portion of human activity.

Defining Consumer Behavior

Before more is said about consumer behavior, it is appropriate to define the scope of the subject as it is treated in this text. Therefore, the following definition is included here to set boundaries. Consumer behavior is defined as:

> . . . the acts of individuals directly involved in obtaining and using economic goods and services, including the decision processes that precede and determine these acts.[4]

This definition has three key parts: (1) " . . . the acts of individuals . . ." This includes such activities as travel to and from stores, in-store shopping, actual purchase, transportation, use, and evaluation of both goods and services available in the market. (2)" . . . individuals directly involved in obtaining and using economic goods and services . . ." This statement identifies the focus of this book—the ultimate consumer. That is, it concentrates on individuals purchasing goods and services for personal consumption by themselves and/or for some other similar unit such as their family or a friend. This latter context would include the homemaker acting as the family purchasing agent as well as someone buying a gift for another person. This part of the definition of consumer behavior also notes that the text does not deal specifically with individuals purchasing for business or institutional usage, even though many of the topics are equally relevant to such activities. (3) ". . . including the decision processes that precede and determine these acts." This statement is included to recognize the importance of the purchase activities of consumers that directly affect their observable market action, for example, contact with salespeople, media and advertising exposure, informal explorations with friends, the formation of evaluative criteria, and the overt acts of identifying and considering alternative purchase decisions.

The diagram in Table 1.1 illustrates the aspects of the study of consumer behavior that are included in the definition. The list of

Processes that are likely to precede the purchase	Purchase act	Activities which often follow the purchase
Clarification of wants	Actual purchase	Who uses the product
Media exposure	Number of items bought at one time	Storing and maintaining the product
Examining alternative products	Timing of the purchase	Setting where the product is typically used
Searching for information	Place where the purchase was made	Evaluation of product's performance
Shopping	Price paid	
Talking with others	How purchased: cash/credit	

Table 1.1
The Study of Consumer Behavior

topics under each aspect is simply examples of what may be given attention.

Historically, the most interest has been shown in the purchase act itself because sales were the major measure of success. However, there is growing awareness among managers that, in order to sustain profitable levels of sales, they must have a broader view because both pre- and post-purchase activities directly affect sales.

An Applied Discipline with Interdisciplinary Roots

The systematic study of consumer behavior has been interdisciplinary from the very start. In fact, some of the first marketing scholars to focus attention on the behavioral dimensions of consumer actions were trained in such disciplines as psychology and sociology. One of the major reasons why consumer behavior is such a rich field of study today is that it continues to rely on both the theoretical and empirical work of a number of other disciplines. For instance, social psychology provides insight into individual behavior in social settings. The work of anthropologists, economists, political scientists, statisticians, and philosophers also contributes to the understanding of consumer decision making.

Despite continued borrowing from other fields, consumer behavior has emerged as an applied discipline much like medicine. In the practice of medicine, the physician uses techniques developed through an understanding of the physical and biological sciences. In the study of consumer behavior, the consumer analyst must be ever aware of the empirical and theoretical underpinnings of the behavioral sciences that support this work.

The study of consumer behavior as an applied field presents some difficulties, the most bothersome of which are set forth in the next section.

Problems Common to the Study of Consumer Behavior

Everyone has expectations as to how people will act under various circumstances, and most people even engage in predicting the behavior of those in whom they have an interest. For instance, most of us are good at predicting who will remember us on our birthday with a gift, and we are probably able to forecast the type of gift we will receive. This suggests that each person has a set of propositions or theories of human behavior, whether recognized or not, that have been developed over his or her lifetime and that, in addition, these propositions are called upon quite often in everyday life as practical aids to living.

Of course, these behavioral propositions are not used only for predicting behavior; they also can be used as an aid to the planning of personal actions. For instance, most of us at some time have tried to influence and shape the anticipated behavior of other people. Frequently, this is to make their future actions more consistent with our own desires. It might be possible to get a friend or family member to be supportive of a desire to move out of a dormitory or to buy a new car. These attempts at influencing people can take on any number of forms but often include carefully selected comments or gestures that are made at "choice" times. As a result of this constant awareness of others, many individuals are tempted to conclude that they really know a lot about people, such as their makeup and what can be expected from them. And in some respects this is true—most of us have a great deal of experience with people because by nature we are social beings. However, this is where some of us begin to get into difficulty. What follows is an attempt to identify the most prevalent and bothersome difficulties that face those who are beginning their study of consumer behavior. These are discussed under the topical headings of myopic view, oversimplification, and the logic trap.

Myopic View of Behavior

There is a great temptation to define the world in terms of personal experiences, that is, from a personal perspective. Although many of us possess a keen insight into our close associates, we often have not had the benefit of long-term exposure to the behavior of many people with whom we eventually must deal or who are of major concern to us—we lack real breadth of experience. Consequently, we are not very good at explaining or predicting actions of these unfamiliar individuals.

An example of a myopic view would be the observation that because you personally enjoyed a local nightclub in your hometown, the college community where you go to school would be an ideal location for a similar facility. The implication is that you are a typical student whose interests are shared by a sizable market segment in the college community and, therefore, such a nightclub would be a profitable business venture. This observation may or may not be correct; it is open to study.

The serious study of consumer behavior requires a constant questioning of the *representativeness* of personal experience and observation and a desire to broaden one's understanding of behavioral processes.

Oversimplification

Another problem many people have is that they oversimplify things, particularly the explanations and/or solutions to complex problems. For instance, to many people today, U.S. inflation and world overpopulation have relatively simple solutions. Reliable sources suggest that this is hardly the case. Consumer behavior has not been spared this urge to oversimplify. We have all heard people classify someone as a status-seeker or show-off. Such labels are sometimes used to explain a particular purchase. For instance: "It's just like Mary to buy that kind of a dress; she is always seeking attention." The implication is that Mary's purchasing behavior is easily explained by this one characteristic.

One way of substantiating this observed tendency toward oversimplification in explaining consumer behavior is to ask yourself what led to your making a particular purchase such as a new suit or a piece of stereo equipment. Then, having noted your response, try to write down the actual series of events and steps that you went through in the process leading to the purchase. Also include a description of your behavior following the purchase that was related to the use or to the evaluation of the item. Obviously this is a challenging task—one that most would dismiss as nonsense or not worth the time involved. Nevertheless, as individuals who have an interest in consumer behavior, you must be willing to recognize the likelihood that much of what may influence observable market behavior has too often gone unrecorded and, therefore, has not been analyzed.

Tucker, in *Foundations of a Theory of Consumer Behavior*,[5] made just this observation. He attempted to call attention to the fact that an understanding of consumer behavior must start with a fundamental appreciation of consumer actions on a microlevel. Therefore, in a very real sense, to expect even limited success in coming to understand consumer behavior at this stage, each student must consciously decide to be more observant of his or her own behavioral patterns as well as those of others. This must be done while keeping in mind the previous warning about myopic views. A decision must also be made to be hesitant in making broad generalizations.

Yet, to a large extent, generalizations will make up a substantial part of what is presented in this book; however, these must be made with care and only after close and insightful observation. It is also helpful to recognize that much of what is stated as a behavioral proposition will have to include some explicit qualifications regarding the circumstances to which it applies.

The Logic Trap

Although intuitive reasoning and logic are useful to everyone in making and evaluating conjectures or assumptions about behavior, they are simply not a substitute for empirical investigation as a means of broadening understanding and of validation. It would be like assuming that because some consumers have been known to use price as a guide to the quality of a product, the highest priced brand will gain the largest market share.

Too frequently the behavioral patterns that are expected to occur logically under some well-prepared marketing plan do not materialize. This is probably due less to consumers being illogical in their actions than it is to a lack of comprehensiveness in behavioral theory.

Providing a warning about the most prevalent difficulties that arise in studying consumers does not necessarily prevent the difficulties from occurring, but it is hoped that the warning builds some resistance to their lure.

The Practical Importance of Studying Consumer Behavior

Despite what has been stated earlier in this chapter about the relevance of consumer behavior, it is still fair for you to ask why you should study this subject. Several reasons are worth mentioning.

Strictly from a personal perspective, there may be at least two reasons.

Intellectual curiosity As an individual becomes better educated and more mature, there is a nurturing of inquisitiveness about his or her environment and what is observable in it. The prominence of market activities is so great that thinking people are going to question what they see and experience. For instance, you might be interested in knowing how brand names are selected, why some television commercials are humorous while others attempt to create fear, or how the appeal of a product such as the Crock Pot could grow so rapidly. These are all reasonable questions whose answers are linked to consumer behavior.

Education for improving personal skills We all learn to become consumers. Most of the training is informal and is acquired over an extended period of time. But a deliberate effort to study consumer behavior as a subject can help one better understand the forces at work around him or her, and, therefore, more effectively cope with these market experiences.

From a professional perspective, there are other reasons for studying consumer behavior. One practical reason for the concentrated study of consumer behavior is to better understand *macromarketing* problems—how a society meets the needs of its people as an aggregate. This involves the study of issues related to broadly based problems of resource allocation, which can take any number of forms. Examples include the preparation of an equitable plan for allocation of a scarce resource, such as crude oil, among alternative users or the development of a comprehensive strategy for the distribution of surplus food commodities among the poor. Those who have had the greatest interest in consumer behavior for macromarketing reasons have most often included government officials, urban planners, economists, administrators of social agencies, and others primarily responsible for the social welfare of a nation.

The concern for solving *micromarketing* problems has motivated others to study consumer behavior. Micromarketing focuses on the problems of administering specific units or entities in any economy, for example, a hotel, supermarket, amusement park, or consumer goods manufacturing plant. The day-to-day concerns of the marketing manager or product manager are primarily those of a micromarketing nature. A typical problem is the allocation of the advertising budget among various media alternatives to maximize effective exposure in a target market. Another is the selection of packing materials that provide adequate physical protection for the product and yet are attractive to the consumer.

What follows is the identification of two key thrusts that draw attention to the variety of practical applications of the knowledge of consumer behavior in both a macro and micro setting. The first considers one of the most widely used ways of utilizing the analysis of consumer behavior in marketing planning—the evaluation of new market opportunities. The second focuses on its use in public policy development.

Evaluating New Market Opportunities

An important reason for studying consumer behavior is the evaluation of consumer groups with unsatisfied needs or desires. To be successful, an organization must not only recognize unmet needs but also understand whether there are clusters of such needs that can be profitably served and what organizational response is required for success in selling to these clusters. Firms that organize their resources capably and flexibly toward unmet needs are sometimes described as consumer-oriented or operating under the "marketing concept."

Evaluation of new markets varies in difficulty according to the affluence and sophistication of a country's economy. In the case of an emerging nation, evaluating new markets may be simply a process of determining how much economic power can be generated and how quantities of basic commodities and services—food, housing, medical care, and so on—can be supplied. When most of the citizens do not have enough basic food to eat, it is not difficult to locate new market opportunities. The best market opportunity is simply the provision of more food, probably of the same types already being consumed. Until a society reaches a point at which a significant number of its members are above a subsistence level, the determination of new market opportunities is fairly obvious.

In an affluent, industrialized society, the most attractive new market opportunities do not ordinarily arise by simply providing more of what is already being consumed. New market opportunities arise because of other reasons, and these reasons make prediction of consumer response somewhat more difficult. Two illustrations follow.

New market opportunities arise through geographic mobility. As consumers move from one area to another, they must reestablish patronage patterns. Financial institutions must be selected; groceries, medical supplies, auto repairs, and gasoline must be purchased in a new setting. In many cases, some of their familiar brands will be less convenient to obtain, and others will not even be available. The consumers' needs and desires in this new environment provide opportunities for local businesses as well as for manufacturers of brands of merchandise available in the new community.

The increasing number of women in the labor force has nurtured new market opportunities. The scarcity of time at home for working women has contributed to the growing interest in convenience foods and even in eating out. Commercial banks, savings and loan associations, and insurance companies have begun to recognize the importance of women as a significant market segment. For example, many women now desire to have salary continuation insurance and life insurance tailored to their professional needs. They also want to establish credit and, in some cases, borrow money on their own for various personal and family needs.

Public Policy Formation

Although most of the attention given to the study of consumer behavior has come from managers in the private business sector, there is a growing awareness among public administrators of the importance of understanding and successfully forecasting the behavior of consumers in nonbusiness settings. What follows is an example of such an application in the public sector.

It is a well-known fact that the American consumer plays an important role in balancing our nation's energy demands with available supplies. About one third of the energy used in the United States is divided between what people consume in their homes (20 percent) and cars (15 percent)—and of the latter percentage, 55 percent is consumed in driving around town. A recent nationwide survey conducted by the Federal Energy Administration (FEA) showed that a majority of the public was aware of the seriousness of the energy problem. The following figures demonstrate the extent of this awareness: 45 percent very serious, 39 percent serious, 5 percent no opinion, and 11 percent not at all serious.[6]

In a similar survey, nearly three quarters of the respondents said that personal conservation efforts can have a real effect on the total amount of energy used. Also, the vast majority indicated that they personally were willing to cut down on their gasoline usage by sharing a ride, using public transportation, and walking to places within one-half mile. Despite the high level of awareness of the problem and a reasonably good idea as to how to contribute to its solution, a follow-up study showed that consumers' actions were not consistent with their views. For instance, only 10 percent had become involved in forming car pools to travel to and from work, and 8 percent had begun to rely upon public transportation. Also, the results of focus group sessions conducted for the FEA suggested that Americans have cultural norms that work against reducing their use of energy. People resented being told that they must forgo the success symbols that, according to American mores, are the just rewards for their work. It was also discovered that even though teenagers were angry at the adult population for creating the energy crisis, the teenagers themselves went about "doing their own thing" and essentially had attitudes toward energy use similar to those of adults.

The results of such a study of consumer behavior should offer key insights into how best to formulate public programs and to implement them effectively. But this is just one situation. There are many similar nonbusiness situations where a fundamental knowledge of consumer behavior could have been useful.

What follows will lay the foundation for systematically studying consumer behavior in various settings.

Developing a Conceptual Basis for Study

Although consumer behavior is complex, the identification of a few basic relationships that capture the essence of modern social science theory can serve to introduce the subject. Furthermore, since consumer behavior is a part of all human behavior, any theory of consumer behavior must be consistent with what is basic to human behavior.

Lewin offers a conceptual view that summarizes the essence of contemporary thinking and portrays human behavior as the result of the interaction among components of what is viewed as one's life space.[7] This can be represented as follows:

$$B = f(\text{life space}).$$

Or, stated another way,

$$B = f(P, E).$$

The life space consists of the total "facts" that psychologically exist for an individual at a given moment. The life space is really the totality of the individual's world as he or she perceives it, and in such a context, a thing exists only if it has demonstrable effects upon behavior.

In the latter formula, (B) represents behavior, (f) function, (P) person, and (E) environment. This expression states that an individual's behavior is the result of the interaction between the individual and his or her environment. The behavior that is being referred to is broad and involves all human actions, including buying behavior. The (P) person in the formula is composed of at least two distinct dimensions. One is heredity; that is, to a large extent individuals are genetically determined entities. For example, some physical characteristics that may set very real limits on one's activity are inherited and cannot be altered. However, at birth humans also begin to acquire information and, thus, learning is another major dimension of the (*P*) person in Lewin's model. The (*E*) environment component recognizes the influence of both the near physical and social settings on behavior.

An illustration of the importance of the social setting is evident in the observation often made today that contemporary man appears to be more "other directed." This uses Reisman's terminology to indicate that people rely more on immediate social stimuli as behavioral cues today than they have done historically. But, of course, this does not deny the impact of the other components on a person's life space.

The life space has also been called a person's psychological field. Figure 1.1 expands upon what is summarized in the Lewinian formula and offers another means of conceptualizing what it is that shapes human behavior.

As Figure 1.1 indicates, a person is moved by basic needs that are internal and exist largely apart from his environment. In this sense, man is similar to many animals. However, as a human being he has a considerable capacity to call upon past experiences and observations as well as to anticipate the future. In addition, man as a social being is profoundly influenced by other people and, of course, is affected by the physical environment, as are other forms of life.

By perceiving a person as being subject to compound and sometimes conflicting motivational determinants, it is possible to recognize the complexity of the forces underlying behavior. Each individual must adapt to his unique psychological field, and to him, as men-

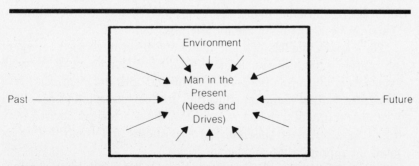

Figure 1.1.
A Person's Psychological Field

Source: James F. Engel, Roger D. Blackwell, and David T. Kollat, *Consumer Behavior*, 2d ed. (New York: Holt, Rinehart and Winston, 1973), p. 21. Copyright © 1973 by Holt, Rinehart and Winston. Reprinted by permission of Holt, Rinehart and Winston.

tioned earlier, this field is reality. He will establish forms of behavior that permit a workable and meaningful pattern of adaptation to his perception of the world. Despite individual uniqueness and the complexity of the forces that affect people, an orderly study of human behavior is possible. The next section discusses the methods used to facilitate the orderly study of behavior and to increase the likelihood of obtaining useful results.

The Orderly Study of Human Behavior

In trying to explain human behavior, social scientists have offered what appears to be an endless number of models of man. *Model* is used here to refer to any simplified representation of some occurrence or phenomenon.

Fundamentally, models aid understanding through simplification. Also, a model can continue to be useful in supplying helpful insights even though it may at times yield some conclusions that are incorrect. For instance, the organization chart of a business firm is an analogue model of a particular entity. As such, it provides a simplified overview of the key divisions and positions and the interrelationships among these units. Ordinarily this will show such things as the formal lines of authority and whether the firm's marketing effort is organized by geographic area or product groups or, possibly, some combination. However, this model of the firm does not typically reflect the true power structure and, in fact, it may lead some observers to draw incorrect conclusions about the firm. Nevertheless, the organization chart can be a useful vehicle for analysis.

The various models of man that have been developed represent alternative hypotheses or theories of human behavior. A *theory* is an explanation of a set of phenomena. This includes the identification of important variables and an indication of their interrelationships. The logical structure of a theory is such that the conclusions derived from it can be interpreted as empirical hypotheses and confirmed or refuted by appropriate testing.

It is not uncommon to hear the comment: "Don't be so theoretical; be practical." Actually, there is nothing more practical than a good theory, that is, a valid theory that focuses on a set of important circumstances. A good theory also builds on the validated hypotheses of previous research and itself becomes a foundation for further investigation. It thereby eliminates the need to expend valuable resources to rediscover what is already known; or, as some might say, it eliminates the need to "reinvent the wheel" each time a new project is undertaken.

What is generally sought by scientists in most areas is a comprehensive or grand theory of the focus of their discipline. This would provide a complete explanation of all the forces under study in the field. For example, a comprehensive theory of sociology would identify all the key variables at work in personal interaction and explain their relationships, including the influence of each upon the others. Such a complete theory would make it possible to be accurate in predicting the outcome of a set of circumstances, knowing the values of the key variables. Although such comprehensiveness is sought, most of what has appeared as theory in the behavioral sciences is more precisely labeled as partial or middle range theory, such as Festinger's cognitive dissonance, Maslow's hierarchy of needs, learning theory, and bargaining theory.

The various models, used as representations of such theories or simply as clusters of hypotheses, have come from numerous sources. What follows in the next two sections of this chapter is a brief summary of how people as consumers have been viewed, first in economic theory and then in marketing.

Economic Perspectives of the Consumer

The role of the consumer differs in microeconomics and macroeconomics; therefore, it is necessary to review each of these areas separately.

A Microeconomic Perspective

The classical economist of the nineteenth century postulated a view of consumer behavior that is still present in contemporary theory, although it has been modified. The basic assumptions are that an individual has complete knowledge of his or her wants as well as all available means of satisfying these wants. In addition, personal preferences are assumed to be independent of the environment at the time in which choice is made as well as unlimited, insatiable, and consistent. The buying decision, then, is simply one of careful allocation of resources to maximize utility or satisfaction. The maximization of utility is thus considered to be the only impetus to buying behavior, and the result is an explicit and elegant theory that lends itself to manipulation using various quantitative techniques.

The classical economist viewed man as behaving in a rational, mechanistic manner with largely the same reactions to a given situation over time. In reality, of course, behavior is seldom predictable to this extent, but little or no attention was devoted to validating the empirical reality of these assumptions. A prime example of this deductive approach is the long-standing assumption that expenditures vary directly with income, increasing as income increases or decreasing as income decreases.

The assumed income-consumption relationship has been challenged by reliable survey evidence, and this is one example of how microeconomic theory has undergone revision to make it more consistent with reality. The Survey Research Center at the University of Michigan has demonstrated that willingness to purchase consumer goods does not invariably bear a direct relation to income; in fact, purchase of durable goods can decline in a period of high and rising incomes. It is recognized that buyers can anticipate the future and that attitudes such as optimism or pessimism concerning one's financial condition in the future can profoundly affect the decision to buy.

The real criticism of the classical economist does not lie in this assumption of rational behavior, because maximization of utility (i.e., value) is a reasonable initial approximation to the fundamental motives underlying buying behavior. The weakness of the classical view for the purposes of systematically studying consumer behavior is its tendency to embrace economics in a moralistic or normative perspective that circumscribes what is so-called "sensible" consumer behavior.

Despite this limitation, it would be an error to include a section on microeconomics without mentioning some of its more positive contributions to the study of consumer behavior. The rigor and exactness of economic theory itself sets a challenging goal for behavioral scientists to strive toward. Furthermore, some of the most comprehensive models of consumer behavior yet developed rely upon concepts used earlier by economists. For example, the study of indifference curve analysis, which incorporates an identification and ranking of consumer wants, is also fundamental to the contemporary models of consumer behavior. In addition, some economists today take a view of the basic components of individual decision making similar to that of the modern consumer analyst, as the following quotation from *Man and Economics* by Mundell illustrates:

> The act of choice is the action of making a decision. A chooser is a decision maker. He confronts aspirations with limitations, preferences with opportunities, intentions with resources.
>
> The act of choice integrates the psychological categories of wants, desires, and preferences with the objective categories of resources, goods, and opportunities. Wants (which are passive) produce desires (which are active), and desires are transformed into preferences; resources produce goods, and goods are transformed into opportunities. Preferences are joined with opportunities in the act of choice.[8]

A Macroeconomic Perspective

Generally, the economist is not directly concerned with the buying choices of individuals, but rather focuses on the choice patterns of large groups over time. Here, the economist's interest may lie in the patterns of behavior pertaining to major decisions such as the allocation of portions of income to savings, that is, the propensity to save versus spend or, in other cases, to the spending on major categories of goods such as consumer durables (e.g., freezers and washing machines). Some economic studies of aggregate demand focus on specific goods like beef, sugar, coffee, automobiles, and housing.

Economists employed in both the public and private sectors have spent considerable time in demand analysis and forecasting. Their theories of aggregate demand are constantly put to the test of empirical relevance and validity, particularly by government. Business firms can use such statistical studies of demand in making sales forecasts. However, one major drawback is that these studies cover industry demand—the demand for automobiles, refrigerators, new houses, and so forth—produced by all of the firms in each of the industries studied. The demand for the products of any one firm depends critically upon its market behavior, which includes such factors as its promotion and general reputation as well as the specific environmental circumstances it faces. Nevertheless, the management of many businesses actively seeks the evidence available from aggregate demand analysis of their own industry. Some businesses even employ their own economists and spend a considerable amount of money in developing econometric models for forecasting demand.

The consumer analyst should not overlook the substantial information base produced from the aggregate demand analysis of economists. Both time-series and cross-sectional economic data-based studies have contributed much to marketing thought by helping to clarify the relationships among purchasing and numerous underlying variables.

Consumer Analysis in Marketing

Marketing thought has undergone dramatic changes because of the post-World War II infusion of behavioral science concepts, and many of the earliest views of buyer behavior have had to yield to new information. As a result, contemporary thought is a blend of the old and the new. But for purposes of clarity, it is helpful to discuss both the traditional viewpoint, because of its historical contributions, and the more recent modifications.

Early Attempts to Understand Buyer Behavior

Consumer behavior as a topic of formal study began to receive attention after World War II. At this time there were two separate and distinct groups interested in it: (1) marketing practitioners and (2) social scientists, for example, sociologists and psychologists. Each group had dissimilar orientations to the subject, used different means of study, and sought results that were consistent with their separate perspectives. Figure 1.2 identifies the variation just described.

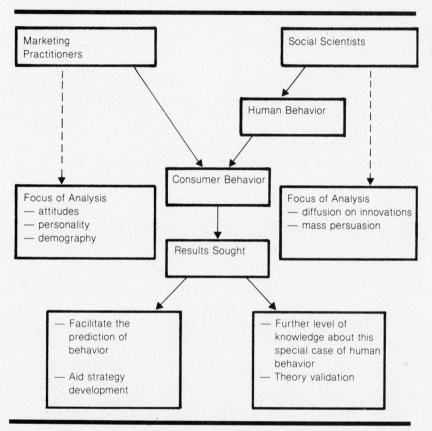

Figure 1.2.
Early Orientations in Studying Consumer Behavior

These early marketing practitioners were essentially pragmatic in their study. They most often focused on variables that had a high degree of face validity in their predictive capacity. For instance, there was generally little disagreement with the proposition that favorable attitudes and selected demographic characteristics influenced buyer behavior. Studies were initiated to demonstrate such relationships and to use these results to predict behavior as well as to aid in strategy development. These studies were not ordinarily tied to any conceptual framework, but were more or less carried on in serial fashion—one after another as a problem arose.

The first social scientists to become interested in consumer behavior after World War II were not motivated by practical needs, but were primarily interested in gaining understanding of this special case of human behavior. Their work was grounded in greater scientific rigor than was the work of marketing practitioners, and they also approached the topic with a number of models that facilitated the identifying of key variables and that postulated fundamental relationships that could be tested—the results of which became the basis for further study.

Recent Contributions to the Study of Consumer Behavior

Only within the last twelve years has real progress been evident in developing integrative-comprehensive theory in consumer behavior. The works of Engel, Kollat, and Blackwell; Howard and Sheth; and Nicosia exemplify this effort. These represent specific attempts at identifying all the significant variables that shape consumer action and the interrelationships among these factors. These works are truly unique accomplishments and have made several noteworthy contributions.[9]

1. They have brought to light the limitations of the attempt to transplant various behavioral theories developed in other disciplines such as psychology and sociology without appropriate modification.

2. Through persistent efforts to formulate comprehensive theories, consumer analysts have gained much self-confidence. Although considerable work remains, there is a feeling of having made some progress.

3. This developmental process in an applied discipline such as consumer behavior has also fostered a demand for comprehensive theory that is grounded in reality—based upon realistic assumptions and verifiable propositions.

Even today, much remains borrowed from other behavioral sciences. Therefore, as a prelude to discussing comprehensive theory development in consumer behavior, it is helpful to briefly trace the developmental process that has been taking place in the study of human behavior. It shows that the accomplishments of the last twelve years in the discipline of consumer behavior were not revolutionary occurrences but evolutionary steps in the study of human behavior.

The evolutionary process has been summarized well by Thompson and Van Houten.[10] They describe three classifications, or models, of man which are representative of the theoretical development that has taken place in the study of human behavior. Their model groupings include: (1) conflict models of man, probably the oldest, (2) machine models of man, and (3) open-system models of man that include the emerging comprehensive theories referred to earlier. Each of these will be discussed briefly in the remainder of this section.

Conflict models of man in their simplest and most primitive form describe human behavior as the result of the struggle between good and evil. The individual is shown basically as a medium through which these forces emerge. Consequently, man is viewed as essentially an innocent bystander who is not responsible for his actions.

The most recent conflict models continue to focus on the struggle between opposing forces that are, however, not necessarily good and evil. For substantiation, Freud's work can be cited. The lines of conflict are laid early in life in what he called the three basic components of personality: the id, the ego, and the superego. The id is the genetically implanted component containing basic cravings or instincts—all that exists at birth. The ego and superego gradually develop and help the individual satisfy these id urges while relating to his environment; hence, the basis for the conflict or struggle.

Conflict models have come principally from clinical psychology. Some of their most prominent authors include Horney, Jung, and Menninger. To a large extent, the theories underlying these models have not met the test of rigorous empirical testing and validation. Nevertheless, they have made a contribution in the developmental process of studying human behavior. A number of direct references have been made to these works in consumer behavior studies. For instance, Lasswell's concept of the "triple appeal" approach to political propaganda formulation relies on Freudian psychoanalytic theory, and Myers and Reynolds suggest that it is applicable to advertising.[11] Lasswell contended that, to be effective, a message should arouse impulses toward such basic drives as hunger or sex, for example, while appeasing the superego by suggesting that the id impulses are justified in some way. Also, the ego should be reached by emphasizing the logic of the proposed action. Cohen's development of the CAD scaling technique for the measurement of personal orientation and behavioral tendencies relies heavily on the work of Horney.[12] Cohen uses Horney's tripartite interpersonal model to help explain a person's perception of his social environment and his action tendencies toward the objects in his life space. The CAD instrument includes three sets of scales, thereby providing a means of measuring a person's compliance, aggressiveness, and detachment. Its use enables the analysts to place individuals into three groups that reflect their most predominant response to others: (1) those who generally move toward other people are considered compliant; (2) those who ordinarily move against others are classified as aggressive; and (3) those who typically move away from people are characterized as detached.[13]

Machine models of man focus upon the S-R (stimulus-response) sequence, meaning that man is essentially Pavlovian. In their most basic forms, these models view a person simply as a physiological machine that responds to genetically implanted drives and environmental stimulation. However, the most complex machine models also recognize the importance of acquired drives. These are drives (needs) which do not exist at birth but are learned throughout life.

In the most simplistic versions of machine models, human beings have drives for biological nourishment and physical safety in relating to their environment—self-preservation in the most basic sense. However, in the more complex models, it is recognized that people acquire the need for social acceptance, self-confidence, and self-fulfillment. The basic logic of this grouping of models is that responses to stimuli are elicited by the expectation of a reward such as satisfaction or pleasure. When the reward is received, the behavior is said to be reinforced and is more likely to reoccur under similar need states and environmental circumstances than unreinforced experiences.

The machine models have ordinarily been associated with the behavioral school of psychology, which includes the works of such well-known figures as Pavlov, Hull, Spence, and Skinner.

Although many modern theories of human behavior, particularly those in the consumer behavior area, have borrowed extensively from the S-R theoretical framework, a person is much more than what machine models represent. This awareness has led in another theoretical direction that goes considerably beyond the scope of what the machine models basically represent. This development is what Thompson and Van Houten call open-system models of man.

The open-system model is an emerging conceptual category of models and, therefore, is not yet highly refined in terms of its boundaries. There are, however, identifiable features that help describe its nature. The most salient feature is that it takes a transactional view of human behavior, meaning that man is no longer considered largely a passive participant in his life space, reacting to stimuli. He is viewed as pro-active. People can and do take initiative.

A second feature of open-system man is that his behavior is purposive. Such a person is capable of having goals or aspirations and of consciously working toward them. Purposive behavior of this type requires such cognitive processes as thinking, planning, and decision making. It also recognizes that deferred gratification is a part of an individual's problem-solving capabilities.

A third feature of this perspective of man is concern for his mental content and how it is acquired. It is assumed that mental content is only understandable in terms of its meaning for the person, and for something to have meaning, it must be perceived and interpreted. Considerable attention has been given to selective perception in consumer behavior, a concept directly related to this dimension of one's being.

Another major emphasis of the open-system model is that man is social. Human activities are often carried out with other people or at least with others in mind. This includes transactional-oriented involvement as well as the use of reference groups. Thus, Thompson and Van Houten characterize open-system man as:

> . . . purposive, as interdependent with the physical and social environment, and as actively involved in transaction with that environment as he pursues his goals. This requires not only that man develop mental processing capabilities—for thinking, deciding, and so on—but also that he acquire information and beliefs which allow him to "know" the persons and things in his environment and to cope with them.[14]

Contributions to this emerging view of human behavior have come from a number of disciplines and individuals too numerous to mention. Certainly consumer behavior theorists have had an input. The work of Lewin, as reflected in his field theory referred to earlier in this chapter, has had a significant impact. Also, a major impetus to this perspective has come from the work done in Gestalt psychology and social psychology.

Chapter 2 presents and discusses the Engel, Blackwell, and Kollat model. Chapter 3 gives specific attention to the usefulness of studying major aggregate trends in consumer behavior.

Summary

Changes in the economic, social, and political environments in this country strongly suggest the need for a broader commitment by businesses to the study of consumer behavior than ever before. Because the focus of this book is upon the market behavior of the ultimate consumer, acts involving the purchasing of goods and services for personal consumption are emphasized. These acts include the processes preceding and following the purchase as well as the purchase act itself.

Three precautions are noted in the application of the concepts of consumer behavior: (1) personal experience may not be representative of the market behavior of larger population segments; (2) oversimplification may lead to surface generalizations and misrepresent what might be revealed after more thorough investigations; and (3) logical reasoning on the personal level may not be universally applicable.

Whether consumer behavior is studied for personal or professional reasons, two key areas of application of this knowledge are identified. One is in the evaluation and planning for new market opportunities and the other is in the development and implementation of public policy.

Whichever the setting, the systematic study of consumer behavior begins with the basic tenets of human behavior, that is, $B = f(P,E)$. The equation portrays an individual's behavior as an effect of the interaction between a person and his or her environment. Although these motivational determinants of behavior are complex, much can be learned about human behavior and, likewise, consumer behavior through an orderly study of important variables at work in any inter-action process.

Several disciplines have contributed to the building of models, or simplified representations, of the theories dealing with how people behave as consumers. From the study of economics, two viewpoints of the role of the consumer can be identified as the micro- and macro-perspectives. Both approaches offer useful information, and the consumer behaviorist can benefit by incorporating these theories into more comprehensive interaction models.

Both marketing practitioners and social scientists contributed to the early study of consumer behavior. Early marketing practitioners focused on variables such as attitudes and demographic characteristics which they felt facilitated the prediction of behavior and aided in strategy development. Social scientists sought to further the conceptual bases of human behavior as it related to marketing operations, but they focused on such subjects as mass persuasion. The more recent study of consumer behavior has benefited from the groundwork laid by these early investigators.

Recent contributions to consumer behavior have developed through an evolutionary process that Thompson and Van Houten have categorized into three groups: (1) conflict models of man, (2) machine models of man, and (3) open-system models of man. Conflict models of man describe human behavior as the result of the struggle between good and evil in which man is viewed as essentially an innocent bystander who is not responsible for his actions. Machine models of man focus on the stimulus and response or Pavlovian-type sequence. The most salient feature of open-system models is that they take a transactional view of human behavior in which man is viewed as pro-active. Three major open-system models are the integrative-comprehensive models of Nicosia; Howard and Sheth; and Engel, Blackwell and Kollat.

Questions and Issues for Discussion

1. Most successful small business owners have never taken a course in consumer behavior nor formally studied the subject. How can this be true?

2. Public agencies such as HEW and DOT should never spend part of their budgets on consumer analysis. Discuss.

3. Providing for consumers' best interests cannot be accomplished by a firm attempting to realize maximum profit. Discuss.

4. Most government services are basically free, that is, they are not obtained by direct payment by the user. Therefore, consumer purchase patterns of such services cannot be studied in a meaningful manner. Discuss.

5. Most consumers can be classified into one of several categories identified by descriptive labels, such as conservative or aggressive, making possible easy prediction of their market behavior. Discuss.

6. How much does the life space of most individuals change over time? Which component, P or E, changes more?

7. The classical economist viewed man as behaving in a rational, mechanistic manner. Are there individuals whom you know who appear to fit this model? If so, is this behavior pattern evident in most of these persons' actions or just in the buying of certain kinds of products?

8. Identify one or two of your personal propositions or theories about consumer behavior, such as how price affects a product's image. What are these propositions based upon?

9. What does it mean to say that a theory is grounded in reality? Why should this be important in the field of consumer behavior?

10. Open-system man has been characterized as purposive. Give an example of purposive action in consumer behavior. Does this characteristic of human behavior simplify or complicate the study of the consumer?

11. The systematic study and analysis of the consumer will likely lead to insights that will permit business to use its resources to control consumer buying behavior. Discuss.

Case 1. Beetleboards

In 1972, Charles E. Bird first used VW Beetles as a medium for advertising. It was initiated on a few college campuses with a handful of

Source: Background information for Case 1 is from "Beetleboards Keep Growing; Enters Caribbean with Foreign Moves Ahead," *Marketing News* April 7, 1978, p. 6.

cars, but it has grown to the involvement of 5200 VWs in the United States today, with plans to expand to 8850 domestically. Large ads for various sponsors are painted on the cars in creative styles. A lot of major advertisers have already experimented with this medium; among them are Bristol-Myers, Eastern Airlines, Kellogg, Levi Strauss, Lorillard, Time, and Sony. Their seriousness is shown by the fact that Brown and Williamson are planning to spend $35 million on Beetleboards during the next five years.

Under the present arrangement, an advertiser pays $175 per month per car, although volume discounts can reduce the cost to about $100. These ads are not casually placed; the demographics and life-styles of a car's driver are matched with the advertised product strategy needs. For example, persons driving VWs advertising White Stag must belong to ski clubs and spend some time driving around skiing areas. Furthermore, the "ad car" must average 42 miles per day.

Several research studies have been undertaken to evaluate this medium. For instance, one reportedly found that R. J. Reynolds generated eleven times as many gross rating points using Beetleboards as they did in thirty sheet outdoor posters.

Assume that you are a research analyst for a sizable advertising agency that represents a variety of clients with a diversified group of products. You have been asked by your research manager to prepare a list of products that could be effectively presented in their target markets by using Beetleboards in the media mixes, that is, as one of a few key means of favorably presenting the products.

Case 1 Questions

1. How would you go about preparing such a list of products? What questions would you need to answer?

2. List a number of products that you believe could be promoted through this medium. Give the rationale for your suggestions.

Case 2. Craigman Company

The energy crisis, more leisure time, concern over health, and "getting back to nature" all have had some effect on the bicycle boom. Of the eight bicycle manufacturers in the United States, none were ready for the increased demand for three-, five-, and ten-speed bicycles by adults in the early 1970s. Each company had a product mix designed primarily for children. Then, in 1973, over half of the bicycle sales in the U.S. were attributed to adults. American manufacturers were unable to meet demand, and imports accounted for one third of total domestic sales.

Sales for bicycles have remained high but producers wonder if this will continue. Craigman, an old established American bicycle manufacturer, is concerned about the future. The company has always produced top quality bicycles and only under the Craigman brand. Because it maintained its high quality standards, Craigman was unable to expand production rapidly during the initial bicycle boom of the seventies.

Another factor that has recently arisen is that some attention is being given to the dangers of various summer sports, including bicycling. For instance, one medical expert said in an interview that a number of cyclists are having knee problems that are directly related to the distances they travel; others should not be bicycling at all.

The impact of these kinds of observations and the competition from alternative activities such as jogging, tennis, and swimming are of growing concern to management. However, future plans must be made. If Craigman were to increase plant capacity, train new workers, and then find a dwindling market for bicycles, the company would suffer financial loss. Craigman could reduce some of its bicycle lines for children and expand adult-designed production, but this would run the risk of another company's capturing the market for new children's models—a field in which Craigman now has a competitive advantage.

Little research has been done on adult bicycle buying trends. A child's bicycle is given a life expectancy of five to eight years. It is unknown how often adults can be expected to replace their bicycles, if at all.

Imported bicycles are viewed in many cases as superior to American-made bicycles. One reason is that when U.S. manufacturers stepped up production in the early seventies to meet demand, quality workmanship was sacrificed. Craigman expects there will be a need for increased advertising if the company steps up production. This is based on the belief that the adult consumer will have to be sold on the idea that the Craigman bicycle is of superior quality and workmanship. Furthermore, the company wants to convey the message that American-made bicycles can be more easily serviced.

Case 2 Questions

1. What are the four or five kinds of information that Craigman will need to have about consumer behavior that could be of major assistance to the management in making their future plans?

2. Rank these from most important to least important and give your rationale for the positioning of them.

Notes

1. "Drugstores See a Boon in Eyeglasses," *Business Week,* No. 2521 (February 13, 1978), p. 116.

2. "Rings on Her Finger, China on Her Table," *Forbes,* Vol. 121, No. 4 (February 20, 1978), p. 76.

3. "Vlasic Foods: Sales Keep Barreling Along," *Sales and Marketing Management,* Vol. 120, No. 1 (January 1978), p. 16.

4. J. F. Engel, R. D. Blackwell, and D. T. Kollat, *Consumer Behavior,* 3rd ed. (Hinsdale, Ill.: Dryden Press, 1978), p. 3.

5. W. T. Tucker, *Foundations for a Theory of Consumer Behavior* (New York: Holt, Rinehart and Winston, Inc., 1967).

6. J. S. Milstein, "Attitudes, Knowledge and Behavior of American Consumers Regarding Energy Conservation with Some Implications for Governmental Action," *Advances in Consumer Research,* ed. by W. D. Perreault, Jr. (Atlanta, Ga.: Proceedings of the Seventh Annual Conference of the Association for Consumer Research, 1976), p. 316.

7. H. H. Kassarjian, "Field Theory in Consumer Behavior," in *Consumer Behavior: Theoretical Sources,* ed. by S. Ward and T. S. Robertson (Englewood Cliffs, N.J.: Prentice-Hall, Inc., 1973), pp. 124–30.

8. R. A. Mundell, *Man and Economics* (New York: McGraw-Hill, 1968), p. 8.

9. J. N. Sheth, *Models of Buyer Behavior: Conceptual, Quantitative, and Empirical* (New York: Harper & Row, Publishers, 1974), pp. 394-95.

10. J. D. Thompson and D. R. Van Houten, *The Behavioral Sciences: An Interpretation* (Reading, Mass.: Addison-Wesley Publishing Company, 1970), pp. 4-13.

11. J. H. Myers and W. H. Reynolds, *Consumer Behavior and Marketing Management* (New York: Houghton Mifflin Company, 1967), pp. 91-93.

12. J. B. Cohen, "An Interpersonal Orientation to the Study of Consumer Behavior," *Journal of Marketing Research* 4 (August 1967), pp. 270-78.

13. J. B. Hernan, "The CAD Instrument in Behavioral Diagnosis," *Proceedings* 2nd Annual Conference, ed. by D. A. Gardner (College Park, Md.: Association for Consumer Research, 1971), pp. 307-11.

14. Thompson and Van Houten, *Behavioral Sciences,* p. 13.

Chapter 2   Consumer Decision Processes

Outline

**Approaches to the Study of
  Consumer Behavior**
Distributive Approach
Decision-Process Approach

**Integrative-Comprehensive Models
  of Consumer Behavior**
Howard-Sheth Model
Engel, Blackwell, and Kollat's
  Consumer Decision Process
  Model

**Using the Model to Explain
  Consumer Behavior**
Purchase of the Volkswagen
  Dasher

Summary

**Questions and Issues for
  Discussion**

Cases

Key Terms

decision-process approach
problem recognition
alternative evaluation
search
choice
outcomes
motives
external stimuli
information processing
active memory
attention
reception
evaluative criteria
beliefs
attitudes
intentions

The preceding chapter drew attention to the importance of theory development in studying consumer behavior and to how this orderly study may be pursued. Special emphasis was given to the contributions made by other disciplines. This chapter provides an overview of the consumer decision process and, in so doing, lays the conceptual foundation for the remainder of the book. First, a discussion of the decision-process approach and the implications it has for the study of consumer behavior is presented. This is followed by a description of the comprehensive decision model developed by Engel, Blackwell, and Kollat, which serves an integrative and organizational function for the remainder of the book. Since most of the following chapters focus on a limited portion of the model, it will be helpful to refer to this chapter from time to time to retain the focus of the overall structure.

Approaches to the Study of Consumer Behavior

Prior to discussing the integrative-comprehensive models of consumer behavior, it is necessary to consider the evaluative processes of the behavioral sciences, focusing on the distributive approach and the decision-process approach.[1]

Distributive Approach

Empirical research on consumer behavior historically has utilized the distributive approach.[2] Consequently, consumer behavior has been conceptualized and studied as an act rather than as a process or series of interrelated acts. Researchers utilizing this approach attempt to determine the relationship between the outcome of consumer decision making and a variety of independent variables such as income, social class, race, and marital status.

Advantages of the Distributive Approach

The distributive approach has been frequently used because it has many advantages. The major advantage is that research utilizing this strategy is relatively simple and typically less expensive than other alternatives. Furthermore, it has been very useful in those instances where the independent variables under study are highly correlated with the purchase of a product. The distributive approach has proven to be somewhat useful in estimating market potential and in making media selection decisions.[3] For example, if the purchase of a particular make of automobile, such as a Porsche, is found to be related to a certain age group, then the number of people who are in that age group might be an excellent estimate of the potential buying units for Porsches. Also, to the extent that people in this age group have distinctive media viewing, listening, and reading habits, the advertising strategy for Porsche may be made more successful by selecting media consistent with these viewing patterns. Clearly, the distributive approach to studying consumer behavior can be very appropriate in certain situations.

Limitations of the Distributive Approach

There are also a number of limitations inherent in the distributive approach. The foremost difficulty is that this approach can, at best, provide only a partial or incomplete explanation of consumer behavior. Consumer analysts now agree that the act of buying a particular product is only a fraction of the relevant consumption behavior; that is, it is important to recognize that the decision to purchase a specific product is preceded by some pattern of conscious and subconscious actions that are a part of decision making. Unless purchase acts (outcomes) are related to these broader processes—and they seldom are—both the decision and the correlates of the decision may be misleading in the sense that they may be true only if certain mixtures of pre-decision processes take place. Furthermore, the distributive approach does not provide the marketing manager with any insight into why the relationship between an independent variable and purchase decisions exists. Because this approach fails to provide information on the sequence of events culminating in a purchase act, it is of limited value in developing effective marketing strategies or in evaluating existing business practices in terms of their relationship to consumer needs. Clearly then, if analysts are to understand, explain, and predict consumer behavior, an approach is needed that is more probing than the distributive approach.

Decision-Process Approach

The decision-process approach to the study of consumer behavior focuses on the means by which consuming units reach a purchase decision. The configuration of this decision process consists of five processes linked in a sequence: (1) problem recognition, (2) alternative evaluation-internal search, (3) alternative evaluation-external search,

(4) purchase, and (5) outcomes. This conceptualization describes the behavioral processes that are operative from the time the consumer recognizes that some decision is necessary to the point at which there is some post-purchase evaluation of the particular purchase.

Reflect for a few moments on a recent purchase that you have made. Perhaps you have bought ski equipment, stereo components, a cassette recorder, a pair of slacks, or an automobile. When did you recognize the existence of a desire for this item? Did you evaluate several alternative brands or models prior to your decision? Were you satisfied with your final choice? In your recall of the purchase, you probably identified some exceptions to the five-stage decision process. First, you may not have been aware that you were passing through these phases. Indeed, most consumers do not consciously state, "I have a problem or a personal desire" or "Now that I have recognized a desire, I had best evaluate the alternatives for satisfying it." Second, you may have omitted one or more of the five decision processes. Finally, you may have observed that your decision process had a time dimension; that is, the decision to purchase may have evolved over several months or, in some instances, the entire process may have involved only a few seconds. It is not that the exact replication of the five processes within a specific time frame is strictly followed but that a similarity in decision patterns does exist among consumers. The decision-process approach to studying consumer behavior has several distinct advantages as well as limitations.

Advantages of the Decision-Process Approach

The decision-process approach has some distinct advantages over the distributive approach. The decision-process approach, as the name implies, views consumer behavior as a *process* and is as concerned with how a decision is reached as it is with the decision itself. Furthermore, the decision approach involves a sequence of processes, including the steps that generally precede the decision, the decision itself, and the course of action that follows the decision. This approach is a more extended and elaborate means of studying consumer behavior than is the distributive approach; therefore, it can ordinarily provide the marketing manager with more relevant information. The identification of the various stages of consumer decision making and the factors that influence the individual at each stage can contribute to the development of more effective marketing strategies and appropriate public policy for the regulation of business practices.)

Limitations of the Decision-Process Approach

There are a number of limitations associated with this approach to studying consumer behavior. In particular, the fact that the decision-process approach is a relatively recent development means that less empirical research has been conducted using this perspective than researchers would like. Furthermore, the research that has been done from the decision-process approach has revealed a considerable amount of variation among consumers in their decision-making behavior. These variations are thought to result from the complexity of interactions arising from the fact that consumers live under many different circumstances. Another difficulty is that very little research has included more than one phase of the decision process, and, therefore, little is known about the relationship among phases or the influence of one phase on another. For example, there are uncertainties as to exactly how internal search leads to external search or what amount of external search typically precedes the purchase decision. Nevertheless, all the stages in the decision process should be included even though some of them do not always occur and the relationships among those that do are not yet fully clear. Finally, despite the fact that there are a number of problems involved in the conceptualization and study of consumer behavior from the decision-process approach, it is increasingly recognized that the advantages outweigh the limitations.)

Integrative-Comprehensive Models of Consumer Behavior

With the emergence of consumer behavior as a subject for intensive study in its own right, researchers and practitioners realized the need for an integrative-comprehensive model. The 1960s produced three such models; one will not be discussed (Nicosia Model)[4], another will be discussed briefly, and the third will be integral to this entire book.

Each of these models attempts to represent the essential qualities of consumer behavior. In effect, each specifies the elements within the black box, the nature of the relationship between them, and the effect they have on consumers' behavior.

Howard-Sheth Model

John Howard proposed the first truly integrative model of buyer behavior in 1963.[5] Howard's model was based on a systematic and thorough utilization of learning theory. Perhaps the most important contribution of Howard's model was the distinction drawn between extensive problem solving, limited problem solving, and automatic response behavior. A major contribution in its own right, this model drew attention to the need for an interdisciplinary approach to clarification of the conceptual basis for such a model and to the need for extensive development of practical implications of buyer behavior models.

The results of the combined efforts of Howard and Sheth provided much of the needed clarification and elaboration of the earlier Howard Model. The Howard-Sheth Model (Figure 2.1) was essentially an attempt to explain brand choice behavior over time.[6] In the development of their model, Howard and Sheth assume that brand choice is not random but is a systematic process and that buyers attempt to make logical decisions, that is, logical within the limits of their cognitive and learning capacities and with the further constraint of limited information.

The Howard-Sheth Model consists of four sets of constructs or variables: (1) input variables, (2) output variables, (3) hypothetical constructs, and (4) exogenous variables.

Each of the variables included in the model and the hypothesized linkages is described in considerable detail in Howard and Sheth's book, *The Theory of Buyer Behavior*. Unfortunately, it is not possible to indicate in a few paragraphs the richness of their theory; however, the essence of the model—the way Howard and Sheth characterize the buying process—can be described briefly.

Howard and Sheth contend that when the buyer is interested in purchasing something, he actively seeks information from his commercial (significative and symbolic) and social environment. The buy-

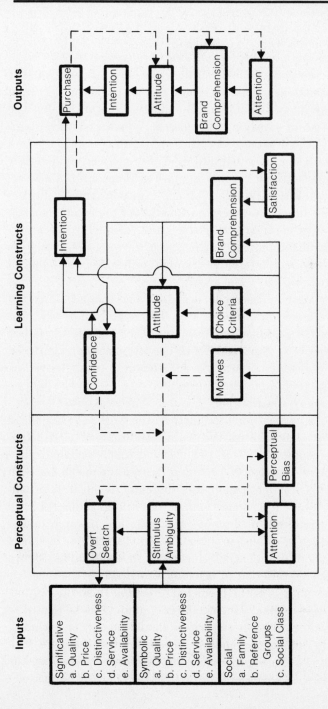

Figure 2.1
Simplified Description of the Howard-Sheth Model of Buyer Behavior

Source: J. A. Howard and J. N. Sheth, *The Theory of Buyer Behavior* (New York: John Wiley and Sons, Inc., 1969). Reprinted by permission of the publisher.

er's perceptual processes limit the information received and modify it so that it is consistent with his own frame of reference. In addition to the process of searching for information, the buyer draws from his learning constructs, such as attitudes and motives. The choice criteria the buyer has developed enable him to choose a brand that has the greatest potential for satisfying his motives. When a buyer's experiences with a brand are satisfactory, the evaluation of it increases and the likelihood of his purchasing that brand of product again increases. If the buyer repeats the decision a number of times, routinized purchase behavior develops. Whether or not a person actually buys a given alternative brand, however, is a function of the comprehension of brand attributes, attitude toward the brand, confidence in the purchase, and individual intention. Furthermore, the exogenous variables help explain individual differences through such factors as financial status, time pressure, and social class.

The great strength of this model lies in the fact that a multiplicity of variables are linked in a precise way. The relationships hypothesized in the model at times approach the rigor of fully developed theory. The work of Howard and Sheth has stimulated and enriched the thinking and research of nearly every student of consumer behavior and promises to do so in the future.

Despite its many contributions, a number of weaknesses are evident in the model, which serve to illustrate the work that lies ahead for the consumer analyst. First, the distinction drawn between hypothetical and measurable variables, while conceptually laudable, introduces unnecessary complexity. A reduced form of the model has been subjected to empirical verification and, therefore, is much more concise in the variables it includes and in the relationships specified among these variables. Furthermore, the empirical research undertaken for purposes of validation has indicated the need for modifications and extensions of the model. In general, the research has shown that the amount of variation in behavior explained by the model is quite low, although it is in the predicted direction. In addition, some variables that were originally included were found not to be related as hypothesized, while others not specified should have been included. The attempts to validate the model have been limited; therefore, such efforts must be continued. In conclusion, it is fair to say that the empirical research to date seems to provide considerable support for the model generally, but it has demonstrated the need for extensive revision.

Engel, Blackwell, and Kollat's
Consumer Decision Process Model

The Consumer Decision Process Model, which serves an integrative and organizational function for the remainder of this book, is the third version of a model developed by Engel, Blackwell, and Kollat. An overview of the model and anecdotal support for it are presented in this chapter. Each phase of the model is developed completely in later chapters along with its theoretical and empirical foundations. This Consumer Decision Process Model is not an end in itself; rather, it is a means to facilitate understanding a very complex phenomenon.

Although the issue as to whether this is the best model remains unresolved, the model does fare well relative to the following criteria:[7]

1. The model conforms well to the rules of logic.
2. The model is internally consistent.
3. The model encompasses relevant theories.
4. The model can be empirically operationalized.
5. The model serves as a basis to derive new propositions.
6. The model is consistent with existing knowledge.
7. The model suggests new directions for research.

Furthermore, the Consumer Decision Process Model provides an excellent framework with which to analyze consumer behavior, as will be demonstrated later in this chapter.

The Consumer Decision Process Model is organized around five interrelated decision-process stages: (1) problem recognition, (2) search, (3) alternative evaluation, (4) choice, and (5) outcomes (see Figure 2.2). These phases are affected by internalized environmental influences, general motivating influences, product/brand evaluations and information processing.

Problem Recognition

Problem recognition occurs when an individual perceives a difference between an ideal state of affairs and the actual state of any given

Figure 2.2
**The Stages in the
Consumer Decision
Process**

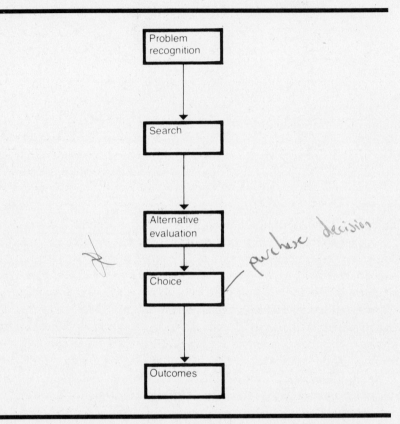

Source: From *Consumer Behavior,* 3rd ed., p. 22, by James F. Engel, Roger D. Blackwell, and David T. Kollat. Copyright © 1978 by Dryden Press, a division of Holt, Rinehart and Winston. Reprinted by permission of Holt, Rinehart and Winston.

moment. The simplified depiction of problem recognition in Figure 2.3 indicates that there are two basic sources of problem recognition: (1) motive activation and (2) external stimuli. Problem recognition, or arousal as it is sometimes termed, can be activated by a number of factors which tend to fall into one of these two categories.

Problem recognition can be activated solely by motive activation without any type of external stimulation. Motives are enduring predispositions to strive to attain specified goals, and they contain both an arousing and a directing dimension. Motive activation causes the individual to become alert, responsive, and vigilant because of the feelings of discomfort produced. The result is the formation of a consciously felt drive that energizes motive-satisfying behavior. For ex-

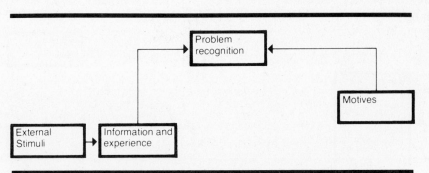

Source: From *Consumer Behavior*, 3rd ed., p. 23, by James F. Engel, Roger D. Blackwell, and David T. Kollat. Copyright © 1978 by Dryden Press, a division of Holt, Rinehart and Winston. Reprinted by permission of Holt, Rinehart and Winston.

ample, thirst is a need that produces physiological discomfort, activates a drive state and initiates appropriate action. The ideal state in this instance is the absence of thirst and the aroused drive signifies that the actual state is short of the ideal state.

Problem recognition can also be activated by external stimuli. Technically, external stimuli affect new information and experience that trigger motive and, in turn, motive activates problem recognition. Figure 2.3 does not have an arrow demonstrating the relationship between information and experience and motive because the objective is simplification and clarity. The following is an example of how an external stimulus can activate problem recognition. Imagine yourself, a long-time pizza lover, walking past a pizza parlor. The aroma of the cooking pizza can activate your consciousness, trigger the hunger motive, and, thereby, introduce a specific behavior. Such an outcome will not occur in all situations because the incoming stimulus can be screened out or distorted if it is inconsistent with one's disposition. For example, the weight watcher may distort the aroma of pizza so that it is no longer appealing, since the consumption of a pizza is inconsistent with the attempt to control caloric intake.

However, not every perceived discrepancy between actual and ideal will result in problem recognition. There is a minimum level of perceived difference that must be surpassed before recognition occurs. The level of perceived difference that is necessary for problem recognition to result will vary among consumers and circumstances. Furthermore, even though problem recognition may occur, action can be constrained by the intervention of external influences. A consumer

Figure 2.4
The Search Process

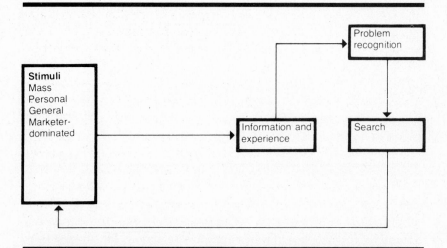

Source: From *Consumer Behavior*, 3rd ed., p. 24, by James F. Engel, Roger D. Blackwell, and David T. Kollat. Copyright © 1978 by Dryden Press, a division of Holt, Rinehart and Winston. Reprinted by permission of Holt, Rinehart and Winston.

may recognize a problem (the perceived need for a new automobile) and make purchase plans. A change in one or more of the external influences, however, can intervene to make this action impossible. That is, an external influence such as available income can constrain or hold the decision-making process—the recognized problem of needing a new automobile remains, but the action is postponed until the constraints are removed. This is consistent with what was referred to as the deferred gratification capacity of the open-system model of man discussed previously.

Search

Once a problem is recognized and no constraints intervene to halt the decision process, the consumer must then assess the alternatives for action. Initially the consumer will search internally to determine whether or not sufficient information is available to make a purchase decision.

If the internal search and alternative evaluation process reveals that alternatives have been well defined and a satisfactory one can be identified, the remaining stages of the decision process will be circumvented, and a purchase decision will be made. This type of response to problem recognition is referred to as routinized response behavior. If the internal search does not prove to be sufficient, however, external search is activated. The process is illustrated in Figure 2.4. While only stored information and experience are depicted in this simplified diagram, several other variables—such as attitudes, beliefs, and personality—also have an impact on the consumer. The impact of these variables will be addressed later. At this juncture the concern is what happens to incoming information as it is processed and evaluated.

Internal search for information occurs instantaneously and largely unconsciously. In many instances, this search is insufficient to permit the consumer to make a decision. A husband and wife, for instance, may have little or no awareness of the advantages and limitations of the competing makes of color television sets. They may not, in addition, know the appropriate criteria to use in evaluating these alternatives. Hence, they might consult friends or relatives or turn to one of the published sources that rate products on technical performance. These are examples of interpersonal and mass communication which are *general* in nature and are not controlled by the marketer. They also no doubt will be influenced by advertisements and personal selling undertaken by the marketer for the express purpose of consumer influence. Search continues until enough information is gathered to permit an enlightened evaluation.

Consumers differ significantly in their willingness and desire to search for purchase-related information. For some consumers, apartment hunting ends when an acceptable alternative is located; for others, a thorough examination of fifteen seemingly suitable available apartments would still be inadequate. These differences exist because some people are cautious and unwilling to act even after careful evaluation of alternatives because of the perceived implications of a wrong decision, whereas others are willing to act largely on hunch and intuition. While there are numerous factors affecting an individual's willingness to search for information, researchers generally maintain that consumers search for information as long as the benefit of the search exceeds the cost of the search.

Information Processing

Information processing refers to the process by which sensory input is transformed, reduced, elaborated, stored, recovered, and used by the consumer. That is, it refers to how consumers "make sense" out of

Figure 2.5
Information Processing

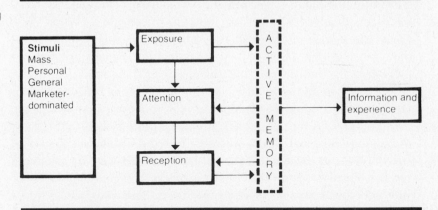

Source: From *Consumer Behavior*, 3rd ed., p. 25, by James F. Engel, Roger D. Blackwell, and David T. Kollat. Copyright © 1978 by Dryden Press, a division of Holt, Rinehart and Winston. Reprinted by permission of Holt, Rinehart and Winston.

incoming information (Figure 2.5). Research has established un-equivocally that consumers are highly selective in the way they process information. In fact, the information loss and distortion can be so substantial that there is very little similarity between the actual content of the message and the content as perceived and retained by the consumer. Information loss and distortion occur as new information is passed through *active memory*. Active memory refers to that portion of the consumer's memory which is used in processing and interpreting incoming information. That is, active memory (depicted in Figure 2.5 with a dotted outline) is a type of filter that controls the flow of information.

Now, how does information processing take place? A homemaker is in a supermarket; she has an extensive shopping list. Yet, she has not written everything down and frequently will use the items on the shelves as a reminder of what she and her family need. As she walks, she scans the shelves and thus is *exposed* to a variety of stimuli. Information processing, then, begins with exposure, at which time the individual is in physical proximity to an informational stimulus such that there is opportunity for one or more of the senses to be activated. This makes the obvious point that the marketer's first task is to get the intended message to the right person at the right point in time.

As she progresses down the aisle, her eye stops at a display of fresh strawberries. Now it can be said that her *attention* has been attracted.

Attention is defined as the active processing of an exposed stimulus such that a conscious impression is made within the active memory. Attention is highly selective, however, and many stimuli are completely filtered out. The key fact is whether or not the stimulus has *pertinence* for that individual.

It is well known that an aroused motive activates an "on-off" mechanism in information processing. We are especially alert to those stimuli which are seen to be relevant in satisfying the aroused drive. Perhaps the homemaker has come to the store with an active recall of her plan to serve fresh strawberries in the near future. Thus, desire to serve pleasing foods could cause the strawberry display to stand out, whereas it might be largely ignored under other conditions.

Attention is a necessary but not sufficient precondition for message *reception*—the accurate comprehension of the meaning of the stimulus and storage of that information in long-term memory. The filtering effect of active memory can distort meaning in such a way that some things are amplified whereas others are diminished or ignored. It is common for a consumer to miss the point of a commercial completely and attribute a meaning that was never intended. Sometimes this distortion occurs to make the perceived meaning more consonant with the individual's own beliefs and preferences. For example, to a consumer with a preference for Coca Cola, Pepsi Cola or R. C. Cola doesn't taste as good.

Not every correctly comprehended message enters into permanent memory, because there also is a tendency to retain only those which are compatible with our present beliefs. Even if the taste-test results for cola beverages were properly understood, the "filter" still can function to block the entry of this new information and thus preserve the existing preference for Coca Cola.

The final stage of information processing as shown in Figure 2.5 is new information or experience which enters into permanent storage. Obviously, it can affect all other things stored within memory and bring about changes. In the context of consumer behavior, however, the greatest changes will be in product beliefs and attitudes, intentions to purchase, and, it is hoped, in actual purchase behavior. More is said about this later.

It should not be inferred from this brief discussion that all attempts at consumer influence will be futile because of selective information processing. If this were the case, $20 billion would not be spent annually on advertising in the United States. The implications of consumer information processing are worth noting. Gaining message exposure is not the marketer's greatest problem, for exposure primarily requires careful media selection. The marketer's real difficulty is to design messages that do not activate the filter in such a way that it prevents further processing or distorts the input. Generally, this will require that the messages be compatible with the consumer's personality and attitudinal components. Thus, even though a 25-year-old bachelor is not likely to attend to messages encouraging saving for retirement, he might very well acknowledge, comprehend, and retain messages urging saving for a new car or a trip to Europe. Selective screening occurs most frequently when the individual is not in a state of active problem recognition and is not engaged in a voluntary search for information. Many advertisements are designed to trigger problem recognition and these are most readily ignored. The person engaged in active search, however, will be far more open and receptive.

Alternative Evaluation

The information that the consumer processes can exert an influence on four key variables within the central processing unit: (1) evaluative criteria, (2) beliefs, (3) attitudes, and (4) intentions. These variables are depicted in Figure 2.6.

Evaluative criteria are the internalized specifications and standards used by consumers to assess and compare alternative products, brands, stores, and other consumption alternatives. They are the desired outcomes from choice and use expressed in the form of the specifications used to evaluate alternatives. Evaluative criteria are concrete, product-specific manifestations of underlying personal goals, typically applied across several products within a product type. For example, the criteria used in judging cola beverages might include taste, amount of carbonation, the presence of an aftertaste, and the price of the product. A beverage like fruit juice may be assessed on entirely different bases, such as nutritional value, texture, and aroma.

Several factors must be kept in mind when considering these evaluative criteria, which are shaped by an individual's personality, stored information, social influence, and the marketing efforts of firms. Furthermore, these criteria change over time. Consequently,

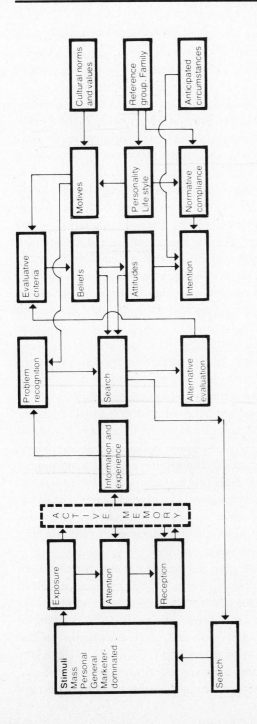

Figure 2.6
**Perceived
Environmental
Influences on
Intentions and
Life-Style**

Source: From *Consumer Behavior*, 3rd ed., p. 30, by James F. Engel, Roger D. Blackwell, and David T. Kollat. Copyright © 1978 by Dryden Press, a division of Holt, Rinehart and Winston. Reprinted by permission of Holt, Rinehart and Winston.

the evaluative criteria relative to any product must be carefully monitored.

Because the marketing manager is committed to developing the most effective marketing program feasible, the determination of the evaluative criteria used by the prospective target market of the product is of fundamental importance. The manager should make certain that the product as perceived by prospective consumers adequately satisfies their relevant criteria. If not, consumers will not consider it as an alternative.

Beliefs represent information that links a given product or brand to evaluative criteria. Whereas evaluative criteria are highly individualized and, therefore, rather resistant to marketer influence, beliefs can normally be influenced by the marketer with little difficulty. For instance, the consumer might specify that decay prevention is the most important evaluative criterion for selecting toothpaste. Marketers' attempts to modify the importance placed on this criterion are not likely to be successful. However, the marketer might, through promotional appeals, help the consumer to believe that one particular brand is superior to all others with respect to decay prevention. In all likelihood, this belief will result in the consumer trying that toothpaste. It is for this reason that the formation and modification of consumer beliefs is considered a major marketing objective.

Attitude can be defined as a learned predisposition to respond consistently in a favorable or unfavorable manner with respect to a given alternative. Marketers frequently interpret an attitude as the assessment a consumer makes regarding the ability a product, brand, or store has to satisfy his or her expectations which, in turn, have been defined by personal evaluative criteria. All things being equal, the alternative choice with the highest rating summed across the evaluative criteria has the greatest probability of being purchased and consumed when a corresponding need exists.

Marketing decision makers now recognize that determining consumers' attitudes toward a brand, product, or store is an essential foundation for the development of effective marketing programs. Fortunately for the users of consumer behavior research, the last decade has been characterized by many substantial developments in the areas of attitude theory and measurement.

Attitudes undoubtedly stand as one of the most analyzed phenomena in general human behavior, and many organizations spend considerable sums of money in trying to change consumer attitudes. Despite this commitment, there is some question about the value of even trying to change attitudes since there is some evidence that attitude change does not necessarily lead to the desired change in behavior. Consumer analysts have recently realized that another variable intervenes between attitudes and behavior—intention.

Intention refers to the subjective probability that a specified action will be undertaken in a particular instance. Thus, it has been concluded that a change in attitude is a necessary, but not sufficient, condition for a change in intention. The change in intention then leads to a change in behavior, unless it is inhibited by an environmental factor. Therefore, attitude change is a valid marketing goal, and the key to an effective marketing strategy is to change the belief structure on which the attitude is based.

Two environmental influences (also depicted in Figure 2.6) that have a particularly pronounced effect on intentions are normative compliance and anticipated circumstances. Normative compliance refers to the existence of perceived social influence on choice plus the motivation to comply with that influence. The sensitivity to comply with such social influence is determined by the individual's personality makeup. Personality is normally considered to be the consistent pattern of responses to environmental stimuli. The term life-style, frequently used interchangeably with personality, refers to the pattern of enduring traits, activities, interests, and opinions which determines general behavior and thereby makes one individual distinctive in comparison with another. It is the product of initial genetic make-up, a lifetime of experiences, and is strongly conditioned by internalized cultural norms and values. Anticipated circumstances refers to a number of factors—the most important of which is personal income— that affect intentions. If sufficient funds are not available, purchase intentions may not be acted upon for a considerable period of time. Knowledge of the status of these two factors can increase substantially the accuracy of predictions of behavior.

Choice and Its Outcomes

The complete model of consumer behavior (Figure 2.7) integrates the portions of the model previously discussed. Furthermore, it depicts

Figure 2.7
**A Complete Model
of Consumer Behavior**

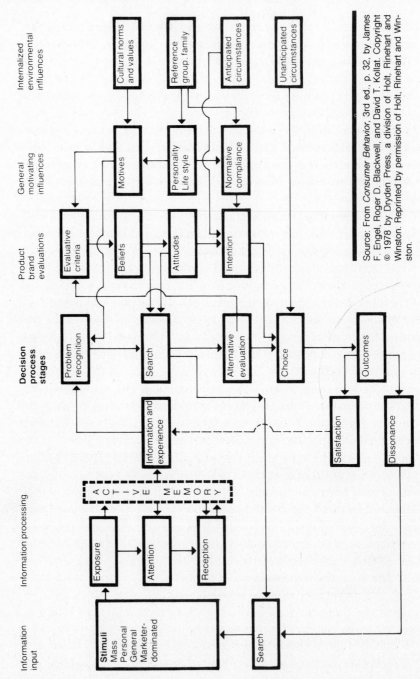

Source: From *Consumer Behavior*, 3rd ed., p. 32, by James F. Engel, Roger D. Blackwell, and David T. Kollat. Copyright © 1978 by Dryden Press, a division of Holt, Rinehart and Winston. Reprinted by permission of Holt, Rinehart and Winston.

choice and outcomes, the last two stages of the decision-making process. Choice generally follows the formation of a purchase intention but perceived unanticipated circumstances can serve as a barrier to such intentions. Examples of unanticipated circumstances are: changes in income, change in family circumstances, and nonavailability of alternatives. In the event that an intended behavior is thwarted, the intention either remains in existence until a later time or the decision-making process begins anew. The choice process includes the selection of the particular retail outlet at which the product is purchased as well as those activities associated with determining the conditions of sale.

The decision to purchase a product or service can, as illustrated in Figure 2.7, result in two types of outcomes: satisfaction and dissonance. If the consumer's post-purchase evaluation indicates that the chosen alternative is consistent with prior beliefs and attitudes, the resultant outcome is satisfaction. The dotted feedback arrow to information and experience indicates that this information becomes stored in memory for use in future purchase decisions. It is likely to have a particularly strong impact on beliefs and, consequently, attitudes. Under similar circumstances, the probability of a repeat purchase in the future is strengthened.

A purchase decision can also produce post-decision dissonance. Post-decision dissonance is a state of doubt motivated by awareness that although one alternative was chosen, the alternatives not chosen also have desirable attributes. Dissonance is especially likely to occur if the purchase is financially burdensome and several attractive alternatives were rejected. The purchaser now might be sensitive to information that confirms the choice and thereby relieves doubt. Therefore, post-decision search for information is not unusual in such circumstances.

Variations in Consumer Decision Processes

The consumer decision process described in the preceding pages is the most comprehensive type of decision making. However, most consumer decision making is not this complex. Indeed, the most common type of consumer decision making—the habitual or routine decision process—is at the opposite extreme. Consumers tend to rationalize their decision making as much as possible to reduce the complexity in their lives. In the case of routinized decision-process behavior, problem recognition will lead directly to a purchase intention and then to a purchase. The consumers' beliefs and attitudes are fixed in the form of brand loyalty, thus simplifying substantially the decision process.

In a sense, extended problem solving and routine behavior lie at opposite ends of a continuum. In between is limited decision-process behavior, which occurs when there is good information about the domain of feasible alternatives but insufficient information about each to permit a sound decision. Thus, there is likely to be a certain amount of search and alternative evaluation.

Obviously, the difference among these types of decision making is more one of degree than of kind. One possible determinant is the presence or absence of perceived risk. Risk may be financial, physical, or social. The consumer is aware that a wrong decision will have undesirable consequences, and often resorts to extended problem solving in the hope of reducing risk to tolerable levels. Many factors, then, are likely to evoke extended decision-process behavior. The extent of decision making varies greatly depending upon the individual, the social environment, and certain product and situation characteristics to be detailed later.

Using the Model to Explain Consumer Behavior

The discussion of the model and its components has, of necessity, been brief, and it is useful to trace a distinctly different buying situation—the purchase of a small automobile.

While the discussion thus far has centered largely on the individual consumer, it is clear that social influences are important. The outcomes from one person's actions can serve as inputs for others. The model, therefore, can easily be utilized to explain the buying process of a family as well as that of an individual.

Purchase of the Volkswagen Dasher[8]

For most people, the purchase of a new and previously unknown make of automobile requires extended problem-solving behavior. Ex-

11/4

Figure 2.8
**Example of
Introductory Print
Advertisement**

Mileage based on German industry test track standards.
©VOLKSWAGEN OF AMERICA, INC.

VOLKSWAGEN INTRODUCES THE PERFECT CAR FOR ITS TIME.

The new Volkswagen Dasher does everything you want
a car to do, and does it on about 25 miles per gallon. That's
why it's the ideal car for today.

Dasher does a powerful 0-50 in only 8.5 seconds. It holds
five comfortably. It has front-wheel drive and gives you
control you've never felt in any conventional car. It has the
amazing Skidbreaker. When one side of the car is riding on
a slippery surface, Skidbreaker forces Dasher to move in a
straight line as you brake. It needs maintenance at only
10,000 mile intervals. And it's covered by the Volkswagen
Owner's Security Blanket.

Nobody else is even _close_.

DASHER
A new kind of Volkswagen.

```
THIS AD AVAILABLE IN 4 SIZES:
1000 lines   33-35-48150
 600 lines   33-35-48160
 400 lines   33-35-48170
 250 lines   33-35-48180
SUPERSEDES INSERT #11/1
```

VW
AUTHORIZED
DEALER

Source: Reprinted by permission of Volkswagen of America. Note, however, that this ad has
been superseded, and the information in it is no longer valid.

perience with the Dasher, introduced to the American public in January 1974 (see the introductory advertisement in Figure 2.8), was limited to awareness of the Volkswagen name. Also, the financial commitment was considerable, and the psychological stakes in selecting the right alternative were high. Almost 300 people who bought Dashers in April 1974 were interviewed. Some of the key findings are presented below.

Characteristics of Purchasers

Dasher buyers tend to concentrate in the following demographic categories:

Married (74.8 percent)

Male (77.1 percent)

Under 35 (42.3 percent)

College educated or beyond (77.2 percent)

Professional occupation (40.1 percent)

Higher income (nearly two thirds beyond $15,000)

Problem Recognition

Problem recognition usually results from factors beyond the marketer's control. In the purchase of a new automobile, for example, a problem becomes recognized most frequently when the currently owned vehicle becomes unsatisfactory for a variety of reasons, such as mechanical wear.

It is interesting to note, by the way, that 34.8 percent disposed of a Volkswagen when they acquired a Dasher. An additional 20 percent disposed of a smaller import or compact American car, thus indicating the presence of a desire to "move up" to a make which offers the advantages of small size along with better performance and the addition of luxury features.

Search

The data in Table 2.1 indicate that television commercials were the major source of initial awareness of the Dasher. Magazine and news-

TV commercial	36.7%	Table 2.1
Articles (magazines/newspapers)	16.4	**Sources of Initial Awareness of the Dasher**
At dealership (showroom/salesmen)	15.7	
Advice of friends/relatives	6.8	
Through Fox/Passat	5.3	
Newspaper ads	4.7	
Advertising (general)	4.6	
Magazine ads	4.2	
Other	5.6	
Total	100.0%	

Source: From *Contemporary Cases in Consumer Behavior*, p. 370, by Roger D. Blackwell, James F. Engel, and W. Wayne Talarzyk. Copyright ©1977 by Dryden Press, a division of Holt, Rinehart and Winston. Reprinted by permission of Holt, Rinehart and Winston.

paper articles were second in importance. The advice of friends and relatives ranked far down the list, undoubtedly because of the newness of this make. Results often are quite different with a more established make.

Alternative Evaluation

The evaluative criteria utilized by Dasher buyers are itemized in Table 2.2. Of these ten, gas mileage proved to be the dominant consideration. Manufacturer's reputation was next in order as might be ex-

Gas mileage	79.7%	Table 2.2
Manufacturer's reputation	28.9	**Evaluative Criteria Mentioned at Least Once as Reason for Purchase of the Dasher**
Quality of workmanship	22.8	
Previous experience with make	21.3	
Warranty coverage	18.2	
Resale value	18.0	
Handling ease	13.4	
Interior room	13.0	
Value for money	6.6	
Exterior styling	6.5	

Source: From *Contemporary Cases in Consumer Behavior*, p. 373, by Roger D. Blackwell, James F. Engel, and W. Wayne Talarzyk. Copyright ©1977 by Dryden Press, a division of Holt, Rinehart and Winston. Reprinted by permission of Holt, Rinehart and Winston.

pected from the large number who traded in a Volkswagen Beetle. Apparently, previous experience with this company had been satisfactory. Quality of workmanship and warranty coverage were the only additional criteria receiving frequent mention.

It is highly revealing to compare the customer's specifications with the sales points mentioned in the dealer's showroom. These appear in Table 2.3. There should be a close match between them, but that apparently did not prove to be the case. Gas mileage did receive the most frequent mention, but there was a large discrepancy from that point on. For example, quality of workmanship rarely was stressed. Little attempt was made to capitalize upon reputation of manufacturer and previous positive experience with Volkswagens. The salesperson tended either to do little or no real selling or to stress perfor-

Table 2.3
**Sales Points Mentioned
at Time of Purchase**

Gas mileage/economy	28.8%
Roominess	17.0
Front-wheel drive	16.2
None (poor salesmanship)	14.8
Handling/ease of driving	14.4
Economy of operation	12.9
Owner's security blanket/computer analysis	8.5
No sales points necessary (presold, knew more than salesman)	8.1
Engine, water-cooled/front-mounted	8.1
Performance	5.9
Design/style	5.5
Features (standard on Dasher but options/accessories on other makes)	5.5
Service	5.5
Quality of workmanship/construction	4.4
Safety	4.4
Engineering	4.4
Other	45.1

Source: From *Contemporary Cases in Consumer Behavior*, p. 370, by Roger D. Blackwell, James F. Engel, and W. Wayne Talarzyk. Copyright ©1977 by Dryden Press, a division of Holt, Rinehart and Winston. Reprinted by permission of Holt, Rinehart and Winston.

mance characteristics that were of less importance to the buyer. It should come as no surprise that initial sales results of the Dasher were far below expectations. The problem may lie at the level of the dealership.

The Dasher carried a higher price tag than the traditional Beetle. Only 15.9 percent of the people interviewed said that the price was about what was expected. Nearly half said that it was a little more than expected, and more than a third said it was a lot more than expected. The justifications given by salespersons for the price are in Table 2.4. Quality of workmanship was stressed most frequently along with general inflation. Quality as an explanation should have been well received given the importance of this factor in the purchase decision.

Quality workmanship	17.7%	
General inflation	17.1	
Didn't (salesman did not attempt to justify)	12.5	
Dollar devaluation	11.8	
Features (standard on Dasher, extra on other makes)	9.2	
No reductions from list price	7.8	
Unique car (superior/new)	6.5	
Couldn't (salesman tried to justify but, according to customer, failed)	6.5	
Increased value of trade-in	5.9	
Low operating cost	5.2	
Value for the money	3.9	
Owner's security blanket	3.9	
Performance	3.9	
Increased production costs	3.9	
Gas mileage	3.2	

Table 2.4
Salesman's Justification for Greater-than-Expected Price of the Dasher

Source: From *Contemporary Cases in Consumer Behavior*, p. 371, by Roger D. Blackwell, James F. Engel, and W. Wayne Talarzyk. Copyright ©1977 by Dryden Press, a division of Holt, Rinehart and Winston. Reprinted by permission of Holt, Rinehart and Winston.

Choice

Part of the choice process is selection of the dealer. The data in Table 2.5 indicate that physical proximity was the dominant consideration,

Table 2.5
**Primary Reason for
Dealership Selection**

Closeness to dealer	40.9%
Previous experience	10.6
Service	8.2
Dealership personnel	7.8
Dealer reputation	7.2
Only one	6.2
Trade-in	5.8
Advice of friends	4.0
Other	9.3
Total	100.0%

Source: From *Contemporary Cases in Consumer Behavior*, p. 370, by Roger D. Blackwell, James F. Engel, and W. Wayne Talarzyk. Copyright ©1977 by Dryden Press, a division of Holt, Rinehart and Winston. Reprinted by permission of Holt, Rinehart and Winston.

with previous experience a distant second. Other factors were of less importance.

Outcomes

Ownership satisfaction is of critical importance in continued loyalty to a given company. In the case of the Dasher, satisfaction was related to reaction to price. If the price was about as expected, the buyer tended to be quite satisfied, whereas satisfaction was much lower when the price was more than expected. (See Table 2.6.)

Table 2.6
**Satisfaction vs. Initial
Reaction to Price**

	Dasher Price Was	
	about what expected	a little/lot more than expected
Completely/very satisfied	70.7%	50.7%
Fairly well satisfied	19.5	26.9
Somewhat dissatisfied	4.9	19.2
Very dissatisfied	4.9	3.2
	100.0%	100.0%

Source: From *Contemporary Cases in Consumer Behavior*, p. 371, by Roger D. Blackwell, James F. Engel, and W. Wayne Talarzyk. Copyright ©1977 by Dryden Press, a division of Holt, Rinehart and Winston. Reprinted by permission of Holt, Rinehart and Winston.

Implications

Sales of the Dasher fell below expectations. Price appeared to be a major factor, and the relationship of reaction to price and buyer satisfaction is a real danger sign. The dissatisfied owner rarely keeps quiet about these reactions and, thus, is bound to affect future sales. Furthermore, the quality of salesmanship at the dealer level reflected a poor grasp of buyer expectations. A reversal of the negative trend will depend in large part on remedial action taken in the marketing program.

Summary

There are essentially two ways to study consumer behavior empirically: (1) the distributive approach, which focuses on behavioral outcomes, and (2) the decision-process approach, which describes the way consumers actually make decisions. Research using the distributive approach is relatively simple and less expensive than are other alternatives; however, this approach can, at best, provide only a partial or incomplete explanation of consumer behavior. The decision-process approach is more advantageous than the distributive approach because it examines the processes preceding the purchase decision, the decision itself, and actions that follow the decision, and by so doing, it ordinarily provides the marketing manager with more relevant information.

This chapter discussed the major comprehensive models but focused on the Engel, Blackwell, and Kollat Model which provides the conceptual framework for the remainder of the book. Its primary purpose has been to clarify the importance of the decision-process perspective. It was pointed out that the consumer decision process has five distinct steps: (1) problem recognition, (2) search for information, (3) alternative evaluation, (4) choice, and (5) outcomes of choice (satisfaction and dissonance). The extent to which each step is undertaken depends upon whether the purchase is of sufficient importance to warrant extended problem solving. Most decisions are based on habit, in which case problem recognition is followed by choice without search and analysis.

Still very valid to this dj.

Many variables affect the decision process. A model of consumer behavior was introduced briefly to delineate the significant variables and to illustrate how they affect the behavioral process. Each is discussed at length elsewhere in the book. The chapter concluded with an example of consumer study where this model was utilized to gain insights into the decision processes and to reveal marketing strategies.

Questions and Issues for Discussion

1. "The distinction drawn between the distributive approach and the decision approach is interesting to the academician but is unimportant to the marketing strategist." Do you agree or disagree? Why?

2. How might the decision-process approach help the manufacturer of high-quality stereo equipment understand how and why consumers purchase his or her product?

3. Paul Smith, an enthusiastic football fan, watched three consecutive football games last New Year's Day. Two weeks later, he recalls the details of every key play, yet he can only recall two of the more than one hundred commercials that were shown during that time period. Both were for a well-known beer. What explanation can you provide?

4. Comment on the following quotation: "The decision-process model can explain deliberate, well-thought-out consumer decision making but cannot explain impulse purchases."

5. Because attitudes have a more direct impact on behavior than do evaluative criteria, marketing strategists are wise to restrict their attention to obtaining information on attitudes. Do you agree or disagree? Explain.

6. "Advertisers are primarily interested in getting potential consumers to understand and remember their advertisements. Therefore, the only relevant consideration in pretesting advertising is how well it is remembered." Comment.

7. The marketing research director of Gant shirts has just determined that 75 percent of the purchases of their product during the last quarter were instances of habitual decision-process behavior. What are the strategy implications of this?

8. Discuss the stages of the decision process, the variations that occur in the decision process, and the underlying determinants of these variations.

9. Assuming all other things equal, what type of decision making would be most likely in each of the following situations:

a. the purchase of a new tennis racket for a beginner; for a touring pro

b. the purchase of toothpaste

c. the purchase of a motorcycle by a student; by a bank vice-president

d. the purchase of a gift for a "special friend."

10. A manufacturer of quality dress shirts located in Los Angeles has recently experienced a decline in sales. The marketing director suspects that the sales decline is due to a change in consumer preferences in dress shirts. The firm decided to hire a marketing research firm to determine how consumers selected dress shirts. The Chicago-based marketing research firm they hired conducted interviews with 200 Chicago homemakers. The research results suggested that consumers liked the appearance of the dress shirts but considered them to be very difficult to care for. The marketing research firm has suggested that the manufacturer modify the fabric used to reduce this problem. The marketing director is not convinced that the research firm has adequately identified the process by which consumers select dress shirts. Based on your understanding of the decision-process model of consumer behavior, what suggestions would you make to the manufacturer? Should the manufacturer follow the marketing research firm's recommendation?

Case 1. Natural Light Beer

In early 1977, Anheuser-Busch, Inc. began to market their Natural Light beer in an attempt to match the success of the Miller Brewing

Source: Some of the information for Case 1 is from "Anheuser-Busch, Miller Battling for Light Beer Market," *St. Louis Globe,* November 2, 1977.

Company, whose Lite beer has been mainly responsible for making Miller the second largest brewer in the industry. Anheuser-Busch was faced with a difficult task since Miller had firmly entrenched its light beer's position in the market with a share of over three quarters. Miller had appealed to the so-called "macho" segment, featuring in television commericals retired, big-name athletes and other rugged-looking fellows enjoying good times over cold Lites. Presumably, this scores high marks with many armchair quarterbacks who are concerned about their expanding, middle-aged tummies. Anheuser-Busch's difficulties were compounded by the fact that Miller's brand name, consisting of just four letters, had virtually become the generic name for this type of product, due in large part to its highly descriptive nature and the very early entry made by Miller into the market.

By the time Natural Light made its entry, several other companies had already put a light beer on the market, notably Schlitz, whose promotional strategy was apparently aimed at outdoing Miller Lite's macho appeal. Schlitz had very limited success, however, suggesting that this type of strategy was of little value to the makers of Natural Light. One study showed that while people remembered the macho image of the Schlitz Light ads, they could not recall the name of the beer being sold.

A major problem for Anheuser-Busch was in the name of its brand. One executive remarked, "A four-word name is a killer. Not many people are going to walk into a bar and say, 'Gimme an Anheuser-Busch Natural Light." The company's position was clearly frustrating. Another executive said, "When someone orders a light beer in a restaurant, he's automatically brought a Miller Lite."

There were, however, several factors working in Anheuser-Busch's favor. The firm has an excellent reputation as a producer of quality beers. It has a highly developed distribution network, which enabled it to move rapidly into the market at a time when other producers were preparing to market their light beers. Both Miller and Schlitz had been cultivating the male market for light beer, and this left Anheuser-Busch with an excellent marketing opportunity. Females, it has been reported, constitute 50 percent of the light-beer market and 35 percent of all beer drinkers. In addition, 60 percent of all beer purchases are made in grocery stores, largely by women. These facts, as well as the rapidly climbing sales in the light-beer market, dispelled all fears at Anheuser-Busch that the demand for this product was nothing more than a fad.

It was decided that the Natural Light ads would be directed at both men and women, with couples taking a "natural break" from leisure activities or after a busy day. Special emphasis was placed on the natural brewing process and the idea that it is for active people of any age or sex.

Miller was well aware of the foothold it had left for other producers who were potential market entrants. It recognized that light beer was originally perceived as women's beer because of its light quality and emphasis on low calories, and were just beginning to test-market a new, lower calorie beer called Players. It, like Natural Light, was designed for both men and women, and had only half the calories contained in Miller's regular beer, as opposed to the "third less" content of Lite. This was all so that Miller could protect Lite's flank— Lite would appeal to men while Players would appeal to women. Officials at Anheuser-Busch did not consider Players much of a challenge to Natural Light. They contended that it sacrificed too much taste and fullness of body to be successful in the market.

Case 1 Questions

1. What might further research reveal to Anheuser-Busch regarding the types of decision processes beer drinkers go through in making their purchases? How could this information assist in planning the marketing strategy for Natural Light?

2. How might Anheuser-Busch trigger a reevaluation by light-beer drinkers of the available alternatives? What components of and variables affecting the consumer decision process are important to understand in order to do so?

3. What could have caused Schlitz's problems in trying to promote its light beer?

4. What should Anheuser-Busch do about the problem of the brand name, Natural Light, and about the fact that consumers think light beer means Lite beer?

Case 2. The Electric Car

Today, concern over long-term sources of energy is widespread. People are recognizing that resources, such as crude oil, are finite and that new alternatives must be developed. Our society has tremendous sunken costs in roads and highways, many of which have depreciable lives of over 60 years. This being so, an abandonment of the automobile as the conventional mode of transportation would be foolhardy. Currently, the best alternative to the gasoline-powered vehicle is the electric car, and Congress has recommended a sum of $160 million to be distributed to firms undertaking research and development in this area.

Of course, at this juncture, most consumers do not view the electric car as being practical, especially for the prices at which many are offered. The National Academy of Sciences (NAS) recently concluded from a market study of electric vehicles that, to compete effectively with geo-powered models, they would need a driving range of up to 200 miles, a cruising speed of 55 mph, and a lower price. Most electric cars available today have a top speed of about 50 mph, but can only be driven 30 to 40 miles before they must be recharged. The most advanced models cost anywhere up to $30,000, and still do not meet NAS specifications.

Progress is being made, however. Sears, Roebuck and Company reports that their Sears DieHard electric car has a realistic range of 60 to 90 miles, depending on driving speed. The car has exceeded 75 mph and will cruise at 65 mph with no difficulty. Recharging cost from complete discharge is from 1 cent to 1.5 cents per mile.

Many say that the key to the electric car's success will be the development of a better battery. Experimental redesign of traditional lead-acid batteries has resulted in a 10-percent gain in watt-hours per pound. Other work is being done on more advanced chemical systems in batteries such as zinc-chlorine and sulfur-based systems. The improved efficiency could greatly broaden the market for electric cars.

Other features are also being made more attractive, such as power seats, windows, and brakes, and air conditioning offered on Electric

Sources: Some of the information in Case 2 is from "Personal Business: What You Get When Buying an Electric Car," *Business Week*, January 17, 1977, p. 75; and "A New Spark Revives Electric Car Makers," *Business Week*, January 17, 1977, pp. 86–87.

Fuel Propulsion Corporation's Transformer I. The body, made by General Motors, resembles that of an Oldsmobile Cutlass or Buick Century. The DieHard electric car is a sporty-looking model, using the body of a Fiat 128-eP. The makers of the Transformer I have even negotiated with the Los Angeles Department of Water and Power to establish a network of 100 recharge stations. The difficulty is that, under present law, only utilities can sell electricity. EFP's president quipped, "Maybe the recharge stations can just sell parking space and give away free electricity."

While Sebring-Vanguard Inc.'s Citicar looks like nothing more than a glorified golf cart, has a top speed of 38 mph, a range of only 40 to 50 miles, and takes 12 hours to recharge the batteries, it sells for a low $3,000 and is quite suitable for commuting short distances. Elcar Corp. is gearing up for production of a car that will come in a variety of fiberglass styles, including a sports model and a van. The Elcar will cruise at about 45 mph with a range of 60 miles and will recharge in about 8 hours. It should cost between $4,000 and $4,500.

An executive of Cleveland's Electric Vehicle Associates, Inc., says there are three main reasons why he expects the market for electric cars to grow rapidly in coming years: "Oil prices are going up, the public is more concerned about noise and air pollution, and internal-combustion cars are getting smaller and more costly." Many fear, however, that present owners bought their electric cars merely for the sake of novelty, and that this motivation will quickly dissipate. Others say, "There is a big risk. If we rush out with any old car, the public might look at it and say 'yuk.' Then five years later, when we do have a good car, people will still have a bad taste in their mouths."

Assume that your firm has just developed an electric car similar to the Elcar, except that its body is made of more substantial material and sells for around $5,500. As marketing director, you must design a strategy for selling this automobile. Do so, using the decision-process model as a guide.

Case 2 Questions

1. What can you do to make sure that your customers will experience a minimum of post-purchase dissonance?

2. One of your competitors, it has been learned, is using the distributive approach in conducting the market research she needs to have done in order to design her strategy. What problems might arise for her?

Notes

1. R. A. Dahl, M. Haire, and P. F. Lazarsfeld, *Social Science Research on Business: Product and Potential* (New York: Columbia University Press, 1959), pp. 103-04.

2. R. Ferber, "Research on Household Behavior," *American Economic Review,* Vol. 52 (March 1962), pp. 19-63.

3. J. A. Patterson, "Buying as a Process," *Business Horizons* (Spring 1965), p. 59.

4. F. M. Nicosia, *Consumer Decision Processes: Marketing and Advertising Implications* (Englewood Cliffs, N. J.: Prentice-Hall, Inc., 1966).

5. J. A. Howard, *Marketing Management: Analysis and Planning* (Homewood, Ill.: Richard D. Irwin, Inc., 1963).

6. J. A. Howard and J. N. Sheth, *The Theory of Buyer Behavior* (New York: John Wiley and Sons, Inc., 1969).

7. Gerald Zaltman, Christian R. A. Pinson, and Reinhard Angelmar, *Metatheory and Consumer Research* (New York: Holt, Rinehart and Winston, Inc., 1973).

8. Adapted from *Contemporary Cases in Consumer Behavior*, pp. 360-74, by Roger D. Blackwell, James F. Engel, and W. Wayne Talarzyk. Copyright © 1977 by Dryden Press, a division of Holt, Rinehart and Winston. Reprinted by permission of Holt, Rinehart and Winston. Courtesy of Volkswagen of America.

Chapter **3**

Macro Perspectives of Consumer Behavior

Outline

Demographics: Aging of the Population

Specific Market Behavior Implications

Social Patterns: Changes in Women's Roles

Specific Market Behavior Implications

Major Market Composition: The Young Single Adult

Specific Market Behavior Implications

Attitudes and Public Opinion: A Longitudinal Study of Public Opinion and Attitudes toward Advertising

Specific Market Behavior Implications

Summary

Questions and Issues for Discussion

Cases

Key Terms

macro perspectives
aggregate factors
demographics
social patterns
attitudes
public opinion
aggregate consumption patterns
behavioral implications
historical consumption patterns
egalitarian
life-style
market composition
discretionary fund
bachelor stage

Horse racing historically has been called the "sport of kings," suggesting that it took a status and affluence to be involved which were beyond the grasp of most. Likewise, the responsibility of aggregate market monitoring and trend watching could be seen as the *noblesse oblige* of top executives. That is, the observation of major influences and changes in the marketplace falls in the domain of those who are fundamentally responsible for shaping the overall course of the organization and who are free from the day-to-day demands of detailed product-line decisions.

The logic of the above suggestion may appeal to some managers, but there are several reasons why professionals functioning at all managerial levels within a firm should broaden their perspectives to include a view of what can be called aggregate market factors. These aggregate factors encompass a wide range of phenomena, from monitoring public attitudes toward business generally or broadcast advertising specifically to identifying long-term expected composition changes in the characteristics of the population itself. The awareness and insights gained by being sensitive to these kinds of circumstances have benefits such as the following:

1. *Present Product-line Effect.* Variation in aggregate trends can have a material impact on micro-market situations. For example, expected increases in the amount of leisure time available have a potential effect on many industries. To mention only a few, such increases could mean more travel, greater interest in spectator sports, added value placed on shopping as a social experience, increased television viewing, as well as a more relaxed adult population that has fewer headaches and, consequently, less need for aspirin. Even marketing managers with a relatively narrow area of responsibility must at least think about how such possible occurrences might be related to their product line.

2. *Clues to New Market Opportunities.* As aggregate circumstances are observed or their occurrences forecasted, new behavioral patterns are often expected to accompany them; as a result, new market opportunities may be seen in their infancy. Of course, it generally takes the most observant and astute professional to note these and to gain a vision as to how to seize the opportunity.

Almost everyone at some time has had an idea for a new product, service, or process that was insightful and ultimately appeared on the market—and may have even been profitable. The typical response seems to be "Why didn't I pursue it earlier? I would have had the opportunity to enjoy this success." Actually, it is doubtful that there is any shortage of "good ideas" like these. To the professional marketer, the kernel of such ideas must be set forth in a way that provides a map of how the best opportunities can become profitable ventures in the future. One cannot begin this process without a heightened awareness of aggregate market phenomena.

3. *Professional Growth for the Individual.* Personal advancement can result from studying the clues found in overall market changes. The keen professional can exercise a degree of control over his or her future by identifying aggregate factors that offer insight into future market opportunities. Generally, marketing managers want to be employed by companies that anticipate growth markets rather than by those that must contend with declining demand and retrenchment of company efforts. The study of aggregate information available and the accompanying interpretation of it offers assistance in planning one's professional future.

In the remainder of this chapter, several aggregate market dimensions are identified and discussed to show what kind of information is available and to point out some of the specific implications of these various findings for those interested in consumer behavior. These are not meant to represent an exhaustive list, but are simply offered as examples of the kinds of aggregate factors worth noting. Although each topic presented is treated separately, there are many interrelationships among them.

Specifically, the following aggregate market dimensions are presented in the sections ahead.

Demographics: Aging of the Population

Social Patterns: Changes in Women's Roles

Major Market Composition: The Young Single Adult

Attitudes and Public Opinion: A Longitudinal Study of Public Opinion and Attitudes toward Advertising

Demographics: Aging of the Population

Demographics generally refers to various, relatively apparent, descriptive characteristics of a group of persons such as their age, sex, ethnic origin, education, and income. These data are ordinarily more readily available than information on personality traits or level of intelligence. The widespread availability of demographic data has had a material impact on its usage even when other information would

Table 3.1
**Median Age of United
States Population**

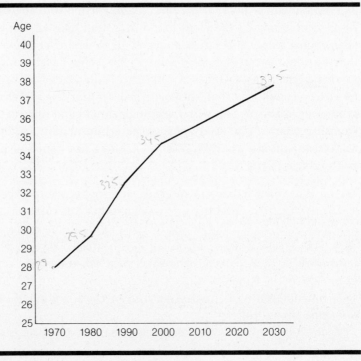

Source: U.S. Bureau of the Census, Census Reports.

have been preferred. The changes expected in one of these character-istics—age—will be discussed in detail.

Even though Americans have liked to think of themselves as youthful, one noteworthy change in our population is that it is growing older. In 1970 the median age was 28 years, by 1981 it will reach 30 years, and by the year 2000 the median age will be 35 years with the expectation that it will be 40 years by 2030.[1] The upward trend in median age is shown in Table 3.1.

The U.S. population has changed already in terms of family formation, births, professional training, and geographic shifts. These changes will materially affect the future and are not subject to significant variation. For instance, all the individuals who will be senior tradesmen, pensioners, or chief executives in the United States in the next 20 years are already born. By carefully identifying who these people are, studying their preferences and attitudes, and gaining an understanding of their skills, business managers and government administrators can learn a great deal about the challenges ahead and the kind of country America will be during the next two decades.[2]

This slow aging process of Americans will most certainly be reflected in aggregate consumption patterns as well as in expressed interests and attitudes. During the next dozen years, the 25- to 44-year-old age group will be the most rapidly increasing segment of the population. Its numbers will swell to 78 million by 1990 from just 58 million today. As a group, these people are the most employable, most productive, and have the greatest purchasing power.[3]

Specific Market Behavior Implications

As a youth-oriented society, it takes some out-of-the-ordinary thought patterns to imagine the possible impact of an aging population. However, such changes can be widespread and of major proportions. The following speculations list some directions this aging pattern could take.

1. Total spending on formal education as a proportion of public funds (elementary through four years of college) is likely to decline. This differs greatly from the trend in the 1950s, for example, when on the average, California opened one school every week. Today many of these schools are no longer needed and some have been closed. Such changes also mean there will be less demand for school supplies, children's clothing, playground equipment, and school lunches.[4]

2. Government and individual spending on crime prevention and home security equipment could slacken as the number of people under 25 years of age declines. This may be practical because certain kinds of crime are most often committed by people in this age group.

3. Geographic shifts in the concentration of the population may slow as the median age becomes older because young adults generally are the most inclined to migrate. This could reduce the need for interstate moving, for Welcome Wagon services, as well as for nationwide real estate listings.

4. The 35- to 44-year-olds buy more new cars than any other group. Furthermore, these middle-age consumers are generally more likely to buy top-of-the-line option-laden models. The rapid increase in the number of people in this age group during the next decade should be encouraging to the automobile industry.

5. Mature, experienced individuals are generally less gullible and less susceptible to social pressure from peers. Therefore, promotional tactics will have to meet the needs of these consumers.

6. As the over-65 segment of the population grows, it will have some special needs.[5]

   a. The demand for medical care will soar. The costs of such care for this older age group averaged $1,360 in 1975—nearly double the amount spent by those under 65 years of age.

   b. Many of these individuals are what has been called the "younger oldies." Often they are cosmopolitan in taste, well traveled, educated, knowledgeable, and very politically active. Many have substantial financial resources, much of which can be spent on nonessentials.[6]

   c. These persons are often substantial consumers of daytime television. Consequently, this medium may grow in attractiveness to advertisers seeking to reach the over-65 segment of the population.

   d. A number of companies have already recognized the purchasing power of the people in the over-65 group. For example, Sterling Drug has begun advertising aspirin for arthritis as well as for headaches. Gerber Products now sells life insurance as well as baby food—with the theme "Gerber now babies the over-50s." And while nobody was looking, the Pepsi generation has broken out in wrinkles and eyeglasses.

Despite all these opportunities to anticipate future changes in consumption patterns resulting from the aggregate population aging process, the logical and readily apparent trends may never happen. Great care must be taken to continue to monitor the impact of such changes on consumer market behavior. It could be very costly to rely strictly on historical consumption patterns related to age. For instance, one recent study undertaken by the Coca Cola Company showed that even though teenagers consume more soft drinks than older adults, persons now in their 40s drink more of these beverages than they did when they were younger. Such findings are certainly encouraging for soft drink bottlers and suggest that traditional youth-oriented products do not necessarily have to suffer declines as their market matures.[7]

Social Patterns: Changes in Women's Roles

Social patterns are the configuration of groups in a society with particular reference to how persons within these groups interact. The
nature of the groups is typically studied including the formal and
informal structures as well as the roles played by the various group
members. Some of the ways that roles assumed by women are changing along with the anticipated impact of these changes will be examined in detail.

Historically, businesses' interest in women as consumers primarily
focused on the roles of wife, mother, homemaker and hostess, or on
that of a single girl preparing to assume one or more of these roles.
Certainly the women's movement of the late sixties and seventies has
made it appropriate to abandon some traditional perspectives while
considerably broadening others. No longer is it safe to assume that
women's personal orientation is essentially toward dependence, association, assistance, and compliance, while characterizing men as aggressively seeking autonomy, high levels of personal achievement,
and dominance.[8]

In support of this, it is worth noting that in 1975, 40 percent of the
women 20 to 24 years old were single, whereas in 1950, only 28 percent of the women this age were single. Actually, the future holds an
interesting phenomenon. It appears likely that there will be a substantial increase in the number of single-female headed households,
as well as an increase in the number of marriages and husband-wife
households.[9]

It has been suggested that as women become more "liberated" and
broaden their social involvement, many changes are likely to occur
that will have an impact on consumer behavior. As would be expected, the following are interrelated, and evidence already exists
that some of these changes are beginning to materialize.

1. The women's movement is a forerunner of significant changes in
social values and in the social system. For example, there is some
evidence showing that more families are becoming egalitarian where
the couples share the traditional husband-father and wife-mother
roles.[10]

2. The life-styles of women will be significantly affected with some
bearing on economic behavior of the consumers at large.

3. Traditional household decision making will undergo significant changes. It is important to keep in mind that this does not necessarily mean more joint decision making. In fact, as persons are pressed for time, it may mean, for example, that the husband assumes the entire grocery shopping responsibility at certain times or that the wife is completely responsible for the maintenance of the car.

4. The economics of the household, especially in the allocation of women's time in processing various products, will change considerably. This could mean rotating the responsibility for meal preparation as well as expressing more interest in eating out and use of carry-out services.

5. As a result of anticipated changes in the life-styles of women, we can expect changes in the life-styles of men. Certainly several of the examples given above suggest this.

Tables 3.2 and 3.3 further illustrate the aggregate changes that have taken place with respect to women in the United States. Table 3.2

Table 3.2
Age Distribution of Women—1950 to 1975, Projected to 2000 (in thousands)

Age Group	1950	1960	1970	1975	1985	2000
Under 15	19,964	27,428	28,395	26,284	26,313	28,545
	(26.2%)	(30.1%)	(27.2%)	(24.0%)	(21.9%)	(21.1%)
15–24	11,232	12,114	17,890	19,902	19,046	19,122
	(14.8%)	(13.3%)	(17.2%)	(18.2%)	(15.8%)	(14.2%)
25–44	23,112	23,965	24,547	27,248	36,030	38,428
	(30.4%)	(26.3%)	(23.5%)	(24.9%)	(30%)	(28.5%)
45–64	15,349	18,428	21,818	22,715	22,836	30,319
	(20.2%)	(20.3%)	(20.9%)	(20.8%)	(19%)	(22.5%)
65 and Over	6,482	9,056	11,650	13,228	15,975	18,558
	(8.5%)	(10%)	(11.2%)	(12.1%)	(13.3%)	(13.7%)
Total Female Population	76,139	90,992	104,300	109,377	120,201	134,973
	(100%)	(100%)	(100%)	(100%)	(100%)	(100%)
Median Age	30.5 yrs	30.3 yrs	29.3 yrs	30.0 yrs	32.3 yrs	36.2 yrs

Source: W. Lazer and J. E. Smallwood, "The Changing Demographics of Women," *Journal of Marketing*, Vol. 41, No. 3 (July 1977), p. 15. Reprinted from the *Journal of Marketing* published by the American Marketing Association.

shows the age distribution of women from 1950 to 1975 and is projected in thousands to the year 2000. Not only has the number of women increased substantially, but there have been some notable changes by age groups. The most striking is the proportion of people 65 and over and the related increase in the median age from 30.5 years in 1950 to a projected 36.2 years in the year 2000.[11]

Table 3.3 summarizes the participation of women in the labor force. One only has to look to the far right columns to see that significant changes have occurred in every age group during the period from 1950 to 1974. Furthermore, the ratio of women to men in the work force has also increased considerably to 63 percent in 1974. It is interesting to recognize that education of women is the demographic characteristic most closely related to their participation in the labor force. That is, it is the highest among women with four or more years of college and lowest for women who are not high school graduates. Furthermore, contrary to some views, generally the greater their husband's income, the more likely they are to be employed.

Age	1950	1960	1970	1974	Change, 1950 to 1974 Number	Percent
16–19	1,714	2,062	3,250	4,005	2,291	133.7
20–24	2,681	2,590	4,893	5,867	3,186	118.8
25–34	4,101	4,140	5,704	7,826	3,725	90.8
35–44	4,166	5,308	5,971	6,354	2,188	52.5
45–54	3,328	5,280	6,523	6,687	3,359	100.9
55–64	1,839	2,986	4,153	4,158	2,319	126.1
65 and over	584	907	1,056	996	412	70.5
Total	18,412	23,272	31,560	35,892	17,480	94.9
Ratio: Women/Men	41%	48%	58%	63%		

Table 3.3
Size of the Female Labor Force by Age, 1950–1974 (in thousands)

Source: W. Lazer and J. E. Smallwood, "The Changing Demographics of Women," *Journal of Marketing*, Vol. 41, No. 3 (July 1977), p. 16. Reprinted from the *Journal of Marketing* published by the American Marketing Association.

Specific Market Behavior Implications

What follows are some possible results of the changes discussed previously. These simply illustrate how persuasive the impact can be on marketing practices:

1. Traditional shopping hours may not be sufficiently convenient to accommodate the households with employed women.

2. Increasingly, shopping is likely to be shared with other household members including the husband as well as sons and daughters.

3. The price of some products may become considerably less important than convenient access to them, availability of good service, and their time-conserving attributes.

4. As women become more cosmopolitan, the sources of product-related information they rely upon will change.

5. As husbands participate more in homemaking and child-rearing, they will need more information about goods and services related to these responsibilities. Traditional male-oriented media have not been a source of this information.

6. Generally, working women affect financial activities. For example, women who work are more likely to have savings accounts, regular checking accounts, and their own credit cards.[12]

7. Working women are travel-oriented and will likely continue to be so. Married working women without children at home have been found to be the best customers for travel services.

8. Although women continue to do less direct automobile purchasing than men, the working woman is more likely to have bought her own car than is the full-time homemaker.

9. There is a growing recognition of the importance of identifying at least four separate segments in what might be called the adult women's market. These include the following, with the proportion of the total adult women shown for each: (1) homemakers: (a) those who intend to continue to stay at home (29 percent) and (b) those who plan to work (20 percent) and (2) working women: (a) those who look at their employment as "just a job" (32 percent) and (b) those who are career-oriented (19 percent).

Age Group	1975 Census		1980 Projections		1985 Projections	
	No. (000)	% of Total Number 18 Yrs. & Older	No. (000)	% of Total Number 18 Yrs. & Older	No. (000)	% of Total Number 18 Yrs. & Older
18–19	8,371	5.7	8,533	5.3	7,338	4.3
20–24	19,226	13.1	20,808	13.1	20,496	12.1
25–29	16,818	11.5	18,933	11.9	20,572	12.1
Total	44,516	30.3	48,374	30.3	48,406	28.6

Table 3.4
1975 Composition of the Young Adult Segment of the U.S. Population (with projections through 1985)

Source: U.S. Bureau of the Census, *Current Population Reports*.

Major Market Composition: The Young Single Adult

Market composition refers to the characteristics that give a market substantive shape and meaning. For example, these characteristics include size in number of units, geographic concentration, growth patterns, income, and identifiable behavioral patterns. There are various markets which have drawn considerable attention. Certainly anything with youthfulness as a dimension has been the focus of at least some of this attention. However, what was learned in the past may need to be modified because the makeup of these various youthful markets are undergoing change. The one given attention here is the young single adult.

The composition of the young adult segment of the population is shown in Table 3.4 with projections through 1985. The size of this market will continue to grow even though it will decline somewhat as a proportion of the total adult population.

As shown in Table 3.5, at every age level, the proportion of young

	1960		1971		1973		1975	
	Men	Women	Men	Women	Men	Women	Men	Women
20–24 Years Old								
Married	46.9%	71.6%	41.6%	61.6%	40.8%	61.7%	39.7%	60.7%
Not married	53.1	28.4	58.4	38.4	59.2	38.3	60.3	39.3
25–29 Years Old								
Married	79.2%	89.5%	73.2%	87.2%	73.3%	87.3%	71.6%	85.2%
Not married	20.8	10.5	26.8	12.8	26.7	12.7	28.4	14.8

Table 3.5
Marital Status among Young Adults Using Selected Years

Source: U.S. Bureau of the Census, *Current Population Reports*.

adults who are single has increased considerably during the past fifteen years. Furthermore, these singles will be a growth market for most of the next decade.

The observed changes just noted are apparently related to a number of circumstances. What follows are some of the more important of these.[13]

1. *Growing prevalence of cohabitation arrangements.* In 1970, for example, there were approximately 143,000 unmarried couples living together.[14] This represented an increase of 80 percent over the 1960 level. It was estimated that this number had reached 750,000 by 1975.

2. *Increasing numbers of women attending college.* This can at least delay marriage.

3. *Growing recognition of the professional achievements of women.* Women are increasingly gaining status through their professional accomplishments. This has taken time and a flexibility that can preclude early marriage.

Of course, it is possible that these are only short-term forces that will be overcome as time passes and that there will again be a return to previous patterns. However, this seems unlikely at this time.

Another phenomenon accompanying the growth in numbers of young single adults is the change in living arrangements that has taken place. Table 3.6 presents data which illustrate this.

Table 3.6
Living Arrangements among Young Single Adults

	1971 Men	1971 Women	1973 Men	1973 Women	1975 Men	1975 Women
20–24 Years Old						
Living at home[a]	75.7%	68.1%	71.0%	65.7%	69.4%	65.6%
Not living at home	24.3	31.9	29.0	34.3	30.6	34.4
25–29 Years Old						
Living at home[a]	50.0%	42.5%	46.1%	38.9%	41.2%	37.7%
Not living at home	50.0	57.5	53.9	61.1	58.8	62.3

[a] Their family's home
Source: U.S. Bureau of the Census, *Current Population Reports.*

Specific Market Behavior Implications

All of these observed changes may have many different effects on consumer behavior. Some examples follow as illustrations.

1. In the short run, it would mean fewer wedding rings and wedding accessories.

2. More single adults will probably mean greater demand for automobiles, oil changes, snow tires, floor mats, downtown parking space, and auto insurance.

3. As single adults move out of their families' homes in growing numbers, the demand for apartments will no doubt increase, as well as the demand for all the household furnishings necessary to make these comfortable. The chances seem good that at least some of these furnishings will be sought as part of the rental arrangement.

4. Singles are generally rather mobile; therefore, they are more likely to use airlines and buses and to take pleasure cruises.

5. The entertainment mix sought by young single adults would be expected to differ from that of the young married person. For example, singles' bars would be more popular as would participant sports.

6. Although single-person households are not likely to have as high an income as households resulting from marriage, the singles often

Table 3.7
Traditional vs. Liberated Life Cycle Stages

| | Purchase Pattern Variations | |
	Traditional	Liberated
Bachelor stage	Car, vacations, recreation; cheap, basic kitchen equipment and furniture	Good kitchen equipment and furniture; television, car, vacations, recreation; some buy a home
Newly married stage	Many household durables; good kitchen equipment, furniture, appliances; car, vacations	Few additional household durables are needed; buy nonessential appliances; buy a home; vacations.

Source: Reprinted with permission from Kay Satow, "Some Comments on Changing Life Styles among Single Young Adults," *Advances in Consumer Research*, Vol. 4, *Proceedings of the 7th Annual Conference of ACR*, p. 336.

have a greater proportion in discretionary funds. This could mean more variation in spending patterns.

7. Some researchers have observed that changing views on being single have made purchase patterns previously associated with the "bachelor stage" absolute for an increasing number of young adults. This new orientation has been referred to as a "liberated" single "who sees the bachelor stage as an active growth stage in which personal identity and credentials are sought." Associated with this is a view of their home as an expression of personal identity. Table 3.7 illustrates some of the variation in purchase patterns that are likely to occur between what has been considered the "traditional" bachelor stage and the emerging "liberated" bachelor stage as well as its impact on the newly married stage that follows it.[15]

Attitudes and Public Opinion: A Longitudinal Study of Public Opinion and Attitudes toward Advertising

Attitude research essentially gives attention to the predisposition of persons toward various objects and topical issues. Investigations into public opinion concern the personal feelings and evaluative judgments of groups of people regarding a wide variety of circumstances as well as specific acts. How individuals form attitudes and how these attitudes are measured are dealt with in detail in a later chapter. The following discussion illustrates one kind of interest in the investigation of aggregate attitude and public opinion monitoring.

Although attitude measures and measures of opinion are typically linked to specific products, to their attributes, and even to the consuming situation surrounding the products, there are still continuous attempts by some prominent organizations to identify and monitor attitudes and opinions in a much broader context. The focus of attention here involves two nationwide studies conducted in 1964 and 1974 sponsored by the American Association of Advertising Agencies on how consumers viewed advertising. The first was essentially a benchmark study done to establish information bases for later comparisons. The 1974 survey was used to note changes in the various measurements over the ten-year period.[16]

The 1974 study was initiated for the following reasons:

1. To learn if there had been any major shifts in publicly held attitudes toward advertising in the ten years following 1964.

2. To develop a reliable means for future tracking of public attitudes toward advertising and related issues that could be used more frequently.

3. To determine specific issues that may contribute to building favorable or unfavorable public opinions of advertising and to identify the kinds of people who hold these various opinions.[17] (This objective was considered the most important.)

Some sample findings from these American Association of Advertising Agencies' studies are presented in the next few paragraphs to further illustrate this kind of approach to attitude and opinion research.

When the three or four topics that people talked about most were identified, it was found that the general public was not as absorbed in issues related to advertising as some headlines suggested. Furthermore, advertising as a topic of conversation ranked far below other subjects such as bringing up children, religion, the federal government, clothing and fashions, and sports. This was true in both 1964 and 1974.

The issue of determining whether people felt positive or negative toward advertising generally was undertaken in a comparative context. That is, their attitudes were researched with respect to five major institutions. As it turned out, the press was given the highest positive endorsement in 1974, with advertising a close second. Labor unions, big business, and the federal government followed in that order.

As indicated earlier, one of the purposes of the 1974 study was to identify opinion groups. These were divided into what were called advertising's critics and its fans. What was found here was consistent with other studies of advertising. The very critical represented a rather small group, 5 percent, with another 16 percent having expressed a "mostly unfavorable" view. Generally, those who were "mostly unfavorable" had above-average education and income; and they were typically in the 30 to 44 age group. This group was found to be quite critical of all institutions.

Those who were called "fans" of advertising represented about one in three persons who were "mostly favorable" toward advertising.

This group tended to be less well educated, less affluent, and generally older than the population as a whole. These were also the persons who viewed television heavily.

It is appropriate to ask how such aggregate findings might affect business and its strategy for reaching the consumer with goods and services through a persuasive informational effort. Some possible answers to this question are presented next.

Specific Market Behavior Implications

What follows simply presents a few ways that the findings from the studies might be used to gain insight with respect to key market issues.

1. These findings provide at least some measure of the likelihood of encountering strong negative public reaction to the use of advertising as part of a firm's promotional mix.

2. The evidence suggests that it would be appropriate to consider varied uses of advertising tactics in attempting to reach consumer groups with divergent orientations toward advertising. For example, a more aggressively stated message may be less likely to arouse a negative reaction among "fans" than "critics."

3. Based on the study findings, some may conclude that, as the population generally becomes better educated and more affluent, the level of criticism toward advertising will increase substantially. If this is expected, it would probably need to be incorporated into a firm's future strategy development.

4. These data may be helpful in planning organized professional opposition to increased government control of advertising. The study offers some evidence with respect to the public's view of the relative importance of the activities of various institutions as well as their evaluative opinions concerning the performance of these same organizations.

Summary

Being sensitive to aggregate market factors that have an impact on buyer behavior has several advantages, such as being able to anticipate the effect on a company's present product line, finding clues to new market opportunities, and plotting one's own professional growth.

In studying aggregate market factors, it is important to identify information sources and also to note specific implications of these data for one's business and personal interests. The market factors given as examples were (1) the increasing age of the population; (2) role changes and modifications in life-styles of women and men; (3) the shift in the composition of the population groups, specifically the single, young adult group; and (4) the changes in public opinion toward advertising during a ten-year period.

Learning to appreciate and apply the many indicators coming from market information sources can be of great use in the study of consumer behavior.

Questions and Issues for Discussion

1. Under what circumstances can a macro perspective assist a marketing manager in carrying out his or her day-to-day responsibilities?

2. Which producers of goods and services are likely to suffer the most from the aging of the population? Which stand to make the most substantial gains? Explain your reasons.

3. How have the changing roles of women generally affected the consuming roles of men? Are these consumption pattern changes likely to persist?

4. Is most of the impact on consumer purchase patterns of the young single adult market essentially short term? That is, does it appear that, after being part of the "young single market," these same persons will go on to be "traditional" adult consumers?

5. What "new" products or services might make their way into the market as the United States population ages?

6. Is it possible for some organization such as the American Association of Advertising Agencies to improve public attitudes toward advertising generally? Why or why not? Illustrate your answer.

7. If a study of consumer attitudes and opinions toward personal selling were to be conducted today, would the results likely be similar to the results of the two studies discussed in the chapter? How might the results of the personal selling study differ?

8. Is it possible for professional marketers to forecast changes in macro market trends? If so, when can management expect to be the most successful in making such forecasts?

9. What sources of information can be used to help identify major market shifts?

10. What aggregate trends are you a part of as a consumer? How are these affecting the manufacturers of consumer durables?

Case 1. Cal Design Construction

Cal Design is a major tract home builder with annual sales exceeding $250 million. Its home office is located in southern California. Typically, the firm buys several hundred acres of land at a time. This land is usually at the outer edge of the suburban area of a major city. A master plan is then developed outlining the whole development including all roads, utilities, parkways, drainage systems, and homes.

Cal Design assumes responsibility for the total development of the area through the actual building and selling of the homes. Historically, the firm has concentrated its building activity west of Denver, although it plans to expand geographically. The houses it has built have primarily had between 1800 and 2200 square feet of floor space with three or four bedrooms. The prices of such houses have generally been from $75,000 to $90,000. These have almost exclusively been sold to white-collar families with the husband in a middle management position.

The company has enjoyed steady growth and has been consistently profitable. This has only come through careful market analysis and excellent engineering and construction know-how. The president, Arthur Riggsby, recently noted the following statement in the *Marketing News* and became concerned over its possible implications.

> One- and two-person households—the single, the widowed, the empty nesters, childless and unmarried couples, and young couples planning to have children later—now account for 59 percent of United States households.[18]

Cal Design typically has built houses that are larger than the average in the local community and also has included a variety of luxury options. In addition, the cost per square foot of these houses has been rising faster than the cost-of-living index and the overall national rate of inflation.

Given factors such as those mentioned above, some members of Cal Design's management were strongly suggesting that the firm move into the construction of low-cost, no-frills homes. These generally have fewer square feet of floor space, can be put on smaller lots, and typically can be completed much more rapidly than the kind of home that Cal Design has been building.

The market for the no-frills home seems to be larger than that for the home of Cal Design's present focus, and it is growing. Furthermore, financing for these smaller houses may be more easily arranged given their lower price as well as the fact that there are several federal assistance programs that offer aid to low- to middle-income buyers.

At this time, Cal Design is formulating its marketing strategy for next year. Its management needs help in analyzing the market trends which may affect its future.

Case 1 Questions

1. What aggregate market trends, if any, come to bear upon the plans that Cal Design is now formulating?

2. Even if there are macro indicators that suggest a changing market composition, is it really necessary for Cal Design to respond to these to be profitable? Explain your reasoning.

Case 2. Interpreting Consumer Views and Regulatory Actions toward Advertising

The 1974 study of public opinion of advertising conducted by the American Association of Advertising Agencies identified some critics. Those who were the most unfavorable toward advertising generally were people with above-average education and income. Furthermore, most critics were between thirty and forty-four years of age.

It is also evident from other aggregate data that the United States population is becoming better educated and more open in its willingness to express itself. As a further attempt to gain an understanding of consumer perceptions of the helpfulness of advertising, R. H. Bruskin Associates undertook a study that specifically inquired about the assistance of ads in providing information.

The Bruskin study gave attention to eight specific product and service categories: food, airlines, automobiles, nonprescription drugs, banks, clothing, insurance, and tobacco products. Consumers were asked whether they felt today's advertising was "more helpful, less helpful, or about as helpful to them as it was five years ago." The findings of this study are shown in Table 3.8.

There has been a growing debate among some advertising professionals as to how such findings should be interpreted. A further complicating factor is the active involvement of the various federal regulatory agencies in the advertising process. For instance, the FTC has recently turned attention toward the use of "preference polls" in advertising. An example of the agency's interest is where it was reported that four out of five dentists surveyed said that "they recommended _____ brand of sugarless gum to their patients who chewed gum." The particular concerns expressed deal with such issues as the appropriateness of the research design used and whether the results may have been presented in a misleading manner.

Table 3.8
Perceived Helpfulness of Ads in 1978 as Compared to Those in 1973

Product/Service Categories	Now More Helpful (percent)	Now Less Helpful (percent)	Now About Same (percent)	Don't Know (percent)
Food	45	7	46	2
Airlines	43	5	49	3
Automobiles	40	9	49	2
Nonprescription Drugs	40	10	48	2
Banks	38	7	53	2
Clothing	35	7	56	2
Insurance	28	9	60	3
Tobacco Products	22	20	54	4

Source: "Are Ads More Helpful? Studies Aren't," *Advertising Age* (July 31, 1978), p. 57. Reprinted with permission from the July 31, 1978, issue of Advertising Age. Copyright 1978 by Crain Communications Inc.

The FTC is not the only agency actively involved in advertising practices. The FCC is reviving its probe into the use of television advertising directed to children. One of its interests is in a possible reduction in the allowable commerical minutes on children's television shows.

To many observers, these regulatory agency activities and the findings of the various studies of advertising just lead to confusion as to what major forces will be shaping the way advertising can and should be used by a firm. This confusion is compounded when one considers the fact that advertising budgets continue to grow and television advertising in particular has enjoyed healthy growth in its revenues and increasingly has attracted local advertisers.

One interested advertiser recently said, "All you can tell for sure is that advertising in one way or another is getting everybody's attention, and that part of this attention is among key consumer buying segments. Therefore, businesses will continue to view it as an important part of their promotional stategy."

Case 2 Questions

1. Do you agree with the last statement? Explain why or why not.

2. Summarize the essence of the meaning of both the American Association of Advertising Agencies' 1974 study and the Bruskin findings. Do these support one another or do they simply deal with different aspects of advertising? Is either set of findings of help to those responsible for planning promotional strategy?

Notes

1. U.S. Bureau of the Census, *Current Population Reports,* No. 704 (Washington, D.C.: U.S. Government Printing Office, July 1977).

2. "Americans Change How Demographic Shifts Affect the Economy," *Business Week* (February 20, 1978), pp. 64-69.

3. U.S. Bureau of the Census, *Current Population Reports,* No. 704 (Washington, D.C.: U.S. Government Printing Office, July 1977).

4. "The Greying of America," *Newsweek* (February 28, 1977), p. 51.

5. Ibid.

6. W. Lazer and J. Smallwood, "The Changing Demographics of Women," *Journal of Marketing,* Vol. 41 (July 1977), p. 15.

7. "Americans Change How Demographic Shifts Affect the Economy," *Business Week* (February 20, 1978), p. 67.

8. A. Venkatesh, "Changing Roles of Women—Some Empirical Findings with Marketing Implications," in *Contemporary Marketing Thought,* ed. B. Greenberg and D. Bellenger, Series No. 41 (Chicago: American Marketing Assn., 1977), p. 417.

9. Lazer and Smallwood, "The Changing Demographics of Women," p. 22.

10. M. Palona and T. Barland, "The Married Professional Women: Study in the Tolerance of Domestication," *Journal of Marriage and the Family,* Vol. 31 (August 1971), p. 535.

11. Lazer and Smallwood, "The Changing Demographics of Women," p. 16.

12. R. Bartos, "The Moving Target: The Impact of Women's Employment on Consumer Behavior," *Journal of Marketing,* Vol. 41 (July 1977), pp. 33-37.

13. L. H. Wartzel, "Young Adults: Single People and Single-Person Households," in *Advances in Consumer Research,* Vol. IV, ed. W. D. Perreault, Jr. (Proceedings of the Seventh Annual Conference of the Association for Consumer Research, 1977), pp. 324-29.

14. K. Satow, "Some Comments on Changing Life Styles among Single Adults," in *Advances in Consumer Research,* Vol. IV, ed. W. D. Perreault, Jr. (Proceedings of the Seventh Annual Conference of the Association for Consumer Research, 1977), pp. 335, 336.

15. Ibid.

16. R. Bartos, "The Consumer View of Advertising—1974," paper from the 1975 Annual Meeting of The American Association of Advertising Agencies (New York: American Association of Advertising Agencies, 1975).

17. Ibid.

18. Marketing Briefs, "New Minority: The 'Average American Family,'" *Marketing News* (February 24, 1978), p. 3.

2 Environmental Influences on Consumer Behavior

The three chapters in this section present an overview of the major environmental influences on consumer behavior. Environmental influences—culture, social class, groups, family—substantially affect consumer behavior. These environmental variables not only influence specific consumer choice but also determine the nature of an individual in ways that influence all decisions of that individual.

These chapters present some of the most important and most interesting, yet often neglected and misunderstood, aspects of the study of consumer behavior. Chapter 4 considers cultural values and norms with emphasis on the importance of values in a cross-cultural setting, both in various nations and in various subcultures.

Chapter 5 addresses the influences that social class and social groups have on consumer behavior. Specific issues are presented such as how important is social class in the American culture, what determines social class membership, how is social class measured, does social class affect consumer behavior, how do groups achieve compliance, and how do groups influence consumer choice.

The final chapter in this section describes family influences on consumer behavior. Families have a substantial influence on consumer behavior and are, in many instances, the actual buying unit. This chapter presents the basic terminology involved in the analysis of family buying and the conclusions suggested by research in family decision making.

Chapter 4 Cultural Influences

Outline

The Nature of Culture

Basic Characteristics of Culture
Culture Is Learned
Culture Is Inculcated
Culture Is a Social Phenomenon
Culture Is Gratifying
Culture is Adaptive

Characteristics of Culture in the United States
Institutions That Affect U.S. Values
Changing Values

Cross-Cultural Analysis of Consumer Behavior
Cross-Cultural Marketing Strategies
Cross-Cultural Marketing Research

The Nature of Subculture
Nationality Subcultures
Religious Subcultures
Geographic Subcultures
Ethnic Subcultures

Summary

Questions and Issues for Discussion

Cases

Key Terms

culture
society
enculturation
acculturation
U.S. values
creative eroticism
cross-cultural analysis
cross-cultural marketing strategies
standardization-localization controversy
subculture
nationality subculture
geographic subculture
ethnic subculture

The shared values of large groups of people influence the means used to satisfy human needs. These values vary substantially among some cultural groupings whereas only inconsequential differences exist among others. For example, research has indicated several differences in the behavior of French and American consumers. Americans are less bound by tradition than the French and, therefore, are more willing to experiment with new products and services.[1] Americans tend to rely more on friends and relatives and on television and print advertising than do the French. Conversely, the French are more likely to notice new products for the first time in the store while passing by than their American counterparts.

Americans are far less willing to save than citizens of any other industrialized nation. The savings rate of Americans, already low, is diminishing, whereas the reverse is true in many other countries. While several tenable explanations can be advanced, it is important that we recognize the impact this has on the consumption behavior of Americans.

This chapter deals with culture and examines the impact of the shared beliefs and values of large groups of people on the behavior of those who are their members. Specifically, these influences are observable in the products made and consumed by various groups of people. Consequently, any thorough study of consumer behavior must include an examination of the effect of large groups on individual decision making. The importance of this kind of group influence is widely accepted in marketing today and has been referred to as *culturalogical,* differentiating it from a psychological orientation that has essentially concentrated on the individual.

The values and influence of smaller groups within the larger culture have been less apparent and less well understood. Nevertheless, these groups, frequently called subcultures, affect consumer decision making and are particularly important in this country because the U.S. population is composed of immigrants and descendants of immigrants from throughout the world. The integrative tendency of cultures that results in similar behavioral patterns is not strong enough in America to produce uniform consuming patterns or responses to all marketers' efforts. Consequently, attention must be paid to the major groups, or subcultures, that comprise the main culture; therefore, an examination of the notion of subculture is included in the second half of this chapter.

The Nature of Culture

In the simplest terms, culture serves an adaptive function; that is, it is a means of helping an individual adapt or cope with the world. A significant part of the importance of culture stems from the influence it has on people's perceptions, attitudes, and values. This leads to the realization that human decision making is greatly affected by the culture in which it operates.

The term "culture" is used to mean the complex set of values, ideas, attitudes, and other meaningful symbols created by humans to shape behavior and the artifacts of that behavior that are transmitted from one generation to the next. Three things should be noted about this definition. First, culture does not refer to instinctive human responses, such as eating when you are hungry. Nor does it include the inventiveness that takes form as one-time solutions to problems, such as automobiles that get better gas mileage. Second, this definition reflects a contemporary view of culture that emphasizes the integrative and learning functions of culture. This definition also stresses the communicative aspect of culture through time, that is, the process of passing on values, beliefs, and artifacts from one generation to the next. Thus, culture can be viewed as the means and methods of coping with the environment that are shared by a large group of people and that are passed from one generation to another. This sharing and then passing on is the result of finding effective means of dealing with common problems and circumstances.

Culture includes both *abstract* and *material elements.* Abstract elements are the values, attitudes, ideas, and personality types, as well as the various combinations of these, such as religion, that can be used to characterize a large group of people. These abstract characteristics are learned over time and are transmitted to succeeding generations. Material elements refer to those objects that are employed by a large group of people in meeting their various needs. As a result, in an advanced society, these take on many different forms. Examples include automobiles, buildings, computers, and advertisements as well as other items that are referred to as the artifacts of a society.

The word *society* was used in the preceding paragraphs to discuss culture, but it was not defined. "Society," as used here, refers to a collection of individuals who share a particular set of symbols and conduct their interpersonal and collective behavior according to the prescriptions of that group of people. Hollander has summarized the relationship between society and culture accordingly: "A culture is a way of life while a society is made up of people who live by its dictates."[2]

The process of absorbing or learning the culture in which one is raised is called *enculturation* or *socialization. Acculturation* refers specifically to the learning of another culture or subculture different from the one in which the person was raised. The social units with which an individual has the most regular and intimate contact include the family, church, and school; these social units have the greatest influence on the cultural values absorbed throughout life. The influence of all other social units is "filtered" by members of the family in the early years of the typical individual. Other human groups, particularly reference groups (which are discussed in the next chapter), are also important transmitters of culture. These groups filter and modify the values of the broader culture to make them consistent with their group values.

Basic Characteristics of Culture

Some people believe the essence of marketing focuses on culture and society because they perceive marketing as the delivery of a standard of living. Certainly those who characterize marketing in this way must be very interested in consumer behavior. Only through studying the consumer's interests and decision-making processes can appropriate goods and services be delivered.

The notion that culture is an important determinant of behavior has caused consumer analysts to examine the fundamental characteristics of culture in order to discover more about its dynamics. Five distinct characteristics, or dimensions, can be identified and described to facilitate understanding culture and its effect on consumer behavior: (1) culture is learned; (2) culture is inculcated; (3) culture is a social phenomenon; (4) culture is gratifying; and (5) culture is adaptive.

Culture Is Learned

Consumer behavior is learned; it is not instinctive. Culture provides the consumer with a framework to recognize a set of stimuli and a set of responses appropriate to those stimuli. For example, consumers are not born with the idea that a hamburger, french fries, and a Coke will satisfy their hunger; they learn it from their culture.

Cultural values learned early in life tend to resist change more strongly than those learned late in life. Fundamental values refer to the ultimate reasons people have for acting as they do; these are intangible and deal with basic aims, aspirations, and ideals. For example, self-oriented values include the right to life and the pursuit of happiness, physical and mental well-being, self-sufficiency, and the right to endeavor to shape one's own life. Once learned and accepted, these values resist change. The appropriate strategy for deeply ingrained, culturally defined behavior is to modify the marketing strategy to reflect the cultural values rather than attempt to modify the culturally determined preferences. It is commonly recognized that, although the family and other social groups contribute most to the socialization process, marketing also can have a significant impact on this process. For instance, there is little doubt that marketing efforts have encouraged the tendency to use whiteness as the primary indicator of the cleanness of laundry.

Culture Is Inculcated

To say that culture is inculcated is simply to say that culture is transmitted from generation to generation. This process is performed mainly by the immediate family, but other groups and institutions contribute to it, also. Ethnic, educational, and religious institutions all participate in the passing on of values, customs, and artifacts from one generation to the next. For example, some religions prohibit the consumption of certain beverages like tea, coffee, and liquor; and, thus, these religious prohibitions have a direct impact on the marketing of such products. The values, norms, and behavioral patterns transmitted are generally idealized. There is, however, considerable disparity between the idealized norm and the norm that is observed in practice. Thus, parents as a rule instill the importance of adhering to laws (idealized norm), yet these same parents may jaywalk, exceed the speed limit, or run a red light. Minor violations of cultural values are permitted, expected, and, occasionally, encouraged, whereas major violations are perceived negatively and are subject to punishment, such as imprisonment.

In a consumer behavior context, such deviations may be less dramatic but, nevertheless, are important to the analyst. Consider the example of a parent who stresses the importance of the performance features of a product, like a stereo, and then obviously buys one because it has a good-looking cabinet. The emphasis on performance characteristics (the idealized norm) is generally more acceptable to society, but this is often not the basis for making a particular purchase decision.

Culture Is a Social Phenomenon

Cultural values, habits, and patterns of behavior are shared by the people living in a particular society. The values consumers have and the consumption behavior they express are group properties; they are not distinctive to the individual consumer. Culture has an effect on all values and behavioral patterns but particularly on those that are basic to social life, such as how to get along with others, the type of food to eat, how to dress, and how to earn a living. The systematic study of culture requires that the marketing strategist focus on groups or segments. Indeed, marketing strategy must be based on assumptions about large numbers of consumers representing sizable market segments. Thus, the planning and directing of marketing operations must be based on similarities of behavior that often result from culturally determined variables.

Culture Is Gratifying

The basic function of culture is to satisfy the needs of the people adhering to its dictates. Only those values, habits, and behavioral patterns that satisfy human needs will be continued through time. Elements within a culture that cease to gratify needs usually become extinguished, at least in the long run. For example, products such as button shoes and hoop skirts are no longer consumed because they do not satisfy consumer needs as well as other styles of the same apparel. The notion that culture reinforces some responses serves as a basis for marketing decision making. Strategists must recognize that the advertising used and the products offered for sale must focus on satisfying needs that society approves.

Culture Is Adaptive

As indicated previously, culture is passed from generation to generation; yet this does not imply that culture is static or endowed with eternal life. Rather, culture adapts to the environment in which it operates and with which it has contact. In the past, cultural change was unbelievably slow. More recently, however, vastly accelerated technological changes and the amazing capabilities of communication are reflected in comparatively rapid cultural adaptation, particularly among the developed nations. For example, consider the speed with which the use of birth control pills and the two-child family have become accepted norms in certain segments of American society. Similarly, the gas-saving economy car, once considered acceptable as a second car, has in a brief time become one of the major product lines for automobile manufacturers.

Characteristics of Culture in the United States

Cultural values in the United States were once thought to be relatively permanent sets of cultural traits transmitted from generation to generation with little alteration. Even though many of these cultural values remain relatively permanent, it is apparent that significant changes in some are occurring at an increasing pace and that the values most in transition have a considerable influence on consumption behavior.

Institutions That Affect U.S. Values

While numerous forces affect values, three institutions in the United States have had a major impact—the family, organized religion, and the schools. These institutions have changed over time and the nature of their influence has been modified.

Family

The relative influence of the family in transmitting American culture has declined somewhat in recent years. The most frequently mentioned reasons for decline in the family's influence on the formation of values include (1) the decrease in parent-child interactions in the formative years from birth to age five, (2) the increasing divorce rate, and (3) the geographical separation of family members. Collectively these changes have resulted in less opportunity for parents to communicate, explain, and justify their values to their children. These changes partially explain why the values of the youthful consumers of the current decade differ from those of their parents.

Religion

Historically, religious institutions in America have played an important role in transmitting basic values from one generation to another. However, there is some indication that church membership and attendance have declined since 1967. There is also considerable evidence that young Americans question the values of organized religion to a greater degree than did the previous generation. If a significant decline in the importance of religious institutions were to take place, the net effect would likely be to establish a more situational or personal set of values, that is, what feels good at a particular time is to be valued or considered appropriate.

Education

Although the importance of the family and organized religion may have diminshed somewhat in shaping values, the part played by educational institutions in this process has increased considerably in recent years. Contributing to this increased influence are (1) the growing enrollments in both preschools and universities during the 1960s and 1970s and (2) the emergence and proliferation of new educational philosophies and techniques. Enrollment in educational institutions began to decline during the latter half of the 1970s and predictions indicate that this decline will continue for nearly two decades. Nevertheless, educational institutions will continue to be a major force affecting U.S. values. Despite declining enrollments, educational institutions have increased their influence on values because of changes in emphasis on learning techniques and teaching methods. The previous emphasis on description and memorization has been replaced by analytical approaches that stress questioning the old and then forming new approaches and solutions. The questioning of traditional "right and wrong" has carried over into everyday life. This trend is exemplified by the increasing number of medical malpractice suits, the growing number of consumer-oriented organizations, and the increasing unionization of white-collar workers. Thus, to an increasing extent, consumers' minds do not operate in black and white but rather in the more realistic and complicated nuances of full color.

Changing Values

Modifications in values emanating from changes in major institutions and other cultural forces in the United States are occurring more rapidly today than they did in the past. Consumer analysts not only must identify these emerging values but also be sensitive to the impact these changes have on consumption behavior. Information on emerging values and their impact will increasingly affect the strategic planning of business organizations, the kinds of goods and services produced, the delivery system used, and virtually every aspect of an organization's operation. Consider the impact of the changes in the following values: youthfulness, religion, creative eroticism, and leisure time.

Youthfulness

The emphasis on youthfulness in recent years reflects a major change in American values and is likely to continue to be important. Individuals, groups, and organizations have and will continue to rely on the creativity of the young to deal with all types of problems. Although not their exclusive domain, the young have more opportunities than their predecessors did to acquire an education and develop creativity. Consequently, the young increasingly are given the responsibilities for running corporations, government agencies, and society in general. Amercian society has placed so much emphasis on youth that many people in all age groups want to be perceived as youthful. Marketing strategists have recognized this and have successfully used a youth-oriented theme to promote products such as clothing, automobiles, home furnishings, and personal grooming items. For example, in attempting to attract the car buyer who is under 30 years of age, a major automobile manufacturer successfully introduced a sporty, small car by emphasizing auto racing and by using young, attractive people in the ads. The manufacturer sold a lot of cars, but the age of the typical buyer was 46 and not 26. Thus, although the youth market in the United States is large in itself, the "youthfulness" influence on the purchase behavior of other age groups is even greater.

Religion

American values have long been shaped by institutionalized religion, particularly the Christian and Jewish faiths. One example of this influence is the impact of the puritan ethic, which dictated that individual and societal needs could only be satisfied through hard work and the accumulation of wealth. In recent years, this value has become less influential, and a movement toward a theology of pleasure has begun. This modern view emphasizes a new type of individuality and release from prohibitions. The concern for pleasure is consistent with a movement toward greater affluence, but until recently this has been constrained by the dominance of the puritan ethic.

Marketing strategists have found such changing conceptions of religious values to be important in facilitating the use of new tactics. Colors and designs can be bright and sensuous; cosmetics and grooming aids can emphasize pleasure of the body; the use of credit can be stimulated with appeals to enjoy products now and pay later; even banks can throw off their stodgy, conservative images with brightly colored logos.

Creative Eroticism

Creative eroticism has emerged as the result of changing American values and has had a significant impact on marketing strategy. Creative eroticism refers to the transition from rigid prohibitions on fun with sex to the present release of such inhibitions. The response of some marketing strategists to this new freedom has become quite apparent. For example, because advertising media have dropped many restrictions about what can be shown, some ad agencies have become innovative in developing sensual themes. The results of these changes are illustrated by the Noxema girl who suggests that the shaver "take it all off," the girl in the Serta mattress ad who seductively demonstrates the comfort enjoyed from that product, and Pete Rose modeling colorful jockey shorts.

The Leisure Life

The increasing importance placed on leisure also reflects a change in American values and has caused some to label the hard-working, industrious person a "workaholic." The growing interest in leisure or recreation has been identified by many as the underlying factor in stimulating the demand for huge quantities of consumer goods. Indeed, American consumers spend approximately 16 percent of their disposable personal income on leisure goods and activities. In order to respond appropriately to this growing interest in leisure, marketing managers must answer questions like: How many hours of each day are allocated among work, nondiscretionary activities such as eating and sleeping, and discretionary activities such as playing tennis and watching television? What products are purchased for use during each type of activity? How much will consumers pay for time-saving products in order to increase the time spent in discretionary activities?

A number of research projects are maintained by business organizations in an attempt to monitor changing values as they affect consumer choices. The most comprehensive of these is called "Monitor" and is maintained through annual surveys of 2,500 persons in a national study by Daniel Yankelovich, Inc. The nature of Monitor and its reasons for existence are described as follows:

> . . . Monitor is a business service designed to provide marketers of consumer goods and services with annual statistical information on the nature of social change in the United States, along with a picture of the way changing social values are affecting people's behavior as consumers. In recent years, marketers have become increasingly sensitized to the importance of changing *social values* as a major influence on consumer behavior. Monitor is a unique service which provides empirically-derived, statistical data on social change, with particular emphasis on how changing social values are impacting on consumer behavior.[3]

Table 4.1, though not comprehensive, identifies a number of important, changing social values that must be taken into account by consumer analysts. In general many of the values appear to be initiated by youth, especially upscale, high-income, educated youth. Furthermore, in several of these trends the initiating force is most often upscale young women. The group *most resistant* to these new values appears to be downscale, older people, especially men. Yankelovich concludes that many of the new values are accepted first by young upscale persons and then picked up by young downscale consumers. Older upscale people then move toward these new values well ahead of the older downscale groups. Thus, instead of moving from older groups in a society and trickling down to younger groups, it appears that social values now *trickle up from young to old* with the upscale (in affluence and education) being the most receptive in both age groups.

Table 4.1
Trends in U.S. Values

Trend	Manifestation
New romanticism	Desire to restore sentimentality, mystery and adventure to life.
Novelty and change	Continuous search for new experiences and avoidance of sameness and repetition.
Sensuousness	Emphasis on sensory experiences— touching, feeling, smelling.
Mysticism	Search for new modes of spiritual experiences and beliefs.
Introspection	Search for self-understanding.
Physical self-enhancement	Expending time, resources, and effort to maintain or enhance one's physical appearance and well-being.
Personalization	Desire to express one's individuality.
Physical health and well-being	Attention to diet, weight, and various aspects of physical well-being.

Trend	Manifestation	
Personal creativity	Widespread creativity in a variety of activities, hobbies, and uses of leisure time.	**Table 4.1 (Continued)**
Meaningful work	Concern for work that is challenging and socially beneficial.	
Rejection of authority	Reluctance to accept the direction of authority.	
Female careerism	Rejection of homemaking as the only career choice for women and increase in number of women in the labor force.	
Living for today	Rejection of traditional values of planning and saving.	
Blurring of the sexes	Decline in the traditional distinctions between men and women.	
Liberal sexual attitudes	Relaxation of sexual prohibitions and de-emphasis on "virtue," especially among women.	
Away from self-improvement	Rejecting the "work ethic" with a regard for "living what you are."	
Return to nature	Concern for the natural and rejection of artificial ingredients.	

Source: Reprinted with permission from Daniel Yankelovich, *The Yankelovich Monitor* (New York: Daniel Yankelovich, 1974), p. 1.

Cross-Cultural Analysis of Consumer Behavior

Cross-cultural analysis—the comparison of similarities and differences among countries in the behavioral and material aspects of their cultures—is vital to the effective development of foreign markets. The perils of cross-cultural ignorance are aptly illustrated by the Western-oriented tobacco company that attempted to introduce filtered cigarettes to an Asian country. Despite warnings of impending failure, the company's managers set up manufacturing and distribution facilities. Unfortunately, the management failed to consider the value placed upon sanitation in the country, the literacy rate, and the short life expectancy. The product was a dismal failure and the loss incurred by the company was considerable.[4]

The failure to recognize differences in information processing among cultural groups can lead to many blunders in advertising and marketing programs where managers are dealing with a culture other than ones with which they are familiar. Colgate-Palmolive introduced Cue toothpaste in French-speaking countries, not knowing that "cue" was a pornographic word in French. General Mills attempted to enter the British cereal market with a package showing an "all-American" youngster. This did not appeal to a culture that holds a more formal view of the role of children. Goodyear Tire and Rubber demonstrated the strength of its "3T" tire cord in the United States by showing a steel chain breaking. When this demonstration was to be included in German advertising, however, it was perceived as uncomplimentary to steel chain manufacturers and regarded as improper.

In Quebec, a U.S. manufacturer of canned fish attempted to market that product through an advertising program that showed a woman in shorts, golfing with her husband, and intending to serve canned fish for the evening meal. The program was a failure. Anthropology studies disclosed that all three of these activities violated the norms of that culture.

Britain's BSR Ltd found that, when it entered the Japanese market, it had to adjust to more than Japan's electric voltage. Instruction manuals, for example, had to be completely rewritten, not just translated, because the Japanese felt that Western manuals were too factual and too cold. The chief executive officer of BSR Ltd's Japanese division observed that Japanese manuals thank the customer for buying the product, describe where the wood came from, how the electronic components were made, and what happens when you turn the product on.[5] BSR Ltd also discovered that products had to have two packages in Japan, one for shipping and one for point-of-purchase display.

Other companies have discovered that marketing products in international markets required some adjustment in their marketing program. Kentucky Fried Chicken found out the hard way that in Japan everything starts in Tokyo. Only after Kentucky Fried Chicken was accepted in Tokyo was satisfactory progress made toward its current level of 150 outlets with sales of over $16 million. Estée Lauder, a New York cosmetic company, found that cosmetics could be successfully marketed to Japanese men only when separate cosmetic departments were established for men and women. Prior to establishing separate departments, 70 percent of the purchases of its men's line were to women, whereas, after the switch, 70 percent were to men; hence, sales rose sharply.

Numerous experiences similar to those presented above have convinced most marketing strategists that executives with cross-cultural competence or those who are foreign nationals are a necessary requirement for the successful development of international markets. This has become increasingly apparent as greater reliance has been placed upon global markets to assure profitability. Consequently, the following conditions have been identified as essential to the successful development of foreign markets:

1. sensitivity to cultural differences;

2. cultural empathy, or the ability to "understand the inner logic and coherence of other ways of life, plus the restraint not to judge them as bad because they are different from one's own ways";

3. ability to withstand the initial culture shock, or "the sum of sudden jolts that awaits the unwary American abroad";

4. ability to cope with and to adapt to foreign environments without "going native."[6]

Cross-Cultural Marketing Strategies

Marketing on a global or international level has increased in importance in recent years, causing a rising concern about the policy of developing strategies and programs that are appropriate across national boundaries. To accomplish such an objective requires much more attention to analysis of the culture which provides the environment for the success or failure of such marketing strategies.

Despite the dominant views listed above, in recent years some marketing strategists have become convinced that it may be possible to standardize marketing programs in a number of areas throughout the world. Although research and practice have identified many obstacles to such standardization, the interest in it continues to increase. The following statement represents the rationale developed by one marketing analyst to support the position that consumers are basically the same. It also illustrates the kind of logic used to encourage this point of view.

> The desire to be beautiful is universal. Such appeals as "mother and child," "freedom from pain," "glow of health" know no boundaries.
>
> In a sense, the young women in Tokyo and the young women in Berlin are sisters not only "under the skin" but on their skin and on their lips and fingernails, and even their hairstyles. If they could, the girls of Moscow would follow suit; and some of them do.[7]

Thus, some contend that consumer behavior theory has universal application and that strategy developed from this theory can be used in any cultural setting. However, empirical research indicates that nearly two thirds of multinational firms find it necessary to employ marketing strategies and programs that reflect local differences. The more emphasis put on cultural similarities, the more likely firms are to emphasize a common strategy rather than a market-to-market approach. In a study of 27 multinational firms operating in the United States and Europe—including General Foods, Nestle, Coca-Cola, Proctor & Gamble, Unilever, and Revlon—Sorenson and Wiechmann found that 63 percent of the total marketing programs were rated as "highly standardized."[8] The results of this study show that, as one would expect, the greater the similarity between countries, the higher the percentage of the marketing program that can be standardized. These authors concluded by describing the importance of cross-cultural (or "cross-border") analysis:

> ... managements of multinationals should give high priority to developing their ability to conduct *systematic cross-border analysis,* if they are not already doing so. Such analysis can help management avoid the mistake of standardizing when markets are significantly different. At the same time, systematic cross-border analysis can help avoid the mistake of excessive custom-tailoring when markets are sufficiently similar to make standardized programs feasible.[9]

A realistic assessment of the standardization-localization controversy is that the management of a firm must be adaptive to some elements of the marketing program that are localized and to others that are standardized. Marketing strategy which is not based on an understanding of cultural realities will have unpredictable success patterns.[10] Yet, there is ample evidence to show that marketing strategies, which are applicable worldwide, can be developed.[11] One study shows that about two thirds of international firms emphasize a localized, decentralized policy.[12] There is a growing number of research and analysis reports indicating that the most effective results are achieved with a high degree of sensitivity to global cultures by home-office executives and a high degree of responsibility and executive flexibility at the local (national) or decentralized levels of management.[13] A firm which is highly centralized in its global operations has been described by some researchers as having an ethnocentric orientation, while a decentralized firm is one having a "regiocentric" or geocentric orientation and that the desirability of the particular orientation depends on the size of the firm, experience in a given market, the size of the potential market, and the type of product and its cultural dependency.[14]

Cross-Cultural Marketing Research

Marketing researchers have begun to conduct cross-cultural studies, but the practice is still embryonic. The previous lack of cross-cultural studies is probably due to lack of familiarity with cross-cultural research methods, the expense of such studies for academic researchers, and the tendency for United States multinational business firms to spend only a minimum amount on marketing research when entering foreign markets compared to their expenditures on domestic markets.[15]

British marketing researchers appear to have a longer history of cross-cultural research and their findings have been tested for applicability to U.S. markets. Ehrenberg and Goodhardt report that mathematical models of repeat-buying habits developed from data on British consumers yield useful results for United States purchasers.[16] This study is important because it lends credence to the belief that consumer models and theories are applicable on a worldwide basis. Other cross-cultural studies have been conducted by Dunn,[17] using the case method of comparison, and Lorimor and Dunn, using the semantic differential and other measures of advertising effectiveness.[18]

In a pioneering cross-cultural study, Sethi found four clusters which he labeled (1) production and transportation, (2) personal consumption, (3) trade, and (4) health and education. After the variables were grouped, countries were classified into clusters according to their scores on the clustered variables. Seven clusters were formed from the 86 countries. For example, countries such as Nigeria, Sudan, Dahomey, Tanzania, and South Vietnam were part of one cluster; Syria, Thailand, United Arab Republic, and the Philippines were some of the countries in another cluster. The United States could not be grouped with any of the other countries.[19] While this study is embryonic and does not yield data corresponding to consumer decisions or marketing strategy, it does provide the basis for much additional development potentially valuable in understanding ways of grouping markets together for common marketing programs.[20]

It is sometimes difficult to overcome language problems in cross-cultural marketing; therefore, a number of techniques have been developed to achieve cross-cultural equivalence in language. A literal translation or a translation by someone who is not familiar with the culture of the language as well as its literal meaning may result in serious marketing mistakes. An example was a widely publicized situation in Canada in which Hunt-Wesson attempted to use the "Big John" family brand name by translating it into French as "Gros Jos," which is a colloquial French expression denoting a woman with big breasts. The incident caused *Playboy* magazine to award its annual "Booby Boo Boo Award" to the company.

When it is desired to use the same name throughout the world rather than translate a brand name, careful research and analysis may determine a brand name that can be used widely without translation. Walter Margulies suggests the following questions be researched or analyzed in the attempt to find an English name that can be used on a cross-cultural basis:

1. Does the English name of the product have another meaning, perhaps unfavorable, in one or more of the countries where it is to be marketed?

2. Can the English name be pronounced everywhere? For example,

Spanish and some other languages lack a "K" in their alphabets, an initial letter in many popular U.S. brand names.

3. Is the name close to that of a foreign brand or does it duplicate another product sold in English-speaking countries?

4. If the product name is distinctly American, will national pride and prejudice work against the acceptance of the product?[21]

The most useful and straightforward technique for overcoming language problems is *back-translation*. In the back-translation procedure, a message (a word or a series of words) is translated from its original language to the translated language and back to its original language by a number of translators. This process is repeated several times with the translated versions being interchanged with the original among the translators. The purpose of the iterations is an attempt to achieve conceptual equivalence in meaning by controlling the various translation biases of the translators.[22]

To conclude this section on cross-cultural marketing research, it is apparent that in some instances, marketing strategists are confronted with cultures quite similar and, in others, with cultures very different. In too many unfortunate cases, what has "worked" in the United States has been applied to a foreign market without understanding if the cultural conditions were the same or not. A marketing strategist can improve the prediction of success by a careful analysis of the cultural conditions in the existing market, followed by another careful analysis of the cultural conditions in the prospective market. Where differences are observed, adjustment in the strategy employed can be undertaken. An outline for systematically analyzing the cultural determinants of success in each market is provided in Table 4.2. This outline is designed to be used either with formal research methods (such as those described above) or, if research is not feasible, as an outline for critical thinking and analysis in the design of global strategy.[23]

---

1. *Determine relevant motivations in the culture*
   What needs are fulfilled with this product in the minds of members of the culture? How are these needs presently fulfilled? Do members of this culture readily recognize these needs?

Table 4.2
Outline of Cross-cultural Analysis of Consumer Behavior

**Table 4.2
(Continued)**

2. *Determine characteristic behavior patterns*
   What patterns are characteristic of purchasing behavior? What forms of division of labor exist within the family structure? How frequently are products of this type purchased? What size packages are normally purchased? Do any of these characteristic behaviors conflict with the behavior expected for this product? How strongly ingrained are the behavior patterns that conflict with those needed for distribution of this product?

3. *Determine what broad cultural values are relevant to this product*
   Are there strong values concerning work, morality, religions, family relations, and so on, that relate to this product? Does this product connote attributes that are in conflict with these cultural values? Can conflicts with values be avoided by changing the product? Are there positive values in this culture with which the product might be identified?

4. *Determine characteristic forms of decision making*
   Do members of the culture display a studied approach to decisions concerning innovations or an impulsive approach? What is the form of the decision process? Upon what information sources do members of the culture rely? Do members of the culture tend to be rigid or flexible in the acceptance of new ideas? What criteria do they use in evaluating alternatives?

5. *Evaluate promotion methods appropriate to the culture*
   What role does advertising occupy in the culture? What themes, words, or illustrations are taboo? What language problems exist in present markets that cannot be translated into this culture? What types of salespeople are accepted by members of the culture? Are such people available?

6. *Determine appropriate institutions for this product in the minds of consumers*
   What types of retailers and intermediary institutions are available? What services do these institutions offer that are expected by the consumer? What alternatives are available for obtaining services needed for the product but not offered by existing institutions? How are various types of retailers regarded by consumers? Will changes in the distribution structure be readily accepted?

The Nature of Subculture

A culture represents a loose agreement on the values, behavior patterns, and symbols it upholds. There are, however, smaller groups within the larger society that have modified these ways of dealing with the environment and with persons enough to be at variance with the general living patterns. These smaller groups are referred to as *subcultures.* More specifically, subcultural influences refer to the norms and values of subgroups within the larger or national culture. Individual consumers may be influenced only slightly by membership in specific subgroups or the subgroups may be the dominant force on the personality and life-style of the consumer.

Some products may be favored specifically by the persons in a particular subculture. The purchase of squid is usually made by those who enjoy the finer points of Italian cuisine, while the appeal of sauna equipment is most likely to be found among those of Finnish descent. However, because sufficient similarities exist among various subcultures, many products are commonly accepted. The appeals of quick-serve eating establishments and motel facilities demonstrate this kind of general acceptance.

Among subcultures there are a number of points of commonness that permit grouping of identifiable characteristics. Four types of subcultures are described below: nationality, religious, geographic, and ethnic. Ethnic subcultures, particularly the black subculture, are given a somewhat more extended analysis in this section because of their importance in contemporary America.

Nationality Subcultures

Nearly every metropolitan area has within its boundaries groups that are relatively homogeneous with respect to nationality. These areas frequently have names, such as Little Italy, Little Poland, or Chinatown, and often distinctive products and/or consumption patterns become associated with the residents. Many times the media, primarily newspapers and radio, develop programs for these markets. Marketing efforts focused on ethnic groups are essential for the success of many firms in metropolitan areas. For example, General Motors is reported to be more successful than its competitors in New York City because of its strong penetration into ethnic markets through a dealer organization built upon subculture realities.

Religious Subcultures

Religious subcultures may exert considerable influence on those members who choose to conform closely to group norms. Mormons, for example, refrain from consuming tobacco, liquor, and certain other stimulants; Christian Scientists restrict their search for information and use of medicines; Seventh Day Adventists abstain from eating meat; many Jews purchase kosher foods on a regular basis; Christians from some denominations avoid ostentatious displays of wealth; and the Amish avoid mechanized life-styles and emphasis on individual personal appearance. Some groups identified with the Jesus movement are creating a subculture based upon emulation of first-century Christianity in contrast to the contemporary practice of conspicuous consumption. It is obvious from these few examples that certain subcultural beliefs and values actually restrict the market for a number of products.

Many conditions can cause the influence of the subculture to decline. Increased mobility, education, and income provide challenges to traditional activities and affect behavior. However, the basic values of a subculture may continue to have an influence on decision making for some time.

Geographic Subcultures

Subcultures develop within different geographic areas of a nation. In the United States, people living in the Southwest appear to have a characteristic style of life that emphasizes the casual form of dress, outdoor entertaining, and unique forms of recreation. Decision making in the Southwest may also be less rigid and perhaps more innovative than the conservative, inhibited attitudes toward new products and programs that supposedly characterize the Midwest. The climate and religious and nationality influences may be highly interrelated with geographic influences, however.

One of the largest and most distinct subcultures in North America is the French-Canadian area of Canada. This geographic subculture accounts for approximately 25 percent of the Canadian population, income, and retail sales. A key concern among marketers is whether or not the same marketing programs can effectively serve both the French-Canadian and English-Canadian consumer. There is some indication, for example, that French Canadians react more to the source of an advertisement than do English Canadians, who are more message oriented.[24] This understanding of the difference in the perceptual processes of these two subcultures indicates the potential for increasing the effectiveness of marketing efforts.

Ethnic Subcultures

The fourth type of subculture is based on ethnic or racial differences and, as mentioned earlier, is given a more extended analysis because of the importance it has in contemporary America. Ethnic subcultures, particularly the black subculture, have been the focus of numerous research efforts in recent years. The black subculture is not synonymous with black skin color. Rather, the black subculture refers to the common heritage of slavery, a history of income deprivation, a shared history of discrimination and suffering, limited housing opportunities, and denial of participation in many aspects of the predominant culture. Consequently, blacks raised as part of the dominant white society may have no more appreciation of the black subculture than any other member of the dominant group.

Although research suggests that there is greater similarity in the purchase patterns of black consumers than there is among whites, black consumption patterns appear to be heterogeneous enough to justify the use of segmentation strategies similar to those used in white markets. For example, there is a growing black middle class, many of whom are well-educated professionals earning sizable incomes and living in quiet suburban neighborhoods. However, the number and purchasing power of black consumers limit the feasibility of using extensive segmentation strategies. Moreover, the processes of acculturation and assimilation are likely to reduce the distinctiveness of the black subculture in future years. This is particularly true if black consumers continue their move toward the acceptance of white middle class values. Even though blacks remain at a disadvantage in their striving toward the goals dictated by these white values, they nevertheless could continue to aspire to achieve them.[25]

Distinctive Characteristics of the Black Subculture

The black subculture has a number of distinctive characteristics that influence the behavior of its members. The major ones are (1) low income, (2) differential family characteristics, and (3) being subject to racial discrimination.

Low income. Members of the black subculture are frequently perceived, and justly so, to have low incomes. In fact, while 10 percent of white households have incomes below the poverty level, more than 30 percent of black households have this unfortunate distinction. Table 4.3 shows the median family income of black families in 1975 to be $9,321 compared to $14,268 for white families. More dramatic perhaps is the proportion of black consumers who live below the poverty level as defined by the U.S. Department of Commerce. As is indicated in Table 4.4, 29.3 percent of all black families were below the poverty level in 1975 compared to 9.7 percent of white families. The differences in income are not attributable only to differences in amount of formal education, because in 1975, 39.3 percent of white families with four or more years of college were in the over $25,000 income category while only 29.4 percent of black families with four years of college were in that category. Such extensive relative deprivation has a direct effect on the values transmitted to all members of the subculture.

Table 4.3
Median Family Income of Black and White Families, 1950 and 1975

	Median Family Income	
	1950	1975
White families	$3,445	$14,268
Black families	1,869	9,321

Source: U.S. Bureau of the Census, *Current Population Reports*, Series P-60, No. 108.

Table 4.4
Persons below the Poverty Level (United States 1960–1975, selected years)

Race	1960 Number below Poverty Level (Millions)	1960 Percent below Poverty Level	1965 Number below Poverty Level (Millions)	1965 Percent below Poverty Level	1970 Number below Poverty Level (Millions)	1970 Percent below Poverty Level	1975 Number below Poverty Level (Millions)	1975 Percent below Poverty Level
White	28.3	18	22.5	13	17.5	9.9	17.8	9.7
Black and other races	11.5	56	10.7	47	7.9	32.0	8.1	29.3
Total	39.9	22	33.2	17	24.3	12.6	25.9	12.3

Note: The poverty threshold for a nonfarm family of four was $2,973 in 1959, $3,968 in 1970, and $5,500 in 1975.

Source: U.S. Department of Commerce, *Current Population Reports*, Series P–20.

Table 4.5
**The Changing Pyramid
of Black Family Income**

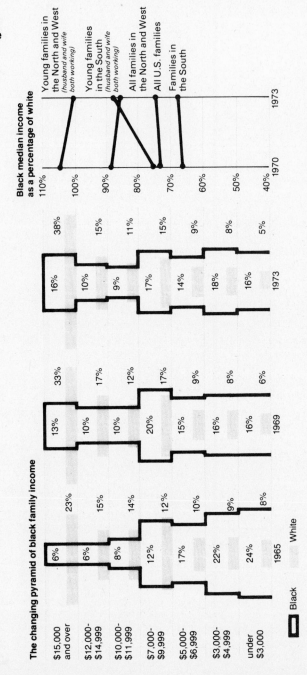

The changing pyramid of black family income

	1965	1969	1973
$15,000 and over	6% / 23%	13% / 33%	16% / 38%
$12,000-$14,999	6% / 15%	10% / 17%	10% / 15%
$10,000-$11,999	8% / 14%	10% / 12%	9% / 11%
$7,000-$9,999	12% / 12%	20% / 17%	17% / 15%
$5,000-$6,999	17% / 10%	15% / 9%	14% / 9%
$3,000-$4,999	22% / 9%	16% / 8%	18% / 8%
under $3,000	24% / 8%	16% / 6%	16% / 5%

■ Black   □ White

Black median income as a percentage of white

1970 — 1973

- Young families in the North and West *(husband and wife both working)*
- Young families in the South *(husband and wife both working)*
- All families in the North and West
- All U.S. families
- Families in the South

110%
100%
90%
80%
70%
60%
50%
40%

Source: U.S. Department of Commerce, Bureau of the Census. Reprinted from "Black America: Still Waiting for Full Membership," *Fortune* (April 1975), p. 162.

It is important to note that, although a predominant cultural fact is income deprivation, there are significant numbers of black consumers who are in middle or upper income groups. Table 4.5 shows the distribution of income for white and black families, revealing 16 percent of American black families with incomes over $15,000 (compared to 38 percent of white families).[26] In spite of increases during the 1960s, however, black families were hit harder by the recessions of the 1970s and much progress was slowed because black families are more likely to be unemployed during recessions than are white families.

Family characteristics. Systematic comparisons of black and white families have indicated that black families are considerably less stable. The traditional indicators of family stability are the proportion living with their spouse, the proportion of illegitimate births, premarital conceptions, and children living with both parents. As would be expected, family stability affects occupational success. A study by the U.S. Department of Labor concluded:

> At the heart of the deterioration of the fabric of Negro society is the deterioration of the Negro family. . . .
> There is probably no single fact of Negro American life so little understood by whites. . . . It is more difficult, however, for whites to perceive the effect that three centuries of exploitation have had on the fabric of Negro society itself. Here the consequences of the historic injustices done to Negro Americans are silent and hidden from view. But here is where the true injury has occurred; unless this damage is repaired, all the effort to end discrimination and poverty and injustice will come to little.[27]

The diversity of some family characteristics of the black subculture can influence their selection and use of products. Conditions such as the high proportion of female-headed households or the large extended network of familial interactions can have a great impact on family consumption. Of course, it must be remembered that some groups of black consumers have family characteristics comparable to society in general. This is particularly true of the growing black middle class referred to earlier.

Racial discrimination. Racial discrimination directed toward the black subculture has been so massive and enduring that it must be considered in the analysis of consumer behavior. Consider, for example, the substantial impact that forced housing conditions has had on the consumption of other goods and services. In some cities, the containment of blacks in a limited number of neighborhoods has had a direct effect on the stores they shop in and the variety of goods purchased.

Of course, discrimination has taken on other forms that shape consumer behavior. For example, because of the location of most public golf courses and the restrictive membership policies of many private clubs, most blacks never have become interested in golf. Consequently, black consumers have not represented an important market segment for golf equipment.

Black consumption patterns. The black subculture results in significant and direct influences on the consumption patterns of black consumers. Research to date indicates that the similarities between black and white consumption behavior are much greater than the differences, but there are some significant differences. In the following pages, the distinctive aspects of the black subculture with respect to search, alternative evaluation, and choice are described.

Search.

1. Black consumers appear to be reached more effectively by general media for products used by both black and white consumers and by black-oriented media for products specifically directed to black consumers.[28]

2. The use of black models in advertising did not increase in the period of 1946 to 1965 (although the social status of blacks in ads has increased) but the proportion of blacks in ads did increase (from 4 percent to 13 percent) from 1967 to 1974.[29]

3. Black consumers react more favorably to advertisements with all black models or integrated models than to advertisements with all white models.[30] Whites in these same studies appear to react to black models as favorably or more so than to white models, although this varies by product category[31] and by amount of prejudice.[32] Black consumers under the age of 30 appear to react unfavorably to advertisements with integrated settings.[33]

4. Black consumers appear to respond (in recall and attitude shift) more positively to advertisements than do white consumers.[34]

5. Black consumers listen to radio more than whites, particularly in the evenings and on weekends, although blacks listen to FM radio less than whites.[35]

6. Black television viewers dislike programs emphasizing white-oriented subjects such as families, organizations, and similar topics and watch more on the weekends in contrast to whites' higher viewing during the week.[36]

7. Participation of blacks in social organizations is higher than that of whites with comparable socioeconomic characteristics, especially in the lowest income groups. Blacks are more likely than whites to belong to church and political groups and equally likely to belong to civic groups.[37]

Alternative evaluation.

1. Blacks save more out of a given income than do whites with the same incomes.[38] Blacks use fewer savings and insurance services, however, and end up with less total financial resources than white families of equivalent income and tend to use the less advantageous types of financial services with the end result that the savings approach of blacks tends to widen the gap of well-being between black and white households.[39] The use of checking accounts by blacks is almost half the rate of use by white families.[40]

2. Blacks spend more for clothing and non-automobile transportation; less for food, housing, medical care, and automobile transportation; and equivalent amounts for recreation and leisure, home furnishings, and equipment than comparable levels of whites.[41]

3. Blacks tend to own more large cars, and perhaps more luxury cars and fewer foreign cars. Ownership of large cars may be required because of the larger size of black families and the need for more pooled transportation.[42]

4. Blacks appear to be more loyal to product brands than equivalent whites.[43]

5. Black families purchase more milk and soft drinks, less tea and coffee, and more liquor than white families. In 1962, blacks accounted for almost one half of all rum consumption in the United States, 41 percent of all gin, over 50 percent of all Scotch whiskies, and over 77 percent of the Canadian whiskies.[44]

6. Blacks spend more time in commuting to work, travel longer distances, and have lower per capita consumption of automobiles than whites.[45]

Choice processes.

1. Black consumers appear to have more awareness of both private and national brands than white consumers and to be better informed about prices than white counterparts.[46]

2. Black consumers appear to respond as well to package design (for beer) designed for white consumers as to packages designed specifically for black consumers.[47]

3. Black consumers tend not to shop by phone or mail order as much as white consumers.[48]

4. Black grocery consumers tend to make frequent trips to neighborhood stores. This may be due to inadequate refrigeration and storage and lack of transportation that would allow carrying large amounts of groceries.[49]

5. Black consumers tend to shop at discount stores, as opposed to department stores, more than do comparable white consumers.[50]

6. Black consumers tend to be unhappier with supermarket facilities and functions than are white consumers (with complaints including poor prices, poor cleanliness, crowded conditions, poor displays, and unfriendly employees).[51]

7. Black consumers place more emphasis on convenience, shopping location, price, quality, and service than on the appeal of buying at black-owned stores, although younger segments of the black community place more emphasis on buying from black-owned firms.[52]

8. Black consumers tend to "shop around" less than white consumers.[53]

A number of studies have been conducted to determine if our retail system discriminates on the basis of ethnic or income characteristics of consumers. The conclusion that seems to be emerging is that retailers generally do not discriminate among buyers on these bases. It has been shown that chain supermarkets do not charge higher prices in the ghetto but, in fact, may charge lower prices about as often as they do higher prices.[54] Sexton found that the costs of operation were actually higher in city areas than in suburban areas and slightly higher in black areas than in white areas but that prices charged were the same in all stores, thus creating a situation whereby suburban residents are actually subsidizing the losses in city areas.[55] In a study of appliance buying, discrimination was not found,[56] nor was it found in a study of mobile home buying;[57] and among automobile salesmen, a pattern was found of charging higher prices to affluent persons.[58]

Even though marketing institutions are not discriminating overtly, this does not guarantee that the poor and ethnic subcultures do not pay more. The shopping behavior of those consumers may create disadvantages that often stem from the environment. In a major study of this problem, Alexis found that poor consumers who shopped in supermarkets were not paying higher prices than more affluent consumers, but that a higher proportion of the poor were shopping in neighborhood, independent stores which charge higher prices than the supermarkets.[59] Most of the studies on this subject have revealed a pattern of smaller, less ably managed, less desirable stores in neighborhoods where poor consumers predominate. Also, consumers may have less access to transportation, less confidence in dealing with retailers outside the neighborhood, less access to credit outside the neighborhood, and other characteristics contributing to problems in purchasing choices. These phenomena may lead to consumer dissatisfaction and unfavorable perceptions that present a substantial public-policy problem in addition to the physical and economic problems.[60]

Summary

Culture can be defined as the complex set of values, ideas, attitudes, and other meaningful symbols created by humans to shape behavior and the artifacts of human behavior, all of which are transmitted from one generation to the next. It includes abstract elements, such as values and attitudes, as well as material elements, such as automobiles, buildings, or other artifacts of a society. Culture has five distinct characteristics. It is learned as opposed to being instinctive. It is transmitted from generation to generation. Cultural values, habits, and patterns of behavior are shaped by people in a society. Culture's basic function is to satisfy the needs of the people. Culture adapts to the environment in which it operates.

American values have undergone some significant changes, and the effect on consumer behavior has been substantial. Changes in three major institutions—the family, organized religion, and education—have instigated these value changes. Four areas illustrate the result of changing American values: Americans of all ages desire to be perceived as youthful; the impact of traditional religious beliefs is decreasing significantly; creative eroticism is met with less and less resistance; and living the leisure life is growing in popularity.

Cross-cultural analysis of similarities and differences is vital to the effective development of foreign markets. Executives who are competent in this area and can recognize the efficacy of a standardized strategy or the need for a localized one are a requirement for a firm's successful development of foreign markets. This chapter presents an outline to assist the marketer in analyzing cross-cultural consumer behavior.

Subcultures are small groups of people within the larger society who have adopted ways of dealing with the environment and with people that are different from the general living pattern. Major types of subcultures are nationality, religious, geographic, and ethnic. The black subculture is particularly important to contemporary America and is characterized by low income, differential family characteristics, and vulnerability to racial discrimination. Differences in black and white consumption patterns are noted with respect to search, alternative evaluation, and choice.

The low-income market recently has been the subject of studies. Although evidence suggests that retailers do not discriminate between buyers on the basis of income or ethnic characteristics, disadvantages—such as lack of transportation and credit—place low-income consumers in situations where they may indeed pay more for goods and services than do the affluent.

Questions and Issues for Discussion

1. Culture is something over which marketers have no control; therefore, the marketing manager's task is to identify basic cultural

values and consumption patterns in light of the products his or her firm distributes. Evaluate this statement.

2. Faced with an annual inflation rate of 50 percent and banks that are reluctant to provide consumer financing for big-ticket items, Brazilians are turning to buying clubs called *consorcios*. The 120 members in each club pool an amount of money each month so that enough is collected to purchase, say, two cars every month. A lottery is then held and two winners receive the cars. Everyone keeps making payments, and lotteries are held for 60 months until enough cars are purchased to satisfy all members. Eventually, then, the club subsidizes the purchases so that the individual members can avoid credit problems and interest charges. Based on your understanding of increased attention toward leisure activities and "buy now, pay later" attitudes of Americans, how would you evaluate the possiblity of aircraft-buying clubs in the U.S.?

3. A door-to-door cosmetic company in the U.S. which has, in the past, designed products solely for American use is now eyeing foreign markets. Although the desire to be beautiful may be universal, what possible problems might the company encounter if it were to use the same marketing strategy overseas as it uses in the U.S.?

4. Sperry Remington Consumer Products has recently begun national distribution of an electric shaver designed specifically for black men's beards. The shaver is priced at $39.80 to $49.95. What should the company know about the black subculture in order to create effective advertising, media, and distribution strategies?

5. What are the essential elements that you would include in the definition of culture?

6. In the U.S., more and more women are joining the work force and many are moving into significantly important executive positions in major corporations. Many life insurance companies, airlines, and hotels are beginning to recognize the female executive as a distinct marketing segment. How might a hotel modify its practices and facilities to better appeal to the female executive?

7. How might information on the culturally based differences between blacks and whites be beneficial to the manager of a new clothing boutique that has just opened in the downtown area of a major city?

8. Many changes are occurring in American values. How will changes such as (1) ecological consciousness and (2) the equality of women affect consumption generally?

9. The soft drink industry foresees problems that will occur in the U.S. in the next decade—the key 13- to 24-year-olds are growing older and the market will shrink by four million persons, or 8 percent. Major strategies include expansion into more overseas markets. However, some estimate that while Americans in this important age category consume 823 cans of soda pop each year, soft drink consumption outside the U.S. probably averages no more than 10 cans per person annually. Many of the consumers overseas also have little discretionary income, and supermarkets have yet to develop in some of the countries. Nevertheless, the soft drink companies are heavily advertising their products and attempting to create goodwill through the sponsorship of sports clinics and games. What potential does the industry see in these markets?

10. Although there is a trend toward a blurring of the sexes in the U.S., many products are still considered "masculine" and "feminine." What marketing strategies might be used to make cigars for women and purses for men culturally acceptable products in this country?

Case 1. Electronic International

You are a new marketing manager for Electronic International, a discount merchandiser specializing in private-label electronic gear. You have been hired to direct overseas operations. You are in a difficult position: the former marketing manager has recently been fired because the company has suffered losses of $17 million in international operations in the past five years, and the future does not look optimistic. His refusal to evaluate possible cultural differences led to overseas fiascos, and it is your job to revamp the marketing strategies.

The first step is to analyze the company's successful strategies in the U.S. market: strategically located stores, a wide product mix sold at discount prices, and heavy advertising—$45 million worth last year.

Your predecessor attempted to use this same marketing strategy overseas, despite warnings from European observers and competitors that Electronic International's discounting methods would not attract European stereo shoppers, who are extremely brand-conscious and quality-oriented. His obstinacy and superficial understanding of European markets, laws, and traditions put the company in its present dilemma.

The first mistake was keeping the discount image in European markets where consumers are willing to pay premium prices for high-quality merchandise. The big-ticket, brand-name items were de-emphasized. The second mistake was in saturating the European market with stores, many of which were poorly located. A total of 419 overseas outlets were haphazardly scattered throughout the countries, with little analysis of population, income levels, accessibility, or competition. In France, an especially "snobbish" market, a minimum of eight stores were built, none of which were located in the Paris metropolitan area. Other blunders included overlooking a Belgian law which requires a government tax stamp on window signs; gearing Christmas promotions in Holland to December 25 while being ignorant of the fact that the Dutch celebrate Christmas on December 6; and being hit with injunctions for violating German laws when giveaway flashlights were used as a promotional tool for the stores. In essence, your predecessor failed to make any attempt to understand the European market, presuming that U.S. successes would guarantee favorable overseas results.

You are aware that other obstacles are present which hinder a rapid pick-up of sales. Britain, Belgium, and Holland ban citizens band radios, which are Electronic International's best-selling item in the U.S. and account for 20 percent of its sales. Also, due to poor hiring and management, your overseas outlets have been experiencing internal theft which has been costing the company several hundred thousand dollars annually.

Case 1 Questions

1. Based on the given information, what strategy would you suggest for increasing sales in the European markets?

2. Would you develop a localized approach to each market, or would you develop a standardized "overseas approach"?

3. Would you change the company's discount image, attempt to make European consumers more price conscious, or develop an alternative strategy?

Case 2. The Ideal Auto

You are a marketing manager for a large automobile company in the U.S. A few years ago, under pressure from the government, environmentalists, and increasing foreign competition, the company introduced a new compact car. The automobile was marketed to white, ecology-minded consumers who were primarily interested in a car that emitted less pollution and economized on gas mileage. The car enjoyed modest success during the first two years in the market; however, last year the car suffered an 8-percent decrease in sales. Consequently, the company is modifying its promotional tactics and is also seeking a secondary target market.

The car itself is a two-door hardtop and is quite sleek in appearance. Its smooth design and low ground clearance could appeal to the sport in anyone. This is confirmed by a consumer survey, in which the sporty appearance tended to be ranked as one of the chief elements of the car's attractiveness. The wide variety of colors offered helps attract a wider range of tastes. The four-seat interior is spacious for a compact, and the deep-pile carpeting and elegant upholstery add to the car's drawing power.

A test drive shows that the car handles beautifully, with astounding agility. It is available with either a short-throw four-speed stick or an automatic transmission. Its rack and pinion steering responds well to the driver's every move. The tight turning radius and front disc brakes also improve its handling and maneuverability. This model's engine is a smooth-running, high-revving, four cylinder with 1400 cc's. It takes the car from 0 to 50 mph in an average of 8.5 seconds. Gas mileage is excellent, with 33 mpg on the highway and 25 mpg for city driving.

Included as standards are power windows, an electric rear window defogger, a tilt steering column, and a 6-way adjustable driver's seat.

Many rich options are available to the buyer, including air conditioning, AM-FM stereo radio, and handsome wire wheel covers. One serious drawback is that luggage space is severely limited, so it was decided that a removable luggage rack be included as an option. This was a wise decision, since nearly 80 percent of all buyers have purchased the optional rack. Currently, the car sells for $5,580, but labor and raw materials costs have risen, and company executives feel that the price should be pushed upward moderately.

Major competition has come from imports, which have made extensive inroads into the U.S. market in the past few years. They were expected to finish 1977 with sales of 2.1 million cars, or slightly less than 19 percent of U.S. car sales. In some western states, they account for nearly 40 percent of the car sales, and an incredible 80 percent of all subcompact sales in some West Coast cities. These sales have been attributed to messages and warnings from the government and environmentalists that Americans must disregard large gas-guzzling cars and opt for the smaller, energy-conserving autos. However, the Americans who are heeding this advice are buying imports instead of domestic cars, because the foreign cars are frequently lower priced, more fully equipped, and are more durable. Some companies have instituted controversial two-tiered pricing schemes and sell their compacts for cheaper prices in areas where foreign competition is keen. Others have developed intensive training sessions for their dealers in an effort to "develop small car specialists." Following these strategies will not help these companies, or your company, unless the poor quality image of American compact automobiles can be overcome.

The company's target market for this model is young, single, or recently married, white consumers in the middle-income category. It is marketed as a comfortable, sporty, yet very economical car. Its first two years on the market were relatively successful ones, due partly to the fact that it was a brand new model and was very heavily promoted. However, the recent sales decline has caused company executives to analyze the situation and develop modified strategies. Part of the decline is attributed to the fact that people who buy compact cars keep them longer; hence, there is a low repurchase rate. Also, a slight majority of American consumers still have a consistent preference for larger cars. Many of the remaining potential customers are being snatched away by the aggressive foreign companies. Therefore, plans for the near future include placing more emphasis on "buying American," increasing the advertising budget by $1.5 million, and adding more standard features to the automobile to enhance competition with the fully equipped foreign models. A major strategy is to appeal to a wider range of consumers by attempting to enter the black market.

The company realizes that the black market may be a tough one to crack, since experts in the industry maintain that blacks prefer larger luxury cars. However, a few compact cars are targeted toward this market, and black consumers especially tend not to purchase foreign automobiles. Consequently, the company feels that it can realize substantial sales if it can establish a niche in this segment. An aggressive advertising campaign is planned.

Based on your knowledge of the black subculture, devise a promotional strategy to sell your firm's compact to this segment. One of your colleagues is skeptical and claims that this proposal represents a waste of promotional dollars. He says that the black middle class is too small in numbers to warrant the expense.

Case 2 Questions

1. Can the car be marketed to low-income blacks and to a low-income market in general? How?

2. Other executives fear that the car's history of appealing mainly to "suburban sports" will continue and thwart these newest plans. Explain how the car can be made more attractive to urbanites.

Notes

1. Robert T. Green and Erick Langeard, "A Cross-National Comparison of Consumer Habits and Innovator Characteristics," *Journal of Marketing*, 39 (July 1975), pp. 34-41.

2. E. P. Hollander, *Principles and Methods of Social Psychology*, 2nd. ed. (New York: Oxford University Press, 1971), p. 307.

3. Daniel Yankelovich, *The Yankelovich Monitor* (New York: Daniel Yankelovich, Inc., 1974), p. 1.

4. J. A. Lee, "Cultural Analysis in Overseas Operations," *Harvard Business Review,* 44 (March-April 1966), pp. 106-14.

5. *The Wall Street Journal,* March 9, 1977, p. 1.

6. Y. H. Furuhashi and H. F. Evarts, "Educating Men for International Marketing," *Journal of Marketing,* 31 (January 1967), pp. 51-53.

7. A. C. Fatt, "The Danger of 'Local' International Advertising," *Journal of Marketing,* 31 (January 1965), pp. 60-62.

8. Ralph Z. Sorenson and Ulrich E. Wiechmann, "How Multinationals View Marketing Standardization," *Harvard Business Review,* 53 (May-June 1975), pp. 38-56.

9. Ibid., p. 48.

10. Montrose Sommers and Jerome Kernan, "Why Products Flourish Here, Fizzle There," *Columbia Journal of World Business,* 2 (March-April 1967), pp. 89-97.

11. Dean Peebles, "Goodyear's Worldwide Advertising," *The International Advertiser,* 8 (January 1967), pp. 19-22 (both good and weak examples are cited in this article); Walter P. Margulies, "Why Global Marketing Requires a Global Focus on Product Design," *Business Abroad,* 94 (January 1969), pp. 22-23; Norman Heller, "How Pepsi-Cola Does It in 110 Countries," John S. Wright and Jac L. Goldstrucker, eds., *New Ideas for Successful Marketing* (Chicago: American Marketing Association, 1966), pp. 700-15.

12. James H. Donnelly, Jr., and John K. Ryans, Jr., "The Role of Culture in Organizing Overseas Operations: The Advertising Experience," University of Washington *Business Review,* 30 (Autumn 1969), pp. 35-41; John K. Ryans, Jr., and James H. Donnelly, Jr., "Standardized Global Advertising, A Call as Yet Unanswered," *Journal of Marketing,* 33 (April 1969), pp. 57-59.

13. Richard M. Bessom, "Corporate Image Strategy for Multinationals," *Atlantic Economic Review* (July-August 1974), pp. 47-51; David Gestetner, "Strategy in Managing International Sales," *Harvard Business Review,* 52 (September-October 1974), pp. 103-08; Howard V. Perlmutter and David A. Heenan, "How Multinational Should Your Top Managers Be?" *Harvard Business Review,* 52 (November-December 1974), pp. 121-32; Harry L. Davis, Gary D. Eppen, and Lars-Gunnar Mattson, "Critical Factors in Worldwide Purchasing," *Harvard Business Review,* 52 (November-December 1974), pp. 81-90.

14. Yoram Wind, Susan P. Douglas, and Howard V. Perlmutter, "Guidelines for Developing International Marketing Strategies," *Journal of Marketing,* 37 (April 1973), pp. 14-23.

15. Support for this statement is provided in a study by Richard H. Holton, "Marketing Policies in Multinational Corporations," *California Management Review,* 13 (Summer 1971), pp. 57-67, at p. 62.

16. A. S. C. Ehrenberg and G. J. Goodhardt, "A Comparison of American and British Repeat-Buying Habits," *Journal of Marketing Research,* 5 (February 1968), pp. 29-33.

17. S. Watson Dunn, "The Case Study Approach in Cross-Cultural Research," *Journal of Marketing Research,* 3 (February 1966), pp. 26-31.

18. E. S. Lorimor and S. Watson Dunn, "Four Measures of Cross-Cultural Advertising Effectiveness," *Journal of Advertising Research,* 8 (1968), pp. 11-13.

19. S. Prakash Sethi, "Comparative Cluster Analysis for World Markets," *Journal of Marketing Research,* 8 (August 1971), pp. 348-54.

20. Robert D. Schooler and Carl Ferguson, "A Model to Determine the Activated Potential of Foreign Markets," *Marquette Business Review* (Fall 1974), pp. 129-36.

21. Margulies, "Why Global Marketing Requires a Global Focus on Product Design," p. 22.

22. Richard W. Brislin, "Back-Translation for Cross-Cultural Research," *Journal of Cross-Cultural Psychology,* 1 (September 1970), pp. 185-216; and Oswald Werner and Donald T. Campbell, "Translating, Working through Interpreters, and the Problems of Decentering," Raoul Naroll and Ronald Cohen, eds., *A Handbook of Method in Cultural Anthropology* (Garden City, N.Y.: The Natural History Press, 1970), pp. 398-420.

23. For an introduction to sources of information about global markets, see David T. Kollat, Roger D. Blackwell, and James F. Robeson, *Strategic Marketing* (New York: Holt, Rinehart and Winston, Inc., 1972), pp. 173-78.

24. Robert Tamilia, "Cross-Cultural Advertising Research: A Review and Suggested Framework," Ronald C. Curhan, ed. *1974 Combined Proceedings,* American Marketing Association, pp. 131-34.

25. R. A. Bauer and S. M. Cunningham, "The Negro Market," *Journal of Advertising Research,* 10 (April 1970), pp. 3-10.

26. "Black America: Still Waiting for Full Membership," *Fortune* (April 1975), pp. 162-72.

27. Office of Planning and Research of U.S. Department of Labor, *The Negro Family: The Case for National Action* (Washington, D.C.: U.S. Government Printing Office, 1965), p. 5.

28. John V. Petrof, "Reaching the Negro Market: A Segregated vs. a General Newspaper," *Journal of Advertising Research,* 8 (April 1968), pp. 40-43.

29. Harold H. Kassarjian, "The Negro and American Advertising, 1946-1965," *Journal of Marketing Research,* 6 (February 1969), pp. 29-39; Ronald Bush, Paul Solomon, and J. F. Hair, Jr., "There Are More Blacks in Commercials," *Journal of Advertising Research,* 17 (February 1977), pp. 21-30.

30. Arnold M. Barban, "The Dilemma of 'Integrated' Advertising," *Journal of Business,* 42 (October 1969), pp. 477-96; B. Stuart Tolley and John J. Goett, "Reactions to Blacks in Newspapers," *Journal of Advertising Research,* 11 (April 1971), pp. 11-17; John W. Gould, Normal B. Sigband, and Cyril E. Zoerner, Jr., "Black Consumer Reactions to 'Integrated' Advertising: An Exploratory Study," *Journal of Marketing,* 34 (July 1970), pp. 20-26; Pravat K. Choudhury and Lawrence S. Schmid, "Black Models in Advertising to Blacks," *Journal of Advertising Research,* 14 (June 1974), pp. 19-22.

31. William V. Muse, "Product-Related Response to Use of Black Models in Advertising," *Journal of Marketing Research,* 8 (February 1971), pp. 107-09; Mary Jane Schlinger and Joseph T. Plummer, "Advertising in Black and White," *Journal of Marketing Research,* 9 (May 1972), pp. 149-53; Ronald Bush, Robert Gwinner, and Paul Solomon, "White Consumer Sales Response to Black Models," *Journal of Marketing,* 38 (April 1974), pp. 25-29.

32. Carl E. Block, "White Backlash to Negro Ads: Fact or Fantasy," *Journalism Quarterly,* 49 (Summer 1972), pp. 258-62.

33. Gould, Sigband, and Zoerner, "Black Consumer Reactions," p. 25; Michael K. Chapko, "Black Ads Are Getting Blacker," *Journal of Communication* (Autumn 1976), pp. 175-78.

34. Tolley and Goett, "Reactions to Blacks in Newpapers," pp. 13-14; Petrof, "Reaching the Negro Market," p. 42.

35. Gerald J. Glassner and Gale D. Metzger, "Radio Usage by Blacks," *Journal of Advertising Research,* 15 (October 1975), pp. 39-45.

36. James W. Carey, "Variations in Negro-White Television Preference," *Journal of Broadcasting,* 10 (1966), pp. 199-211.

37. Anthony M. Orum, "A Reappraisal of the Social and Political Participation of Negroes," *American Journal of Sociology,* 72 (July 1966), pp. 32-46; Marvin E. Olsen, "Social and Political Participation of Blacks," *American Sociological Review,* 35 (1970), pp. 682-96.

38. Marcus Alexis, "Some Negro-White Differences in Consumption," *American Journal of Economics and Sociology,* 21 (January 1962), pp. 137-48.

39. S. Roxanne Hiltz, "Black and White in the Consumer Financial System," *American Journal of Sociology,* 76 (1971), pp. 987-99.

40. Edward B. Selby, Jr., and James T. Lindley, "Black Consumers—

Hidden Market Potential," *The Bankers Magazine* (Summer 1973), pp. 84-87.

41. Alexis, "Some Negro-White Differences in Consumption"; also, James Stafford, Keith Cox, and James Higginbotham, "Some Consumption Pattern Differences between Urban Whites and Negroes," *Social Science Quarterly* (December 1968), pp. 619-30.

42. Fred C. Akers, "Negro and White Automobile Buying Behavior: New Evidence," *Journal of Marketing Research,* 5 (August 1968), pp. 283-90; Carl M. Larson and Hugh G. Wales, "Brand Preferences of Chicago Blacks," *Journal of Advertising Research,* 13 (August 1973), pp. 15-21.

43. Frank G. Davis, "Differential Factors in the Negro Market" (Chicago: National Association of Market Developers, 1959), p. 6 (privately published report based upon data collected by *Ebony* magazine).

44. Data from Bernard Howard and Co., Inc., and *Ebony,* reported in Raymond O. Oladipupo, *How Distinct Is the Negro Market?* (New York: Ogilvie & Mather, 1970), pp. 30-34.

45. James O. Wheeler, "Transportation Problems in Negro Ghettos," *Sociology and Social Research,* 53 (January 1969), pp. 171-79.

46. Robert L. King and Earl Robert DeManche, "Comparative Acceptance of Selected Private-Branded Food Products by Low-Income Negro and White Families," in Philip R. McDonald, ed., *Marketing Involvement in Society and the Economy* (Chicago: American Marketing Association, 1969), pp. 63-69.

47. Herbert E. Krugman, "White and Negro Responses to Package Design," *Journal of Marketing Research,* 3 (May 1966), pp. 199-200.

48. Keith K. Cox, James B. Higginbotham, and James E. Stafford, "Negro Retail Shopping and Credit Behavior," *Journal of Retailing,* 48 (Spring 1972), pp. 54-66.

49. Donald F. Dixon and Daniel J. McLaughlin, Jr., "Shopping Behavior, Expenditure Patterns, and Inner City Food Prices," *Journal of Marketing Research,* 8 (February 1971), pp. 960-99.

50. Similarity between blacks and whites was, however, reported in Cox et al., "Negro Retail Shopping and Credit Behavior," p. 60.

51. John V. Petrof, "Attitudes of the Urban Poor toward Their Neighborhood Supermarkets," *Journal of Retailing,* 47 (Spring 1971), pp. 3-17.

52. Dennis H. Gensch and Richard Staelin, "The Appeal of Buying Black," *Journal of Marketing Research,* 9 (May 1972), pp. 141-48; Dennis Gensch and Richard Staelin, "Making Black Retail Outlets Work," *California Management Review,* 15 (Fall 1972), pp. 52-62.

53. Donald E. Sexton, Jr., "Differences in Food Shopping Habits by Area of Residence, Race, and Income," *Journal of Retailing,* 50 (Spring 1974), pp. 37-48.

54. U.S. Bureau of Labor Statistics, *A Study of Prices in Food Stores*

Located in Low and Higher Income Areas of Six Large Cities (Washington, D.C.: U.S. Government Printing Office, 1966).

55. Donald E. Sexton, Jr., "Grocery Prices Paid by Blacks and Whites: Further Findings," *Journal of Economics and Business,* 25 (Fall 1972), pp. 39-44.

56. Norman Kangun, "Race and Price Discrimination in the Marketplace: A Further Study," *Mississippi Valley Journal of Economics and Business,* 5 (Spring 1970), pp. 66-75. This study includes Indian families as well as black families.

57. Waylon D. Griffin and Frederick D. Sturdivant, "Discrimination and Middle Class Minority Consumers," *Journal of Marketing,* 37 (July 1973), pp. 65-68.

58. Gordon L. Wise, "Automobile Salesmen's Perceptions of New Car Prospects," *Bulletin of Business Research,* 46 (February 1971), pp. 2-6.

59. Marcus Alexis, "The Effects of Race and Retail Structure on Consumer Behavior and Market Performance," in Jagdish Sheth and Peter L. Wright, eds., *Proceedings of a National Conference on Social Marketing* (Urbana-Champaign: University of Illinois, 1974), pp. 205-40.

60. Gerald E. Hills, Donald H. Granbois, and James M. Patterson, "Black Consumer Perceptions of Food Store Attributes," *Journal of Marketing,* 37 (April 1973), pp. 47-57.

Chapter 5

Social Class and Group Influences

Outline

Social Class Defined
Social Class Determinants

Measurement of Social Class

Social Class Distribution in the United States

Effect of Social Class on Consumer Behavior

Social Groups

Types of Social Groups

Functions of Groups
Socialization
Compliance to Group Norms
Groups and the Self-concept

Reference Groups
Functions of Reference Groups
Marketing Analysis of Reference-Group Influence

Summary

Questions and Issues for Discussion

Cases

Key Terms

social class
social class determinants
social class measurement
reputational method
subjective method
objective method
social class distribution
social groups
social aggregates
primary groups
secondary groups
formal groups
informal groups
socialization process
compliance
norms
self-concept
reference group
normative function
comparative function

People generally tend to associate with those whom they consider to be like themselves. Frequently they have similar occupations and levels of formal education and are likely to live in comparable circumstances. Under such arrangements, fundamental values and viewpoints about life are shared. There is a particular social consciousness associated with these shared characteristics and a social status attached to them. A hierarchy among status groups has developed because some are regarded as having more social prestige and are, therefore, superior to the others.

Historically, sociologists have been particularly interested in the phenomenon of social structure for its own sake. Consumer analysts, on the other hand, have become attentive to social stratification because it can significantly influence consumer behavior. This section of the chapter pays specific attention to social class as one form of social stratification. Social class will first be defined briefly—with its dimensions identified and discussed—and will include a representation of the social class structure in the United States. The final part of this section will draw attention to the issue of the relative importance of social class and income in explaining and predicting consumer behavior.

There is a reluctance to recognize the prevalence of social classes in the United States, and because of our heritage there is a tendency to dismiss visible symbols of social status, particularly ascribed status. The enlightened approach is to acknowledge the existence of social classes and understand their impact on consumer behavior.

Social Class Defined

Social classes are relatively permanent and homogeneous divisions in a society into which individuals or families sharing similar values, lifestyles, interests, and behavior can be categorized. Of course, it is much easier to provide such a definition than it is to operationalize it. There are no absolute boundaries separating social classes; consequently, there has been considerable disagreement as to where one social class ends and another begins.

Social classes are multidimensional, hierarchical structures that tend to restrict the behavior of members of a particular social class. That is, a number of variables—power, prestige, influence, wealth, and income—combine to create a social class. Social class is not the same as income, although it is often treated as such. Furthermore, people tend to rank, frequently on an intuitive basis without reference to specific people, the various strata or social groupings. This ranking into relatively homogeneous groupings tends to restrict the behavior of the individuals within each social class.

Social Class Determinants

Social classes take shape through what have been called determinants—those characteristics that differentiate the members of one social class from another. Although there are a number of ways that can be used to determine a person's social class, there is considerable similarity among the various approaches. One of the more helpful approaches follows. It concentrates on five dimensions of social class. These five include occupation, personal performance, personal interactions, possessions, and value orientation.

Occupation

Many believe that an individual's occupation is the best single clue to his or her social class membership. This appears to be true because a person's life's work has a substantial influence on the way he or she lives. For instance, in many cases the wardrobe that an individual begins to assemble upon taking his or her first job reflects the expectations associated with this new position. This can be illustrated by considering what clothing would most likely be purchased by a young accountant working for a public accounting firm as compared to clothing bought by a young commercial artist. A man who is a young accountant would probably begin by purchasing conservative suits, while the male artist may buy distinctive sport shirts and slacks.

Occupations may also be ranked according to the prestige, honor, and respect associated with them by members of society. Surprisingly to some, the resulting rankings are quite stable over time.

Personal Performance

Individual achievement is also related to social class status. Ordinarily this is concerned with occupational accomplishments, but it may involve non-job performance as well. These latter accomplishments include service to various community groups or even superior family role performance.

Such community participation includes functioning as a successful United Fund chairperson, member of the local board of education, member of the chamber of commerce, or member of the city council. These organizations demand a great deal of time and usually pay no salary to their members, but each position offers considerable public visibility and attention. Consequently, people active in community service develop the behavioral pattern expected of them by the public. These influences are of interest to the consumer analyst because they may affect purchasing patterns—first, among the individuals who hold these positions and then, more important, among those who use public figures as references. For example, it is reasonable to expect a leading member of the local chamber of commerce of a community that is very economically dependent on the automobile industry to drive an American-made car. Also, the visibility of people holding such community-service positions puts their taste in clothing on open display.

Personal Interactions

Personal interactions are particularly important in determining social status. Whom one relates to on a regular basis, how one is treated, and how one treats those with whom he or she interacts serve to identify the social class to which he or she belongs. Indeed, having frequent and intimate relationships with other members of a particular social class is considered essential to the maintenance of one's social class.

There are rather rigid barriers to social interaction among members of different social strata. In the United States, these rarely take the form of explicit restrictions, but they are effective nevertheless. For example, a lodge or club may require that a new member be sponsored by a current member, or it may be that the initiation fee is sufficiently high to limit membership to the desired group. Perhaps the most obvious example of restricted interaction is the existence in several U.S. cities of a Social Register which incorporates very rigid criteria for gaining admission to intimate interactions in the top social classes.

Such memberships result in interaction that directly affects consumer decision making. For instance, who one uses as a source of information about product brands or stores often comes from the ranks of those individuals with whom one associates on a day-to-day basis.

Possessions

Personal possessions are often used as indicators of social status. The old idea of keeping up with the Joneses implies a social consciousness of quantity and quality of consumption. Also, Veblen's theory of conspicuous consumption draws specific attention to the practice of some people who engage in buying to verify their newly acquired wealth. However, while possessions are necessary conditions for class membership, they are not sufficient. Further, the importance of possessions relates not only to the amount of possessions that an individual has but also the nature of his or her choices.

Historically, a number of products have been especially attractive as symbols of status for members of the mass market. The automobile has been one of the most visible, although its importance in this respect has faded in recent years. Other products have replaced it. For example, the ownership of a vacation home, a third car, a pleasure home, or a backyard swimming pool has special connotations for some middle class Americans. This does not mean that these items are not purchased for their functional features; it does suggest that, in promoting them, special attention should be given to their capacity to offer a status appeal. Decisions about possessions and their relation to social class are questions of extreme importance to the consumer analyst.

Value Orientations

Fundamental values are interpreted and applied differently; consequently the value orientations of individuals are important determinants of social class. The members of a social class tend to share a common set of abstract convictions that organize and relate many specific values, and, therefore, it is intuitively appealing that social class should substantially affect consumption behavior.

For example, identifiable differences in beliefs among members of different social classes about family formation, child rearing, the home, and work affect market behavior and may even provide a basis for market segmentation. Several of these differences and their impact on marketing strategy development are discussed in the next chapter.

Measurement of Social Class

Several methods have been developed for measuring social class. The three principal methods are (1) reputational, (2) subjective, and (3) objective. In considering these methods, it is important to remember that the marketer's primary reason for measuring social class is to identify market segments that manifest similar consumption behavior.

The *reputational method* basically considers a social class as a social group characterized by common modes of thinking and member interaction. People are ranked into social classes by having individuals within a particular community group the people they know into various classes. While this method is useful in predicting social interaction in small and moderate sized communities, the variability in peoples' perceptions of different social classes limits its usefulness, particularly in large cities. There is some indication that conjoint analysis, a procedure that analyzes the relative importance of various socioeconomic characteristics in judgments about social class, offers considerable potential in understanding the structure of social class.[1]

Subjective methods of determining social classes ask respondents to rate themselves on social class. Such methods have been used on occasion but are of limited use for consumer analysts for two reasons: (1) respondents tend to overrate their own class position (often by one class rank) and (2) respondents avoid the connotative terms "upper" and "lower" classes and thus exaggerate the size of the middle classes. The value of subjective methods to date appears to be minimal due primarily to the absence of a simple, self-administered rating scale to identify social classes without simply asking the respondent his or her social class. When such a scale is developed, this method may prove to be quite useful.

Objective methods of determining social classes rely on the assigning of classes (or status) on the basis of respondents' possession of some value of a stratified variable. The most often used variables are occupation, income, education, size and type of residence, ownership of possessions, and organizational affiliations.

Most consumer research uses some objective methods for classifying because they yield quantitative results and obviate subjective interpretation. Objective methods can be divided into those that involve single indexes and those that use multiple indexes.

While occupation is widely accepted as the best single indicator of social class, there are a number of multiple-item indexes, most of which relate to Warner's Index of Status Characteristics.[2] The most frequently used variables in this classification process are occupation, income, education, size and type of residence, ownership of personal possessions, and organizational affiliations.

Even though some of the application procedures are technically detailed and intellectually intriguing, the resulting classifications are only approximations. However, these groupings of individuals generally are sufficiently different from each other to be helpful to the analyst and manager.

For example, the manager of a public agency responsible for state employment services may find it helpful to vary his or her agency's efforts in matching applicants and job opportunities when dealing with people from different social classes because of the variation in their values and interests.

Social Class Distribution in the United States

The exact distribution of individuals into separate categories of social class depends upon the definitions used. The mainstream of social

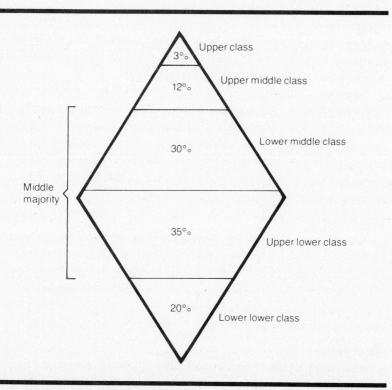

Figure 5.1
Social Classes in the United States

Upper class
3%

Upper middle class
12%

Lower middle class
30%

Middle majority

Upper lower class
35%

Lower lower class
20%

Source: Charles B. McCann, *Women and Department Store Newspaper Advertising* (Chicago: Social Research, 1957), p. 94. Reprinted by permission.

research has commonly used a six-class system. One representation of the distribution of the United States' population by these six classes is shown in Figure 5.1, with the upper and lower divisions of the upper class combined. The accuracy of this class distribution has been supported in numerous studies.[3]

The lower middle and upper lower classes are the largest groups of consumers in the United States. This is the so-called "mass market" or "middle majority" to which most business organizations, political parties, and others direct their attention. To illustrate the differences that exist among the various social classes, it is useful to consider the key elements of social class behavior. Figure 5.2 is a skeleton outline of some of the most important identifying characteristics of each social class and its consumption patterns. These generalizations are based on a number of studies.[4]

Figure 5.2
Social Class Behavior in America

Upper Upper

Upper uppers are the social elite of society. Inherited wealth from socially prominent families is the key to admission. Children attend private preparatory schools and graduate from the best colleges.

Consumers in the upper upper class spend money as if it were unimportant, not niggardly but not with display either, for that would imply that money is important. For some products, a "trickle-down" influence may exist between social classes. That is, some products gain acceptance among upper classes before winning popularity in lower social strata. The social position of these individuals is so secure that they can deviate from class norms if they choose to without losing status.

Lower Upper

Lower uppers include the very-high-income professional people who have "earned" their position rather than inherited it. They are the *nouveaux riches,* active people with many material symbols of their status. They buy the largest homes in the best suburbs, the most expensive automobiles, swimming pools and other symbols of conspicuous consumption, making them innovators and good markets for luxury marketing offerings.

Upper Middle

The key word for upper middles is "career." These careers are based on professional or graduate degrees for a specific profession or the skill of

Figure 5.2
**Social Class Behavior
in America (continued)**

business administration. Members of this class are demanding of their children in educational attainment.

The *quality* market for many products is the upper middle class; gracious living in a conspicuous but careful manner characterizes the family's life-style. The home is of high importance and an important symbol of the family's success and competence.

Lower Middle

Lower middle class families are "typical" Americans, exemplifying the core of respectability, conscientious work habits, and adherence to culturally defined norms and standards. They believe in attending church and obeying the law and are upset when their children are arrested for law violations. They are not innovators.

The *home* is very important to the lower middle family, and they want it to be neat, well-painted, and in a respected neighborhood. They may have little confidence in their own tastes and adopt "standardized" home furnishings—perhaps from Levitz or Wickes. This is in contrast to the upper middle homemaker who feels freer to experiment with new styles and new arrangements and to the upper lower homemaker who is not very concerned about the overall plan for furnishing the home. The lower middle homemaker reads and follows the advice of the medium-level shelter and service magazines in an attempt to make the house "pretty."

The lower middle class homemaker "works" more at shopping than other homemakers and considers purchase decisions demanding and tedious. He or she may have a high degree of price sensitivity.

Upper Lower

Members of upper lower social classes—the largest segment of society—exhibit a routine life, characterized by a day-to-day existence of unchanging activities. They live in dull areas of the city, in small houses or apartments. The "hard hats" are included in this class, with many members working at uncreative jobs requiring manual activity or only moderate skills and education. Because of unions and security, many may earn incomes that give them considerable discretionary income.

The purchase decisions of the working-class woman are often impulsive. Nevertheless, she may have high brand-loyalty to "national" brands. Buying them is one way to "prove" her knowledge as a buyer, a role in which she feels (probably correctly) that she has little skill. She has little

Figure 5.2
Social Class Behavior in America (continued)

social contact outside the home and does not like to belong to civic organizations or attend church activities. Social interaction is limited to close neighbors and relatives. If she takes a vacation, it will probably be to visit relatives in another city. Upper lowers are concerned that they not be confused with the lower lowers.

Lower Lower
The lower lower social class contains the so-called "disreputable" people of the society who may try to rise above their class on some occasions but usually fail to do so and become reconciled to their position in society. An individual in the lower lower class often rejects middle class morality and "gets his kicks" wherever he can—and this includes buying impulsively. This lack of planning causes purchases which cost too much and may result in inferior goods. This person pays too much for products, buys on credit at a high interest rate, and has difficulty evaluating the quality or value of a product.

Prior to concluding this section, a precautionary note is necessary. There has been and undoubtedly will continue to be some discontent with the usefulness of social class as a means of explaining consumer behavior. There are two major sources of this discontent, neither of which has proven to be valid: (1) the emergence of the massification theory and (2) the income versus social class dispute. Massification theory, the contention that social class differentiation was diminishing in the United States, has proven to be without valid foundation.[5] The second source of discontent, that income is a better correlate of consumption behavior than social class, has also been negated in recent years.[6] Consequently, there is every reason to believe that social class will continue to be an important determinant of consumption behavior.

Effect of Social Class on Consumer Behavior

Consumer researchers have conducted a number of studies to determine the influence of social class on consumer behavior. The following generalizations indicate the impact social class has on consumer behavior and provide an understanding of how such information can be incorporated into marketing decision making.

1. The kind, quality, and style of clothing an individual wears is related to that individual's social class. While all social classes are interested in clothing fashions, the upper classes pay greater attention to fashion information.[7]

2. The evaluative criteria a family uses to select a home are affected by social class.[8] There is some indication that traditional living-room furniture is preferred by the established upper class, whereas modern living-room furniture is preferred by the upwardly mobile within the current generation, that is, the nouveaux riches.

3. The percentage of family income spent on leisure, independent of income, does not vary between social classes, but the evaluative criteria used in selecting type of recreation is heavily influenced by social class. For example, the heaviest users of both commercial leisure facilities and public facilities (such as parks, museums, and swimming pools) are the middle classes.[9]

4. The lower classes tend to use bank credit cards for durables and necessities, whereas the upper class tends to use them for luxury items.[10] Furthermore, the higher social classes have a more favorable attitude toward credit usage.[11] The most frequent users of charge cards are higher income, better educated, middle-age people with professional occupations.[12]

5. The amount and type of search undertaken by an individual varies by social class as well as by product and situation.[13] Upper class individuals have far more access to media information than do their lower class counterparts.[14] Lower class individuals tend to rely on relatives and close friends for information about consumption decisions, whereas middle class individuals put more reliance upon media-acquired information and actively engage in external search for the media.

6. Lower class individuals tend to prefer to shop at local, face-to-face places where they are confident they will receive friendly service and easy credit. Upper middle class individuals tend to be more confident in their shopping ability and shop at a broader range of stores. The discount store especially appeals to the middle class because they are careful and economy-minded in their buying.

Social Groups

Social groups have a massive impact on all human thought and action. Groups serve as the mechanism by which we learn the values, norms, and behavior patterns that are required by the society in which we live. Therefore, a meaningful analysis of consumer behavior must take into account the functioning of groups as a factor affecting consumption decisions. Furthermore, it is sometimes appropriate to focus on a group as a consuming unit rather than simply on individuals as consumers. For instance, many industrial purchasing decisions are made by groups rather than by individuals. Similarly, it is frequently necessary to consider the family as the consuming unit.

Social groups are formed and maintained in three basic ways.[15] The first is that of a collection of people occupying the same approximate space. Membership in this type of group does not include personal interaction; the people involved are largely unaffected by the presence of the others in this group environment. Examples of this type of group are the riders on a bus or the shoppers in a store. In most instances, shoppers have no personal interaction and relatively little effect on each other. The second form is a collection of people who are basically different from one another but have some commonality. The shared characteristic may be demographic, psychological, or socioeconomic. For instance, a purchaser of a Rolls Royce and the purchaser of a Pinto would be considered to be members of the same group (automobile owners), yet they may have little else in common. The third form that a group can take is a collection of people who interact regularly and communicate among themselves in such a manner that the group itself takes on a unique character. The notion of a group character suggests that the group is something more than the sum of its parts; it becomes an entity by itself. Fraternities, basketball teams, and bridge clubs are examples of this third type of group.

The first two forms are appropriately termed "social aggregates" because they do not possess the vital element of member interaction, which is the distinguishing factor of a true group. This is not to say that social aggregates should not be the object of study by consumer analysts. Members of aggregates may have common attitudes and behavioral patterns even though they do not purposefully meet and exchange information. However, the group that is characterized by regular contact and exchange of information is believed to have a greater impact on behavior than the other type of group. Fortunately for consumer analysts, social psychologists have done extensive analyses of social groups that provide insight into why groups are formed, how they function, and how they influence member behavior.

Types of Social Groups

Most people are members of several groups. Some of these groups have a greater effect on values and behavior than do others. For instance, church membership may have a greater impact on an individual's values and behavior than membership in a flying club. In order to permit some generalization about the relative influence of various groups, attempts have been made to distinguish among them. Such differentiation follows.

Primary groups are aggregates of individuals that are small and intimate enough so that all members can communicate regularly with each other on a face-to-face basis. These generally include the family, friendship groups, and small work groups. *Secondary groups* are all the other groups to which people belong and have significantly less face-to-face exchange, such as professional associations, university classes, and many community service organizations. Increased mobility and modern communications systems have somewhat blurred the distinction between primary and secondary groups. However, marketers maintain a strong interest in those primary groups characterized by considerable interaction among members because they tend to have a more pronounced and lasting effect on consumer behavior than do most secondary groups. For instance, parents of young children often allow them to eat the same types of candies that they ate as children, possibly resulting in a similar allowance years later, when the next generation comes along.

A second fundamental distinction frequently made among groups is based on structure and membership requirements. *Formal groups* are those characterized by an explicit structure, specified membership requirements, and, typically, a specified goal. The membership requirements may be minimal, such as the payment of dues, and the structure limited, but the requirements exist. A ski club, for instance, may require the payment of dues and student status and may have only a president. Yet, such a group can have a considerable impact on the type of equipment that members purchase and the locations at which they ski. *Informal groups* that usually develop on the basis of proximity, common interests, or similar circumstances have no explicit structure or membership requirements. The groups exist solely for the satisfaction of the members. Both formal and informal groups affect consumer decision making; however, formal groups have been the object of more research because they are easier to identify.

Recognizing the fact that it is often more meaningful to study consumers as members of groups rather than as isolated individuals has strengthened the analyst's understanding of consumer behavior. The task is usually complex, though, because each consumer is a member of several groups and all may influence a person's behavior.

Functions of Groups

From a consumer behavior perspective, groups perform three functions that are worth noting. First, groups have a substantial influence on the awareness of and preference for behavioral alternatives and the resulting life-styles. Second, groups serve society as conformity-enforcing mechanisms. Third, groups are important forces in the establishment and maintenance of an individual's self-concept. Each of these functions will be developed in the following paragraphs.

Socialization

Groups develop member awareness of and preference for certain consumption behavior through the socialization process. The *socialization process* refers to the manner in which a new member learns the value system, the norms, and the required behavior patterns of the groups and organizations into which he or she is entering.[16] The socialization of children occurs through the influence of family and playmates in the neighborhood as well as through institutional groups such as the schools. For instance, the family influences the child in such diverse areas as what to eat for breakfast, how much television to watch, and whether drinking alcoholic beverages is to be restrained or not. There is a particularly high interest among consumer researchers in understanding the socialization process of children within the family and as they are affected by the media. This interest stems from the hope that understanding the process among children will contribute to our understanding of adult behavior and also because of its importance to public policy formulation.[17]

At one time it was thought that the childhood socialization experiences were the only really important ones, but in recent years it has been recognized that adult socialization can also occur and markedly influence decision making. Such learning and adaptation frequently occur when adults change jobs, marry, or move to a new location.

Groups serve an important function in attitude formation and change. Individuals are not born with certain attitudes, nor are they developed in a vacuum.[18] Most attitudes are acquired by relating oneself to a variety of groups. Consumer analysts have established the existence of a relationship between an individual's attitudes and the attitudes of groups of which he or she is a member, but the precise nature or strength of the relationship has not been fully explored. The task of studying the nature of this relationship is complicated by the fact that consumers are members of many groups and differentially accept influences of each.

Compliance to Group Norms

Groups serve a normative function in that they cause members to comply with certain norms, that is, to behave in similar patterns. Marketing analysts are particularly interested in the normative function of groups because it is of assistance in determining whether or not a product will be accepted by a large enough group to make it a successful venture.

Norms Defined

Norms are statements or beliefs of the majority of group members that define what the activities of group members should be. These may be said to exist when the individuals involved agree, either explicitly or implicitly, that all members will regularly behave in a certain manner. The behavior prescribed may be consequential, such as renouncing material wealth as in the case of religious groups, or insignificant, such as not wearing a necktie.

When a new member wishes to join a group, that person receives pressure to conform to the group's standards. Although a group member may deviate from some norms while accepting others, he or she will find that conforming is often rewarded by the rest of the group, while nonconforming results in a withholding of rewards or even in sanctions. Thus, norms become stable expectations held by a consensus of the group concerning the behavioral rules for individual members.

Why People Conform to Norms

Once it has been established that members do conform to the norms of groups, it is necessary to consider why such conformity occurs. Homans' theory of social exchange is based on the premise that the behavior of one individual responding to another is more or less reinforcing or punishing to the behavior of that individual.[19] If, for example, you are invited to join another person on a shopping trip, there will be rewards (companionship, esteem accorded by the invitation, etc.), but there may also be costs (time lost, giving up association with others, etc.). The nature of interactions with another individual or group will be determined by a person's perception of the profit derived from the interaction. Homans defines this in familiar economic terms:

$$\text{Profit} = \text{Rewards} - \text{Costs}.$$

Based on this premise, individuals can be seen as arranging their social relations so as to maximize total profit. Thus, the groups an individual chooses to belong to and the degree to which there is adherence to the norms of that group are both based upon the net profit figure and not on rewards or costs alone. This view of conforming to norms provides the consumer analyst with a set of tools (concepts) to understand the formation of the group, the formation of group norms, and the extent of influence that results.

Conformity to Group Norms

A group dimension of particular interest to marketing analysts is the tendency of individuals to conform to group norms. Asch demonstrated the group pressure phenomenon in a situation where two sets of individuals were asked if there was a difference in the length of two lines. In a normal setting, there was no difficulty in correctly getting the answer that the lines were of equal length. But when wrong answers were deliberately given by three cooperating students, 37 percent of the other respondents also gave the wrong answer.[20]

The extent to which an individual conforms to a group's standards is a function of several variables. For instance, the study described above suggests that the pressure to conform increased as the number of agreeing individuals increased, but only up to a point. That is, increasing the number of agreeing individuals does not create a progressively greater impact.

The stability and cohesiveness of a group also affects the extent to which individuals accommodate the requirements. For instance, Festinger demonstrated that the more stable and cohesive a group is, the more likely it is to have conformity power over deviant members.[21]

In an experimental setting, Venkatesan demonstrated the effect of group pressure on the decision-making process of its members.[22] It was shown that when the superiority of one product among alternatives was not obvious, individuals tended to choose the preference of the majority.

Groups and the Self-concept

The way individuals perceive themselves has great relevance for marketing managers. People will attempt to purchase items that fit the interpretation they have of themselves or that will improve their self-concept.

This notion of self-concept involves the attitudes and perceptions one uses to define his or her personhood. The self is considered to have five components:

> The first component is an organized set of motivations. The second component of the self is a series of social roles to which the person is

committed, along with a knowledge of how to play them. Social roles are clusters of norms that are related to particular positions that a person occupies. The third component of the self is a more general set of commitments to social norms and their underlying values. The fourth component of the self is a set of cognitive abilities, including the ability to create and understand symbols, which guide response to the intended meanings of others in social interaction and provide a "map" of the physical and social setting in which the person finds himself. The fifth and final component of the self is a set of ideas about one's qualities, capabilities, commitments, and motives—a self image—that is developed by the individual in the course of his socialization.[23]

The symbols that people use to form and express their self-concept include the goods and services they buy and the way they use them. It is helpful at times to see these consumption patterns as being consistent with some internalized view that may be a combination of what one actually perceives him or herself to be and what he or she is striving to be.

The self-concept of an individual is also related to how that person believes others see him or her. The life-style adopted by a man or woman includes the selection and use of items in a manner that will reflect his or her perceived status among others.

The importance of the self-concept to marketing analysts is illustrated in Figure 5.3. Assume that an individual *A* perceives himself as being thrifty, economical, and practical. He may purchase a Volkswagen as a symbol of these qualities, thereby achieving internal self-enhancement. The audience *B* may include peers, family, and significant others. The doubleheaded arrows *b* and *c* in Figure 5.3 indicate that the Volkswagen is attributed meaning by *A* and that the audience *B* is also attributing meaning to it. If the Volkswagen *X* has a meaning common to *A* and *B*, communication of self has occurred, and the reaction of *B* will provide self-enhancement to individual *A*. Empirical support for the process of establishing congruence of self-concept and brand/store choice now permits marketing analysts to be concerned with the development of marketing strategies from such a base. The clothing store that wants to focus on the avant-garde type customer must offer a product line and store design that enhance self-concept for customers.

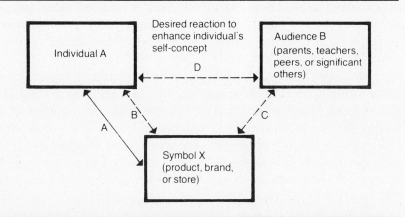

Figure 5.3
**Relationship of the
Consumption of Goods
as Symbols to Self-
concept**

Source: E. L. Grubb and H. L. Grathwohl, "Consumer Self-concept, Symbolism and Market Behavior: A Theoretical Approach," *Journal of Marketing,* 31 (October, 1967), p. 25. Reprinted from the *Journal of Marketing* published by the American Marketing Association.

Reference Groups

Although the impact of the group has long been recognized, confidence in the ability of group theory to explain consumer attitudes and behavior has been shaken by the reporting of contradictory evidence. For instance, members of a particular group may have similar preferences for automobiles but not for clothing. Confidence in the basic force, however, has been renewed by the development of reference-group theory. Reference-group theory was developed as a result of the recognition that not all groups to which an individual belongs exert the same influence or hold the same relevance for him or her. In fact, some groups of which the person is not even a member may be of considerable influence.

Functions of Reference Groups

Reference groups perform a normative and comparative function. The *normative function* refers to a group having a consensus of opinion with which the individual agrees and in which the individual seeks to gain or maintain acceptance. That is, such reference groups serve as a source of individual norms, attitudes, and values. Religious sects are an obvious example of performance of the normative function. The *comparative function* refers to the means by which the individual uses a group to establish his or her frame of reference for value formation and decision making. In this sense, the group itself serves as an actual standard. Consider the long-time member of a society for the advancement of the classical arts, who views with much disdain the rock music cult. These two forms of influence—that is, the normative function and the use of the group as a frame of reference for the individual—are the most meaningful for consumer analysts. These reference groups may differ greatly in size, composition, structure, and purpose, but their most important characteristic is the degree of influence they have over the consumer.

A particularly appealing dimension of reference-group theory is the fact that it incorporates both membership and nonmembership groups. Consumers may select as a reference group a nonmembership group to which they aspire to belong and begin to conform to the perceived norms. For instance, if one wishes to join a tennis club, there may be certain kinds of equipment that are considered appropriate and, therefore, necessary. Consumers may even use as a reference a group to which they can never belong. That is, even when there is no possiblility of attaining membership, a consumer may adopt those attitudes and behaviors of a group that are reasonably consonant with the realities of his or her own personal world. The fact that this does occur is one basis for having Bob Griese advertise men's clothing or Billie Jean King endorse tennis rackets.

Marketing Analysis of Reference-Group Influence

Various marketing analysts have described the importance of reference-group influences on consumer behavior, but researchers have given only limited empirical attention to the area. The research that has been done can be placed into two categories: (1) studies establishing that reference groups do influence consumption decisions and (2) studies to determine the consumption situations affected by reference groups.

The fact that reference groups influence consumption decisions has been demonstrated in a number of studies. One of these studies was an experiment that simulated the purchase of bread. Homemakers were required to choose a loaf of bread from four alternatives identified only by a letter on the wrapper. The study demonstrated that the preferences formed for each "brand" as represented by a different letter of the alphabet as well as the identifiable variation in preferences could be attributed to the influence of the consumer's reference group.[24]

The amount and nature of reference-group influence on individual consumption decisions appears to be affected by the product category involved and the characteristics of the group. The following two sections discuss the nature of these two dimensions.

Product Categories

Several studies have shown that the amount of reference-group influence upon consumption is related to the type of product involved. Using this perspective, Bourne differentiated among products subject to strong and weak group influences. The results of Bourne's analysis are summarized in Table 5.1. The Product +, Brand + category refers to those products that have significant specifications among friendship groups. Products such as automobiles, cigarettes, beer, and drugs are subject to strong norms that affect specific brands selected as well as the product purchased. Conversely, the Product −, Brand − category includes items such as soap, canned fruit, and radios, which are not subject to the influence of reference groups with respect to either the product or the brand purchased.

Bourne's analysis established four categories dealing with the varying effects of reference groups on consumer behavior:

1. Product +, Brand +. Reference groups influence whether or not the product itself is purchased and, if it is purchased, what brand is selected (automobiles, cigarettes).

2. Product +, Brand −. Reference groups influence whether or not the product is purchased but not which brand is selected (instant coffee, air conditioners).

3. Product −, Brand +. Reference groups do not influence the purchase of the product but do influence the brand selected if a purchase is to be made (clothing, furniture).

4. Product −, Brand −. Reference groups generally have no influence on either the purchase of the product or the brand selected (soap, canned fruit).

The research done by Bourne and others suggests that reference-group influence is strong when a product is a conspicuous expression of personal tastes; that is, the ability of a product to attract attention significantly contributes to whether or not it is susceptible to reference-group influence. Products are conspicuous when they are noticed and identified by others.[25] Reference groups also tend to have a particularly pronounced influence when the consumer has little knowledge about a product.

Group Characteristics

The amount of reference-group influence is determined partially by the characteristics of the group. Specifically, some studies have dem-

Table 5.1
Reference-Group Influence on Product Decisions

	Weak −	Strong +		
Strong +	Clothing Furniture Magazines Refrigerator (type) Toilet soap	Cars Cigarettes Beer (prem. vs. reg.) Drugs	+	Brand or Type
Weak −	Soap Canned peaches Laundry soap Refrigerator (brand) Radios	Air conditioners Instant coffee TV (black and white)	−	
	− Product +			

Source: Foundation for Research on Human Behavior, *Group Influence in Marketing and Public Relations* (Ann Arbor, Mich: The Foundation, 1956), p. 8. Reprinted by permission of the publisher.

onstrated that the more cohesive the group is, the greater the group influence is likely to be on individual choices. Cohesiveness appears to have its most important function in providing an agreeable environment in which informal leaders can effectively operate.[26] More important, it has been concluded that the higher the degree of brand loyalty exhibited by the group leader, the more likely the other members are to prefer the same brand and the more likely they are to become brand loyal.

When the marketing strategist attempts to apply the reference-group concept, two problems must be overcome. First, it must be determined if the purchase of the product and its brand is influenced by reference groups. Second, if the reference-group concept is relevant, it must be determined which reference groups will have an influence. The concept of research groups is of obvious significance in understanding consumer behavior. However, the attempts so far to apply the concept to marketing problems have been less than totally productive.

Summary

Social classes are relatively permanent and homogeneous divisions in a society into which individuals or families sharing similar values, lifestyles, interests, and behavior can be categorized. A helpful method for differentiating social classes makes use of a member's occupation, personal performance, personal interaction, possessions, and value orientation. An objective method for measuring social class most frequently uses the following variables: occupation, income, education, size and type of residence, ownership of personal possessions, and organizational affiliations. The most common class distribution in the United States is Warner's six-class system, which ranges from an upper upper class to a lower lower class. From a marketing perspective, the following three classes are the most important: upper middle class, lower middle class, and the upper lower class. There have been two major sources of discontent with the usefulness of social class as a means of explaining consumer behavior. These are the emergence of the massification theory and the contention that income is a better correlate of consumption behavior than social class. Both of these have been neglected in recent years. A skeleton outline of some important identifying characteristics and consumption patterns of each social class is presented, and some generalizations indicating the impact social class has on consumer behavior are also provided.

Social groups can be classified as primary or secondary and formal or informal. Primary groups have more influence over their members than do secondary groups. Formal groups have explicit structure, membership requirements, and specified goals, while informal groups do not. Groups perform three significant consumer behavior functions. First, they have a substantial influence on the awareness of and preference for behavioral alternatives and their resulting life-styles. Second, groups serve a normative function by causing members to comply with certain norms. Third, groups are important forces in the establishment and maintenance of an individual's self-concept.

Reference groups perform normative functions by serving as a source of individual norms, attitudes, and values. They also perform comparative functions when individuals use a group to establish a frame of reference for value formation and decision making.

The amount and nature of the influence that reference groups have on consumer behavior is determined by product category and group characteristics. Product categories that lend themselves to strong reference-group influence are those products that are readily noticed and identified by others and those about which the consumer has little knowledge. Group characteristics tend to have significant influence on consumer behavior when the group is a cohesive one and when the group leader exhibits a high degree of brand loyalty.

Questions and Issues for Discussion

1. What is the relationship between social class and income? Is income a better indicator of a person's potential to consume than is social class?

2. In a study conducted by A. C. Nielsen Company in 1976, 35.7 billion coupons were distributed in 1975, up from 29.8 billion in 1974. The survey revealed that upper-income families are the most frequent users of coupons, and that as income falls, so does the use of coupons. Why might this be so?

3. According to a *Business Week* article (April 11, 1977), aggregate income of the lower-middle class (income of $5,000–$15,000) has been growing more slowly than that of groups at both extremes of the income distribution. It contended that a "tiering" between luxury and staple consumer markets has been intensifying throughout the 1970s. One pollster remarked, "If you sell to the luxury market, the Rolls Royce drivers, or to the poor, say baked beans, you'll do well. But the middle class is standing still or losing." Do you agree or disagree?

4. A large manufacturer of recreational equipment is interested in increasing his penetration in existing markets and expanding to new markets. Why would information on social class be of assistance to this firm?

5. A successful fast food chain would like to widen its market by appealing to what is becoming the "new affluent," that is, young, married couples of which both partners enjoy professional careers. It has been reported that these couples dine out four nights of the week. What methods could the chain use to make its food service more palatable to this segment of diners?

6. The self-concept is interesting and, perhaps, relevant to certain types of purchases (automobiles, clothes), but the concept is of no value to the producers of soft drinks, television sets, hardware, and in fact, most product purchases. Discuss. Do your comments also hold true for the purchase of services?

7. Identify each of the following groups as (1) primary or secondary, and (2) formal or informal:

(a) A crew working for the Department of Highways

(b) Concert-goers

(c) American Marketing Association members

(d) 200 relatives attending a family reunion

(e) Gong Show panelists.

8. Identify three reference groups that are important to you. Are these the same three you would have identified five years ago? Are these three groups of equal influence on your values and behavior?

Name at least one norm of each group. Discuss how each of these norms is enforced.

9. How might a reference group influence your purchase of (1) an education for your child, (2) motor oil, (3) an in-car stereo, (4) an engagement ring, and (5) the purchase of a gift to be presented to a former teacher at her retirement dinner? What reference group would be important in making each decision?

10. How could a labor union use the group concept to formulate a strategy for attracting new members? Could the Environmental Protection Agency or the Department of Energy use the group concept to better perform their tasks? How?

Case 1. Johnson Stores Incorporated

Johnson Stores Incorporated, a large national retailer, is presently taking a fashion gamble which is being eyed by analysts and competing retailers with skepticism. In its 90-year history, it has been identified as a retailer to "small-town America," appealing to price-conscious consumers in bargain basement surroundings. Its reliance on low-priced, private-label software recently cost the store its long-held high position in retailing when T. G. Jones surpassed it. In the past three years, it has lost market share in 50 percent of the markets in which it operates. It is not the dominant retailer in any of its ten major markets. The stores' location in many shopping malls has hurt sales because of the intense competition of the more fashion-conscious stores. Nevertheless, it is trying to win back its high position in the retailing industry. The strategy is to concentrate on brand-name women's apparel and fast-paced fashion whims in an effort to attract a less price-conscious clientele. Observers are wary because the same move was tried a few years ago by Sears, Roebuck & Company and proved to be a failure. Johnson's chairman, however, contends that the image change will be effective because finding the right item is the main consideration of the customer. Price has become secondary.

In a 1975 survey of 5,000 regular Johnson customers, it was found that women purchased Johnson's lingerie and underwear, but patron-

Source: Some information in Case 1 is from "J. C. Penney's Fashion Gamble," *Business Week,* January 16, 1978, pp. 66–74.

ized competing department stores to buy high-markup lines of sportswear, coats, and dresses. The customers desired higher priced, better quality garments than were available at Johnson's. A second interview revealed that of Johnson's three categories of customers—juniors, conservatives, and contemporaries (the largest group who spend the most money on apparel)—only one third of the all-important contemporaries rated the chain highly for its women's merchandise. The group perceived Johnson's as being an old-fashioned store that attracted lower-class customers. Also, many were even unsure as to whether the chain was oriented to women. This was the catalyst for Johnson's realization that it was neglecting many of its customers' needs. Now it intends to fill the vacuum between the discount stores' merchandise and the more expensive merchandise in upgraded department stores by providing moderately priced items.

Johnson's is undertaking a research project in five of its major markets: Atlanta, Houston, Pittsburgh, St. Louis, and Seattle. Nineteen outlets in these cities have been chosen for the "fashion pilot project." The stores' layout, merchandise mix, buying and pricing structure, advertising, and personnel are being changed significantly. The former racks of polyester goods that were displayed under starkly lit fluorescent tubes have been replaced by softly lit and carpeted women's apparel departments that feature cashmere sweaters, wool skirts, soft-style silk blouses, and a few enticing mink coats.

The major problem facing Johnson's is whether or not the company can "trade up" its image and prices and still keep its present clientele. At the same time, it will be difficult to attract fashion-conscious consumers to a store that also sells and heavily promotes paint and hardware. Johnson's management argues that the convenience offered to women will overcome this problem; instead of women shopping at Johnson's for men's and children's wear and housewares and then driving to another store for their own apparel, they will now be able to meet all of their shopping needs in one store.

Besides the risk of keeping its present customers and attracting new ones, Johnson's could also feasibly encounter supply problems. The demanding buying and selling schedules for fashion goods will require more expertise than Johnson's has needed in the past. Also, the chain does not have a guarantee that it will be able to obtain all of the brand name goods it wants, because suppliers are reluctant to sell to chains for fear of lowering the impact of their brands and annoying their department store accounts. One supplier admits that he does not want to be the first or even the third company to supply the store. He wants to wait until fifty or more brand manufacturers are supplying it. His reasoning is that if Johnson's tries a brand for a season and then dumps it, the supplier is finished. He'll have offended his department store accounts for nothing.

In spite of the potential risks, Johnson's is aggressively overhauling its pilot stores. Brand-name goods now constitute 25 percent of the merchandise in the store. Instead of contracting for $15 skirts, $35 to $40 skirts are being sought. The stores also carry dresses in the $80 price range. However, not all of the stores are conscientious about protecting the fashion and glamour image. In one store, smoke detectors and coffee makers were displayed next to the women's apparel. In another, $4500 mink coats and $750 raccoon jackets were next to a candy counter and a popcorn machine. And none of the stores strategically placed mirrors next to the expensive furs to tempt the customers into trying them on and admiring themselves.

Case 1 Questions

1. Using your knowledge of social class and its effect on consumption behavior, explain why Johnson's will have difficulty attracting a more distinguished clientele to its women's apparel department.

2. What restraints might the social-class determinants impose on Johnson's efforts to gain the acceptance of this segment?

3. In your estimation, can a store effectively cater to both price-conscious and fashion-conscious consumers simultaneously? What methods could Johnson's employ to do so?

Case 2. The Tennis Shoe Market

Over the past several years, the leading United States athletic shoe manufacturers have decidedly lost ground to foreign competition. This is especially true in what is known as the upper tier of the sneakers race—the leather- or nylon-topped division. Considered the

Source: Some Information in Case 2 is from "Sneaker Makers Are Set to Pursue the Athletes at Summer Olympics," *Wall Street Journal*, April 23, 1976.

most lucrative segment of the athletic shoe market in the United States, the share belonging to foreign producers has reached almost 60 percent and is rising. There is very much at stake in this struggle for buyers. In 1975, it is estimated that retail sales of all types of athletic shoes in the United States alone amounted to over 1.25 billion dollars, slightly less than double the total of seven years before. Worldwide, the figure approached $5 billion in 1975.

Sales of expensive white canvas and rubber sneakers, long preferred by small boys, have been the slowest growing. It is significant, however, that sales of athletic footwear worn by youngsters between the ages of 10 and 17 add up to $39.4 million annually. Sneakers experiencing the real growth in sales, though, are the leather- or nylon-topped models mentioned above. These typically sell for over $20, are available in a dazzling variety of colors, and sport dashing emblems of the makers. Many of those who wear these high-priced models do so not for purposes of engaging in sports, but just to look sporty. So the growth in demand for these shoes is as much a function of style as anything.

Mothers have for a long time been fearful that athletic shoes are bad for the feet, but this has proven to be a fallacy. There is even some question as to whether the costlier varieties are superior to canvas types in terms of functional attributes. Says one pediatrician, "Leather uppers might provide more stability for the foot in heavy competition, but this is counterbalanced by the fact that canvas-topped models usually offer better ventilation."

Adidas of West Germany, whose emblem of three diagonal stripes has become a well-known commercial symbol, has raced to the top of overall United States athletic shoe sales since the 1968 Olympics with its extensive television coverage. It now makes shoes for almost every sport, and is making good headway in former U.S. strongholds such as baseball, basketball, and tennis. "Those damn three stripes," gripes one American shoe man, "they stand out on a track like a Rolls Royce in a used car lot."

Undoubtedly, U.S. manufacturers are seeking some means of reversing this trend. Both Kipper's and Monroe's, the two largest U.S. shoemakers, were slow to introduce their leather-topped models and are now trying desperately to make comebacks. Kipper's has marketed a line of jogging and leisure shoes called "Zooms," and has recently offered a $5 rebate to buyers of their traditional shoes. Monroe's donated substantial sums to amateur athletics and has begun advertising during telecasts of such athletic events. But the foreign competition knows that such athletic events, especially the Olympics, offer a splendid opportunity to display their merchandise. Pony, a Japanese brand, scored a victory by lining up the Canadian team, which had one of the largest contingents for the Montreal games. Adidas contracted with the overall Olympic organizing committee to outfit all ushers, timers, and other officials with shoes and leisure suits.

Endorsements by professional athletes are also very important to these firms. Standouts in nearly every sport can be seen and heard promoting someone's shoes. Converse, for example, signed New York Nets ace Julius Irving ("Dr. J.") to wear its All-Star brand (promoted as "lim-o-zeens for the feet") and conduct summer clinics in basketball. Adidas, however, uses a saturation tactic, outfitting whole professional teams—and the entire American Basketball Association— free. Their promotions director explains, "Every pro athlete is a hero in his hometown at least, and we feel that helps us more than a few big names."

Case 2 Questions

1. Using your acquaintance with reference-group theory, explain its relevance to the situation described above.

2. In a recent survey, teenage boys were asked about their participation in team sports: 74 percent of the boys said they enjoy football; 72 percent, basketball; and 71 percent, baseball. In making their purchasing decision for sports equipment, 53 percent of the respondents said they rely on the advice of their parents. How might the producers of Kippers or Monroes make use of this information in their marketing programs?

3. Discuss the roles that teammates might play in influencing the purchasing decisions of a young athlete.

4. Explain the self-concept's role in an individual's decision to purchase a pair of athletic shoes or some sports equipment.

Notes

1. Arun K. Jain, "A Method for Investigating and Representing Implicit Social Class Theory," *Journal of Consumer Research*, Vol. 2 (June 1975), pp. 53–59.

2. W. Lloyd Warner, Marchia Meeker, and Kenneth Eels, *Social Class in America: A Manual of Procedure for the Measurement of Social Status* (Chicago: Science Research Associates, 1949), pp. 56-57.

3. James M. Carman, *The Application of Social Class in Market Segmentation* (Berkeley, Calif.: Institute of Business and Economic Research, University of California Graduate School of Business Administration, 1965); W. L. Warner, J. O. Low, P. S. Lune, and L. Srole, *Yankee City* (New Haven, Conn.: Yale University Press, 1963), p. 43; August B. Hollingshead and Frederick C. Redich, "Social Stratification and Psychiatric Disorders," *American Sociological Review*, Vol. 18 (1953), pp. 163-67; Arthur J. Vidich and Joseph Bensman, *Small Town in Mass Society* (Princeton, N.J.: Princeton University Press, 1958, Anchor Edition, 1960), p. 52.

4. Pierre Martineau, "Social Classes and Spending Behavior," *Journal of Marketing,* Vol. 23 (October 1958), pp. 121-30; Sidney Levy, "Social Class and Consumer Behavior," Joseph W. Newman, ed., *On Knowing the Consumer* (New York: John Wiley and Sons, 1966), pp. 146-60; Phillip Kotler, "Behavioral Model for Analyzing Buyers," *Journal of Marketing,* Vol. 29 (October 1965); Richard P. Coleman and Bernice L. Newgarten, *Social Status in the City* (San Francisco: Jossey-Bass, 1971).

5. Norval D. Glenn, "Massification Versus Differentiation: Some Trend Data from National Survey," *Social Forces,* Vol. 46 (December 1967); Norval D. Glenn and Jon P. Alstop, "Cultural Distances Among Occupational Categories," *American Sociological Review,* Vol. 33 (June 1968).

6. R. D. Hisrich and Michael Peters, "Selecting the Superior Segmentation Correlate," *Journal of Marketing,* Vol. 38 (July 1974), pp. 60-63.

7. Stuart U. Rich and Subhash C. Jain, "Social Class and Life Cycle as Predictors of Shopping Behavior," *Journal of Marketing Research,* Vol. 5 (February 1968), pp. 41-49.

8. Edward O. Laumann and James S. House, "Living Room Styles and Social Attributes: The Patterning of Material Artifacts in a Modern Urban Community," *Sociology and Social Research,* Vol. 54 (April 1970), pp. 321-42.

9. An excellent discussion of the problems in defining social class, stratification, and status and of the theoretical perspectives that exist in status research is found in Thomas E. Lasswell, *Class and Stratum: An Introduction to Concepts and Research* (Boston: Houghton Mifflin Co., 1965), Chapters 1-4.

10. H. Lee Mathews and John W. Slocum, Jr., "Social Class and Commercial Bank Credit Card Usage," *Journal of Marketing,* Vol. 33 (January 1969), pp. 71-78.

11. John W. Slocum, Jr., and H. Lee Mathews, "Social Class and Income as Indicators of Consumer Credit Behavior," *Journal of Marketing,* Vol. 34 (April 1970), pp. 69-74.

12. Joseph T. Plummer, "Life Style Patterns and Commercial Bank Credit Card Usage," *Journal of Marketing,* Vol. 35 (April 1971), pp. 35-41.

13. Gordon R. Foxall, "Social Factors in Consumer Choice: Replication and Extension," *Journal of Consumer Research,* Vol. 2 (June 1975), pp. 60-64.

14. James S. House, "Why and When Is Status Inconsistency Stressful?" *American Journal of Sociology,* Vol. 81 (1976), pp. 395-411.

15. S. Asch, *Social Psychology* (Englewood Cliffs, N.J.: Prentice-Hall, Inc., 1957), Chapter 6.

16. Edgar H. Schein, "Organization Socialization and the Profession of Management," David A. Kolb, Irwin M. Rubin, and James M. McIntyre, eds., *Organizational Psychology* (Englewood Cliffs, N.J.: Prentice-Hall, Inc.,1971), pp. 1-14, at p. 3.

17. Scott Ward, "Consumer Socialization," *Journal of Consumer Research,* Vol. 1 (September 1974), pp. 1-14.

18. T. M. Newcomb, "Attitude Development as a Function of Reference Groups: The Bennington Study," E. E. Maccoby, T. M. Newcomb, and E. L. Hartley, eds., *Readings in Social Psychology* (New York: Holt, Rinehart and Winston, Inc., 1958), pp. 265-75.

19. G. Homans, *Social Behavior: Its Elementary Forms* (New York: Harcourt, Brace, Jovanovich, Inc., 1961), Chapters 3 and 4.

20. S. E. Asch, "Effects of Group Pressure Upon the Modification and Distortion of Judgements," H. H. Kassarjian and T. S. Robertson, eds., *Consumer Behavior* (Glenview, Ill.: Scott, Foresman and Company, 1973), pp. 215-324.

21. L. Festinger, "Informal Social Communication," *Psychological Review,* Vol. 57 (1950), pp. 271-92.

22. M. Venkatesan, "Experimental Study of Consumer Behavior Conformity and Independence," *Journal of Marketing Research,* Vol. 3 (November 1966), pp. 384-87.

23. John P. Hewitt, *Social Stratification and Deviant Behavior* (New York: Random House, 1970), pp. 32-33.

24. J. E. Stafford, "Effects of Group Influence on Consumer Brand Preferences," *Journal of Marketing,* Vol. 3 (February 1966), pp. 68-75.

25. Foundation for Research on Human Behavior, *Group Influence in Marketing and Public Relations* (Ann Arbor, Mich.: The Foundation, 1956), p. 10.

26. Stafford, "Effects of Group Influence," pp. 68-75.

Chapter 6   The Family in
Consumer Behavior

Outline

Family Forms

Family Influences on Individual Members

Values

Interpersonal Attitudes

Self-perception

Daily Life Routine

Concluding Comment: Family Influence on Individual Members

The Family as a Buying and Consuming Entity

Alternative Models

The Family as a Dynamic Entity

Family Role Structures

Additional Concepts of Role Structure

Children in Family Decision Making

Summary

Questions and Issues for Discussion

Cases

Key Terms

family

nuclear family

extended family

family of orientation

family of procreation

household

social class

influencing function

mediating function

values

interpersonal attitudes

self-perception

daily life routine

decision-process model

family life cycle

target market

role dominance

role specialization

syncratic decision

gatekeeper concept

role accumulation

role transition

passive dictation

The family as an institution has been receiving increasing attention from a broad spectrum of researchers and policymakers. Some of them question whether the family is in transition, in trouble, or even able to survive, while others convey an optimistic assessment of its future.[1] However the changes in values and the traditional familial responsibilities, stability, composition, and roles are approached, it is evident that government, business, and the academic community have become more committed to studying the approximately 57 million living units defined as families.

In focusing on the family as it relates to consumer behavior, at least two perspectives may be used. First, the family may be viewed as an agent that influences the behavior of its individual members. This involves an awareness of the effect that various beliefs, life-styles, socioeconomic status, and patterns of interaction among members have on an individual member's market behavior. The family is, therefore, seen as a reference group. The second perspective focuses on the family as a unique entity. The family is viewed as a unit that has specific identifiable characteristics and an existence beyond a simple summation of the behavior or outlook of its individual members. The uniqueness of the consumption patterns of the family entity is often a product of the intimacy of shared concerns and priorities, and these result in behavioral patterns worthy of special study.

Before these perspectives can be elaborated, it is well to consider several circumstances that are very likely to affect these influencing and consuming functions of the family.

1. The Women's Liberation Movement. Not only have the efforts for equal opportunity in employment and legal matters made an impact on family life in general, so has the magnitude of the number of women in the labor force bringing the demands of their new life-styles to the marketplace. Some of the results of these forces were noted in Chapter 3.

2. The "New" Freedom in Sexual Conduct. Persons who identify with this trend may have greater expectations and fewer inhibitions in seeking self-fulfillment generally. This pattern has fostered strong interest in personal hobbies, self-expression in clothing selection, and participation in sports such as racketball and tennis.

3. New and Emerging Forms of the Family with Different Perceptions of the Bearing and Rearing of Children. A declining birth rate, an increasing divorce rate, postponement of marriage, alternative living arrangements, and a growing skepticism toward having children are among the issues surrounding the family. These also can have a measurable impact on consumer behavior. For example, having children later in the life of a family typically means bringing a child into a more affluent environment. The household will be more well established and can commit greater resources to child-oriented spending.

A recent news release from the Bureau of Labor Statistics revealed that only 13 percent of the people in the United States were living in the traditional "typical" family of parents and children (still at home) with one wage earner.[2] Percentages of persons in other family living arrangements were as follows: 21 percent, single-person households; 16 percent, single-parent families; 23 percent, married, but no children; 16 percent, married with children and two wage earners; 6 percent, extended families; 4 percent, experimental families; and 1 percent, others.

There are many ramifications of these conditions and trends. The shifts in household composition and size could have a substantial impact on the level of demand for a vast array of products and services including housing, education, and health care. The increase in the frequency with which families pay for services to carry out routine household tasks also means other changes in the marketplace. Several examples are more varied meal patterns and the use of professional house cleaners and lawn-care services. Much more could be said, but at this point it is sufficient to remember that these conditions do have some effect on the manner in which the family serves as an influencing agent and a unique consuming unit.

In approaching the study of the family, it is also useful to identify and define several alternative configurations of the family. These include the nuclear family, extended family, family of orientation, family of procreation, and the household. This brief review draws attention to the nature and roots of family behavioral patterns that can arise from different interpersonal relationships. For instance, a recent study of banking practices in a medium-sized community showed that the experiences of specific members of the extended family had a substantial influence on adults' selection of their primary bank.

Family Forms

There are important variations in what have been called families or family groups that must be differentiated for increased clarity and understood as offering overlapping circles of influence. What follows is not an attempt to be exhaustive, but an attempt to deal with the more common forms that the family takes.

First, the term *family* generally refers to a group of people who are related by blood, marriage, or legal adoption. Individuals who simply live together in an apartment or dormitory as roommates are not considered a family in the customary use of the term. This general definition does not delineate the family entity sufficiently to permit identification of the influences and interactions that are important to the consumer analyst. Considerable clarification can be achieved by distinguishing among the following: the nuclear family, the extended family, the family of orientation, and the family of procreation. It will also be helpful to differentiate between a family and a household.

Nuclear family refers to the immediate kinship group of father and/or mother and their offspring or adopted children who ordinarily live together. A temporary separation of a member does not dissolve this kinship. For example, a son or daughter away at college is still part of the nuclear family. The members of a nuclear family have considerable face-to-face contact on a regular basis. This living together and the intimate sharing that takes place over time are major characteristics of the nuclear family. It is also the family grouping that has been studied the most.

The *extended family* includes the nuclear family plus other relatives, such as grandparents, uncles, aunts, cousins, and in-laws. As a focus of attention in terms of their possible influence on the family members' behaviors or the behavior of the family unit, there is a practical limit as to who is included for study. The extent to which a relative is considered a part of the extended family is essentially determined by the regularity and intimacy of the interaction with the family members.

The family that one is born into or adopted into is called the *family of orientation*. This family group typically initiates the enculturation process that continues throughout life. The interpretation of family roles, various help patterns (exchange of money, advice, gifts, and services), and fundamental values are identified and passed on to offspring by this family. The family of orientation essentially begins with the nuclear family but ordinarily is expanded over time and becomes the extended family.

The *family of procreation* is established when one marries; that is, this represents the formation of a new family unit capable of existence as a separate entity.

All families are households; however, not all households are families. The term *household* refers to a living unit or entity for consumption purposes, and in the United States about 80 percent of these units are families. A person living alone represents a separate, fully functioning living unit and is also considered a household. Nevertheless, a single person does not consititute a family because the term *family* is used to refer to at least two related people. Nor would two single men or women living together in an apartment be referred to as a family, although they do constitute a household.

The purpose of this chapter is to concentrate on families. Generally, they are more permanent, demonstrate greater interdependency among members, and have historically assumed more significant roles in society than have nonfamily households. Furthermore, the nuclear family in particular is the optimum unit of study because of the following reasons.

1. The family is the accumulating unit, the inventory of acquisitions over time being a nuclear family inventory. The items accumulated include various possessions such as cooking utensils, furniture, books, an automobile, and usually some form of real estate.

2. The nuclear family is typically the decision-making unit in asset accumulation and consumption.

3. The nuclear family is more accessible for study than are its competitors and more easily definable for purposes of study than is the household, for example, which may include lodgers who have little part in family acquisition.[3]

Although these points essentially draw attention to the family as a consuming unit, it is also important to recognize the impact of the family as a socializing influence on its members. Even though these two dimensions of the family are interrelated, it is helpful to separate them for discussion. Therefore, the next section will give specific attention to family influences on its members.

Family Influences on Individual Members

Because of the nature of humans, a young person must be cared for and nurtured both physically and psychologically; most often this is handled in a family environment. Parsons and Bales contend that no society has found an effective substitute arrangement for the family.[4]

Even in the kibbutz, where a community-oriented structure exists, the basic socialization responsibilities remain with the parents. That is, the family continues to exist as a distinct unit. Because the socialization process begins at birth, the family's influence on the behavior of the individual member can be significant.

Furthermore, with all that has been said about changing family composition and the pressures that have been affecting the relationships among family members, one might expect growing disenchantment with family experiences. This is not the case. The level of satisfaction that adults in the United States obtained from their family relationships has not deteriorated over the last several years. This is reflected in the findings summarized in Table 6.1 from the results of nationwide studies conducted by the National Opinion Research Center. Actually, there has been some slight increase in the positive direction concerning the level of satisfaction with family life from 1973 through 1975.

The family shapes its members' personality characteristics, attitudes, and evaluative criteria, that is, the way its members look at the world and how they relate to it. To a large extent, this influence is informal and exerted on the individual over an extended period of time. Part of this influence includes the acquiring of a consumer outlook. As Boyd and Levy have contended, ". . . people are born with apparently insatiable needs and desires. From their first moments they are learning what specific things to consume and the ways to consume them, and, quite as important, what not to consume."[5]

Table 6.1
Satisfaction with Family Life: 1973–1975

	1973	1974	1975
A very great deal	43.0%	43.3%	44.1%
A great deal	31.3%	33.5%	32.9%
Quite a bit	9.8%	10.6%	10.5%
A fair amount	8.6%	6.9%	6.6%
Some	3.4%	2.4%	2.5%
A little	2.2%	2.0%	1.6%
None	1.7%	1.3%	1.9%

Source: U.S. Department of Commerce, Bureau of the Census, *Social Indicators 1976: Selected Data on Social Conditions and Trends in the United States* (Washington, D.C.: Government Printing Office, 1977), p. 68.

In describing similar circumstances, Riesman and Roseborough stated that what children learn from their parents is a kind of basic set of domestic arrangements, for instance, a view of furniture as specific functional items to acquire rather than as a stylistic concept and, consequently, the need for home furnishings such as ranges, refrigerators, and television sets. The same individuals are likely to learn styles and moods of consumption from their peers.[6]

The amount of influence the family has will vary at different periods of its members' lives. For example, a very young child may have

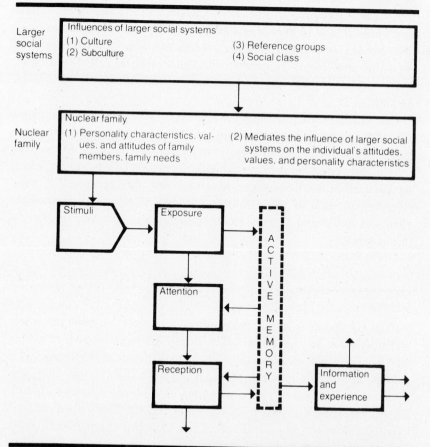

Figure 6.1
Family Influences on Individual Information and Experiences

relatively little contact outside his or her immediate family environment until the age of four or five years. Typically, the number of socializing agents increases substantially upon entering school with the regular nonfamily contact with teachers and schoolmates.

Figure 6.1 illustrates the relations among larger social systems, the family, and the individual. It can be noted that the nuclear family plays two important roles. First, the interaction among family members helps shape individual personalities, evaluative criteria, and attitudes. Second, the nuclear family often performs a mediating or interpretation function in exchanges among members, particularly as these relate to resolving differences concerning the needs of the family as a whole. These two functions are stimuli or inputs into the individual's central control unit and are subject to the complex processes of exposure, attention, comprehension, and retention. As such, they have varying degrees of influence on an individual's psychological makeup.

One example of these family influences in action is the impact that a family's social class can have on its life-style and, subsequently, on its members' buying behaviors. The differences that arise from social class membership basically are reflected in variations in values, interpersonal attitudes, self-perceptions and daily life routines.[7] A brief reference to each of these four factors will illustrate their possible effect on individual family member behavior and some marketing implications.

Values

Values are deeply internalized personal feelings that generally affect one's behavior and judgments. The family plays an important role in the development of personal values, which can vary across social classes. For example, some research suggests that people from low socioeconomic classes value personal advancement and self-sufficiency less than do middle class people. This difference can have a significant impact on an individual family member's personal desire for education, his or her motivation while in an educational environment, and even his or her attitude toward providing financial support for education as a taxpayer. Furthermore, any such influence on educational attainment may have a life-long effect on an individual's market behavior. For example, better educated people are generally more astute shoppers. They are also more likely to show an interest in the arts, the public park system, and sports like golf and pleasure boating.

The value placed on time as a scarce resource also varies from one social class to another. The middle class has generally placed the most value on the careful planning and budgeting of time. This is consistent with the high achievement orientation of middle class people. The high valuation of time also affects consumer behavior. For instance, the willingness to engage in prepurchase search for information, the specific sources used, as well as one's interest in labor-saving products are influenced by the perceived value of a person's time.

The role of values in the market behavior of consumers has not received much attention. Adding the knowledge of consumer value orientations, especially in the family framework, to the already used demographic and psychographic (life-style) variables could help marketing management operations become more effective. Some of the most promising avenues for research and application of the knowledge of values include market analysis and segmentation, product planning, promotional strategy development, and public policy formulation.[8]

For example, market identification might include a segment made up of consumers who highly regard imaginativeness, an exciting lifestyle, and independence. Such a grouping could be defined as a market segment of consumers concerned with individuality and self-expression. These consumers may be more receptive to products that can be tailored to their individual desires through the use of added accessories and styling options. Certainly, automobile producers have provided such product flexibility as have some clothing manufacturers.[9]

Interpersonal Attitudes

Interpersonal attitudes refers to the predisposition of family members to interactions among themselves as well as with those outside the family. Differences in interpersonal attitudes exist across social classes and shape individual family member behavior. For instance, middle class husbands and wives are more likely to jointly pursue various family functions—such as decision making in child rearing, family budgeting, and expenditures for major purchases—than those in lower class families. As a result, a middle class woman may be more likely to postpone a purchase decision until she has obtained her husband's views than is a woman from a lower socioeconomic class.

Also, middle class families generally relate socially to more people than do lower class families. This includes having more nonfamily members into the home for meals, entertainment, and socializing. This kind of interpersonal interaction has a long-term effect on children and a more immediate impact on other members' market activities. Middle class individuals are more likely to seek information from others when making a major purchase decision than are individuals from lower social classes.[10] This latter behavioral pattern may substantially alter the information base from which one operates in his or her prepurchase deliberation.

Self-perception

Levy found that the way one thinks of or perceives him or herself also varies by social class.[11] For instance, lower class women understand their own bodies less well and have more taboos about them than do middle class women. Lower class women were also found to have more traditional views of interpersonal relations. Masculinity and physical strength were found to be of more concern to lower class men than they were to middle class men.

Lower class people generally have less self-confidence and feel less in control of their own destiny.[12] Consequently, they are more likely to believe that if they get ahead, it is the result of chance or luck rather than the result of personal effort. These views are shared among family members and are passed on from one generation to the next. Their influence on family members' market behavior can take on many forms. For example, such a prevailing family view may lead to a discouragement of a member's efforts for self-improvement through technical training or enrollment in a self-development course such as that offered through adult education programs. It may also encourage a greater interest in gambling such as that which is available through state-sponsored lotteries.

Daily Life Routine

Each family develops its own routine to cope with the daily demands placed upon it. In fact, an interesting exercise for each of us is to attempt to set down in some detail the way our family handles the responsibilities of a typical day.

In most families, this routine varies between weekdays and the weekend and, to some extent, by season. The record of such a routine would at least include the time when family members arise; how meals are prepared and eaten (e.g., in some families the meals are prepared jointly while more typically this responsibility falls upon one member—the wife); when members leave for work, school, other regular activities; how much time is spent apart, together, and in what activities; and how the family closes the day.

The word "routine" is used to imply a regular pattern. The awareness of this regular pattern continues over time and, coupled with what is known about learning theory, strongly suggests that the daily family life routine can have an important impact on the individual family member's behavior. The strong interest of other family members in certain sports, for example, may shape one's interests also. Furthermore, what food is served at home and how it is served affects younger members' eating patterns outside the home and their meal preparation and entertainment style when they establish their own families later in life.

Concluding Comment:
Family Influence on Individual Members

As an individual interacts with other family members, he or she simultaneously influences these individuals as he or she is being influenced by them. Furthermore, no other single group or individual ordinarily has as many opportunities for shaping a person's behavior as does his or her family. As mentioned earlier, the nuclear family is a primary group with frequent face-to-face contact among its members. It also shares a common pool of financial resources as well as consumption needs. Therefore, family members tend to be more alike in their thinking and behavioral patterns than they would be if they were not in the same family.

The Family as a Buying and Consuming Entity

As pointed out in the introduction to this chapter, the family, particularly the nuclear family, is a very significant economic and social unit in most societies. Personal goals and expectations are brought together, shared, and shaped by family members in such a way that the family itself takes on a set of characteristics that reflect those of its members but which, nevertheless, are unique to it. Decisions regarding the purchase and use of goods and services are made by a family through the interaction of its members. Consequently, it can be said that family decision making, similar to that of individuals who act on their own behalf, can be characterized by a decision-process model.

Families and family behavior have been studied extensively by social scientists in many disciplines including sociology, social psychology, anthropology, home economics, consumer psychology, economics, and marketing. However, as Ferber has pointed out, relatively little attention has been given to bringing together the various dimensions of consumer behavior within the framework of the family to provide a more realistic explanation of economic behavior.[13]

Alternative Models

Ferber has developed what he calls a simplified decision-making framework with specific attention given to family saving and spending.[14] This is shown in Figure 6.2. The basis for the framework is the division of family economic decisions into two types—financial and nonfinancial. Those decisions in the financial grouping include decisions dealing with money management, savings, spending, and asset management. Because this framework was used primarily to discuss

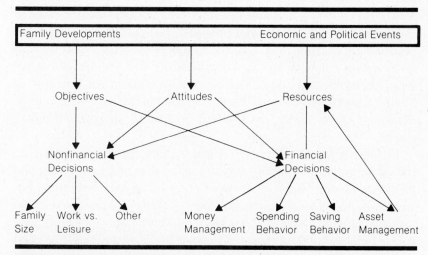

Figure 6.2
Interrelation of Saving and Spending Decisions

Source: R. Ferber, "Family Decision Making and Economic Behavior," in *Family Economic Behavior: Problems and Prospects*, ed. E. B. Sheldon (Philadelphia: J. B. Lippincott Company, 1973), p. 31. Reprinted by permission of the publisher.

financial decisions, all other decisions that a family may make are grouped together under what is called nonfinancial.

One can quickly note in Ferber's framework that both financial and nonfinancial decisions are affected by the available financial resources of the family, by the objectives or goals of the family, and by the attitudes of the family members. The family's objectives and attitudes relate to a wide variety of topics and, therefore, encompass both the material and the nonmaterial goals of the family in both the short and long run. Attitudes include expectations and outlooks of the different family members on economic and related issues as well as their system of preferences and value judgments concerning alternative types of economic behavior.

This framework takes note of the fact that family decisions in some instances are dominated by influences that are external and not under the family's control. In particular, these include economic and political events in the community in which the family lives and personal experiences of the individual family members such as births, deaths, marriages, and accidents.

Other, more detailed models of family decision making have been developed. One of the most recent contributions has been made by

Sheth. He offers a comprehensive model of family decision making in consumer behavior. The model presented in Figure 6.3 is a representation of his attempt to specify the nature of family decision making in consumer behavior and to bring together the findings of various social scientists in a comprehensive representation. An overview of Sheth's theory is presented here, but the details may be found in *Models of Buyer Behavior: Conceptual, Quantitative, and Empirical.*[15]

In viewing the Sheth model, it can be noted at the far right that the consumption of a family is classified as that of (1) the individual members, (2) the family as a whole, and (3) the household unit. Examples of individual members' consumption include their use of shaving cream, which may just be used by the father (husband), nail polish by the mother (wife), and comic books or toys by the child (children). However, various food items and hand soap, for example, are consumed by everyone in the family. Furthermore, certain goods and services (e.g., utilities such as water, electricity, and natural gas) as well as such items as paint, wallpaper, and the living-room furniture are used by the family indirectly in the process of living together in the same residence. The latter fit into Sheth's third category of consumption. This approach to classifying family consumption points out that the demand for goods and services may be collective and direct, collective and indirect, or individual.

In Sheth's theory, as represented by the model shown, family consumption is considered to follow family buying decisions. This indicates that gifts, rentals, and acquisitions by means other than buying are not explicitly taken into account. This seems appropriate because these latter forms represent a small proportion of the goods and services consumed by most families.

Family buying decisions are identified as either autonomous—made by a single member—or joint—made by at least two members of the family. The theory as a whole has four major subsections that can be observed in the model:

1. Individual members of the family, their predispositions, and the underlying buying motives and evaluative beliefs about products and brands

2. Determinants of the motives and beliefs of the individual members that are both external and internal

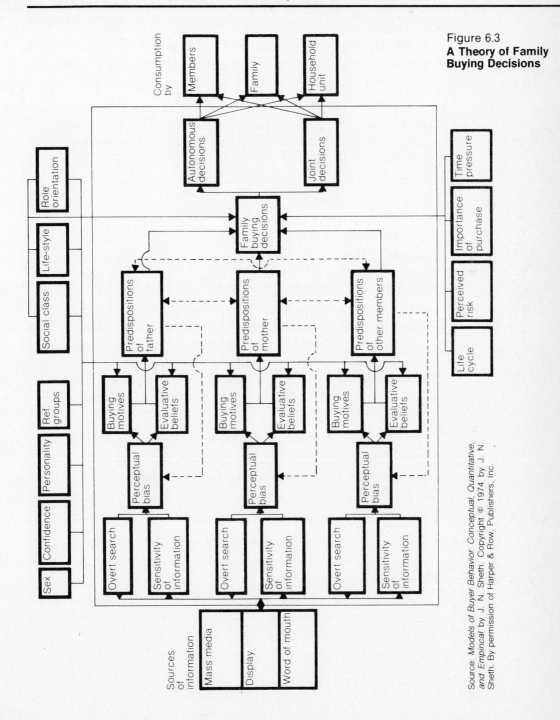

Figure 6.3
**A Theory of Family
Buying Decisions**

Source: *Models of Buyer Behavior: Conceptual, Quantitative, and Empirical* by J. N. Sheth. Copyright © 1974 by J. N. Sheth. By permission of Harper & Row, Publishers, Inc.

3. Determinants of autonomous versus joint family decision making

4. The process of joint decision making, with consequent intermember conflict and its resolution.

Although the Ferber and Sheth models differ substantially, each draws attention to the importance of focusing on the family as a unique consuming unit. The next section specifically takes note of the fact that families change over time, that is, that the family is a dynamic entity.

The Family as a Dynamic Entity

For many reasons, family composition changes over time, and this may substantially alter the family needs, its decision-making process, and its market behavior (where it shops and what it buys). One way of viewing these changes that has proven helpful is through what has been called the *family life cycle*. A common representation of this follows below. It should be noted, however, that in this categorization there are three listings included here as a representation of the usual format, although they are not families but nonfamily households. Furthermore, these three nonfamily households represent pre- and post-family entities.

1. Bachelor State: young single people not living at home (nonfamily household)

2. Newly Married Couples: young with no children

3. Full Nest I: young married couples with youngest child under six

4. Full Nest II: young married couples with youngest child six or over

5. Full Nest III: older married couples with dependent children

6. Empty Nest I: older married couples, no children living with them, household head in labor force

7. Empty Nest II: older married couples, no children living at home, household head retired

8. Solitary survivor in labor force (nonfamily household)

9. Solitary survivor, retired (nonfamily household)

This scheme takes note of the fact that changes in family composition are likely to be more important in terms of market behavior than age or simply the aging process of the family members. To illustrate the importance of family composition to consumer behavior, a brief summary is presented of the major dimensions of four of the above listed stages in the life cycle and some of their marketing implications.

Bachelor Stage

Although earnings are low in relation to what they will be later in one's career, this income is subject to few rigid demands; so consumers in this stage have substantial discretion over how they spend their money. Part of this income is typically used to purchase a car and basic household equipment. People at this stage also tend to be more fashion- and recreation-oriented, spending a substantial proportion of their income on clothing, entertainment, food away from home, vacations, leisure-time pursuits, and other products and services involved in the mating game.

Recent trends suggest that this stage is extending over a longer period of time. Furthermore, older singles are increasingly purchasing items formerly bought almost exclusively by married couples, such as single-family houses and all the household items necessary to furnish them.

Newly Married Couples

Newly married couples without children are usually better off financially than they have been in the past or will be in the near future because frequently both husband and wife are employed. To illustrate the economic importance of changes in the family life cycle, attention may be given to the results of establishing this new family, that is, the movement from stage one, Bachelorhood, to stage two, Newly Married—no children.

As Wattenberg observed, ". . . it is . . . no secret that when a young man and young woman decide to get married they trigger a vast chain of intense economic activity unmatched in the human life cycle."[16] He illustrated this point by referring to a 1972 study by Trendex that dealt with the brief six-month period surrounding a marriage—the three months before a couple's wedding and the first three months after it. Couples at this stage in the family life cycle comprised only 2.5 percent of all U.S. households; however, they represented substantial sales to a number of industries. The following are examples:

58% of the total for sterling flatware

41% of stereo and hi-fi equipment

27% of sewing machines

25% of total bedroom furniture

16% of vacuum cleaners

13% of clothes dryers

13% of refrigerators

11% of hard-surface floor coverings.

For marketing managers in these industries, this segment of the population represents one that deserves considerable attention.

Full Nest II

At this stage, the youngest child is six or older and in school; the husband's income has ordinarily improved; and if the wife has not been employed, she often returns to work outside the home. As a result, the family's financial position improves. Consumption patterns during this time continue to be heavily influenced by the children's needs. Consequently, a number of different products and services are purchased in relatively large quantities, including doctors' services and medicines, tennis shoes, laundry detergent, snack foods, bicycles, music lessons, and school supplies.

Empty Nest II

By this time the family head has retired and so the couple usually suffers a substantial reduction in income. Although it is increasingly popular for a retired person to take on some part-time work, it ordinarily does not make up the difference between preretirement income and retirement income. Expenditures on the home and related items are scaled down, and apartment living may begin. Unfortunately, a sizable number of the couples in this group will be forced to live at a level approaching subsistence. Furthermore, health concerns receive more attention, and some even move to more agreeable climates or retirement centers in their area.

Concluding Comment and Marketing Implications

The words "typically" and "ordinarily" have been used throughout this last section on the family life cycle. This does not mean that all families fit neatly into one of these developmental stages. In fact, everyone knows of other configurations of family life; we may even have grown up in one. One of these other family groupings is the single-parent family with young children. To a large extent these families' needs and behavioral patterns follow those in the Full Nest I stage. However, to meet these needs the remaining parent will likely be employed and probably make more extensive use of day care facilities and babysitters than would be the case if both parents were in the family. Also, in many such families the expenditures for child care are substantial and, therefore, force the family to live at a somewhat lower level than would be necessary if it had two adults present.

The special needs and desires of families at each stage of the family life cycle offer unique market opportunities; that is, these needs and desires offer opportunities for governmental agencies, nonprofit organizations, and businesses to be of service. Specifically, the life cycle concept can be used to:

1. *Identify Target Markets.* Studies of consumer expenditures reveal that the consumption of many products and services varies significantly by stage in the family life cycle. This provides a means of identifying specific groups of consumers within the broader consumer market that have the greatest interest in certain products or services. As a result, marketing efforts to provide for these needs and desires can be more effective and efficient. For instance, with a target market clearly identified, products can be tailored to the consumers' requirements, distribution provided in convenient outlets, and advertising undertaken in media that reach the target market with a minimum of wasted coverage.

2. *Forecast Demand.* The Bureau of the Census publishes estimates of the future size and age structure of families in the United States. The data in Table 6.2 show such projections. For example, the projected increase in female-headed families is considerable from 1970 to 1990.

Table 6.2
**Families by Type
1970, 1975, 1980,
1985, 1990**

Year	Husband/Wife		Male Head, No Wife Present		Female Head, No Husband Present	
	No. (Mill.)	Percent	No. (Mill.)	Percent	No. (Mill.)	Percent
1970	44.8	86.8	1.2	2.4	5.6	10.8
1975	47.8	85.0	1.4	2.6	6.9	12.4
1980	51.8	84.5	1.6	2.6	7.9	12.9
1985	55.7	83.9	1.7	2.6	8.9	13.5
1990	59.0	83.2	1.9	2.7	10.0	14.1

Source: U.S. Department of Commerce, Bureau of the Census, *Social Indicators 1976: Selected Data on Social Conditions and Trends in the United States* (Washington, D.C.: Government Printing Office, 1977), p. 64.

It is also possible to obtain consumption rates of products and services broken down by life cycle, age, and other demographic data. Table 6.3 summarizes such expenditure patterns by selected family income groupings. By identifying the consumption patterns of those family segments that are predicted to expand significantly, it is possible to single out product and service groupings that are likely to enjoy above-average growth rates in the future.

Table 6.3
**Weekly Per Capita
Expenditures on Food
for Selected Family
Income Groups**

Item	$3,400 to $5,000	$6,900 to $8,749	$10,500 to $12,549	$15,200 to $19,474
Food at Home	$7.64	$8.11	$8.32	$7.64
Cereal and bakery	.93	.94	.99	.91
Meats	2.10	2.34	2.49	2.21
Poultry	.33	.34	.32	.33
Fish and seafood	.20	.21	.21	.21
Dairy products	1.27	1.28	1.31	1.22
Fruit and vegetables	1.06	1.18	1.22	1.12
Sugar and other sweets	.23	.26	.25	.24
Fats and oils	.21	.20	.20	.20
Nonalcoholic beverages	.62	.65	.63	.58
Miscellaneous prepared foods	.69	.71	.69	.63
Food away from Home	$2.48	$2.98	$3.84	$2.81

Source: U.S. Department of Labor, Bureau of Labor Statistics, *1972–73 Consumer Expenditure Survey*, Release No. 75-276 (Washington, D.C.: Government Printing Office, 1975).

Family Role Structures

This section is concerned with the role and influence of family members in the decision-making process. Family role structure refers to the behavior of nuclear family members at each stage in the decision-making process. One means of gaining an understanding of family role structure is by studying the various forms of role specialization that occur in families.

Role specialization within the family can affect both the decision-making process and the decisions made. This specialization takes a number of forms; two are used here to illustrate the importance of role specialization and the nature of its influence. First, role dominance will be discussed, followed by the gatekeeper concept.

Role Dominance

Role dominance refers to the extent to which one member of a family has greater influence in the family decision-making process than do other members. Typically, husband-dominant or wife-dominant decision making has been the focus of attention. These are decisions involving both spouses but where the ideas of one have greater impact. There have been a number of studies conducted to identify patterns of dominance and the circumstances that foster such dominance. Marketing and advertising managers are particularly interested in determining which spouse has the most influence in various types of decisions so that promotional strategy can be oriented accordingly.

A person's background can contribute to role dominance. There is evidence to indicate that the degree of dominance by one member can vary among groups with differing cultural backgrounds. Also, several researchers have found evidence to suggest that husband dominance appears to be more likely when the husband is successful in his occupation. The wife's influence increases with age and is generally greater if she is employed.[17] It is important to note, too, that existing evidence also shows that dominance by one family member depends upon the particular type of decision being made; that is, a family cannot ordinarily be classified as being wife-dominant or husband-dominant, because when confronted with certain decisions the wife will have the greater influence, and in other situations the husband will be dominant. For example, Davis found that the husband is more influential in the decision to purchase the family car, while the wife has considerably greater relative influence in furniture purchasing decisions.[18]

To many families, the fact that the husband or the wife dominates (has the greater influence) in certain decisions is simply the result of conscious role specialization. The wife, because of her formal and informal training as well as her interests, is more knowledgeable in particular decision areas. Her dominance is the recognition of this expertise. In other decision areas, the husband is the recognized family authority, and he dominates for similar reasons. However, this role specialization may also be the result of the acceptance of traditional masculine/feminine roles. Family decisions of a particular type made most often by both husband and wife exerting equal influence have been called *syncratic.*

Using a sample of 73 Belgian households, Davis and Rigaux studied the average relative influence of husbands and wives, the extent of role specialization for each decision, and the similarity among decisions in terms of marital roles.[19] Figure 6.4 positions 25 decisions in terms of two axes. The first is a scale of the relative influence between husband and wife. Average relative influence for a decision when aggregated over families can range along a continuum from 1 (all respondents reporting husband-dominance) to 3 (all respondents reporting wife-dominance). The second axis is a scale of the extent of role specialization as measured by the percentage of families reporting that a decision is jointly made.

This type of analysis has practical implications for managers. For example, the classification of a decision into one of the four types of influences—wife-dominant, husband-dominant, autonomic, or syncratic—suggests the need for unique communication strategies. When a decision is either husband- or wife-dominant, messages must be designed in reference to the designated spouse. A syncratic decision pattern calls for messages developed to appeal to the couple as an entity. Decisions that are generally autonomic—family decisions made most often by either the wife or the husband—require yet another approach. In this latter case, there are really two separate audiences—one consisting of wives and the other of husbands.

The Davis and Rigaux study also focused on the changing "decision unit" during the decision-making process. The family decision-making process was divided into three phases, including problem recognition, search for information, and final decision. Using this format,

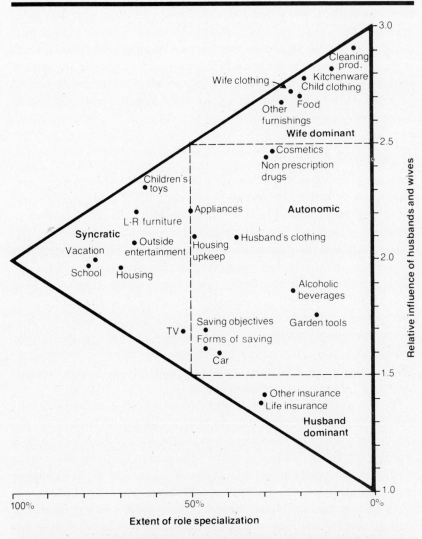

Figure 6.4
**Extent of Role
Specialization: Marital
Roles in 25 Decisions**

Source: Reprinted with permission from H. L. Davis and B. P. Rigaux, "Perceptions of Marital Roles in Decision Processes," *Journal of Consumer Research,* Vol. 1 (June 1974), p. 54.

it was possible to show that some changes in husband and wife influence do occur from the time a problem is recognized until a final decision is made. This, too, has implications for managers in their strategy development. It may be necessary, for example, to initiate problem recognition by directing one's message to the husband and wife (syncratic), while at a later point the decision is essentially wife-dominant.

Gatekeeper Concept

Another form of role specialization is what a number of consumer analysts have called the *gatekeeper concept.* The "gatekeeper" refers to an individual who acts as a valve and filter affecting the flow of information coming into the family. In a number of families, the homemaker still illustrates this concept at work. The fact that she is at home more than other members, as well as her concern for the general well-being of the family, puts her in a position to receive, screen, and sort incoming messages. For instance, as the mail arrives she may sort out and at times discard "junk mail" that was addressed to the "occupant" or even to other specific members of the family. Salespeople who call during the day are also subjected to her gate-keeping action. In a business setting, a manager's secretary or assistant may function in a similar capacity.

To the consumer analyst, such role specialization must be identified and understood because it can have a substantial impact on consumer behavior. For example, when a homemaker functioning as a family gatekeeper discards a mailer intended to motivate the family member most responsible for lawn weed killer, and if that member were the husband, the message would never reach its destination. Obviously, it has no impact on him. Under these circumstances the firm marketing the new weed killer probably should have used another medium to deliver its message or should have modified the mailer substantially to increase its chances of reaching the desired destination.

Additional Concepts of Role Structure

Further insight into the market behavior of families as they pass through various stages in the life cycle can be explained through the concepts of role accumulation and role transition. Role accumulation is a way of describing some of the effects of experience upon the ongoing processes of purchasing and consuming through the years.

In the early years of marriage, many couples make the money management and record-keeping process a joint venture. When Ferber and Lee conducted an investigation of the feasibility of identifying a family financial officer in young married couples, they found that immediately after marriage about half of the couples in the study acted jointly in handling financial matters. But, by the end of the second year of marriage, only about one third continued to act jointly and the shift was more often toward the wife assuming the most responsibility. The change to the wife was more likely if she demonstrated greater concern than her husband for quality and economy.[20] It is reasonable to assume that, as the experience and perceptiveness about finances continues to grow in one spouse, a further allocation of responsibility would likely be designated to this marriage partner.

The concept of role transition becomes relevant in relating to the changes in patterns of husband-wife-children involvement in product purchases. Much research into the changes occurring in marital role relationships shows several interesting trends in role transition in product decision making. In one study covering the period 1955–1973, the following decision transitions were noted. How much to spend on groceries became more of a wife-dominated decision, while the decision on life insurance became more husband-dominated. In regard to automobiles, housing, and vacation purchases, families moved toward more joint decision making than in the earlier study period.[21]

The transition can be explained in part by the entry of wife-mothers into the labor force and the concomitant involvement of both sexes in nontraditional activities.

What is evident is that family decision roles have been changing, and the marketing of products must take these trends into consideration.

Children in Family Decision Making

There is little doubt that children attempt to influence their parents in purchasing goods and services. Of course, this is particularly obvious in places such as the ready-to-eat cereal aisle in the supermarket and the toy section of the local discount store. Furthermore, advertisers have long recognized the potential influence of children. This is exemplified by the fact that in 1975 alone, advertisers spent nearly $90 million to present their messages directly to these younger family members.[22]

Unfortunately, most of the published research dealing with family decision making has given sole attention to the relative involvement and personal exchanges between husbands and wives. However, the neglect of the influence of children among researchers has begun to pass.

One recent study found, for example, a high degree of adult and child interaction in all stages of the decision-making process involved in selecting a fast food restaurant. This included initiation of the purchase idea, provision of information on alternatives, and the final decision. In fact, over 80 percent of the family situations studied involved adult and child interaction. These findings suggest that it might be appropriate for fast food advertising to portray adults with children, or the family as a group, participating in the choice process.[23]

Besides the direct requests that children make of their parents, there are other, more subtle, forms of influence. These often get through to parents by way of what has been called "passive dictation."[24] For instance, mothers can observe what foods their children will eat as well as those they won't eat. Also, favorite clothing items often are worn excessively, while others are consistently left in the closet. Even some types of games and toys attract more attention than others. Research has shown that mothers rely heavily on their observations to select products when there is no other evaluative criterion. Consider the following examples of the nature of children's influence on their mothers.

—Children-centered mothers were more likely to be influenced by their children than were family-oriented mothers and mothers from closely knit families.

—Mothers who reviewed television programs with their children were more likely to yield to their children's purchase influences. This was found to be particularly true for products advertised on these television programs.[25]

Summary

The family can be studied from two standpoints in consumer behavior: (1) as an agent that influences the behavior of each member and (2) as a unit having specific identifiable characteristics including unique patterns of consumption. Both perspectives are needed to present the impact of the family in the marketplace.

The family is more interrelated than other living units and through its decisions an inventory of assets is accumulated over time which portrays as well as affects the life-style of its members. These collective and individual impacts are reasons for using family—particularly nuclear family—instead of nonfamily households in the study of consumer behavior.

Part of the influence of the family on its members is affected by the social class to which it belongs. Social class can affect values, interpersonal attitudes, self-perceptions, and daily life routines. Interaction among family members results in similarities in thinking and behavioral patterns that would not exist if the individuals were not in the same family.

The family decision-making models of Ferber and Sheth focus on the family as a buying and consuming entity. Ferber's model displays the interrelation of financial and nonfinancial decisions with key influential variables. Sheth's model, which is more detailed, divides family consumption into three groups: family, individual, and household consumption. The theory depicts in four major subparts family buying decisions made either jointly or by single members.

The family life cycle is used to study how the family's consumption patterns are altered over time as family composition and position change. The special needs and desires of families at each stage of the family life cycle offer unique market opportunities for organizations and businesses. The family life cycle can be used by the marketer to identify target markets and to forecast demand.

Family role specialization, as seen in role dominance and the gatekeeper concept, can affect the decision-making process. Research has shown that buying decisions can be scaled as husband-dominated, wife-dominated, and joint decisions and that role dominance can change during different phases of the decision process. The gatekeeper concept is important because the family member acting as gatekeeper can prevent marketing information directed at other family members from reaching them. Finally, it should be noted that researchers are beginning to study the important area of children's influence on their parents, particularly their mothers. Research shows that mothers are influenced not only by the direct requests of children but also by more subtle influences such as passive dictation.

Questions and Issues for Discussion

1. The family composed of parents and children still living at home is no longer the "typical" American family. What errors in marketing strategy development would probably be made by companies in the following industries missing this change in family composition?

(a) furniture

(b) packaged convenience food

(c) automobiles

(d) clothing.

2. Is it reasonable to conclude that, once a woman marries, her family of orientation generally has little or no effect on her buying behavior? Discuss.

3. How can firms selling the following products and services make use of the family life cycle concept in identifying their target market and planning appropriate advertising strategy?

(a) home movie cameras

(b) airline travel

(c) life insurance

(d) mobile homes.

4. Do fundamental values change with the times so that what families hold to be important today will probably not last through this generation? How are changing values likely to alter family purchasing patterns?

5. What effect will the increasing number of women in full-time employment have upon the usefulness of the gatekeeper concept in studying family decision making?

6. To what extent does the family influence its members' individual buying behaviors with respect to each of the following?

(a) the brand of notebook paper purchased by a high-school student for use in school

(b) preferences for various snack foods

(c) movies attended by students away at college

(d) the first car that a young woman buys.

7. How does the role of the child in family decision making ordinarily change over time? Can this change affect family buying patterns? If so, give some examples.

8. Assume that the information given in the chart that follows has just been obtained from a major consumer research study. It lists several types of purchases and indicates that they were found to be syncratic, wife-dominant, or husband-dominant. How could this information be used by a marketing manager in the development of marketing strategy?

Product/Service Purchased	Dominant Influence in Purchase Decision
(a) Household cleaning products	Wife-dominant
(b) Family vacations	Syncratic
(c) Stereo equipment	Syncratic
(d) Ready-to-eat cereal	Wife-dominant
(e) Over-the-counter sleep aids	Husband-dominant
(f) Bank credit cards	Syncratic

9. The style of living that a family chooses has a greater influence on its purchase patterns than does its social class status. For example, some families are very casual in their style of living; consequently, the products and services they buy reflect these interests. Furthermore, such a family can take on this casual style while being a member of any social class. Is this a true statement? Discuss.

10. Referring to the data in Table 6.1, "Satisfaction with Family Life," what implications do these findings have for the creation of advertising appeals or for the settings used for ads to promote various consumer products?

Case 1. Vantage Machines, Incorporated

Vantage manufactures cleaning and maintenance equipment for industrial users. During its 50 years of operation, the management has developed a line of machines that can sweep, dry and wet vacuum, scrub, dry polish, and shampoo the variety of floor surfaces used in commercial establishments. The company operates under the philosophy that industrial and commercial users will quickly realize that the right mechanized cleaning and maintenance equipment can pay for itself by providing safety, sanitation, and effective cleaning for floors and other surfaces.

Vantage's production is consolidated at a single facility in which the components of all individual models are design-engineered, manufactured, and shipped to distributors. Sales and servicing are handled through well-established industrial equipment dealers in about 300 U.S. cities. Demand has been increasing at this level, but recently the company has become aware of the possibility of expanding into the consumer market.

The life-styles and living environments of many families strongly suggest the need for versatile and effective floor and furniture cleaners. Although some of the current models would not be appropriate, many small models could be used in the home setting. These would include a 16-inch wide upright vacuum cleaner, a 12-inch wide dry-foam rug shampooer and vacuum, and the 5- or 8-gallon tank-type dry and wet vacuum with attachments.

To help in the decision on whether to enter the consumer market, management has set down a number of advantages and disadvantages.

Advantages

1. Highly effective cleaning ability that is superior to most current consumer vacuums.

2. Quality components and production as well as reputable servicing that have given them a "good" name.

3. Versatility in job performance that minimizes the need for multiple equipment pieces. Example: A wet and dry tank vacuum can be used for general cleaning in the house and garage as well as for water extraction after shampooing or when water problems occur. It is also capable of picking up small pieces of debris as well as dirt and dust.

2. How can Eldercare go about determining how decisions are made in the selection of a retirement center?

Notes

1. Mary Jo Bane, *Here to Stay: American Families in the Twentieth Century* (New York: Basic Books, 1976); Urie Bronfenbrenner, "The Disturbing Changes in the American Family," *Search* (Fall 1977); F. George Day, *The Family in Transition* (New York: John Wiley and Sons, Inc., 1972); Walter F. Mondale, "Government Policy, Stress and the Family," *Journal of Home Economics* (November 1976); "The Amercian Family, Can It Survive Today's Shocks?" *U. S. News and World Report,* October 27, 1975.

2. News release from the Bureau of Labor Statistics, March 8, 1977.

3. R. Hill and D. M. Klein, "Understanding Family Consumption: Common Ground for Integrating Uncommon Disciplinary Perspectives," E. B. Sheldon, ed., *Family Economic Behavior: Problems and Prospects* (Philadelphia: J. B. Lippincott Company, 1973), p. 4.

4. T. Parsons and R. F. Bales, *Family: Socialization and Interaction Process* (New York: The Free Press, 1955).

5. H. W. Boyd, Jr. and S. J. Levy, *Promotion: A Behavioral View* (Englewood Cliffs, N.J.: Prentice-Hall, Inc., 1967), pp. 48–49.

6. D. Riesman and H. Roseborough, "Careers and Consumer Behavior," L. Clark, ed., *Consumer Behavior: The Life Cycle and Consumer Behavior,* Vol. II (New York: New York University Press, 1955), p. 3.

7. T. S. Robertson, *Consumer Behavior* (Glenview, Ill.: Scott, Foresman and Company, 1970), p. 3.

8. D. E. Vinson, J. E. Scott, and L. M. Lamont, "The Role of Personal Values in Marketing and Consumer Behavior," *Journal of Marketing,* Vol. 41 (April 1977), p. 48.

9. Ibid., p. 49.

10. C. E. Block, "Prepurchase Search Behavior of Low-Income Households," *Journal of Retailing,* Vol. 48 (Spring 1972), pp. 3-15.

11. S. J. Levy, "Social Class and Consumer Behavior," J. W. Newman, ed., *On Knowing the Consumer* (New York: John Wiley and Sons, Inc., 1966), pp. 150-52.

12. E. Herzog, *About the Poor: Some Facts and Some Fictions* (Washington, D. C.: U. S. Department of Health, Education, and Welfare, Social and Rehabilitation Service, 1967), pp. 40-43.

13. R. Ferber, "Family Decision Making and Economic Behavior," E. B.

Sheldon, ed., *Family Economic Behavior: Problems and Prospects* (Philadelphia: J. B. Lippincott Company, 1973), p. 29.

14. Ibid., pp. 30–38.

15. J. N. Sheth, *Models of Buyer Behavior: Conceptual, Quantitative, and Empirical* (New York: Harper & Row, Publishers, 1974), pp. 18–33.

16. B. J. Wattenberg, "The Forming-Families: The Spark in the Tinder, 1975–1985," R. C. Curhan, ed., *1974 Combined Proceedings: New Marketing for Social and Economic Progress and Marketing's Contributions to the Firm and to the Society* (Chicago: American Marketing Association, 1975), p. 53.

17. L. E. Ostlund, "Role Theory and Group Dynamics," S. Ward and T. S. Robertson, eds., *Consumer Behavior Theoretical Sources* (Englewood Cliffs, N.J.: Prentice-Hall, Inc., 1973), p. 263.

18. H. L. Davis, "Dimensions of Marital Roles in Consumer Decision Making," *Journal of Marketing Research,* Vol. 7 (May 1970), pp. 168–77.

19. H. L. Davis and B. P. Rigaux, "Perceptions of Marital Roles in Decision Processes," *Journal of Consumer Research,* Vol. 1 (June 1974), pp. 51–61.

20. R. Ferber and L. Choa Lee, "Husband-Wife Influence in Family Purchasing Behavior," *Journal of Consumer Research,* Vol. 1 (June 1974), pp. 49–50.

21. I. C. M. Cunningham and R. T. Green, "Purchasing Roles in the U.S. Family, 1955 and 1973," *Journal of Marketing,* Vol. 38 (October 1974), p. 64.

22. S. Mehrotra and S. Torges, "Determinants of Children's Influence on Mother's Buying Behavior," W. Perreault, ed., *Advances in Consumer Research,* Vol. IV (Annual Proceedings, Association for Consumer Research, Chicago, Illinois, 1977), p. 56.

23. G. J. Szbilla and A. Sosanie, "Family Decision Making: Husband, Wife and Children," W. Perreault, ed., *Advances in Consumer Research,* Vol. IV (Annual Proceedings, Association for Consumer Research, Chicago, Illinois, 1977), p. 49.

24. W. Wells, "Communicating with Children," *Journal of Advertising Research,* Vol. 5 (June 1965), p. 3.

25. Szbilla and Sosanie, "Family Decision Making," p. 60.

Part 3

Intrapersonal and Interpersonal Determinants of Consumer Behavior

The four chapters in this section give specific attention to what are essentially considered internal factors that influence and shape an individual's buying behavior. Some of these factors are often thought to be what truly differentiate one person from another; personality, for example, is such a dimension.

Also, some of the variables treated in these chapters have more direct operational meaning in terms of day-to-day consumer buying patterns than others. Evaluative criteria, for instance, have specific relevance to how alternative brands are compared and finally selected. Consequently, particular marketing tactics might be developed to take advantage of such knowledge. Personality, however, is an internal factor which has less direct known linkage to the actual brand selection process. But this does not mean that one of these variables is necessarily more important than another in gaining a comprehensive understanding of consumer behavior.

The relative amount of scholarly research that has been undertaken in the study of the interpersonal factors discussed in this section has varied widely. For example, the formation and composition of attitudes and their relationship to actual behavior have been studied extensively during the last five years. The process of learning has also been a subject of considerable study, which has resulted in useful theories and information. Evaluative criteria, however, have received very little attention; hence their use to consumer analysts is still minimal.

Each of these subjects—personality, life-style, learning, evaluative criteria, and attitudes—offers insights into the buying process which are fundamentally important because, without them, any analysis of consumer behavior would be purely speculative and superficial.

Chapter **7**   Personality and
Life-styles

Outline

Personality Theories in Consumer Behavior
Psychoanalytic Theory
Social Psychological Theory
Trait-Factor Theory

Personality and Product Choice

Implications for Marketing Strategy

Marketing Applications of Personality Research
Consumption-Related Personality Inventories
Personality as a Moderator Variable
Personality as an Intervening Variable

Life-style Concept
Life-style Influences on Consumer Decisions

Forces Shaping American Life-styles
Marketing Strategy and Programming—A Case Example

Application of the Life-style Concept

Summary

Questions and Issues for Discussion

Cases

Key Terms

personality

psychoanalytic theory

id

ego

superego

motivational research

social psychological theory

compliant

aggressive

detached

trait-factor theory

moderator variable

intervening variable

life-style concept

psychographics

Personality Theories in Consumer Behavior

Personality is a frequently used and reasonably familiar term. Most people have at various times characterized someone as having a pleasant personality or, perhaps, an obnoxious personality. While this use of the word "personality" typically conveys meaning, it lacks the precision necessary for application in marketing strategy and planning. Actually, there is little agreement on what the components of personality are and how these components become organized into a meaningful whole. Thus, an examination of the major personality theories is essential to acquiring an appreciation of the potential contribution of this concept.

Most definitions of personality are general, and the term is frequently used in different ways. Nevertheless, the common element of all definitions of personality is the notion that personality is a consistent pattern of responses to environmental stimuli. This consistent pattern of responses permits the categorization of people in a number of ways, such as stuffy, methodical, or egotistical. A consumer's reaction to a need, a routine situation, or new stimulus is determined by his or her normal mode of coping with the environment. Marketing strategists' fascination with personality stems from the belief that this consistent mode of behaving will enable marketers to understand consumer behavior. The assumption is that if they really understand a consumer's personality, they will understand why a person consumes the way he or she does and then, perhaps, they can effectively influence that consumption behavior.

Psychoanalytic Theory

Psychoanalytic, or Freudian, theory posits that personality is composed of three systems of interdependent psychological forces or constructs: the id, the ego, and the superego.[1] The interaction of these three systems determines the person's behavior. The *id*, the original source of all psychic energy, seeks to achieve immediate gratification of all biological or instinctual needs. Thus, a consumer's instinctive cravings, needs, and desires originate in the id. If all the pleasure-seeking impulses emanating from the id were openly expressed, the consumer would quickly violate society's norms, rules, and regulations. Indeed, proponents of the psychoanalytic theory would contend that uncontrolled behavior that directly satisfies all instinctive needs and desires is inherently bad. The *superego,* the internal representative of society's norms and values, acts to inhibit the impulses emanating from the id that would be contrary to society's norms and values. Thus, the superego can be thought of as the consumer's conscience or moral arm that serves to direct behavior. The *ego* functions to control and direct the id's impulses so that gratification can be achieved in a socially acceptable manner. The ego controls behavior by selecting the instincts that will be satisfied as well as the manner in which they will be satisfied. This is accomplished by integrating the often conflicting demands of the id and the superego. According to psychoanalytic theory, the id is entirely unconscious and the ego and superego partially unconscious, resulting in an unconscious determination of behavior. Consequently, only the highly trained professional psychiatrist is capable of identifying the consumer's true personality by means of projective techniques and in-depth interviews.

Psychoanalytic theory has provided the conceptual basis for motivational research. Consumer behavior, according to motivational researchers, is the result of unconscious consumer motives that can only be determined through the use of indirect assessment methods that include a wide assortment of projective techniques. The following are some motivational research explanations of consumer behavior:[2]

1. A man buys a convertible as a substitute mistress.

2. A woman is very serious when she bakes a cake because unconsciously she is going through the symbolic act of birth.

3. Men want their cigars to be odiferous in order to prove that they (the men) are masculine.

4. Men who wear suspenders are reacting to an unresolved castration complex.

Some of the difficulties inherent in proving these and similar generalizations are illustrated by the well-known case in which conflicting interpretations of the prune industry were advanced by two prominent motivational researchers. One researcher found that people disliked prunes because prunes aroused feelings of old age and insecurity. The other motivational researcher concluded that Americans had an emotional block about prunes' laxative qualities. Which interpretation is (or, for that matter, whether both are) operative cannot be determined by motivational research procedures.

These subjective interpretations of consumer motivations, although perhaps atypical, highlight the danger of using a personality model developed in and for a clinical setting to explain consumer behavior. The individual focus characterizing psychoanalytic theory is frequently inappropriate to the marketing analyst whose interest is in groups or segments of consumers. Indeed, even if individual information could be obtained, its application by the marketing strategist is not readily apparent. While psychoanalytic theory has been extensively and justly criticized, few would deny that it had a tremendous impact on marketing in the 1950s and 1960s and, to a lesser extent, in the 1970s.

Social Psychological Theory

Social psychological theory developed as a reaction to the psychoanalytic theory's rigid adherence to the biological determinants of personality. Social psychological theorists contend that social variables, not biological ones, are the most important determinants of personality. Humans are conscious of their needs and wants; consequently, their behavior is directed toward satisfying them. The following are representative needs considered to be basic determinants of personality by proponents of the social psychological orientation: the striving for superiority, freedom from loneliness, security, satisfying human relationships, and coping with anxiety.

One paradigm reflecting this orientation suggests that consumer behavior results from three predominant interpersonal orientations—compliant, aggressive, and detached. A psychological instrument—the CAD scale—has been developed to measure these three basic orientations.[3] The *compliant* person wants to be appreciated, wanted, loved, and included in the activities of others. The compliant person is so other-oriented that he or she becomes overgenerous, overgrateful, and overconsiderate. For example, the compliant person seeking reassurance of acceptance by others is likely to seek the security afforded by personal grooming products. The *aggressive* person seeks success, prestige, and the admiration of others. The aggressive person values other people only if they are useful to achieving a goal. He or she considers everyone to be motivated by self-interest and shows concern for others only to cover up his or her real goals. For example, the aggressive person seeking a separate identity will be more concerned with distinctive brands of personal grooming products. The *detached* person seeks freedom from obligations, independence, and self-sufficiency. The detached person does not want to be influenced or to share experiences with others; rather he or she seeks to maintain or establish an emotional distance from others. For example, the detached person will probably not be concerned with products (such as personal grooming products) or brands that ensure acceptance by others.

The marketer of personal grooming products can reach two conclusions from the research on the CAD personalities. First, the interpersonal goals and values of consumers will result in different degrees of acceptance of personal grooming products. Second, a consistent, focused marketing program emphasizing a specific set of interpersonal values can attract a large number of consumers of a particular personality type.

A summary of the results obtained from applying the CAD to a number of items is presented in Table 7.1. The results obtained not only were consistent with the theory's predictions, but also provided valuable input to marketing decision making.

Trait-Factor Theory

According to trait-factor theory, an individual's personality is composed of a set of traits or factors. The relatively enduring and distinctive ways in which consumers differ from one another are referred to as *traits*. Therefore, traits can be considered consumer difference variables. Proponents of trait-factor theory contend that consumers have relatively stable traits that produce similar effects on behavior, regardless of the situation. Furthermore, although a trait is common to many individuals, there is considerable variation in the degree to which one consumer expresses that particular trait.

Three critical assumptions serve as the basis for the use of trait-factor theory.

Assumption 1: Traits are common to many individuals and vary in absolute amounts among individuals.

Assumption 2: Traits are relatively stable and exert fairly universal effects on behavior regardless of the environmental situation.

Assumption 3: A consistent functioning of personality variables is predictive of a wide variety of behavior.

Table 7.1
Summary of Product and Brand Study

Product	Within-trait comparison[a]	Brand or category	N	Percent of high grouping in each brand or product category		
				C (n = 66)	A (n = 67)	D (n = 75)
Cigarettes	NS	Smoker	47	40	40	32
		Nonsmoker	83	60	60	68
Men's dress shirts	NS	Arrow	26	20	15	22
		Van Heusen	21	16	25	20
		Brand not known	15	8	5	12
		Other	67	56	55	46
Mouthwash	Compliant	Used	91	74	64	56
		Not used	54	26	36	44
Men's deodorant	Aggressive	Old Spice	33	34	41	24
		Right Guard	53	45	38	52
		Other	33	21	21	24
Men's cologne and after shave lotion	Aggressive	At least several times a week	119	88	91	82
		Several times a month or less	25	12	9	18
Toilet or bath soap	Compliant	Dial	50	47	36	31
		No preference	39	19	23	38
		Other	46	34	41	31

Men's hair dressing	NS	Not used	46	41	43	39
		Other	65	59	57	61
Toothpaste	NS	Crest	77	61	60	60
		Colgate	28	16	24	20
		Other	29	23	16	20
Razors	Aggressive	Electric	48	38	25	38
		Manual	92	62	75	62
Beer	NS	Coors	54	41	49	35
		Not consumed	29	19	19	24
		Other	60	40	32	41
Tea	Detached	At least several times a week	41	26	22	33
		Several times a month or less	116	74	78	67
Wine	Compliant	At least several times a month	38	35	33	23
		Several times a year or less	119	65	67	77
Metrecal and similar diet products	NS	At least a few times a year	18	15	12	11
		Never	139	85	88	89

Table 7.1 (continued)

| Product | Within-trait comparison[a] | Brand or category | N | Percent of high grouping in each brand or product category | | | |
				C (n = 66)	A (n = 67)	D (n = 75)
Gasoline	NS	Standard	32	17	23	19
		Shell	32	28	18	23
		Other	83	55	59	58
Headache remedies	NS	Bayer aspirin	44	32	38	30
		Other aspirin	33	13	23	21
		Bufferin	23	18	11	15
		Other remedy	47	37	28	34

[a]High and low groupings on each trait were compared using the chi-square test. Differences significant at the .05 level are reported by trait designation.
Source: J. B. Cohen, "An Interpersonal Orientation to the Study of Consumer Behavior," *Journal of Marketing Research, 4* (August 1967), p. 276. Reprinted from the *Journal of Marketing Research* published by the American Marketing Association.

The consumer analyst who adheres to this orientation typically selects one of the many personality inventories (for example, the California Personality Inventory, Edwards Personal Preference Schedule, or Gordon Personal Profile) and attempts to find a statistical relationship between a set of personality variables and some type of consumer behavior. In many instances, borrowing a standard scale developed for clinical purposes has produced less than gratifying results. Indeed, a more effective procedure is to modify a standard test to make it more reflective of the consumer behavior context, such as is

Sociable

I am always glad to join a large gathering.

I consider myself a very sociable, outgoing person.

I find it easy to mingle among people at a social gathering.

When I am in a small group, I sit back and let others do most of the talking.

I have decidedly fewer friends than most people.

I am considered a very enthusiastic person.

Relaxed

I get tense as I think of all the things lying ahead of me.

Quite small setbacks occasionally irritate me too much.

I wish I knew how to relax.

I shrink from facing a crisis or a difficulty.

Internal Control

Sometimes I feel that I don't have enough control over the direction my life is taking.

Many times I feel that I have little influence over the things that happen to me.

What happens to me is my own doing.

Becoming a success is a matter of hard work; luck has nothing to do with it.

Getting a good job depends mainly on being in the right place at the right time.

Table 7.2
Test Items in the Modified Personality Instrument

Source: Reprinted with permission from Kathryn E. A. Villani and Yoram Wind, "On the Usage of 'Modified' Personality Trait Measures in Consumer Research," *Journal of Consumer Research*, Vol. 2 (December 1975), pp. 223-28.

presented in Table 7.2. Modified tests of this type have provided reliable measures of traits such as "sociable, relaxed, and internal control."[4]

Trait-factor theory has been used almost exclusively as the conceptual basis of marketing personality research. In this research, the typical study attempts to find a relationship between a set of personality variables and assorted consumer behaviors such as purchases, media choice, innovation, fear and social influence, product choice, opinion leadership, risk taking, attitude change, and so forth.[5] Personality has been found to relate to specific *attributes* of products.[6] Research also indicates that people can make relatively good judgments about other people's traits and how they relate to such choices as automobile brands, occupations, and magazines.[7]

Personality and Product Choice

The consumer analyst's fascination with personality stems from the belief that a consumer's personality significantly influences consumer behavior. Many consumer analysts would contend that consumption patterns are an expression of a consumer's personality and, consequently, knowledge of a consumer's personality is strategic to the marketing decision maker. The rich literature of personality in psychology and the inherent intellectual appeal of the concept have, however, produced unrealistic expectations regarding its capacity to explain behavior.

Consumer analysts have made numerous attempts to demonstrate the relationship between personality and product or brand choice. For example, an attempt to demonstrate the relationship between personality and brand of automobile purchased proved unsuccessful.[8] There is, however, some indication that personality is related to the type of automobile owned; that is, the owner of a convertible appeared to be more aggressive, impulsive, sociable, and somewhat less stable and reflective than the owner of a standard or compact car. A number of marketing analysts also have found a relationship between personality and product use. For example, there appears to be a tendency for women who are enthusiastic, sensitive, and submissive to be more prone to purchase private brands than women who do not have these traits.

In general, when marketing analysts have employed more sophisticated analytical techniques, they have found that a relationship exists between personality and certain types of products (for instance, convenience products).[9] Thus, even though the unsuccessful attempts to relate personality and consumer behavior outnumber the successful ones, the consumer analyst's interest in personality continues to be strong.

Implications for Marketing Strategy

In order to market a product effectively, the marketing manager must frequently segment the market; that is, the marketing manager must adapt his or her marketing effort to the demands of relatively homogeneous groups that make up the market. Traditionally, marketers used such demographic dimensions as age, income, occupation, and social class to identify consumer groups. Many marketing managers, however, contend that demographic variables lack the richness needed to accurately focus marketing efforts. The speculation is that personality captures much of the richness not present in demographic variables.

The marketing strategist must address the issue of whether personality variables provide an effective basis for allocating marketing effort. Most attempts to base marketing strategy on personality have not been unequivocally successful. In order for personality information to aid the marketing strategist, a few basic conditions must prevail. First, consumers with common personality dimensions must be homogeneous with respect to such demographic factors as age, income, and location so that they can be communicated with economically through the mass market. This is necessary because data on media patterns are typically available in terms of demographic characteristics. In the absence of identifiable common characteristics, there is no practical means of focusing on a specific market segment. Second, personality differences must reflect clear-cut variations in consumer preferences that can be focused on through modifications in marketing effort. In other words, consumers may have different personalities and still prefer the same products. If this is the case, personality information contributes little, if anything, to effective marketing decision making. Third, the market segments identified by personality measures must be of sufficient size to be reached economically. Thus, even though personality may enable successful identification of a segment of consumers, the segment must be of sufficient size to be profitable.

Most marketing strategists would contend that these criteria have not been sufficiently met and, thus, personality has not been demonstrated convincingly to be a significant input to marketing decision making. There is no reason to assume, for example, that individuals with a given personality profile are homogeneous in other respects; nor does it seem reasonable to expect that they have enough in common to be reached easily through the mass media without attracting a large number of nonprospects.

Therefore, it appears that future research that attempts to predict buyer behavior or identify market segments based on personality dimensions is destined to a low practical payout. The next section, however, focuses on select recent developments that provide considerable cause for optimism.

Marketing Applications of Personality Research

Several recent marketing research efforts have produced useful results for marketing strategists. In particular, three major modifications in the use of personality research have been made that have contributed substantially to the usefulness of personality information to marketing decision makers. These modifications are: (1) consumption-related personality inventories, (2) use of personality as a moderator variable, and (3) use of personality as an intervening variable.

Consumption-Related Personality Inventories

Consumer analysts now believe that much of the disappointment with personality information resulted from the use of standardized inventories designed for use in the psychological clinic and that the improper application of these standardized inventories may have obscured the value of personality information. It seems obvious that better results should be expected when personality measures related directly to the process of buying and consumption are used.

The construction of consumption-related personality inventories is difficult and tedious but offers considerable benefits. Consider five dichotomous orientations of homemakers toward housework that served as the basis for a personality inventory developed specifically to distinguish views toward household cleaning.

1. *Flexible versus rigid.* This dimension focused on the need to maintain a flexible or strict cleaning schedule and organization of time to this end.

2. *Evaluative versus nonevaluative.* To what extent is cleaning central to a homemaker's evaluation of herself and others in the role of wife and mother?

3. *Objective versus family role.* This dealt with the degree to which cleaning is seen as essential to family nature as opposed to being a necessary utilitarian task. In other words, is cleaning an "act of love"?

4. *Emancipated versus limited.* The emancipated homemaker was defined as the woman who holds the point of view that she can participate in a larger social context outside the home.

5. *Appreciated versus unappreciated.* This dimension showed the homemaker's perception of the extent to which her husband and children appreciate her efforts on their behalf.

When the personality inventory based on these five dimensions was administered to 300 homemakers, it suggested the following results. The emancipated, nonevaluative, objective, and flexible homemaker does not consider cleaning to be a measure of her worth or an expression of her love; whereas the traditional, restricted, evaluative homemaker views cleaning as a measure of her worth and an expression of love.[10]

The results of this research effort suggest that the strategist who wants to focus on these segments must develop different products, packages, and designs and must communicate differently with these two segments. The differences observed in these homemakers suggest that the marketing strategist must develop totally different marketing strategies for each segment; the failure to do so might result in the loss of both segments. For instance, the marketer of kitchen appliances could stress to the less traditional homemaker the convenience and time savings afforded by his or her products, while communicating to the traditional homemaker the appreciation her family would show for the exciting dishes these appliances would enable her to serve.

Personality as a Moderator Variable

Consumer analysts now realize that personality interacts with other variables, particularly the environment, to determine behavior; that is, personality may permit accurate predictions of behavior in some situations but not in others. Because certain groups are differentially affected by certain personality traits, these personality traits are said to moderate the situation. Predictions that specify the situation should be more accurate if they are to be useful to marketing strategists. Suppose that the distributor of a name brand of bourbon attempts to determine the relationship between personality and the purchase of his bourbon. This distributor would very likely determine that the socially concerned person would purchase name brand bourbon to serve to guests but purchase inexpensive house brands for his or her personal use. Thus, if the marketing strategist can identify the key situations, personality information can be a valuable input to strategy development.

The application of moderator variables to increase the accuracy of predictions about the impact of personality on consumer behavior is, however, somewhat limited by the difficulty inherent in selecting moderator variables. The use of personality as a moderator variable shows promise as a means of explaining conflicting results. It is, however, an area that needs much more research before a definitive assessment can be made.

Personality as an Intervening Variable

Personality may be useful if the market is first segmented in subgroups on some objective variable other than personality. Then each isolated subgroup is studied to determine any differences in psychological attributes. Any number of variables could be used for the initial market segmentation, including age, income, degree of product use, or others, depending upon the nature of the problem. One approach that has proved useful is to differentiate buyers by the extent to which they use both the product and the brand. Then the inquiry focuses on why one person uses the brand and others do not.

Consider the case of the Flavorfest Company, which demonstrates the use of personality as an intervening variable.[11] The Flavorfest Company manufactures and distributes a well-known bottled condiment product. The firm has long dominated the market for this product line, which includes other spices and seasoning items. Flavorfest could base a marketing program on the assumption that all potential customers are equally valuable prospects, but such an assumption should be verified by research. Actually, it is more likely that substantial consumer differences exist. The research summarized below disclosed the existence of three distinct market segments.

1. Heavy Users (39 percent of the market)

a. Demographic attributes: homemakers aged 20-45, well educated, higher income categories, small families with most children under five, concentration in northeast and midwest regions and in suburban and farm areas.

b. Motivational attributes

(1) Strong motivation not to be old-fashioned and a desire to express individuality through creative action and use of exciting new things.

(2) The traditional role of homemaker is viewed with displeasure, and experimentation with new foods is done to express her individuality—not to please her family.

(3) The image of Flavorfest suggests exciting and exotic taste, and the product is reacted to favorably in terms of taste, appearance, and food value. It is highly prized in experimental cooking; hence, there is substantial compatibility between user's values and product image.

2. Light to Moderate Users (20 percent of the market)

a. Demographic attributes: homemakers aged 35-54, large families with children under 12, middle-income groups, location primarily in the southeast, Pacific states, and southwest regions.

b. Motivational attributes

(1) A strong desire to express individuality through creative cookery, which is constrained somewhat by a conflicting desire to maintain tradition and subvert herself to her family's desires.

(2) The desire to experiment with new foods is also constrained by a lack of confidence in the results of her experimental cooking.

(3) The image of Flavorfest is favorable. The product is liked in all respects, but it is confined largely to use with one type of food. It is viewed as unacceptable in other uses; hence, her vision is limited regarding new uses of Flavorfest.

3. Nonusers (41 percent of the market)

a. Demographic attributes: older homemakers, large families, lower income brackets, location primarily in the eastern states and some parts of the South.

b. Motivational attributes

(1) A strong motive to maintain tradition and emotional ties with the past; identification with her mother and her role in the home.

(2) A conservative nonventuresome personality.

(3) Her role as mother and homemaker discourages experimental cookery, and Flavorfest is thus looked on unfavorably. The image of Flavorfest connotes flavors and a degree of modernity that is unacceptable.

(4) No interest is expressed in new uses and experimentation with Flavorfest, for the product does not represent the values embraced by these homemakers.

This research clearly indicates that there are important demographic and motivational differences between users and nonusers of Flavorfest. The findings summarized above indicate that the heavy-user segment is relatively large, and Flavorfest products are well regarded by the homemakers in this segment. Furthermore, the potential exists for stimulating greater use in this segment because of the product's use in experimental cookery.

The nonuser segment, on the other hand, requires a different marketing strategy. This segment is large but is made up of people with relatively low purchasing power, living in areas where population growth is stagnant. The negative values expressed toward Flavorfest suggest that there is little opportunity for stimulating the sale of Flavorfest in this market segment.

The light-to-moderate-user segment represents the greatest opportunity for increased sales. The desire for creative cookery is present but is constrained by a desire to maintain tradition and by a lack of confidence in the results of experimental efforts. However, the favorable opinion of Flavorfest suggests that sales could be stimulated by demonstrating the compatibility between pleasing the family and creative cookery.

As an intervening variable, personality is more properly categorized as it should be—a variable that accounts for individual differences within broader categories of economic and social influence. As such, it may be a significant variable in a total model of consumer behavior in some buying situations and, consequently, should be measured and studied in more detail in consumer research.

Life-style Concept

During the 1960s, a new concept called "life-style" began to take shape. The concept of life-style resulted from a merging of the objectivity of the personality inventory (trait-factor theory) with the rich, consumer-oriented, descriptive detail of the qualitative motivation research investigation (psychoanalytic theory).[12] In recent years, this rich concept has captured the interest and imagination of academicians and practitioners alike.

The concept of life-style has become widely diffused in the marketing literature and among marketing practitioners even though its use was not common until about 1970. Although there are numerous definitions of life-style (one researcher has identified 32 different definitions),[13] there is general agreement that life-style refers to the patterns in which people live and spend money and time. Life-style embraces a wide range of content including activities, interests, opinions, needs, values, attitudes, and personality traits. Precoded, objective questionnaires which are amenable to complex multivariate statistical analysis are used to measure each of these dimensions.

Life-style Influences on Consumer Decisions

The process of life-style influence on consumer decisions is shown in Figure 7.1. Life-styles are learned by individuals as the result of many influences such as culture, social class, reference groups, and the family. More specifically, however, life-styles are derivatives of consum-

Figure 7.1
**Life-style Influences on
Consumer Decisions**

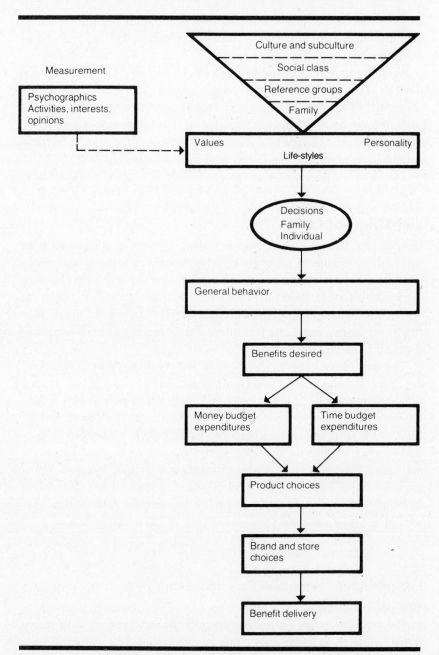

Source: James F. Engel, Roger D. Blackwell, and David T. Kollat, *Consumer Behavior*, 3rd ed. (Hinsdale, Ill.: Dryden Press, 1978), p. 175. Copyright © 1978 by Dryden Press, a division of Holt, Rinehart and Winston. Reprinted by permission of Holt, Rinehart and Winston.

ers' personal value systems and personalities. Thus, there is great overlap in meaning among the terms values, personality, and life-style. Life-style can be considered a derivative concept combining the influences of personality and social values that have been internalized by an individual.

The theory of life-styles is based on a theory of human behavior proposed by George Kelly which states that people try to predict and control their lives.[14] To do this, people form constructs, or patterns, to construe the events happening around them and use such constructs to interpret, conceptualize, and predict events. Some persons have constructs or patterns for interpreting their universe that are different from other individuals'—accounting for differences in life-styles. Kelly noted that this construct system not only is personal but also is continually changing in response to a person's need to conceptualize cues from the changing environment to be consistent with his or her personality.

People develop their sets of constructs *to minimize incompatibilities or inconsistencies*. Therefore, a person who agrees with the statement "I buy many things with a credit card" is also likely to agree with the statement "I will probably have more money to spend next year." Although less obvious, perhaps, this "construct" theory also explains why the same person is likely to agree with the statements "A husband and wife should not conceive more than two children" and "The use of marijuana should be made legal." Only a limited part of a person's life-style is visible to or measurable by the consumer researcher, but from the portion that is measured, conclusions are made about the type or overall pattern. The failure to comprehend fully or measure the whole life-style may account for apparent inconsistencies in a person's style of life or pervasiveness in the person's personality. This, of course, complicates prediction of consumer choices related solely to life-style measures.

The term life-style has come to mean about the same as psychographics, or AIO (activities, interests, opinions). The three major components of life-style—activities, interests, and opinions—have been defined as follows:

> An *activity* is a manifest action such as viewing a medium, shopping in a store, or telling a neighbor about a new service. Although these acts are usually observable, the reasons for the actions are seldom subject to direct measurement.

An *interest* in some object, event, or topic is the degree of excitement that accompanies both special and continuing attention to it.

An *opinion* is a verbal or written "answer" that a person gives in response to stimulus situations in which some "question" is raised. It is used to describe interpretations, expectations, and evaluations—such as beliefs about the intentions of other people, anticipations concerning future events, and appraisals of the rewarding or punishing consequences of alternative courses of action.[15]

In addition to measures of activities, interests and opinions, use of the life-style concept includes variables such as income, life cycle, education and other demographics. That is, the measurement of life-style includes "measures of people's activities in terms of (1) how they spend their time; (2) their interests, what they place importance on in their immediate surroundings; (3) their opinions in terms of their view of themselves and the world around them; and (4) some basic characteristics such as their stage in life cycle, income, education, and where they live."[16]

Forces Shaping American Life-styles

Through the process of socialization, an individual's behavior, or what some might call "personality," is shaped and influenced. The influences continue throughout a lifetime, causing people to adopt general values (thrift, pleasure, honesty) which, in turn, influence consumption. These life forces also produce specific preferences—such as color preferences, packaging and convenience preferences, preferred hours of shopping, characteristic interactions with salespersons, and so forth.

Values, as indicated previously, are generalized beliefs or expectations about behavior. Values are important determinants of life-styles and are broader in scope than attitudes or the types of variables contained in AIO measures. Values serve as a basic, integrating framework for our attitudes.

Individuals are not born with their values. Rather, values are learned or passed on from generation to generation in a society or from member to member in a subculture group. (See Chapter 3.) Many values are relatively permanent from generation to generation but others are undergoing considerable change in the contemporary environment. The values most in transition frequently are of most interest to marketing strategists because they provide the *basis for differences between life-style market segments*. They may hold the key to growth for marketing strategists seeking to understand and predict future opportunities or challenges for a particular company or industry.

Two types of forces may be isolated and analyzed in understanding values in a society. The first type of value source is the triad of institutions—family, school, and religion. As long as these institutions are stable, the values transmitted are likely to be relatively stable. When these institutions change rapidly, however, the values of consumers also change somewhat rapidly, causing serious discontinuity in the effectiveness of communication and marketing strategies.

The second source of values is early lifetime experiences, which include the range of diverse experiences that occur as a person is growing up and forming values. "Every person is a product of his or her environment" is a familiar truism. A less familiar one is that "people strive to achieve as adults what they feel they were deprived of in early stages of life." These generalizations suggest another reason why values are changing—namely, that the lifetime experiences of young consumers are fundamentally and qualitatively different from those of previous generations.

From an analysis of intergenerational influences, it would be predicted that the market for products could be segmented to some extent on the basis of values derived from lifetime experiences. Consumers who grew up during the Great Depression should place greater emphasis on material things, financial security, and economic criteria, whereas younger consumers should place greater emphasis on interpersonal or relationship values, noneconomic criteria, and immediate rather than future pleasure. In a study related to this topic, Vinson and Munson measured the values of students and compared them to similar measures of values of parents, particularly as they related to product attributes in an automobile. The results confirmed the above analysis and the researchers concluded that parents emphasized attributes signifying utilitarian or functional characteristics associated with automobile ownership (quality of warranty, service required, handling) while students were more concerned with aesthetic and socially observable features (styling, prestige, luxury interior).[17]

Marketing Strategy and Programming—A Case Example

Values affect life-styles in very substantial ways. Although it has been recognized for some time that values have a pervasive influence on consumer life-styles and consumption patterns, it has been difficult for marketing executives to relate these broad-based values to the specifics of marketing strategy and programming.

Table 7.3 is presented as a case example of how changing values are manifested in life-styles specific enough to be used for developing marketing programs. This table is presented in the next several pages of the text and requires the reader to expend considerable effort to study the relationship between life-style and marketing strategy. It would be possible to describe in general terms that strategies can be based on life-styles, but we believe you will grasp how this is done more readily with a comprehensive case example than with an abstract description.

The case example presented in Table 7.3 contains descriptions of key life-styles emerging as a result of the forces described in the preceding pages of this text. The trends were measured through repeated measures in surveys conducted by national polling services amplified by a psychographic study of 10,000 households selected from families in the Market Facts panel base. The names given the trends are significant only to the extent that they help communicate in a few words the meaning of the trends to the executives who must make marketing strategy decisions. This particular study, which is representative of similar projects by other organizations, was funded by the Home Furnishings Market Institute, to be used by a number of its member firms.

Many observations can be made after studying this case example. Perhaps the most important, however, is the possibility of an *integrated marketing program* based on information about consumer life-styles. Table 7.3 gives examples of how both *manufacturers* and *retailers* can develop strategies from life-style data. Additionally, the reader should note, in the third and fourth columns, the range of marketing decisions that is affected by life-style trends. These decisions include product, price, and advertising elements of the program as well as many distribution elements.

Table 7.3
Case Example of Marketing Strategy and Programming Based on Life-style Trends

Trend	Description of Trend	Illustrative Product Implications for Manufacturers and Retailers	Illustrative Additional Manufacturer Strategy Implications	Illustrative Additional Retailer Strategy Implications
More Casual Life-styles	Desire to live a less traditional, conservative, formalized life-style in terms of behavior, dress, eating, entertainment, and so on.	Potential increase in sales of furniture that is more comfortable. More casual, perhaps rugged, case goods. Potential long-term reduction in sales of formal living and dining room furniture. Good growth prospects for indoor/outdoor furniture.	Consider advertising featuring furniture and home furnishings in more realistic and casual life-style settings. Think about emphasizing comfort where appropriate.	Same as manufacturer.

Table 7.3 (continued)

Trend	Description of Trend	Illustrative Product Implications for Manufacturers and Retailers	Illustrative Additional Manufacturer Strategy Implications	Illustrative Additional Retailer Strategy Implications
Desire for Elegance and Personalization	Growing interest in a personalized life-style that is different from others and consistent with one's self-concept.	Growing market for uniquely designed furniture that is visibly different from what is widely available. Growing market for old, second-hand furniture, including antiques. Increasing tendency to mix styles between and/or within rooms. Potential increase in sales of "refinish-it-yourself" furniture, including kits.	Consider advertising featuring unique furniture and furniture settings that mix styles and designs harmoniously. Evaluate distribution through retailers having a reputation for uniqueness; brochures and sales promotion pieces that recommend what goes with what.	Consider devoting some inventory dollars to unique and unusual merchandise that is not available elsewhere. Some room settings and advertising might mix styles and designs harmoniously.
Flexibility of Roles/Women's Liberation	Men and women perform multiple roles—mother, hostess, wife, maid. Greater exchange of many roles between sexes.	Growing market for interchangeable (room-to-room) furniture as well as furniture that can serve a variety of purposes (multiple purpose).	Consider advertising and sales promotion featuring the interchangeability and multiple-purpose features of appropriate items.	Same as manufacturer. Add interchangeability and multiple-purpose features to sales presentations where applicable. Avoid double standards (male, female) in extending credit.

Instant Gratification	Living more for today and planning and living less for the future. Desire for instant standard of living, instant career achievement. Interest in "solutions to problems" rather than parts of problems. Growing intolerance of incompetence—waiting in line, etc.	Enlarging market for low cost/reasonable quality and well-designed furniture and home furnishings—analogously, the Mustang (or "fun watches"). Greater interest in groupings (packages) of furniture that go together—not necessarily the same style.	Continue to re-evaluate delivery time. Evaluate advertising and sales promotion for complete rooms using themes like "decorate your family room by bedtime."	Same as manufacturer. Also consider trying to speed up the time required to process a customer transaction. For regular customers, think about maintaining a file containing room layout, items purchased, including swatches, and so on.
Theology of Pleasure	Interested in having fun and in products, services, and other experiences that make life fun. This is a reaction to the boredom of life emanating partly from job tedium and dissatisfaction.	Favors unique, interesting furniture and furnishings that are conversation pieces. Also fun items like bean bag chairs and water beds.	Consider advertising and promoting furniture and furnishings in unique, fun settings. Evaluate distribution through retailers having a unique, fun image.	Create store excitement through unique displays. Re-evaluate how frequently they are changed. Consider music and other techniques that are consistent with your market. Think about establishing a play area for children, refreshment center, etc. Advertise and promote furniture in unique, fun settings.

Table 7.3 (continued)

Trend	Description of Trend	Illustrative Product Implications for Manufacturers and Retailers	Illustrative Additional Manufacturer Strategy Implications	Illustrative Additional Retailer Strategy Implications
Simplification	Removing or reducing the time and/or energy required to perform what are perceived by some to be mundane, undesirable tasks. Examples include self-cleaning ovens, trash compactors, power lawnmowers, etc.	Furniture and home furnishings that are easy to care for, easy to repair, and require less frequent cleaning, dusting, and so on. Minimum maintenance wall coverings. Opportunity for services such as furniture and carpet cleaning and repair, complete interior cleaning, painting, refurbishing, and so on.	Consider advertising and promoting easy maintenance features.	Same as manufacturer.

Changing Morality	Growing tendency to believe that premarital sex, homosexuality, etc. are not morally wrong. Increasing tendency to live together without being married.	Creates new needs for "temporary" furniture and home furnishings, including rental. Growing market for modular sofa and chair units that can be pushed together to create a large "lounging area." Opportunity for unique beds, headboards, and bedroom furniture designs that create atmosphere and facilitate "lounging" as well as sleeping. Emphasis on products of minimum deterioration or obsolescence for rental programs.	Think about advertising and promoting the modular features of sofa and chairs, if applicable. Also emphasize the "lounging" features of beds and bedroom furniture. Feature bedroom and other furniture in tastefully sensual settings. Potential opportunity for diversification into furniture rental.	Same as manufacturer, depending upon local market characteristics and opportunities.

Table 7.3 (continued)

Trend	Description of Trend	Illustrative Product Implications for Manufacturers and Retailers	Illustrative Additional Manufacturer Strategy Implications	Illustrative Additional Retailer Strategy Implications
Concern about Appearance and Health	Partial outgrowth of youth orientation. Concern about health, weight, physical appearance—often youthful appearance. Illustrations include wigs, hair dye, face lifts, vitamins, bust development, diet foods, etc.	Potential market for health and exercise equipment that has good design and is like furniture so that it looks good in bedrooms and/or other furnished areas, or which can be marketed as an accessory item, to be attached to or used with some item of furniture.		

Novelty, Change, and Escape	Reaction to the perceived boredom of life, resulting partly from the absence of meaningful work. Interest in products, services, and experiences that provide for novelty, change, and escape.	Potential market for less long-lasting, relatively low-priced, furniture and furnishings provided they are well-designed—i.e., the Timex concept. Growth potential for novelty items. Growing market for furniture and home furnishings for camping, camping vehicles and trucks, second homes, and so on. Potential opportunity for multiple coverings for upholstered goods.	Through advertising and promotion, evaluate positioning the home (apartment) as a place to "get away from it all." Also show how furniture and furnishings can be rearranged to create a fresh change and new feeling.	Same as manufacturer. Also include in merchandise presentations and sales presentations.

Table 7.3 (continued)

Trend	Description of Trend	Illustrative Product Implications for Manufacturers and Retailers	Illustrative Additional Manufacturer Strategy Implications	Illustrative Additional Retailer Strategy Implications
Naturalism	Growing desire to have the best of both worlds—the advantages of technology and the standard of living that it makes possible on the one hand—and naturalism, return to nature on the other. Rejection of artificial forms of behavior and dress.	Continuing market for natural woods and other materials. Earth tones should be popular. Designs that facilitate "openness" and "bring the outdoors" inside should do well. Less demand for wall-to-wall carpeting; more for area and throw rugs. Potential growth of patterns and materials using natural scenes and outdoor living.	Through advertising and sales promotion, consider featuring the natural characteristics of the product—natural woods, natural wool, etc.	Same as manufacturer. Include naturalness in sales presentations. Consider expanding assortment of area rugs.

Personal Creativity	For reasons of economy and/or self-expression, desire to make selected things and perform certain functions that have historically been purchased—i.e., crafts, home sewing, home repair and improvement, etc.	Growing market for products that allow final accessorization by the purchaser. Sales of unfinished furniture should increase, including higher quality furniture and knock-down pieces that require finishing as well as assembling. Growing market for used furniture that is unique. Opportunity for carpeting and floor covering products with "do-it-yourself" installation. Limited, but growing, opportunity for high cost gourmet cookware. Opportunity for "do-it-yourself" wall covering kit.	Advertising and promotion that shows consumers how to finish, assemble, refinish, upholster, reupholster furniture, install carpeting, wall coverings, etc. Potential theme might be: "If we can do it, so can you."	Same as manufacturer. Consider offering refinishing, reupholstering, cleaning, and similar services to customers. Also consider conducting classes in things like finishing and upholstering and sell kits.
Changing Attitudes toward Credit	Expectation that credit will be available to finance the "good life."	Increasing stability of sales.		Process credit applications quickly and politely. If third parties are involved, develop a mechanism to make the transition as smooth as possible.

Table 7.3 (continued)

Trend	Description of Trend	Illustrative Product Implications for Manufacturers and Retailers	Illustrative Additional Manufacturer Strategy Implications	Illustrative Additional Retailer Strategy Implications
New Work Ethic	Having fun is not bad and is not necessarily something to be minimized. Trend toward "working to live" rather than "living to work."	More time at home to enjoy furniture. Growing market for in-door/outdoor casual furniture and furnishings.	Think about advertising and promotion emphasizing "you deserve to relax." Utilize background settings in which people are relaxing and having fun. Where possible, adjust personnel policies to changing work ethic—flexible work hours, limited night and weekend commitments, and so on.	Same as manufacturer.
Institutional Reliance	Reliance on institutions—particularly government and business—to solve society's "problems" and a growing number of consumption needs.	Potential increase in the number of furniture and home furnishings items that are built in at the time of construction.	Consider developing working relationships with large builders, developers, architects, etc.	Same as manufacturer.
Eroding Confidence in Institutions	Dramatic reductions in the confidence people have in major institutions, particularly business.		Develop consumerism program.	Same as manufacturer.

Consumerism	Increasing concern over price/quality/quantity relationships. Increasing product and service expectations.	Growing need to tighten quality control. Guarantees and warranties will become more important.	Use guarantee/warranty cards to monitor who is buying your product(s) and where. Set up system to encourage customer complaints and to respond honestly and fairly. Periodically conduct studies of your customers and other people to measure your image.	Same as manufacturer. Also think about encouraging salespeople to talk in "customer-oriented" rather than technical terms. For example, the difference between wool and nylon carpeting is___. What this means to you, Mrs. Consumer, is___.
International Orientation	Gradual emergence of a "one world" orientation resulting from political and trade relationships and increasing travel, education, and communications. Early manifestations likely to be the gradual assimilation of selected Western European traditions and life-styles—particularly among younger, higher educated, more affluent segments.	Monitor trends in Europe to identify items that are popular there, particularly those that appeal to people under 35 years of age. Pay particular attention to furniture and home furnishings in countries having high density and smaller size (square footage) housing—such as Sweden and Holland.		

Table 7.3 (continued)

Trend	Description of Trend	Illustrative Product Implications for Manufacturers and Retailers	Illustrative Additional Manufacturer Strategy Implications	Illustrative Additional Retailer Strategy Implications
Energy/ Ecological/ Environmental Orientation	Gradual proliferation of energy conservation ethic which in turn may be generalized into natural resources conservation, and then into "anti-waste" in general.		Consider publicizing how your company buys wood only from resources that have an acceptable restoration program. Follow same policy for other natural resources that you use—including energy.	Same as manufacturer.
Price/Value Orientation	Emanating from the loss of real income and rising prices, growing concern about the value received for the price.	Products should have "visible" price-quality relationships. Greater attention should be placed on engineering products that give good value for the price. Warranties and guarantees will become more important. Potential decline in middle price points compared to upper and lower.	Think about emphasizing that furniture and many other home furnishings are one of the best investments that can be made. Re-evaluate pricing strategy in the context of achieving a "visible" price-quality relationship. If applicable to your company, develop a contingency strategy for the potential erosion of middle price points.	Same as manufacturer.

Eclecticism	Trend away from homogeneous fashion and life-styles toward the acceptance of a multiplicity of acceptable styles. Decline of fashion and life-style dictatorship toward more individualistic, often peer group influence.	Eclectic product line and assortment (that goes together) may become more effective. Comfort may become a more important criterion in selecting items. Growing market for accessories based on astrology, the occult, mysticism. Also accessory collections—medals, stamps, etc.	Through advertising and promotion show eclectic furniture groupings and dramatize comfort. Where appropriate, emphasize maintenance/durability aspects; for example, "(brand name) lets kids be kids."	Same as manufacturer.
Time Conservation	Growing recognition that time is a critical resource and constraint in many consumers' lives.	Furniture and home furnishings that are easy to care for, easy to repair, require less frequent cleaning, dusting, and so on.	Consider featuring ease of cleaning and maintenance in advertising and promotion.	Same as manufacturer. Also include in sales presentations. Also, improve ability of consumer to buy some items without visiting store.

Source: David T. Kollat, *Profile V Management Report* (Columbus: Management Horizons, Inc., 1976); David T. Kollat and Roger D. Blackwell, *Direction 1980* (Columbus: Management Horizons, Inc., 1970) and other related materials. © Management Horizons, Incorporated, 1976. Reprinted by permission.

Application of the Life-style Concept

The application of the life-style concept has become rather widespread because it involves one of the more direct methodologies of consumer research. Generally, the application of the life-style concept involves having fairly large samples of people respond to a series of questionnaire items on a "Likert Scale." That is, respondents indicate that they strongly agree, agree, are neutral, disagree, or strongly disagree with each item on the questionnaire. The typical questionnaire includes questions on activities, interests, opinions, and demographics (Table 7.4). An example of the specific format for questions and categories of response is provided in Table 7.5. Most life-style studies use some multivariate techniques of analysis in addition to cross-classification. Typically, factor analysis is used to reduce a great amount of data to a more basic structure. Factor analysis is a mathematical procedure for analyzing the high amount of correlation almost always existent in items into its most basic components or "factors." An example of the output of such analysis is presented in Table 7.6. This consolidation into eight male groups is based on about 300 psychographic questions completed in a national sample of 4,000 respondents.[18] This tremendous quantity of data must be reduced into a concise form to be useful to managers, and techniques such as factor analysis are useful in such situations.

Table 7.4
Life-style Dimensions

Activities	Interests	Opinions	Demographics
Work	Family	Themselves	Age
Hobbies	Home	Social issues	Education
Social events	Job	Politics	Income
Vacation	Community	Business	Occupation
Entertainment	Recreation	Economics	Family size
Club membership	Fashion	Education	Dwelling
Community	Food	Products	Geography
Shopping	Media	Future	City size
Sports	Achievements	Culture	Stage in life cycle

Source: Joseph T. Plummer, "The Concept and Application of Life Style Segmentation," *Journal of Marketing*, Vol. 38 (January 1974), p. 34. Reprinted from the *Journal of Marketing* published by the American Marketing Association.

Table 7.5
An Example of AIO Questions, Classified by Sex

Activity statements	Females (N = 594)					Males (N = 490)				
	SA	A	N/O	D	CD	SA	A	N/O	D	CD
Vacation related										
Our family travels together quite a lot	38%	30%	7%	16%	9%	37%	33%	7%	15%	8%
A cabin by a quiet lake is a great place to spend the summer	44	28	10	11	7	45	30	9	11	5
On a vacation, I just want to rest and relax	31	30	7	23	9	34	30	4	21	11
I like to spend my vacations in or near a big city	6	13	12	30	39	4	10	11	28	47
On my vacations, I like to get away from mechanization and automation	23	33	16	19	9	28	37	14	16	5
Vacations should be planned for children	17	39	16	20	8	18	38	19	18	7
Entertainment related										
Television is our primary source of entertainment	26%	26%	6%	23%	19%	24%	31%	6%	19%	20%
I would rather spend a quiet evening at home than go out to a party	24	30	8	25	13	30	31	8	23	8
We do not often go out to dinner or the theater together	20	22	8	19	31	15	25	6	22	32
Sporting related										
The best sports are very competitive	13%	21%	31%	21%	14%	28%	28%	20%	15%	9%
I prefer to participate in individual sports more than team sports	11	18	39	18	14	16	29	25	17	13
Whenever possible, I prefer to participate in sporting activities, rather than just watch them	15	27	15	19	24	25	29	12	18	16
I like to go and watch sporting events	18	40	13	15	14	34	37	10	12	7

Table 7.5 (continued)

Activity statements	Females (N = 594)					Males (N = 490)				
	SA	A	N/O	D	CD	SA	A	N/O	D	CD
Leisure time related										
I have enough leisure time	14%	23%	8%	28%	27%	13%	14%	8%	31%	34%
I tend to spend most of my leisure time indoors	16	35	6	29	14	7	22	7	32	32
Basically, I'm satisfied with my present leisure time activities	21	45	7	20	7	25	39	7	22	7
My leisure time tends to be boring	4	14	8	26	48	4	12	8	27	49
Specific activity related										
I do a lot of repair work on my car	1%	4%	23%	7%	65%	24%	24%	5%	16%	31%
I often work on a do-it-yourself project in my home	37	34	15	7	7	36	31	13	11	9
I am active in one or more service organizations	12	11	19	17	41	8	10	23	18	41
General statements										
When it comes to my recreation, time is a more important factor to me than money	23%	29%	17%	21%	10%	25%	30%	15%	19%	11%
When it comes to my recreation, money is a more important factor to me than time	9	19	16	34	22	10	20	18	34	18
I watch television more than I should	21	28	7	23	21	20	29	9	24	18
My major hobby is my family	49	30	9	9	3	35	32	14	14	5

Note: SA = Strongly agree; N/O = Undecided or no opinion; D = Disagree somewhat; CD = Completely disagree.
Source: Douglass K. Hawes, W. Wayne Talarzyk, and Roger D. Blackwell, "Consumer Satisfactions from Leisure Time Pursuits," M. J. Schlinger, ed. *Advances in Consumer Research* (Chicago: American Marketing Association, 1975), p. 833. Reprinted by permission.

Group I. *"The quiet family man"* (8% of total males)

He is a self-sufficient man who wants to be left alone and is basically shy. Tries to be as little involved with community life as possible. His life revolves around the family, simple work, and television viewing. Has a marked fantasy life. As a shopper he is practical, less drawn to consumer goods and pleasures than other men.

Low education and low economic status, he tends to be older than average.

Group II. *"The traditionalist"* (16% of total males)

A man who feels secure, has self-esteem, follows conventional rules. He is proper and respectable, regards himself as altruistic and interested in the welfare of others. As a shopper he is conservative, likes popular brands and well-known manufacturers.

Low education and low or middle socioeconomic status; the oldest age group.

Group III. *"The discontented man"* (13% of total males)

He is a man who is likely to be dissatisfied with his work. He feels bypassed by life, dreams of better jobs, more money, and more security. He tends to be distrustful and socially aloof. As a buyer, he is quite price conscious.

Lowest education and lowest socioeconomic group, mostly older than average.

Group IV. *"The ethical highbrow"* (14% of total males)

This is a very concerned man, sensitive to people's needs. Basically a puritan, content with family life, friends, and work. Interested in culture, religion, and social reform. As a consumer he is interested in quality, which may at times justify greater expenditure.

Well educated, middle or upper socioeconomic status, mainly middle aged or older.

Group V. *"The pleasure oriented man"* (9% of total males)

He tends to emphasize his masculinity and rejects whatever appears to be soft or feminine. He views himself a leader among men. Self-centered, dislikes his work or job. Seeks immediate gratification for his needs. He is an impulsive buyer, likely to buy products with a masculine image.

Low education, lower socioeconomic class, middle aged or younger.

Table 7.6
Eight Male Psychographic Segments

Table 7.6 (continued)

Group VI. *"The achiever"* (11% of total males)

This is likely to be a hardworking man, dedicated to success and all that it implies, social prestige, power, and money. Is in favor of diversity, is adventurous about leisure time pursuits. Is stylish, likes good food, music, etc. As a consumer he is status conscious, a thoughtful and discriminating buyer.
Good education, high socioeconomic status, young.

Group VII. *"The he-man"* (19% of total males)

He is gregarious, likes action, seeks an exciting and dramatic life. Thinks of himself as capable and dominant. Tends to be more of a bachelor than a family man, even after marriage. Products he buys and brands preferred are likely to have "self-expressive value," especially a "man of action" dimension.
Well-educated, mainly middle socioeconomic status, the youngest of the male groups.

Group VIII. *"The sophisticated man"* (10% of total males)

He is likely to be an intellectual, concerned about social issues, admires men with artistic and intellectual achievements. Socially cosmopolitan, broad interests. Wants to be dominant, and a leader. As a consumer he is attracted to the unique and fashionable.
Best educated and highest economic status of all groups, younger than average.

Source: William D. Wells, "Psychographics: A Critical Review," *Journal of Marketing Research,* Vol. 12 (May 1975), pp. 196-213. Reprinted from the *Journal of Marketing Research* published by the American Marketing Association.

The most frequent and perhaps useful application of life-style measurement currently is for market segmentation strategies. This application is based on the premise that the more you know and understand about customers, the more effectively a communications and marketing program can be developed to reach that target market. Plummer analyzes the value of market segmentation and concludes that it provides a new view of the market, assists in product positioning, leads to more effective communication, helps develop total marketing and media strategies, suggests new product opportunities and, in general, helps explain the "why" of a product or brand situation.[19]

Overall, life-style research is most appropriate for products whose function includes psychological gratification or whose performance cannot be evaluated objectively—products with high involvement, products that are designed for a minority market segment, and products that are relatively expensive or symbolic.[20] Life-style research is particularly helpful where advertising is a major tool in the product's marketing mix, where consumers are willing to switch brands when they are not completely satisfied, and where the category is not dominated by one or two brands. It is not so appropriate for commodities, for products that are purchased primarily on the basis of price, or for products that have low involvement on the part of consumers.

For appropriate products and market segments, the most productive use of marketing programming based on life-style research is probably in determining the style of communications, in developing new products, in positioning them, or in developing new packaging.[21]

Summary

Personality can be thought of as a consistent pattern of responses to environmental stimuli. Three major personality theories are examined. The psychoanalytic, or Freudian, theory determines a person's behavior through the interaction of three systems of interdependent psychological forces—the id, the ego and the superego. Social psychological theory considers social variables, not biological ones, to be the important determinants of personality and contends that people consciously direct their behavior toward need satisfaction. According to trait-factor theory, one's personality is composed of a set of traits or difference variables, the implication being that types of consumer behavior can be statistically related to a set of personality variables. Consumer analysts' attempts to show that personality substantially influences consumer behavior have resulted in more unsuccessful trials than successful ones.

On the basis of difficulties with market segmentation and related problems, most marketing strategists would contend that personality has not been demonstrated to be a significant input to marketing decision making. However, recent research efforts have produced three major modifications in the use of personality theory that may make it useful. First, consumption-related personality inventories have been constructed to replace standardized inventories specifically designed for use in the psychological clinic. Second, personality has been found to act with other variables as a moderator to determine behavior. Third, personality has become meaningful as an intervening variable accounting for individual differences within broader categories of economic and social influence.

The life-style concept refers to the patterns in which people live and spend money and time. Life-styles are learned by individuals as the result of various social influences and are the derivatives of social values and personality. The three major components of life-style, or the psychographic variables, have been defined as activities, interests, and opinions. Life-style also takes into account demographic variables.

Values are generalized beliefs or expectations about behavior and are important determinants of life-style. Many values remain stable from generation to generation, but others are undergoing considerable change in the contemporary environment. Marketing strategists are especially interested in changing values because they provide the basis for differences among life-style market segments. Two sources of values are institutions (the family, schools, and religion) and early lifetime experiences. A case example is presented that contains descriptions of key life-styles currently emerging as a result of changing values and that illustrates how manufacturers and retailers can develop strategies from the life-style data.

The most frequent and perhaps useful application of life-style research currently is for market segmentation strategies. According to Plummer, market segmentation provides a new view of the market, assists in product positioning, leads to more effective communication, helps develop total marketing and media strategies, suggests new product opportunities, and helps explain the "why" of a product or brand situation. Suggestions are given for product types most conducive to life-style application.

Questions and Issues for Discussion

1. What are the basic differences among the three major personality theories? How might the marketing strategies developed by proponents of each of these theories differ from one another? Which of the theories is likely to provide the greatest contribution to the marketing strategist?

2. Now that the FCC has permitted telephone subscribers to buy their phone instruments, decorator phones and gadgetry have become a novelty. New products range from extension phones shaped like Mickey Mouse to those that feature automatic answering, dialing, call timing, and built-in radio-alarm clocks. The possibilities are immense, and people in the industry are anticipating installing anywhere from four to six phones per home. How might an understanding of personality traits be of use to the companies in designing new telephones? How important is the influence of personality in choosing a decorator phone?

3. Why do consumer analysts continue to consider personality a central concept despite the many disappointing experiences marketing strategists have had with it?

4. You are a book publisher and have recently agreed to publish a series of thriller mysteries. Do you think it is possible to segment the market for the novels on the basis of information obtained from a CAD scale? What reservations would you have in doing so?

5. Billy Biggs is a college student who makes jewelry in his spare time for a local jewelry store. While working in the store, he has observed that the male students who buy jewelry for themselves are outgoing, dress fashionably, and seem to be very self-confident. However, the majority of the males who enter the store with female companions find men's jewelry unacceptable because of the fear that it detracts from their masculinity. They admit that some items are attractive but would not consider purchasing them for themselves, even when females assure them that men's jewelry is socially acceptable. Which modification in personality theory would enable Billy to better understand why these men are reluctant to purchase and wear jewelry? Explain. What strategy could Billy use in appealing to the tastes of these males?

6. Marshall Field, the nation's largest independent full-service department store, is known as the "sleeping giant of retailing." In its

125-year history, it has catered solely to the "well-heeled" mature woman and has neglected the changing tastes of its potential customers. Now the store realizes that it must recognize changing life-styles by appealing to a wider, younger and less affluent clientele. What psychograhic information would be useful to the store to better enable it to appeal to this market segment?

7. The magazine industry has been relatively unsuccessful in using the "unisex movement" to its advantage. Few publishers have been able to appeal to both male and female readers with a single magazine. What recommendations would you make, based on your understanding of life-style trends?

8. For what types of products is life-style research most appropriate? In what ways would a marketing manager make the most productive use of information received from life-style research?

9. A study of consumerism in the United States has reflected a vote of no confidence in business. A recent Harris poll revealed that 59 percent of the respondents agreed with the statement that companies are "too concerned about profits to care about quality." How do you suppose these expectations and beliefs about the behavior of business firms is affecting life-styles? Some companies have set up consumer affairs departments in the last few years, but consumer advocates have regarded such moves as public relations ploys. Officers of these firms, however, claim that the departments have given their customers "real corporate clout." One executive says, "Whether customers buy from us or the competition can often depend on how they perceive our treating them." What measures could the consumer affairs department of a major oil company recommend to help better serve consumers, thus increasing confidence in the organization and profits?

10. Fancy Sweets, a maker of "adult candies," has lines of boxed chocolates including such unusual sweets as "chocolate-covered ants." These lines have experienced a decline in sales over the last five years, which top executives attribute to the "diet craze." How should this firm go about trying to reverse this decline in sales? Can you think of some other popular trend that could be advantageous in the product development and positioning of Fancy Sweets?

Case 1. Warner Communications, Inc.

The idea of a TV service that charges customers for the programs they view was conceived in 1929. Since that time, many companies have lost millions of dollars in their efforts to make such a system attractive to television viewers. However, pay-TV systems that charge customers a flat rate per month to view recent movies and sports events that are uninterrupted by commercials have encountered relative success in recent years. Out of the approximately 11 million viewing homes that pay a monthly rate of $7–$10 for the clear reception offered through cable TV service, slightly more than one million homes are subscribing to the movie service. No guarantee exists, though, that a system can attract enough subscribers to make it a profitable operation. Home Box Office, the Time, Inc. subsidiary that supplies pay-TV programs to some 800,000 cable TV homes, has its subscribers split among more than 200 different cable systems. Other problems exist also: there is a 2- to 3-percent turnover of subscribers each month, a severe shortage of films, and a highly fluctuating acceptance rate among cable TV subscribers—anywhere from 10 to 90 percent in each of its cable systems. Despite the potential problems, however, many are convinced that a pay-TV system can be highly profitable in high-density urban markets and are spending millions of dollars to prove it.

The young industry has been split over a dispute between per program vs. monthly charges. One advocate of the per-program charge notion is Warner Communications, Inc., which has developed a new kind of cable system called QUBE (pronounced "cube"). The system differs from other pay-TV operations in that it does not offer a known quantity of TV programs to subscribers who pay a flat amount each month for the service. Instead, subscribers pay a $9.95 installation charge and then buy "on impulse" the programs that are of interest to them. This is done by pressing buttons on a hand-held QUBE control unit that sends a message to a computer to transmit a specific movie, play, educational course, audience-participation quiz game, or

Sources: Some of the information in Case 1 is from "Still Pitching for Pay-TV," *Business Week*, April 11, 1977, pp. 111–114; and "The Cable-TV Industry Gets Moving Again," *Business Week*, November 21, 1977, pp. 154–158.

public affairs lecture to the TV. Different prices are charged for the various programs. For example, a production of the opera "Cavalleria Rusticana" costs $2.50, a Frank Sinatra concert costs $2, and movies range in price from $1 for *High Noon* to $3.50 for *Network*. When a customer "orders" a program, the computer records its title and the time and date it received the message; the information is then processed and a monthly bill is sent to the customer. Although a few similar systems are in existence in some test markets, Warner believes that its system provides features the others lack. For instance, QUBE will allow viewers to "talk back" to the studio by pushing certain buttons on their control devices. These buttons enable them to place bids for items shown at an auction, select optional football plays that a quarterback should run, "vote" on civic questions, or choose answers in courses given for school credit. As a truly unique feature, Warner has built elaborate studios in the city where it is being test-marketed and plans to produce costly original programs. In the future, the company intends to offer fire and burglar alarm services through the system.

Warner admits that it has no clear idea of the revenues to be made from a QUBE installation. A subscriber could possibly run up a $14 bill in one day for several movies or sports events. However, the company has doubts as to whether customers will be that free with their money. In addition, it is feasible that the company could heavily promote a film or event that is expected to be a blockbuster and instead turns out to be a "flop." It would decidedly lessen viewer confidence. Nevertheless, Warner is estimated to have spent close to $12 million in developing the system for its test market. Competitors question the large expenditure because of the limited size of the city. Furthermore, even if the system does prove to be successful in the test market, it may be difficult to expand to other areas because many cities already have a system established or are in the process of developing one.

Case 1 Questions

1. Do you think that a personality inventory would reveal a significant relationship between certain personality traits and purchase of a pay (per program) TV system? If so, which personality traits might influence the purchase?

2. How should the market be segmented demographically?

3. What appeals should Warner make to convince TV viewers that the benefits of QUBE exceed the costs?

Case 2. Homestead Bros.

Homestead Bros., a producer of household decorator, maintenance, and kitchen products, and, more recently, cookbooks and home care and decorator manuals, has been looking for fresh ideas and improvements in its segmentation strategy and marketing mix. Prompted by reports from some regional managers that there seemed to be a substantial increase in the number of males making inquiries about its products, especially in certain geographic areas, Homestead hired Hayes & Neutzel Consultants to research the matter. What follows are excerpts from their analysis of what they call a major trend in lifestyles, which they think may be the vanguard of the restructured "new family of the eighties."

While female participation in the labor force has increased markedly in the last decade or so, there have also been some interesting changes in the work habits of males. Indeed, these changes are worth noting. According to 1976 Bureau of Labor Statistics figures, there has been over a 26-percent increase since 1967 in the percentage of married women who work, but in this period, the number of men outside the labor force rose a remarkable 71 percent. Some 2.2 million men in 1976 neither held nor sought jobs. Over half of these men were disabled, but the number of able, prime working-age males in this category is nonetheless startling.

Among work-force dropouts ages 25 to 34, 63 percent have working wives, and many of these males may reenter the job market sooner or later. A large number of young married students or men—many of them black—manifest the discouraged worker effect: today's unemployment rate is so high and the prospects of finding good work are so

Source: Some information in Case 2 is from "The Great Male Cop-out from the Work Ethic," *Business Week*, November 14, 1977, pp. 156-161.

dismal that these men would rather not undertake job search. There is evidence to show that the male dropout phenomenon is not a temporary one, however. Census Bureau data support the conclusion that the proportion of men who say they will seek work within a year "drops sharply with increased employment in the period of inactivity." And some economists hold that increases in the level of structural unemployment (unemployment due largely to imperfect communication and mobility) has pushed upward the "full employment rate of unemployment."

A more supportive social atmosphere, exemplified by new government- and corporate-financed alternatives to working for a living, has helped encourage what some choose to call a "male liberation." Many young husbands and middle-aged men are letting their wives earn the paychecks while they stay at home and attend to domestic chores. One former $30,000-a-year Philadelphia executive claims that he "found out where the clean socks come from" and elected to become a househusband.

In the last decade, books such as the *Greening of America* have expressed and inspired widespread questioning of the work ethic. Words such as "workaholic" have crept into our vocabulary, reflecting a growing disaffection with the old morality. "I wouldn't go back to the corporate ulcer factory under any circumstances," says a former vice president of a large midwestern brewery. He adds, "I'm perfectly satisfied that making more money is not so all-important." This changing attitude towards work has been confirmed as quite prevalent by experts in the field and was expressed repeatedly by respondents to a *Business Week* survey. It doubtless has contributed to the rising number of househusbands in the United States.

A good example of the growing number of househusbands is provided by a 31-year-old holder of two masters' degrees in education, who says he has been content to stay at home doing the cooking and washing for the past five years, while his wife, a physician, acts as the breadwinner. "If I ever do work, I will create the job," he asserts. "I'm not willing to play the politics of getting a job organized to deliver what I want it to."

Men such as this, who are not disabled and not in school, are a third of all male nonworkers among both blacks and whites. Many of them are actually on-and-off workers. Most of the time the work is legal, such as carpentry and driveway sealing, but in some instances it is illegal, such as selling drugs. One way or the other, these men work as unofficially and occasionally self-employed persons, thus eluding labor force statistics.

Another "house person" says that when he quit his job as a warehouseman six years ago, he enjoyed his new role so much that he decided not to look for another job. He points out, however, that "it's definitely still work." In addition to his routine of seeing the kids off to school, cooking, cleaning, shopping, doing the laundry, and maintaining a $75,000 home, he must carry on with the male-oriented tasks of fixing cars and chopping wood, making his a 24-hour responsibility. He says he thinks about a regular job towards the end of every month, "when the money around here starts getting pretty thin."

In some areas of the country, work-force dropouts have begun to constitute a substantial percentage of the population. In the Florida Keys, for example, an entire subculture of boat dwellers has sacrificed regular employment for a life of fishing, sailing, and odd-jobbing. Two new recruits are a husband and wife, both in their thirties, who left a combined income of $19,500 they earned at a southern university. He seriously doubts that they will ever return. "I'll just play it by ear and see," he says. "My only regret is that I didn't do it years ago."

Case 2 Questions

1. With the regional managers' reports having been confirmed, you, as a Homestead Bros. marketing manager, must develop a strategy covering all aspects of the marketing mix for immediate implementation in those geographical areas where this trend has gained the widest acceptance.

2. Using Figure 7.1 as a reference, discuss the influence of these changing attitudes toward work and the exchange of traditional family roles between husbands and wives on consumer decisions.

Notes

1. W. D. Wells and A. D. Beard, "Personality and Consumer Behavior," S. Ward and T. S. Robertson, eds., *Consumer Behavior: Theoretical Sources* (Englewood Cliffs, N.J.: Prentice-Hall, Inc., 1973), pp. 141-99.

2. P. Kotler, *Marketing Management* (Englewood Cliffs, N.J.: Prentice-Hall, Inc., 1976), p. 76.

3. J. B. Cohen, "An Interpersonal Orientation to the Study of Consumer Behavior," *Journal of Marketing Research,* 4 (August 1967), pp. 270-78.

4. Kathryn E. A. Villani and Yoram Wind, "On the Usage of 'Modified' Personality Trait Measures in Consumer Research," *Journal of Consumer Research,* 2 (December 1975), pp. 223-28.

5. H. H. Kassarjian, "Personality and Consumer Behavior: A Review," *Journal of Marketing Research,* 8 (November 1971), pp. 409-18.

6. Mark I. Alpert, "Personality and the Determinants of Product Choice," *Journal of Marketing Research,* 9 (February 1972), pp. 89-92.

7. Paul E. Green, Yoram Wind, and Arun K. Jain, "A Note on Measurement of Social-Psychological Belief Systems," *Journal of Marketing Research,* 9 (May 1972), pp. 204-08.

8. F. B. Evans, "Psychological and Objective Factors in the Prediction of Brand Choice," *Journal of Business,* 32 (October 1959), pp. 340-69.

9. D. L. Sparks and W. T. Tucker, "A Multivariate Analysis of Personality and Product Use," *Journal of Marketing Research,* 8 (February 1971), pp. 66-70.

10. I. S. White, "The Perception of Value in Products," J. W. Newman, ed., *On Knowing the Consumer* (New York: John Wiley & Sons, Inc., 1966), pp. 90-106.

11. James Engel, Hugh Wales, and Martin Warshaw, *Promotional Strategy,* 3rd ed. (Homewood, Ill.: Richard D. Irwin, Inc., 1975), pp. 170-72. © 1975 by Richard D. Irwin, Inc.

12. William D. Wells, "Psychographics: A Critical Review," *Journal of Marketing Research,* 12 (May 1975), pp. 196-213.

13. Ibid., p. 196.

14. George A. Kelly, *Th   Psychology of Personal Constructs,* Vol. I (New York: N. W. Norton & Co., 1955). The following discussion is drawn heavily from Fred Reynolds and William Darden, "Construing Life Style and Psychographics," William D. Wells, ed., *Life Style and Psychographics* (Chicago: American Marketing Association, 1974), pp. 71-96.

15. Reynolds and Darden, "Construing Life Style and Psychographics," p. 87.

16. Joseph T. Plummer, "The Concept and Application of Life Style Segmentation," *Journal of Marketing,* 38 (January 1974), pp. 33-37, at 33.

17. Donald E. Vinson and J. Michael Munson, "Personal Values: An Approach to Market Segmentation," Kenneth Bernhardt, ed., *Marketing: 1776–1976 and Beyond* (Chicago: American Marketing Association, 1976), pp. 313-17.

18. Wells, "Psychographics."

19. Plummer, "Concept and Application of Life Style Segmentation."

20. Rudolph W. Struse, "Lifestyle Research Inappropriate for Some Categories of Products," *Marketing News,* 10 (June 17, 1977), p. 9.

21. Ibid., p. 9.

Chapter **8**   The Role of
Learning

Outline

The Study of Learning

Learning in Consumer Behavior

The Learning Process
Learning Defined
Learning to Become a Consumer

The Components of the Learning Process
Drive
Cue
Response
Reinforcement
Retention

Further Notions from Learning Theory as Applied to Consumer Behavior
Semantic Generation
Semantic Satiation
Covert Involvement and Vicarious Practice
Aha Experiences
Mental Completing

Summary

Questions and Issues for Discussion

Cases

Key Terms

learning

classical conditioning

instrumental conditioning

conditioning stimulus

symbolic learning

consumership

cognitive development theory

socialization orientation to learning

drive

primary drives

secondary drives

cues

generalization

response

reinforcement

retention

semantic satiation

covert involvement

vicarious practice

aha experience

mental completing

closure

The learning process is fundamental to most aspects of consumer behavior; consequently, it is an extremely important topic to understand. The nature of learning as it relates to consumer behavior can be illustrated by examining three examples of things that American consumers have learned recently that have already had noticeable market impact. This type of consumer learning will continue and the potential influence will be considerable.

1. With increasing food costs, sizable numbers of consumers have learned that some attractive savings can be obtained by those who

are willing to make a break with their national brands of canned goods by selecting what have been called "no-name, no-frill, plain-wrap, and generic" products. These are popular grocery items available in stripped-down packaging. Wrappers are typically plain white with a stark black legend such as "Whole Kernel Corn," "Syrup," or "Yellow Cling Peaches."[1] In a limited price survey, for example, Consumers Union found savings of an average of 30 percent over name-brand products of essentially equal quality. CU attributes the savings to the lack of big-budget advertising. Many food chains have quickly moved to offer such no-frill items, including Jewel Food Stores, A & P, Big Bear, Food Marts, and Giant Food Stores.[2]

2. American consumers have learned that there is a "new" alternative mode of individualized transportation available to them—the moped. The moped is a hybrid motorcycle-bicycle combination that uses very little fuel and generally provides flexible low-cost transportation to those who are willing to tangle with traffic and road hazards at under 30 miles per hour. Sales in the United States have already exceeded 150,000 per year and are expected to increase rapidly. Even though the moped is new to the domestic market, it is certainly not new to many European and Asian consumers.

3. A few years ago, consumers generally had no idea that a smoke detector was important to have in their homes. As an indication of how much has been learned about its desirability, the manufacturers of First Alert recently advertised their brand of detector as an ideal Mother's Day gift. There is no doubt that in a relatively short time, many consumers have become aware of this product's usefulness and have moved in great numbers to purchase it. Whether it is actually a good Mother's Day present remains to be learned. If asked, many would probably have some reservations.

A limited number of other manufacturers have had similar success in convincing consumers of the desirability of owning selected products that historically have had little demand in the mass market. For instance, Homelite, through a concerted marketing effort, substantially contributed to making the chain saw an everyday consumer good. Homelite is now planning a similar strategy in an attempt to build demand for its line of gasoline-powered generators. Their effort is primarily aimed at the owners of homes valued at over $50,000. If successful, they expect to sell 5,000 units the first year; the top of their line generator sells for $1800.[3]

The Study of Learning

Historically, much of the research that focused on learning as a formal process concentrated on simple, mechanical learning. This typically included what have been called *classical conditioning* and *instrumental conditioning*.[4] Classical conditioning theory had its origin in the work of Pavlov and is often exemplified by referring to the salivation of a dog at the sound of a dinner bell. In a learning situation such as this, the relevant action follows some triggering event. In instrumental conditioning the reverse is true. The sought response or action precedes what is called the *conditioning stimulus*.

In a consumer behavior context, instrumental conditioning has been called trial-and-error learning; that is, a consumer recognizes a personal desire for a particular product or service and proceeds to determine the most preferred one by trying in turn what appear to be reasonable alternatives.[5] It is not unusual to find consumers using this method of selection when buying such products as cough medicine, cake mixes, dog food, and hand lotion.

Most of the work in both classical conditioning and instrumental conditioning has involved experimental psychologists using various animals, particularly rats. The assumption made by these researchers is that the learning process in its simplest form occurs in all species, including man. Stated more simply, it is basically the same wherever it is found. However, the more complex process of symbolic learning—the involvement of what has been called thinking or ideation—is unique to man.[6] This complex form is of greatest interest to the consumer analyst and is being studied seriously. But, this symbolic learning is also the most difficult to study.

Learning in Consumer Behavior

As a way of introducing the subject of learning and of illustrating the variety of circumstances where it is involved in consumer behavior, the hypothetical situations included in Table 8.1 are offered as instances of consumer learning. Each of the topics identified is important to the consumer analyst because it relates specifically to market behavior and subsequently to the success of a firm's marketing strategy. Nevertheless, the situations have been substantially condensed to facilitate their usage here.

Actually, each situation described in Table 8.1 represents a rather complex phenomenon, such as brand loyalty as portrayed by the consistent buying of Kodak film. A number of factors were influential in shaping the observed behavior. The following descriptions identify some of these details:

Some basic interest in photography is involved, and this was learned. The interest was probably developed over an extended period of time, with the nuclear family probably having had some impact on nurturing it.

The depth of one's interest also develops over time and contributes to formulating the criteria used to evaluate the picture-taking process.

Attention has been given to determining when it is appropriate to take pictures as well as the kind of equipment and supplies to use for obtaining acceptable results. In most cases, these decisions were made over time by gathering information using a number of means including: observing others; discussions with various people; reading, listening, and/or viewing advertisements; and personal trial and error.

Experience in shopping may also influence the brand of film purchased. The relative importance of patronage factors varies among consumer groups but usually includes convenience, product line, service, and price level.

Table 8.1
Instance in Consumer Learning

Consumer Behavior Topical Issue	Situation Observed among Some Consumer Groups	What Was Learned
1. Brand loyalty	Consistent buying of Kodak film	Among brands of film considered, this brand has proven to be most satisfactory in terms of price, quality, and availability.

Table 8.1 (continued)

Consumer Behavior Topical Issue	Situation Observed among Some Consumer Groups	What Was Learned
2. Brand switching	Changing brands of toothpaste	The brand previously used has been found to be less desirable in terms of taste and texture than the new brand now being purchased.
3. Promotional message retention	Recall of the slogan of a well-known company, e.g., "Have it your way."	The advertising theme was associated with a particular fast food restaurant and the service feature of the firm.
4. Store or establishment loyalty	Visiting the same service station regularly for auto-related products	Over time, alternatives were considered, and this station was found to be the most preferred in terms of the evaluative criteria used.
5. Changing evaluative criteria	Starting to shop at a discount supermarket where prices are consistently lower on selected items	Shopping at this store is helpful in holding down family food expenditures.

As time passes and an individual accumulates experience in purchasing and using a product, such as photographic film, that person ordinarily will attempt to simplify the decision process and the actual act of buying. What this typically leads to is the learning of a behavioral set through the integration of several basic elements of behavior into a meaningful group. In a nontechnical sense, three major components make up this behavioral set. These are shown in Figure 8.1.

Figure 8.1
Elements of Behavioral Set

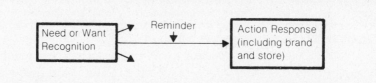

When a personal need or want is recognized (frequently this involves an external reminder such as an advertisement or someone saying, "Let's go on a picnic and don't forget to bring your camera"), a pattern of action quickly comes to mind. This often includes the brand of film to buy as well as where to make the purchase. What has been learned over time has greatly simplified the purchase process and shortened the amount of time that is needed to complete the act of buying. Some analysts have called this "routinized buying behavior."

Actually, nothing is quite as important in predicting what choice will be made by a consumer as knowledge of past behavior in similar situations. This fundamental role of learning in economic behavior is described by Katona:

> Learning, in the broadest sense of the term, is a basic feature of any organism. The human organism acquires forms of behavior, it acquires forms of action, of knowledge, or emotions. What has been done does not necessarily belong only to the past and is not necessarily lost. It may or may not exert influence on present behavior. Under what conditions and in what ways past experience affects later behavior is one of the most important problems of psychology.[7]

The whole model of the consumer decision process is shown again in Figure 8.2 as a reminder of the pervasiveness of learning. Each aspect of the model has components that, in one way or another, either contribute to what is learned or rely on what has been learned and processed.

Before proceeding further, a formal definition of learning must be set forth. It is also important to identify the key components of the learning process.

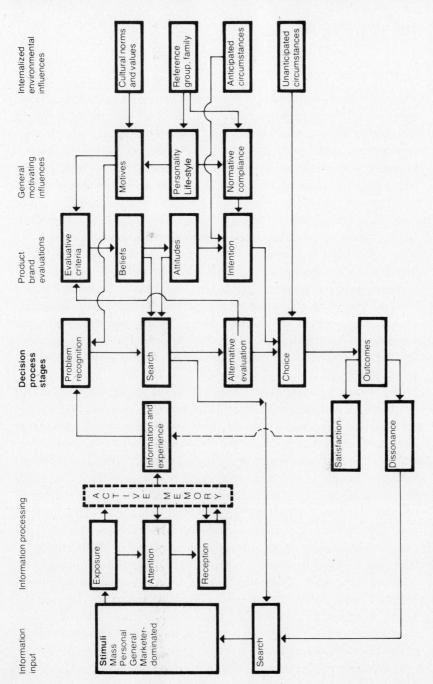

Figure 8.2
**A Complete Model of
Consumer Behavior**

Source: James F. Engel, Roger D. Blackwell, and David T. Kollat, *Consumer Behavior*, 3rd ed. (Hinsdale, Ill.: Dryden Press, 1978), p. 32. Copyright © 1978 by Dryden Press, a division of Holt, Rinehart and Winston. Reprinted by permission of Holt, Rinehart and Winston.

The Learning Process

Learning Defined

There are many definitions of learning, but one in particular is most appropriate to the subject of this book. As used throughout the text, *learning* is defined as those changes in responses and response tendencies that result from the effects of experience. This definition acknowledges that learned behavior must include changes in attitudes, emotions, evaluative criteria, and personality as well as the more easily observed variations in physical behavior that have taken place over time due to individual experience. Some of these changes are often difficult to detect, as illustrated in the following example.

In 1972, Charles Dawson bought a new Chevrolet. The car was a four-door top-of-the-line model with AM/FM radio, air conditioning, power brakes, and power steering. This was Charles' first new car and he knew very little about automobiles. Even though he felt somewhat uncomfortable about the decision he had made, two facts made the purchase acceptable to him: (1) his neighbor had recently purchased the same model and (2) the features that were pointed out by the dealer salesman.

During the next six years, Charles' interest in cars heightened and he became a real auto buff. As a result, he read whatever he could on the new cars and discussed his ideas with equally knowledgeable friends. Then in 1979, he decided it was time to buy another new car. After rather intensive searching and shopping at various dealerships, he again bought a new Chevrolet, which was essentially the same model as his first car with nearly identical equipment. Certainly Charles Dawson had learned a great deal about cars since his first purchase. Nevertheless, there was no observable change in actual purchase behavior; that is, he made the same choice in 1979 as in 1972. However, if his attitudes or buying intentions had been measured at both points in time, there would have been a marked difference in results. Furthermore, the confidence that he had at the time of the second purchase would also have been much greater.[8] Therefore, it is appropriate to acknowledge that learning took place without a change in the purchase outcome.

It should be noted that the definition of learning that we are using excludes changes in behavior and response tendencies resulting from physiological factors such as natural growth, deterioration due to the aging process, fatigue, or drugs.[9] Of course, it is quite appropriate to take these physiological factors into consideration when one is attempting to affect the learning process. For example, observable changes in the motor capacity of young boys aged nine or ten from one summer to the next may greatly alter their ability to learn to catch and throw a baseball. This change due to the natural physical maturing process can increase their self-confidence and, as a result, make them more interested in the game of baseball and the equipment that goes along with it.

As pointed out in Chapter 1, the models of man of most help to the consumer analyst have consolidated work done in a number of areas and have moved toward a more comprehensive theory. In the learning area, this is exemplified by the declining interest in simple, mechanistic, S-R (stimulus-response) type explanations to recent efforts which pay more attention to the internal processes of individuals such as thinking and problem solving. These latter processes are recognized as an intricate part of the S-O-R relationship, where the (O) represents the internal state of the individual.[10]

Learning to Become a Consumer

No one is born with instinctive consumer skills, nor, at some designated moment in time, such as on a fifteenth birthday, is one immediately transformed into a fully functioning mature consumer. Even though little research has been done on how a person becomes a capable consumer, it is obvious that such skills are acquired over time through personal experiences, the observation of others, and by exposure to various kinds of information from a wide variety of sources. The complete process is made up of many individual learning experiences beginning at a rather early age. An experience such as a mother showing her son how to "squeeze test" a loaf of bread for freshness helps build an elementary repertoire of consumer skills.[11]

Despite the importance and pervasiveness of buying and consuming in all affluent countries, the general view of what might be called consumership—the individual performance of the functions of buying and consuming—is a casual one. This view is implicitly unique for the following reasons.

1. The Importance of Consumership

   a. Buying and consuming is a process that is continued throughout one's lifetime; typically it increases as a household gains more disposable income, grows in size, and faces persistent changes in the needs of its members.

   b. The actual carrying out of the process of buying and consuming has a profound effect on one's level of living as well as on that of members of one's family; furthermore, what a person buys and uses can materially influence his or her physical and mental well-being.

2. Attitudes and Generally Accepted Consumership Procedures

   a. Typically no explicit, well-formulated goals are set down by individuals or families as to what they expect to gain from their buying and consuming experiences.

   b. There are no formal tests of competency or published standards of performance. Success is essentially measured in terms of personal and family satisfaction derived from the consumption experiences, the perceived status acquired from accumulated personal possessions, and the casual evaluative comments received from others.

Even though the above circumstances exist, researchers are expressing considerable interest in how children acquire skills, knowledge, and attitudes relevant to their functioning as consumers. These researchers are particularly interested in the establishment of a conceptual basis that can be used for assembling what is discovered in some meaningful manner. The prevailing view of the progress that has been made in developing this conceptual framework is summarized in the following two paragraphs.

Developing a Frame of Reference

Cognitive development theory assumes that children are active participants in their own development as mature adult consumers. This means that through natural maturation and interactions with his or her environment, the child moves through a series of stages in being able to organize market information and experiences along with his or her thoughts about these. The stages and their content are the result of the interaction of personal factors, such as one's rate of maturing, and environmental factors, such as the child's personal, family experiences. It is important to note that research does show that cognitive skills are related to age and generally increase with a child's age. Therefore, the learning process for children at varying ages, as well as what is learned, may be quite different.[12]

The assumption made in this chapter is that the cognitive development perspective is more accurate in identifying the actual learning process than are other explanations, such as those found in socialization research. The socialization perspective views the child as being relatively passive in the learning process. The position of those who support the socialization orientation is to study what and how the various forces in the environment, such as television advertising, affect children. As a result, the child's behavior is essentially considered a function of forces acting upon him or her. This view is not consistent with the open-system model of man introduced in the first chapter and, consequently, is not particularly helpful in explaining how children proceed to become functioning consumers.

Change in the Learning Process

A major complicating factor in attempting to understand the process by which children learn is the fact that many changes have been taking place in the setting within which children grow up. For instance, public concern for the impact of television in shaping the desires that children have for various products has heightened considerably and become quite controversial during the past few years. It has even involved a personal attack from the chairman of the Federal Trade Commission. However, Urie Bronfenbrenner, a noted scholar in family studies, has pointed out that the primary danger of television viewing lies not so much in the behavior it produces but in the behavior that it prevents from occurring—family talks, group games, family festivities, as well as arguments among family members through which much of the child's learning takes place and his or her character is formed.[13]

Another factor that is modifying the manner in which children learn is the changing physical environment of the home. Again, the modern home environment generally is providing less opportunity for personal interaction. One manifestation of this change is a product called the "cognition crib," which comes equipped with a tape recorder that is activated by the sound of the infant's voice. The crib is also built so that programmed play modules for practice in sensory and physical skills can be inserted into the sides. These modules come in sets of six and the parent is encouraged to change them about every three months to keep pace with the child's development. Other crib accessories that are available as options include various mobiles, an aquarium, a piggy bank, and ego-building mirrors. Also, because "faces are what an infant sees first, six soft plastic faces . . . adhere to the crib window." The only active role parents appear to play here is as purchasers.[14]

The product just described is not yet sweeping the country, but it does illustrate the kinds of change that are occurring in the manner in which children acquire the skills and basic information necessary to function as adults. There is no doubt that such environmental circumstances influence a child's consumer attitudes and patterns of market behavior. For example, the more children become accustomed to looking to mechanical or electronic devices for entertainment (television and electronic games), assistance in their school work (electronic calculators), or even help in meal preparation (microwave ovens), the more these same individuals may be willing as adults to accept increasing use of self-service retailing and electronic banking equipment, shopping by telephone, and accepting prepackaged products from vending machines.

The Components of the Learning Process

As indicated earlier, the learning process can be broken down into several key components. These include drive, cue, response, reinforcement, and retention. The nature of each of these will be discussed in this section.

Drive

Drive refers to any strong internal stimulus that impels action. It is a force that arouses an individual and keeps him or her ready to respond and, thus, is the basis of motivation. A motive is also an internal stimulus. However, it is directed toward a specific goal, whereas a drive is a more general state of being aroused.

Traditionally, drives have been classified as either *primary* or *secondary*. Primary drives are essentially based on innate physiological needs such as thirst, hunger, pain avoidance, and sex. However, more recently these drives have been recognized to reflect also the need for curiosity, exploration, or novelty.[15] Secondary drives are learned; that is, they are acquired over time through experience.

An individual is subject to many drives of both types, the intensity of which will vary from time to time. In some cases, this changing intensity is easy to explain, while in others it is not. For instance, it is relatively easy to understand that one's thirst will generally heighten with physical activity or with the heat of the day. Observation of this change in drive intensity has definite market implications. When the thirst drive is strong, consumers are more receptive to a suggestion to have a cold drink. Furthermore, if this thirst is satisfied with a cold glass of Nestea iced tea, for example, this may provide sufficient impetus to try this brand again when similar circumstances arise.

At times it may be possible for a firm to simulate an experience such as that just described in an advertisement and realize some of the same impact on the consumer as the actual experience would have had. If the consumer can "see himself in the staged episode," learning can take place. Generally, this is consistent with human learning: Individuals often benefit from the experiences of others with whom they can identify. Using this idea in advertising reduces the need for the firm to attempt to time the placement of its ads to correspond with the greatest intensity of a particular consumer drive.

Nevertheless, it is still a reasonably common practice for some retailers to attempt to retain sufficient flexibility in inserting on short notice ads for selected special-purpose products. The intention is to choose times that are likely to correspond to the highest level of drive intensity among consumers in their target market. For example, rain coats, ice-and-snow-melting products, snow shovels, and umbrellas are frequently shown in advertisements that are prepared under pressure of last-minute deadlines imposed to take advantage of changing weather conditions. Some department stores have felt these kinds of opportunities to be sufficiently important for them to employ private weather-forecasting services.

Cue

Cues, as the term is used here, are stimuli that occur externally to the individual and can emanate from any environmental source. To be relevant in consumer behavior, they must affect individual market actions or response tendencies. This effect can arise through visual perception or through any of the other human senses. It is frequently the marketing manager's desire to create cue stimuli that trigger a move to action that culminates in buying some specific good or service as well as in visiting a particular store.

Although it is necessary to focus attention on the cue in consumer behavior, it should not be forgotten that in most situations the object of primary concern to the manager is the desired response. For instance, it may take considerable money, time, and creative talent to develop an interesting and attractive advertisement. This may be extremely important in gaining attention, but if the ad does not contribute to moving the members of the target market toward purchasing the product or service involved, more than likely it has failed. This perspective is also consistent with consumer interests. As the results of the American Association of Advertising Agencies' 1974 study, *The Consumer View of Advertising,* show, the most important issue to consumers in their perception of advertising is the communication of product benefits; that is, consumers perceive advertising as cue stimuli that provide them with information including product features, availability, and price.[16]

Most firms make use of a concept called *generalization* in their use of cue stimuli. Generalization refers to the process that enables the individual to respond to a new stimulus as he or she has learned to respond to a similar but somewhat different one in the past.[17] The use of a variety of ads with a common theme in a promotional campaign has been an attempt by advertisers to employ the generalization concept and to reduce consumer boredom. In some cases, for example, this can be facilitated by simply shortening 60-second television commercials to 30 seconds. The appeal of this approach is enhanced because of its economy.

Response

Response refers to the outcome or what occurs as the result of the interaction among drive, cue, the variables of the internal decision-making process, and environmental forces. The definition of learning referred to earlier stated that the outcome can take several forms of interest to the consumer analyst. These include consumer attitude change. This objective may be illustated by an example from the public sector. A school board that has experienced a series of defeats of its request for additional operating funds may believe that public attitudes toward the local schools need to be altered before voter approval can be obtained. Such an evaluation of the situation by the board could lead them to initiate an informational campaign. This effort may be directed toward supplying influential citizen groups with critical data on the current state of the schools and program plans for the coming year. In this situation, the desired outcome of the action undertaken—the informational effort—is positive attitude change, the assumption being that more favorable public attitudes will lead to subsequent success in passage of the operating levy.

Many other responses can be used to illustrate what is relevant to those interested in consumer behavior. Some examples include the modification of consumer perception of a hardware store's image, the gaining of consumer awareness of Kellogg's new Corny Snaps, the addition of a previously excluded brand of hand soap to the list of those considered when purchasing this generic product, the association of a new logo with its sponsor by an important customer group, the trial of a new brand of nonpetroleum-based lubricant by a significant number of race car drivers, and the increase of voter registration in an area by a specified amount.

In a scientific sense, it is easier to study simple responses such as eye movement or changes in an individual's pulse rate following some stimulus than it is to focus on more complex market situations. However, most business managers and public administrators are only interested in changes in eye movement patterns or pulse rates if the observed results can be linked to relevant market behavior. Unfortunately, progress in most disciplines is usually slow in moving from laboratory experimentation to field application; although some success can be claimed, consumer behavior has been no exception.

Reinforcement

Reinforcement involves the matching of the consequences or outcomes of a response with the anticipated benefits; that is, it is the extent to which the actual benefits of a response coincide with what is considered acceptable, given the reason for action. Generally, the better the match between expectation and outcome, the greater the probablity that the same response will be made under similar circumstances in the future. For example, assume that upon getting the urge to consume a candy bar you try a bar that you have never eaten before. If this is a satisfying experience, it increases the likelihood that under similar conditions at some future time you will buy this same candy, or stated more formally by Bayton, "When consumption or utilization of the goal-object leads to gratification of the initiating needs there is reinforcement."[18]

It is necessary to keep in mind that the phrase "under similar circumstances" was used above. Sufficient variation can occur to cause the consumer to deviate from what was learned previously. This variation can be brought about by any number of variables. For instance, the consumer may simply feel differently, once his or her drive state has been modified, or it may be that the cue was different. Still another source of variation in the circumstances is the response alternatives open to the consumer. For instance, the unavailability of the consumer's favorite brand of golf balls because it is out of stock could lead to the unplanned purchase of a competitive brand. The out-of-stock condition is an inhibitor to carrying out the planned buying action. It is important to consider what possible effects this condition can have on future purchases of this product.

Retention

The remembering of learned material and experiences over time is called *retention*. That which is not retained is considered forgotten. The human ability to remember is of considerable importance to those interested in consumer behavior.

Although there is substantial disagreement about the nature of the forgetting process, most analysts agree that some forgetting does take place and, all other things being equal, the more time that has passed since learning something, the less likely it is going to be remembered. For example, assume that two different yet rather similar promotional letters were sent to you, a non-savings-and-loan saver. Each was from a different savings and loan association in your community urging you to open a savings account at its institution. Also assume that you received one of these letters on January 1 and the other on January 15. On February 1, it is more likely that you will remember more details from the second letter, all other things being equal.

Having read the previous paragraph, one is quickly tempted to respond that "all other things" are ordinarily not equal. For instance, one of the two savings and loans referred to above may be located more conveniently to your home. Because convenience of location has consistently emerged as a major determinant in consumer selection of a savings and loan association for a new savings account, this alone may have substantially affected your retention of the two messages.

A number of other factors can also affect retention. Some of these include the clarity of the message, the similarity of competing messages, the individual's interest in the subject, and the extent to which what was learned was consistent with one's values and previous experience.

Despite the multiplicity of influences on retention, once something is learned, it appears that it is never completely forgotten. Therefore, to say that a response tendency has been extinguished merely means that the response in question has been repressed (generally through nonreinforcement), or it may have essentially been displaced by the learning of an alternative that is incompatible with the original response.[19] An example of this latter situation is the successful effort of convincing consumers to purchase a new product in place of one they have used satisfactorily before. There are a number of these situations in the men's shaving product area. Just think for a moment of all the alternative shaving systems now on the market. The male consumer has not been asked to forget his current method of shaving but to realize the added benefits of using the "new" shaving system offered. To some extent, the same approach has been used in amateur photography. Both Kodak and Polaroid have been very innovative in making new, improved means of picture-taking available to the amateur.

In summary, the interrelationship of the five key components of the learning process is shown in Figure 8.3. What follows in the next section are examples of some more notions from learning theory that are applicable to consumer behavior.

Further Notions from Learning Theory as Applied to Consumer Behavior

This section is not meant to be an exhaustive treatment, but simply a way of illustrating that there are many possible applications of learning theory to the consumer in the market. The concepts discussed include semantic generation, semantic satiation, covert involvement and vicarious practice, aha experiences, and mental completing.

Semantic Generation

Semantic generation refers to the process of establishing meaning for words that essentially have no meaning. Some firms have intentionally sought to develop brand names or corporate names that have had no previous meaning. This enables the firm to create an appropriate meaning. Standard Oil of New Jersey, for example, went to considerable expense and took three years to create the name EXXON. J. Kenneth Jamieson, chairman, said to the employees,. "EXXON is unique, distinctive, and it's all ours."[20] Several years ago, Pontiac coined the word "pizazz" as a product feature. It had no meaning apart from that which consumers associated with it via their encounter with the advertising for Pontiac automobiles, dealers, and the car itself. Another familiar use of semantic generation is by Midas Mufflers in its creation of "Midasize."

The employment of semantic generation can be very useful in the communication process in that it enables an organization to exercise greater control over what is associated with its corporate name, brand, or advertising campaign. Of course, some firms take an entirely different strategy and attempt to capitalize on what they perceive to be well-established words, that is, words that elicit strong, deeply seated meaning. These include such brands as Mr. Clean household cleaner, Ultra Brite toothpaste, Prime dog food, Love cosmetics, and Sweetheart dishwashing liquid.

Figure 8.3
Learning Process

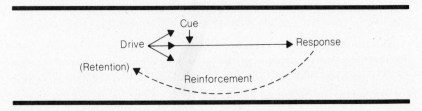

Semantic Satiation

Semantic satiation refers to the fact that continued use of a meaningful word can make is less meaningful. It signifies the general weakening and increase in ambiguity of what is associated with the word. For example, the meaning of the word "discount" to many people has become weak through overuse in referring to a wide variety of marketing practices. The usage pattern of the term "cut rate" had a similar history and consequently became meaningless.

One might say that brand names that have become generic terms have experienced semantic satiation as a unique designation for one firm's product offerings. These include such familiar products as aspirin and nylon that were once names of brands. Some people contend today that popular brand names, such as Scotch Tape, Kleenex Tissues, and even Coke, have nearly lost their usefulness as distinctive brand names. Nevertheless, the companies that own them strongly disagree and continue to remind people that they are their brands.

With the extensive use of the broadcast media, particularly television, by some consumer goods' manufacturers, semantic satiation can occur more quickly. Part of what has been expressed as consumer boredom may be a symptom of semantic satiation.

Covert Involvement and Vicarious Practice

Covert involvement encompasses the internal responses to stimuli, in other words, mental or emotional feelings. By this means a consumer may experience some of the benefits from a product or service by simply thinking about it.[21] This might be as exciting as the thrill of a ride on a fast-moving snowmobile in northern Minnesota or the feeling one gets from a refreshing drink of iced tea on a hot day.

Dichter called this phenomenon a mental rehearsal of the anticipated experience.[22] In this way, the individual can learn about the results of his or her action before actually engaging in it. Some firms have been particularly skillful in facilitating covert involvement through their commercials. For example, television commercials for Nestea show various people taking a cooling plunge into a pool upon drinking a glass of Nestea. Coca-Cola and Pepsi have also been shown in pleasure-filled settings that can be easily identified with and mentally rehearsed. Furthermore, the benefits of purchasing certain products are more emotional than physical, and they may never be experienced in a real-life setting. Consequently, the benefits are part of a mental fantasy.

Vicarious practice is closely associated with the concept of covert involvement. Learning is generally strengthened by seeing the object of attention in use. This permits an individual to visualize its use and is therefore sometimes referred to as observational learning or modeling.

It may be practically impossible to learn how to use a new fishing lure skillfully by watching a commercial that demonstrates it, but the observation process does enhance an individual's comprehension of how he or she might catch more desirable fish by using the lure.

Aha Experiences

The *aha experience* typically refers to a problem-solving situation where there is one correct or acceptable response. It is like saying "Yes, I remember now." Britt characterizes this as follows:

> The discovery in the "aha" experience is the result of a trial-and-error method in which the person attempting to solve the problem emits the most obvious response. This process continues until he finds the correct solution; and when he does, he feels as though he has "hit upon it."[23]

This concept may be applied, for example, to the area of unplanned purchasing. The two instances that follow are illustrations of practical situations where this concept may be operational.

Reminder impulse buying: This is a situation in which a shopper sees an item and remembers that he or she needs the product.

Suggestion impulse buying: This is when a shopper sees an item and then visualizes a need for it, even though no previous thought has been given to the product.

Supermarket checkout areas are a favorite setting to use in applying this idea.

Mental Completing

Mental completing refers to the human tendency to remember incomplete patterns better than complete patterns. This involves the process of *closure*—the tendency of an experience to be organized into a whole or continuous figure or vision.

This concept was used in advertising Salem cigarettes. Salem commercials were built around the jingle "You can take Salem out of the country, but you can't take the country out of Salem." In broadcast advertising, the jingle was played one and one-half times. The silence after the second "You can take Salem out of the country, but . . ." encouraged the listener to complete the message. Even to the non-smoker there was a compelling urge to complete the jingle.[24]

This section has shown that various learning concepts developed elsewhere have useful applications in consumer behavior. However, there has been some risk in offering them—the tendency to oversimplify both the concepts and their usefulness. Even if such concepts are appropriately used, they do not guarantee success to the marketing manager for a number of reasons. For instance, it would be extremely difficult to determine the impact on generating profitable sales of Salem cigarettes that resulted from the clever use of closure noted above. Furthermore, what first meets the eye as an opportunity may actually be deceiving to the strategist.

In order to motivate people, it may take the recognition of deep emotional feelings or anxieties and a creative approach to soothing them. A good example of this comes from the appeal once made by the Red Cross to the patriotism of possible blood donors which proved to be a dismal failure.[25] This failure was due to the fact that abstract, ideological appeals rarely result in immediate action. In researching the problem, it was determined that giving blood arouses unconscious anxieties. This was found to be especially true of men, by whom it was equated with giving away part of their personal strength and virility.

Consequently, these underlying feelings squelched the impact of the information about the critical need for blood and the information concerning the rapid regeneration of blood in the body. Therefore, to get men to give blood it was vital to make them feel more masculine; that is, it is important to show that a man has virility to spare and that the personal sacrifice actually is a sign of his masculinity. This was accomplished in part by giving each donor a pin in the form of a white drop of blood, the equivalent of a wounded soldier's Purple Heart medal. The recommended changes in tactics resulted in a sudden and dramatic increase in blood donations.

Summary

Learning has been defined as changes in responses and response tendencies that result from the effects of experience. Evidence of learned behavior includes changes in attitudes, emotions, evaluative criteria, and personality as well as the more easily observed variations in physical behavior that have taken place over time due to individual experience.

One cannot study consumer behavior without relating the role of learning to the purchase process. Although little research has been done on the evolution of a mature and fully functioning consumer, several observations can be made about the consumership process. Consumership is an important and ongoing process that has substantial impact on an individual's and a family's life-style, including their physical and mental well-being. Also, acceptable consumership procedures often do not involve explicit, well-defined goals or standards of performance; personal and familial satisfactions are usually measures of success.

Researchers have expressed considerable interest in how children acquire skills, knowledge, and attitudes relevant to their functioning as consumers. The conceptual framework which has been developed to assemble what is being discovered on this subject is called the cognitive development theory. The theory assumes that a child is an active participant in his or her own development as a mature adult consumer. This means that through natural maturation and interactions with his or her environment, the child moves through a series of stages in the ability to organize market information and experiences along with his or her thoughts about these. A major complicating factor in attempting to understand the process by which children learn is the fact that so many changes have been taking place in the setting within which children grow up.

The learning process can be broken down into five key components: drive, cue, response, reinforcement, and retention. *Drive* is any strong internal stimulus that impels action, such as hunger, thirst, or one that is acquired through experience. A *cue* is an external stimulus from an environmental source that affects individual market actions or response tendencies. *Response* is the result of the interaction of drive, cue, the variables of the internal decision-making process, and environmental forces and can take several forms. *Reinforcement* occurs when the outcome of a response matches the anticipated benefits, satisfying the initial needs. *Retention* is the remembering of learned material and experiences over time.

Many learning theory concepts can be applied to consumer behavior. The creation of meaning for words such as "EXXON" that essentially have no meaning is a concept known as *semantic generation*. Continued use of a meaningful word, causing it to become less meaningful, is *semantic satiation*. *Covert involvement* is the consumer's internal response to stimuli, such as feeling the benefits to be gained from a product by just thinking about it. *Vicarious practice* can occur when the consumer sees an object of attention in use. *Aha experiences* occur in problem-solving situations where there is one correct or acceptable response, such as unplanned purchasing. *Mental completing* is the human tendency to remember incomplete patterns better than complete ones. Indeed, the learning process is fundamental to consumer behavior.

Questions and Issues for Discussion

1. Because learning is basic to human existence, is it an appropriate area for marketing managers or other executives to attempt to manipulate? Explain your answer.

2. Identify several ways in which personal and familial consumership affect one's physical and mental well-being.

3. How is the open-system model complementary to the cognitive development theory? Why is it not compatible with the socialization approach to learning?

4. Many consumer goods are sold in a highly competitive environment in which competing promotional messages are plentiful. Under such circumstances, how can one firm use any learning concept to its own advantage? Give an example.

5. Identify each of the following as a drive, cue, response, reinforcement process, or evidence of retention. Be able to defend your answers.

(a) shopping at J. C. Penney's

(b) gaining enjoyment from attending a professional baseball game

(c) recommending to a friend that she try your preferred brand of shampoo

(d) being concerned about one's personal health

(e) telling a friend about an ad for 7-Up.

6. Is there reason to believe that, because children generally have had much less experience than adults, they are likely to be more receptive to the use of vicarious practice in advertising appeals? Explain the reasons for your answer.

7. Give an example to illustrate the use of each of the following learning concepts in attempting to appeal to the consumer to conserve energy:

(a) semantic generation

(b) covert involvement

(c) aha experience

(d) mental completing.

8. How can consumer learning generally work to the disadvantage of a particular firm? Give an example to illustrate your answer.

9. Describe a purchase experience that you personally have been engaged in recently. Identify how learning was involved in this experience. Is it possible to determine what was the drive, cue, response, and reinforcement in this situation?

10. Do consumers ever become so set in their ways that learning a new idea is nearly impossible? If so, give an example to illustrate how this could happen.

11. Is it possible to "unlearn" something? Does this affect consumer behavior? Explain.

12. Can a fear appeal be used successfully in advertising to get consumers to learn the benefits of a particular product or service? Give an example to support your answer.

Case 1. The United States Department of the Treasury

In April 1976, after a 38-year lapse, the government began printing $2 bills again. Because of inflation and higher prices on many items, the reach of the $1 bill was more limited than ever before; therefore, the decision to reintroduce the $2 bill seemed reasonable. Fewer of this higher denomination of currency would be needed by the public and the savings on printing to the government was estimated at $9 million a year.

By August 1978, 647 million $2 bills had been issued but were not an active part of the money flow. Most of these bills were sitting in dresser drawers, bank vaults, and other places where speculators or curiosity collectors had them safely tucked away. Some banks reported that they could not get customers to accept them at all.

Several other clues provide insight into the public's reluctance to accept and use $2 bills. Many cashiers and bank tellers feel inconvenienced because their cash drawers do not have enough slots to accommodate this bill. There is also a myth that the $2 bill carries a curse. This may or may not be related to its past history of use at race tracks. Those who used it at other public places were apt to be associated with attendance at the track.

As a maneuver to put vitality into the use of the $2 bill, the United States Department of the Treasury plans to print a $1 copper-nickel coin which will replace the Eisenhower dollar and will be somewhat larger than the quarter. Both the director of the Bureau of Printing and Engraving (which makes bills) and the director of the Mint (which makes coins) feel that if the coin gains public acceptance, so will the bill. The dollar coin will be used more readily as pocket change and this will influence people to carry the $2 bill as a small denomination unit of currency.

Government officials admit that, in 1976 when just the $2 bill was introduced, it was not properly promoted. They also feel that it usually takes five to eight years to circulate a new type of currency. Yet bankers are not convinced of the appropriateness of either form of tender. Many believe the public will reject the coin as well as the bill.

Case 1 Questions

1. How do you feel about these new forms of tender?

2. Based on the concepts presented in this chapter, what strategy could the Treasury officials use to encourage people to adopt the $1 coin as well as the $2 bill?

Case 2. Subliminal Systems, Inc.

The use of subliminal communication has been revived by two behavioral scientists who believe that messages played just below the level of conscious audibility can be effective deterrents to shoplifting. These men formed a company, Subliminal Systems, Inc., and have developed devices which send messages mixed with the background music piped into retail establishments. The scientists claim impressive results from sending hidden suggestions such as "I am honest" or "I won't steal." In several stores in an East Coast chain, theft losses were reported to have declined by one third during a nine-month period in which these below-consciousness messages were sent.

Back in the 1950s, much controversy erupted over the use of subliminal suggestions in advertising. One widely publicized case involved a movie theater that discovered more refreshments were sold after 1/3000 of a second messages, such as "Hungry? Eat popcorn. Drink Coca-Cola," were flashed on the screen. There was much negative reaction to these hidden advertisements because of the belief that they manipulated human desires and could cause people to buy certain products. Furthermore, the research methodology used to validate the early use of this concept has since been criticized by social scientists. There were no laws passed to prohibit this method of advertising and there is no way to know just how widely the technique was practiced.

Now the issue has been revitalized and the limited success of these subliminal, anticrime persuaders may encourage more grocery and department stores to adopt similar devices to reduce losses from theft. Only time can determine what other uses for this type of promotion will be advocated.

Case 2 Questions

1. Assume that you are a part of a marketing support staff in a large department store that has been approached by an independent firm marketing the use of subliminal antishoplifting systems. What are the five or six key questions that you believe should be asked about the system before this is presented to top management? Give the rationale for each question suggested.

2. What type of learning is taking place through this application of a subliminal system? How could this be explained to the "average person" who is not familiar with learning theory?

Notes

1. "Shopping-Cart War: 'No Frills' Food Shops Attract Customers, Unsettle Supermarkets," *Wall Street Journal* (April 27, 1978), p. 1.

2. "Big Savings in Small Packages," *Consumer Report,* Vol. 43 (June 1978), pp. 315, 317.

3. "Marketing Observer," *Business Week* (March 13, 1978), p. 114.

4. M. L. Ray, *Psychological Theories and Interpretations of Learning: Technical Report* (Cambridge, Mass.: Marketing Science Institute, 1973), pp. 2–3.

5. F. Hansen, *Consumer Choice Behavior: A Cognitive Theory* (New York: The Free Press, 1972), p. 126.

6. B. R. Berelson and G. A. Steiner, *Human Behavior* (New York: Harcourt Brace Jovanovich, 1964), pp. 133–34.

7. G. Katona, *Psychological Analysis of Economic Behavior* (New York: McGraw-Hill Book Company, 1951), p. 30.

8. P. D. Bennett and G. D. Harrell, "The Role of Confidence in Understanding and Predicting Buyers' Attitudes and Purchase Intentions," *Journal of Consumer Research,* Vol. 2 (September 1975), p. 116.

9. Berelson and Steiner, *Human Behavior,* p. 135.

10. Ray, *Psychological Theories,* p. 18.

11. R. L. Moore and L. F. Stephens, "Some Communication and Demographic Determinants of Adolescent Consumer Learning," *Journal of Consumer Research,* Vol. 2 (September 1975), p. 81.

12. D. B. Wachman, E. Wartella, and S. Ward, "Learning to Be Consumers: The Role of the Family," *Journal of Communication,* Vol. 27 (Winter 1977), pp. 138-41.

13. Urie Bronfenbrenner, "The Next Generation of Americans," Paper from the 1975 Annual Meeting of the American Association of Advertising Agencies (Dorado, Puerto Rico: American Association of Advertising Agencies, 1975), pp. 28-29.

14. Ibid.

15. Ray, *Psychological Theories,* p. 28.

16. R. Bartos, *The Consumer View of Advertising—1974* (New York: American Association of Advertising Agencies, 1975), pp. 38-41.

17. Hansen, *Consumer Choice Behavior,* p. 124.

18. J. A. Bayton, "Motivation, Cognition, Learning—Basic Factors in Consumer Behavior," *Journal of Marketing,* Vol. 22 (January 1958), p. 288.

19. Bereleson and Steiner, *Human Behavior,* pp. 137-38.

20. "Name Change Brings Excedrin Headaches and Costs Approximately $100 Million," *Wall Street Journal* (January 9, 1973), p. 34.

21. S. H. Britt, "Applying Learning Principles to Marketing," *MSU Business Topics,* Vol. 23 (Spring 1975), p. 9.

22. "Dichter Gives 10 Points for Effective Ads," *Advertising Age,* Vol. 42 (November 22, 1971), pp. 57-61.

23. Britt, "Applying Learning Principles," p. 11.

24. Ibid., p. 10.

25. P. Zimbardo and E. B. Ebbesen, *Influencing Attitudes and Changing Behavior* (Reading, Mass.: Addison-Wesley Publishing Co., Inc., 1970), pp. 109-10.

Chapter 9   Evaluative Criteria

Outline

Variability in Evaluative Criteria
Differences in Criteria among
  Consumer Groups
Individual Use of Different Criteria
**How Evaluative Criteria Are
  Formed**
Personality and Life-style
Social Forces
Demographic Factors
Market Forces
**Evaluative Criteria Are Not Always
  What They "Ought to Be"**
**How Evaluative Criteria Can Be
  Identified**
Direct Questioning
Indirect Questioning
**Other Practical Considerations in
  Focusing on Evaluative Criteria**
Summary
**Questions and Issues for
  Discussion**
Cases

Key Terms

evaluative criteria

variability

**conditions causing criteria
  variations**

accumulated information

personal motives

personality

life-style

voluntary simplicity

social forces

market forces

salient characteristics

in-depth probing

direct questioning

indirect questioning

Few areas of consumer behavior have more operational significance from a manager's point of view than the bases used by those in a target market to judge an organization or its product offerings. This chapter concentrates on evaluative criteria—those specifications used by the consumer to compare and evaluate goods and services, brands, and places of business.

The place of evaluative criteria in the consumer's decision-making process is shown in Figure 9.1. As can be seen here, the actual evaluation of alternatives must include the application of these criteria— even though at times these may not be well formulated or stable.

Figure 9.1
**The Functional
Relationship among
Evaluative Criteria,
Beliefs, Attitudes,
Intentions, and Choice**

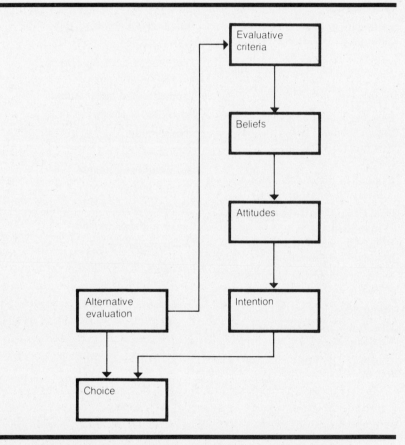

Source: James F. Engel, Roger D. Blackwell, and David T. Kollat, *Consumer Behavior,* 3rd ed. (Hinsdale, Ill.: Dryden Press, 1978), p. 367. Copyright © 1978 by Dryden Press, a division of Holt, Rinehart and Winston. Reprinted by permission of Holt, Rinehart and Winston.

Figure 9.1 also points out that in the process of applying their evaluative criteria, consumers form beliefs that include such things as what minimum features a given product should have, attitudes or biases with respect to how well particular brands or stores will satisfy their desires, as well as specific purchase intentions. With respect to intentions, for instance, one might find the following. After a quick trip to a couple of local clothing stores and a brief conversation with a friend, a young woman concludes that she will have to visit a nearby major city to find the style of evening dress that will be most flattering to her. This is one form of expressing purchase intentions, even though no specific women's shop or brand has been mentioned. Of course, in many situations where one's experience base is great, there would be little doubt as to what brand would be sought.

To be usable to a business in any real sense, consumer purchase intentions expressed for its brands must be converted into profitable sales. For example, Chem-Source, a Suffern, New York, company, recently developed a new fishing bait called "Instant Worm." These imitation worms are available in various colors, flavors, and scents and are made from such natural ingredients as sugar, fiber, and fats. They are dispensed conveniently when needed from an aerosol can like the kind used for shaving cream. The product was introduced to the market through print media which reached fishing enthusiasts. However well this innovation is perceived to meet the evaluative criteria of a substantial number of such enthusiasts—even to the point of their expression of strong buying intentions—sufficient actual purchases at profitable prices must be made to keep both the manufacturer and its dealers involved in the market. As most business men and women realize, the chances of success are low for virtually any new product. Such low levels of expected success make it extremely important to be as accurate as possible in one's assessment of each aspect of the evaluative process.

Actually, evaluative criteria are a group of product features or performance characteristics, such as price and dependability, that consumers value and expect to find in a particular product, brand, retail outlet, or other organization with which they anticipate dealing during some reasonable period of time. The use of such criteria is not limited to those situations where a product or service is being considered for purchase; the criteria are applied more broadly in decision making. For instance, administrators of charitable organizations have considerable interest in the criteria used by their prospective donors in deciding which causes to support and the amount of the contribution that will be made. Political candidates also try to identify those issues or factors that are the most instrumental in voting decisions. This, too, is an attempt to determine and be sensitive to the relative importance of evaluative criteria used by individuals in comparing alternatives in a decision-making situation.

Determining evaluative criteria is necessary but not sufficient. The consumer analyst must also identify and understand the evaluative criteria as they are perceived by the consumer. For example, if price is found to be important to consumers, does this mean that the very lowest price is sought or is some target price considered fair and appropriate? As mentioned earlier in the text, the consumer's reality is his or her perception of surrounding circumstances. This includes perceived features in whatever it is he or she is interested in—motorcycles, automobiles, tennis shoes, restaurants, clothing, books, and so forth. Therefore, a manager's knowledge is inadequate if it only includes determining what features or performance characteristics are sought by important market segments and is not clear as to what these mean in an operational sense or how the product is viewed in terms of these criteria. Furthermore, it is of major importance that a manager know how well his or her product offering compares to competitive brands in the eyes of the consumer.

An example of the importance of knowing the makeup and meaning of the evaluative criteria can be related to the purchase of suntan preparations. Assume that research has shown that ease of application is one of the most sought-after features and that the branded products available can be easily grouped in terms of how they are applied. One group of products is creams available in either tubes or jars. The other major group of products is packaged in aerosol cans. The producers of all these products believe they are easy to use, and in a functional sense, this may be true. However, if consumers in the primary target market only associate ease of application of a suntan preparation with a creamlike substance, this is the reality that must be dealt with. This does not necessarily suggest that aerosol cans should be abandoned, but it does pose a difficult belief to overcome and would affect the marketing strategy used. Just such a difficulty as this appeared when toothpaste was made available in aerosol cans as an alternative to tubes.

Variability in Evaluative Criteria

The features or performance characteristics sought in a product or service vary among different market segments as well as for a given individual under different circumstances. For instance, it is safe to say that what a typical teenager seeks in entertainment is different from what most older people expect. Also, teenagers' entertainment desires may vary in different situations. On a warm summer afternoon, their entertainment desires may only be fulfilled by a picnic at the park with friends, while on another evening, attending a movie alone is a most satisfying experience.

Differences in Criteria among Consumer Groups

Various consumer groups may use substantially different evaluative criteria in assessing any given product. These differences, once identified, can become the basis for the formation of unique marketing strategies to be used in appealing to the respective market segments. This is illustrated by the situation in the following paragraph.

Several years ago it was discovered that women held two major views with respect to their reason for using perfume. One group viewed perfume as something that enhanced natural beauty. The other group considered perfume a means of covering up unpleasant or offensive odors.[1] It is very likely that different evaluative criteria will be used by women in each of these two major segments in comparing alternative brands of perfume. For instance, a mild fragrance would probably be sought by the first market segment, while a bolder scent would be pleasing to the latter group. The importance of price is also likely to vary between these two customer groups. Differences like these can be incorporated in a firm's advertising strategy, package design, brand name selection, pricing scheme as well as other phases of its marketing program.

Individual Use of Different Criteria

The evaluative criteria used by an individual and the relative importance of the contents of the criteria at some point in time can change under different circumstances. This variation is discussed under two possible conditions: (1) purchasing for personal consumption versus buying for others and (2) the impact of environmental situations.

Purchasing for Personal Consumption versus Buying for Others

When a person is buying an item for personal use that he or she has had experience with, a particular evaluative criterion is usually called to mind. This is then used in the process of choosing among alternative brands. However, if the same individual is making a purchase for someone else, such as a gift, a somewhat modified set of evaluative criteria is likely to be employed. This will probably include an attempt to consider what the recipient would look for in the product, but it is also likely to include some price limit as to the maximum amount that can or should be spent on this gift. The following situation illustrates such an occasion.

If you were to buy a flower arrangement for a table decoration for a party that you are giving, certain criteria would come to mind that you would use in making the selection. These would include your personal preferences for particular flowers as well as the colors that would complement the table decorations. However, if these flowers were intended as a gift for a parent's birthday and they were to be sent FTD, a different set of criteria would be used.

The same kind of variation in criteria can be observed when a father is purchasing an item such as golf clubs for himself and also for his young son or daughter. If the father is buying a set of clubs for himself and is an experienced golfer with a serious interest in the sport, the quality of the clubs will probably be considerably more important than the price. However, if the clubs are for a son or daughter who is just a beginner, price may be quite important. Under these latter conditions, the parent is uncertain as to whether the interest will continue and, consequently, wants to limit his investment while still providing an opportunity for the young person to learn something about the sport.

The Impact of Environmental Situations

Research shows that it is ordinarily possible to identify a list of what might be called ideal or preferred product features or operating characteristics for whatever product a firm markets. One study found, for example, that homemakers in one major market sought the following attributes in a cake mix: ease of use, economy, consistent results, and tastiness.

These are listed in the order of importance to the homemakers studied. As such, these four characteristics represent their evaluative criteria under "normal" circumstances. However, if some of these homemakers were faced with the responsibility of making a cake for a very special occasion, such as a wedding, some variation might take place. In the situation posed, it is likely that the fourth characteristic—tastiness—would move to the top as the most important consideration.

Tables 9.1 and 9.2 summarize some of the actual findings from a recent study of grocery shopping patterns in a major midwestern city. Each table presents two sets of data. First, the information on the left side shows reasons why persons who use each store for buying most of their groceries do so, and on the right are reasons why other persons shop at the respective two stores for fill-in items. These data were assembled by one store's management to determine the criteria used by consumers who shop the two stores for most of their grocery needs as well as the reasons given for using each store for supplemental shopping.

In studying these findings, the major chain store, for example, is shown to have had a strong price appeal among both groups of shoppers. However, the quality of meat at the independent store was a dominant criterion in selecting this store for fill-in items. It is also worth noting how much importance was placed on convenient store location among grocery shoppers generally. This latter finding is typical of most grocery shopping studies. The store that sponsored the

Table 9.1
Ranked Reasons for Shopping at One Major National Chain Store

Rank	Reasons for Using for Most Shopping	Percent	Rank	Reasons for Using for Fill-In Shopping	Percent
1	Overall low prices	63.0	1	Attractive specials	42.9
2	Convenient location	59.3	2	Overall low prices	42.9
3	Overall selection	29.6	3	Good produce	37.1
4	Well stocked	18.5	4	Good meat	34.3
5	Good meat	16.7	5	Convenient location	31.4
6	Good produce	9.3	6	Overall selection	20.0

Source: Carl Block and Earl Wims, unpublished research report, Marketeam Associates, St. Louis, Missouri, 1978. Reprinted by permission.

Table 9.2
Ranked Reasons for Shopping at One Local Independent Store

Rank	Reasons for Using for Most Shopping	Percent	Rank	Reasons for Using for Fill-In Shopping	Percent
1	Convenient location	65.5	1	Good meat	80.0
2	Overall low prices	41.4	2	Convenient location	70.0
3	Friendly, helpful personnel	31.0	3	Overall selection	50.0
4	Good meat	24.1	4	Attractive specials	40.0
5	Independently owned	17.2	5	Good produce	20.0
6	Good produce	13.8	6	High quality dairy products	20.0

Source: Carl Block and Earl Wims, unpublished research report, Marketeam Associates, St. Louis, Missouri, 1978. Reprinted by permission.

research used the findings to further build on their perceived advantage while attempting to show how they could effectively meet their competitors' offerings.

The consumer lives in an environment that poses many different circumstances, and to make the assumption that, once established, the evaluative criteria become rigid and not subject to change is inconsistent with reality. Nevertheless, it is possible to identify the evaluative criteria used by consumers in various market segments in the majority of buying situations. These criteria represent the most consistently used means of comparing alternatives and can greatly assist the marketing manager in developing strategy that will emphasize them.

How Evaluative Criteria Are Formed

Figure 9.2 shows by way of a diagram how evaluative criteria are formed. The factors that most directly affect the criteria are (1) accumulated information and experience and (2) personal motives. These two variables, in turn, are shaped by an individual's personality and his or her chosen life-style as well as by a range of social forces surrounding him or her, including cultural norms, values, and the demographic characteristics of personal circumstances.

People who are responsible for developing marketing strategy are wise to become aware of the nature of these identified variables and

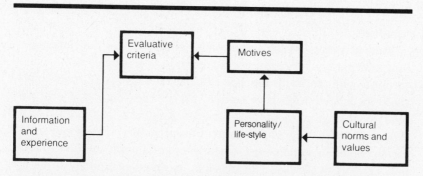

Figure 9.2
**The Determinants of
Evaluative Criteria**

Source: James F. Engel, Roger D. Blackwell, and David T. Kollat, *Consumer Behavior,* 3rd ed. (Hinsdale, Ill.: Dryden Press, 1978), p. 368. Copyright © 1978 by Dryden Press, a division of Holt, Rinehart and Winston. Reprinted by permission of Holt, Rinehart and Winston.

their patterns of influence because this can be of considerable value in providing direction for marketing efforts. Much advertising, for example, is intended to affect the consumer through changing his or her information base as well as in stimulating action by way of arousing his or her motives. To be successful at advertising to a designated target market, one would at least need to know such things as consumers' dominant values and personal demographic characteristics.

The next few paragraphs discuss how personality and life-style, along with social forces, can come to bear on the formulation of evaluative criteria. Following this, it will then be appropriate to focus on how information and experience and personal motives can be affected by marketing efforts which then help to shape evaluative criteria.

Personality and Life-style

Personality is the individuality that is observed in the form of rather consistent modes of behavior that are characterized in various ways such as aggressive, persuasive, innovative, and complacent patterns of behavior. (See Chapter 7 for a detailed discussion of personality.) Such individuality can influence the content of a person's evaluative criteria. Some people, for instance, are more willing to assume risk than others. This willingness to assume risk, in turn, can have a substantial effect on how they make choices. For a stockbroker, it could be beneficial to group prospective customers using this characteristic because it helps shape the evaluative criteria people use in selecting securities.

Innovativeness is also a personality characteristic that has important implications for consumer behavior. It, too, is likely to be related to one's willingness to assume risks of various kinds, particularly those associated with new product usage. For those who are truly innovators, it may mean that newness itself is a key component of their evaluative criteria. It appears that considerable personal gratification comes to some people when they are among the first to try a new product or service. Nevertheless, newness is unlikely to be the only basis for making any buying decision.

Life-style represents chosen patterns of living that express an individual's personality and value structure, including how he or she spends time and money as well as personal attitudes held concerning a variety of consumption-related issues such as family formation, living arrangements, work, and leisure, all of which in time are reflected, in buying behavior. One Stanford research study revealed how a change in life-style could have a material impact on evaluative criteria. This research focused on what was called "voluntary simplicity," or VS. It was found that VS consumers searched for products that were consistent with the following criteria: (1) durable, (2) nonpollutant, (3) used little energy, and (4) were made simply. Typically, these consumers prefer natural foods, clothing that can be mended and handed down, simple appliances, and cars that they themselves can repair and maintain easily. The study estimated that as many as 25 percent of the adult population may be VS consumers by 1985. It had already reached an estimated 5,000,000 by early 1977.[2]

The importance of life-style research today in planning marketing strategy is illustrated by the fact that the Leo Burnett Ad Agency was reported to have spent $100,000 to study the tennis market for the Wilson T2000. The investigation was a life-style segmentation analysis. The results showed that there were four types of tennis players who can be classified in this manner: beginners, 30 percent; socializers, 25 percent; competitors, 25 percent; buffs, 20 percent. The buffs were the most serious group and were composed equally of men and women. They were identified as players who would do virtually anything for a winning edge. Therefore, the "extra power" claim made for the T2000 was a benefit sought by tennis buffs and would be reflected in the evaluative criteria they used to select a tennis racket.[3]

Social Forces

Each of the major social forces has been discussed in earlier chapters. However, it is important to visualize the relevance of these social forces in shaping the criteria used by individuals to evaluate alternative goods and services.

A good example, which illustrates the persistence of outmoded historical practices or norms in society, comes out of a businesslike setting rather than a consumer choice situation, but has parallels in the consumer market. When most people think of a fire truck, they are likely to picture a red vehicle with the various necessary equipment. However, the continued use of the red color by many communities is essentially the result of strong tradition rather than research. In fact, visibility studies conducted by ophthalmologists and fire safety researchers have shown that the color of a fire truck can make a substantial difference in its ability to stand out visually. As can be seen in Table 9.3, the traditional red fire truck came out on the bottom of the visibility scale. Such strong traditional practices are also found in the use of color and design of consumer goods as well as in their packaging. Consequently, what may have been found to be "best" in a scientific sense may not be consistent with consumers' evaluative criteria shaped by traditional practices.

Other social forces that can have a substantial impact on how products or services are assessed include the influence of friendship groups, social class norms, the work environment, and opinion leaders.

Table 9.3
The Impact of Color Variation in Visibility

Color	Finding
Lime-yellow	Research shows this range on the color spectrum is most visible to the human eye.
Red	Traditional red is ranked with other dark colors as least visible to the eye.
White	Outdoors it is often difficult for motorists to see white in snow, dust, and fog.
Omaha Orange	This color ranks on the high visibility portion of the color spectrum.

Source: Phil McPeck, "Why a Yellow Firetruck?" *Vibrations* (February 29, 1976), p. 10. Reprinted by permission.

Demographic Factors

As noted in Chapter 3, a large proportion of marketing research effort has sought to differentiate prospective customers on the basis of demographic characteristics. These typically include age, education, sex, household income, occupation, household size, and geographic place of residence. As mentioned earlier, the development of the family life cycle concept has resulted from the combining of selected demographic variables into groupings that provide further insight into behavioral patterns.

From the illustrations used in Chapter 6, it is apparent that evaluative criteria are subject to variation as family composition changes over time. However, even a single demographic variable can have an effect on the content of one's evaluative criteria. For instance, the amount of formal education completed can have a substantial impact on an individual's ability to read and comprehend information. As a result, people with very little formal education generally rely more on radio and television media for information and may not develop very sophisticated evaluative criteria.[4] The consequences of this may show up in many ways, for instance, in their inability to include any nutritional factors in the criteria they use in food selection and meal planning.

Income, too, can have a direct and noticeable effect on evaluative criteria. For example, the concept of a fair price for a product may vary considerably across income groups. Furthermore, price considerations are likely to be among the most important selection criteria for

	Size of Household		
Attractiveness	1 or 2 Person	3 or 4 Person	5 or More Person
Very appealing	25.3%	27.5%	37.2%
Somewhat appealing	56.0%	47.5%	44.2%
Somewhat unappealing	14.7%	15.0%	13.9%
Very unappealing	4.0%	10.0%	4.7%
	100.0%	100.0%	100.0%

Table 9.4
Overall Appeal of Savings Plus by Household Size

Source: Earl Wims and Carl Block, unpublished research report, Marketeam Associates, St. Louis, Missouri, 1978. Reprinted by permission.

low-income groups. It is not uncommon for older people living on social security to use price rather than style or color as the most important factor in assessing alternative brands of women's clothing.

The data presented in Tables 9.4 and 9.5 are from a study designed to measure consumer interest in and likelihood of usage of a new financial service called "Savings Plus." This service is being offered by a large metropolitan savings and loan and makes it possible for consumers to obtain substantial discounts from participating merchants by paying in cash or by check at the time of purchase. Discounts range from 2 percent on grocery items to 20 percent on furniture and appliances. The consumer simply opens a savings account at the sponsoring savings and loan, presents the "Savings Plus" card, pays the full cash price, and the discount appears in his or her savings account by the 10th day of the following month. The preliminary concept testing of the service brought the responses shown. One can quickly see that household size had affected the criteria people used to evaluate the benefits of such a service. These findings among others were then used to formulate promotional strategy which most effectively communicated the benefits of the service to the respective market segments. It was also designed to resolve the questions and reservations held by some consumers.

Market Forces

The efforts of business firms and other organizations can have a substantial impact on the formation of an individual's evaluative criteria.

Table 9.5
Likelihood of Opening a Savings Account at Sponsoring Savings and Loan by Household Size

| | Size of Household | | |
How Likely	1 or 2 Person	3 or 4 Person	5 or More Person
Very likely	18.7%	16.2%	30.2%
Somewhat likely	30.6%	35.0%	37.2%
Somewhat unlikely	24.0%	23.8%	18.6%
Very unlikely	26.7%	25.0%	14.0%
	100.0%	100.0%	100.0%

Source: Earl Wims and Carl Block, unpublished research report, Marketeam Associates, St. Louis, Missouri, 1978. Reprinted by permission.

For instance, environmental groups, such as the National Wildlife Federation, the Audubon Society, and the Sierra Club, have encouraged consumers to avoid clothing and other products that make use of rare species of animals. In other situations the influence has come from organizations such as the Better Business Bureau, Consumers Union, and the Consumer Product Safety Commission (CPSC). One significant promotional effort undertaken by the CPSC in cooperation with private business encouraged consumers to exercise great care in using their rotary lawn mowers and to purchase only rotary mowers that meet minimum safety requirements. Of course, advertising and other marketing efforts that business firms employ also influence the criteria consumers use to assess products and places of business. The area of influence subject to the greatest control by marketing managers or public administrators is their marketing strategy and the tactics they use in its implementation. Therefore, this effort is discussed in some detail in the following paragraphs.

In addressing this subject, Boyd, Ray, and Strong indicate that a manager has two possible strategy alternatives that focus on the evaluative criteria used by consumers in a firm's target market.[5] These two are presented below with illustrations of their application.

Add Characteristic(s) to Those Considered Salient for the Product Class

Through the use of salespeople, advertising, or publicity, a firm can make potential customers aware of one or more product features or attributes that were not previously considered; some may be entirely new features. This strategy has been successfully employed in a number of situations. For example, such a method has been used in promoting additives in gasoline, fluoride in toothpaste, vitamins in cereals, bleach in detergents, and butter or other fats in turkeys to make them self-basting.

This strategy has been used most frequently when a product is in the maturity stage of its life cycle—that is, when it has enjoyed considerable market success and competitive brands have begun to look very similar. Such a strategy is often combined with a modification in the physical features of the product. The combined efforts of altering the physical product and employing promotional strategy to encourage the consumer to notice this change with the intent of their considering it as an important buying criterion can extend the profitable life of the product. Of course, it is extremely important to keep in mind that the basic assumption made by the firm using this approach is that its brand is superior with respect to the product feature or attribute being promoted. For instance, it would be absurd for an oil company to promote a de-icer additive as an important product feature if its brand of gasoline had an inferior de-icer compared to that of its competitors.

Increase or Decrease the Rating for a Salient Product Class Characteristic

A firm that learned its brand rated well on a product characteristic that was not of great importance to consumers can try to change the weight given this characteristic. It may be, for example, that one brand of ice cream has all natural ingredients, but this feature does not appear to be too important to consumers. The firm that produces all-natural ice cream may wish to try to increase the weight placed upon this product feature. This could be a particularly attractive strategy if key competitors could not make the same claim.

Under some circumstances, a firm may choose to try to reduce the importance that consumers place on a certain product feature or operating characteristic because of its brand's inability to show up favorably on this dimension. For example, in promoting some of their full-size models, U.S. auto manufacturers have played down the importance of fuel economy and emphasized the roominess of the standard-size models.

Evaluative Criteria Are Not Always What They "Ought" to Be

Almost everyone has an opinion about what to look for when buying commonly used products and services, and from time to time we are asked for our advice as to what these important features include. A number of rather objective criteria are typically offered in response to such an inquiry. Frequently these include some statement about a product's price, durability, range of features, warranty, adaptability, and ease of obtaining service. In many product purchases, these kinds of features are undoubtedly key considerations in consumers' minds. Also, consumers as a whole probably believe that these are what evaluative criteria ought to be.

However, there are other evaluative criteria that are hardly ever discussed among consumers and it is likely that many consumers would even deny their existence. These latter criteria are essentially subjective in nature; that is, they are much less well defined and more difficult to measure. Nevertheless, there is sound evidence to show that consumers do include dimensions such as eye appeal, style, status, aesthetics, and prestige when evaluating many products. Furthermore, it is not difficult to understand why these are relevant because some are the kinds of things that enrich life and raise an experience above the ordinary.

For a consumer analyst, it would be naive to simply focus on either the objective or subjective criteria to the exclusion of the others. The real challenge is to correctly identify the whole set of evaluative criteria of prospective customers and to determine the relative importance of each of its components.

How Evaluative Criteria Can Be Identified

There are essentially two ways of determining the evaluative criteria that are used by important market segments. These are direct questioning and indirect questioning. Each of these may be employed with some or considerable in-depth probing.

Direct Questioning

Direct questioning involves a series of inquiries that ask in a straightforward manner on what basis the person being questioned makes a particular buying decision, that is, what product features or performance characteristics he or she seeks in a given product or service. For instance, a number of studies have been done in an attempt to determine what prospective students and their parents look for in a college or university. Through direct questioning of a representative group, it may be that the curricula offered, the geographic location of the school, and the tuition emerge as the three most important issues. However, this list itself does not completely specify the content of the evaluative criteria for selecting a school. This point can be illustrated with respect to the location dimension. It may be that, all other things being equal, parents and prospective students may have a strong preference for schools within a 150-mile drive from their home. This information now gives practical meaning to the specification of location as a criterion.

Another illustration can be used to illustrate a different dimension of the content issue. The term *convenience* often appears among evaluative criteria but not always with the same meaning intended. For instance, "convenience" as a criterion in the selection of a fast food restaurant may mean a location close to home or possibly the minimum distance a person is willing to travel to find such a restaurant whenever he or she is hungry for a hamburger and french fries. Still another meaning could focus on the speed of the service received once a person is in the door.

To properly identify the evaluative criteria and accurately determine their relative importance by direct questioning takes careful planning and structuring of the questions used. It may also require a series of questions to get to the real meaning of each dimension, as the above examples illustrate.

Indirect Questioning

Some experienced analysts believe that consumers are often unable to list accurately the bases they use in the selection of products or services. Proponents of this argument contend that what may happen is that a list of evaluative criteria is given by the consumer when he or she is asked, but that it represents socially acceptable reasons for buying a product—not necessarily the real reasons. Furthermore, some products and services are particularly difficult to discuss openly and, therefore, any inquiry regarding them must employ some indirect approach.

As a means of avoiding these kinds of difficulties and of obtaining the actual evaluative criteria, various indirect questioning procedures can be used. One approach that has been successful is to ask those being questioned what they believe others they know seek in the product. For example, "What do your neighbors look for in a house paint? In other words, on what basis do they judge the various brands available to them?" The assumption made in following this procedure is that people will reveal their own feelings even though they are being asked about someone else's behavior. A similar approach to the one just described frames the questions in yet another way: "What would you suggest that a new family in your community look for in selecting a church?"

Questioning individuals in small groups can also facilitate the discovery of their evaluative criteria. An experienced moderator can ask probing questions that nurture personal interaction and the discussion of deeply held ideas and notions. For instance, it may be discovered that color and texture preferences serve as subconscious bases for the evaluation of packaged goods. Obtaining such information could stimulate interest in reviewing packaging schemes for a firm's product line.

This indirect questioning procedure could also take the form of asking people to compare brands of products on various attributes. Their responses can then be scaled for more precise comparisons. The most recent work of this nature uses multidimensional scaling and offers considerable promise as a means of more accurate differentiation of important evaluative criteria. However, this subject is beyond the scope of this book.

Usually, indirect questioning procedures are used to supplement or check the accuracy of the results obtained from the more direct methods of inquiry. It is important to keep in mind that considerable expertise is necessary to make good use of this approach.

Other Practical Considerations in Focusing on Evaluative Criteria

The points that follow cut across several topics discussed earlier in this chapter. They also serve as a final reminder of the operational significance of evaluative criteria to the marketing manager.

1. Although the number of features used to compare alternative brands of a product may be unlimited, consumers usually have about five or six key considerations that they rely on.

2. Evaluative criteria are usually formed over an extended period of time and are always subject to change based on new information and consumer experience. Nevertheless, criteria remain reasonably stable from year to year. In other words, rapid change in what people seek in particular products, services, and business establishments is not typical.

3. Obtaining some measure of the relative importance of each item in the evaluative criteria is essential. Some product features or operating characteristics may be considerably more relevant than others. The relative importance of various elements of the criteria is probably more subject to change over short periods of time than is the substance of the criteria itself.

4. In some product groups, competitive brands or business establishments are perceived to be very similar on most features that consumers seek; therefore, characteristics of lesser importance become the real basis for differentiation. For example, when a consumer is selecting a drugstore to fill a doctor's prescription, assume that he or she is looking for a high level of professional expertise and judgment in the pharmacist, a fair pricing policy, and a convenient location. To many consumers, pharmacists may be perceived to be of essentially equal competence because of state licensing laws with requirements to use fresh, quality ingredients and to charge about the same price for prescription drugs. If consumers believe this, then convenience of location emerges as the key differentiating characteristic and, consequently, the basis for their selection of a drugstore.

5. When consumers cannot judge a product's features directly, surrogate or substitute means of evaluation are frequently used. For example, national brand names may be relied on for quality. One of the reasons some people buy St. Joseph brand of aspirin is because they seek high quality in such drugs and apparently believe that they can trust national brands.

Some consumers also use price as a guide to quality; that is, they believe that you essentially get what you pay for in a purchase.

6. It is not unusual to find circumstances in which a consumer's evaluative criteria are so specified that only one brand meets the features sought. This is particularly true when subjective criteria are involved. For instance, to some people, their required product features and subjective considerations such as style and prestige in an automobile can be met only by a Volvo. If there are no major constraints on their purchasing a Volvo, they are likely to be very loyal buyers.

Some manufacturers of multiple product lines have tried to encourage the situation described above by specifying the use of one of their products with another. Kraftco, for instance, specifies on the box of its macaroni dinner that Parkay margarine be used in preparing it, hoping that consumers will use only this recommended brand.

7. Evaluative criteria may be applied in steps; that is, some consumers go through a rough screening of alternative brands using relatively general criteria preceding their making finer comparisons based on more rigorous standards. For instance, some individuals will only buy domestically produced products; consequently, their initial comparisons will quickly sort out products with a foreign origin. This will be followed by a judging of the remaining brands on their features and performance characteristics such as price, durability, and aesthetic appeal.

Summary

This chapter concentrates on a portion of the central control unit—evaluative criteria. These are specifications used by the consumer to compare and evaluate goods and services, brands, and places of business. As alternative purchase choices are evaluated and the criteria applied, beliefs, attitudes, and intentions enter in to affect the choice made. The use of such criteria is not limited to purchase situations; it can be applied to other areas such as political and social choices. In addition to determining evaluative criteria, the consumer analyst must identify and understand these judgment guidelines as they are perceived by the consumer and consider those conditions which cause variations in the criteria.

There are two factors that most directly affect the formation of criteria: (1) accumulated information and experience and (2) personal motives. These variables, in turn, are shaped by an individual's personality and his or her chosen life-style as well as by a range of social forces surrounding the individual.

The area of influence subject to the greatest control by marketing managers is their marketing strategies and the tactics they use to affect the evaluative criteria a consumer uses in selecting a product or service. These efforts by a firm are called market forces; and their influence may be implemented (1) by adding characteristics to those considered salient for the product class or (2) by increasing or decreasing the rating for a salient product class characteristic.

Evaluative criteria are not always objective but can include many subjective dimensions such as eye appeal or status.

Direct questioning can be used to identify a consumer's evaluative criteria if the questions are planned carefully and reveal true, complete answers. Indirect questioning by asking a consumer for his or her perception of another consumer's evaluative criteria can often reveal the original consumer's own criteria.

Questions and Issues for Discussion

1. Are evaluative criteria generally well formulated in the minds of consumers? What products or market circumstances are likely to foster the development of clearly stated evaluative criteria?

2. What are some common evaluative criteria used to assess the following goods and services?

  (a) chewing gum

  (b) color television

  (c) original art work

  (d) a medical doctor.

3. Assume that you wanted to be the true "economic person," that is, someone who might be called perfectly rational. What criteria would you personally use to evaluate the following?

  (a) automobile

  (b) college

(c) auto mechanic

(d) breakfast cereal.

4. Since evaluative criteria vary among people assessing the same good or service, how can a marketing manager use these in planning his or her marketing strategy?

5. Are there situations in which evaluative criteria are developed after the purchase is made? If so, give an example.

6. Can consumers be taught what are "good" evaluative criteria in buying specific products? For instance, can a book on "buymanship" be helpful to a person in selecting a new electric range?

7. How is the experience that one has had with a product likely to affect the evaluative criteria used to assess its replacement? Give an example.

8. What are some products or services that are evaluated strictly on a subjective basis? Why is this the case?

9. Do consumers usually get what they pay for? When is price the most important criterion in selecting a product?

10. Give some examples of products that are evaluated today on bases substantially different from those used five years ago.

11. Using the data presented in Tables 9.1 and 9.2, discuss the differences in appeals of the two stores. How might these results be used in the development of promotional strategy for the local firm?

Case 1. A Shift in Eating Habits

"It's good-bye, TV dinner, hello, boeuf bourguignon in millions of homes these days. U.S. eating habits are changing as cooking becomes an avocation, not a chore."[6] This statement summarizes a back-to-basics shift that seems to be occurring in food preparation.

Cooking is becoming a creative outlet and a means of self-expression for men and women. The popularity of articles and radio programs, such as "Meet the Cook," which feature reliable and tempting recipes and solid preparation techniques supports this trend. Last year, over 450 new cookbooks came on the market. Not only are cooking classes in adult education programs well attended, but also cooking schools are becoming a business venture in such places as supermarkets. One independent food chain in the Midwest recently built an elaborate demonstration kitchen in one of its stores. As many as twenty budding food artists of all ages can sit at one time and observe local chefs reveal their cooking specialties.

Recessionary periods and the ongoing increase in the price of food have also caused people to reconsider how they budget for food and to re-evaluate the criterion of convenience. Many Americans are no longer willing to pay for the cost of minimizing their culinary efforts by using frozen and packaged main dishes, vegetable combinations, and desserts. The 10- to 20-percent decrease each year in sales tonnage of frozen vegetables with butter illustrates this trend.

Alert food processors are watching shifts such as this in the marketplace and are adjusting their operations accordingly. Small-appliance manufacturers are also aware of the possibilities for their products. One company conducted an extensive behavioral study into the shopping and cooking habits of couples. The investigation of its sample was analyzed in the following way.

Love-to-Cooks made up 60 percent of the households studied. The couples tended to be young, affluent, and educated. Eating out and cooking at home were both shared experiences.

Hate-to-Cooks made up 30 percent of the sample. These couples had demographic characteristics which were similiar to the first group's, but they seemed more concerned about dieting, health, and nutrition. They tended to depend on fast foods and convenience during the week but indulged in fine restaurant eating on the weekends.

The remaining 10 percent were called Couldn't-Care-Lesses. Their age and economic and social status varied. Their menus were strictly from the prepared food section of the grocery store.

The prediction is that the first group would expand although the makeup of the group would probably be altered.

Case 1 Questions

1. This change in cooking and eating habits can have an impact on the operations of a number of firms and institutions. Suggest ways in which each of the following might be affected:

(a) grocery stores

(b) restaurants

(c) small-appliance manufacturers

(d) colleges and universities

(e) housewares departments in stores.

2. Select one of the classifications in the behavioral study. What evaluative criteria would you use in purchasing

(a) an electric food processor

(b) food for "brown-bagging" lunches

(c) frozen "gourmet-style" vegetables?

Case 2. The Medi-Diagno Clinic

Health care costs have been skyrocketing and every segment of the economy—industry, labor, government, and consumers—is searching for ways to slow their acceleration speed. When figured as a percent of GNP, the total cost of health care in 1977 was nearing 9 percent of all expenditures. This proportion has doubled since 1950 and is predicted to rise to 10 percent by 1983.[7]

A great portion of current health care costs is related to advancements in diagnostic, surgical, and therapeutic technology which have made possible an expanded level of service. The results are gratifying when the success of devices such as pacemakers and operations such as hip replacements are considered. But, the new cures and service expansions have triggered a cyclical impact on costs.

Insurance has become the means of spreading the cost of health care and reducing the expense to any one individual family. The government is a major insurer and provides health care for many persons through Medicaid and Medicare. Business firms have also paid for a major portion of health care bills through insurance benefits provided for their employees.

The future cost of these medical plans is a great concern to employers and more and more are willing to provide their employees with access to preventive health care clinics and medical information programs. Although the cost of a regular medical check-up or some other service is high, lives and money can be saved in the long run.

The management of Medi-Diagno Clinic wants to develop contractual agreements with large companies and unions whereby regular use of their facilities would become an employee or member benefit. Various diagnostic packages are available through a series of about a dozen medical testing stations known as multi-phasic screening. The clinic's staff of paramedics, who operate the equipment, and physicians, who review any irregularities in a patient's medical profile, can provide diagnoses on specific body systems such as respiration or perform the more general medical check-ups. The efficient operation of the clinic permits a large number of patients to pass through daily with a visit lasting about an hour. The cost of a diagnostic package is several hundred dollars less than hospital-based tests with the hours for patients' visits being much more extended than in other facilities performing these same services.

Case 2 Questions

1. As the management of Medi-Diagno approaches an industry or union, what information should it have available in order to sell the program and what facts and opinions about the employees should it obtain from the firm or organization before beginning to negotiate a contract?

2. As a health-care consumer, what evaluative criteria would you use in deciding whether to go to a private physician or to a Medi-Diagno Clinic? As an owner of a small company, what evaluative criteria would you use in comparing a group insurance plan to a program of preventive health care?

Notes

1. D. Yankelovich, "New Criteria for Market Segmentation," P. Kotler and K. K. Cox, eds., *Readings in Marketing Management* (Englewood Cliffs, N.J.: Prentice-Hall, Inc., 1971), p. 97.

2. "Change in Social Values Could Mean Trouble to Manufacturers," *St. Louis Post-Dispatch* (February 6, 1977), p. 9F.

3. "Psychographics: Ads That Try to Get Inside Your Head," *The National Observer* (February 26, 1977), p. 1.

4. C. E. Block, "Prepurchase Search Behavior of Low-Income Households," *Journal of Retailing,* 48 (Spring 1972), pp. 12–13.

5. H. W. Boyd, Jr., M. L. Ray, and E. C. Strong, "An Attitudinal Framework for Advertising Strategy," *Journal of Marketing,* 36 (April 1972), pp. 29–33.

6. "The Kitchen: America's Playroom," *Forbes* (March 15, 1976), p. 24.

7. "Unhealthy Costs of Health Care," *Business Week* (September 4, 1978), p. 59.

Chapter **10**   Attitudes

Outline

The Meaning of Attitudes
The Classical Psychological Model
The Multi-attribute Models

Attitudes toward Alternatives: Expectancy-Value Models
The Rosenberg Model
The Fishbein Model
An Application of the Expectancy-Value Model

Extending the Expectancy-Value Model

Implication for Marketing Strategy

Attitude Change Strategies
Changing a Consumer's Belief (B) about a Product
Changing the Evaluation of a Belief (a) about a Product
Adding a New B-a Combination

Foundations for Managing Attitude Change
Functions of Attitudes
Organization of Attitudes
Consistency among Attitudes

Managing Attitude Change
Message Discrepancy
Message Content
Message Structure
Source Credibility

Summary

Questions and Issues for Discussion

Cases

Key Terms

attitude
cognitive component
affective component
behavioral component
hierarchy of effects
multi-attribute models
evaluative criteria
beliefs
intention
expectancy-value models
attribute adequacy models
conjunctive models
disjunctive model
lexiographic model
Rosenberg Model
Fishbein Model
adjustment function
ego-defensive function
value-expressive function
knowledge function
centrality
message discrepancy
fear appeals
unstructured message
distraction
two-sided messages
primacy
recency

The concept of attitude is one of the most prevalent and important concepts in consumer behavior, indeed, in the social sciences generally. Interest in attitudes emanates from the belief that knowledge of attitudes permits accurate prediction of consumer behavior. "Attitude" will be defined precisely in the next section, but generally a consumer's attitudes can be thought of as his or her basic orientation for or against various alternative products, services, retail outlets, and the like. Because attitudes form a coherent system of evaluative orientations, they are an important component in any model of consumer decision making.

The Meaning of Attitudes

Everyone has, on occasion, been asked to express his or her assessment of something. For example, "How do you like your new Vega?" or "How do you feel about free checking?" or "How do you feel about the use of sex in advertising?" Thus, although few can provide a precise definition of "attitudes," most have a reasonably clear intuitive understanding of what they are. Interestingly enough, even though there is general agreement on the meaning of "attitudes" at the intuitive level, there is little agreement at the theoretical level.

An attitude is an abstract concept in that its structure or makeup cannot be directly observed. Thus, the nature of attitude fosters alternative views regarding the underlying structure of attitude and, consequently, alternative definitions.

The Classical Psychological Model

The classical definition is that an *attitude* is a mental and neural state of readiness to respond which is organized through experience and which exerts a directive and/or dynamic influence on behavior.[1] It soon became popular to adopt the classical psychological model which theorizes that attitudes are made up of three basic components: (1) cognitive, (2) affective, and (3) behavioral.[2] In terms of consumer behavior, the *cognitive* component refers to the manner in which a consumer perceives information about a product, service, advertisement, or retail outlet. This component includes beliefs a consumer has about the support services a retailer offers as well as beliefs about the relative merits of the product. In other words, this attitude component includes considerations such as whether Coke or Pepsi tastes better, which has more carbonation, which has a better aftertaste, and which is a better thirst quencher.

The *affective* component is the consumer's overall feeling of like or dislike for an attitude object (that is, a product, service, advertisement, retail outlet). Generally, marketing analysts use verbal statements to measure the affective component. Statements such as "I really like the taste of Gatorade," and "The slacks look great, but I just don't like the way they fit me" illustrate consumer expressions of the affective component. The affective and cognitive components are considered to be highly correlated; that is, consumer analysts have observed that a consumer's beliefs and feelings toward a particular product are typically consistent.

The *behavioral* component is the consumer's action tendency or expected behavior, that is, his or her intention. This "likelihood-of-buying" component is relevant to the product's normal purchase cycle. Thus, if a consumer indicates an intention to buy a Yamaha motorcycle, it is only reasonable to expect her to buy that brand the next time she buys a motorcycle. Marketing strategists have been particularly concerned about developing accurate and timely measures of the behavioral component because of the relationship between a consumer's action tendency and his or her actual purchase behavior.

The idea of attitudes being comprised of three major components has had considerable impact on the thinking of consumer analysts and an especially pronounced impact in the area of advertising. The classical psychological model provided the basis for a conception of advertising effectiveness called the "hierarchy of effects" hypothesis.[3] This model became widely accepted because it provided a concise and lucid, although not completely valid, explanation of how attitudes were changed through advertising. The relationship between the three attitudinal components and the consumer's movement from unawareness to purchase is illustrated in Figure 10.1. Essentially, this model suggests that not only are attitudes made up of three components, but also these components are arranged in a particular order; that is, a consumer must have awareness and knowledge of a product (cognitive component) before a liking and preference (affective component) for it can occur. The validity of this model has been the subject of extensive research and debate.[4] There is, for example, some indication that an alternative hierarchy of effects may exist under certain consumption situations. The fact remains that the hierarchy of effects model is conceptually founded on well-established psychological theory. Furthermore, this model, highly regarded by practitioners, has provided considerable direction for the development of promotional strategy. For example, cigarette manufacturers, who are under intense pressure from the FTC to reduce the tar and nicotine contents of their cigarettes, need to aggressively promote their new low-tar brands to consumers who enjoy the "full-flavor" brands such as Marlboro, Winston, and Kool. In order to facilitate acceptance of the brands (ignoring the obvious ethical issue), the companies must first create awareness of the cigarettes and knowledge about their relative "health" attributes. Next, the companies must create a liking and preference for the brands until consumers are convinced of the advantage of smoking milder cigarettes. Finally, the company can seek trial and repurchase of the brands.

Figure 10.1
Hierarchy of Effects Model

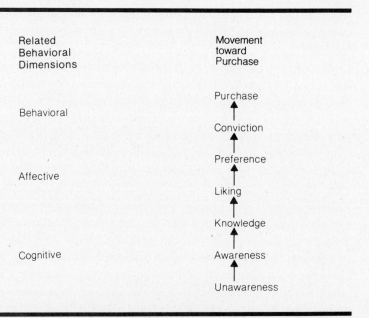

Source: R.J. Lavidge and G.A. Steiner, "A Model for Predictive Measurements of Advertising Effectiveness," *Journal of Marketing*, 25 (October 1961), p. 61. Reprinted from the *Journal of Marketing* published by the American Marketing Association.

The Multi-attribute Models

The past decade has been characterized by the emergence of multi-attribute models of attitudes.[5] Although several models have been developed, the work of Fishbein has perhaps had the greatest impact. Fishbein introduced beliefs as the cognitive foundation on which attitudes are built. Attitudes are functionally related to intentions, according to Fishbein, which, in turn, predict behavior. The relationship of belief, attitude, and intention is illustrated in Figure 10.2. Because the remainder of this chapter makes extensive use of these variables, it is appropriate to provide a clear definition of these variables.

1. *Evaluative criteria:* desired outcomes from choice or use of an alternative expressed in the form of the attributes or specifications used to compare various alternatives.

2. *Beliefs:* information which links a given alternative to a specified evaluative criterion, specifying the extent to which the alternative possesses the desired attribute.

3. *Attitude:* a learned predisposition to respond consistently in a favorable manner with respect to a given alternative.

4. *Intention:* the subjective probability that beliefs and attitudes will be acted upon.

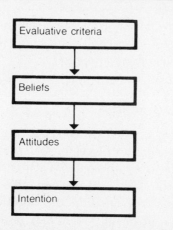

Figure 10.2
The Relationship of Evaluative Criteria, Beliefs, Attitudes, and Intention

Source: James F. Engel, Roger D. Blackwell, and David T. Kollat, *Consumer Behavior*, 3rd ed. (Hinsdale, Ill.: Dryden Press, 1978), p. 389. Copyright © 1978 by Dryden Press, a division of Holt, Rinehart and Winston. Reprinted by permission of Holt, Rinehart and Winston.

The multi-attribute models that have been developed to explain the process by which consumers form beliefs and attitudes fall into two major categories, compensatory and noncompensatory. Compensatory models—such as the expectancy-value model and the attribute adequacy model—are models in which a weakness of one attribute may be compensated for by strengths of another attribute. Noncompensatory models—such as the conjunctive model, disjunctive model, and lexiographic model—are those models in which a weakness of one attribute is not compensated for by strength of another attribute. A brief explanation of the major compensatory and noncompensatory models is presented below.

Compensatory Models

Expectancy-Value Model. This model assumes that each alternative will be evaluated on more than one attribute. Judgments are based on beliefs about whether or not an object actually possesses an attribute and the evaluation of the "goodness or badness" of those beliefs. Each brand is evaluated individually on all attributes and the total evaluation is the sum of the ratings of each attribute. The consumer selects the brand with the highest overall evaluation.

Attribute Adequacy Model. In the attribute adequacy model, an evaluation is arrived at in a manner similar to that discussed above, with the exception that an explicit assessment is made of the differences between "ideal and actual" of each attribute possessed by the object under consideration.

Noncompensatory Models

Conjunctive Model. In the case of this model, the consumer establishes a minimum acceptable level for each product attribute. A brand is determined to be acceptable only if each attribute equals or exceeds that minimum level. A lower than acceptable rating of one attribute will lead to a negative evaluation and rejection of the product. For example, a stereo component system may be evaluated as completely satisfactory in terms of sound reproduction and appearance but be rejected because it is not compact enough in size.

Disjunctive Model. The disjunctive model suggests that consumers establish one or more attributes as being dominant. A brand will be evaluated as acceptable only if it exceeds the minimum specified level of these key attributes. To continue with the example of the stereo component set, assume that sound reproduction and mechanical characteristics are the dominant considerations. Any set measuring up to expectation on these attributes will be regarded as acceptable no matter what its size, color, and so on.

Lexiographic Model. According to the lexiographic model, the consumer ranks product attributes from most important to least important. The brand that dominates on the most important criterion receives the highest evaluation. If two or more brands tie, the second attribute is examined and so on until the tie is broken.

While there is a distinct possibility that consumers use each of these models in certain circumstances, there is growing evidence that the expectancy-value model holds the greatest promise. The next section contains a detailed description of the two dominant expectancy-value models.

Attitudes toward Alternatives: Expectancy-Value Models

The dominant focus of consumer researchers in explaining attitudes toward alternatives has been the expectancy-value model, particularly the Rosenberg Model and the Fishbein Model.

The Rosenberg Model

The Rosenberg Model considers attitudes to contain two variables: (1) values (approximately equivalent to "evaluative criteria") and their importance in arriving at an attitude and (2) perceived instrumentality (the degree to which the taking of a point of view or following an action will either enhance or block the attainment of a value).[6]

For example, if "low price" is an important value (evaluative criterion) and the consumer has come to believe that brand A offers a low price, then the perceived instrumentality of brand A would be high. Rosenberg's model is expressed as follows:

$$A_O = \sum_{i=1}^{N} (VI_i)(PI_i)$$

where:

A_O = the overall evaluation of the attractiveness of alternative O;

VI_i = the importance of the ith value;

PI_i = the perceived instrumentality of alternative O with respect to value;

N = the number of pertinent or salient values.

In its pure form, the Rosenberg Model calls for the measurement of value importance on a scale of 21 categories ranging from "gives me maximum satisfaction" ($+10$) to "gives me maximum dissatisfaction" (-10). Using our earlier example, "low price" might receive a rating of $+10$. Perceived instrumentality is assessed using 11 categories ranging from "the condition is completely attained through a given action" ($+5$) to "the condition is completely blocked through undertaking the given action" (-5). Perhaps brand A in the above example would be given a score of $+5$ on this variable.

The Fishbein Model

The Fishbein Model is similar in many ways to Rosenberg's formulation, but there are subtle differences.[7] His first component is belief, defined as the probability that an object does or does not have a particular attribute. The second component is an "affective term," normally stated in terms of "good or bad." It specifies whether or not the possession or lack of possession of the attribute in question is positive or negative. Fishbein's model is expressed as follows.

$$A_O = \sum_{i=1}^{N} B_i a_i$$

where:

A_O = attitude toward the object;

B_i = the ith belief about the object;

a_i = the evaluation of the belief;

N = the total number of beliefs.

That is, the formula calls for belief (B_i) and evaluation (a_i) scores to be multiplied for each belief. Then these scores are summed to arrive at a single attitude ranking.

This initial formulation by Fishbein was later revised to reflect the results of major research efforts. The revised Fishbein model stated below has had a dramatic impact on the research and application of attitudes in consumer behavior.

$$A_{act} = \sum_{i=1}^{N} B_i a_i$$

where:

A_{act} = attitude toward the act under consideration;

B_i = the ith belief toward the act;

a_i = the evaluation of the ith belief;

N = the total number of beliefs.

The differences between A_O and A_{act} are not in the formulation but in the questions utilized to assess B and a components. The questions here focus on one specific purchase-and-use situation and attempt to evaluate the consequences. Belief may now be interpreted as the probability that a product attribute will exist or that the act of purchase will give certain consequences. The a_i component evaluates that belief along a "good-bad" dimension.

An Application of the Expectancy-Value Model

Most of the marketing applications have not strictly followed either the Rosenberg Model or the Fishbein Model. Rather, the applications have used some modification of them. Consider, for example, the following application.[8]

$$A_o = \sum_{i=1}^{n} W_i B_{ib}$$

where:

A_o = attitude toward a particular alternative o;

W_i = weight or importance of evaluative criterion i;

B_{ib} = evaluative aspect or belief with respect to utility of alternative b to satisfy evaluative criterion i;

n = number of evaluative criteria important in selection of an alternative in category under consideration.

In this formula, W_i is the weight or importance of the evaluative criterion, and B_{ib} is the evaluation of the alternative along that criterion. This rating is performed for each evaluative criterion, and the summed score is attitude toward the alternative.

The determination of evaluative criteria was discussed in the preceding chapter. It will be recalled that the usual procedure is first to isolate the appropriate dimensions and then to assess the importance of each W_i on some type of scale. The next step is to measure beliefs about the utility of individual brands through use of a scaling technique. The score for each individual consists of the sum of his or her rating for each brand on each criterion B_{ib} times the importance of that criterion W_i.

			Very Satisfactory			Very Unsatisfactory	
Decay	Brand A	1	2	3	4	5	6
Prevention	Brand B	1	2	3	4	5	6
Taste	Brand A	1	2	3	4	5	6
	Brand B	1	2	3	4	5	6

Data from one study utilizing this formula appear in Table 10.1. Five brands of mouthwash were rated along five criteria, of which germ-killing power and effectiveness were perceived as being of greatest importance. No summary score of A_b is provided, but the detailed ratings often are of greater use in marketing planning. From these data, for example, it is apparent that Listerine holds first place in preference, and, correspondingly, it has the highest ratings on the two most important evaluative criteria. Cepacol, on the other hand, is least preferred and has consistently the lowest ratings across all criteria. Additional data from this study showed that Cepacol is most preferred by those with postgraduate degrees but, unfortunately, mouthwash consumption is lowest in this segment. Management now must determine what must be done to improve these ratings. If the product, in fact, is competitive in terms of germ killing and the other attributes, the solution may be to advertise this fact. In any event, useful information has been provided for marketing planning.

**Table 10.1
An Example of Brand Attitudes Computed as a Rating along Evaluative Criteria**

(a) Frequency of Attribute-Importance Ranking

Attribute	Ranking (in percent)				
	1st	2nd	3rd	4th	5th
Kills germs	49.3	31.9	11.9	5.9	1.0
Taste/flavor	15.1	22.6	43.0	18.5	0.7
Price	4.7	12.2	22.9	52.8	7.4
Color	0.2	0.3	1.1	9.3	89.1
Effectiveness	30.9	33.1	21.0	13.4	1.6

(b) Average Consumer Ratings of Mouthwash Brands on Relevant Attributes

Brands	Average Score on				
	Kills Germs	Taste/ Flavor	Price	Color	Effective- ness
Micrin	2.22	2.46	2.60	1.85	2.21
Cepacol	2.40	2.92	2.70	2.29	2.36
Listerine	1.63	2.86	2.29	2.27	1.64
Lavoris	2.31	2.38	2.50	1.81	2.27
Colgate 100	2.35	2.52	2.68	1.87	2.32

Source: James Engel, Hugh Wales, and Martin Warshaw, *Promotional Strategy*, 3rd ed. (Homewood, Ill.: Richard D. Irwin, 1975), pp. 170-72. © 1975 by Richard D. Irwin, Inc.

Extending the Expectancy-Value Model

Consumer behavior researchers came to the realization that the accuracy of prediction could be increased by extending the expectancy-value model to include situational influences,[9] group and family influences,[10] and anticipated and unanticipated circumstances. The resulting general model appears as follows:

$$B \approx BI = (A_{act})w_o + (NB)(Mc)\,w_1$$

where:

B	= overt behavior;
BI	= behavioral intentions;
A_{act}	= attitude toward undertaking a given action in a particular set of circumstances;
NB	= normative beliefs (those norms that govern the situation);
Mc	= the individual's motivation to comply with those social norms active in the situation;
$w_o\ w_1$	= the weights reflecting the importance of each component (derived statistically through a regression analysis);

A_{act}, NB, and Mc all must be measured, whereas the weights reflecting the importance of these factors are estimated statistically.

For purposes of illustration, assume that a consumer is about to purchase a camera and is involved in alternative evaluation. Assume, further, that "ease of use," "guarantees good pictures every time," and "price" are known to be the most frequently utilized evaluative criteria among those in this particular market segment. The belief statements appear as follows based on this prior knowledge:

The camera does not require me to make my own settings for light and distance.

The camera works in such a way that I cannot overexpose or underexpose a picture.

The camera costs $150 or less.

Attitudes toward the act of purchasing brand X now would be evaluated with scales such as these:[11]

Brand X does not require me to make my own settings for light and distance.

(B_i)   Probable .... Improbable

(a_i)   Good... Bad

Brand X works in such a way that I cannot overexpose or underexpose a picture.

(B_i)   Probable .... Improbable

(a_i)   Good... Bad

Brand X will cost less than $150.

(B_i)   Probable .... Improbable

(a_i)   Good... Bad

The attitude now is derived by multiplying the B_i and a_i components for each belief and then summing across the total number of beliefs (N). The a_i component must only be measured once, whereas the B_i component must be measured for each brand.

Social norms have been discussed extensively in an earlier chapter, and they were defined, in general, as internalized, socially sanctioned forms of behavior. The existence of such norms, however, is of no consequence unless the individual is motivated to comply with these social pressures. There are a number of ways to measure normative beliefs, and the following are only illustrative questions for the camera-buying example:

The local camera club believes that brand X offers the best buy for the money.

        Probable .... Improbable

Most of the better photographers in the camera club use brand X and consider all other brands inferior.

        Probable .... Improbable

My best friends and picture-taking partners believe that brand X is the best brand to buy and use.

        Probable .... Improbable

Motivation to comply would be revealed by questions such as these:

I intend to follow the thinking of other members of the camera club.

        True .... False

I intend to follow the leadership of the better photographers in the camera club.

      True . . . . False

I intend to follow the advice of my picture-taking friends.

      True . . . . False

The second component of the extended model is computed now by multiplying the two values for each normative statement and summing them across all possible statements. The total estimate of behavioral intention is the combined sum of these two factors.

The efforts to apply the extended expectancy-value model to predict intentions and behavior have produced reasonably good results.[12] Indeed, the results are far better than those obtained with any competing model. The accuracy and value of the extended expectancy-value model can be increased further by taking into account the full range of situational influences, even though A_{act} can be situationally specific and the normative component is included. For instance, *anticipated circumstances* such as financial status, availability of goods, access to retail stores, and general attitudes of optimism or pessimism toward the future financial picture all function to shape intentions. A change in any of these will result in a change in intentions. Thus, anticipated circumstances should enter as a factor in the *BI* equation along with A_{act} and the normative component. Similarly, *unanticipated changes* in any of these considerations and others will prevent the fulfillment of intentions. Choice, then, is a function of both intention and unanticipated circumstances. The total model of the belief, attitude, and intention relationship is presented in Figure 10.3. This model is, of course, a part of the basic model presented in Chapter 3.

Notice, first, that beliefs are a function of evaluative criteria and information and experience. Attitudes, in turn, are a function of beliefs (plus, of course, the evaluative aspect) as Fishbein claims. Finally, intention is a function of attitude (A_{act}), normative compliance (computed as specified in the Fishbein extended model using measures of both the existence of norms and the motivation to comply), and anticipated circumstances. Normative compliance, by the way, also is affected by life-style, since motivation to comply is a personality variable.

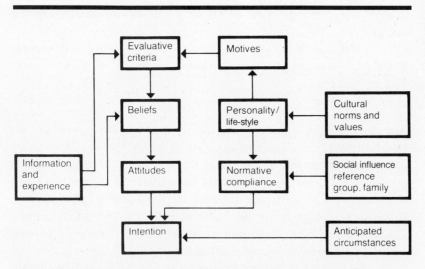

Figure 10.3
A Model of the Relationships among Beliefs, Attitudes, and Intentions

Source: James F. Engel, Roger D. Blackwell, and David T. Kollat, *Consumer Behavior*, 3rd ed. (Hinsdale, Ill.: Dryden Press, 1978), p. 404. Copyright © 1978 by Dryden Press, a division of Holt, Rinehart and Winston. Reprinted by permission of Holt, Rinehart and Winston.

Implication for Marketing Strategy

The various forms of expectancy-value models, ranging from the more simple A_O model to the complex extended Fishbein conceptualization, all can be of value in marketing planning. While the subject of change in beliefs and attitudes is considered in depth in the next section of this chapter, it is helpful here to discuss briefly a marketing implication.

Returning to the example of a camera purchase, assume that the a_i computations show that two attributes are most important in the purchase:

The camera does not require me to make my own settings for light and distance.

The camera works in such a way that I cannot overexpose or underexpose a picture.

Assume further that most people in the market segment of interest rated brand X as follows:

Brand X does not require me to make my own settings for light and distance.

Probable - X Improbable

Brand X works in such a way that I cannot overexpose or underexpose a picture.

Probable - X - - - - Improbable

Management now is faced with a dilemma. Consumer perceptions are clearly unfavorable. The first question to ask is "Are we, in fact, failing to measure up in product design to meet the attributes desired by our market?" If the answer is "yes," then there are at least two possibilities. One is to shift to a different market segment which will respond more favorably to the brand as it is. The second is to make major changes in the existing product or to introduce an altogether new product to become more competitive.

If the answer to the above question is "no," then the problem is one of market awareness. The strategy now is to use advertising, personal selling, and other forms of promotion to change the B_i values on these two evaluative criteria in a more favorable direction. Some of the procedures for changing beliefs, attitudes, and intentions are discussed in the following section of this chapter.

One possible approach is to convince the consumer that he or she is using the wrong evaluative criteria. Here an attempt would be made to change the a_i rating for the two important attributes. It was shown in the last chapter that this is a near impossibility for the business firm. However, it can be done most readily through consumer education. Consider the case of a retailer of relatively high-priced, quality kitchen appliances who discovered that consumers base most of their appliance purchase decisions on price and easy credit, two criteria on which he is ranked rather unfavorably. He should attempt to instill in the consumers the importance of purchasing products that meet all safety standards and of patronizing a store that offers excellent repair service, criteria on which his store is rated highly.

Attitude Change Strategies

Recall that attitudes in the expectancy-value model can be changed in these ways: (1) changing an existing B element, (2) changing an existing a element, and (3) adding a new B-a combination.[13] For the purpose of simplicity, the A_O model is used here as opposed to the more complex extended model.

Changing a Consumer's Belief (B) about a Product

Returning once again to the camera-buying example used in the previous section, recall that there were two important beliefs underlying attitudes and that brand X received an unfavorable evaluation:

Brand X does not require me to make my own settings for light and distance.

Probable- X Improbable

Brand X works in such a way that I cannot overexpose or underexpose a picture.

Probable - X - - - Improbable

It was suggested that the first problem always must be to verify whether or not consumer perceptions are true. If so, changes may be called for in product design. If they are not true, however, the company faces the problem of remedying a weakness in awareness on these important dimensions.

Here the goal would be to undertake a strategy with the objective of moving a large number of people in a more positive direction on both attributes. Usually it is possible to state such objectives in quantifiable terms. An example might be "to convince 60 percent of the people in this market segment that brand X does not require them to make their own settings for light and distance." A similar goal might be set for the second attribute. Changes then would be detected by actually measuring the number of prospects rating these statements as being highly probable after the marketing strategy has been implemented.

This type of objective is quite common in advertising management. It is based on the premise, first of all, that the attributes in question are salient to the individual. If not, it matters little whether or not movement in the desired direction occurs because attitudes and behavior will remain unchanged.

Changing the Evaluation of a Belief (*a*) about a Product

The manufacturer in our camera example could perhaps examine the poor ratings on the belief statements and conclude that the best strategy is to tell prospects that it is wrong to purchase a fully automatic camera that prevents overexposure or underexposure. The message might read like this: "The really expert photographers always make their own settings. In that way, they know the picture is their own creation. Brand X allows you to achieve this high degree of fulfillment."

Such a strategy may completely overlook that evaluative criteria often have their roots in life-style, and that they are a reflection of important motives. In this case, the average prospect may, in effect, be manifesting real fear that he or she cannot operate a complex camera. In this case, such an appeal is likely to fall on deaf ears because of the difficulties any manufacturer faces in trying to change evaluative criteria. Usually they are strongly held and must be taken as given.

Adding a New *B-a* Combination

Another strategy could be to attempt to introduce an altogether new attribute in the hopes of increasing the overall attractiveness of the brand. This assumes, of course, that such benefits do, in fact, exist. One example might be to feature the company's camera brand as having small size and lighter weight. This previously may not have been a criterion used by the prospect, but it easily could be, especially if the messages stressed "automatic performance and fool-proof pictures" as well as small size and light weight.

Foundations for Managing Attitude Change

A meaningful understanding of how to manage attitude change involves an understanding of why consumers hold the attitudes they do and the purposes that attitudes serve. Attitudes traditionally have been viewed as serving four functions: (1) the adjustment function,

(2) the ego-defensive function, (3) the value-expressive function, and (4) the knowledge function.[14] Each of these will be discussed in the following paragraphs, as well as how attitudes are organized.

Functions of Attitudes

The *adjustment function* emphasizes the adaptive tendency of consumers. Consumers tend to adapt or adjust their attitudes to reflect the behavior viewed as favorable by their friends and associates. As a result of this adaptive tendency, consumers develop favorable attitudes toward products, brands, and retail outlets that provide the expected level of satisfaction and unfavorable attitudes toward those that do not provide the expected level of satisfaction. In this manner, a consumer learns to adjust to his or her environment and develop somewhat enduring response patterns that enable him or her to enhance the satisfaction experienced from consuming products and services. For example, a new soft drink may be perceived as having a good taste. If the drink lives up to the consumer's expectation, he or she may develop a favorable attitude toward the soft drink and decide to drink it regularly. Thus, the consumer's attitudes tend to provide direction to the behavior that provides satisfaction.

The *ego-defensive function* refers to the human tendency to avoid situations or forces that are inconsistent with one's ego or self-image. Consumers develop and maintain attitudes toward products, brands, and retail stores that protect them from acknowledging their limitations. For instance, even the purchaser of a product that proves to be inferior maintains an attitude toward that product that permits his or her self-image to remain intact.

The *value-expressive function* refers to attitudes that reflect a consumer's values, that is, attitudes that express to society those values that are consistent with the consumer's self-image. Whereas the ego-defensive attitudes tend to protect the consumer, the value-expressive attitudes tend to enhance the consumer's self-image. For example, if Gant shirts connote high quality, workmanship, and styling, the consumer who prefers that brand expresses his preference for that value to society when he buys them. Furthermore, consumers who consider that value important will probably be loyal to Gant shirts.

The *knowledge function* of attitudes is to provide consistency and stability in the way an individual perceives the world around him or her; that is, attitudes serve the function of providing a stable frame of reference for understanding and adapting to the chaotic world. Consumers are simply not able to engage in conscious problem solving with respect to every purchase decision; consequently, the knowledge function of attitudes can be instrumental in the formation of routine product evaluations and purchase decisions. Although a homemaker may hear claims from every producer of a pain reliever that their brand is superior, for various reasons she probably has a more favorable attitude towards one of these brands than all others. As far as she is concerned, that brand is the best headache remedy. This knowledge enables her to maintain consistency and reduce the problem of selection to a matter of the appropriate number of tablets to purchase.

Organization of Attitudes

"Jonathan Whiteshed, a self-proclaimed wine connoisseur, has long preferred French wines because of their superior aroma, body, and taste. An associate of Jonathan's recently gave him a copy of *Wines Internationale,* which contained the most recent ratings of wines by international experts. Despite the low ratings received by Jonathan's favorite French wines, he continues to prefer them to all others."

Was Jonathan's refusal to change his attitudes unusual? Not at all. Consumers' attitudes are characterized by an enduring tendency to maintain consistency and resist change from influences of various types. Moreover, the basic components of attitudes (the cognitive, affective, and behavorial dimensions discussed earlier) also must maintain consistency. Most consumers appear to have a tendency to maintain consistency. In fact, most people have the psychological ability to screen out and distort reality in order to maintain this consistency. Thus, for a marketing strategist to effectively utilize his or her marketing effort, it is necessary to understand the process by which consumers maintain consistency among the components of an attitude and among various attitudes. Research into the internal organization of an attitude suggests that most individuals can tolerate

only limited inconsistency between the affective and cognitive components.[15] When consistency is attained between the cognitive and affective components, the attitude is said to be in a stable state which
persists over time. If the information a consumer receives about a
product (cognitive component) is contrary to his or her beliefs about
that product (affective component), inconsistency will result. Although most consumers can tolerate some inconsistency, reorganiza-
tion of attitude components must occur at some level of inconsistency. Consistency among attitude components can be achieved by
(1) rejecting the stimulus input that introduced the inconsistency, (2)
modifying the stimulus input to make it consistent with the other
component, or (3) making some sort of accomodation so that a new
attitude emerges with internal consistency. For instance, the consumer who purchased an aluminum tennis racket may experience
inconsistency after reading an advertisement claiming aluminum
rackets to be inferior to wood rackets. The consumer can relieve this
inconsistency by rejecting the validity of the claim or by modifying
the claim (for example, by believing the claim is true only for some
brands).

Consistency among Attitudes

Every consumer maintains basic values and social relationships that
are considered to have high personal goal relevance. Each of these can
serve as a significant anchor for attitudes in that only the dispositions
that reflect a positive orientation to the consumer's self-concept are
formed and retained.

Attitudes that are closely related to the consumer's self-concept
and basic values are said to have centrality. Attitudes with central
anchoring points, in turn, tend to become organized so that a change
in one affects the others. Therefore, a person strives to attain balance
in his or her attitudinal structure, making attitude change difficult.

Insofar as a person's attitude toward something is imbedded in a large
latticework of attitudes—and such things as the amount of stored information about the object, its personal goal relevance and psychological

centrality are all indicators of such imbedding—any attempt to change the attitude must come to grips with the fact that this attitude is anchored by the other attitudes in the system. Such an attitude does not exist in a vacuum; if it changes, then other compensatory changes must follow to restore balance.[16]

A striving toward maintenance of balance (resistance to change), on the other hand, is greatly reduced when attitudes are peripheral to self-concept, basic values, and other significant focal objects. Thus, although a professor's attitude toward the importance of higher education may be highly resistant to change, his or her attitude toward Budweiser beer may be readily changed.

The question may be asked as to whether attitudes toward products and services ever attain such a degree of centrality that change is resisted. This can happen on occasion, although it must be admitted that products and services generally reflect far less personal commitment than do attitudes with high personal goal relevance, such as religion and family. However, some marketing strategists would contend that attitudes toward brands of coffee often attain high centrality. They assume that many homemakers believe that their competence as cooks and even as wives is determined in part by the quality of the coffee they serve. When one brand is perceived as being satisfactory, the resulting attitude is probably so imbedded that change is unlikely.

The probability of change varies inversely with attitude strength. In addition to centrality, the other basic determinant of strength is the amount of stored information and past experience that underlies the rating of the alternative. In other words, "attitudes about an object are more subject to change through contradictory incoming information when the existing mass of stored information about the object is smaller."[17] On the other hand, when centrality and stored information both are high, attempts to bring about change may well result in selective attention, comprehension, and retention. The driver of a loud hot rod, who attends to all the maintenance requirements of his car, has probably witnessed the admiration of numerous peers for his "wheels." It could be safely said that he considers the hot rod part of himself, or at the very least an integral part of his image. This fellow will in all likelihood screen or distort appeals from the EPA to reduce noise pollution.

Managing Attitude Change

Consumer attitudes tend to be relatively stable, especially if they are strongly held. However, they are not static; thus, much marketing effort is expended to change consumer attitudes. Marketing effort can result in consumer attitude change, but such change can also result from nonmarketing factors. For example, consumer attitudes toward economy cars have changed considerably since the energy shortage and the accompanying increases in gasoline prices. The purpose of this section is to discuss some of the most important ways in which marketing-controlled efforts, particularly mass communication, can contribute to attitude change. The topics discussed here are those that appear to have the greatest significance to marketing managers.

Message Discrepancy

The manager who wishes to change attitudes must answer several basic questions in order to develop an effective strategy. For instance, should an advertisement assert that the product in question is superior in every respect or should a more moderate position be taken? To what extent can an advertisement deviate from a consumer's own position and still induce attitude change? A decade ago, consumer analysts would have contended that the more a message deviated from the receiver's own position, the greater the likelihood that the consumer's attitudes would change in the desired direction. However, this position has been modified in recent years. Research now indicates that attitude change can be enhanced by advocating a discrepant position; but, beyond some point, increasing discrepancy will actually decrease attitude change. For example, an advertisement claiming that Ford automobiles are quieter and less expensive than Mercedes may very well produce attitude change regarding the quality of Ford automobiles. However, if the advertisement were to claim Ford cars to be superior in every respect (performance, durability, workmanship), the discrepancy between the claim and the existing attitude might be beyond the consumer's limit and, consequently, inhibit attitude change. Thus, the marketing strategist must conduct research to determine a discrepancy limit and make certain that the message stays within that boundary.

Consumer analysts have also found that attitude change is affected by the credibility of the communicator. Consumers seem to place greater confidence in a trustworthy source; that is, they are more receptive to a credible source, even when the message is substantially discrepant from their own position. The importance of having a highly credible source is particularly pronounced in advertising because the source is considered anything but impartial and unbiased. For instance, the maker of Jockey briefs effectively used baseball star Lou Brock, football hero Craig Morton, and hockey player Vic Hadfield to model its bikini, peekaboo mesh, and flower-printed briefs in an effort to ward off traditionalists' fears of appearing unmasculine when wearing them.

Message Content

Fear Appeals

The marketing strategist seeking to change attitudes has considerable latitude in the message content employed. For example, the message can be designed to arouse the anxieties or fears of the consumer (fear appeals). Early research on fear appeals suggested that a marketer's attempt to stress the unfavorable consequences of not using a product would have an adverse effect on a consumer's attitude. In recent years, research has suggested that there is a positive relationship between fear and persuasion—but only in certain instances. That is, a favorable attitude toward a product can be developed by emphasizing the adverse consequences of not using the product in question *only* when consumers do not perceive themselves as part of the market for the recommended product or brand.[18] Further, it now appears that an increased threat of physical or social consequences enhances persuasion only when the credibility of the source is high. When this is not the case, counterargumentation seems to be generated, with the outcome that the source is rejected as being biased. Fear appeals have been used in recent years to promote such diverse products and services as mouthwash, toothpaste, candy mints, automobile seatbelts, antismoking campaigns, planned parenthood counseling, and informative booklets on the prevention of social diseases.

The credibility of advertising, in general, is not high. This fact in itself should be a warning to those who would use the fear appeal indiscriminately. Furthermore, the credibility of manufacturers varies greatly. Hence, the credibility of both medium and communicator must be established before serious consideration is given to this strategy. For instance, the maker of expensive record cleaning fluid and paraphernalia might determine that, among magazines bought by music lovers, *Stereo Review* and *High Fidelity* have the highest credibility ratings. Ads in these magazines featuring a popular jazz musician who believes that failure to use the brand in question is the acceptance of "less than perfect quality in sound" may have a profound effect on readers and cause them to at least give this product a trial run. However, this producer may confound his plans if he does not select his medium with great caution or if his choice of communicator proves to be unwise. It may be, for example, that the musician, chosen as a result of his widening commercial appeal, is viewed by more articulate listeners as having bastardized jazz as an art form. Consequently, this marketer would have lost considerable ground in his target market.

Unstructured Message

The amount of change advocated in the message has been found to have an effect on attitudes. The structured advertisement that tells a complete story logically and sequentially with a definite conclusion stated appears to be quite effective for many groups, at least in the short run. However, the unstructured advertisement that permits the audience to draw its own conclusion may be more effective in the long run, particularly with a highly intelligent audience. Thus, the marketing manager of a bank attempting to develop an image of friendliness would find the unstructured message to be more effective.

Humor

During the 1950s and 1960s, there was a tendency to avoid the use of humor in marketing communications on the pretext that it can quickly overwhelm the product message and, thus, fail to achieve creative objectives. In recent years, humor has been widely used by marketers. In fact, approximately 15 percent of television ads use some form of humor.[19] Some of today's great product successes reached a dominant market position through humor. Most North American readers will quickly identify these product themes:

"With a Name Like Smucker's . . . "

"Flick My Bic . . . "

"Please Don't Squeeze the Charmin . . . "

"Butter . . . Parkay . . . "

"The Noisiest Potato Chip in the World . . . "

Research clearly indicates that humor can produce above-average attitude change in brand preference if certain precautions are observed.[20]

1. The brand must be identified in the opening ten seconds, or there is the real danger that humor can inhibit recall of important selling points.

2. The type of humor makes a difference. Subtlety is more effective than the bizarre.

3. The humor must be relevant to the brand or key idea. Recall and persuasion both are diminished when humor and the key idea are not linked.

4. Humorous commercials that entertain by belittling the potential user usually do not perform well. A better strategy is to make light of the brand, the situation, or the subject matter.

Distraction

People develop counterarguments against a message that contradicts their present attitudes; thus, change is impeded. Any strategy which serves to interfere with or reduce counterargumentation is worthy of consideration from the perspective of ensuring correct comprehension. However, the potential for deception and consumer manipulation is high, and the authors would be hard put to defend such a strategy from an ethical point of view.

There is some evidence that counterargumentation can be reduced if distraction of some type is introduced during exposure. For example, this can be done through the use of humor or competing stimuli such as background music or noise. Unfortunately, distraction in an advertising context can reduce attention and reception and thereby overpower any positive effect on attitude itself. For instance, a commercial promoting a dietetic cat food that utilizes comical cats who "talk" or make human gestures may be very effective in gaining attention, but the distraction caused by the cats may be so overwhelming that viewers remain oblivious to the actual message content of the ad.

Message Structure

Two-sided Messages

Advertising messages traditionally have been one-sided; that is, they have emphasized only the strengths of the advertised brand and have avoided the brand's weaknesses as well as the strengths of competing brands. Some recent evidence, however, suggests that under certain conditions two-sided messages may actually be more effective in changing consumers' attitudes. Thus, the advertisement promoting deodorant by comparing the strengths and weaknesses of the brand being promoted as well as those of the competing brands may be more effective than the advertisement that only discusses the strengths of the brand in question. In recent years, the Federal Trade Commission has repeatedly urged advertisers to name competitors when comparisons are made in advertisements.

With regard to a somewhat related phenomenon, it is interesting to point out that the policy of corrective advertising instituted by the Federal Trade Commission in 1971 may have some unintended effects. The basic premise of the policy is that manufacturers should be required to admit blame publicly in their advertisements once they have been found guilty of false and misleading appeals. This admission in a certain percentage of their future messages presumably will serve to offset past misleading efforts. There is evidence that counteradvertising works in this way.[21] The opposite also can happen in that the admission of blame will enhance the present credibility of the advertiser in the consumers' eyes and hence increase promotional effectiveness. This, of course, would be contrary to the result intended by the Federal Trade Commission.

Order of Presentation

There now is a considerable body of evidence on the subject of the order in which dominant appeals should be presented. This assumes, of course, that there are two or more main arguments in the appeals that are either related to each other or opposed to each other (pro and con). Some say that the argument presented first will prove to be most effective (primacy), whereas others say that the most recently presented argument will dominate (recency). Research investigations have focused on the order of two-sided appeals and on the order of major arguments in a one-sided message.

While the research conducted to date is somewhat equivocal, it is possible to develop some guidelines for strategy development. On the one hand, initial presentation of the strongest argument may have a stronger effect on attention attraction and receptiveness to subsequent arguments. Material presented first usually is learned best. On the other hand, presentation of successively weaker arguments may tend to diminish the overall persuasive effect of the message. Therefore, saving the strongest arguments for last may boost reception when it is most needed.

Repetition

The benefit of repetition is a fundamental tenet of learning theory. Most authorities agree that repetition of a persuasive message generally is beneficial. It is argued that preceding advertisements may have made too weak an impression to stimulate much buying interest; therefore, later ads can effectively strengthen the original weak impressions, with the result that a prospect's disposition to think and act favorably is enhanced.

In addition, markets are not static; people continually enter and leave. Therefore, a repeated message will reach new prospects. If this fact is overlooked, a firm can quickly experience erosion of its market share as previously loyal buyers diminish.

Although there is a great deal yet to be learned about the effect of repetition, it is possible to develop some tentative generalizations to guide the development of marketing strategies.

1. Due to situational distractions or because of message complexity, it may be necessary to repeat a message a number of times before information is completely processed.[22]

2. Repetition creates a new belief linking attribute and brand, which in turn functions to change attitude.[23]

3. The continued pairing of an attribute and a brand through repetition increases strength of belief.[24]

4. The increased frequency of an exposure tends to result in diminishing returns per exposure due to the strong effects of the initial exposures.[25]

5. Repetition can result in increased liking for a stimulus.[26] It seems to be especially effective in ads that contain jingles.

6. Repetition has a somewhat greater effect on brand evaluation and purchase intention than it does on buying behavior.[27]

Source Credibility

As noted above, it has been found that there can be a greater discrepancy between a prospect's present belief position and the message if the source is perceived as being credible. In other words, people seem to place greater confidence in a trustworthy source and, hence, are more receptive to what is said, even when there is a substantial deviation from their own position. Similarly, there is a marked reduction in willingness to accept a discrepant message when the source is of moderate or low credibility.

The moderating effect of source credibility has distinct managerial significance. It is difficult to make an advertisement credible when it is obvious that the intent of the message is to persuade. The receiver generally recognizes that the source or sender of the message is anything but impartial and unbiased. Therefore, a message that deviates substantially from the receiver's own belief is likely to be screened out as he or she processes the stimulus.

Admittedly, much about source credibility is pure speculation not based on research undertaken under natural field conditions using commercial messages as the variable. Nevertheless, the importance of impartiality is verified. Undoubtedly the image of certain commercial spokesmen is largely attributable to their reputations of impartiality. Arthur Godfrey, for example, is often mentioned as a credible source who would not recommend a product that does not perform as claimed. Spokesmen who capitalize upon credibility, however, are infrequent in the mass media. In light of a recent consent agreement between the FTC and Pat Boone, the credibility of celebrity endorsements may be enhanced in the future. The singer agreed to pay 2.5 percent of any restitution that the FTC ordered when it was discovered that he had promoted an acne treatment's false claims of its ability to cure and eliminate the cause of acne. The agreement indicates that the FTC will insist that endorsers be accountable for the claims they make, which may have considerable impact on the willingness of celebrities to take this risk.

Given that marketing communications usually are not perceived as highly credible, the message should deviate only to a small extent from the attitude position of members of the target audience. Attitude change is best achieved by successive exposures, each of which encompasses only small discrepancy. This generalization is especially critical when consumers' attitudes are based on ego involvement.

Summary

An attitude is a learned predisposition to respond consistently in a favorable manner with respect to a given alternative. Two models exemplify current views of the structure of attitudes. The most widely accepted model, the classical psychological model, utilizes cognitive, affective, and behavioral components. It provides the basis for the "hierarchy of effects" hypothesis, which portrays how attitudes can be changed through effective advertising. Multi-attribute models illustrate the relationship among consumers' evaluative criteria, beliefs, attitudes, and intentions. The two main categories of multi-attribute models are compensatory models (such as the expectancy-value and attribute adequacy models) in which a weakness of one attribute is compensated for by strengths of another attribute, and noncompensatory models (such as the conjunctive, disjunctive, and lexiographic models) in which a weakness of one attribute is not compensated for by strength of another attribute. Evidence suggests that the expectancy-value model holds the greatest promise. A detailed explanation of the Rosenberg and Fishbein models is given.

Consumer behavior researchers have come to believe that accuracy of prediction can be increased by extending the expectancy-value model to include situational influences, group and family influences, and anticipated and unanticipated circumstances. Efforts to apply this extended model to predict intentions and behavior have produced reasonably good results.

Consumer attitudes tend to be relatively stable, but are not immune to change through marketing efforts. Three marketing strategies for changing consumer attitudes are mentioned: changing a consumer's belief about a product, changing the evaluation of a belief about a product, and introducing a new belief about a product.

Attitudes traditionally have been viewed as serving four functions: adjustment, ego-defensive, value-expressive, and knowledge. Consumers tend to maintain a degree of consistency in their attitudes. Topics that have the greatest significance to marketers who desire to change consumer attitudes are: message discrepancy, message content (fear appeals, structured vs. unstructured messages, the use of humor, and distraction), and message structure (two-sided messages, order of presentation, repetition, and source credibility).

Questions and Issues for Discussion

1. Describe the interaction that might take place among the three basic attitudinal components of an individual who practices middle-of-the-road politics, upon hearing a speech by a politician who may be considered an "extremist." How might this interaction differ if the politician were far less extreme, but held views which were nevertheless discrepant from this individual's position?

2. How might the hierarchy of effects model help the manufacturer of distinctive women's fashions to develop an effective promotional strategy?

3. Distinguish between the classical psychological model and the multi-attribute model. Which model holds the greatest promise for the marketing strategist?

4. Describe in detail how the multi-attribute model might provide useful direction in the following instances:

(a) decision as to whether or not to remodel a night spot located in an affluent suburban area.

(b) decision as to whether or not to modify the taste of carbonation of Dr. Pepper.

(c) development of a promotional campaign for the Salvation Army.

5. Discuss the extended expectancy-value model and how its various components might function to shape the intentions of consumers who buy distinctive brands of personal grooming products. What type of strategy would you recommend to the marketer of these products on the basis of your conjectures?

6. What are the major functions served by attitudes? Identify an example of each function. How can an understanding of these functions served by attitudes help the marketing strategist?

7. A large, nationally known insurance company is considering a promotional campaign stressing the unfavorable consequences of not having adequate life insurance. Would you encourage the use of such a campaign? Why or why not?

8. The White Mountain Company, producer of Winged Majesty bicycles, has decided to discontinue its current advertising program. The company is considering the following two campaigns. The first would feature a well-known athlete on a series of television commercials. Each commercial would be in a different setting and would emphasize the enjoyment bicycle riders experience. The second campaign would feature various typical bicyclists who would discuss the fine qualities of Winged Majesty bicycles. They would, for example, indicate that the Winged Majesty bicycles, although slightly more expensive than other brands, are of the finest craftsmanship. How might an understanding of consumer attitudes and attitude change aid in selecting the most effective campaign? Which of the two campaigns would you recommend that White Mountain adopt for its bicycles?

9. A marketing research study undertaken for a manufacturer of televisions indicated that twenty percent of the target market planned on purchasing a color set within the following six months and five percent planned on purchasing a black and white set. How much confidence should be placed in the predictive accuracy of such intention measurements? Why?

10. Indicate whether you think humor, a two-sided message, or repetition is appropriate in each of the following instances. In each case, explain why.

(a) promotion of product safety by the Consumer Product Safety Commission.

(b) advertisements for a breakfast cereal marketed as a health food.

(c) promotion of the local or regional professional soccer team.

Case 1. Budson Yogurt

Edgar Allen III, marketing manager of Budson, a regional manufacturer of Yogurt, has just finished examining a report of Budson and industry-wide sales figures of the food product. Although the product has not been an instant success in the U.S., the figures reveal that many people have come to appreciate the tart Yogurt. Industry sales have surged from $27 million in 1967 to $300 million in 1975, and the trend is expected to continue. However, Mr. Allen is slightly dismayed at Yogurt's success relative to that of a major competitor: only 23 percent of all households are regular purchasers of Yogurt in contrast to the 65 percent of households that regularly buy cottage cheese.

Yogurt has been a staple of the Middle Eastern countries for centuries but was not sold in the U.S. until 1930. Its flavor comes from two

Source: Some of the general information in Case 1 is from "Yogurt Makers Try a Mass-Market Recipe," *Business Week*, November 8, 1976, pp. 91–92.

strains of bacteria on homogenized, pasteurized milk. However, the product did not encounter much success in the U.S. until 1947, when some producers started adding fruit to the Yogurt to counteract its acid taste. Nevertheless, many Americans still harbor unfavorable attitudes toward the product. An industry spokesman recently remarked that the basic problem facing Yogurt producers is to "get people around their taste apprehension." Unfortunately, additional obstacles exist which inhibit widespread marketing success of Yogurt. Manufacturers are hindered by distribution problems and the limited shelf life of the product, because it can remain fresh only for approximately 21 days. Yogurt makers also have difficulties in finding a niche in the marketplace. One company promotes its product as a nutritious snack; another stresses the convenience of the food product. Many manufacturers, though, have rejected previous low-calorie and "natural" claims, due to labeling laws that have forced them to reveal the product's contents.

These, and several other problems, face the Budson Company. The Yogurt industry is dominated by approximately a dozen specialized regional manufacturers; hundreds of local dairies also produce it. However, at least one of the competitors is attempting to attain nationwide distribution within the coming year. Budson would like to do the same, but recent sales of its Yogurt have not kept pace with its major competitors, which has hampered the company's confidence in making such a drastic move. Instead, it intends expanding into the relatively undeveloped Southern market, while simultaneously implementing a new marketing strategy in its home market.

Budson's current marketing strategy is based on the following data:

1. The American market for Yogurt is largely untapped. Only 10 percent of all consumers eat Yogurt at least once a week, and nearly 50 percent of the population refuses to try it.

2. The heaviest consumers of Yogurt are young, white, urban people who have incomes exceeding $15,000.

3. The more children there are in a family, the less likely the family is to purchase Yogurt. This could be attributed to the relatively high cost of an 8-oz. container—prices range from $.52 for private label supermarket brands to $.88 for branded products.

Budson's Mr. Allen is unsure of how to reposition the product to gain the widest acceptance by consumers. The current strategy depicts Yogurt as a snack food, but competition is very keen. He has considered marketing Yogurt as a dessert, but diet-conscious consumers perceive that to be a "dirty word." He does not feel that the product is substantial enough to be promoted as a light meal either.

In an effort to clarify his understanding of consumer attitudes toward Yogurt, Mr. Allen conducted a survey of single males and females in both the Midwest and Southern markets. The survey revealed that a majority of the respondents were aware of the caloric aspect of Yogurt and its bacteria culture content which aids in digestion. However, few of the respondents (both users and nonusers) perceived these attributes to be as important as taste. Obviously, Yogurt eaters (46 percent of the respondents) perceived it to have a good taste, and nonusers (54 percent of the respondents) perceived it to have a bad taste. Of the noneaters, however, 65 percent had never tasted Yogurt. Despite these perceptions, an amazing 85 percent of the total respondents believed Yogurt to be a nutritious product.

Case 1 Questions

1. How should Budson reposition its Yogurt in light of the information from the survey?

2. How might an understanding of the hierarchy of effects model contribute to an effective advertising campaign?

3. What advertising strategies should the company implement to enhance the product attributes?

Case 2. Great Midwestern Trade Bank

The Great Midwestern Trade Bank (GMTB), which has branches in several large and medium-sized cities, has set out to solve what its marketing director, Alex Heyward, has called an "identity crisis." The

Source: Some information in Case 2 is from "Marketing Research in Banking," *Bank Marketing*, May 1975, pp. 28-33.

crux of Heyward's argument is that his bank (and, in fact, banking institutions in general) has never sought to identify and effectively communicate its character and image within its market. Any attempt on the part of a commercial bank to differentiate itself in the eyes of existing and potential customers will be wrought with difficulty, and there are several reasons for this discussed below. Heyward points out, however, that it can be done and that a financial institution, like any other business enterprise, has an identity that is real, and as such it should be judiciously planned and managed, in the same sense that more tangible assets are administered.

Construction and management of identity for GMTB is made difficult by a multitude of problems, many of which are endemic to the banking industry as a whole. One such problem is the quickly changing populations within many regions. The number of people in migration is unprecedented, and has caused the character of towns and neighborhoods to change dramatically over brief spans of time. Several GMTB branch managers have said that their customer turnover is so high that faces have become unrecognizable and are changing from month to month. Heyward fears that these branches may be attracting new customers merely on the basis of convenience of location and that the entry of an additional competitor could shrink deposits to a less than adequate level.

A second difficulty, according to Heyward, is that the roles played by financial institutions and the rights accorded them by the government are "meshing and melding now as never before." This has been the cause of much confusion among consumers as to whether, for instance, a full-service bank, savings and loan, savings bank, or credit union will be most consonant with their banking requirements. The issue is further clouded by developments such as Electronic Funds Transfer Systems, demand accounts at savings and loans, a narrowing of interest rate differentials and various service innovations. Banks can no longer rely primarily on tradition and personal relations to draw customers.

Heyward feels that another source of GMTB's identity crisis has been its expansion through the acquisition of a number of smaller banking institutions in its region. Finding one day that their bank's name has changed and that they must now deal with strangers can cause resentment on the part of consumers and destroy long-held

GMTB has a lower charge per check than most other banks.

	C	N	C	N	C	N	C	N	C	N	C	N	
Probable	5	7	7	15	19	41	31	24	25	8	13	5	Improbable
Good	78	87	12	8	10	5	0	0	0	0	0	0	Bad

GMTB's loan policy is a very stringent one.

	C	N	C	N	C	N	C	N	C	N	C	N	
Probable	15	37	16	29	23	19	30	15	15	0	1	0	Improbable
Good	0	0	1	0	3	2	20	22	31	30	45	46	Bad

The people at GMTB are always friendly and courteous.

	C	N	C	N	C	N	C	N	C	N	C	N	
Probable	11	10	26	25	25	34	23	19	13	7	2	5	Improbable
Good	91	96	9	4	0	0	0	0	0	0	0	0	Bad

GMTB deals harshly with customers who overdraw their accounts.

	C	N	C	N	C	N	C	N	C	N	C	N	
Probable	16	17	30	28	28	24	17	20	9	7	0	4	Improbable
Good	12	14	18	17	29	28	26	25	11	10	4	6	Bad

GMTB is a trustworthy financial institution.

	C	N	C	N	C	N	C	N	C	N	C	N	
Probable	34	18	27	20	19	22	18	25	2	8	0	7	Improbable
Good	100	100	0	0	0	0	0	0	0	0	0	0	Bad

GMTB can completely provide for anyone's banking needs.

	C	N	C	N	C	N	C	N	C	N	C	N	
Probable	7	4	10	9	21	23	44	27	12	20	6	17	Improbable
Good	97	98	3	2	0	0	0	0	0	0	0	0	Bad

loyalties. Making demands with these people can be a delicate process, and a clearly defined identity could be expeditious for GMTB in these matters.

The competitive strategies of banking institutions have been noted for their imitative propensity by many marketing experts. Says Heyward, "As soon as one bank adopts some innovation, it diffuses through the industry as fast as you can say 'blue chip.'" This may be a necessary result of a heightened consumer orientation and energetic competition, but, to the consumer, the net effect is a blurring of these institutions and their offerings.

Heyward has concluded that his bank can maintain its strong position successfully only if it discovers how consumers perceive their institution, and whether or not these perceptions are well matched with consumers' social and psychological needs and desires. With the help of a consumer analyst from a local university, Heyward constructed a survey designed to measure the attitudes of consumers towards GMTB. He then distributed copies of the survey to branch managers who were able to administer the survey to a total of 300 GMTB customers and 175 noncustomers. The results of selected items from the survey are given on page 359. The percent (rounded) on the left for each rating category indicates frequency of response for GMTB customers (C), while that on the right indicates response frequency for noncustomers (N).

Case 2 Questions

1. Evaluate the results given above that describe the importance to consumers of each attribute and the extent to which GMTB measures up on these.

2. Are the differences in response between GMTB customers and noncustomers significant to strategy development?

3. In light of GMTB's difficulties and the survey results, discuss the three basic attitude change strategies and suggest to Heyward the strategy or combination of strategies you think is most appropriate for GMTB to implement, and how this might be done.

Notes

1. G. Allport, "Attitudes," C. Murchison, ed., *Handbook of Social Psychology* (Worcester, Mass.: Clark University Press, 1935), pp. 798–884.

2. D. Krech, R. S. Crutchfield, and E. L. Ballachey, *Individual in Society* (New York: McGraw-Hill Book Company, 1962), pp. 137–269.

3. R. L. Lavidge and G. A. Steiner, "A Model for Predictive Measurements of Advertising Effectiveness," *Journal of Marketing,* 25 (October 1961), pp. 59-62.

4. K. S. Palda, "The Hypothesis of a Hierarchy of Effects: A Partial Evaluation," *Journal of Marketing Research,* 3 (February 1966), pp. 13-24.

5. Martin Fishbein and Icek Ajzen, *Belief, Attitude, Intention and Behavior: An Introduction to Theory and Research* (Reading, Mass.: Addison-Wesley, 1975), p. 12.

6. Milton J. Rosenberg, "Cognitive Structure and Attitudinal Affect," *Journal of Abnormal and Social Psychology,* 53, (1956) pp. 367-72.

7. Martin Fishbein, "An Investigation of the Relationships between Beliefs about an Object and the Attitude toward That Object," *Human Relations,* 16 (1963), pp. 233-40.

8. W. W. Talarzyk and R. Moinpour, "Comparison of an Attitude Model and Coombsian Unfolding Analysis for the Prediction of Individual Brand Preference," paper presented at the Workshop of Attitude Research and Consumer Behavior, University of Illinois (December 1970).

9. Russell W. Belk, "Situational Variables in Consumer Behavior," *Journal of Consumer Research,* 2 (December 1975) pp. 157-64.

10. Herbert C. Kelman, "Attitudes Are Alive and Well and Gainfully Employed in the Sphere of Action," *American Psychologist,* 29 (May 1974), pp. 310-24.

11. See Fishbein and Ajzen, *Belief, Attitude, Intention and Behavior.*

12. David T. Wilson, H. Lee Mathews, and James W. Harvey, "An Empirical Test of the Fishbein Behavioral Intention Model," *Journal of Consumer Research,* 1 (March 1975), pp. 39-48.

13. All three of these options were suggested by Lutz. See Richard J. Lutz, "Changing Brand Attitudes through Modification of Cognitive Structure," *Journal of Consumer Research,* 1 (March 1975), pp. 49-59.

14. D. Katz, "The Functional Approach to the Study of Attitudes," *Public Opinion Quarterly,* 24 (Winter, 1960), pp. 160-204.

15. M. J. Rosenberg, "Inconsistency Arousal and Reduction in Attitude Change," *Current Studies in Social Psychology,* I. D. Steiner and M. Fishbein, eds. (New York: Holt, Rinehart and Winston, 1965), pp. 123-24.

16. T. M. Newcomb, R. H. Turner, and P. E. Converse, *Social Psychology* (New York: Holt, Rinehart and Winston, 1965), p. 136.

17. Ibid., p. 91.

18. J. J. Wheatley, "Marketing and the Use of Fear-or-Anxiety-Arousing

Appeals," *Journal of Marketing,* 35 (April 1971), pp. 62-64; B. Sternthal and C. S. Craig, "Fear Appeals: Revisited and Revised," *Journal of Consumer Research,* 1 (December 1974), pp. 22-34.

19. J. Patrick Kelly and Paul J. Solomon, "Humor in Television Advertising," *Journal of Advertising,* 4 (Summer 1975), pp. 31-35.

20. Harold L. Ross, Jr., "How to Create Effective Humorous Commercials, Yielding above Average Brand Preference Changes," *Marketing News* (March 26, 1976), p. 4.

21. H. T. Hunt, "Measuring the Impact and Effectiveness of Counter Messages" (Conference on Advertising and the Public Interest, American Marketing Association, May 1973); and Michael B. Mazis and Janice E. Adkinson, "An Experimental Evaluation of a Proposed Corrective Advertising Remedy," *Journal of Marketing Research,* 13 (May 1976), pp. 178-83.

22. Andrew A. Mitchell and Jerry C. Olson, "Cognitive Effects of Advertising Repetition" (Working Paper no. 49, College of Business Administration, The Pennsylvania State University, October 1976).

23. Ibid.

24. Ibid.

25. Alan G. Sawyer, "The Effects of Repetition: Conclusions and Suggestions about Experimental Laboratory Research" (Paper presented at the Workshop on Consumer Information Processing, University of Chicago, November 1972).

26. Ibid.

27. Ibid.

Part 4

Consumer Decision Process: Analysis and Applications

The six chapters in this section focus on the consumer decision process. Chapter 11 is concerned with problem recognition. Problem recognition is the point at which customers recognize that some decision is necessary. The nature and determinants of problem recognition are discussed and illustrated, followed by an analysis of procedures and techniques used for measurement and appraisal. This chapter also addresses the issue of marketers' attempts to trigger problem recognition.

Chapter 12 deals with the issue of how information is processed into usable form. A considerable body of research indicates that the consumer, to a great extent, sees and hears what he or she *wants* to see and hear. Significant implications of this fact for marketing planning will be stressed in other chapters in this section.

Chapter 13 centers on how consumers obtain information in order to learn about and to evaluate the characteristics and attributes of the alternatives available as potential solutions to the problem. Particular emphasis is given to those conditions and factors that are likely to precipitate information search and the information sources most frequently used.

The immediate choice situation, Chapter 14, focuses on the purchase act itself and the encounters that occur during the act of buying as well as the immediate surroundings of the act of buying. The chapter also examines the consumer's selection of a store and the in-store purchasing processes.

Choice and the outcomes of choice are the last stage in the decision process. Chapter 15 examines choice in both a retail store and in-home purchasing environment. It also focuses on postdecision dissonance and satisfaction—two of the most important outcomes. Satisfaction, in particular, assumes relevance in the context of the consumerism movement, which has risen in large part to remedy the important causes of dissatisfaction.

The final chapter, on choice patterns, serves as an integration of much that has been previously discussed. There is a vast literature on this subject, and marketing implications of choice patterns abound.

Chapter **11** Problem
Recognition

Outline

The Nature of Problem-Recognition Processes

Ideal State

Actual State

Outcomes of Problem-Recognition Processes

Types of Problem-Recognition Processes

Simple Problem-Recognition Processes

Somewhat Complicated Problem-Recognition Processes

Highly Complex Problem-Recognition Processes

Unique Aspects of Problem-Recognition Processes

Determinants of Problem-Recognition Processes

Factors Affecting the Ideal State

Factors Affecting the Actual State

Marketing Implications of Problem Recognition

Measurement of Problem-Recognition Processes

Using Information on Problem-Recognition Processes: An Illustration

Attempts to Trigger Problem Recognition

Summary

Questions and Issues for Discussion

Cases

Key Terms

problem recognition

ideal state

actual state

simple problem recognition

somewhat complicated problem recognition

highly complex problem recognition

awareness

factors affecting ideal state

novelty

motive activation

factors affecting actual state

purchase-probability scale

The preceding chapters have focused on various aspects of consumer decision processes. The key environmental influences on consumer decision making—culture, subcultures, social class, groups, and the family—and their influences on consumer decision making were discussed in Chapters 4, 5, and 6. Subsequent to this, consumer information processing and the elements that comprise the individual consumer's psychological makeup were examined. In the discussion of each of these topics, it was assumed that the consumer wanted to purchase a product. But how do consumers recognize the need to purchase a particular product or service? How does the consumer's unique psychological makeup influence the recognition of a problem? Do environmental influences such as culture or social class affect the process of consumer problem recognition?

These questions and many others must be addressed if consumer analysts are to understand fully the mechanism that triggers consumer action. In other words, because the consumer must perceive a problem before a purchase is enacted, it is necessary to understand first the process whereby a problem is recognized, and then the action that results from the recognition. Unfortunately, problem recognition is not a simple act. Rather, it is a complex process that involves, and occurs as the result of, many variables.

The Nature of Problem-Recognition Processes

The first stage in decision-process behavior is problem recognition—the perceived difference between an ideal state of affairs and an actual situation that is sufficient to arouse and activate the decision process. When problem recognition occurs, the human system is energized, and goal-oriented behavior ensues. Seemingly unrelated activities now become organized to satisfy this state of arousal, and the individual becomes distinctly more sensitive to relevant information from the environment. In short, the system is "turned on" and triggered to engage in purposeful activity.

The abbreviated model of the consumer decision process in Figure 11.1 depicts two principal determinants of problem recognition: (1) motives and (2) information and experience. Motives are enduring predispositions to strive to attain specified goals and hence determine, to a large degree, the "ideal" for an individual at any point in time. New information, on the other hand, often serves to reveal the extent to which the present circumstance deviates from the ideal. Once this perceived deviation reaches a certain point, the individual is aroused to restore the disturbed balance.

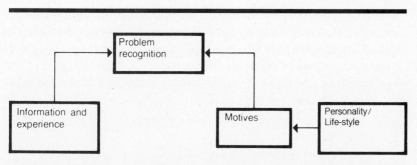

Source: James F. Engel, Roger D. Blackwell, and David T. Kollat, *Consumer Behavior*, 3rd ed. (Hinsdale, Ill.: Dryden Press, 1978), p. 215. Copyright © 1978 by Dryden Press, a division of Holt, Rinehart and Winston. Reprinted by permission of Holt, Rinehart and Winston.

Figure 11.1
**Determinants of
Problem Recognition**

Statements such as "I need a Coke" or "I need a new sweater" are clear instances of a consumer expressing recognition of a problem. In the first instance—"I need a Coke"—the desired state is the absence of thirst. The actual state is a feeling of discomfort resulting from a physiological need for liquid. The recognition of the discrepancy between the ideal state and the actual state will cause the consumer to initiate behavior to alleviate this discrepancy. In the second instance—"I need a new sweater"—the ideal state and actual state are less clear. The individual may actually need a new sweater to keep warm; however, most likely the statement reflects the consumer's perception that a different, more stylish sweater would more accurately reflect the "real me."

Ideal State

The ideal and actual states are quite complex, involving a number of variables. First, consider the ideal state. By definition, there are one or more motives underlying this state. The prominent motives and the behavior perceived as having the potential to satisfy these motives are affected by personality characteristics, attitudes, values, and evaluative criteria. Since the consumer's decision processes are affected by culture, subculture, social class, group, and family, these variables, albeit indirectly, affect the ideal state. Furthermore, there are instances in which the condition or performance characteristics of the product or service being used affect the ideal state. For instance, the owner of a 1979 Mercedes can develop a considerably higher expected level of performance for automobiles (ideal state) than can the owner of a five-year-old Chevrolet. The ideal state is also affected by the consumer's resources, including current and expected income, and by marketing efforts, such as advertising, personal selling, and product demonstration.

Actual State

The actual state refers to the way the consumer perceives the existing state of affairs. The consumer's perception of the existing state of affairs involves many variables interacting in complex ways. In fact, the variables that affect the actual state are the same variables that influenced past purchases and might affect the ideal state. Thus, the actual state is affected by variables, such as environmental constraints on decision making, and by marketing efforts. Take, for example, the owner of a new sports car who finds out that the car he thought was performing perfectly is, by industry standards, performing below expectations. This redefinition of reasonable performance is a change in the actual state of affairs.

Outcomes of Problem-Recognition Processes

Problem recognition can result in two major types of outcomes: (1) no action, or hold, and (2) search. The no-action or hold outcome results when the consumer perceives a discrepancy between the actual and ideal states but the difference is not of sufficient magnitude to affect behavior. That is, a minimum level of perceived difference must be surpassed before the problem recognition that triggers behavior change occurs. For instance, the consumer's ideal state with respect to a bank's checking service may be totally free checking at a convenient location. The actual state may be low-cost checking at a conveniently located bank. There is clearly a difference between ideal and actual states of affairs, but the discrepancy (low-cost checking) is probably not of sufficient magnitude to trigger search for a different bank. If the actual state were high-cost checking at an inconveniently located bank, the discrepancy might be sufficient to cause the consumer to search for an alternative bank.

The level of perceived difference that is necessary to initiate search behavior varies among consumers and circumstances. The retired consumer with considerable free time might not be disturbed by an inconveniently located bank or long waiting lines in the lobby. However, the working mother of three young children might find the same distance and delay intolerable. Special circumstances can also affect the perceived discrepancy between actual and ideal states of affairs. For instance, the possibility of a hamburger and french fries at a "greasy spoon" restaurant might normally produce a significant discrepancy between actual and ideal places at which to dine; yet when very hungry and pressed for time, many people find such "cuisine" palatable and even gratifying.

The hold outcome can also occur when a significant discrepancy between ideal state and actual state is perceived but further problem-solving behavior is precluded. Such a condition can result from a lack of financial resources, time, energy, or the availability of appropriate alternatives. For instance, if the working mother of three young children had no alternative bank available, she would necessarily continue to do business with that institution; that is, even though considerable discrepancy exists between the ideal and actual bank service, the fact that no alternative bank is available would preclude any change in behavior.

Many consumers have, on occasion, experienced problem recognition only to have further action constrained by the intervention of an external influence. A consumer may perceive considerable discrepancy between an actual state (ownership of a 1961 Ford) and an ideal state (ownership of a 1979 Porsche) only to have further action (purchase of the Porsche) constrained by a lack of available income.

Similarly, behavior can be constrained by time, energy, and the availability of appropriate alternatives. For instance, the household with both adults employed full time outside the home might perceive a significant discrepancy between the meals they actually prepare and the meals they would like to prepare. In this instance, the behavior to eliminate this discrepancy might be precluded by available time.

The second type of outcome that can result from problem recognition is search. As was described in detail in Chapter 3, search is followed by alternative evaluation, choice, and outcomes. Both types of outcomes are stored in the individual's memory component. Thus, some problem-recognition processes are learned while others are not. In the case of learned problem-recognition processes—for example, those involving a physiological need such as thirst—the problem recognition becomes programmed and automatic. In the United States, a considerable segment of the population is programmed to reach for a Coca-Cola, Pepsi, or 7-Up when thirsty; that is, those people have learned and stored the information that when they recognize a discrepancy between their actual state (thirst) and ideal state (absence of thirst), Coke, Pepsi, or 7-Up will eliminate that discrepancy. Frequently problem-recognition processes are not this automatic; indeed, they can be quite complex.

Types of Problem-Recognition Processes

The preceding discussion attempted to explain the nature of the problem-recognition process. Implicit in this discussion was the notion that problem recognition varies substantially in relation to the extent of complexity involved. Problem recognition can be simple, somewhat complicated, or highly complex. The amount of complexity is considered to be a function of (1) the time period involved, (2) the urgency of the need, (3) the number of influencing factors, and (4) the intensity of the consumer's attitudes and motives.

Simple Problem-Recognition Processes

Simple problem recognition refers to those strongly learned, highly programmed, and automatic processes. Although perhaps not arising in the same way, the consumer has typically experienced this situation in the past. Assume, for example, that you are driving down the highway, 100 miles from your destination, when you notice the gas gauge is on empty. Gasoline is clearly necessary for the continuance of your journey. Because there is a significant discrepancy between the actual state (an empty gas tank) and the ideal state (an adequate supply of gasoline), a problem is recognized. This type of problem recognition (depletion of existing solution) occurs frequently. In fact, many of the problems that consumers recognize result from the depletion of the product being utilized to satisfy the problem.

Somewhat Complicated Problem-Recognition Processes

This type of problem-recognition process is characterized by more time, more influencing factors, and, perhaps, more intense consumer attitudes. In brief, this problem-recognition process is more complex than the simple process. Assume an individual has had a Harman-Kardon stereo system for a few years and has been completely satisfied with it. This individual reads a magazine advertisement for Pioneer stereo systems but does not think much about it and continues to be satisfied with her present system. During the next few weeks, she continues to read advertisements on Pioneer systems. While visiting a friend, she listens to his Pioneer stereo system and finds it to be superior to her own in several respects. Her friend indicates that he has been very pleased with the system's performance. On her next shopping trip, she stops at a stereo shop and finds that Pioneer stereo systems have been reduced in price by 40 percent. The factors described above might not have affected the ideal state of this consumer. However, this consumer's ideal state may have changed dramatically because of these impinging factors. There is no doubt, however, that the problem-recognition process is considerably more complex in this situation than in the previous one.

Highly Complex Problem-Recognition Processes

Highly complex problem-recognition processes refer to those infrequent, unprogrammed processes that involve a considerable period of time, are affected by many factors, and involve strongly held attitudes. Assume that several years ago a consumer purchased a 1971 Chevelle. The car has performed well and the consumer is satisfied with it. He has seen advertisements for the new compacts (Pinto, Vega) but considers them too small and too expensive. One evening a friend gives him a ride home in his recently purchased Vega. He is amazed at the room in the Vega and likes the car. His feeling is intensified considerably during subsequent weeks when his 1971 Chevelle will not start, and he is forced to walk eleven blocks in a rainstorm. During the next few months, he pays closer attention to the cars he sees. He also pays closer attention to advertisements for cars and on two occasions visits automobile dealers for trial runs and price information.

Finally, he comments to his wife about the high price of gasoline, the impending repairs on his "old" Chevelle, and the possibility of a sporty compact. She reacts negatively, pointing out that the family has one car (a 1976 wagon) that is in excellent condition and that a new car is too expensive. She would prefer to save the money or use it for a nice vacation. Besides, she observes, he would be healthier if he walked to work—a routine that would eliminate the need for a second car.

A few weeks later, the 1971 Chevelle breaks down, and the mechanic estimates that it will cost $200 to repair it. The husband points out that spending $200 on that old junker is just wasting money. During the next few weeks, the family gets by with one car and both husband and wife become somewhat irritated because of the inconvenience this causes. The next day the husband finds out he has received a $50-a-month raise, and that evening he informs his wife of the raise. They discuss the matter at some length and eventually decide to buy a new car.

In this hypothetical, although not unrealistic, situation, problem recognition is far more complex than in the previous two cases. Problem recognition occurred over a considerable period of time as the result of the interaction of many factors, including marketing efforts (advertisements, dealership, price), environmental factors (price of gasoline), the ability to purchase ($50 raise), and the difficulty with the old car ($200 repair cost).

Unique Aspects of Problem-Recognition Processes

The nature of problem recognition and the examples just cited indicate that these processes differ in many respects from the concepts discussed elsewhere in this text. An explicit discussion of the unique aspects of problem recognition is necessary for a clear understanding of the nature of the process.

First, it is apparent that problem-recognition processes may simultaneously involve many variables, including perception, learning, attitudes, personality characteristics, and various reference-group influences. The concepts involved vary considerably from situation to situation, as illustrated by the increasing complexity of the three examples presented above. In this sense, problem recognition may be a more comprehensive process than many concepts discussed previously.

Second, it is obvious that problem recognition is a more complex process than motivation. Although problem recognition involves motives, it may also involve attitudes, values, and other influences. Therefore, problem recognition is not another name for motivation; it embraces many other concepts and processes.

Third, problem recognition may involve complex comparisons and weighing of such things as the relative importance of various needs, attitudes about how limited financial resources should be allocated to alternative uses, and attitudes about the qualitative level at which needs should be satisfied. Moreover, these need hierarchies and attitudes may differ from one family member to another, so that conflict-resolution processes may be necessary before problem recognition occurs.

Finally, as used here, problem recognition differs from the concepts of awareness and interest that are used in many studies of consumer behavior, particularly the diffusion of innovations. Problem recognition involves an awareness of a difference between an actual and an ideal state. The consumer may or may not be aware of products and brands, and an awareness of or exposure to products and/or brands may or may not precipitate problem recognition. Thus, "awareness" is a much more general term than "problem recognition" and, as such, bears no necessary relation to this phenomenon. Similarly, the concept of interest is not necessarily related to problem recognition. Problem recognition can occur without any interest on the part of the consumer in a product or brand. Or the consumer can be interested in a product or brand without recognizing a problem (a new car or home being among the more common examples).

Determinants of Problem-Recognition Processes

The preceding discussion of problem recognition has illustrated the complexity of the phenomenon and has demonstrated that numerous factors affect the processes. The type and number of factors that affect problem-recognition processes vary from situation to situation. The number of factors that can affect problem-recognition processes in general is large, but, in any given situation, a single factor or a few

Figure 11.2
Determinants of Problem-Recognition Processes

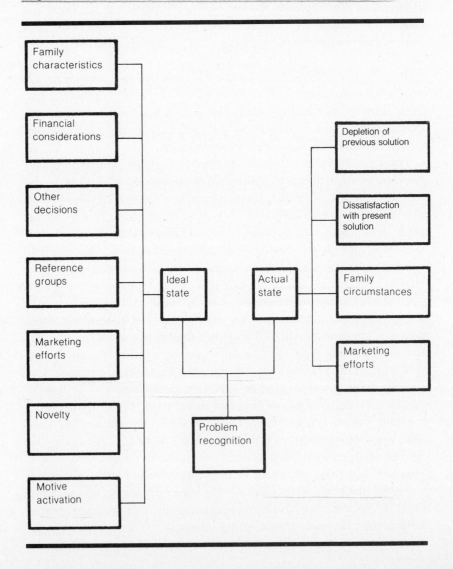

factors are the primary contributors to problem recognition. Detailed discussion of all possible determinants of problem recognition is impossible; however, detailed discussion of the primary determinants is necessary and appropriate.

Some determinants produce problem recognition by affecting the consumer's ideal state of affairs, whereas others affect the consumer's actual state of affairs. Certain determinants can, of course, affect both ideal and actual states. The primary determinants of problem recognition and the state of affairs on which they are believed to have the greatest impact are presented in Figure 11.2.

Factors Affecting the Ideal State —▷ bs exterior   EXTERNAL FACTORS

There is perhaps an infinite number of factors that affect a consumer's ideal state of affairs. The most important factors affecting the consumer's ideal state (Figure 11.2) are (1) family characteristics, (2) financial considerations, (3) other decisions, (4) reference groups, (5) marketing efforts, (6) novelty, and (7) motive activation.

① Family Characteristics

Perhaps no factor that affects the ideal state has so monumental and lasting an effect as changes in family characteristics. When a person marries, significant changes occur in the ideal state with respect to housing, home furnishings, leisure activities, and numerous other things.[1] The birth of a child substantially alters the needs and attitudes of the nuclear family and produces considerable changes in the ideal state of affairs.[2] Indeed, new needs and commensurate redefinitions of ideal states continually occur as the size and composition of the family change. For instance, as the older couple's children "leave the nest," redefinitions of the ideal automobile, ideal home, and ideal club memberships may follow.

② Financial Considerations

Financial considerations, such as changing financial status and financial expectations, can affect a consumer's ideal state and, thus, trigger de ae ucade uor. problem recognition. A salary increase, inheritance, or some other windfall can cause a consumer to substantially alter his or her ideal state of affairs.[3] Such a change in financial status can, for example, cause the ideal state to become ownership of a new Cadillac when the prewindfall ideal state might have been a three-year-old Ford. Similarly, a financial disaster can precipitate a change in the ideal state of comparable magnitude in the opposite direction. The marketing strategist, obviously, cannot influence a consumer's financial status. However, changes in the financial status of sizable market segments can present an opportunity to increase profit by adjusting the market offerings. For example, changes in the financial status of farmers can affect changes in the desired equipment on pickup trucks. Such a change might be met by producing trucks with fewer options and frills. Consumers' expectations regarding their financial status can also affect their ideal state of affairs. The purchase of a new automobile by the second-semester college senior frequently results from a change in the student's ideal state of affairs that is triggered by financial expectations upon graduation. Marketing analysts have clearly documented the importance of expectations in the period preceding the purchase of many durable goods.[4]

Other Decisions

Problem recognition, chiefly through changed perception of the ideal state, is often the result of other purchase decisions. For example, the purchase of a new stereo system can affect the consumer's perception of the desirability of records or tapes currently owned. In other words, the consumer can become dissatisfied and alter the ideal state of one product because of the recognition of problems in related areas. Marketing strategists frequently group or display related products in reasonable proximity where such a phenomenon may occur. For example, washers and dryers, beds and bedding, and furniture and carpeting are frequently displayed together.

Reference Group

The state of affairs perceived to be ideal can be affected by changes in reference groups. For example, a college graduate quickly learns that there is a marked difference between the clothing that is appropriate on a college campus and the clothing appropriate for a career in busi-

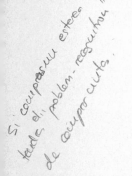

ness. The change in reference groups from fellow students to aspiring executives influences the consumer's ideal state of affairs and, consequently, the consumer perceives the existence of a problem.

Marketing Efforts

Finally, various marketing efforts—including advertising, product displays, and personal selling—can affect a consumer's perception of the ideal state of affairs and thus trigger problem recognition. An advertisement informing the television viewer of certain distinctive product features can, for example, affect the viewer's ideal state of affairs. If the ideal state of affairs is perceived to be significantly discrepant from the actual state, the advertisement has triggered problem recognition. For example, a person who prides himself on taking the time to jog each day to keep in shape and who is exposed to some ads for a newly opened health spa in his locality may recognize that jogging alone is boring and that the spa would offer opportunities for using gymnastic equipment and meeting friends. Indeed, the marketing strategist's objective may be to focus marketing efforts in order to stimulate problem recognition among certain market segments.

Promotion often is designed to appeal to a dominant motive or set of motives, which then reinforces the ideal state and triggers problem recognition. Aside from the obvious benefits of financial protection for one's family, one study disclosed an interesting pattern of motivations underlying the purchase of life insurance.[5] First, such a purchase represents an emancipation from childhood and thereby serves as a mark of entry into the adult world. In addition, it is alleged that life insurance symbolizes adult love, which circumvents selfishness of youth and even extends beyond death. Large amounts of insurance may, in addition, enhance feelings of potency and power in the consumer in much the same manner as boasting of sexual achievements. Finally, insurance purchased during the years of striving is a positive achievement, a symbol of power and success, so to speak, representing that one's family will be provided for adequately.

Novelty

Novelty, or the desire for change, is a frequently overlooked factor in the determination of problem recognition. There is some indication, for example, that approximately one third of those who purchase a new brand do so simply because they want a change.[6] Furthermore, they purchase these new brands even though they are satisfied with their present brand. The estimates of the number of people who purchase a new brand because of a desire for something new vary from 15 percent to nearly 30 percent. Clearly, then, the desire for novelty and change has a significant effect on the ideal state of affairs.

Motive Activation

A lifetime of learning and experience obviously will serve to reinforce certain patterns of behavior which are beneficial either in giving pleasure or in reducing discomfort and pain. These, in turn, become embedded in one's personality as motives—enduring predispositions that direct behavior toward attaining certain goals. Motives function both to arouse behavior initially and to direct it toward desired outcomes.

To underscore the significance of motives, it should be stressed that *purposeful behavior is motive-satisfying behavior.* The implication of this premise is that motive patterns are not likely to be changed through persuasive activity of any type, especially that undertaken by the commercial marketer. One essential task for marketing research, therefore, is to uncover dominant motives and thereby provide clues for the development of products and sales appeals which will be regarded as motive satisfying by the consumer. For instance, young artists concentrated in a district of a large city may be motivated to somehow express their individuality. The owner of a boutique in this district might take advantage of this motive by offering a wide range of unusual and "arty" products, thereby enhancing her store's image and increasing sales.

Psychologists and marketing people alike have tried their hand at classification and have devised lists, some of which are exceedingly long. This list-making often is little more than an exercise in ingenuity, however, because 100 people no doubt would produce 100 different lists. An attempt to determine motive patterns on a more analytical basis is a different matter. Abraham Maslow, whose thinking is based more on an intuitive than on an empirical foundation, has significantly helped to clarify this difficult question.[7]

Maslow hypothesizes that motives are organized to establish priorities and hierarchies of importance (prepotency). Through this means, internal conflict is avoided by one motive taking precedence over another. The following classification was suggested, proceeding from the lowest order to the highest:

1. *Physiological*—the fundamentals of survival, including hunger and thirst.

2. *Safety*—concern over physical survival, ordinary prudence which might be overlooked in striving to satisfy hunger or thirst.

3. *Belongingness and love*—striving to be accepted by intimate members of one's family and to be an important person to them. This also can include nonfamily members.

4. *Esteem and status*—striving to achieve a high standing relative to others, including desires for mastery, reputation, and prestige.

5. *Self-actualization*—a desire to know, understand, systematize, organize, and construct a system of values.

Three essentially different categories are comprehended in this classification: (1) motives related to survival needs, (2) motives related to human interaction and involvement, and (3) motives related to competency and self. Each higher order of motive will not function until lower levels are satisfied, at least to some degree. The hungry person will care little about understanding nuclear physics. Undoubtedly, some motives in each category are never fully satisfied and thus remain continued sources of problem recognition. A strong desire for status, for example, can be virtually insatiable.

It is unlikely that a classification such as Maslow's will prove very useful in explaining the specific motives in a given purchase. But prepotency (ordered relationships of motive strength) is of conceptual value. It has been verified that prepotency is reflected in consumer buying to the extent that previously ignored desires often exert themselves only after a purchase has satisfied a predominant (and perhaps lower order) motive.

A consumer's motives are integrated by his or her self-concept into a purposeful pattern that is reflected in purchasing behavior. For example, cranberry sauce has long been a staple of the American diet, especially at Thanksgiving, Christmas, and other holidays. The heavy user of this product, however, uses it throughout the year as well. Through marketing research, the heavy user was found to have a very interesting self-concept and life-style. The core of her self-concept was found to lie in service to her family, and the same had been true of her mother and grandmother. Not surprisingly, her dominant values are highly traditional, and she adamantly rejects the modern liberation movement. The image of cranberry sauce, in turn, is remarkably consistent with her outlook on life in that it connotes tradition and engenders happy associations of family life, well-being, and the "horn of plenty." Use of the product, then, represents highly self-approved behavior.

Quite an opposite life-style was found when the nonuser of cranberry sauce was studied. Her values reflect the now familiar concept of the liberated woman, even though this study was undertaken prior to the onset of the feminist movement. Traditional values, by and large, are rejected, and cranberries are rejected as well because of their old-fashioned image. Here is an example of a contradiction between self-concept and product image that will not be overcome through marketing effort, no matter how skillful. It is interesting to note, however, that this same person proved to be a heavy user of cranberry juice, which reflects quite a different image. Its values in nutrition, dieting, and modern cookery make it compatible with the life-style of those in this market segment.

The contribution that understanding of consumer motives makes to effective marketing is evidenced by the experience of a leading publishing house with *The Living Bible*. Initially this Bible, a modern language version of the traditional Bible, was to be marketed to the nonchurchgoing public.[8] It was discovered that interest in the Bible in general and *The Living Bible* in particular was highest among homemakers in the middle income and average education bracket with children still living at home. The psychographic profile revealed a basically conservative outlook toward life characterized by a traditional value profile and a high premium placed on the family and child raising. *The Living Bible,* thus, was presented as an ideal guide for the concerned parent in raising children as they should be in today's world. *The Living Bible* quickly outdistanced its competition and found its way into nearly 40 percent of American homes.

Factors Affecting the Actual State

A consumer's actual state of affairs can be affected by the depletion of the previous solution, dissatisfaction with the previous solution, family circumstances, and marketing efforts. Although other factors can affect the consumer's actual state of affairs, these four factors are the most important determinants.

Depletion of the Previous Solution

Perhaps the most frequent determinant of problem recognition is the depletion of the previous solution to a problem. Familiar examples are running out of gasoline, food, beer, and toothpaste. The depletion of an existing solution to a problem produces problem recognition only if the consumer recognizes the depletion and if the underlying need still exists. Thus, the depletion of an ample supply of golf balls would not produce problem recognition if you have decided never to play golf again. However, the depletion of an ardent golfer's supply of golf balls would produce a state of problem recognition. The marketing analyst must estimate the likely depletion time of various market segments and the pattern of behavior used to replenish the depleted supply in order to assure availability of the product. Determining when users of a certain type of product will replenish supply is crucial to adjusting marketing efforts to encourage repeat purchases by users and to stimulate trial by nonusers.

Dissatisfaction with the Present Solution

Problem recognition can also result from a consumer's dissatisfaction with the present solution to a problem. That is, when a product breaks, wears out, or otherwise becomes unsatisfactory, a consumer's desired state of affairs can be affected.[9] The purchase of a new automobile is, for instance, frequently triggered by the failure of the consumer's present automobile. A consumer can also become dissatisfied with the present solution to a problem because of the solution's price. For example, the high cost of renting a house or an apartment frequently triggers the problem recognition that precedes the purchase of a house. The marketing analyst must monitor the satisfaction that consumers experience with his or her products in order to accurately focus marketing efforts.

Family Circumstances

Problem recognition often occurs as the outcome of changes within the nuclear family. The birth of a child, for instance, results in modified requirements for food, clothing, furniture, and perhaps a house instead of an apartment. New needs and redefinitions of actual states (in reality, both actual and desired states are affected) thus occur as the size and age composition of the family change. Even a change in the husband's or wife's place of employment can affect the desirability of the present home, thereby evoking problem recognition.

A changed financial status or anticipated change also can have the same effect. Salary increases, tax refunds, temporary or unusual employment, cash gifts, and the payment of debts all serve to activate a new set of desires. Of course, the opposite also can happen. In addition, financial expectations are quite important in the period immediately preceding the purchase of durable goods because a favorable financial outlook is an incentive for purchase and vice versa.

Marketing Efforts

Marketing efforts can also affect the consumer's actual state and, consequently, trigger problem recognition. An advertisement informing consumers that a lawn mower once believed safe is actually unsafe may affect the consumer's perception of the actual state and thus result in considerable discrepancy between his or her ideal and actual states.

Marketing Implications of Problem Recognition

The preceding observations on the determinants of problem recognition suggest certain guidelines for the marketing strategist. First, the marketing strategist must determine the unique aspects of problem-recognition processes for the specific product in question because the determinants of problem recognition are different for automobiles, sport shirts, and soft drinks. Consequently, the marketing strategist must identify the relative importance of the various determinants of problem recognition and then focus marketing efforts to achieve the firm's objective. Second, the marketing strategist must recognize that consumers differ substantially in their sensitivity to the factors that affect problem recognition. Therefore, the marketing strategist must identify the prominent problem-recognition processes associated with the purchase of a particular product by relevant consumer segments.

Suppose that the Coca-Cola Company identifies depletion of the previous solution as the primary determinant of problem recognition relative to the purchase of Coke by people between the ages of 16 and 21. This determination and the recognition that Coke is a convenience-type product would suggest that an intensive distribution strategy would be appropriate; that is, since dissatisfaction with the product is not a major factor triggering problem recognition, the company need not attempt to convince consumers of the relative benefits of its product. Rather, the company should concentrate on making the product available at as many locations as possible. However, the Coca-Cola Company might find that the primary determinant of problem recognition in another consumer segment is dissatisfaction with the previous solution. The marketing strategy appropriate for this segment would differ considerably from that appropriate for the youth segment.

Measurement of Problem-Recognition Processes

Consumer analysts now believe that problem recognition can best be measured by obtaining information on purchase intentions. As discussed in Chapter 10, purchase intentions have been recognized as the intervening variable between the attitudes and the behavior that are operative when a problem is recognized. Thus, a consumer's indicated intention to purchase can be interpreted as an acknowledgment that a problem has been recognized and that the consumer is in the early stage of problem-solving activity. A consumer's expressed intention to purchase a product indicates that the consumer perceives a discrepancy between the ideal and actual states, and, as a result, will be seeking to facilitate resolution of the problem.

Consumer analysts have used a variety of techniques to measure consumer purchase intentions.[10] The technique that has provided marketing strategists with the most accurate information on problem recognition is the purchase-probability scale.[11] The purchase-probability technique requests that consumers estimate the probability that they will purchase a particular product or brand within a designated time period on the following type of scale.

The predictive accuracy of this method is largely attributable to the fact that it sensitively distributes consumers with different levels of purchase intentions. Consumer analysts have demonstrated that purchase-probability scales provide marketing strategists with accurate measures of problem recognition for numerous product categories, such as automobiles,[12] household appliances,[13] low-priced convenience items,[14] and several grocery-product categories.[15] The usefulness of purchase-intention information depends upon the specific product and brand in question.

Using Information on Problem-Recognition Processes: An Illustration

An executive of the General Electric Company has very ably demonstrated the usefulness of information on problem recognition in formulating marketing strategy.[16] Measures of problem recognition were obtained from members of the General Electric Consumer Panel by means of purchase-probability scales. This information was then used to identify promotional targets and allocate promotional efforts. First, the purchase-probability scale must be grouped into larger categories.

La escala de
prob. de compra

One of several possible groupings is illustrated in Table 11.1. Once the categories have been determined, the marketing analyst estimates the percentage distribution of consumers across the five categories for the firm's brand and the major competing brands. In other words, General Electric must determine what percentage of its customers are in Category I, Category II, and so on. Then, for each category, the marketing analyst must:

1. Specify the evaluative criteria used by consumers
2. Indicate the relative importance of the evaluative criteria
3. Specify the evaluation of each brand on the evaluative criteria
4. Multiply the relative importance of each criterion times the brand's rating on that criterion.

The marketing analyst uses this information to estimate the potential economic value (i.e., potential profit) of each category. If a particular category evaluated the product in question high on the evaluative criteria considered important to consumers in that category, then that category would have a higher potential than if it had evaluated the product low on those evaluative criteria. The same procedure can be used to assess the value of each category.

Once the marketing analyst has estimated the economic value of

Category	Purchase Probability Scale
I	Certain, practically certain (99 in 100)
	Almost sure (9 in 10)
II	Very probably (8 in 10)
	Probably (7 in 10)
III	Good possibility (6 in 10)
	Fairly good possibility (5 in 10)
	Fair possibility (4 in 10)
IV	Some possibility (3 in 10)
	Slight possibility (2 in 10)
V	Very slight possibility (1 in 10)
	No chance, almost no chance (1 in 100)

Table 11.1
Grouping Purchase-Probability Scales

each category, media-usage profiles can be constructed for each category and then promotional plans can be developed for specific categories. Media can be directed toward the objective of moving people up one or more category levels. Copy can be conceptualized and developed to refer to differences in brand ratings on specific evaluative criteria between users and nonusers at each category level for the firm's brand as well as for competing brands. Finally, after the marketing program has been executed, purchase-intention information can be evaluated to determine if the program has effectively moved people to a higher category of purchase intention.

The preceding discussion has illustrated how information on problem-recognition processes can be used to direct marketing efforts more effectively. The increasing competition for organizational resources will undoubtedly lead to the development of yet more sophisticated means of utilizing this information.

Attempts to Trigger Problem Recognition

It has been pointed out that marketing efforts can play a role in triggering problem recognition either by highlighting the ideal state or by showing the inadequacies of the actual state. Nevertheless, the stimulation of problem recognition through any type of marketing activity is far more difficult than it might seem from the discussion thus far. Keep in mind that each person has the ability to be completely oblivious to persuasion, that is, to see and hear what he or she *wants* to see and hear. In fact, filters tend to be closed when problem recognition is not active. The existence of an aroused motive per se makes one decidedly more responsive to relevant information. The reverse is also true.

In the final analysis, problem recognition most frequently is triggered by factors beyond the control of the marketer. Advertisements and other forms of promotion assume their greatest effectiveness following problem recognition. The best strategy, then, is to find consumers who, for one reason or another, are dissatisfied with present solutions and are receptive to something different. Then appropriate changes can be introduced in product, package, price, promotion, and distribution to capitalize on a responsive segment of prospective customers. The payout from this approach usually is greater than that achieved by attempts to stimulate problem recognition in a frequently indifferent consumer audience that is bombarded by persuasion from all sides.

Summary

The first stage in decision-process behavior is problem recognition—a perceived difference between an ideal state and an actual state of affairs. Two determinants of problem recognition are (1) motives and (2) information and experience. Following problem recognition, the consumer may "hold" and take no action or may begin the search process. Types of problem-recognition processes vary substantially in complexity. Simple problem-recognition processes are strongly learned, highly programmed, and automatic. Somewhat complicated processes are characterized by more time, more impinging factors, and more intense consumer attitudes. The highly complex processes are the infrequent, unprogrammed type that involve a considerable period of time, are affected by a number of factors, and involve strongly held attitudes.

This chapter addresses the primary factors involved in the problem-recognition process. The factors affecting the actual state are (1) the depletion of a previous solution to a problem, (2) dissatisfaction with the present solution to a problem, (3) family circumstances, and (4) marketing efforts. The factors affecting the ideal state of affairs are (1) changes in family characteristics, (2) financial considerations, (3) other decisions, (4) changes in reference groups, (5) marketing efforts, (6) novelty, and (7) motive activation. Marketers can measure problem-recognition processes by using the purchase-probability scale as shown in an example of how the General Electric Company used problem-recognition processes to improve its marketing effort.

The stimulation of problem recognition in consumers through marketing efforts is a difficult task. Because consumers have the ability to be completely oblivious to persuasion and are most responsive to relevant promotional information when they recognize a problem, the best marketing strategy is to locate those who are dissatisfied with their present solution and are open to something different.

Questions and Issues for Discussion

1. "Problem recognition is something over which marketers have no control. Therefore, the marketing manager's task is to identify the problem-recognition patterns relevant to his or her products." Do you agree?

2. The First Friendly Bank, located in Library, Michigan (population 50,000), has experienced a declining market share for the past three years. The marketing director knows that Library has a very mobile population and that First Friendly has not gotten its share of new residents, but is perplexed as to what action to take. How might an understanding of problem recognition help the marketing director?

3. Describe the problem recognition processes that might occur relative to the following products:

(a) bar soap

(b) breakfast cereal

(c) medical examination

(d) camera.

4. How does problem recognition differ from motivation, needs, and product awareness?

5. A major producer of golf clubs has just determined that the principal factors affecting problem recognition for sporting equipment products are (1) changing financial characteristics and (2) dissatisfaction with the present solution. How might the information help the producer more effectively allocate his marketing effort?

6. The Energy Research & Development Administration (ERDA) was instituting a $175,000 advertising campaign in Denver advocating the use of energy-efficient household products. The ads encouraged consumers to consider energy costs along with product costs. Denver merchants were preparing tie-in ads in the hopes that they would make consumers conscious of the cost of operating products such as hairdryers and toasters. Explain how a knowledge of the problem-recognition process could better enable the ERDA and the merchants to promote this program effectively.

7. Give two examples of desires you became aware of only after a purchase had satisfied a previous desire.

8. The National Institute for Occupational Safety and Health recently reported that a new study of beauticians and cosmetologists shows that they have a higher-than-expected incidence of six kinds of cancer. Consequently, the Food & Drug Administration is proposing that a warning label be placed on permanent hair dyes that contain the harmful substances. Although consumers are becoming increasingly concerned over the issue, the publicity has yet to lead to decreased sales. How can you explain this? One drug chain's marketing vice-president stated that younger people seem more concerned than established users. How can the FDA stimulate problem recognition in these users?

9. Identify the factors that affected problem recognition for your most recent purchase of a nondurable product, a durable product, and a service. Were the factors that affected problem recognition the same in all three instances?

10. Merit Brothers, a successful producer of quality outer apparel, recognizes that continual growth will require its penetration into new markets. The company has developed a complete line of men's leisure suits but is uncertain as to whether it can market them successfully. Explain how a purchase-probability scale can be used to give the company guidance in its marketing strategy.

Case 1. Albany Incorporated

Albany Incorporated produces a complete line of televisions that is sold throughout the United States. In the past ten years, the TV industry has experienced considerable growth that is expected to continue for some time. Over ten million units are expected to be sold this year, and Albany wishes to improve upon last year's market share of 9 percent of total dollar volume. Much to the surprise of many top management personnel, however, combined sales of Albany's 19-, 21-, and 25-inch models declined by over 14 percent in the first two quarters, causing their share of the market to drop below 8 percent. After much research, hard work, and soul-searching with his staff, Bob Monroe, Albany's marketing director, was able to identify the chief causes of his firm's unusually poor performance of recent months.

Source: Some of the information in Case 1 is from "TV Sales Are Booming, with Christmas Ahead," *Business Week*, November 21, 1977, p. 62

Of 71.2 million households in the United States, 77 percent already have color sets, and almost 32 million households have two or more working sets. Although this leaves considerable room for continued growth, pessimists conclude that total industry sales will plummet in the not-too-distant future. Monroe believes, however, that these pessimists are far from correct. First of all, he says that even though the replacement market for sets seems to have stagnated, it is likely that disposable income will continue to increase, and consumer confidence remains quite high. Second, he anticipates a surge in sales through the latter part of the year, since, historically, sales of televisions have done well as the Christmas season approaches. The replacement market, in fact, should have much potential. According to some of the research conducted by Monroe's staff, 28 million color sets now in use are at least 5 years old. Owners of these televisions are ripe prospects for current, solid state models, such as Albany's 25-inch set featuring such electronic gadgetry as wireless remote control channel switching and tuning and digital clock readouts on the picture tube. Indeed, the replacement market is the cause of much optimism in the industry. Monroe's staff estimates that 58 percent of current sales of color sets are to customers replacing their older models. Their study shows that many potential buyers are certain that new models will out-perform their older sets with greatly improved reliability. The new electronic features offered by most manufacturers have caught the attention of consumers, causing them to view their old sets as outmoded.

Monroe does not think that the problems his firm has encountered have anything to do with the overall demand for TV sets. Demand should be sufficient to sustain further growth in which Albany would like to share. Rather, he suspects that Albany's troubles lie in changes in specific demand patterns, ill-advised budget policies, and modifications in the sales strategies of rival producers.

With the advent of electronic video games, some of Albany's competitors began to induce customers to buy a new TV set by offering the game unit below cost as a "sweetener." This is one example of how some sales possibly have been lured away from Albany. Another is the "trade-in" program instituted by one giant American producer. This firm reimbursed dealers for offering $50 to $150 for any old set, operative or not, to purchasers of its 25-inch model. Two million dollars were spent on promoting the program, which apparently had devastating effects on the sales of Albany's larger models. In general, Albany's advertising budget has not kept pace with that of other producers. Despite Monroe's earlier warnings, a majority of directors, perhaps a bit euphoric over the original success and subsequent growth in sales of their television sets, decided to channel outrageous sums into the development of stereo systems, not taking into account the dangers of resting on their laurels in such a highly competitive industry. Most other American producers realized a problem that had severely threatened their positions. This was the influx of and growth in demand for foreign sets, particularly Japanese, many of which are small-screened portables and initially retailed at about $300. The price has long since risen, but, as one store manager told Monroe, even when the foreign brands are higher priced, they outsell the familiar American brands because they offer "very, very high quality."

Monroe is mindful of the small set trend. His staff report shows that the person who buys a portable set today is out of the market for the next three to four years. A small set can be conveniently moved from living room to kitchen to pool-side by the viewer. The buyer of a large console, however, is unable to move the heavy unit and will soon want a second set to move about the home. Monroe's figures indicate that the purchaser of a large set will reenter the market for a portable within 18 months.

Case 1 Questions

1. With approval from the board finally secured, Monroe and his staff plan to develop an intense promotional campaign for use in the fall through the early spring of next year. Make a recommendation to Mr. Monroe, explaining how he might use the concept of problem recognition in designing Albany's campaign. Be sure to discuss the key variables involved in problem-recognition processes, and how techniques designed to measure problem recognition can be used in the development of strategy and in monitoring the success of the campaign.

2. Identify those market segments that would probably experience problem recognition first.

Case 2. Stoko Company

The Stoko Company, a leading manufacturer of vacuum cleaners, is currently weighing the possibility of consumer acceptance of a new vacuum cleaner it wants to market, called "Soft Sweep." This product has a decibel level which is 50 percent lower than the company's other vacuum cleaners. The desire to market the product stems from the Environmental Protection Agency's (EPA) dissatisfaction with noise pollution in the home resulting from appliances.

After the EPA cracked down on the amount of noise made by portable air compressors and heavy trucks in 1975, it steered its emphasis toward the level of noise in the home. Following an investigation, it proposed to the FTC that manufacturers of home appliances, such as blenders and dishwashers, be required to label the products with the amount of noise, or decibel level, each emits. The EPA's contention was that if consumers are exposed to noise level labels, they will demand and purchase quieter brands of appliances. One spokesman declared, "For many Americans, the insidious noise associated with various labor- and time-saving devices has long been endured as an inevitable by-product of the convenience era." However, the labeling proposal is expected to change that.

The Stoko Company has recently developed its "quiet" vacuum cleaner in anticipation of the labeling proposal's acceptance, since, at the time, consumer sentiment was running 3 to 1 in favor of the program. Other manufacturers of appliances, though, are wary of the program. They question the assumption that consumers care whether one brand of appliance is noisier than another. Also, perception differs among consumers; consequently, what noise seems jarring to one consumer may not irritate another consumer at all. The manufacturers contend that consumers are more interested in utility than noise. The consequence of passage of this proposal, as they see it, is a trade-off between noise and efficiency. The manufacturer who opts to compete on the basis of noise will be forced to develop larger, bulkier products and incur increased costs. This is due to the fact that most appliance noise is the result of air circulating over the motor parts to keep them cool. If the flow of air is reduced, some compensation will have to be made to prevent overheating. The manufacturers fear the costs and burdens of additional testing or certification should the proposal be passed. EPA officials agree that appliance prices may rise due to the cost of administering the program and testing the noise levels of the products, but they argue that an efficiently designed and produced appliance need not be bulky nor contribute to the higher prices.

Manufacturers also attribute much of their reluctance to produce quieter appliances to a psychological factor—consumers tend to equate noise with power. They point out that a certain brand of vacuum cleaner was marketed in 1962 on the merits of its quietness but proved to be an utter failure because consumers thought it lacked cleaning power. They cite another case of a vacuum cleaner manufacturer who, concerned about a clicking noise in his product, surveyed customers and found that the users did not mind the noise at all; instead, they perceived the noise to be a sign that the vacuum was working.

The EPA acknowledges that consumers correlate power with noise, but asserts that consumers are also disturbed by noise. Government studies attest that 16 million Americans suffer from some degree of hearing loss directly caused by noise. Hearing specialists are becoming increasingly concerned about the amount of noise to which consumers are exposed, especially in the home where the combination of garbage disposals, mixers, and other appliances can raise the decibel level to the 80–90 range—approximately the level encountered near a major airport.

The Stoko Company realizes that it still is under no obligation to manufacture or market a less-noise vacuum cleaner. The FTC needs to work out the ground rules, such as which appliances need labeling, the information the labels should contain and how they should be displayed, and whether or not to rely initially on voluntary industry cooperation. Even if the proposal is passed, appliance manufacturers will not be mandated to produce quieter products, but will only be inconvenienced with competition in the form of noise levels. However, according to rumors, one of the first two products likely to be proposed for labels is vacuum cleaners. Also, the FTC is leaning toward a color coding or numbering system to facilitate easy comparison shopping for the average consumer. Based on this information, the Stoko Company has been confident that its new vacuum cleaner will be a success because it will be the first, or one of the first, "quiet" vacuums on the market. The company knows of no other vacuum cleaner manufacturer who is in the process of developing such a product. Thus, while other companies compete on the basis of a two- or three-decibel difference in their products, Stoko will establish itself as the leader in the "quiet" appliance trend.

To investigate more recent consumer attitudes toward less-noise appliances, the company enlisted the services of a consulting agency. The agency undertook a survey of 900 homemakers in an eastern metropolitan area in an effort to determine whether or not the homemakers had an understanding of decibel levels, if they were indeed bothered by noisy appliances, and if they would consider purchasing a relatively quiet vacuum cleaner. The following are the results of the survey.

Response	Percent of Homemakers
1. Certain or almost certain to buy a "quiet" vacuum cleaner.	4
2. Very probably or probably will buy a "quiet" vacuum cleaner.	8
3. Good, fairly good, or fair possibility of buying a "quiet" vacuum cleaner.	30
4. Some or slight possibility of buying a "quiet" vacuum cleaner.	36
5. Very slight possibility or almost no chance of buying a "quiet" vacuum cleaner.	22

The survey also revealed that 60 percent of the homemakers were aware of the decibel level encountered near an airport, but only 10 percent could estimate the approximate decibel levels of home appliances. Responses also indicated that 70 percent of the homemakers were not bothered by noisy appliances because they had learned to "tune them out." However, when the homemakers were informed by the interviewers of the noise levels of certain appliances, a majority of them showed signs of amazement and concern.

Case 2 Questions

1. How should the Stoko Company interpret the information from this survey?

2. Considering the expense of educating consumers about noise levels and the financial risk the company will incur with the introduction of "Soft Sweep," can and should Stoko attempt to stimulate problem recognition in vacuum cleaner users? Explain.

3. Identify the market segment having the most potential for initial acceptance of this product.

Notes

1. R. Ferber, "Family Decision Making and Economic Behavior," E. B. Sheldon, ed., *Family Economic Behavior: Problems and Perspectives* (Philadelphia: J. B. Lippincott Company, 1972), pp. 29-61.

2. W. D. Wells and G. Gubar, "The Life Style Concept in Marketing Research," *Journal of Marketing Research,* 3 (November 1966), pp. 355-63.

3. F. T. Juster and P. Wachtel, "Uncertainty Expectations and Durable Goods Demand Models," B. Strumpel, J. N. Morgan, and E. Zahn, eds., *Human Behavior in Economic Affairs* (San Francisco: Jossey-Bass, Inc., 1972), pp. 321-45.

4. E. Mueller, "The Desire for Innovations in Household Goods," L. Clark, ed., *Consumer Behavior: Research on Consumer Reactions* (New York: Harper & Row, Inc., 1958), p. 37.

5. Ernest Dichter, *The Strategy of Desire* (New York: Doubleday, 1960), pp. 215-20.

6. M. Venkatesan, "Cognitive Consistency and Novelty Seeking," Scott Ward and Thomas S. Robertson, eds., *Consumer Behavior: Theoretical Sources* (Englewood Cliffs, N.J.: Prentice-Hall, 1973), pp. 354-84.

7. A. H. Maslow, *Motivation and Personality* (New York: Harper & Row, 1954).

8. See Roger D. Blackwell, James F. Engel, and W. Wayne Talarzyk, *Contemporary Cases in Consumer Behavior* (Hinsdale, Ill.: The Dryden Press, 1977), pp. 350-59.

9. D. H. Granbois, "A Study of the Family Decision Making Process in the Purchase of Major Durable Household Goods," Unpublished doctoral dissertation (Bloomington, Ind.: Indiana University Graduate School of Business, 1962), p. 84.

10. F. T. Juster, *Consumer Buying Intentions and Purchase Probability* (New York: National Bureau of Economic Research, 1966).

11. D. H. Granbois and J. O. Summers, "On the Predictive Accuracy of Subjective Purchase Probabilities," in *Proceedings of the Third Annual Conference of the Association for Consumer Research* (Chicago: American Marketing Association, 1972), pp. 502-11.

12. Ibid., p. 506.

13. R. W. Pratt, Jr., "Understanding the Decision Process for Consumer Durables: An Example of the Longitudinal Approach," P. D. Bennett, ed., *Marketing and Economic Development* (Chicago: American Marketing Association, 1965), pp. 244-60.

14. A. Gruber, "Purchase Intent and Purchase Probability," *Journal of Advertising Research,* 10 (February 1970), pp. 23-27.

15. S. Banks, "The Relationship between Preference and Purchase of Brands," *Journal of Marketing,* 15 (October 1950), pp. 145-57.

16. R. W. Pratt, "Consumer Buying Intentions as an Aid in Formulating Marketing Strategy," R. L. King, ed., *Marketing and the New Science of Planning* (Chicago: American Marketing Association, 1968), pp. 296-302.

Chapter 12 Information Processing

Outline

The Foundation of Information
  Processing
The Dynamics of Information
  Processing
Exposure
Attention
Interpreting Stimuli
Sensory Overload
Reception
Comprehension
Acceptance
Response
Controlling Information Processing
Selective Information Processing
Summary
Questions and Issues for
  Discussion
Cases

Key Terms

information processing
memory
active memory
long-term memory
exposure
attention
reception
preliminary classification
analysis for pertinence
cognitive consistency
discrimination without awareness
sensory overload
novelty and contrast
comprehension
acceptance
response
selective exposure
selecive attention
selective reception

Consumers are regularly exposed to a variety of stimuli from a number of sources. In fact, the stimuli, or sensory inputs, that confront a consumer are so numerous that some would contend that processing these inputs is one of our most encompassing activities. Interpreting these stimuli and assigning them meaning is a complex process that must be understood in order to function effectively in the contemporary marketing environment.

Consider the following situation. A ruggedly handsome man perched high on his horse overlooks the cattle-branding taking place in the distance. He slowly, deliberately puts a cigarette to his lips, draws deeply, and exhales, exuding satisfaction. The music, the setting, the man, even his steady gaze, combine to suggest a macho experience associated with smoking this brand of cigarettes. This advertisement with numerous variations has contributed to the tremendous success of a well-known brand of cigarettes. Yet there is another market segment, a rapidly growing one, that abhors such advertisements. Slogans such as "I don't spit in your face, please don't blow smoke in mine" and "smoking should be confined to consenting adults in private" have emerged among this segment. Further evidence of this segment's reaction is the fact that nearly all 50 states, over 100 cities, 25 counties, and 15 universities have some kind of ban on smoking. How can two segments have such totally different reactions to the same stimulus?

Consider the experience of CBS when, in the early 1970s, it introduced "All in the Family" featuring Archie Bunker. Assuming that the program would be perceived as a satire on bigotry, it seemed reasonable to predict that most people would see Archie for what he is—highly prejudiced and narrow minded. Yet, an audience survey indicated that many saw Archie as a hero.[1] These people, on the whole, embraced the same patterns of prejudice, whereas those who were not prejudiced had quite an opposite reaction.

Now what happened here? Both groups received exactly the same message, but their responses were polar opposites. One thing becomes clear immediately—the audience is *not* just a group of passive recipients. Each person actively processes and interprets information in a unique way. In fact, people tend to see and hear what they want to see and hear, as is demonstrated by the fact that only 44 percent of those exposed to the thousands of print advertisements analyzed by the Starch readership service noticed a particular ad, 35 percent read enough to identify the brand, and only 9 percent said they read most of the ad.[2] Obviously, only a small proportion of advertising is fully perceived at any given point in time, thus demonstrating the *selectivity* of information processing.

Information processing refers to the process by which a sensory input is transformed, reduced, elaborated, stored, recovered, and used by a consumer. This complex process begins with exposure and progresses to attention, message reception, and attitudinal or behavioral change. Moreover, it will be demonstrated that the individual is quite capable of resisting persuasion and that there is no "magic power" available for the seller or advertiser to use.

The Foundation of Information Processing

Memory, long recognized as an important cognitive process, is now considered to provide the basic foundation for consumer information processing. The central processing unit, reproduced in Figure 12.1, in effect, depicts memory in its totality. The component labeled active memory functions as a temporary storage. Active memory is similar to a desk top. All sorts of things are assembled on the desk surface when a person is working on a problem and later are put away. In active memory, incoming information and the information stored in long-term memory are brought together. It is here that new input is categorized and interpreted.

Not everything contained in long-term memory is available for use in active memory. There appear to be two basic factors determining

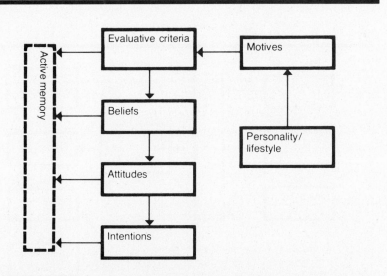

Figure 12.1
The Components of a Consumer's Memory

Source: James F. Engel, Roger D. Blackwell, and David T. Kollat, *Consumer Behavior*, 3rd ed. (Hinsdale, Ill.: Dryden Press, 1978), p. 338. Copyright © 1978 by Dryden Press, a division of Holt, Rinehart and Winston. Reprinted by permission of Holt, Rinehart and Winston.

what information is used in active memory. First, there are differences in the extent to which new information is analyzed. The more extensively a consumer analyzes information, the higher the probability that the information will be retained in long-term memory.[3] The second factor is the extent to which the contents of memory are recirculated and used both in problem solving and the interpretation of new information.[4] The less an item is used, the more difficult it becomes to retrieve that item.

The important consideration for anyone concerned with influencing consumer behavior, whether for purposes of education or for commercial gain, is to ascertain that the information presented does move from active memory into long-term memory where it has a chance to shape future behavior.

The Dynamics of Information Processing

Information processing, depicted in Figure 12.2, consists of four interrelated stages. The first stage is the actual *exposure* and activation of sensory processes. *Attention,* the second stage, has been attracted

Figure 12.2
**The Stages in
Information Processing**

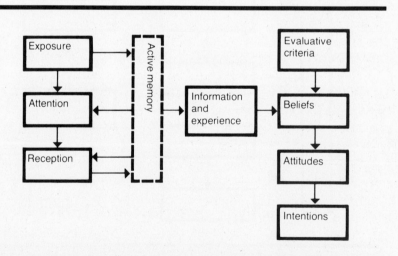

Source: James F. Engel, Roger D. Blackwell, David T. Kollat, *Consumer Behavior,* 3rd ed. (Hinsdale, Ill.: Dryden Press, 1978), p. 339. Copyright © 1978 by Dryden Press, a division of Holt, Rinehart and Winston. Reprinted by permission of Holt, Rinehart and Winston.

when a stimulus moves into conscious active memory. Attracting attention is a necessary but not sufficient condition for a message to be received and comprehended *(reception)* in the manner intended by the sender. In fact, the item that enters long-term memory may differ substantially from the item that was sent because of the consumer's capacity to modify it. The fourth stage, *response* (depicted in Figure 12.2 as new information and experience), refers to the change that occurs in beliefs, attitudes, or intentions.

Exposure

Exposure, the initial phase of information processing, occurs when an individual is confronted with a stimulus that activates his or her senses. The senses transport the stimulus energy to the brain, which generates the sensations of sight, hearing, smell, touch, or taste. This phenomenon seems simple enough and the application for the marketing manager straightforward. Unfortunately, this is not the case. The principal difficulty confounding exposure is that people selectively expose themselves to stimuli. That is, consumers do not indiscriminately expose themselves to stimuli; rather, they are selective about the information to which they permit themselves to be exposed. The marketer's efforts to disseminate information to consumers is further complicated by the fact that selective exposure is particularly pronounced in the case of persuasive communications. For example, research has indicated that there is a relationship between whether or not a person smokes and the reading of articles that expound a relationship between smoking and cancer. In one study in particular, 67 percent of the nonsmokers, versus 44 percent of smokers, claimed high readership of the articles.[5]

Exposure occurs from physical proximity to a stimulus input such that the individual has direct opportunity for one or more senses to be activated. This very commonsense principle of media selection is more difficult to implement than it might appear, however, because the first step is a very precise definition of target audience. It will not do, for example, to say that the target market for Friskie's dry cat food is all families that have a cat as a pet. Obviously any consumer has a variety of options in feeding a pet, and it will be necessary to determine beforehand exactly the types of people who prefer both dry food and this particular brand. Next, research must disclose which media will actually reach this particular audience. The data might reveal that the best prospects for Friskie's dry cat food are owners of "alley" cats, have relatively large families, reside in suburbs, prefer the convenience of dry cat food, and are heavy viewers of family-oriented television shows. With this information, all things being equal, the marketer at least stands a chance of delivering the message to the potential customer.

Consumer analysts are not in agreement as to the reason consumers selectively expose themselves to communications. Some consumer analysts contend that selective exposure results from the consumer's desire to avoid information that is inconsistent with existing beliefs and dispositions.[6] Other analysts contend that factors such as education and background cause people to process information selectively. In any event, selective exposure is a problem with which the marketing strategist must contend, because the actual audience almost always is smaller than the desired audience. Thus, the marketing strategist must carefully evaluate the media exposure patterns of his or her target market to achieve the greatest possible exposure for the firm's communications.

Attention

Attention is defined as the conscious end product of a complex process whereby an incoming stimulus is categorized and given initial meaning. More formally, attention is the active processing of exposed information stimuli such that a conscious impression is made.

Interpreting Stimuli

Stimuli that consumers are exposed to enter active memory for further processing. This processing consists of two stages: (1) preliminary classification and (2) analysis for pertinence. Preliminary classification is based primarily on sensory factors, whereas analysis for pertinence accepts or rejects stimuli on the basis of their utility to that consumer at that point in time.

Preliminary Classification

Preliminary classification refers to the triggering of an initial response when a consumer is presented with a new stimulus. This triggering may take the form of a turning direction, a growing sense of alertness, and so on. That is, preliminary classification prepares the consumer for contending with a new stimulus and mobilizes him or her for action. Essentially, then, it is the process by which stimuli are analyzed for meaning largely on such physical properties as loudness, pitch, and so on.[7] This preliminary analysis is assisted by learned tendencies to organize and categorize stimuli based on physical properties.

Figure 12.3 is an illustration of the tendency consumers have to organize stimuli. Does the illustration contain rows of dots or columns of dots? Because the dots are closer together in the horizontal direction, most people report seeing rows; that is, the horizontal dots are recognized as being in closer proximity. There is a widespread tendency to organize objects in proximity and to interpret them in this manner.

Figure 12.3
An Illustration of Proximity

An understanding of preliminary classification can substantially benefit the marketing strategist. For example, the marketer must realize that consumers tend to assign similar quality evaluations to products in proximity. Thus, if a low-quality product is stocked by a retailer to offer a low-price alternative to the consumer, that product may affect the evaluations of other merchandise in the store's product line. Indeed, if maintaining a high-quality evaluation is desired, it may benefit the merchant not to handle the low-quality product or perhaps to separate it physically or, in some manner other than just price, distinguish the low-quality product from the high-quality product line. This is a partial explanation for why many department stores set aside whole floors for their "bargain" merchandise.

Analysis for Pertinence

Analysis for pertinence refers to the process of determining whether or not a stimulus is pertinent to a consumer. Countless stimuli vie for classification at any given moment. One authority gives the following estimates: (1) information comes into the central nervous system from over 260 million visual cells alone; (2) 48,000 cells are available for auditory perception; (3) the other senses each have at least 78,000 receptor cells; and (4) it would take a brain the size of a cubic light-year to process the information received by the eyes alone.[8] Obviously, there are distinct limits on processing capacity, and the analysis for pertinence functions to restrict entry only to those stimuli that have relevance.

After a stimulus has undergone preliminary classification, it is further processed to determine its pertinence for the consumer. Whereas preliminary classification is an almost automatic and undirected screening, the evaluation of a stimulus' relevance to a consumer is internally directed and more complex. The stimuli that emerge from this analysis are those perceived pertinent to the consumer given the present circumstances. Consumer analysts have identified numerous factors that affect the determination of pertinence; however, the following are particularly important.

1. The influence of need states. The consumer's predominant needs, both physical and psychological, substantially affect the stimuli perceived to be important and, consequently, to require further processing. For example, hungry people are most likely to give food-related responses when ambiguous stimuli are seen or heard. Furthermore, the hungry consumer will more readily attend to food advertisements than will a nonhungry counterpart. Similarly, an appeal to social acceptance through avoidance of body odor will be more readily noticed by those who fear social rejection.

Thus, the marketing strategist should, to the extent possible, identify market segments that are experiencing a high need state for his or her generic product or perhaps identify conditions that are associated with a high need state. A household with a new baby typically experiences a high need for the many products required to provide proper care. Marketing communications about such products, which are directed to this consuming unit, will have a better chance of being attended to and, thus, a better possibility of being comprehended.

2. *The influence of values.* The consumer's values have a substantial effect on whether or not a stimulus is passed on for further information processing. Researchers have demonstrated that stimuli consistent with a consumer's values are more quickly recognized and more likely to be attended to than are stimuli inconsistent with a consumer's values. Thus, the marketing strategist might reasonably conclude that preferred brand names will be recognized more quickly than nonpreferred brands.[9] This explains why certain advertisements are noticed more quickly than others. The key appears to lie in the extent to which the brand name is featured. Whereas a stimulus that is consistent with an individual's values is likely to be evaluated as pertinent and, consequently, attended to, a stimulus that reflects something with low value is likely to be avoided. In other words, consumers establish barriers to prevent or inhibit their attending to stimuli that have little or no value for them. Thus, if a consumer has a low regard for foreign-made automobiles, he or she will be less likely to notice advertisements featuring foreign automobiles than those featuring domestically produced automobiles. The marketing strategist must carefully direct communications to focus, to the extent possible, on segments that have assigned a favorable value to the brand.

3. *The influence of cognitive consistency.* The components within the central processing unit interact to form an individual's cognitive structure. This cognitive structure functions to enable the individual to cope with his or her environment by attending to stimuli that are consistent with the central processing unit. For example, assume that a consumer opposed to the consumption of alcoholic beverages is exposed to an advertisement urging him or her to consume Budweiser beer. Even though such an advertisement may receive preliminary classification, the consumer is fully capable of screening out this stimulus, probably on the grounds of no pertinence. Attending to this ad could produce a state of inconsistency that would be psychologically uncomfortable and, thus, contrary to the consumer's tendency

to maintain consistency with the components of the central processing unit.[10]

In summary, the marketing strategist must recognize that consumers selectively attend to marketing stimuli. The consumer may observe an advertisement out of the "corner of his eye," engage in preliminary classification, and then redirect attention accordingly. The consumer may be committed to a brand or store and, hence, resist a challenge to his or her preference. Consequently, the effective allocation of marketing effort necessitates an understanding of the needs, values, and attitudes of the consumers for whom the effort is intended. For instance, the National Society for the Prevention of Drug Abuse would be wise to study these aspects among potential drug abusers in order to determine the types of messages and communicators to which this segment of society would listen.

Discrimination without Awareness

Discrimination without awareness, more technically called subliminal perception, refers to the contention that consumers can be influenced by stimuli of which they are not consciously aware. The first test of this in an advertising context was in the late 1950s. The words "Drink Coke" and "Eat Popcorn" were presumably flashed on a movie screen at speeds well beyond the conscious awareness of audience members. Technically, it would be said that the presentation was subliminal or below the threshold at which conscious discrimination is possible—hence the term subliminal perception. The sale of Coca-Cola allegedly increased 57.7 percent, whereas the sale of popcorn increased 18.1 percent. In reality, these findings have unanimously been dismissed as being invalid, and all attempts at replication of that particular experiment have failed. Although the notion of subliminal perception was soundly rejected in the 1960s, some researchers and social critics still maintain that subliminal perception is a reality.[11] The mere mention of influencing consumers at a subconscious level raises images of "Big Brother" and the specter of the "hidden persuaders." These fears of unconscious manipulation of people are groundless. Indeed, it is possible for us to engage in preliminary classification and the analysis for pertinence without conscious awareness of being so engaged. However, the entry of unwanted stimuli is still barred, which should put to rest any fears.

Sensory Overload

As Alvin Toffler pointed out so graphically in *Future Shock,* this is an overcommunicative era in which persuaders of all types outdo themselves to attract attention.[12] Literally, the consumer is bombarded on all sides. Estimates of the number of commercial messages confronting the average individual each day range from 250 to 2000, giving rise to what is known more technically as *sensory overload.* It is quite possible that a given message will not capture attention simply because it is "lost in the noise."

The sensory overload problem is accentuated by the fact that most advertisers use the technique of repetition. One recently conceived tactic of increasing the exposure of advertising messages to the public is the use of miniature billboards that are strategically placed on shopping carts to serve as last-minute "reminders" to consumers. Perhaps the most blatant use of repetition, however, is the broadcasting of radio commercials in supermarkets. This method has been unsuccessful in the past, but one company is optimistic that it has finally developed the technology to make this approach feasible.

To avoid being lost in the crowd, the advertiser often must exercise creative ingenuity. Various attention-attracting devices may, on the surface, appear to be gimmicks, but their sole purpose is to do nothing more than capture attention. Once attention is attracted, the message itself takes over and determines the degree of success in the remaining stages of information processing. Three such devices are (1) novelty and contrast, (2) manipulation of intensity through variations in size and position of the message, and (3) use of color.

Novelty and Contrast

One well-known example of the use of novelty and contrast is the Chiquita brand banana advertisements, which usually depict the banana in such a way that it stands out clearly against its background. By using the novelty of standing the banana on end, for example, the advertiser is more likely to capture consumers' attention. This, of course, says nothing about the persuasive power of the message. The following are a few techniques of using novelty and contrast.

1. A black-and-white advertisement featuring an unusual amount of white space with no print or illustration can stand out clearly when competitive messages are in color.

2. An unusually shaped package captures attention when all others on a shelf are similar in design, shape, and color.

3. The announcer's voice advertising a product during a break in a classical music program is likely to be noticed because of the sharp contrast in stimulus.

Size and Position

Size and position of communications are also frequently used to enhance message reception. Research on the impact of size and position suggest the following generalizations for marketing strategists:

1. Increasing the size of an advertisement increases its impact, but less than proportionately.[13]

2. Readership of newspaper and magazine advertisements is not related to the side of the page (left or right) on which an ad appears.[14]

3. The greatest readership in magazines is usually attracted by advertisements on the covers or in the first 10 percent of the pages, but beyond this point, location is a minor factor.[15]

4. Position on the page has no effect except when there are many competing advertisements on that page, in which case the upper right-hand position offers an advantage in newspapers.[16]

Color

Marketing strategists have also come to recognize that, if used effectively, color can enhance message reception considerably. For example, color television commercials are, on the average, 50 percent more effective as measured by message recognition than are the same television commercials in black and white. Similarly, color newspaper advertisements have a much higher readership than do black and white advertisements. Consider the following generalizations:

1. Contemporary social trends have encouraged experimentation with color in all phases of life, ranging from the factory to the home. Thus, people have become responsive to innovative color stimuli.

2. Most products (especially food) look better in color.

3. Color can be used to create moods, ranging from the somber appeal of dark colors to the freshness of greens and blues.

Attention can be measured in a number of ways. The most common method involves exposing prospects to one or more messages under conditions that range from three or four advertisements in some type of booklet to full-scale exposure to the actual media. Respondents are then asked to indicate the messages they recall. While this method actually measures retention, it is argued that everyone who recalls an advertisement must have attended to it. Therefore, this method yields a conservative estimate of attention to a stimulus, since more people attend to a stimulus than recall it. Almost anyone can verify this assertion by considering the number of occasions in which he or she has been told witty jokes and has been unable to remember them a short time later.

Among the methods designed to measure attention more directly, the galvanic skin response (GSR) and the pupil dilation response (PDR) are attracting the most attention. GSR measures two phenomena: (1) the decline in the electrical resistance of the skin to a passage of current and (2) the change in the potential difference between two areas of body surface.[17] When GSR increases upon exposure to a stimulus, it is considered an indicator of *arousal*. PDR, on the other hand, measures minute differences in size as the pupil dilates and contracts. Recent studies document that PDR is a sensitive measure of the amount of information or load processed within the central processing unit from the incoming stimulus.

Reception

The fact that a stimulus has successfully attracted attention does not mean that it will be processed further in the manner intended by the sender. Whether or not it will actually be received and processed into long-term memory depends upon the accurate comprehension and acceptance of the stimuli.

Comprehension

The comprehension of marketing stimuli is affected substantially by the fact that consumers frequently assign meaning to a stimulus in a way that deviates from objective reality. That is, a consumer can attend to a marketer's communication and yet obtain ideas substantially different from those intended to be conveyed. Although there are many ways in which this can take place, two are particularly important to marketing strategists: (1) distortion of physical stimuli properties and (2) miscomprehension of communication message content.

Several studies in the past 25 years have indicated that consumers cannot distinguish among the physical properties of cola beverages (Coca-Cola, Pepsi Cola, and R. C. Cola) when the brand name is not identified.[18] Even when lesser known brands were included, consumers were unable to identify correctly the well-known brands. However, when the brand name of a cola beverage is identified, consumers contend that they can detect taste differences and frequently express strong brand preferences. Similar results have been obtained with respect to products such as beer[19] and turkey.[20] This research indicates that consumers can attend to a marketer's communication or even consume a product and yet comprehend only the information consistent with their central processing unit. In other words, consumers modify or distort information they attend to in order to make it more consistent with their personal preferences and, therefore, less disruptive.

This type of distortion frequently occurs in consumer decision making. For example, when the soft drink Twink was introduced, the company experienced sales well below the estimated potential.[21] A taste test was conducted in which labeled and unlabeled samples of this brand and competitive brands were compared. The findings indicated that Twink received excellent ratings in comparison with others when it was unlabeled. The ratings were completely reversed, however, when the brands were identified. It appears that the product image, name, or some other consideration affected taste ratings. As a result, the promotional program was totally revamped while the product formulation was left unchanged. The marketing strategist must be aware of the distortions that are likely to take place with respect to his or her product and develop the product name, image, and promotional program accordingly.

We all have expectations about the content of the stimuli confronting us, and frequently our reaction to a stimulus reflects the expectation rather than the stimulus itself. For example, a liquid cold remedy was introduced in a test market in an attempt to make inroads into the market share of Vicks Nyquil. The advertisements used in the promotional campaign were very similar to those employed by Nyquil, and there was considerable evidence that consumers thought that they were viewing Nyquil ads. Their familiarity with Nyquil produced certain expectations, and, as a result, they miscomprehended the competitor's promotional efforts. The miscomprehension of message content frequently occurs to prevent disturbance of existing preferences and dispositions, particularly if consumers are reasonably satisfied with the brand they are now using. The numerous mechanisms that produce this distortion require that the marketer identify the market segment for which the message is intended and then pretest the message to determine if the target market has a tendency to miscomprehend the message being given.

Acceptance

The correct comprehension of a marketing message does not guarantee that the message will be accepted into long-term memory by the consumer. Acceptance is, of course, a vital stage since a message must be accepted into long-term memory to affect the consumer's behavior. There is convincing evidence that acceptance is more likely when the consumer's beliefs and attitudes are consistent with those contained in the message. When the position advocated in the marketing communication is contrary to that held by the consumer, many outcomes are possible. For example, a long-time smoker may simply discredit the validity of the American Cancer Society's claims that cigarette smoking causes cancer.

The two components of reception—comprehension and acceptance—are measured separately. Comprehension is widely tested by advertisers through some type of recall procedure. The preferred method is to place test messages within, for example, a magazine or television program and then to allow for exposure under completely natural conditions. Recognition or recall is assessed at some period after exposure, usually within 24 hours.

One well-known advertising agency uses a magazine created to duplicate the format of a general-interest magazine. Interviewers place it in homes and people are asked to read it at their leisure. Follow-up interviews are designed to measure recall and comprehension. Recall is measured by the percentage of respondents who give aided or unaided identification of the brand and demonstrate some knowledge of the message. Comprehension is measured by the respondent's ability to state the actual intended message of the advertisement.

Response

The final stage of information processing is the entry of new information into long-term memory. (See Figure 12.2.) As was true with the three previous stages of information processing, consumers are highly selective about the information they retain. Only a limited amount of information that is attended to and comprehended is retained in the consumer's memory. Consumer analysts have determined that the factors influencing the consumer's decision to retain information are basically the same as those affecting the decision to attend to information. Perhaps the key factor affecting the decision to retain information is the pertinence the information has for the consumer. Only information that is judged to be pertinent to the consumer's needs and existing dispositions is retained, and even such information will be forgotten without some reinforcement. As a result, information that the consumer judges to be threatening to his or her cognitive consistency can easily be kept from permanent, or long-term, memory. Thus, the marketing strategist who seeks to get consumers to retain a message about a brand other than their preferred brand faces an imposing task.

There is no question that marketing stimuli are rapidly forgotten after the initial exposure. For example, only 24 percent of respondents in a study could name at least one advertised product on a television show; fewer than one third could identify a commercial appearing within less than two minutes prior to an interview; and residual recall of commercial content after a longer period levels off at 12 percent or less.[22] This is not surprising because advertising stimuli, by and large, are only marginally pertinent to the consumer in most viewing or listening situations. It is also possible that existing brand or product preferences are protected through failure to recall contradictory stimuli, in which case prevention of cognitive inconsistency could be another explanation, but this failure is likely to function in only a minority of situations.

Controlling Information Processing

Perhaps the aspect of information processing of greatest concern to consumers is the notion that propagandists can control what information is actually processed. From the discussion thus far, it is apparent that consumers control their information processing and have an effective system of defense against unwanted persuasion. The key point to note is that consumers resist change in strongly held beliefs and attitudes and do so through selective information processing. Consumers are particularly selective about information relative to strongly held beliefs and attitudes, which are likely to exist when the subject matter is related to an individual's self-concept (high commitment). The response can be quite different under conditions of low commitment.

Selective Information Processing

Selective information processing is most likely to occur when a consumer is confronted with a large number of distinguishing characteristics among the available alternatives and when these characteristics are particularly important.[23] Under these conditions, the consumer's active memory functions as a filter and triggers selective information processing; that is, it triggers selective exposure, selective attention, and selective reception.

Selective Exposure

Contrary to the fear of many consumer advocates (and the desire of many advertisers) consumers avoid, filter out, and, in general, resist information contrary to their beliefs and attitudes by simply not exposing themselves to it. That is, consumers shield their beliefs and attitudes from contrary information and seek out supportive information. For example, the consumer who considers professional boxing a brutal, dehumanizing "sport" does not watch it on television or subscribe to *Ring* magazine.

Selective Attention

Consumers selectively attend to information, particularly when the information is in the form of advertising. Indeed, many advertisements register either a negative impression or no impression at all.[24] Consider, for example, the case of Beth Johnson who, at one time, was considering the purchase of a microwave range but has recently become concerned about the adverse publicity regarding possible radiation effects. Such publicity would undoubtedly have an adverse effect on Beth's beliefs and attitudes about radar ranges. What is likely to happen when she is exposed to the advertisement in Figure 12.4? While the advertisement is likely to receive preliminary processing for its physical properties, the analysis for pertinence would very likely prevent further information processing. This would occur because, like most consumers, Beth would like to maintain cognitive consistency.

When beliefs and attitudes are strongly held, as is assumed to be the case here, there is little the communicator can do to overcome selective attention. This is especially true when mass media are used because there is no way to modify the message and, in effect, try again. In face-to-face communication, on the other hand, there is instant feedback of response and the opportunity to rephrase the content. A skillful salesperson, then, can be successful in countering a strongly held belief, but this success is not possible through advertising.

The logical strategy for the mass marketer is to direct efforts, insofar as possible, to people who already are neutral or even sympathetic toward the content and to avoid those who are not. The probability of inroads into this latter group usually is not worth the effort. This fact is the underlying rationale for the concept of market segmentation. Another possibility is to search for those consumers whose beliefs are wavering for one reason or another. Perhaps there is dissatisfaction with a competitor because of poor performance. This could underscore

Figure 12.4
**Appeal to Strongly Held
Beliefs and Attitudes**

the Roper Microwave does it all . . . your way!

WARMS
LO-SIMMERS
HI-SIMMERS
ROASTS
RE-HEATS
DEFROSTS

Step right into the exciting world of microwave magic . . . but don't change your cooking style! The Roper Micro-Select control matches the cooking speed to what your recipe calls for . . . to make fast microwave cooking even more efficient. You can warm rolls, sandwiches, snacks in seconds. Lo-simmer your soups. The browning dish gives steaks and chops that beautifully-browned appearance. Special defrost cycle makes freezer-to-table preparation fast . . . with no fuss or muss. Big, bright interior even holds a 22-pound turkey. If you haven't experienced the delightful difference of microwave magic . . . try the Roper Microwave, *your way!*

Your Roper Dealer has three countertop Roper Microwaves, a combination wall oven, and an eye-level Microwave with a self-cleaning lower oven to show you.

*America's cooking specialists
with a century-plus tradition
for quality and reliability!*

KANKAKEE, ILLINOIS 60901

Source: Reproduced by permission of Roper Sales Corp., Kankakee, Illinois.

a profitable market opportunity and signify an "open perceptual fil-ter."

Another way for marketing organizations to overcome the problem of selective attention is through the practice of what might be called "controlled exposure." With this technique, consumers are placed in situations in which they have little or no choice but to give their attention to the message. In one such example, a real estate firm invites potential customers to a free meal and then makes a highly concentrated presentation during the meal concerning real estate de-velopment in Florida. The consumer is in a room with no windows and few distractions other than the sales presentation itself. While this tactic may be highly debatable from an ethical point of view given the frequency of fraudulent real estate deals, many variants exist in the form of beauty seminars, cooking schools, sewing classes, and the like in which consumers must attend to the message because of the situation. Indeed, some presentations can be made highly at-tractive to consumers, such as a recent series of breakfast seminars launched by Bonwit Teller in an effort to lure new women customers to its Manhattan store. The seminars featured such notable personal-ities as the editor-in-chief of Vogue magazine and designers Diane von Furstenberg and Bill Blass. Tickets were sold out quickly, indi-cating an enthusiasm about the presentation that would aid in con-sumer receptivity to the promotional messages.

Selective Reception

Consumers also maintain control of their information processing by selectively accepting and comprehending information. This is accom-plished by regularly comprehending information consistent with their viewpoint and misinterpreting information discrepant with their viewpoint. In certain instances, consumers reject the message source, the content, or both as being biased.

Returning to our consumer, Beth, and the ad for microwave ranges, it is possible that Beth will attend to the ad but will com-pletely distort the message in order to conclude that the product is inferior. Moreover, acceptance certainly could be prevented if she were to conclude that "advertisers are always biased anyway." Thus, exposure and attraction of attention by no means insure that the message will be perceived as the advertiser intends.

The extent of selective information processing is clearly documented in the data reproduced in Table 12.1. Does this selection occur because consumers are protecting their beliefs and attitudes against cognitive inconsistency? That is, does a consumer avoid or misperceive an advertisement, such as Figure 12.4, because he or she is committed to a competitive brand? The point is that commitment in the sense discussed above is not present in all or even most consumer buying situations. Some experts would contend that consumer apathy and outright boredom are more tenable explanations for the ineffectiveness of advertisements. Clearly, many messages are rejected because of indifference. Remember that hundreds of commercial stimuli are vying for consumers' attention each day. Many of them are simply lost in the noise because of consumers' limited ability to process information.

Magazines		Television	
Number of Ads	Recall Range %	Number of Ads	Recall Range (%)
Tires			
13	0– 3.9	13	0– 3.9
21	4– 7.9	5	4– 7.9
11	8–11.9	5	8–11.9
2	12–15.9	4	12–15.9
3	16–19.9		
2	24–27.9		
2	28–31.9		
Automobiles			
20	0– 1.9	49	0– 1.9
33	2– 3.9	29	2– 3.9
47	4– 5.9	19	4– 5.9
27	6– 7.9	6	6– 7.9
12	8– 9.9	4	8– 9.9
7	10–11.9	2	10–11.9
7	12–13.9	2	12–13.9
1	14–15.9	4	14–15.9
1	16–17.9	1	16
1	18–19.9		
3	20–21.9		
3	22–23.9		
1	24		
Life insurance			
24	0– 1.9	8	0– 1.9
23	2– 3.9	13	2– 3.9
10	4– 5.9	7	4– 5.9
2	6– 7.9	5	6– 7.9
1	8– 9.9	3	8– 9.9
		1	10–11.9
		1	14–15.9
		1	18–19.9
			20–21.9

Table 12.1
Registration of Featured Idea: Recall after 24 Hours

Table 12.1
(continued)

Magazines		Television	
Number of Ads	Recall Range %	Number of Ads	Recall Range (%)
TV sets			
5	0– 1.9	6	0– 1.9
6	2– 3.9	9	2– 3.9
4	4– 5.9	4	4– 5.9
4	6– 7.9	3	6– 7.9
3	8– 9.9	1	8– 9.9
1	10–11.9	3	10–11.9
2	12–13.9	2	12–13.9
1	14–15.9	1	14–15.9
1	18–19.9	3	16–17.9
Aftershaves, colognes			
2	0– 3.9	7	0– 3.9
10	4– 7.9	4	4– 7.9
3	8–11.9	3	8–11.9
1	12–15.9	2	12–15.9
1	16–19.9	1	16–19.9
1	20–23.9	3	24–27

Source: *Advertising Age* (April 12, 1971), p. 52. Reprinted with permission from the April 12, 1971, issue of *Advertising Age.* Copyright 1971 by Crain Communications, Inc.

Summary

Information processing refers to the process by which a sensory input is transformed, reduced, elaborated, stored, recovered, and used by a consumer. Memory, now considered to provide the basic foundation for consumer information processing, consists of a long-term component for more permanent storage and an active component where incoming information and the information stored in long-term memory are brought together and the new input is categorized and interpreted. The extent to which new information is analyzed and the intent to which the contents of memory are recirculated for use in problem solving and interpretation of new information determine what information is retained and used in active memory. To someone concerned with influencing consumer behavior, the important consideration is whether or not the information presented moves from active memory into long-term memory where it can act to shape future behavior.

Exposure, the first phase of information processing, occurs when an individual is confronted with a stimulus that activates his or her senses. Consumers may selectively expose themselves to stimuli. Thus, the marketing strategist must precisely define the target audience and its media exposure patterns to achieve the greatest possible exposure for the firm's communications.

Attention, the second phase of information processing, is the active processing of exposed information stimuli such that a conscious impression is made. This processing consists of two stages. The first, preliminary classification, is the process by which stimuli are analyzed for meaning largely on the basis of physical properties. The second, analysis for pertinence, refers to the process of determining whether or not a stimulus has relevance for the consumer. Some important factors that affect the determination of pertinence are the influences of need states, values, and the consistency of the consumer's cognitive structure.

Discrimination without awareness, or subliminal perception, refers to the contention that consumers can be influenced by stimuli of which they are not consciously aware. This notion was strongly rejected during the 1960s, but those who maintain that it is a reality should bear in mind that the consumer is able to bar unwanted stimuli from further processing during the analysis for pertinence of stimuli to which he or she is exposed.

The average individual is confronted with 250 to 2000 commercial messages each day. This is known technically as sensory overload. Its significance for marketers is that messages may not capture attention simply because they are "lost in the noise." Repetition can erode the ability to attract attention, but three devices that marketers can use in their messages to attract attention are the use of novelty and contrast, size and positioning of the communication, and the use of color. Attention can be measured in a number of ways. The most widely used method involves exposing prospects to one or more messages under varying conditions and then asking them to indicate which ones they recall. This method, albeit indirect, yields a conservative measure of attention to a stimulus. More direct measures include the galvanic skin response (GSR) and the pupil dilation response (PDR).

Attracting attention is a necessary but not sufficient condition for a message to be processed further in the manner intended by the sender. Further processing depends on accurate comprehension and acceptance of the stimuli. That is, the marketer must ensure to the fullest extent possible that his or her target market will not assign a meaning to the communication which deviates from the intended meaning, and that the consumer will accept the message into long-term memory.

Response, the final stage of information processing, refers to the change that occurs in the beliefs, attitudes, and intentions of the consumer. It should be kept in mind that consumers are capable of a high degree of selectivity at all stages of information processing. They are able to block all stages of information processing. For example, they are able to block unwanted stimuli through selective exposure, attention, reception, and selective control over the entry of new information into long-term memory. This is especially true where strongly held beliefs and attitudes are related to the subject matter.

Questions and Issues for Discussion

1. Comment on the following statement: "Because exposure is the initial stage of consumer information processing, the marketing strategist should focus most of his or her efforts on it to achieve maximum exposure."

2. Shasta Beverages, Inc., wants to increase its 3-percent share of the soft drink market to 12 percent by 1983. Even though it competes on price with private-label and regional brands, its nationwide distribution forces the company to compete with Coke, Pepsi, 7-Up, Dr Pepper, and R. C. Cola. The company wants to increase consumer awareness of its full line of flavors as an alternative to cola and lemon-lime products. How can an understanding of consumer information processes help the company develop an effective promotional strategy? How can consumer selectivity hinder Shasta's attempts at increasing awareness of its brand?

3. In a recent consumer survey on the believability of company slogans, over 50 percent of the respondents rated "Kodak makes your pictures count" and Hallmark's "When you care enough to send the very best" as being credible. Those not scoring well included J. C. Penney's "The last battery your car will ever need" and Pan Am's "We go further than anyone to please our passengers." To what information processing factors can this poor reaction be attributed? How can J. C. Penney and Pan Am increase the believability of their slogans?

4. Describe three strategies that a marketer could implement to overcome selective attention by consumers toward his or her product.

5. Consumers are becoming increasingly irritated with the airline industry because of jammed telephone reservation lines that are the result of a baffling array of discount fares offered with complex restrictions. The multitude of complicated fares confuses many customers and is causing increased discontent among those who spend half an hour on the telephone trying to understand which fare offers the best bargain. How can the airline industry use a knowledge of consumer information processing to develop a more effective program?

6. Discuss the fears of some people that consumers can be manipulated by propagandists who can control what information is actually processed. Do you think this would be possible for a group who decided to advocate its collectivist philosophy through the mass media in the United States? Would it be possible for the manufacturers of children's toys?

7. Charles Johnson, advertising director of a small savings and loan company in Chicago, has recently introduced an advertising campaign modeled after the campaign of a very large and successful Chicago bank. Based on your understanding of consumer information processing, is the campaign likely to be successful? Why or why not?

8. Matchbook advertising, which is felt by its proponents to offer excellent and nearly continuous exposure of an advertising message, has been adopted by a machine tool manufacturer. Boxes of the matches will be distributed to the firm's potential clients by its salespeople as they make their rounds. How would you appraise this strategy? What could this firm do to augment the effectiveness of this strategy?

9. Pancake Syrup Incorporated has recently developed and introduced a totally new pancake syrup called "Sweet-n-Thick." The laboratory taste tests indicated that the product would be well received by consumers. Unfortunately, this has not been the case. What possible explanations are there for the disappointing performance of this new product? How might an understanding of consumer information processing help explain this situation?

10. Explain the importance and action of memory in consumer information processing. What conditions would make it highly probable that a consumer will retain a piece of information in long-term memory?

Case 1. Flame & Fume Watchman

In 1973, when the much heralded smoke alarms first began to gain popularity, Ron Fischer and some friends were discussing the devices over a meal. Fischer was cynical and said, "I've got a nose like a bloodhound. Why should I spend money on a piece of junk that I can out-perform with my schnoz?" Being a rather mulish fellow, for the next several years he dismissed the information he was exposed to on smoke alarms as irrelevant to his or his family's needs. One day his son, who had listened to the local fire chief advocate smoke alarms in a talk at his school, came home saying, "We're really dumb not to have a smoke alarm," and was sharply reprimanded. However, on a cold night in the winter months of 1978, Ron went to bed after drinking more than a few beers, leaving three smoldering logs in the fireplace. As the house filled with smoke, his "schnoz" proved less than what he had cracked it up to be. Fortunately, none of the Fischers were permanently injured that night, but Ron and one of his sons were hospitalized for smoke inhalation.

With his house under repair, Ron returned to a motel room upon his release from the hospital, swearing he'd never again leave the safety of his family and home to chance. He immediately began to inquire about smoke alarms, and to look into the feasibility of installing a sprinkler system in his home. After gaining control of his impulses, Fischer decided against a sprinkler system, partly because of cost considerations and partly because his wife feared the consequences of a malfunction or false alarm. "It isn't the type of thing we'd want to test regularly," she said.

Sources: Some of the information in Case 1 is from "Sales of Home Smoke Alarms Catch Fire, Fueled by Support from Nearly Everyone," *Wall Street Journal*, March 17, 1977; and "The Fiery Debate over Smoke-Alarm Efficiency," *Business Week*, September 26, 1977, pp. 95–98.

Ron was a bit confused about which smoke alarm was best suited for his requirements. This is understandable in light of the fierce debate among manufacturers, government, and consumer groups over which type of smoke alarm is the most effective. Fischer consulted an Underwriters Laboratories report and found, much to his dismay, that 98 brands of smoke alarms met its standards. He then obtained technical literature on the two basic types of smoke alarms so that he could appraise them himself.

The more traditional type of alarm, an ionization detector, works by bombarding the air in a small chamber with radioactive particles. This "charges" the air so that a weak electric current is carried through the chamber; smoke particles interfere with the current's flow and trigger the alarm. Photoelectric units, on the other hand, utilize a light source and a photo receptor, which are unaligned so that normally the receptor "sees" no light. When smoke particles enter the chamber, they scatter the light, "splashing" some of it onto the receptor, thus setting off the alarm.

Regrettably, this information did not do very much to help Fischer make up his mind. He asked the advice of a friend, who happened to own an ionization unit. His friend told him that "the ionization types are supposed to respond before any visible signs of smoke appear" and showed him an advertisement of one large manufacturer. The ad claimed that "in fires that break out and spread fast—the really dangerous fires—seconds count, not minutes. Ionization detectors are much faster than those slow-acting photoelectric units in flaming fires, so you better put your life on one of the best—the Flame & Fume Watchman."

Fischer was tired of searching, so his friend brought him to the retailer where he had purchased his Flame & Fume Watchman. The ad had convinced Ron to do the same. But as they waited for service at the dealer's, Ron picked up a copy of a magazine in which there was a full-page advertisement for a photoelectric model smoke alarm. The ad included the results of a study conducted by the manufacturer which found that ionization detectors did respond more quickly to flaming fires. "On the other hand," it said, "photoelectric units are much faster to respond to smoldering fires. In fact, in smoldering fires, the photoelectric detectors gave 11 to 12 minutes more escape time, on a weighted average." The ad went on to explain that an ionization detector will sound its alarm when smoke obscures vision at a rate of

4 percent per foot when it is 2 feet away from a fire. Thus, if the smoldering fire is 10 feet away, the ionization detector may not respond until smoke obscures vision at a rate of 20 percent per foot, a potentially lethal level. This advertisement also claimed that smoke is the only universal signal in all dangerous fires and is the lethal factor in 90 percent or more of all home fatalities. The ionization alarms detect invisible particles of combustion, not smoke, it said.

Fischer was a bit confused by these contradictory claims. Understandably, he wondered which to believe. He was convinced that either type of alarm would allow his family to reach safety in the event of another fire. He was also concerned with possible damage to his home and property, having spent over $13,000 for repairs from the fire that spread from his fireplace. With 11 to 12 minutes of additional escape time, he thought, the fire department could be reached that much sooner, potentially saving him thousands of dollars. He also knew that if he could somehow prove this to his insurance company, he could save more than 6 percent on his future premiums. It angered him somewhat to recall that the ad his friend had shown him for the Flame & Fume Watchman had sounded rather condescending to the photoelectric models, whereas the second ad he was exposed to seemed to be more objective.

When the salesman finally approached Fischer, his friend was astounded to hear him order two photoelectric units of the kind in the advertisement. "What made you decide to do that?" his friend asked. Fischer replied, "With two, I know I'll be safe, plus I'm sure to get the discount on my insurance premiums!"

Case 1 Questions

1. In detail, describe the nature of Fischer's information processing before and after the fire that prompted him to turn 180 degrees on his stand concerning smoke alarms.

2. What did the makers of the Flame & Fume Watchman do wrong, and how could an understanding of selective information processing have enabled them to avoid such difficulties?

3. The fire commissioner of a large northeastern city says that technical improvements are bringing down the price of smoke alarms while increasing their effectiveness. Equally as important, he says, the alarms are breaking down public apathy about fire safety. Why do you suppose the public has been apathetic about fire safety? How do you think smoke alarms have reversed this tendency?

Case 2. Metro Mobile Home Sales

Bernard Dutcher, owner of Metro Mobile Home Sales, is dismayed at the lack of interest consumers have been showing in mobile homes. The townhouse and condominium markets have been flourishing, and he has been told that 40 to 45 percent of the sales are made to single men and women. Dutcher perceives this segment of the market to be substantial and is afraid that if he fails to stimulate a demand for his mobile homes, he may be forced out of business. To understand more fully the present and potential impact of the "single" market, Dutcher hired two consultants to survey the population and buying habits in the southern metropolitan area where his business is located. The following is a compilation of their findings.

Single residents account for 21 percent of the households, up from 17 percent in 1970. The number of people living alone has increased by 43 percent, compared to a 6 percent increase in married households. This increase can be attributed to later marriage, higher divorce rates, and a widening gap between the life expectancies of men and women. Half of the women between the ages of 20 and 24 and two thirds of the men are single. Many of these young adults view living alone as a good transition in their lives and some see it as a necessary preparation for marriage. This young singles segment is the the fastest growing one. Widows account for one third of the single market; people who are divorced make up the rest. These consumers purchased 13 percent of the homes in the previous year, and women appear to be the fastest growing segment of the home-buying market. Many singles are spending upwards of $47,000 for their homes. The majority of the buyers, however, favor townhouses and condominiums.

After receiving this information, Dutcher contemplated his past promotional strategies and sales. Three years ago, Metro Mobile Home Sales had the second largest share of the market with 23 per-

Source: Some of the information for Case 2 is from "A Living-Alone Trend Affects Housing, Cars and Other Industries," *Wall Street Journal*, November 16, 1977.

cent (the leader had a 40 percent share, and three other competitors split the remaining 37 percent of the market). Recently, though, and for no apparent reason, Dutcher's market share dropped to 17 percent, despite the fact that he increased his advertising budget by 15 percent. Most of his budget had been placed in spot television commercials. He had never really advertised to a specific demographic segment of the market; instead, he aimed his messages at all consumers who were potential home buyers and mainly emphasized the cost-savings of a mobile home as opposed to a detached home. The ads were typical of a local retailer or dealership—a rapid, hard-sell pitch that included mention of the business name and location three times. During the next few weeks, Dutcher paid close attention to his competitor's mobile home advertisements. The competitor used a hard-sell approach also, but placed less emphasis on price and more on other advantages of mobile homes, such as their obvious mobility, coziness, and lower heating and cooling bills. Dutcher disagreed with this approach but was losing confidence in his own judgment. Therefore he commissioned the same two consultants to survey consumers again. This time he was interested in consumer perception of his advertising and perceptions about the mobile home industry in general.

The survey was designed to measure the difference of opinion among married, single, divorced, and widowed consumers. In many instances, the responses were similar. For example, an average of 60 percent of the respondents in each group were aware of advertisements for Metro Mobile Home Sales. However, only a scant 15 to 20 percent of respondents listened to the ads. Of those who did (a majority of whom were over the age of 35), an even smaller 5 percent could recall the ads. Differences did exist in each group's perception of the ads. Young, single consumers perceived the ads to be shoddy and the messages to be obnoxious and irrelevant. Married consumers perceived the ads as having no pertinence to their needs. Divorced and widowed customers were a little more favorable toward the ads but admitted the ads were inferior to the competitor's ads.

Most of the respondents held mobile homes in low regard. Young, single consumers perceived mobile homes as being low-quality housing. They disliked trailer courts because they tended to be run-down and offered little privacy. Married respondents said that mobile homes were too compact, offered no privacy, and were not stable.

Divorced and widowed customers feared that the mobile homes offered less security than detached homes.

Case 2 Questions

1. To what would you attribute Mr. Dutcher's decrease in market share?

2. Dutcher's repetitious ads have contributed to sensory overload, and a majority of the consumers are choosing to ignore them. How can he increase exposure, attention, reception, and response of the single market to his mobile homes?

Notes

1. Neil Bidmar and Milton Rokeach, "Archie Bunker's Bigotry: A Study in Selective Perception and Exposure," *Journal of Communication,* 24 (Winter 1974), pp. 36–47.

2. Herbert Krugman, "What Makes Advertising Effective?" *Harvard Business Review,* 53 (March–April 1975), pp. 96–102.

3. See Michael J. Watkins, "Concept and Measurement of Primary Memory," *Psychological Bulletin,* 81 (October 1974), pp. 695–711.

4. F. I. M. Craik and R. S. Lockhart, "Levels of Processing: A Framework for Memory Research," *Journal of Verbal Learning and Verbal Behavior,* 11 (1972), pp. 671–84.

5. C. Cannell and J. C. MacDonald, "The Impact of Health News on Attitudes and Behavior," *Journalism Quarterly,* 33 (Summer 1956), pp. 315–23.

6. J. Mills, "Interest in Supporting and Discrepant Information," R. P. Abelson et al., eds., *Theories of Cognitive Consistency: A Sourcebook* (Chicago: Rand McNally & Co., 1968), pp. 771–76.

7. Hershel W. Leibowitz and Lewis O. Harvey, Jr., "Perception," Mark R. Rosenzweig and Lyman W. Porter, eds., *Annual Review of Psychology,* Volume 24 (Palo Alto, Calif.: Annual Reviews, Inc., 1973), pp. 200–40.

8. Wilbert J. McKeachie and Charlotte L. Doyle, *Psychology* (Reading, Mass.: Addison-Wesley Publishing Company, Inc., 1966), p. 171.

9. Homer E. Spence and James F. Engel, "The Impact of Brand Preference on the Perception of Brand Names: A Laboratory Analysis," P. R. McDonald, ed., *Marketing Involvement in Society and the Economy* (Chicago: American Marketing Association, 1970), pp. 267–71.

10. M. J. Rosenberg, "Inconsistency Arousal and Reduction in Attitude Change," I. O. Steiner and M. Fishbein, eds., *Current Studies in Social Psychology* (New York: Holt, Rinehart and Winston, Inc., 1965), pp. 123–24.

11. Norman F. Dixon, *Subliminal Perception—The Nature of the Controversy* (Maidenhead-Berkshire, England: McGraw-Hill Publishing Co., Ltd., 1971); and Ezra Stotland and Lance K. Canon, *Social Psychology: A Cognitive Approach* (Philadelphia, Pa.: W. B. Saunders, 1972), Chapter 3.

12. Alvin Toffler, *Future Shock* (New York: Random House, 1970).

13. R. Barton, *Advertising Media* (New York: McGraw-Hill, 1964), p. 109.

14. "Position in Newspaper Advertising: 2," *Media/Scope* (March 1963), pp. 76–82.

15. Ibid., pp. 76–82.

16. "Position in Newspaper Advertising: 1," *Media/Scope* (February 1963), p. 57.

17. R. D. Blackwell et al., "Laboratory Equipment for Marketing Research" (Dubuque, Iowa: Kendall Hunt, 1970), p. 42; "Oculometer Is Finding Out What Viewers See in Those TV Commercials," *Advertising Age* (April 11, 1977), p. 56; and the following two papers presented at the annual meetings of Division 23 of the American Psychological Association, September 5, 1976: Norman B. Leferman, "Current Uses of the Tachistoscope in Advertising Research," and Edmund W. J. Faison, "Validating Recognition Speed as an Indicator of Package Design Effectiveness."

18. F. J. Thumin, "Identification of Cola Beverages," *Journal of Applied Psychology,* 46 (November 1962), pp. 358–60.

19. R. I. Allison and K. P. Uhl, "Brand Identification and Perception," *Journal of Marketing Research,* 1 (August 1964), pp. 80–85.

20. J. C. Makens, "Effect of Brand Preference upon Consumers' Perceived Taste of Turkey Meat," *Journal of Applied Psychology,* 49 (August 1965), pp. 261–63.

21. "Twink: Perception of Taste," R. D. Blackwell, J. F. Engel, and D. T. Kollat, eds., *Cases in Consumer Behavior* (New York: Holt, Rinehart and Winston, Inc., 1969), pp. 38–43.

22. L. Bogart, *Strategy in Advertising* (New York: Harcourt Brace Jovanovich, 1967), Chapter 5.

23. Thomas S. Robertson, "Low-Commitment Consumer Behavior," *Journal of Advertising Research,* 16 (April 1976), pp. 19–26.

24. Leo Bogart, "Where Does Advertising Research Go from Here?" *Journal of Advertising Research,* 9 (March 1969), p. 6.

Chapter **13** Information
Search

Outline

Search Defined
Search in the Decision Process
Internal Search
External Search
The Propensity to Engage in External Search
Phases of External Search
Factors Affecting the Impact of External Sources
How to Increase Consumer Receptiveness to Messages
Summary
Questions and Issues for Discussion
Cases

Key Terms

exposure

social inhibitors

search

internal search

external search

sensory memory

short-term memory

permanent memory

brand comprehension

connotative meaning of a brand

brand confidence

direct marketing

clarifiers

simplifiers

perception of problem

modes of tension reduction

risk-handling style

preliminary search

evoked set of alternatives

medium image

vehicle image

personal or organizational image

testimonials

communication

consumer responsiveness

timing

frame of reference

psychographics

message formulation

The American consumer, more than any other in the world today, is exposed to information from numerous sources. The following are a few statistics which illustrate the volume and extent of this exposure.

About 24 million pieces of direct mail advertising are sent to Americans in a year. According to a U.S. Postal Service survey, 63 percent of all such pieces are opened and read.[1]

In a typical day, 40 million people turn to the classified sections of their newspaper: 45 percent look at ads for merchandise, 42 percent go over real estate listings, 35 percent pay attention to automobile offerings, while 33 percent look at employment opportunities.[2]

Approximately 106 million adults, 20 years of age and older, turn to the Yellow Pages to locate some good or service over 4 billion times a year.[3]

Despite such mass exposure, considerable evidence shows that, when it comes time to make a purchase, relatively little deliberate search is undertaken for purchase-related information. For example, in one study it was found that about one consumer in ten checked advertisements before shopping for shoes or personal accessories. Even when more costly items are sought, such as a television set or household furniture, there is evidence to show that only about half of the consumers look at ads before shopping. Another study revealed that small-appliance purchasers visited only one store and made their buying decision in about a week.[4]

Most of what has been observed and reported above should not be used to characterize the American consumer as an irrational, frivolous person. Actually, there are several explanations for such behavior. First, exposure to information and persuasive messages is a continuous process. This constant flow of information enables people to accumulate knowledge about various goods and services even before they need or want it. Furthermore, this exposure also helps consumers clarify what it is they might want or what product could conceivably assist them in resolving some particular problem, should it ever arise. This means that consumers are in a state of readiness to buy many different products before they are specifically sought.[5] For most of us, it is not difficult to recall some situation where this readiness was consciously noted, for instance, finding out that an all-night drugstore located conveniently to your home now carries a few grocery items, including bread and milk. The chances are that these products will only be purchased there at some off hour when a pressing need arises. Nevertheless, the information is stored and available for quick recall when necessary. Outdoor advertising along the highway often serves this same function. It is not unusual in some areas to see a sign that reminds you that there is a Howard Johnson's restaurant 75 miles ahead. The sign may be noted briefly in passing without interest. However, 65 to 70 miles later, the restaurant is sought as an opportunity for a refreshing break.

There are several other logical explanations of why consumers appear to engage in little search prior to making a purchase. Such information gathering can add substantially to the cost; for example, trips to various stores and the studying of ads and searching through catalogs takes considerable time and even money for direct expenses, such as gasoline and parking. Furthermore, because these activities take time, their consideration forces postponement of the purchase. This delay can be bothersome if there is an urgent need for the item or if there is a strong desire to have it. To some, wedding rings would be in this category, while to others it would be a motorcycle or a new dress.

The gathering of information can add to personal frustration in yet another way. Consumers can become overloaded with facts, figures, and persuasive statements to the point that they distract from consumers' ability to make a satisfying purchase decision. Consequently, some people allot little time to gathering information beyond some minimum level.

At times, there are also social inhibitors to the search for information. For example, in a study of the purchase of funeral services in a major metropolitan area, over 80 percent of the 500 households surveyed stated that they considered it entirely proper to contact several funeral homes for the purpose of comparing the services offered and their prices. However, approximately 40 percent of this same group of respondents indicated that they personally would be very uncomfortable making such contacts and, consequently, this became a barrier to their search. In the face of such evidence, it may be appropriate for private citizens' groups like the Memorial and Planning Funeral Society, concerned professionals from the funeral industry, and government agencies to work to reduce the perceived difficulty. Nevertheless, social inhibitors, such as those underlying the behavioral patterns of shopping for funeral services, are slow to change.

Despite the likelihood for limited search, there was an encouraging finding in the above study concerning consumer knowledge of one key purchase dimension—costs of services. Although a substantial number of the "inexperienced" funeral buyers (those who had not arranged or helped arrange a funeral within the previous five years) felt they needed more price information, their perceptions of the cost of funerals were very close to the actual costs paid by "experienced" funeral buyers in their area. Again, this illustrates the point made earlier, that information about various goods and services is accumulated over an extended period of time. Therefore, what is called search in a technical sense is only the more deliberate action of information gathering within a reasonable period of time prior to the anticipated purchase.[6]

Before going further, it is appropriate to introduce more formally the subjects covered in this chapter. As the title suggests, this chapter focuses on two closely related aspects of consumer behavior—prepurchase search and the evaluation of alternatives. To the extent that it is possible, each of these topics is integrated into all of the major sections of the chapter.

Search Defined

Search, as used in this text, is the purposeful attention given to the gathering and assembling of information related to the satisfaction of some perceived need, want, or desire. Search results when existing beliefs and attitudes are found to be inadequate, that is, when they are based on insufficient information. It is a prepurchase action in that it takes place before the product of interest is bought. The search process is proactive; that is, it is deliberate and has a certain momentum to it. Search may be either internal or external. *Internal search* is essentially a mental review of what an individual has experienced or has been exposed to and what has been learned and remembered. *External search* is the act of seeking information from any outside source by the individual who is engaged in the search process.

Search in the Decision Process

It can be noted in Figure 13.1 that the search process follows problem recognition. This means that some need or want has been consciously identified. Problems and the search they precipitate come in many forms. Three brief examples are given below to illustrate the relationship between problem recognition and search.

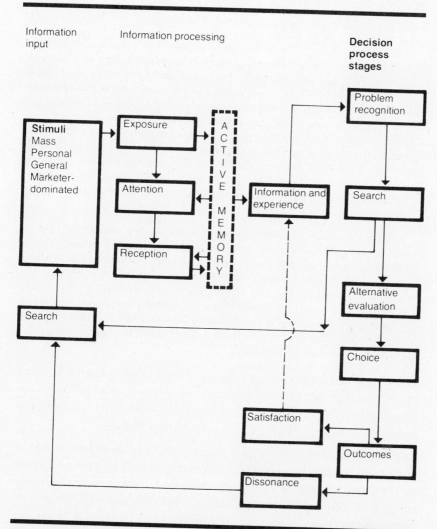

Figure 13.1
**Information Search
Process**

Source: Adapted from James F. Engel, Roger D. Blackwell, and David T. Kollat, *Consumer Behavior*, 3rd ed. (Hinsdale, Ill.: Dryden Press, 1978), p. 32. Copyright © 1978 by Dryden Press, a division of Holt, Rinehart and Winston. Reprinted by permission of Holt, Rinehart and Winston.

Having noticed that the window air conditioner in his bedroom has been running excessively, a man checks the filter and finds that it needs to be replaced. By this means, he acknowledges that a purchase must be made. In this case the product cost is low, and the most likely concern in the search process is to locate the most convenient store where the filter of the correct size can be purchased. This does not mean that the search process will take little time; it depends on the availability of the filter and the consumer's ability to locate it.

During the fall semester, a university student has become discontented with dorm life and has decided to move into an apartment in town. She has never had her own apartment but has observed the advantages that it has provided her friends. The problem she has recognized is that of dissatisfaction with dorm life and the resulting need to move. However, the search is likely to be considerably more complex and time-consuming than in the previous situation described. For instance, initially she will have to decide what kind of apartment she wants. Then, through external search, she will be able to discover what is actually available in the town and obtain information regarding such issues as rental costs, lease arrangements, required security deposits, and whether she might be able to share an apartment with someone.

A local independent trucker who owns his own rig has just decided that he wants a new CB radio for his personal car. He purchased his first CB radio two years ago for his truck and has found it very helpful in cases of emergencies and in monitoring road and weather conditions. Although the product is somewhat complex and technical in this situation, the trucker has experience to rely on. Nevertheless, the search process may take him a substantial amount of time and involve the consideration of alternative product types and brands as well as comparison of the prices and service available at various retail outlets.

These three situations illustrate some of the variation that is likely to occur in search behavior and alternative evaluation as different circumstances arise. A number of factors directly affect the nature of the search process itself. These can be categorized as follows.[7]

1. *The uniqueness of the object sought, that is, the extent to which acceptable substitutes exist.* This can be illustrated by again referring to the three situations previously described. In the case of the air conditioner filter, there is considerable similarity among alternatives. Therefore, once one is found, it will probably be purchased. However, the trucker faces more variety and, consequently, a greater need to engage in search. The manufacturers of CB radios and the retail outlets that stock them can have a substantial effect on this process by means of their promotional efforts. For instance, the issuance of a catalog can reduce the need to visit some stores.

2. *The strength of the motivation that precipitated the search activity.* In the case of the university student who has become dissatisfied with

dorm living arrangements, there is really no explicit indication given as to her level of discontent. If, for example, she is very unhappy and this dissatisfaction is reinforced by her parents after they see her grades, she will be inclined to expend considerable effort in the search process. However, if the situation is quite different and her discontent is related to one particular situation that has essentially been resolved, her propensity to look for alternative in-town rental units may be extremely low.

Firms can play a direct part in stimulating a willingness to search. The heavy advertising of new products, for instance, can cause discontent with those currently used or at least encourage the consumer to consider alternatives. If one gives a quick thought to the breakfast cereal or snack food offerings currently available, this point is confirmed.

3. Previous experience in searching for similar products or services. The extent of the search that the trucker will engage in as he seeks to find a CB radio for his car will be affected by the fact that he already owns one and has had the benefit of the first purchase experience. For example, he may already know which stores carry equipment of the quality he is most interested in owning. He may also have catalogs from these outlets describing their product lines and showing current prices.

4. General predisposition toward search. None of the situations described earlier offer any details about the individual's willingness to personally engage in search. However, differences among consumers do exist, and to a large extent the observed variation has been related to perceived risk. For example, two people with similar backgrounds and experience facing essentially the same situation often approach it differently. In a number of instances, this can be explained by the fact that some people are simply more willing than others to assume a given amount of risk. In other cases, two individuals will perceive varying amounts of risk in a given situation and, hence, behave differently.

The impact of variation in perceived risk can be illustrated by observing two mothers who each face the same problem of needing to treat what looks like poison ivy on their young children. One mother is very apprehensive about using any over-the-counter drug before checking with her doctor. She fears a possible reaction in the child and is deeply concerned as to whether her diagnosis is correct. The other mother, who faces the same situation, simply goes to the drugstore and then, after reading the labels of several branded lotions for the treatment of poison ivy, purchases one and applies it according to the directions.

In order to reduce risk, consumers often adopt one of several behavior patterns. Some of the most common are identified below.[8] Consumers may buy only:

1. a specific brand
2. nationally advertised brands
3. the cheapest brand
4. the most expensive brand
5. a certain amount of the product
6. products with a plain and simple design.

As a means of further examining the consumer search process, the next two sections will deal first with internal search and then with external search.

Internal Search

Internal search is the conscious recall and consideration of specific information and experiences that appear to be relevant to the recognized problem that the consumer faces. In some situations, this search is nearly instantaneous, while in others, thinking and pondering of ideas takes place over a considerable period of time. A simple illustration will explain how the latter occurs.

Assume that it is a Saturday morning and you have just recalled that next Monday is your mother's birthday. You are 225 miles from home. You have a gift in mind and rush out to the store to buy it. Things are going quite well, and at your first stop you are able to buy what you want and have it gift wrapped. You then hurry home to prepare the package for mailing. You do this as quickly as possible, but by now it is 11:45 A.M. Although the post office is only about a 10-minute drive away, in Saturday traffic it takes you nearly 20 minutes, and upon arriving you find the post office closed. This is a frustrating moment; you do not know what to do except to drive home. You sit down and relax, trying to think of some way of getting that package to its destination by Monday. In a few minutes, you have thought of two alternatives. First, there is a post office substation in a local supermarket that is still open, and second, you could send the gift by Greyhound Package Service. You recall having heard an advertisement for this service on the radio.

Almost everyone has had this kind of experience. In this situation, the two alternative means for getting the package to its destination on time were in memory but were not recalled without conscious effort and the lapse of some time.

It is important to keep in mind that nearly everyone in our economically advanced society is exposed to vast amounts of information, some of which is retained and available for recall at a later time. The way in which this information is dealt with and retained is of major concern to the consumer analyst. What is retained may have a lasting effect on an individual's behavior as a consumer. Consequently, managers of all organizations that are interested in consumer behavior must necessarily become aware of the information selection and retention process.

Specifically, the success and general helpfulness of internal search to the consumer is dependent on what information is retained. No one is receptive to and retains all that he or she sees, hears, touches, smells, or tastes. For example, there is evidence to show that during about 50 percent of television advertising, the average consumer tunes out the entire commercial.[9]

In terms of effectiveness as an information receiver and storage facility, a human being compares poorly to equipment such as a tape recorder. But a human's coding ability—the capacity for insight, judgment, and the ability to identify meaningful patterns in messages—is superb. To a great extent, this remarkable ability is the result of a systematic selection of information and not a random process. People generally seem to have a unique set of rules and operating procedures enabling them to select information, keep it manageable, and still meet their needs.

Howard has offered a model of this selection process that includes three phases or steps in information handling.[10] (See Figure 13.2.) Each phase has a separate function described below:

Figure 13.2
**Information Reception
and Storage**

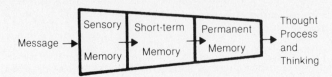

Sensory memory. Sensory memory receives all information to which it is exposed. Although this memory component is large and comprehensive at any point in time, total retention is extremely short. If the information in the sensory memory is not transferred from it to short-term memory in a matter of milliseconds, it is dissipated and lost.

Short-term memory. This component retains its content somewhat longer than does sensory memory before it is lost. Some evidence suggests that if the message is transferred to long-term memory within 18 seconds, it can be satisfactorily stored.

Permanent memory. This is the component that affects consumer behavior. Another way of describing it is to think of this phase of memory as being made up of all the coded stimuli received from the various messages that penetrated the sensory and short-term memory components. These come from many sources including products, packages, advertisements, and personal encounters with salespeople as well as with friends and family members.

The coded stimuli stored in long-term or permanent memory are what is recalled when internal search is undertaken. However, this does not explain why some information gets into long-term memory and other information does not. There are several factors that can affect what impressions and experiences move into long-term memory. Three of these are identified here.

1. The capacity of the individual. This is influenced by such characteristics as the person's intelligence, maturity (for example, children cannot process information as fast and as accurately as adults), personality, education, and social class. The last two factors may contribute to message receptiveness through their effect on an individual's language capacity. For example, the better educated member of the upper middle class probably has a vocabulary larger than that of the average member of the lower class. As a result, the former is better able to interpret messages.

2. Familiarity with the subject. The more familiar a topic or product, the more likely the individual is to already have some memory base for it. For instance, toasters are a familiar household product to nearly everyone, whereas a multipurpose kitchen appliance branded as La Machine by Moulinex Products is comparatively less well known. All other things being equal, familiarity contributes to the ease of movement of information into long-term memory.

3. Relevance of the subject or product. This refers to the extent to which some bit of information is related to the individual's perceived needs, wants, or desires. In short, consumers are more likely to give attention to what they believe they need to know and less or no attention to other information. Ad headlines that promise cost savings or increased miles per gallon attempt to attract attention by making the message appear extremely relevant.

There is evidence to show that consumers develop brand concepts in their long-term memory. These concepts are made up of: (1) *brand comprehension,* which is the denotative or literal meaning of a brand (Ivory as a brand of hand soap, including its physical attributes); (2) *attitude or connotative meaning of a brand* (the subjective feelings that an individual has about a brand, such as its status appeal); and (3) *brand confidence,* which refers to the extent to which the consumer is comfortable or certain about his or her evaluation of the brand.

Internal search usually produces one of three outcomes. First, if the process generates satisfactory results, that is, an acceptable resolution to the recognized problem, the consumer will likely forgo external search and proceed to the purchase stage. Second, internal search may convince the consumer that there is no feasible way of solving the problem, and so the process is halted. The third outcome is the recognition by the consumer that there is a need for further information and, therefore, it is necessary to undertake external search and further evaluation.

External Search

As indicated earlier, external search is the expenditure of deliberate effort to seek information from various outside sources. This phase of search is a means of supplementing the consumer's existing knowledge. Any source may be used, but there are several that are most frequently consulted. These include salespeople, advertisements, packages, showroom visits, and friends and family members. The propensity for an individual to engage in such search is discussed in the following section.

The Propensity to Engage in External Search

The energy expended by an individual in external search is dependent on several factors. The following are some of the most important.[11]

Individual Reactions to a Given Problem

Some problems appear to need immediate attention. To certain individuals, for example, the loss of their watch would require quick action. They may simply feel unable to function without it. To others, seeing their automobile gasoline gauge register one quarter full will precipitate a similar feeling of urgency. In this same sense, the use of the brand name Die-Hard for a Sears' auto battery quite likely has a special appeal to some people because of their fear of not being able to start their car.

The success of what has been called "direct marketing" is evidence of a desire of many persons to simplify the physical search process. One industry source defines direct marketing as follows:

> Direct marketing is a marketing system which offers products and services to present and potential customers/prospects through the use of various promotional media singly or in combination, in order to effect a direct action response by mail, telephone, or personal visit.[12]

Some examples of the diversity and volume of products sold through this approach are given below.

● United States oil companies sell approximately $100 million of non-petroleum-related merchandise to their credit card holders through direct mail.

In 1975 alone, nonprofit charitable, religious, educational, and public-interest organizations raised $21.4 billion through the mail.

● About $200 million worth of photographic film is processed simply through mail contact directly with the supplier.[13]

A *Better Homes and Gardens* study gives further focus on the principal reasons why consumers who shop by mail do so. These findings are summarized in Table 13.1.

Modes of Tension Reduction

Some personal tension always accompanies problem recognition, but the methods people use to relieve this internal stress vary among individuals and, to some extent, vary with the situation. Some consumers, upon recognizing a need for a particular product, must actively begin going from store to store in search of the product and related information to ease their tension. The very act of getting out into the market relieves their stress. A careful study of newspaper ads appears to ease the tensions of some homemakers as they face the weekly grocery shopping.

To other consumers, it seems as if their tension is lessened only by making a purchase. Any time expended in search is simply seen as a delaying action and, consequently, may even increase the level of anxiety.

The differing natures of problem situations precipitate varying patterns of relieving tension. For example, any delay in the choice of a dentist when you have a toothache is probably going to be avoided.

Table 13.1
Why Consumers Shop by Mail

Reasons Given	Percent
Can't find items elsewhere	44.6
Convenience	36.5
Fun	9.5
Price	6.8
Better quality	1.3
Other	1.3

Source: Adapted from R. J. Listman, "An Overview of the Field of Direct Marketing" (New York: The Direct Mail/Marketing Educational Foundation, Inc., 1978), pp. 10–11. Reprinted by permission.

Therefore, search may amount to no more than calling a friend for the name of her dentist or frantically calling each dentist in the telephone directory until one is located who will see you immediately.

Perception and the Handling of Risk or Uncertainty

As mentioned earlier, the ability and willingness of people to assume risk varies considerably. Inability to resolve a recognized problem through internal search will result in different behavioral patterns.

Research has suggested that some consumers can be characterized by their risk-handling styles and the means they use to reduce their perceived risk. Two such consumer groupings classified by risk-handling styles have been identified as *clarifiers* and *simplifiers*. Clarifiers, when confronted with some confusion, seek additional information in order to understand better the context in which a decision can be made. Simplifiers, facing the same amount of confusion, selectively screen out information that is not consistent with their predispositions, thus simplifying the context within which the decision is to be made.[14]

The use of brand names that strongly suggest specific product benefits may be particularly helpful to the simplifier. They are short and to the point. This can be illustrated by considering the brand names of several sedatives and stimulants including Sleep-Eze, Cope, Compōz, and No Doz.

As the result of some personal initiative and considerable encouragement from government agencies, consumer interest groups, and Congress, business firms have taken several significant steps to reduce perceived risk among consumers by facilitating search and the evaluation of alternatives. Three of the more recent examples are given below.

Unit Pricing. A considerable number of grocery stores are now providing shelf-pricing information that gives price per some standard unit, such as per ounce or per pound. This can be helpful to consumers in making price comparisons among brands of a given product such as canned green beans, cooking oil, and dry milk. It also provides a quick means of determining how much of a premium, if any, is being paid for national brands. Also, it is a way of finding out just how economical the "super size" is over the "large" of some brand.

Nutritional Labeling. A list of the nutrients contained in a serving of many processed foods is now available on their labels. Such information can serve as a means of determining how each food item can be used to build a balanced diet through meal planning and careful shopping.

Interest Rate Information. As the result of federal legislation, interest rates must be communicated in a uniform manner to each consumer by the financial institution involved before a loan is made. Although many questions remain as to the total effect of this effort, it has been a substantial step in the direction of more openness.

Phases of External Search

The external search process can be divided into two parts based on how the search experience takes place.[15] This is illustrated very simply in Figure 13.3 and is then discussed in the paragraphs that follow. The process is shown as being funnel-shaped to emphasize that it is a means of beginning with broad considerations and then gradually refining the search and evaluation process until a satisfactory conclusion is reached.

Preliminary Search

The search that is initiated after it is recognized that internal search has not resolved the problem is called preliminary search. The length of this phase varies depending upon the circumstances faced, but it typically produces the following results.

Figure 13.3
**Phases of External
Search**

1. A redefinition of the desired product or service attributes. This often occurs because there is a reconciliation between what may be called the idealized product or service—what was conceived of as being sought—and what is observed as being available in the market.

This includes becoming aware of specific product features and operating characteristics as well as other dimensions such as warranties, available credit terms, and the service that can be expected from the supplier. In planning their product and service offerings, firms that practice this marketing concept have sought to identify consumer preferences in terms of what is perceived to be the "ideal product." This has been followed by the use of strategy in producing and positioning their offerings in the market to deliver the most acceptable product to the identified market. Quite obviously, some "ideal products" are not profitable to produce and market, while others require some modifications before marketing. For example, some French-designed clothing for women would be very appealing to the mass market in the United States, but it usually cannot be produced and distributed profitably to the American consumer until it is modified. Some modifications are often required so that the items can be mass-produced and sold at acceptable price levels through stores such as J. C. Penney's, Macy's, Famous Barr, and Sears.

2. Consumers' first acknowledgment that there are constraints imposed in the search process. These constraints come in various forms. For example, in some communities there are only one or two retail outlets that carry certain merchandise. It may be that the item of interest is a small household appliance, such as a personal-size television set with a 10-inch screen. Prior to beginning the external search process, it was assumed that all appliance stores and the local discount house carried these sets. However, upon visiting several of these stores and calling the others, only two stores were found to stock them.

Another constraint may be the terms available. It is possible that a young couple looking for their first home soon discovers that every bank and savings and loan association in their town requires a 20-percent down payment as a condition of securing a loan. This poses a considerable obstacle given their housing preferences. This may be reconciled by deciding to wait until some future time with the idea that additional savings can be accumulated, assistance can be sought from their parents in the form of a short-term loan to supplement their savings, or possibly their housing preferences can be modified.

3. More concise assessment of personal resources available. This includes a recognition of the time and energy necessary to carry out the search activity as well as those resources needed to obtain the product or service sought.

It is often hard to estimate what it will take to adequately search for information about a product or service that is being considered for purchase. But once the search process gets under way, one begins to realize the number of alternative brands available, which stores should probably be shopped, and just how much time this could take. It seems as though most people are likely to underestimate what it takes to engage in a satisfying search experience.

For instance, a student arrives on the campus of a large state university with plans to purchase a 10-speed bicycle. This will help him greatly in getting around the campus. However, the student is new in the community and, furthermore, has never owned a 10-speed. His plan is to make this purchase the first day or two after he arrives. He considers this a major investment and has set aside $150 for this purpose but hopes to spend less. In this case, extensive search is probably going to be necessary to identify where bicycles are sold, the models and makes available, and the features of greatest importance; to gather pricing information; and to inquire about warranties as well as the service that can be expected. This student soon realizes that two days are not enough time to accomplish what he wants to do and that his $150 may not even be adequate.

Business firms assist in resolving such consumer problems by various means including advertising, placing stores in convenient locations, publishing catalogs that can be kept at home for quick reference, providing salespeople to point out and explain product features, and labeling and designing packages that allow a full view of the product while still protecting it. It is through exposure to these sources during the preliminary search that many consumers clearly formulate some order in their preferences regarding specific product features. In addition, it is common for the consumer to add some features to those sought initially and to drop others from further consideration.

It is also during this preliminary search process that consumers assemble the range of brands that can feasibly be looked upon as true alternatives. This list of alternatives has been called a consumer's *evoked set* or *consideration group*. This group nearly always is a subset of all the brands available. For instance, a young man looking for motor oil at a discount house quickly observes that there are over a dozen different brands on the shelves in the automotive section. Upon giving this some thought, he eliminates all but the recognized national brands. He reasons that this is for his new car and he wants to be sure of the quality. Furthermore, by changing the oil himself, he can save considerable money, more than enough to buy what he considers to be a top-quality product. Not only has this young man eliminated the private brands, but also he has implicitly excluded any national brand that is not on the shelf at the discount house.

This concept of the formulation of an evoked set or consideration group has important implications for the marketing manager. First, in a very real sense, if the firm's brand is not in the consumer's consideration group, it will not be given any attention. Therefore, an important marketing strategy objective is to move a given brand into the evoked set of more consumers. This is a measurable objective to establish. For example, it is possible to develop a research study that asks members of an identified target market which brands they ordinarily consider before making a purchase of a particular type of product. The question could be just as easily framed in terms of selecting a store. For instance, "Which stores are you likely to visit when you are looking for a new pair of dress shoes?"

Another important factor to acknowledge regarding the evoked set is that those brands in the set represent the real competition. Again, if a brand is not in a consumer's evoked set, it is not given attention. Therefore, not only must a firm work to establish its brand as one that is ordinarily considered when purchasing that type of product, but also the firm must recognize its competitors in the mind of the consumer.

Concluding Search Effort and Alternative Evaluation

After the preliminary efforts have been expended in external search, the process itself must be drawn to a close. As in preliminary search, there is no uniform amount of time or effort given to this concluding phase. This will vary depending upon the circumstances. However, there are several possible identifiable results of this latter phase.

1. The consumer has identified an acceptable product or service that resolves the recognized problem. This means that whatever needs, wants, and desires are present, apparently these can be satisfied in some acceptable manner by making a purchase of a particular item. At this point a decision is usually made to discontinue the search process; often this is followed quickly by a purchase.

2. The consumer has not been able to locate an acceptable product, service, or store alternative given the evaluative criteria used. However, a decision is made to discontinue search anyway. This may be the result of simply running out of time or patience or recognizing that there are no acceptable alternatives currently available.

3. No acceptable alternative is found but a decision is made to continue searching. In some cases, the complete search cycle is repeated; that is, internal search is again undertaken with the possibility of it being followed by further external search and alternative evaluation.

Factors Affecting the Impact of External Sources

There is almost no limit to the number and variety of sources consulted during external search. However, several factors can be associated with the impact of the messages received. Some of the most important are discussed in the following paragraphs.

Perceived Image of the Source

There are at least three ways in which the perception of the source can influence its impact. These are considered under the topics of medium image, vehicle image, and personal or organizational image.

Medium Image. Medium is the means or channel used to reach the consumer. Television, radio, salespeople, and newspapers are media. Various studies have been undertaken in an attempt to determine what differences in consumer perceptions exist with respect to the overall effectiveness of various media. The results from one such study are reported here to illustrate some of the findings.

Table 13.2
**The Relative
Desirability of Media**

Most Want to Keep	12/59 %	11/63 %	1/67 %	1/71 %	11/72 %	11/74 %
Television	42	44	53	58	56	59
Newspapers	32	28	26	19	22	19
Radio	19	19	14	17	16	17
Magazines	4	5	3	5	5	4
Don't know or no answer	3	4	4	1	1	1

Source: Television Information Office, *Trends in Public Attitudes toward Television and Other Mass Media: A Report by the Roper Organization, Inc.* (New York: Television Information Office, National Association of Broadcasters, 1975), p. 5. Reprinted by permission.

The findings summarized in Table 13.2 were obtained in a series of nationwide surveys conducted over a 15-year period by Roper Research, Inc., for the Television Information Office, a television industry trade association.[16] These data show that consumers have different expectations with respect to various media. For example, in an effort to measure the relative desirability of four major media, the following question was asked: "Suppose that you could continue to have only one of the following—radio, television, newspapers, or magazines—which one of the four would you *most* want to *keep*?"

The growing attractiveness of television as an advertising medium is illustrated by the data presented in Table 13.3, which show the change in spending in local markets by the top four department and discount stores for the first quarter of 1978 as compared to that of 1977.

Table 13.3
**Top Four Department
and Discount Stores:
Local Television
Advertisers
(First Quarter
Comparisons 1978
versus 1977)**

Store	1977 (millions)	1978 (millions)	Percent Change
Mobil Oil Company (Montgomery Ward and Jefferson Stores)	$4.47	$6.99	+56
Sears, Roebuck and Company	4.63	4.79	+ 3
J. C. Penney Company	2.45	4.33	+77
Federated Department Stores	2.92	4.19	+44

Source: "Stores Boost Spending in TV for First Quarter," *Advertising Age*, Vol. 49 (June 12, 1978), p. 62. Reprinted with permission from the June 12, 1978, issue of *Advertising Age.* Copyright 1978 by Crain Communications Inc.

Vehicle Image. The term *vehicle,* as used here, refers to a specific source such as the *Wall Street Journal* or *Business Week.* Quite obviously, all magazines are not alike; neither are all newspapers or all television programs. Consequently, these perceived differences can have an impact on the receptiveness of consumers to their messages. For example, the major news magazines such as *Newsweek, Time,* and *U.S. News and World Report* have a certain authoritative manner. Their total character is substantially different from that of *Woman's Day* and *Family Circle.*

As the result of such differences, consumers expect to obtain certain kinds of information from each vehicle. Furthermore, some products and services are out of place in some media. For instance, the news magazines previously mentioned are more likely to be perceived as appropriate sources of information on such topics as life insurance and books to read than they are as sources of information on food items or fabric softeners.

Personal or Organizational Image. Individuals and organizations that are engaged in communicating with consumers precipitate an image or characterization in the mind of their audience. This, too, can affect the impact of their message.

Testimonials—the inclusion of product or service users in promotional messages—have been a favorite technique of many businesses. The intent of the sponsor in using such a technique varies widely. However, a few common reasons can be cited briefly. First, the technique provides an endorsement of the product or service by a source that is generally considered to be more credible than the sponsor. In a sense, it is also a way of personalizing the product and its benefits. In addition, it can be a means of suggesting the product's superiority. For example, the racing car driver's use of STP may vividly illustrate to the average consumer the operational significance of his expertise in selecting an oil treatment. Some consumers might conclude that if he uses STP, it must be good. Nearly everyone can recall the success in using Joe DiMaggio to promote Mr. Coffee. The Ted Bates Advertising Agency arranged this and is hoping for equally good fortune in the use of Sophia Loren in television commercials for Filter Fresh, a water filtration system being introduced by North American Systems. The reasons for selecting her were given as "she's highly credible, speaks very well, has done cookbooks and is known as a housewife and a mother as well as an actress."[17]

The concern for accuracy and truthfulness in advertising has recently led the FTC to propose guidelines for using testimonials.

The use of individuals in promotion is not the only time when the image of the message source is of importance. Business organizations also have images. Firms such as IBM, Xerox, General Electric, and Hallmark have worked hard to establish and maintain a favorable public image. Consequently, slogans such as that used by Hallmark— "When you care enough to send the very best"—can have real market benefits in terms of message receptiveness.

The public endorsement of some products by certain associations, groups, or professional organizations can increase the receptiveness of consumers to the respective messages. For instance, the American Optometric Association name has been used in conjunction with the promotion of Quasar's television control mechanism for automatically adjusting the brightness of the television picture as room lightness changes. The American Dental Association's endorsement has long been used on Crest toothpaste, and the NFL has licensed various firms to use the league's name on specific "official" products.

The Consumers Union has an outstanding record of testing products, publishing the results in *Consumer Reports,* and making "best buy" recommendations. Although firms are forbidden from mentioning the Consumers Union findings in their promotional messages, millions of Americans have used *Consumer Reports* as a source of product- and service-related information.

However, the impact of the "no-name" generic products, mentioned in Chapter 8, may substantially affect the long-run usefulness of such tests. One of the fundamental reasons for branding has been that a brand name ties the quality of the product offered to the source and provides the consumer with a convenient indicator of consistent properties. Then, typically, as a consumer's experience demonstrated that one brand best met his or her evaluative criteria, the given brand was sought in the future when these same features were considered desirable. As brand names are removed, however, the consumer will have to rely on the retailer's reputation to supply consistent quality. This is what consumers faced many years ago in buying from the general store.

Various magazine and newspaper columnists have earned reputations as extremely reliable sources of information regarding a number of different goods and services. For example, sports writers' comments and recommendations have proven helpful to consumers in selecting such products as fishing lures, ski equipment, and tennis shoes. It is just as likely for a home and garden writer to suggest that certain products be used in protecting bushes from insects.

The fact that consumers frequently seek prepurchase information from friends and relatives reflects their concern for the image of the source. These personal sources are relied on for several reasons. The more important include their perceived credibility, the fact that they are readily available, there is little or no cost associated with their use, and because these personal sources offer an opportunity to discuss features of the product or service that may be of particular interest to the prospective buyer. The extent to which these same benefits can be found in a commercial source will greatly enhance its value to the consumer.

Clarity of the Message Presented

The word communication comes from the Latin word *communis,* which means common. When we attempt to communicate with someone or some group, we are trying to establish a "commonness" with them, and language is the currency of human communication.

In this process of communication, the likelihood that the keynote idea as perceived by the source—for example, the business firm—will get to its destination is determined to some extent by the effect of certain obstacles it faces en route. For instance, there is usually some unwanted interference that comes to bear upon the message. This includes audible noise, such as static on the radio or the distraction resulting from a doorbell ringing during a television commercial. It can also result from what is typically called "clutter." In the broadcast media this term refers to the unwanted distractions from nonprogram material: other commercials, promotional announcements, credits, and public service announcements.

The extent of this latter kind of interference was brought to light by a spot-check conducted in December 1971 by the American Association of Advertising Agencies. The Association found 50 percent more commercials and 33 percent more commercial minutes at that time than was found in a similar study conducted in 1963. Under these conditions, it is appropriate for advertisers to question the capacity of their messages to affect behavior in the intended way. A study conducted by Daniel Starch and Staff, Incorporated, draws specific attention to the appropriateness of this concern. In the Starch study, the recall of commercials was measured in 1971 and found generally to have dropped an average of 22 percent from that determined in a comparable study done a year earlier.[18]

The clarity of a message is also influenced by the extent to which the message source and destination have common frames of reference.[19] Figure 13.4 illustrates the importance of this.

The communicator as the source can only form a message out of his or her experiences, and the intended receiver can only understand and interpret a received signal in terms of his or her own experience. The area of commonness shown in Figure 13.4 is where a meaningful exchange can take place. For example, the benefits of a quartz crystal watch or a videodisc machine (the visual equivalent of the phonograph) could not be presented effectively to anyone who has never before heard either of the terms.[20]

How to Increase Consumer Receptiveness to Messages

Business firms and other interested organizations can influence receptiveness to their messages in several ways. Three of the most important means are appropriate timing, media selection, and message formulation.

Timing Considerations

Timing, as the term is used here, refers to getting the message to the target market at times when it is likely to have a significant impact. Important factors in timing are the natural buying cycles and at what stage the consumer is in the purchase process.

For example, in considering a buying cycle, products such as garden seeds and Christmas cards are seasonal items and, for the most part, are purchased during relatively short, identifiable periods. For

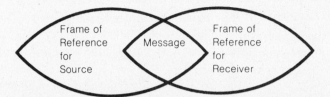

Figure 13.4
The Importance of Commonality

seeds, catalogs typically are mailed during the winter while Christmas cards must be promoted and sold in the late fall.

Another aspect of timing that is more difficult to deal with focuses on the position of the consumer in the buying process. For instance, if the purchase process is viewed simply as a hierarchy of effects including awareness, interest, desire, and action, it is ordinarily appropriate to deliver different messages to consumers at each of the various stages. In some cases it is possible to segment a market on the basis of stages of the purchase process. Using information from an organization such as Welcome Wagon can pinpoint families that are not aware of the services that some firms offer in their new neighborhood.

Media Selection

There is considerable evidence to show that various media have different audiences, meaning that they reach different groups. Without even obtaining any specific figures, most people would expect to find substantial variation between the readers of *Redbook* and *Popular Mechanics*. There may be less confidence in one's personal ability to specify differences among the viewers of Lawrence Welk's program and Monday night football, but differences would be expected nevertheless.

Many magazines have been developed with very specific audiences in mind. For example, recently a new special-interest magazine aimed at Jewish consumers who eat only kosher foods at home has been announced by Adar Communications, Inc. The publication will be called *Kosher Home* and it will seek the makers of more than 10,000 food products certified as kosher as its primary advertisers. However, the magazine's management does not intend to overlook houseware manufacturers since Jewish consumers often have up to four sets of dishes, flatware, and cookware because of their need to separate milk and meat products in the preparation and serving of meals. The publisher expects to have a circulation of 500,000.[21]

Fortunately, considerable data are available to managers who need to make media selection decisions. For instance, the Standard Rate and Data Service publishes a wealth of information about media reach and related cost data. A. C. Nielsen does continuous ratings of television programs, and many radio and television stations as well as most magazines and newspapers provide information to prospective advertisers on their respective audiences.

Other forms of analysis have provided a more vivid picture of the relationship between product usage and media exposure patterns. Psychographics—the study of the interrelationship among consumer activities, interests, and opinions—offers an interesting example. One such study focused on eye makeup users.[22] It found that users tended to be young and well educated and to live in metropolitan areas. Product usage rates were much higher for working women than for full-time homemakers and substantially higher in the western part of the United States than elsewhere. Further analysis showed the person also to be a heavy user of other cosmetics such as liquid face makeup base, lipstick, hair spray, perfume, and nail polish. She also turned out to be an above-average cigarette smoker, gasoline purchaser, and long-distance telephone user. With respect to media, the eye makeup user was found to like television movies and the "Tonight Show," but she did not like panel programs or westerns. She read fashion, news, and general-interest magazines, but did not read publications such as *True Confessions*.

Studies of this nature add an important dimension to the way in which various media are evaluated. There is no doubt that an audience's quality, as well as its size, should be considered. In using psychographic analysis, one study found the *Playboy* reader, for example, to be basically the male counterpart of the eye makeup user, while the man who read *Reader's Digest* emerged as the essence of conservative middle-class values—pro-business, anti–government welfare programs, anti–union power, and politically active. In the same study, the *Time*-only reader, as compared to the *Newsweek*-only reader, emerged as less concerned about job security, less worried about government and union power, less worried about threat of communism and generally more favorably disposed toward advertising.[23]

The concern for effectiveness in reaching a particular audience has led to considerable innovativeness on the part of some nonprofit organizations. For example, the development and distribution of *True to Life* magazine was the result of the efforts of the staff and students of the Emory University Family Planning Program.[24] In a unique approach to health education, they used a confession magazine format for a health information aid. Two titles from the table of contents illustrate the approach: "Mama Made Me Do It, but She Wouldn't Tell Me Why!" and "How I Spent My Summer Vacation—and Nearly Died Three Months Later!"

The *True to Life* magazine presented information about birth control and other health and social issues. The characters woven into the stories demonstrate how individuals can take control of their own lives. *True to Life* was distributed to high schools, hospitals, Planned Parenthood affiliates, and other health, social, and educational agencies.

Even though the above examples focus on the mass media, it should not be assumed that these are the only alternatives. Certainly the use of salespeople is a medium of major importance. In fact, more money is spent in personal selling than in advertising or other forms of promotion. Salespeople must be carefully integrated into a firm's marketing effort. Also, the use of dealers and their representatives are another channel through which information reaches the consumer. In the move toward self-service, there has been a tendency for some people to overlook the significance of personal sources of information. Even the major discount houses and supermarkets that epitomize American self-service retailing have clerks available for answering customer questions and for aggressively selling products such as appliances and furniture.

Message Formulation

It has been said, "The medium is the message," and some people do believe that the environment within which a message is offered is so important that often it overwhelms what is actually written or said. If this were true, it would simplify the preparation of messages. However, it is not true.

Prepared messages become a critical part of what the consumer receives and moves into memory; therefore, they must be formulated with great care. For instance, there is little doubt that some positive responses have been effected by the simple statements "Look, Ma, no cavities" used by Procter and Gamble in their Crest toothpaste ads, and from "Only a dentist can give her a better fluoride treatment," used by Colgate-Palmolive. They may even have contributed to the dominance of these two brands of the $600-million toothpaste market.

It is interesting to note the creative strategy that was used by Lever Brothers to penetrate this market with Aim toothpaste. In 1971, Crest and Colgate had 73 percent of the total market when work was begun on Aim. After considerable study and market analysis, it was decided that there were several differentiating features of the Aim brand that would be important to consumers. However, these needed to be communicated effectively to a target audience essentially made up of mothers with children living at home. The tone of the message needed to be serious, informative, and authoritative because tooth decay, dental health, and dentist bills are major family concerns. It was then decided that attention would be focused on the fact that Aim was new, contained a therapeutic level of stannous fluoride, was in a modern gel form, and had more brushing incentives. These incentives included a pleasing color, flavor, texture, and appearance.[25]

The decision was made to use a slice-of-life setting for the message to create as nearly as possible the situation that was likely to occur in many Crest-user homes. The message theme used was "Take Aim against cavities"—a strategy that proved very successful. By 1978, Aim had captured about an 11-percent share of the toothpaste market.[26]

An equally challenging task faced Burger King in its attempt to gain on the giant McDonald's. Briefly it was a task of taking one simple fact uncovered through consumer research—that fast food customers hate to wait for special orders—and turning it into an opportunity. A simple, direct message seemed most effective, and "Have it your way" was promoted in a memorable campaign.[27]

Of course, getting the message across was not the only critical marketing task. The total strategy had to demonstrate to the public that, no matter what they might order at Burger King, it would be served promptly in a pleasant manner. This message was delivered to consumers through television advertising, restaurant signs, and printing on packages as well as through personnel. The 38-percent sales jump in one year suggests that Burger King's prime prospects—people 18-49 years old, many of whom live in families with children age 12 and under—liked the idea.

Summary

The volume of product information made available for consumers is considered substantial; yet, evidence suggests that at the time of a purchase there is likely to be little deliberate search. There are several explanations for this behavior. Exposure to information and persuasive messages is a continuous process enabling people to accumulate a reserve of knowledge which could assist in making a purchase at another time. Information gathering can be an added cost in time and money and can also add personal frustration in terms of an overload of facts, figures, and statements that reduce the consumer's ability to make a satisfying purchase decision. There are also social inhibitors which make it difficult to change certain behavior patterns.

Information search is the purposeful attention given to the gathering and assembling of information related to the satisfaction of some perceived need, want, or desire. In the consumer decision process, search follows problem recognition. Several factors significantly affect the search process: (1) the uniqueness of the object sought, (2) the strength of the motivation that caused the search activity, (3) previous experience in searching for similar products or services, and (4) one's general predisposition toward search.

The consumer search process is a prepurchase action which is carried on both internally and externally. *Internal search* is the conscious recall and consideration of specific information and experiences that appear to be relevant to the problem. This information is drawn from the long-term or permanent memory that Howard describes in his information reception and storage model. Internal search and alternative evaluation will cause the consumer to either proceed to the purchase stage, decide not to purchase, or commence external search and further evaluation.

External search is the deliberate effort to seek information from various outside sources. The extent to which the consumer engages in external search depends upon (1) the way the individual looks at a given problem, (2) his or her modes of reducing the tension that accompanies problem recognition, and (3) his or her ability and willingness to assume risk. Two phases make up the external search—the preliminary search effort and the concluding search effort. The preliminary search typically produces (1) a redefinition of the desired product or service attributes, (2) a firm acknowledgment by the consumer that there are constraints imposed in the search process, and (3) a more concise assessment of available personal resources. The concluding search effort can result in the consumer's either finding the problem-solving product or service, not finding it and discontinuing the search, or not finding it and continuing the search.

The impact of the external search is affected by the consumer's perceived image of the source (communicator) and by the clarity of the message. The image of the source is influenced not only by the person or organization doing the speaking or writing but also by the images of the vehicle and medium used. An important contributor to message clarity is the field of experience common to the source and the receiver. Consumer receptiveness to messages can be increased by (1) timing the message to reach the market when it is most likely to have significant impact, (2) selecting the media that the target audience is most likely to be using, and (3) formulating the message with great care.

Questions and Issues for Discussion

1. Some contend that change takes place so rapidly in our society today that it makes most product information obsolete soon after the consumer receives it. To what extent is this true? How is the constant introduction of new products likely to affect the consumer's search process?

2. A U.S. Postal Service survey was cited at the beginning of this chapter. It indicated that 63 percent of all direct mail pieces are opened and read. How could a nonprofit organization such as Planned

Parenthood develop a direct mail piece that could be expected to obtain a much higher level of readership?

3. How successful could a firm expect to be if it concentrated on making the best possible product for a price no higher than that of its competitors and if it relied strictly on its satisfied customers and its label to tell of the product's superiority? Consider this question with respect to each of the following products: mouthwash, musical instruments, homemade candy, and cameras.

4. How would the prepurchase search process probably vary for families at different stages of the family life cycle? Answer this question for each of the following situations:

Product/Service	Stages of Family Life Cycle
(a) Medical doctor in a new town	Newly married couples; full nest II
(b) Family clothing store	Full nest I; full nest III
(c) Living-room furniture	Full nest II; empty nest I
(d) Supermarket	Bachelor state; solitary survivor, retired

5. Is it reasonable to say that most people make poor choices of products and services if we compare their decisions to the "best buy" available in their community? Explain your answer.

6. Assume that you are responsible for teaching a class in how to be a good shopper. How would you go about explaining to your students how to carry out their prepurchase search and the evaluation of alternatives? Would these suggestions vary by product, age of students in your class, the income of the students, or how much experience they have had with the product?

7. How can the following buying patterns reduce the risk that a consumer takes in making a particular purchase?

  (a) Consistently buying one brand

  (b) Selecting the cheapest brand available

  (c) Buying the most expensive brand available

  (d) Purchasing only products with a plain and simple design.

8. How helpful and practical would each of the following be in assisting consumers in their search for information and in their evaluation of various competitive brands?

(a) Many products would be packaged in uniform amounts (for example, all soup cans would contain $10\frac{3}{4}$ oz., peanut butter jars $18\frac{1}{4}$ oz., and canned corn $12\frac{1}{3}$ oz.).

(b) All containers would have even amounts in them (the soup referred to above would be either 10 oz. or 11 oz.), but different brands could have varying amounts in their packages.

(c) The federal government would test and rate all consumer goods with a retail price over $10.00, with the resultant rating appearing on the product.

9. How appropriate would each of the media listed below be for promoting Preparation H (hemorrhoid treatment), memorial monuments (grave markers), and Jockey brand men's underwear? Give reasons for your answers.

(a) *Wall Street Journal*
(b) *Reader's Digest*
(c) National television
(d) Salespeople
(e) *Esquire*
(f) *Field and Stream*
(g) Billboards
(h) Local radio
(i) *Seventeen*
(j) Direct mail

10. Testimonials are often used to promote goods and services as well as political candidates and charitable causes. If you were asked to suggest three or four simple rules of thumb that would assist in making testimonials successful, what would you offer? Give reasons for your suggestions.

Case 1. Mutualco Life Insurance

At the beginning of 1976, Mutualco Life Insurance was the tenth largest life insurance company in the United States, but research found it to be twenty-fourth in unaided awareness tests among life insurance buyers. That is, 23 other life insurance companies came to mind more often than Mutualco when consumers were asked to name as many insurance companies as they could recall. These share-of-mind findings were not pleasing to the company's management, who set out to alter the situation.

Initially, consumer behavior research, commissioned by Mutualco, was undertaken using focus groups to explore the underlying feelings and beliefs held toward life insurance companies and the claims they make in their promotional strategy. Several findings were uncovered.

1. There was intense skepticism about life insurance claims generally.

2. Skepticism often led the consumer to ignore individual ad claims and the company placing the ad.

3. The term "mutual" as part of a company's name was vague and hard to understand; it also fostered more negative than positive feelings.

4. Many consumers felt that all life insurance was the same.

In further analyzing the research results, Mutualco management concluded that one major problem was that many life insurance ads promised benefits in terms that reflected company interests—not consumer interests. However, Mutualco's approach of taking the position that "people had many pressing uses for their money and buying life insurance at best was just one of them" was found credible. That is, this view accurately reflected consumers' true feelings. In addition, Mutualco had been successful in alleviating the fear among its policyholders of being oversold. These latter findings gave the company the idea of calling itself "The Concerned Company." This was believed to be a good way of asserting its non-hard-sell approach.

Armed with these findings and the desire to improve consumers' awareness of it, Mutualco decided to move away from its historical dependence on print advertising and sales promotion. The decision was made to participate in sponsoring the television broadcasting of the World Series. This was the company's first venture into television. Mutualco ran 10 commercials a total of 45 times during the 1978 series. The first results came in the way of letters, notes, and phone calls from policyholders, agents, the general public, and even from a few competitors—virtually all of them were positive. Follow-up research showed a high level of consumer awareness of the ads as well as a high level of willingness on the part of policyholders to recommend the company.

Case 1 Questions

1. Mutualco Life Insurance, like most similar companies, depends upon its agents to sell its life insurance policies. How can these agents capitalize on the success of this campaign and the research findings presented earlier to sell more life insurance?

2. Is it possible that "The Concerned Company" theme could produce some negative effects among prospects? If so, what might these be?

Case 2. Midwest Advertising Agency Assembly

The growing involvement of women in the labor force has brought considerable challenge to people who are responsible for assuring a high level of effective reach in a firm's promotional efforts. Furthermore, there is little disagreement among advertising executives about the fundamental importance of attempting to reach a well-defined audience in most advertising campaigns.

With a diminishing number of women assuming traditional homemaker roles, women generally can no longer be reached as easily as they once could via daytime television. A number of changes have appeared in response to this recognition.

1. "Sit-coms," television programs through which a working woman can gain relief from the day's tensions by sitting down for a short time in front of the television, show more working women in principal roles.

2. New special-interest magazines have appeared that are oriented toward the employed woman, such as *Working Woman, MS., New Woman,* and *Working Mother.*

3. Changes have occurred in traditional women's magazines such as *Good Housekeeping, Redbook,* and *Ladies' Home Journal.* These publications have varied their editorial content to include the interests and concerns of working women.

4. Women have begun appearing in commercials in fewer stereotyped roles.

5. There is a greater offering of television specials that are capable of attracting the "light" television viewer, many of whom are working women.

6. Fringe viewing and listening time periods are increasingly being experimented with as possible means of reaching a combination of the women who are employed outside the home as well as those who still are assuming the more traditional homemaker role.

With the above trends in mind, the Midwest Advertising Agency Assembly, a trade group serving ten states, has decided to hold a conference for business and agency executives who are responsible for dealing with "women as a key target market." The Assembly's desire is to emphasize discussion of how the changing roles of women are affecting the means of reaching women as consumers. This is to be a conference where serious exchanges of ideas can take place. The plan is to have half the conference sessions focus on media selection issues and half on topics concerning the development of appealing messages.

Case 2 Questions

1. Assume that you are responsible for developing a first draft of a proposed conference program. This should include the specific topics to be included as titles of four round-table discussion sessions for each of the two major aspects of the conference.

2. Identify two or three people, by name, from your local area who could be used as effective luncheon speakers on a topic consistent with the orientation of the conference. Give your reasons for suggesting each of these persons.

Notes

1. "The New World of Advertising," *Advertising Age,* 44 (November 21, 1973), p. 119.

2. Ibid., p. 64.

3. *The Yellow Pages in Marketing and Advertising* (New York: American Telephone and Telegraph Company, 1970), p. 17.

4. S. H. Chaffee and J. M. McLead, "Consumer Decisions and Information Use," S. Ward and T. S. Robertson, eds., *Consumer Behavior: Theoretical Sources* (Englewood Cliffs, N.J.: Prentice-Hall, Inc., 1973), pp. 386–87.

5. J. D. Clarton, J. N. Fry, and B. Portis, "A Taxonomy of Prepurchase Information Gathering Patterns," *Journal of Consumer Research,* 1 (December 1974), p. 35.

6. C. Block, E. Wims, and B. Kellerman, "An Empirical Test of Behavioral Propositions Set Forth in a Proposed Trade Regulation Rule by the FTC," Unpublished research paper (Columbia, Mo.: University of Missouri, 1978), p. 5.

7. R. F. Kelly, "The Search Component of the Consumer Decision Process—A Theoretic Examination," R. L. King, ed., *1968 Fall Conference Proceedings: Marketing and the New Science of Planning* (Chicago: American Marketing Association, 1969), p. 276.

8. J. F. Engel, D. T. Kollat, and R. D. Blackwell, *Consumer Behavior,* 2nd ed. (Hinsdale, Ill.: Dryden Press, 1973), p. 379.

9. J. A. Howard, "New Directions in Buyer Behavior Research," F. C. Allvine, ed., *Combined Proceedings: 1971 Spring and Fall Conferences* (Chicago: American Marketing Association, 1972), p. 376.

10. Ibid., pp. 376-77.

11. Kelly, "The Search Component," p. 278.

12. R. J. Listman, "An Overview of the Field of Direct Marketing" (New York: The Direct Mail/Marketing Educational Foundation, Inc., 1978), p. 1.

13. Ibid., pp. 10-11.

14. D. F. Cox, "The Influence of Cognitive Needs and Styles on Information Handling in Making Product Evaluation," D. F. Cox, ed., *Risk Taking and Information Handling in Consumer Behavior* (Boston: Division of Graduate School of Business, Harvard University, 1967), pp. 370-93.

15. Kelly, "The Search Component," p. 276.

16. Television Information Office, *Trends in Public Attitudes toward Television and Other Mass Media: A Report by the Roper Organization, Inc.* (New York: Television Information Office, National Association of Broadcasters, 1975), pp. 4-5.

17. "Sophia Loren Makes U.S. TV Commercial Debut," *New York Times* (November 21, 1977), p. 56.

18. P. Webb and M. L. Ray, *The Effects of Television Clutter: An Experimental Investigation* (Cambridge, Mass.: Marketing Science Institute, 1974), p. 3.

19. W. Schramm, "How Communication Works," L. Richardson, ed., *Dimensions of Communication* (New York: Appleton-Century Crofts, 1969), p. 6.

20. "Videodiscs: The Expensive Race to Be First," *Business Week* (September 15, 1975), p. 58.

21. "Marketing Briefs," *Marketing News,* Vol. XI (June 16, 1978), p. 2.

22. W. D. Wells, and D. J. Tigert, *Activities, Interests, and Opinions Working Paper* (Chicago: Graduate School of Business, University of Chicago, September, 1969), pp. 3-4.

23. Ibid., p. 8.

24. M. Crow, ed., *True to Life* (Atlanta: Emory University School of Medicine, Department of Gynecology and Obstetrics, Division of Research and Training in Maternal Health and Family Planning, September, 1970).

25. C. Fredericks, "Aim Toothpaste vs. Crest and Colgate," *How Do You Tackle the Leaders: Paper from the 1974 Regional Convention of the American Association of Advertising Agencies* (New York: American Association of Advertising Agencies, 1975), pp. 3-13.

26. "Close-up, Aim Not Ovate, but They Were Gold Eggs for Lever: Johnson," *Marketing News,* Vol. XI (June 2, 1978), p. 8.

27. R. Mercer, "Burger King vs. McDonald's," in *How Do You Tackle the Leaders: Paper from the 1974 Regional Convention of the American Association of Advertising Agencies* (New York: American Association of Advertising Agencies, 1975), pp. 27-39.

Chapter **14**

Immediate Choice Situation

Outline

Store Selection as a Purchasing Process

General Determinants of Store Choice

Store Image as a Factor in Consumer Decision Making

In-Store Purchasing Processes

Serving as a Reminder

Creating a Favorable Atmosphere

Resolving Questionable Issues

Gaining Closure

Summary

Questions and Issues for Discussion

Cases

Key Terms

purchasing processes

store selection

patronage routine

store image

buyer-seller relationship

functional utility

emotional utility

atmospherics

closure

This chapter draws attention to the circumstances associated with the consumer-retailer encounter. The situations that comprise the immediate surroundings of the act of buying are called purchasing processes. In a fundamental sense, a number of these latter activities are the final phase of the search process, but because they are so closely associated with making a purchase, they will be given special attention. Often these purchasing processes can be described simply as consumer-retail environment interactions. These include, for example, what one encounters upon entering a service station to buy gasoline or a sporting goods shop to purchase a volleyball net.

A number of retail firms have been very skillful in attracting large masses of people and continuing to serve them successfully, for example, fast food chains, such as McDonald's and Wendy's; Midas Muffler shops in auto repairs; and K-Mart in general merchandise. Certainly none of the goods offered by the firms just mentioned are especially unique. What has been particularly attractive to consumers is the delivery system of these firms as compared to that of their primary competitors. They have all built distinctive images and reputations for performance that today are often used as criteria for judging others. Consequently, the patterns of consumer-retailer interaction are well worth studying.

Figure 14.1 shows the complete consumer behavior model and clearly identifies the choice situation in relation to search, alternative evaluation, and outcomes. To a large extent, these outcomes are actual purchases. Consequently, purchasing processes involve the final aspects of the refinement of the evaluative criteria and their application by the consumer in a market setting where there is an awareness not only of what is desired, but also of what is available.

In treating the subject of purchase processes, the chapter is divided into two major sections. The first focuses on the selection of a store or place of business where the consumer intends to make a particular purchase. The second part of the chapter pays attention specifically to the in-store environment and how it can influence consumer behavior.

Store Selection as a Purchasing Process

Choice of a store or other business establishment is one of the important decisions that consumers make as they approach the final act of buying. Store selection itself is a purchase process, and Figure 14.2 is a conceptualization of how consumers go about making such selections. Essentially, four sets of variables are involved: (1) evaluative criteria, (2) perceived characteristics of the stores under consideration, (3) the comparison processes, and (4) the classifying of stores as either acceptable or unacceptable. The actual choice is the result of the process of comparing perceived store characteristics with the consumer's evaluative criteria.

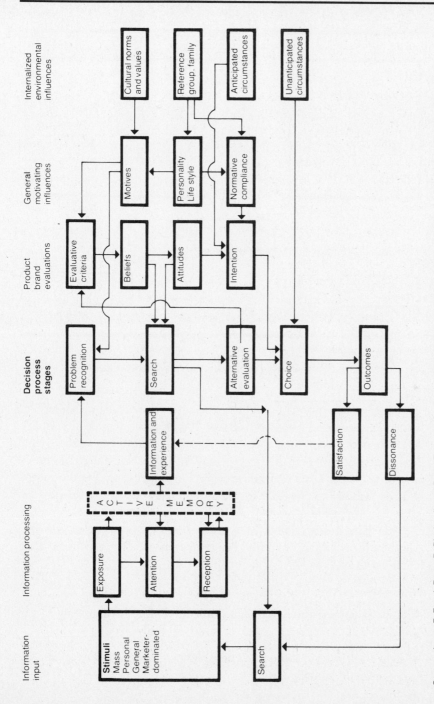

Figure 14.1
**A Complete Model of
Consumer Behavior
Showing Purchasing
Processes and
Outcomes**

Source: James F. Engel, Roger D. Blackwell, and David T. Kollat, *Consumer Behavior*, 3rd ed. (Hinsdale, Ill.: Dryden Press, 1978), p. 32. Copyright © 1978 by Dryden Press, a division of Holt, Rinehart and Winston. Reprinted by permission of Holt, Rinehart and Winston.

Figure 14.2
**Store-Choice
Processes**

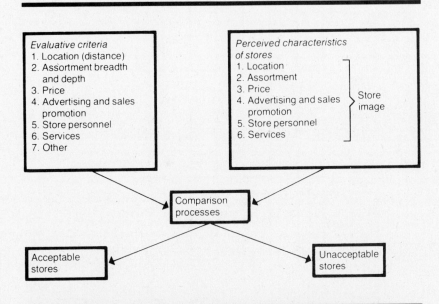

Consumer expectations brought to the retail store must be identified and monitored over time. A study of 600 Houston female supermarket shoppers, 73 percent of whom classified themselves primarily as homemakers, revealed the perceptions in Table 14.1 about the ideal amount of time to spend in the grocery store each week. Furthermore, a large number of the women indicated that they try to spend less time in a supermarket now than in previous years.[1]

This same research showed a greater expression of dislike or displeasure for shopping than had been anticipated. The reasons for this included the following:

● overwhelmed by the vastness of merchandise selection

● worked outside the home and didn't have time for shopping

● little to show for time spent

● didn't see why it should be their responsibility when everyone in the household benefited.

Time	Percent
Less than 30 minutes	12.8
30 to 45 minutes	37.5
About one hour	38.7
About one and one-half hours	6.2
No opinion/other response	4.8

Table 14.1
Perceptions of Ideal Amount of Weekly In-Store Grocery Shopping

Source: P. L. Burr, "Female Supermarket Shopping: Some Behavioral Reflections," C. D. Schick, ed., *Challenge of Change to Advertising Education: Proceedings of the 1976 American Academy of Advertising* (Austin, Texas: American Academy of Advertising, 1976), pp. 173, 174. Reprinted by permission.

As consumers make store choices and proceed to patronize those selected, learning is going on. That is, if the shopping experience within the "acceptable stores" is satisfactory, the choice will be reinforced. As a result, over time the need to search for particular types of stores is greatly reduced. It can reach the point where certain need arousal sends the consumer to one of a very limited number of stores. For instance, it is not unusual for consumers to develop a pattern of regularly patronizing a particular dry-cleaning establishment. This may have been the result of a long trial-and-error process or of simply finding an acceptable cleaner on one trial. Whatever the initial selection process involved, at some particular point there was the feeling that, on the basis of the given evaluative criteria, this one establishment was satisfactory. It is likely that regular patronage will continue as long as the relationship continues to be satisfactory.

Store loyalty of this sort is rather widespread. It is often possible to find considerable customer loyalty as reflected in regular visits to a specific supermarket, beauty salon, barber shop, clothing store, auto repair shop, and drugstore. Medical doctors and dentists also enjoy a very high level of patient loyalty. *Patronage routine*—regularly returning to a given store or service outlet—can appeal to the consumer because it reduces uncertainty and the time necessary to complete a purchase as well as enhancing the general feeling of belonging. Such benefits pose a formidable competitive challenge. Therefore, it is usually much easier for a merchant to maintain his or her present customer base than to attract business from competitors.

General Determinants of Store Choice

The specific evaluative criteria used in store choice vary significantly, depending on the type of product or service being sought. For instance, the criteria used to select a photo shop where a new camera is to be purchased are usually much more varied than those employed in seeking to buy a can of spray enamel for repainting an old desk. Nevertheless, certain determinants are used more than others. These include (1) location, (2) depth and breadth of assortment, (3) price, (4) advertising and word-of-mouth communications, (5) sales promotion, (6) store personnel, (7) services, (8) physical attributes, and (9) store clientele, that is, who else shops there.

The operational impact of these various determinants is affected by consumer perceptions. These perceptions form what has been called store image. Put simply, *store image* is a composite of the dimensions that consumers perceive as the store or service establishment; it is often what makes one business different from its competitors in the eyes of the consumer.[2] The next section pays specific attention to what has been called "image" and to the importance of this phenomenon in studying consumer choice processes.

Store Image as a Factor in Consumer Decision Making

The dimensions whose presence and importance compose an image vary from one store to another. Tangible dimensions typically involve such factors as having low prices, adequate parking, and sufficient salespeople. Intangibles that are not easily measured but are of importance are characterized by descriptions such as "a friendly store," "a place where I feel comfortable," and "an exciting place to shop." How these dimensions are actually put together to form an image of a particular establishment and the relative importance of each dimension depend on the store's management and on the views of the consumers who shop there. For example, the way in which one type of customer perceives Neiman-Marcus or Macy's can be markedly different from the manner in which others view them. In today's consumers' market, it is impossible to be "all things to all people." A firm's management must decide which segments of the consumer market it can successfully serve and then try to develop an image that is consistent with the preferences of those consumers.

Two short cases are presented here to illustrate what is meant by a retail store's image and how this image can be related to a firm's market success. These cases include a composite of experiences of several different organizations that have been combined into two representative situations. They employ the analysis framework suggested by May.[3]

Case 1

Subject Area: Sewing Machine Sales and Service Department Image

Type of Company: A major midwestern department store in a large metropolitan area. Its direct competition included three other full-line stores, all of which were significantly larger in total size.

Issue: A sizable number of customer complaints were being received with respect to the store's sewing machine sales efforts and their related service operation. The complaints were steadily increasing, and specific references were being made to the use of bait-and-switch tactics.

Objective: To determine the image of the sewing machine sales and service department among recent customers (those who had done business with the department during the previous six months) as well as among noncustomers.

Research Methods: A sample-survey procedure was used to reach a representative number of both recent customers and noncustomers. Telephone interviewing was employed. A series of questions was included to determine how people chose among departments offering these products, what were the most important considerations, and how all four department stores in the area compared on these evaluative criteria.

Findings: The research findings revealed the following about the store studied.

1. It had a considerably poorer sewing machine service image than did its major competitors.

2. The store's salespeople in this department were considered aggressive and often rude.

3. The sales area and its displays were poorly arranged and messy as compared to the competitors' facilities.

4. Phone calls to the department were frequently met with long delays as people waited for answers to simple questions.

5. Its prices were considered the lowest in town.

Conclusion: Further analysis of the sales and service volume of this department showed that its sewing machine sales were greater than those of its three competitors combined. In addition, it appeared that most complaints came from people who had purchased a machine during November or December and from those who had sought warranty work. It was also discovered that their competitors had recently experienced some increase in the number of complaints in their sewing machine and service departments.

Action: Management decided to take no immediate action. This department had shown one of the best growth and profitability records in the whole store. It was hoped, however, that in the future additional space could be allocated to this department.

Case 2

Subject Area: Image of Young Women's Ready-to-Wear and Related Merchandise

Type of Company: A women's specialty store in a southern university community of about 60,000.

Issue: A lower level of sales in various accessory departments of this shop as compared to the sales of similar items in two local competitive stores. These accessories included such items as jewelry, scarves, hosiery, and handbags.

Objective: To determine the image of the three women's ready-to-wear shops and to compare them. Some explanation was sought for the lower level of accessory sales in the store sponsoring the study.

Research Methodology: A sample-survey was conducted using a questionnaire inserted in the local newspaper followed by personal interviews of members of selected sororities at the university.

Findings: The study revealed that:

1. Both customers and noncustomers of the sponsoring store found the two competitors to have a more appealing store layout. People could better visualize the interrelationship among the display items in these stores.

2. The two competitors' lines were considered to be more complete. A shopper was just more likely to find what she wanted.

Conclusion: The store that initiated the study was larger and had divided its offerings into separate departments, each having a clerk who was responsible for its displays and sales. This had led to the development of these departments into rather separate entities. Consequently, even though the selection was the largest in town, the customer was not able to see the merchandise as parts of a coordinated whole.

Action: The individual departments were disbanded and consolidated into one coordinated unit, making use of various display areas for different accessories. The store manager assumed responsibility for developing display themes throughout the store that emphasized the interrelatedness of the merchandise.

The impression might be conveyed by these cases that once an image is determined, management can proceed to deal with other matters. This is not possible because store image is a dynamic concept; that is, even maintaining an existing image takes effort. If, for example, a men's apparel store is noted for its fashion leadership, its merchandising practices must be consistent with this character.

Management's failure to develop a responsive strategy to meet changing consumer preferences can be disastrous. Abercrombie and Fitch made its mark in retailing by catering to elitist clientele attracted by its unique assortment of expensive sports equipment, apparel, and gift items. Among its long list of well-known customers were Theodore Roosevelt, for whom it outfitted African safaris, and Admiral Richard Byrd, who obtained the necessary equipment for his expedition to Antarctica from Abercrombie and Fitch. Even though it broadened its line and expanded into a chain with branches in nine cities, it never truly became a modern-style retailer capable of appealing to members of a more budget-conscious generation who gave their loyalty to mass-merchandising discounters. Abercrombie and Fitch's sales peaked at $28 million in 1968 and then began to falter until the company filed for voluntary bankruptcy in 1976.[4]

In a recent article, Williams, Painter, and Nicholas presented a policy-oriented typology of grocery shoppers based upon their research that provides suggestions for marketing strategy development, which can be useful in formulating marketing efforts to influence particular market segments.

Figure 14.3 identifies four consumer buying styles represented by each of the four cells. The labels used are descriptive of what variation in store offering that respondents in each segment seek as typified by their evaluation of their favorite grocery store. In this scheme, service practices are basically store location and shopping convenience.[5]

Figure 14.3
**Grocery Shopper
Buying Styles**

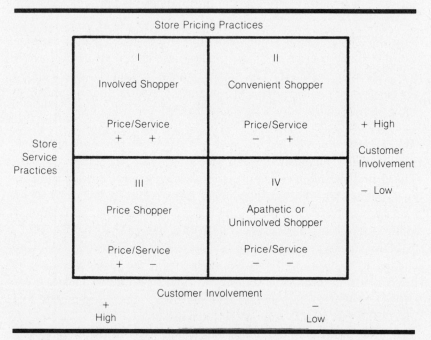

Source: R. Williams, J. Painter, and H. Nicholas, ''A Policy-Oriented Typology of Grocery Shoppers,'' *Journal of Retailing*, Vol. 54 (Spring 1978), p. 29. Reproduced by permission of the *Journal of Retailing*, New York University.

As can be noted from Table 14.2, Group IV customers essentially evaluated everything in a negative manner. Group II customers perceived the prices at their favorite store as being too high. However, they consciously made trade-offs of price for convenience; they con-

Image Dimensions	I Involved Shopper	II Convenient Shopper	III Price Shopper	IV Apathetic Shopper
Prices	low	high	low	high
Advertising	good	neutral	good	bad
Quality	high	neutral	neutral	low
Convenience	high	high	low	low

Table 14.2
How Favorite Stores Were Evaluated

Source: R. Williams, J. Painter, and H. Nicholas, ''A Policy-Oriented Typology of Grocery Shoppers,'' *Journal of Retailing*, Vol. 54 (Spring 1978), p. 33. Reproduced by permission of the *Journal of Retailing*, New York University.

sidered their favorite store to be very convenient. Group III customers considered the prices they paid at their favorite store to be low; but the store's convenience was also rated rather low. Group I customers evaluated both service and price dimensions favorably.

It was found that convenience-oriented shoppers tended to be loyal to the store where they shopped. Consequently, they were generally more profitable customers. To attract this type of customer, it would be important to emphasize the ease and speed of shopping. Price shoppers, however, have an economic orientation and even go out of their way to obtain low prices. These latter customers are likely to be attracted by newspaper ads and coupon distributions. Management must become aware of the relative size of the various market segments because it may be difficult for one chain to appeal equally well to each of the possible segments.

Once consumers select a business establishment, they move closer to the purchase act. The next section pays specific attention to these latter encounters.

In-Store Purchasing Processes

As a way of drawing attention to the fundamental components of the in-store buyer-seller relationship, a model developed by Sheth is introduced here. This conceptual framework is presented in Figure 14.4 and is intended to provide a comprehensive means of studying the key variables in the buyer-seller interaction. A brief overview of the model will be given with the hope that those who have further interest will go to the original source for greater detail.

Figure 14.4
A Conceptual Framework of Buyer-Seller Interaction

Seller

	Compatible Process	Incompatible Process
Compatible Content	Ideal Transaction	Inefficient Transaction
Incompatible Content	Inefficient Transaction	No Transaction

Seller

Style of Communication
1. Task Oriented Style
2. Interaction Oriented Style
3. Self-Oriented Style

Content of Communication
1. Functional Utility
2. Social-Organizational Utility
3. Situational Utility
4. Emotional Utility
5. Curiosity Utility

Buyer

Content of Communication
1. Functional Utility
2. Social-Organizational Utility
3. Situational Utility
4. Emotional Utility
5. Curiosity Utility

Style of Communication
1. Task Oriented Style
2. Interaction Oriented Style
3. Self-Oriented Style

Product-Specific Factors
- Technology and Competition
- Market Motivations
- Buyer-Seller Plans

Organizational Factors
- Org. Objectives
- Org. Style
- Org. Structure

Personal Factors
- Personal Background
- Personal Life Style
- Role Orientation

Source: J. N. Sheth, "Buyer-Seller Interaction: A Conceptual Framework," G. Zaltman and B. Sternthal, eds., *Broadening the Concept of Consumer Behavior* (Chicago: Association for Consumer Research, 1975), p. 133. Reprinted by permission of Association for Consumer Research.

today. He checked with his sales manager and found that the lowest acceptable price was $3695. Upon hearing this, the young woman thought for a moment and said, "All right, I will take it for $3695."

This brief encounter and the purchase that followed include several activities and circumstances that make up the purchasing process. These are identified below:

1. Deciding to go back to this particular Ford dealer

2. Going into the showroom and looking for Gil Crawford, the salesman

3. Observing the interior atmosphere of the dealership, including taking notice of the various signs

4. Sitting down in the lounge area and reading the article in the *Ford Times*

5. Looking at the car that the salesman said he thought she would like

6. Asking for the salesman's best price

7. Making a counter offer to the salesman

8. Deciding to purchase the car shown to her

9. Giving the salesman the deposit.

> *Situation II:* An elderly man enters the Safeway supermarket near his home. Just a short distance from the entrance, he notices several shopping carts filled with various canned goods. Attached to the carts are signs that identify these items as weekend specials. He stops for a moment looking over the sale items and then proceeds on into the main part of the store. There is the soft sound of music in the background, and as he moves down the first aisle, he sees fresh strawberries in pint containers displayed along with shortcake and whipped topping. These berries are certainly appealing, for they are the first of the season. However, what he really came in for was a quart of milk and some luncheon meat. He picks up these two items and also a container of strawberries and then makes his way to the checkout. He pays for these groceries with food stamps. The items are put into a bag and he leaves.

Here, too, there are a number of dimensions to the purchasing process that are identifiable.

1. Entering the Safeway store

2. Taking notice of the canned goods on sale as well as the display of strawberries and related items

3. Being aware of the background music

4. Selecting the three items for purchase

5. Choosing among the available brands of milk and luncheon meat

6. Going through the checkout

7. Paying for his purchases with food stamps

8. Having his purchases put into a bag.

Situation III: It is September, and the Sears Christmas catalog, called the *Wish Book,* has just arrived in the Daugherty home. The children can hardly wait to study the toy section. One child has a birthday coming up in mid-October and, therefore, she wants to get her list of gift suggestions together quickly. This is soon done and brought to the attention of the rest of the family during dinner.

She has been careful to separate her suggestions into three groups, according to their costs. She has done this because she knows from experience that her mother and father are willing to buy her a gift more expensive than what her younger brother could afford. Furthermore, it was strongly suggested that she make only modest requests of her aunts and uncles.

Shortly after these suggestions are made known, her mother and father decide to call the Sears catalog department and place their order. This is done, and the two items ordered are picked up later in the week at the local store and charged to their account.

Here, as in the previous two situations, there are several aspects of the purchasing process that can be noted:

1. The child's looking over the catalog and making a list of suggested gifts

2. The discussion of the various gift suggestions during dinner

3. The parents' selection of two items from their daughter's list

4. Calling the local Sears store and placing the order

5. Picking up the items and charging them to their account.

Each of these three situations has described a set of circumstances that portray a consumer-retailer encounter following individual problem recognition, the formulation of evaluative criteria, and varying amounts of search. These circumstances include a cluster of factors and related interactions that make up the immediate or near environment within which the actual purchase takes place. Because each of these factors and accompanying interactions may have had some influence on the purchase outcomes, they are of considerable interest to the consumer analyst. The ways in which the various aspects of these purchasing processes affect consumers can be summarized under the following topics: (1) serving as a reminder, (2) creating a favorable atmosphere, (3) resolving questionable issues, and (4) gaining closure. Each of these will be discussed in the following sections, and examples from the three situations will be used to illustrate their possible impact.

Serving as a Reminder

It would make it easier for the consumer analyst and probably for the consumer, too, if all or most purchases were made as the result of a clearly identifiable sequence of steps. Such a sequence would include the conscientious recognition of a particular problem and a deliberate pattern of action to resolve it in some practical manner. Although it is recognized that consumer behavior is essentially reasoned, or purposeful, behavior, often the consumer needs some nudge or other assistance in directing him or her toward want-satisfying action.

Consumers may need to be reminded that they actually need or want some particular product. For instance, to certain shoppers the layout of their favorite supermarket serves as a shopping list of a sort. Going up and down the aisles and noting what is in each section of the store brings to mind items that have not been explicitly written down on a list but that, nevertheless, are desired. Just glancing at the cash register in the beverage store may remind you to buy some snack food that you had nearly forgotten. The very act of browsing through a clothing store can bring to your attention the desire to buy a new tie to match a shirt received recently as a gift or remind you that those favorite brown slacks are showing wear and should be replaced.

Each of the three buying situations described earlier included reminder factors. Furthermore, a number of these are subject to the direct control of the merchant and, consequently, can be modified to vary their possible effects on the consumer. In Situation I the various hanging banners and signs in the Ford dealer's showroom reminded the young woman that this was the time to buy—cars were on sale. Even the placement of a magazine like *Ford Times* in the lounge area could have contributed favorably to moving the consumer closer toward making a purchase. The article she read reminded her of the fun she should have traveling in her new car. The salesman's pleasant greeting may have brought to her mind that this was a friendly and cordial place, one that she would likely get good treatment from after the purchase. This latter experience could have served to strengthen her feeling that this was a wise stop to make.

In Situation II the elderly man took note of the canned goods on sale as he entered the store. This may have reminded him of a need for these items. Although he did not buy any of them on this trip, he could return later and do so. These sales displays may also have served to remind him of the fact that the prices at the supermarket are low as compared to others nearby. The display of fresh strawberries did bring to his mind how good these can taste, and they were sufficiently attractive that he made the purchase. However, even though he noticed the shortcake and topping on display with the berries, no purchase was made. Retail experience shows that such combination displays can often promote greater interest in all items in the display.

Some of the purchase processes in Situation III also served as reminders. The receipt of the *Wish Book* itself is a reminder to begin planning for Christmas. Its arrival in September served to encourage the Daugherty girl to put together a list of gift suggestions if she wanted to express her preferences to her family. Using the catalog in this way again brought to the attention of this family that a large number of items can be purchased from the convenience of their home.

Many companies take very seriously the opportunities that exist within the store to remind the customer to buy their brand. This interest is substantiated by the fact that United States firms spent an estimated $2 billion on point-of-purchase advertising in 1973. The following figures note the estimated annual expenditures of five major firms on point-of-purchase advertising:[7]

General Motors	$44,000,000
Procter and Gamble	9,000,000
Coca-Cola	16,000,000
Bristol Myers	7,942,000
General Foods	4,000,000

The possible impact of in-store reminders is exemplified by considering the findings from one study of the buying behavior of 6795 shoppers in 16 mass-merchandising stores in several geographic areas. Unplanned purchases were made by 30 percent of all shoppers. Of these unplanned purchases, 81 percent were a national or regional brand; 24 percent of these items were first-time purchases; and 48 percent were of a brand that had not been bought before.[8]

Some merchants have become very creative in developing reminder techniques. One display for a baking products company utilized a device that released the pleasant odor of its cinnamon cake inside the supermarket. This allowed the shopper to make a buying decision after having had the opportunity to inspect the package, note the price, read the point-of-purchase advertising, and smell the product's aroma.

Creating a Favorable Atmosphere

The environment within which goods are offered for sale or services are rendered can be a substantial part of what interests the consumer. For example, nearly everyone likes to try a new restaurant, often just to sample the experiences that are available there.

In a very real sense, the environment or atmosphere is a part of what the consumer buys. Too frequently the businessperson has neglected atmosphere as a viable marketing technique. According to Kotler, *atmospherics* involves the conscious designing of space and its various dimensions to effect certain responses in buyers.[9] Of course, consumers perceive an atmosphere in a business establishment whether or not one has been consciously developed.

In Situation I the perceived atmosphere was apparently one of friendliness that nurtured a feeling of confidence in the dealership. This perception may even have included the belief that the salesman had the consumer's best interest in mind. In Situation II the supermarket was probably like many others; yet it most likely had some characteristics that set it apart from its competitors in the area. Factors that can contribute to atmospheric differences among supermarkets include the general cleanliness of the store, the quality and freshness of its meat and produce, the width of the aisles, the extent to which the shelves are well stocked, the helpfulness of the employees, and even the background music and the color of the interior walls.

One might be tempted to conclude that Situation III has no atmospheric dimensions. However, this is not the case. The format of the catalog itself creates a unique environment for shopping. In addition, the mailing of the *Wish Book* makes use of the home as part of the purchasing atmosphere. In recognizing this opportunity, some catalog merchandisers have even suggested that a person sit down in front of the fireplace or some other comfortable spot and browse through the offerings. If children grow up with fond memories of paging through such catalogs, this may have a substantial impact on their purchasing patterns later in life. Consequently, even the atmosphere created by a catalog can be a powerful marketing tool.

Atmospheres are likely to be most important under certain conditions. Four of these are identified below.[10]

1. Atmospherics is a relevant marketing technique primarily in situations where the product is purchased or consumed and where the seller has design options. For example, atmospherics are more likely to be important to a restaurant with sit-down facilities than to one that only has a carry-out service. Also, manufacturers of consumer goods are less likely to be able to use atmospherics than are retailers.

2. Atmospherics becomes an important marketing tool as the number of competitive outlets increases. This becomes another means by which one business can be differentiated from another. Furthermore, this kind of competitive action is more difficult for competitors to counter than are price changes or even assortment carried.

3. Atmospherics is a more relevant marketing tool in industries where product and/or price differences are small. Savings and loan associations often seek differentiation through the use of atmospherics because regulatory requirements necessarily result in considerable similarity among them. Their efforts typically take shape through the skillful use of interior decor and related promotional strategy.

4. Atmospherics can be a helpful technique when a firm's offerings are aimed at a distinct social class or at buyers with particular lifestyles. The May Company basement, with its unique merchandising strategy, is likely to appeal to the working class. Consequently, its atmosphere must be consistent with bargain-basement retailing. This environment is in considerable contrast to other departments in the very same store that cater to a more upper-middle-class clientele.

Resolving Questionable Issues

The retailer-consumer interaction offers a unique opportunity to deal with unresolved questions that the consumer might have about the product or service under consideration. As pointed out in the last chapter, the search process can bring the consumer to the realization that initial expectations must be modified in light of what is available and personal resource limitations. Such confrontation with reality can be disturbing and can raise doubts as to whether certain personal needs or desires can be satisfied.

The retail store is often the only place where these questions can be answered. The consumer needs assistance to resolve these difficulties. Such assistance may be provided by the merchant through salespeople, product usage and care labels, and assembling an assortment of products for customer inspection and visual comparison as well as through point-of-purchase advertising.

In Situation I the young woman who entered the local auto dealership had some specific questions in mind. These were quickly answered to her satisfaction by the salesman. In neither Situation II nor III were specific questions identified, although there were implicit questions nevertheless. In Situation II, for example, the elderly man's entering the supermarket with two items in mind poses the question as to whether his preferred brands or enough variety will be available. Furthermore, in this specific situation he no doubt had some definite price expectations because he was using food stamps to make his purchases. In Situation III there apparently was considerable excitement on the child's part as she approached the catalog expecting to find a number of acceptable gift possibilites. The issue as to whether any acceptable items could be found in the catalog could only be resolved by searching through it. However, past experience with the Sears catalog as well as the attractive cover and related promotion by the company suggest that this is a gratifying way to shop.

Unfortunately, it is not an unusual experience for consumers to enter business establishments with specific questions in mind only to find no satisfying means of resolving them. The striving for greater efficiency in mass retailing has led many firms toward greater emphasis on self-service, which in turn has made the retailer-consumer encounter more impersonal. Consequently, the consumer has had to depend on point-of-purchase advertising, package descriptions, personal inspection of the product, or even on the opinion of someone else to help make the final evaluation. In some cases, where clerks have been made available in large mass-merchandising outlets, the service has been so poor that customers buy in spite of the "assistance" and not because of it.

An important point for businesspeople to be aware of is that people who enter their establishment are frequently serious prospects; they have been through a self-selection process. For example, most of those who walk into a shoe store are acknowledging that they have an interest in the shoes in that store.

Gaining Closure

Closure refers to the process of bringing consumers to the point where the evidence before them conclusively suggests that the product or service being offered should be bought. Or stated more simply, it is moving the consumer to the point where he or she says, "Yes, I'll take it."

To the business firm, all expenditures of time and money to get the prospective customer to the point of a "near sale" are wasted if a satisfactory level of profitable sales is not generated. This suggests that there is some truth in the old saying that "Nothing happens until somebody sells something."

However, gaining closure does not mean selling people goods or services that they do not want. It is quite the contrary; it means providing the consumer with exactly what is wanted and proving so beyond a doubt. This is consistent with the marketing concept.

Gaining closure is so important that some businesses have specialists who take over from the regular salespeople after there is evidence that the consumer is nearing a final decision. Other firms help their sales staff develop closing techniques through extensive sales training.

Of course, obtaining closure takes more than a salesperson's asking for the order. It is presenting goods or services in such a way that the prospect will find that what is being given attention represents the culmination of the search process. As a result, the purchase act becomes a natural step to take.

To a large extent, the whole series of events in Situation I that occurred after the young woman entered the auto dealership seemed to move her toward the purchase. This included the pleasant atmosphere, the point-of-purchase advertising, the friendliness shown her, the way in which her questions were answered, and the salesman's showing her the car that he believed she would like. It appeared as if it was quite natural for her to say, "All right, I will take it."

In Situations II and III closure has also been obtained but in a more subtle manner. In the supermarket, for example, having the desired items conveniently available and in an attractive setting at an acceptable price contributed to gaining closure. The special display of three related products also encouraged the elderly man to purchase one item that he apparently had not planned to buy when he entered the store. In Situation III the catalog format, the extensive selection of merchandise, the ease with which orders could be placed, and the apparent knowledge from past experience that orders would be filled promptly and satisfactorily are all likely to have contributed to gaining closure.

Summary

Purchasing processes include the purchase act itself and those encounters which are a part of the circumstances that make up the immediate surroundings of the act of buying. This chapter examines the consumer's selection of a store and the in-store purchasing processes.

Store selection itself is a purchasing process involving the comparison of the store's perceived characteristics against one's evaluative criteria and then the classification of the store as either acceptable or unacceptable. Common criteria used are location, depth and breadth of assortment, price, store personnel, etc. The image of a store should be made consistent with the preferences of the consumer group that the store management desires to serve.

As consumers make store choices which satisfy them, store loyalty can be developed. For the consumer, having a patronage routine can reduce uncertainties and time necessary in completing a purchase. To the businessperson, store loyalty represents a competitive challenge.

Once the store is selected, the in-store purchasing processes commence. A model developed by Sheth is introduced as a means of studying the key variables in the buyer-seller interaction. This transaction can have multiple outcomes that perform any of five functions described earlier. Sheth believes that a satisfactory interaction can only occur between the buyer and seller if they are compatible with respect to both the content and style of the communication between them. These communication variables are affected by a number of personal, organizational, and product-related factors.

It is appropriate to note the effect that various aspects of these purchasing processes have on the consumer. First, techniques to serve as a reminder to the consumer, such as point-of-purchase advertising, are quite effective and precipitate many unplanned purchases. Second, creating a favorable atmosphere for purchase is effective, especially under certain conditions. For example, when the product or price differences are small, atmospherics can be the deciding factor for the consumer. Third, the retailer-consumer interaction can be beneficial to both parties by resolving questionable issues that the consumer has in mind. Last, gaining closure is proving beyond a doubt to consumers that they have been provided with exactly what they want and having them acknowledge, "Yes, I'll take it."

Questions and Issues for Discussion

1. Is it reasonable to assume that a store's image is similar to an individual's personality and that neither changes very much over time?

2. How could atmospherics contribute to the creation of the following:

(a) A budget men's shop

(b) A feeling of security as well as friendliness and customer concern in a bank

(c) An exclusive health spa.

3. Identify the major components of the purchasing process, assuming you have been the buyer of each of the products or services:

(a) a small convenience good, such as a newspaper;

(b) auto repair service;

(c) a small appliance when brand was an important consideration.

4. Is it in the best interest of the public to have firms create an image of their retail establishments? Shouldn't they just try to serve their customers in the best possible manner? Explain.

5. How can the layout of a store or of a particular department in it contribute to generating profitable sales? Describe what you would call a good layout of a sporting goods shop. Give reasons for your suggestions.

6. Closure is a concept that has operational significance in a number of aspects of marketing. Give an example of how closure could function in each of the following:

(a) In an advertisement for sunglasses

(b) As part of a display in a hobby shop

(c) When a door-to-door volunteer calls for contributions to the Heart Fund.

7. How could one go about determining the evaluative criteria that consumers use to select particular stores in which to shop? Is it likely that these criteria are well established in the consumer's mind?

8. How true is the following statement? "During inflationary periods with high unemployment, consumers generally will sacrifice store atmosphere for low prices."

9. Some say that, today, the package, serving as the "silent salesman" in self-service retailing, is probably the most influential component of the purchasing process. Evaluate this observation.

10. Some large retailers appear to spend millions of dollars on advertising to get the consumer into their store only to lose the sale because of the poor expertise of their salespeople. What is their rationale in following this practice?

Case 1. Booneville Mailback, Inc.

Booneville Mailback, Incorporated, is a mail order supplier that has specialized in selling gift items through catalogs sent to business executives. The primary market has been firms that typically send gifts to their key customers during the Christmas season as a thank you for the year's orders. Over the last ten years, the firm has grown from $1 million annual volume to $10 million. BMI's line includes office novelties, decorative household and office products, and a limited line of packaged candies and cheeses. Their prices range from $10.95 to $99.95. Most business gifts purchased through BMI averaged $30 each and were typically ordered in lots of two dozen.

The company recently experimented with a pre-Christmas limited mailing to a select group of 400 executives' wives whose names and addresses were obtained through a purchased mailing list from a list broker. The results were encouraging. Approximately 5 percent of those contacted made purchases averaging $25 each.

These findings became available at the same time as a report prepared by Maxwell Sroge Company, a Chicago-based consulting firm. The following are some of the statistics offered in the Sroge report:[11]

1. Mail order sales volume increased to $19.2 billion in 1976, a 13.8 percent increase over 1975.

2. There were about 8000 firms in the mail order business in 1976.

3. The major lines sold in order of importance were:

    (a) ready-to-wear clothing—$2 billion in sales

    (b) insurance—$1.19 billion in sales

    (c) magazine subscriptions—$975 million in sales

    (d) books—$966 million in sales.

4. Profits as a percentage of sales were considerably higher in the mail order business than in manufacturing or retailing generally.

Consumer use of purchase-by-mail opportunities were expected to continue to grow. A number of factors will contribute to this: the flow of women into the job market, the aging of the population as a whole, and increasing real income.

BMI management believes that these and other factors will make traditional in-store shopping less appealing. They also feel that their generous return policy will further assist them in successfully entering the consumer side of the mail order business.

Case 1 Questions

1. What are the strongest reasons that can be given for BMI to enter the consumer mail order market?

2. What are the major drawbacks that BMI faces in entering the consumer mail order market?

3. How could a firm like BMI compete successfully with Sears, Ward's, Penney's, Aldens, and Spiegel in the direct marketing field?

Case 2. Skatesite Parks

Skatesite is a firm with 30 commercial areas in 10 states designed specifically for skateboard enthusiasts. Each site has about one acre of of land including parking, clubhouse, and a safe skating environment essentially designed for kids. To the ordinary person, these parks look like a series of concrete bowls. But actually, they are protected skating areas where, for $2.50 plus 75 cents for safety equipment rental, a child or adult can skate for 2½ hours. On weekdays, between 60 and 90 people use each park; on weekends this averages 100 people each day.

Skatesite has been quite successful for a relatively new and rather small company. At this time the clubhouse at each Skatesite Park is primarily a place where one can purchase snack foods and soft drinks. These items have sold rather well; nevertheless, the Skatesite management saw opportunities to augment this by selling skateboards and accessory items such as T-shirts. These seem to be natural choices to add. The best-selling models of skateboards sell for between $20 and $35, but they actually range in price from $6 to $125 each. Mark-up is about 50 percent on retail.

Several factors about the skateboard market make it increasingly attractive.[12]

1. There are an estimated 20 million skateboarders in the U.S.

2. The equipment available is far superior at this time as compared to the skateboard craze of the mid 1960s.

3. Skateboards appeal to a broad age group, essentially 7 to 25 years old.

4. The use of safety equipment has made the skateboard much more attractive to parents. In 1975, the U.S. Consumer Products Safety Commission estimated that there were about 28,000 skateboard injuries nationally. This ranked it 25th in terms of being dangerous. However, bicycles were ranked first in terms of frequency and severity of injury.

The real marketing issue of interest to Skatesite is how to take full advantage of the sales opportunities that exist among park customers. Not only do children come and spend several hours at their skateboard parks, but also parents often spend an hour or two there.

The management does not want to overcommercialize their parks, but neither do they want to pass up attractive profit potential.

Case 2 Questions

1. What considerations in addition to those mentioned above should Skatesite management give attention to before substantially changing its offering of supplemental sales items?

2. How could the buying interests of skateboard users be explored? To what extent are parents likely to be important in this setting?

Notes

1. P. L. Burr, "Female Supermarket Shopping: Some Behavioral Reflections," C. D. Schick, ed., *Challenge of Change to Advertising Education: Proceedings of the 1976 American Academy of Advertising* (Austin, Texas: American Academy of Advertising, 1976), pp. 173, 174.

2. E. G. May, *Management Applications of Retail Image Research: Marketing Science Institute Working Paper* (Cambridge, Mass.: Marketing Science Institute, 1973), p. 21.

3. Ibid.

4. "Abercrombie's Problem Was Image," *Marketing Executive's Digest* (January 1978), p. 4.

5. R. H. Williams, J. J. Painter, and H. R. Nicholas, "A Policy-Oriented Typology of Grocery Shoppers," *Journal of Retailing,* 54 (Spring 1978), pp. 28-40.

6. J. N. Sheth, "Buyer-Seller Interaction: A Conceptual Framework," G. Zaltman and B. Sternthal, eds., *Broadening the Concept of Consumer Behavior* (Chicago: Association for Consumer Research, 1975), pp. 131-40.

7. H. S. Gorschman, "New Dimensions in Unhidden Persuasion," *Journal of the Academy of Marketing Science,* 1 (Fall 1973), pp. 110-11.

8. Ibid., p. 113.

9. P. Kotler, "Atmospherics as a Marketing Tool," *Journal of Retailing,* 49 (Winter 1973-74), p. 50.

10. Ibid., pp. 52-53.

11. " '76 Mail Order Sales Rose 13.8% to $19.2 Billion, Sroge Reports," *Marketing News* (November 18, 1977), p. 3.

12. Fran Arman, "Wobbling Out on Wheelies and Heelies," *The National Observer* (July 3, 1976), p. 12.

Chapter **15** Choice and Its Outcomes

Outline

The Nature of Consumer Choice

The Effect of Unanticipated
    Circumstances on Consumer
    Choice

Understanding Unplanned
    Consumer Choice

Nonretail Store Consumer Choice

The Outcomes of Consumer
    Choice
Satisfaction
Dissonance

Managerial Implications of the
    Outcomes of Consumer Choice

Summary

Questions and Issues for
    Discussion

Cases

Key Terms

choice

outcomes of choice

unanticipated circumstances

unplanned consumer choice

nonretail store shopping

satisfaction

dissatisfaction

dissonance

re-evaluation of alternatives

postdecision information search

Joe Martin strolled leisurely across the campus, reflecting on recent events. Seven weeks ago, Joe had received a job offer from General Foods. As soon as the offer was firm, Joe had decided to buy a new car. He read numerous automotive magazines, *Consumer Reports,* talked with friends, and test drove every type of car in his price range. Joe liked the appearance, handling, and EPA gas mileage ratings of the Pinto. Both local Ford dealers offered to sell Joe the Pinto he wanted at approximately the same price. Joe decided to purchase the Pinto from the Vern Wilson Ford dealership because he heard that Vern Wilson had a good service department. Once Joe had selected the car, only a few details remained to complete the transaction. In particular, Joe had to select a bank to obtain financing and an insurance company and agent to obtain auto insurance. The ancillary aspects of the transaction required more effort than Joe had anticipated, but he finally completed the transactions.

As he approached the student union, Joe saw Charlie Stallers sitting on the steps. Charlie, who was also graduating next month, had recently purchased a Vega. "Hey, Charlie," Joe said, "how's the Vega?" "Hi, Joe. The Vega's running great. I drove to Chicago last weekend and got 35 miles per gallon." "Hey, that's great, Charlie. I'm not even getting 30 miles per gallon with my Pinto."

The situation described in the preceding paragraphs illustrates that the consumer decision process does not culminate with the selection of a preferred alternative. Therefore, this chapter focuses on the last two phases of the consumer decision process: choice and the outcomes of choice. Choice, the selection and purchase of an alternative, occurs in both a retail and nonretail (in-home) purchasing environment. The initial section of this chapter deals with consumer choice. The latter section focuses on the outcomes of choice, specifically on the two major forms of choice outcomes: satisfaction and postdecision dissonance.

The Nature of Consumer Choice

The previous chapter described in detail how consumers select a particular retail store and the effect that certain aspects of the store environment have on consumer choice. Choice, as depicted in Figure 15.1, is the result of two determinants: intentions and unanticipated circumstances. The notion of intentions has been discussed previously; consequently, the primary concern here is the effect that unanticipated circumstances have on purchase intentions.

The Effect of Unanticipated Circumstances on Consumer Choice

A list of unanticipated circumstances could, of course, be endless; however, a number of circumstances are more likely than others to

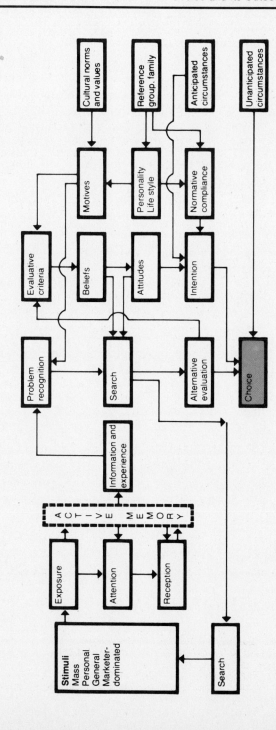

Figure 15.1
The Choice Process

Source: James F. Engel, Roger D. Blackwell, and David T. Kollat, *Consumer Behavior*, 3rd ed. (Hinsdale, Ill.: Dryden Press, 1978), p. 480. Copyright © 1978 by Dryden Press, a division of Holt, Rinehart and Winston. Reprinted by permission of Holt, Rinehart and Winston.

affect consumer intentions and, thus, consumer choice. The nonavailability of funds might, for example, cause a consumer to abort the decision process or to substitute a different brand. Furthermore, the influence of a normative reference group does not cease when intentions have been formed. Finally, store managers may utilize a number of in-store influences to promote brand substitution. Brand substitution, the purchase of a brand that differs from the one a consumer intended to purchase before entering the retail store, varies widely from one product type to the next and is usually less than ten percent of all purchases. The major reasons for brand substitution in supermarkets and drugstores are listed in Table 15.1. Brand substitution occurs in drugstores because customers see the merchandise or a display; whereas the brand display, a lower price, and desire for a change are the major determinants of brand substitution in supermarkets.

In order to understand consumer choice, or, more specifically, brand substitution, it is important to note how brand substitution occurs. That is, what happens to a consumer who enters a store intending to purchase two six-packs of Miller's and emerges from the store with a case of Coors and a bottle of Lancer's Rosé. One possible explanation is that she was exposed to display information about

Table 15.1
Reasons for Brand Substitution as Determined by Respondents' Self-Assessments

Reason(s) Stated by Respondent	Type of Retail Outlet	
	Drugstore[a] %	Supermarket[b] %
Saw merchandise	48	Not used
Display	30	25
Less expensive, on sale	9	21
Wanted a change	Not used	19
Usual brand out of stock	2	7
Recommended by family or friends	2	9
All other	9	19

Sources: [a]*Drugstore Brand Switching and Impulse Buying* (New York: Point-of-Purchase Advertising Institute, 1963), pp. 22–23. Reprinted by permission.
[b]"Colonial Study," *Progressive Grocer* (1964), p. C-118. Reprinted by permission.
Reprinted from James F. Engel, Roger D. Blackwell, and David T. Kollat, *Consumer Behavior*, 3rd ed. (Hinsdale, Ill.: Dryden Press, 1978), p. 481.

Coors that caused her to re-evaluate established beliefs and attitudes, with the result that her previous intention changed. An alternative explanation is that the brand substitution (from Miller's to Coors) occurred as a result of a lower price. If lower price caused the substitution, the change may not be a lasting change in beliefs and attitudes. It is common for consumers to have a set of acceptable alternatives, and when the price of a brand within the set is reduced, a temporary shift in choice results. The restoration of relative price parity often results in a return to the preferred brand, all other things being equal.

Out-of-stock conditions, another unanticipated circumstance that affects consumer intentions, are an important consideration in the planning of retail merchandise assortments. The various types of out-of-stock conditions can, of course, result in different responses by consumers.[1] For example, nearly half (42 percent) of supermarket shoppers are unwilling to buy a substitute brand when their preferred brand is out of stock. This type of behavior varies widely by product category, however. For example, 62 percent would not buy a substitute brand of toothpaste, compared with only 23 percent for toilet tissue.

As would be expected, brand substitution is not as likely to occur when the unanticipated circumstance confronting the consumer is the unavailability of the preferred size. Approximately 80 percent of supermarket shoppers readily substitute for a different size when the preferred package is out of stock. The willingness to substitute package size varied from 75 percent for coffee to 87 percent for toilet soap.

Many consumers are uncompromising when it comes to desired product colors. For example, one out of ten refused to buy a substitute for desired color in toilet soap and toilet tissues. Although strong brand loyalty seems to exist in these product categories, about 28 percent of toilet tissue purchasers and 17 percent of toilet soap purchasers said they switch brands because of color preference.

Profit-conscious retailers are interested in increasing profit per square foot and are, therefore, more interested in product category sales rather than brand sales, unless competing brands have widely varying profit contributions. The expenditures of time, money, and space that result in brand substitution rather than increased sales are wasteful. Hence it is advantageous for the retailer to understand the nature and determinants of brand substitution.

In contrast, the manufacturer is interested in maximizing substitutions to his or her brand and minimizing substitution to other brands. A thorough understanding of why brand substitution occurs, who substitutes away from the brand, and who substitutes to the brand is a prerequisite to designing successful marketing programs. For instance, if the producer of a malodorous household insect killer determines that the less conventional, experimenting homemaker is switching away from his brand in favor of "pleasant scented" bug sprays and that traditional homemakers, who are less flexible in habit, are switching to his brand because the strong smell gives them confidence in its ability to kill pests, he may be able to alter his strategy to reflect these preferences. He might place more emphasis in his promotion on the strength of his brand ("You can tell by the smell") and perhaps market a spray whose smell is more agreeable, thus broadening the appeal of his offerings.

Understanding Unplanned Consumer Choice

Unplanned consumer choice, frequently referred to as impulse purchasing or unplanned purchasing, is believed to be quite widespread. This phenomenon is formally defined as *a buying action undertaken without a problem previously having been recognized or a buying intention formed prior to entering the store.* The extent of unplanned purchasing is widely disputed, but some estimates suggest that nearly a third of variety store and drugstore purchases are such.

Consider the example of the woman who purchased a case of Coors and a bottle of Lancer's Rosé. Suppose that prior to when she entered the retail store, we asked her what she planned to purchase. If she had indicated two six-packs of Miller's and then emerged with a case of Coors and a bottle of Lancer's wine, we could conclude that she made two unplanned purchases. There are at least two tenable explanations for this unplanned purchasing. First, she may have been exposed to a new in-store influence, such as an actual display of the product or an in-store promotional technique, that triggered problem recognition and thereby led to an on-the-spot decision to purchase. A second tenable explanation is that the measure of purchase intention used was incomplete. That is, this consumer may have articulated an incomplete listing of intended purchases, thereby answering our question with a minimum expenditure of her time and mental effort.[2]

The shopper also may be *unable* to itemize purchase plans for a variety of reasons. First, most studies of unplanned purchases force the shopper, in the absence of a shopping list, to rely strictly on memory. Therefore, it is highly probable that measured plans will deviate to some degree from actual plans. Second, the shopper may know what he or she intends to purchase but may be unable, in the absence of a list, to relate these intentions regardless of the interviewing method used. That is, without exposure to in-store stimuli, the customer may be unable cognitively to construct and relate intended purchases.

Allegedly retailers, especially supermarket managers, use unplanned purchasing as a criterion for their decisions. Indeed, there is some indication that certain store layouts, shelf locations, and types of displays are particularly conducive to stimulating unplanned purchasing. For example, one tactic is to place an assortment of novelties, candies, and other items around cash registers in supermarkets and discount stores for customers to inspect as they wait to check out. Although this may have some results, the disparate definitions of unplanned purchasing, measurement difficulties, and inconsistent research findings suggest that such claims are overly optimistic.

Nonretail Store Consumer Choice

Thus far the discussion has focused on consumer choice within the retail environment. Consumer choice does, however, occur outside the retail context. In fact, nonretail store sales, including sales by mail, telephone, home visits, catalogs, and direct response advertising, account for approximately twelve percent of the consumer market.

Nonretail store shoppers vary widely in demographic and life-style characteristics and purchase motivations.[3] However, there are no meaningful demographic differences between them and consumers who shop only within the retail setting.[4] Nonretail store shoppers are characterized as being (1) venturesome,[5] (2) self-confident,[6] (3) innovative,[7] (4) price-conscious,[8] and (5) cosmopolitan.[9]

The most common factors motivating nonretail shopping are convenience, product assortment, price, and the availability of unique products. Nonretail store shoppers cannot be considered a "captive" market, consisting of those actively avoiding retail stores. Rather, this type of purchasing is often discretionary. Avoiding an extra trip to pick up a needed item and buying in response to an advertisement frequently serve to trigger such consumer choice. Most nonretail store shoppers also consider themselves to be active retail store shoppers as well. They do not consider in-store shopping to be difficult or unpleasant. Rather, they are flexible in their choice of shopping alternatives; they are not bound by shopping traditions; and they perceive little risk associated with nonretail store buying.[10] These consumers would be the ones most likely to respond to one national advertiser's invitation to "Call toll-free for delivery by your nearest dealer." Prospects are urged to shop by telephone twenty-four hours a day and charge the purchases to their credit cards. Through a computerized system, the customer's zip code and credit card numbers are matched against the listed dealers and then the nearest dealer makes the delivery.

The Outcomes of Consumer Choice

The decision to purchase a product can, as illustrated in the complete model of the consumer decision process (Figure 15.2), result in two types of outcomes: satisfaction and dissonance. Both outcomes of consumer choice can exercise a strong effect on future choice behavior.

Satisfaction

A consumer purchase decision normally triggers some form of post-purchase evaluation whereby a consumer assesses the result of that decision. This evaluation results from the fact that consumers make purchase decisions that frequently involve substantial amounts of money and insufficient information. Because the purchase decision is normally made on the basis of insufficient information, the consumer cannot be certain that his or her decision was the best possible one. Furthermore, consumers frequently lack the technical knowledge necessary to thoroughly evaluate alternative products available in the

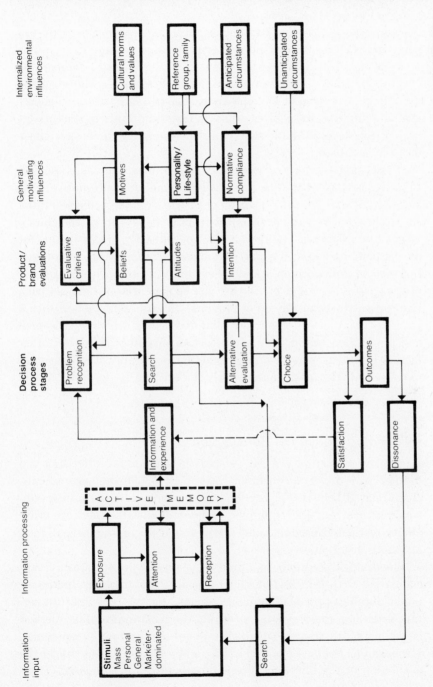

Figure 15.2
**The Complete Model of
Consumer Decision
Processes Showing the
Outcomes of Choice**

Source: James F. Engel, Roger D. Blackwell, and David T. Kollat, *Consumer Behavior*, 3rd ed. (Hinsdale, Ill.: Dryden Press, 1978), p. 492. Copyright © 1978 by Dryden Press, a division of Holt, Rinehart and Winston. Reprinted by permission of Holt, Rinehart and Winston.

marketplace. Few consumers, for example, possess an adequate understanding of electronics to intelligently evaluate alternative brands of color televisions. Thus, the assurance of complete, comparable product information will not assure that the consumer will select the best alternative. The lack of the knowledge necessary to intelligently evaluate product alternatives results in uncertainty about the correctness of the decision made and, thus, the tendency for postpurchase decision evaluation.

If the purchase decision evaluation determines that the chosen alternative is consistent with prior beliefs about that alternative, consumer *satisfaction* results. Consumer *dissatisfaction* occurs when the chosen alternative is inconsistent with prior beliefs about the chosen alternative. Notice in Figure 15.2 that an evaluation of satisfaction (or dissatisfaction) becomes a part of long-term memory, and, hence, it can exert an influence on brand beliefs and attitudes. The probability of engaging in a similar buying act will be increased if there are positive consequences in the act of purchase and use. Satisfaction with a purchase decision will positively reinforce beliefs, which will develop and strengthen brand loyalty. In certain instances, however, other factors intervene to affect buying action or, simply, the consumer may seek novelty and, consequently, brand loyalty does not always result.

Influencing Consumer Satisfaction

A number of factors directly related to the purchase decision can dramatically affect a consumer's satisfaction. Three types of purchase-related behavior of particular importance in determining consumer satisfaction are (1) purchase-related financial outlays, (2) availability of related products and services, and (3) product installation and use considerations.

The decision to purchase a product or service precipitates a financial outlay that, for some purchase decisions (automobiles, homes, or major durables), present genuine problems for the consumer. In certain instances, the decision concerning the most appropriate method of payment can trigger extended problem solving for the consumer. For example, the decision to purchase a stereo system can trigger the evaluation of the following alternative methods of financing: (1) installment credit, (2) bank financing, (3) personal sources, and (4) complete payment at the point of purchase. The decision with respect to financial payment is among the most important decisions that are confronted in many buying situations. The tremendous success of bank cards (Master Charge, VISA, and the like) and retailer-sponsored installment credit (Sears, Penney's, Ward's) suggests that consumers prefer to simplify the financial payment decision as much as possible.

A second type of further purchase-related behavior that can be triggered by a planned purchase decision is the interest in related products and services; that is, the planned purchase of a particular product can generate interest in the purchase of related products. For example, the planned purchase of a new sofa can trigger the recognition that other furniture items, such as chairs, tables, or lamps, are necessary to properly coordinate the entire room. The recognition of this phenomenon by marketing strategists has resulted in the existence of home furnishing centers rather than furniture departments. In other words, marketing strategists frequently provide consumers with the opportunity to procure related product items at the same time the major purchase decision is being made.

The third major type of further purchase-related behavior that directly affects satisfaction is product installation and use considerations. Once a consumer decides to purchase a product, the product must be prepared for use. For many types of products the preparation for use is a simple task. For example, the purchase of a shirt typically requires the consumer to simply remove the shirt from the package, remove any tags, and, perhaps, iron it before use. The preparation for use can, however, be considerably more complex. As most parents can attest, the preparation of products for use that occurs on birthdays and holidays can provide a formidable challenge to the most able "engineer." Even after a product is prepared for use, a period of learning may be necessary to acquire the skills necessary for proper use. A bicycle, for example, must first be assembled and then, in the case of the novice, the consumer must learn to ride it. Each of these situations can require considerable time, thought, and effort, to say nothing of the consternation that can result if inadequate directions are provided.

The major focus—in many instances, the sole focus—of marketing managers has been the consumer's purchase decision. All too frequently the outcomes of the consumer decision are ignored. The marketing manager can have a great deal of impact on whether the consumer experiences satisfaction or dissatisfaction. The recognition that a consumer's concern over financing and credit arrangements can be a barrier that delays or even prevents a purchase dictates the development and implementation of aggressive marketing practices. Retailers have become aware of this fact, and many offer such a variety of convenient credit arrangements that the need for problem solving by the consumer relative to financing is virtually eliminated. The introduction and widespread use of the various bank cards further attests to the consumer's preference for simplifying the financial payment decision. However, there are differences in how bank cards are used by different market segments. For instance, consumers in the higher income categories tend to use them for convenience purposes, while lower income consumers tend to use the cards as installment credit.[11] In essence, then, the marketing strategist must determine the financial payment alternatives preferred by the relevant consumer segments and, to the extent possible, make them available. Such action will enhance the likelihood that the consumer will experience satisfaction with the purchase decision.

As indicated previously, the purchase decision can trigger an interest in related products and services. Even though few marketing analysts would deny that this presents considerable opportunity to the perceptive decision maker, many opportunities are not capitalized on because decision makers fail to recognize the extent to which one purchase can lead to another. One strategy might be to prepare accompanying literature that suggests possible accessories, companion products, and so on. For example, the camera manufacturer might include information on the advantages of certain film, attachments, and additional camera lenses. The automobile dealer should recognize that the purchase of a car triggers numerous other purchases such as a state or local inspection sticker, licenses, insurance, and financing. Even if the auto dealer is not able to provide all of these related items for the consumer, the dealer's assistance in obtaining them could certainly contribute to the consumer's satisfaction. The dealer might offer to arrange for the state inspection as well as obtain and pay for the car license. Although the activities suggested would result in a minor increase in cost, they might add substantially to the satisfaction experienced by the consumer, producing favorable word-of-mouth communications to friends and relatives.

The recognition of a decision that triggers the purchase of related products can provide considerable opportunity for increasing a firm's profitability. The purchase of a tent, for example, will typically trigger the purchase of related products such as camping stoves, lanterns, sleeping bags, air mattresses, special pots, pans, and dishes, tent heaters, and many other items. The Coleman Company of Wichita, Kansas, recognized this some years ago and is now a leading producer of virtually every product associated with camping. In essence, then, the marketing analyst must identify the various related products that might be associated with the purchase of a given product. The identification of such can assist considerably in the development of a growth strategy, new product opportunities, and more effective merchandising of existing product lines.

Manufacturers all too frequently assume that their responsibilities to the consumer terminate with the decision to purchase. There is, however, considerable indication that prompt, proper installation and adequate instruction in the proper use of a product can contribute significantly to the satisfaction experienced by a consumer. Furthermore, the lack of these purchase-related activities can result in consumer dissatisfaction and, consequently, negative word-of-mouth communications about the product to friends and relatives. Consider, for example, the dissatisfaction experienced by the consumer who purchases central air conditioning to make the months of July and August somewhat tolerable for his or her family only to have the company delay installation to September. The probability of this consumer recommending this company to friends or neighbors, if not zero, certainly approaches zero. Contrast that with the sailboat company that includes, as a condition of sale, free instructions in the operation and maintenance of sailboats. The satisfaction a consumer derives from the purchase of a sailboat is directly related to his or her use of that product and increases the likelihood of having satisfied consumers.

The marketing effort should be based on an awareness of how the product fits into the consumer's life-style and of the essential conditions of product use. On this basis, the seller should facilitate the consumer's efforts to the extent possible in order to maximize the satisfaction gained from the product.

When Marketers Fail—Consumer Dissatisfaction

For a period of time, it seemed that consumer satisfaction was not a relevant issue. However, in the last decade, businesses have undertaken the necessary remedial action. Consider the following statement by Thomas A. Murphy, chairman of the General Motors Corporation:

> . . . public sentiment is clearly against big business. . . . It has been building for many years, and for a number of reasons—but principally, in my judgment, because business has been falling short of customer expectations. And today's customer dissatisfaction is both the sorry evidence and the sad result. . . . We simply are not being believed. . . . We move in the right direction every time we emphasize quality as well as quantity in our products, every time we welcome criticism and act upon it rather than avoid it and condemn it. . . . We are going to have to fulfill the businessman's first, last, and always responsibility: the responsibility to satisfy these customers—today, right now, not tomorrow.[12]

Marketing strategists must determine consumer desires as well as product capabilities. Advertisement and selling messages, then, should be designed to create expectancies that will be fulfilled by the product insofar as is possible. The extent to which this seemingly commonsense precaution is violated through the use of "cute" exaggerations and other forms of creative gimmickry in advertisements is, at times, appalling and can lead to serious complaints and, possibly, legal action taken against the manufacturer. (See Chapter 17 for a discussion of deceptive advertising.)

Similarly, product designers should be keenly aware of the way in which a product fits into the consumer's style of life by considering what it means to the consumer and how it is used. The product should be designed and promoted so that performance will be satisfactory under conditions actually experienced in the home. Many homemakers, for example, use electric toasters for English muffins, rolls, and other forms of baked goods besides bread. If the toaster will not handle these items satisfactorily, disconfirmed expectancies and buyer dissatisfaction are the probable result.

Many consumers, in turn, become quite vocal when they are dissatisfied and do not hesitate to spread unfavorable word-of-mouth communication. One low-priced brand of automobile seems to have been particularly damaged in this fashion by product performance that violated its advertising claims. This, in turn, becomes compounded in that those who become aware of this fact will tend to "screen out" advertisements for this make. Thus, little opportunity exists to turn these people into prospects.

The extent of consumer dissatisfaction, as indicated by consumer complaints, varies substantially among product areas. Five problem areas were especially prevalent in the purchase of food and clothing:[13]

1. Discovery of unexpected low quality in prepackaged items
2. Finding grocery stores to be sold out on advertised product specials
3. Finding bread and dairy products to be stale, broken, or spoiled
4. Purchasing shoes that fall apart or wear out in a short time
5. Purchasing a defective clothing item.

The incidence of these complaints ranges from 45 percent who discovered a clothing item to be defective to 70.7 percent who found the quality in prepackaged foods to be lower than expected. The only real bright spot is that most of the consumers indicated satisfaction with retailer remedies.

Dissonance

Postchoice dissonance refers to the doubt that is motivated by awareness that one alternative was chosen and to the existence of beliefs that the unchosen alternatives also have desirable attributes. A consumer experiences dissonance when two cognitions or beliefs do not fit together, resulting in a state of psychological discomfort. This discomfort can be reduced by (1) re-evaluating the desirability of the unchosen alternatives in favor of the choice he or she has made or (2) searching for information to confirm his or her choice.

Extensive information search and alternative evaluation can result in the consumer's having to choose from among several attractive alternatives. The consumer must choose the one alternative perceived to be the most desirable. Selection of the most desirable alternative, however, is not an easy task because available information seldom eliminates all uncertainty. Consequently, when a consumer selects the alternative perceived to be most desirable, other desirable alternatives must be forgone. Information on desirable alternatives, particularly new information, can trigger postpurchase doubt.

Suppose that a consumer recognizes the need to purchase a dishwasher. After considering the many alternatives, the consumer reduces the number of alternatives under consideration to three, all of which appear equally desirable. After several weeks of evaluating alternatives, the consumer selects brand A. Five days after the purchase, the consumer becomes aware of a *Consumer Reports* which contains the results of tests of the five major brands. Brand B was evaluated superior to brand A (the brand purchased) on nearly every relevant product feature. This new information about an available alternative can cause postpurchase doubt that can affect the satisfaction the consumer derived from this purchase. Postdecision doubts of these types are most probable when:[14]

1. A certain minimum level of dissonance tolerance is surpassed. Individuals can live with inconsistency in many areas of their lives until this point is reached.

2. The action is irrevocable.

3. Unchosen alternatives have desirable features.

4. A number of desirable alternatives are available.

5. The individual is committed to his or her decision because of its psychological significance.

6. Available alternatives are qualitatively dissimilar—that is, each has some desirable unique features (referred to in the terminology of dissonance theory as low "cognitive overlap").

7. Perception and thought about unchosen alternatives is undertaken as a result of free will (volition) with little or no outside applied pressure. If pressure is applied, the individual will do what he or she is forced to do without letting personal point of view or preference really be challenged.

Consumers have at their disposal two means by which dissonance can be reduced: (1) re-evaluation of alternatives and (2) postdecision information search.

When dissonance occurs, it can be reduced by re-evaluation of alternatives, that is, by increasing the perceived attractiveness of the chosen alternative and/or downgrading the desirability of those that were not chosen. In addition, it is possible to accomplish the same result by concluding that all alternatives are essentially identical, even though this was not felt to be true during prepurchase deliberations. By so doing, of course, none would stand out over others, and doubts would be removed.

Doubts following purchase also can be reduced by postdecision information search—searching for additional information that serves to confirm the wisdom of the choice. In the purchase of an automobile, for example, dissonance cannot be reduced by changing the behavior and admitting a mistake because of great financial loss if the car is returned to the dealer. Also, most people are reluctant to admit that they made a wrong decision and to live with the knowledge of their error. Therefore, it is more likely that a person experiencing such dissonance will buttress choice through procuring additional information than it is that the person will both admit and accept the fact that he or she made a wrong decision.

Given this knowledge of postdecision doubts, how should a marketer promote consumer products? The evidence to date suggests that promotional messages need to create realistic expectation.[15] Promotional efforts that create unrealistic expectations for products can result in consumer dissatisfaction with the purchase and use of the products. The importance of developing realistic consumer expectations is evident in a recent Ford Motor Company advertising campaign. The campaign compares the Ford Granada to two more expensive luxury cars (the Mercedes 280 and the Cadillac Seville) on two evaluative criteria. The advertisement reports that the Granada consistently ranked first or second on one criterion but was always second on the other criterion. The ad, of course, stresses that this performance is achieved despite the substantially lower price of the Granada. The promotional campaign is obviously designed to convince the audience that the Granada performs about as well as two luxury cars on certain dimensions even though it is lower in price. If the promotion asserted product superiority on every dimension, the likelihood of unconfirmed expectations might be great.

It is a reasonable extension of the discussion thus far to predict that a consumer who is not especially confident in his or her choice would be receptive to advertisements and other literature provided by the manufacturer. The selling arguments and points of alternative superiority stressed there could prove useful in bolstering a perception that the decision was wise and proper. Some evidence has confirmed this hypothesis, but none of it has conclusively verified that dissonance reduction is the motivation for postdecision information search.[16] It is equally possible that a new owner will be "set" to notice advertisements simply because of the fact that an important new product has entered his or her life. For example, the proud father who receives home movie equipment as a birthday present from his family will pay particular attention to ads pertaining to such equipment because of his newly developed interest in home-movie filming. This is a common phenomenon unrelated to dissonance.

Managerial Implications of the Outcomes of Consumer Choice

The managerial implications of the outcomes of consumer choice are apparent. The marketing analyst must regularly monitor consumers' evaluation of the product to be certain the product continues to receive favorable evaluations on evaluative criteria, beliefs, and attitudes. The activities of Ford Motor Company relative to the Granada provide an illustration of how one major corporation uses postpurchase information.

If the evaluation of choice results in complete dissatisfaction being transmitted to long-term memory, two types of outcomes can result. First, the consumer can discontinue this type of purchase behavior. Discontinuance of purchase behavior can result when the current solution is unsatisfactory and no other acceptable solution is available. For example, a consumer with a strong preference for Italian food might, after unsatisfactory experiences at all available restaurants, simply discontinue his or her purchases of Italian food. The second type of outcome that can result is a change in purchase behavior. The consumer might continue his or her search for a satisfactory solution in other locations, re-evaluate the alternative solutions, or redefine the problem to increase the likelihood of locating a satisfactory solution. Thus, the connoisseur of Italian food might decide to experiment with Italian restaurants outside the immediate area, change his or her evaluation of one of the available restaurants, or decide that a 24-hour heartburn is not a valid indicator of the quality of Italian food.

If the feedback to the consumer's long-term memory is partial satisfaction, the outcome might be (1) discontinuance of the purchase behavior; (2) continuance of the purchase behavior but with some reservations; or (3) modification of the purchase behavior.[17] If partial satisfaction was experienced with respect to the solution of a one-time problem, the purchase behavior, will, of course, be discontinued. A consumer might be only partially satisfied and yet continue the same purchase behavior because the product is an inconsequential one or because the best available alternative is presently being used. A post-purchase evaluation that results in partial satisfaction for the consumer may cause a modification in purchase behavior. The modification can result from a change in the consumer's problem recognition or from the alternatives available to the consumer. Consider the case of three consumers who are heavy users of coffee, but who react differently when the prices of coffee skyrocket. One consumer refuses to buy any coffee until the price declines. Another continues to purchase coffee because she considers it to be a necessity, although she is very dissatisfied with the price. The third consumer opts for a coffee substitute, such as Postem, because it offers a flavor similar to that of coffee for a lesser price.

Postpurchase evaluations that result in partial satisfaction or dissatisfaction present particularly appealing opportunities to the marketing analyst. A method of identifying and subsequently converting consumer dissatisfaction and partial satisfaction into marketing opportunities has been suggested by the director of research for Batten, Barton, Durstine & Osborn, Inc., who made the following observation:

> If you ask consumers what they want in a canned dog food, they tell you they want a food the dog will eat and it should be good for the dog. If you ask a housewife what problems she has with canned dog food, she will tell you that it is too expensive and smells bad.[18]

The statement was made to illustrate the difference between *benefit research,* which focuses on consumers' evaluations of the benefits provided by a product, and *problem research,* which focuses on the features of a product that bother consumers. Problem research can be of considerable value in identifying a partially satisfied or dissatisfied consumer and converting that consumer into a marketing opportunity. The Problem Detection System, developed by BBD&O, has consumers list all possible problems associated with the use of a particular product.[19] This enables the researcher to identify those problems that can be converted into marketing opportunities. Once the marketing analyst has identified the consumer problems, new product concepts must be developed to solve these problems.

In 1970, General Motors made the decision to call back 4.9 million cars to check for safety defects. GM's decision, estimated to have cost the company $50 million, might have been influenced by proposed warranty legislation.[20] Regardless of GM's motivation, the decision underscores the urgent need for manufacturers and distributors to devote adequate attention to postpurchase considerations. Adequate attention to postpurchase considerations provides substantial profit opportunities to business organizations—opportunities that only a few firms currently recognize.

Summary

The last two phases of the consumer decision process are choice and the outcomes of choice. Choice is the selection and purchase of an alternative and occurs in both a retail and nonretail purchasing environment. Outcomes of choice are satisfaction and postdecision dissonance.

Choice is the result of intentions and unanticipated circumstances, which include: (1) the nonavailability of funds, (2) the influence of a normative reference group, (3) brand substitution (the purchase of a brand that differs from the one a consumer intended to purchase before entering a retail outlet), and (4) out-of-stock conditions. Unplanned consumer choice is a buying action that is undertaken without a problem previously having been recognized or a buying intention formed prior to entering a store. Consumer choice can also occur outside the retail context. Nonretail sales include sales by mail, telephone, home visits, catalogs, and direct response advertising. Nonretail store shoppers have been categorized as venturesome, self-confident, innovative, price-conscious, and cosmopolitan. Factors such as convenience, product assortment, price and the availability of unique products motivate consumers to engage in nonretail shopping.

Postpurchase decision evaluation is normally triggered when a consumer makes a purchase decision. Satisfaction results if the evaluation determines that the chosen alternative is consistent with prior beliefs about that alternative. Dissatisfaction occurs when the chosen alternative is inconsistent with prior beliefs about the chosen alternative. Satisfaction positively reinforces beliefs that develop and strengthen brand loyalty. Three factors of particular importance in determining consumer satisfaction are (1) purchase-related financial outlays, (2) availability of related products and services, and (3) product installation and use considerations. Marketers can enhance consumer satisfaction by offering financial payment alternatives, identifying and providing purchase-related products and services, and providing prompt, proper installation and adequate instruction in the proper use of a product. Dissatisfaction can be reduced if the marketer determines consumer desires and product capabilities and designs advertisements that create expectancies which the product can fulfill. Also, products should be designed and promoted so that performance will be satisfactory under conditions actually experienced in the home.

Postpurchase dissonance refers to the doubt that is motivated by awareness that one alternative was chosen and to the existence of beliefs that the unchosen alternatives also have desirable attributes. This psychological discomfort can be reduced by (1) re-evaluating the desirability of the unchosen alternatives in favor of the choice made or (2) searching for information to confirm the choice.

Marketing analysts must regularly monitor consumers' evaluation of products. If consumers are dissatisfied, two outcomes can result: (1) discontinuance of the purchase behavior or (2) a change in purchase behavior. When consumer postpurchase evaluations result in partial satisfaction or dissatisfaction, benefit research and problem research can aid the marketer in converting the consumer into a marketing opportunity.

Questions and Issues for Discussion

1. Some consumer analysts believe that an understanding of further purchase-related behavior can provide considerable opportunities to the astute marketing manager. Explain how this might be the case.

2. L'Emptor Caveat, a seller of antique furniture and decorations, gets a lot of one-time customers. The store is a hodgepodge of items of different styles and from different eras. How could the store benefit if management understood the purchase-related behavior of consumers?

3. Research indicates that consumers were very surprised to discover the quality of sound reproduction of a particular stereophonic system. Would you say this finding is favorable? Explain.

4. "A store's business may be good for the bank cards, but it is unclear whether the bank card business is good for the stores," says an executive of a large chain of department stores that wants customers to use no credit card but its own. Evaluate the executive's statement and the position the store has taken.

5. What are the implications of postpurchase decision evaluation providing a partially satisfactory feedback to long-term memory? Will a consumer continue to purchase a product that regularly receives a partially satisfactory evaluation?

6. The Johnson Company produces and distributes ski equipment; it has experienced sales declines for the past three years while the industry as a whole has been booming. Expert skiers have reported to Johnson that their skis were slightly more difficult to break in, but after the break-in period, they rated them as comparable to the best skis available. This was encouraging since Johnson skis were less expensive than most of its competitors' lines. A market research study of current users of Johnson's product lines revealed considerable variation in the evaluation of the skis. One of the more interesting findings of the study was that while over 80 percent of the skiers who rated themselves "advanced" said they would recommend Johnson skis to a friend, only 60 percent of the intermediate users said they would do the same, and the figure was below 30 percent for beginners. Based on your understanding of the outcomes of choice, how might you explain Johnson's declining sales? How might an understanding of further purchase-related behavior aid Johnson's management in overcoming their disappointing sales performance?

7. What is the distinction between further purchase-related behavior and postpurchase decision evaluation? How might one affect the other?

8. A study by *Progressive Grocer* magazine shows that many consumers cannot guess correctly the prices of items which they regularly buy. Subtle quantity and price changes made by manufacturers can obviously contribute to this seemingly widespread ignorance. Explain the relevance of these price misconceptions to unplanned consumer choice.

9. What functions does postpurchase decision evaluation serve? How do positive and negative evaluations affect evaluative criteria and attitudes?

10. Research shows that only about one fourth of the nonprice problems that consumers perceive with products or services are satisfactorily resolved. What could businesses do to increase this percentage?

Case 1. Avon Products, Inc.

A 20-year-old female, dressed somewhat casually and holding a beige carrying case, approaches a house in a typical suburban residential area and knocks on the door. A middle-aged woman greets her and invites her into the house. Half an hour later, she leaves the house and crosses the street to repeat the procedure. The female is one of 895,000 Avon Ladies around the world, who, in their spare time, peddle more than 600 items door to door.

Avon Products, Inc., is the world's largest cosmetics and toiletries merchandiser. In the late 1800s, a door-to-door bookseller hired a woman to distribute free samples of perfume to potential customers as premiums to help sell the books. She eventually abandoned the line of books and began recruiting women to sell the perfume. Over the years, products such as face cream, lotions, soap, lipstick, and

Source: Some of the information used in Case 1 is from "Cosmetics Firm Makes a Strong Comeback from a Recession Dip," *Wall Street Journal*, April 6, 1977.

toothpaste were added. Now the company offers men's grooming products, a line of cosmetics specifically for blacks, and costume jewelry (in fact, Avon is currently the largest costume jewelry distributor in America). Although the company is optimistic, some financial analysts are speculating how long the company can maintain its high sales ranking and somewhat "old-fashioned" approach in the presence of aggressive competitors such as Revlon, Max Factor, and Alberto-Culver. Their conjecture is that door-to-door selling may become obsolete in the near future.

The number of self-employed, unsalaried Avon Ladies is greater than the total personnel of J. C. Penney, Montgomery Ward, and Sears combined. These ladies work approximately 15 to 25 hours every two weeks at their own pace. They usually buy the merchandise at 60 percent off the list price and then add on 40 percent for their gross profit. They are advised to use a soft-sell approach, and the Avon Ladies often become so chummy with their customers, that the time is spent drinking coffee and conversing. Employee turnover is high, with 50 percent of them quitting each year.

Financial analysts foresee a twofold problem for Avon. First, they anticipate a lack of consumer response to the Avon Ladies. The analysts base this forecast on three factors: (1) Because of the rising crime rate in both cities and suburbs, housewives are less willing to welcome strangers into their homes. (2) Many housewives enjoy the convenience of driving to a store for their needs instead of waiting for the Avon Lady to visit them. (3) The number of working women is growing, which limits the number of customers who can be reached during the day. The second problem is recruiting women who will take the risk of walking hazardous streets and entering strangers' homes. This is more of a gamble in today's society than it was in the past.

Avon counters that most city Avon Ladies do not carry their Avon portfolios, thus preventing an invitation to robbery. As for a potential lack of consumer response, one Avon executive contends that its line of cosmetics for blacks receives high brand loyalty. Also, 50 percent of its sales are to working women, who tend to be heavier users of cosmetics and have more money to spend on them. In fact, office workers are being recruited as Avon Ladies and, in New York City, they are exposed to advertisements in subways saying, "Do Three Things During Your Lunch Hour: 1. Eat Lunch. 2. Shop. 3. Earn Money, Sell Avon."

It is apparent that Avon is trying to alter what it calls its "dowdy" image. In order to compete more aggressively with the large cosmetic companies that distribute their products through retail outlets and to make its merchandise more attractive to a wider spectrum of consumers, Avon introduced Emprise, a $60-an-ounce perfume. Although it turned out be the company's third most successful new-product introduction, sales results were below expectations. This was an indication to company executives that an image change might be impractical.

Case 1 Questions

1. What explanations can you offer for Avon's remarkable success as a door-to-door distributor of cosmetics?

2. What benefits does a company receive by using a door-to-door selling approach as opposed to distribution through a retail outlet?

3. Using your understanding of the outcomes of choice, unplanned consumer choice, and nonretail store consumer choice, evaluate the success of Avon's selling technique.

Case 2. Steady Mark, Incorporated

Steady Mark, Incorporated, makes all kinds of household appliances and controls its own chain of distributors. In late 1977, the stockholders' wrath finally caught up with the managerial regime. Citing an average six percent decline in earnings for the previous three years, rapid turnover of line and lower-tier staff employees, an apparently stagnant research and development department, and burgeoning files of customer complaints, the owners discharged over 15 high-level

Source: This case is adapted from Roger D. Blackwell, James F. Engel, and W. Wayne Talarzyk, *Contemporary Cases in Consumer Behavior* (Hinsdale, Ill.: Dryden Press, 1977), Case 34, pp. 309–318. Copyright © 1977 by Dryden Press, a division of Holt, Rinehart and Winston. Reprinted by permission of Holt, Rinehart and Winston.

managers, including the firm's president and its vice-president in charge of marketing. "We need a shake-up," said the largest stockholder. "I'd call the state of this corporation deplorable."

Larry Chapman, formerly an executive of a large automobile manufacturer and in academia for the last several years, was persuaded to take the reins of Steady Mark. The first task, he said, was to direct the energies of the firm toward the consumer. "This firm has tremendous capabilities, and the main reason it is now in this position is that it has steadily lost contact with the consuming public, including its own customers, and has increasingly failed to satisfy their needs and requirements." Chapman first issued a memo to managers at all levels, stating that building a favorable image in the minds of consumers should always be the top priority. To Steady Mark's retail distributors, he said, "A short-term advance in sales is never as valuable as the creation of a lifetime customer and favorable word-of-mouth communication. Don't view service after the sale as a problem. In the long run, you'll appreciate its advantages. We want customers to enjoy their experience with our organization and its products. The prerequisite is provision of prompt, efficient, and courteous service."

Chapman instituted a bold incentive plan for personnel of every profit center within the organization. For production centers, the plan was based on cost per unit of output with a stipulation that quality control standards must be met. If the standards were exceeded, bonuses would also increase, according to a formula. At the retail level, the bonus formula was based mainly on sales and customer complaints. To ensure the accuracy of the latter bonus-allocation variable, a short letter was to be mailed to all purchasers of Steady Mark appliances, thanking them for their business and encouraging them to direct any and every complaint concerning retailer relations and service after the sale to Steady Mark corporate headquarters, where it would be given timely consideration. Customers were also told that their retailer would graciously accept any constructive criticisms they might have. The distributors were told to consider the criticisms as a unique opportunity to sell more appliances, obtain repeat business, and increase profits. "Be responsive to these criticisms," Chapman's memo said, "and do not let short-run costs be a barrier to action."

Technical, managerial, and marketing consultants were called in for advice and assistance in all phases of the operation. Retailers were provided with funds to increase their service forces. Each service man or woman (16 percent of the force are females) was given extensive technical training and is now practiced in the art of field decision making before ever reaching the field.

A consumer affairs division was organized to further assure the responsiveness of Steady Mark to customers. Among the duties of the department are to redress all grievances, answer any consumer inquiries, and monitor the company's image. As an added check on poor quality of service, the division receives a copy of the job ticket for every service call made. A representative sample of the customers who have received service is then chosen, and members of the sample are contacted for a report on the quality of the service rendered. This control has other benefits besides monitoring service quality. Such control provides a feedback system, giving early warning of product defects to production and quality control personnel. If there is a problem, operations can alter processes and eliminate a major source of consumer dissatisfaction.

The consumer affairs division provides a toll-free "hot-line" which, besides the important function of linking customers with Steady Mark in a personal way, has generated benefits such as excellent publicity in the press, word-of-mouth advertising, and favorable reactions from government and consumer advocates. The good will that results from the "hot-line" is as valuable as any asset on the Steady Mark balance sheet.

Steady Mark has also invested in consumer education projects. The first step was to rewrite all instruction manuals in the "consumer's language" with colorful illustrations and warnings in bold type. Now, it is the sponsor of educational films for schools, civic groups, and theaters on how to buy, use, and get service for appliances. Steady Mark also sponsors television specials of cultural interest. A guide is published by Steady Mark called "Buying Appliances: What You Need to Know," which again is written in the "consumer's language" and provides simple tips on appraising technical specifications and general product features.

According to Larry Chapman, "The results have been stupendous! Profits have bounced back like a rubber ball. Earnings per share are up by 35 percent, and our stock is in very heavy demand on the exchanges. The morale within the firm has really skyrocketed. It just goes to show that you can't say enough about a consumer orientation on the part of private business. It's good for both parties."

Case 2 Questions

1. Evaluate the Steady Mark program and Chapman's understanding of the outcomes of choice.

2. Steady Mark has a number of competitors that also manufacture high-quality appliances. Chapman is concerned with the dissonance Steady Mark's customers may experience, since it could lead to dissatisfaction and impede repeat business, despite the steps the firm has taken. What suggestions could you make to Chapman regarding a further strategy designed to minimize dissonance? Include in your suggestions some possibilities for research that (1) could aid Steady Mark in identifying those features of their products and service provision which consumers evaluate favorably; (2) could be emphasized in their promotional strategy; and (3) could aid Steady Mark in the development of new products.

Notes

1. See "Out-of-Stocks Disappoint Shoppers, Force Store Switching," *Progressive Grocer* (November 1968), pp. S-26–S-23.

2. David T. Kollat, "A Decision-Process Approach to Impulse Purchasing," Raymond M. Haas, ed., *Science, Technology and Marketing* (Chicago: American Marketing Association, 1966), pp. 626–39.

3. Peter L. Gillett, "In-Home Shoppers—An Overview," *Journal of Marketing,* Vol. 40 (October 1976), pp. 81–88.

4. Ibid., p. 86.

5. Fred D. Reynolds, "An Analysis of Catalog Buying Behavior," *Journal of Marketing,* Vol. 38 (July 1974), p. 48.

6. Ibid.

7. Christie Paksoy, "Lifestyle and Psychographic Analysis of Catalog Shoppers," presented at American Council of Consumer Interests, 1975.

8. Ibid.

9. Isabella C. M. Cunningham and William H. Cunningham, "The Urban In-Home Shopper: Socio-economic and Attitudinal Characteristics," *Journal of Retailing,* Vol. 49 (Fall 1973), p. 42.

10. Gillett, "In-Home Shoppers."

11. H. L. Mathews and J. W. Slocum, Jr., "Social Class and Commercial Bank Credit Card Usage," *Journal of Marketing,* Vol. 33 (January 1969), pp. 71–78.

12. Thomas A. Murphy, "Businessman, Heal Thyself," *Newsweek* (December 20, 1976), p. 11.

13. John O. Summers and Donald H. Granbois, "Predictive and Normative Expectations in Consumer Dissatisfaction and Complaining Behavior," William D. Perreault, ed., *Advances in Consumer Research,* Vol. 4 (Atlanta: Association for Consumer Research, 1977), pp. 155-58.

14. M. T. O'Keefe, "The Anti-Smoking Commericals: A Study of Television's Impact on Behavior," *Public Opinion Quarterly*, Vol. 35 (1971), pp. 242-48; and H. B. Gerard, "Basic Features of Commitment," R. P. Abelson *et al.*, eds., *Theories of Cognitive Consistency: A Sourcebook* (Chicago: Rand McNally, 1968), pp. 456-63.

15. R. E. Anderson, "Consumer Dissatisfaction: The Effect of Disconfirmed Expectancy on Perceived Product Performance," *Journal of Marketing Research,* Vol. 10 (February 1973), pp. 38-44.

16. William H. Cummings and M. Venkatesan, "Cognitive Dissonance and Consumer Behavior: A Review of the Evidence," *Journal of Marketing Research*, Vol. 13 (August 1976), pp. 303-08.

17. C. G. Walters, *Consumer Behavior: Theory and Practice,* 2nd ed. (Homewood, Ill.: Richard D. Irwin, Inc., 1974), p. 560.

18. "Light Says Problem Research Will Give More Benefits Than Benefit Research," *Marketing News,* Vol. 9 (September 26, 1975), p. 12.

19. Ibid., p. 12.

20. G. Fisk, "Guidelines for Warranty Service after Sale," *Journal of Marketing,* Vol. 34 (January 1970), pp. 63-67.

Chapter 16   Choice Patterns

Outline

The Meaning of Brand Loyalty
Brand Choice Sequences
Proportion of Purchases
Preference Purchase Definition

Explaining Brand Loyalty

Understanding Brand Loyalty

Managerial Implications of Brand Loyalty

Importance of Understanding the Diffusion of Innovations
Product Life Cycle
New Product Development

Elements of the Diffusion Process

Diffusion of Innovations and the Adoption Process
Adoption Decision-Process Model
Innovation Decision-Process Model

Identifying Innovativeness

Summary

Questions and Issues for Discussion

Cases

Key Terms

brand loyalty

undivided loyalty

divided loyalty

unstable loyalty

proportion of purchases

preference purchase

stochastic models

deterministic models

Markov models

diffusion of innovations

product life cycle

innovation

continuous innovation

dynamically continuous innovation

discontinuous innovation

Adoption Decision-Process Model

awareness

legitimation

trial

adoption

Innovation Decision-Process Model

Understanding consumer behavior, although an intriguing subject in its own right, is fundamental to the development and execution of effective marketing programs in a developed economic system. Consider the following marketing programs:

> BMW thinks that its luxury car, which sells for between $14,000 and $18,000, has not achieved the market penetration it could in the United States. As a result, BMW recently kicked off a national media campaign in U.S. magazines with high-income readerships. The U.S. subsidiary of the Bavarian company hopes to experience a 20-percent increase in unit sales of the car it refers to as the "ultimate" car.[1]

Morton Foods, a small potato-chip and salad-dressing producer in Dallas, has developed a marketing program that combines old-fashioned service with country music. Morton Foods, recently purchased by a group of Dallas businessmen, experienced considerable difficulty under its previous owners, W. R. Grace & Co. Morton's new president attributes the difficulties to Grace's decision to discontinue business to small outlets in rural Texas that were buying less than $15 worth of merchandise per week. These small outlets were the core of Morton's business before Grace bought the company, and the new owners have developed a marketing program featuring door-to-door service and country music to attempt to regain their business.[2]

The Gulf Oil Company has adopted the slogan "where the automotive runaround ends" for its new auto parts and service centers. The Gulf stores will handle a complete line of auto parts, tires, and accessories and complete mechanical service but no gasoline. Each outlet will handle an $80,000 inventory and operate seven days a week. The firm's objective is to satisfy all the motoring public's automotive repair and service needs in a single outlet.[3]

Ten religious denominations in Atlanta, Dallas, Kansas City, Los Angeles, and Philadelphia are participating in a project whereby a member can authorize that his church contribution be made automatically through his checking account, or debited against his credit card (VISA or Master Charge). The church member must simply authorize his bank to make a regular transfer of funds or make a charge against his credit card. The objective of the new service is to provide the churches involved with a more stable cash flow.[4]

These four illustrations, albeit quite varied, have a common element—they all illustrate the importance of developing marketing programs that are based on an understanding of consumer behavior. The widespread adoption of the marketing concept that includes as its basic precept a consumer orientation has had a subtle yet pervasive impact on marketing decision making. The result has been that virtually every decision made by marketing strategists includes an analysis of consumer behavior. The analyses range from subjective judgment to comprehensive market study, but the consumer's behavior is almost always a key consideration.

The remainder of this chapter focuses on the two consumer choice patterns that are particularly important to the marketing decision maker. These choice patterns, commonly known as brand loyalty and diffusion of innovations, have captured the interest of researchers and marketing strategists alike because of the tremendous potential they have to facilitate marketing decision making. *Brand loyalty* refers to the tendency of consumers to consistently purchase a particular brand over time. *Diffusion of innovations* refers to the spread of a particular product, brand, or idea throughout the consumer market. The following discussion considers these two choice patterns in detail.

The Meaning of Brand Loyalty

Brand loyalty is one of the most widely established and instinctively appealing concepts in consumer behavior. Unfortunately, it is also one of the most controversial and misunderstood. The controversy and misunderstanding result from the fact that brand loyalty has been conceptualized as both the result of consumer choice and the cause of consumer choice. An adequate understanding of brand loyalty requires some consideration of the development of the concept.

Brand Choice Sequences

Consumer behavior researchers and marketing practitioners initially considered brand loyalty to be the sequence of purchasing a particular brand. Using consumer choice patterns for products such as coffee, orange juice, soap, and margarine, consumers were grouped in the following categories:

1. *Undivided loyalty*—consumers who consistently purchase the same brand, that is, consistently purchase brand A or brand B or brand C

2. *Divided loyalty*—consumers who regularly purchase two brands, thus manifesting the choice pattern ABABAB

3. *Unstable loyalty*—consumers who purchase a product several times then switch to another brand for several purchases, thus manifesting the choice pattern AAABBBCCC

4. *No loyalty*—consumers who consistently purchase different brands.

Based on this classification, consumers' brand loyalty varies substantially (from 54 to 95 percent) among different types of products.[5]

Proportion of Purchases

Dissatisfaction with the difficulties inherent in the brand-choice sequence definition of brand loyalty resulted in the development of the proportion of purchases definition. Using this definition, brand loyalty is considered to be the proportion of total purchases within a given product category devoted to the most frequently purchased brand or set of brands.

The use of this definition of brand loyalty facilitated the development of the concept of *multibrand* loyalty in various forms. For example, *dual-brand* loyalty would be the percent of total purchases devoted to the two most favorite brands; *triple-brand* loyalty refers to the three most favorite brands. The consumer who purchases only Coke or Pepsi when he or she purchases soft drinks would be considered to be dual-brand loyal.

Preference Purchase Definition

The concept of brand loyalty is truly useful only if it includes consumers' preferences and purchases. That is, brand loyalty is considerably more than repeat purchase behavior, and explicit recognition must be made of the difference between intentional loyalty and spurious loyalty.

Perhaps the most useful and complete definition of brand loyalty is the following: "Brand loyalty is (1) the biased (i.e., non-random) (2) behavioral response (i.e., purchase) (3) expressed over time (4) by some decision-making unit (5) with respect to one or more alternative brands out of a set of such brands, and is (6) a function of psychological (i.e., decision-making, evaluative) processes."[6]

This definition of brand loyalty is consistent with the decision-process approach to the study of consumer behavior and it delineates brand loyalty as a special choice pattern for analysis. The two major strengths of this definition are: (1) it distinguishes repeat purchase behavior, which focuses only on behavior, from loyalty, which encompasses the antecedents of behavior, and (2) it emphasizes that the unit of analysis must be the "decision-making unit."

Explaining Brand Loyalty

A substantial amount of consumer research has attempted to explain brand loyalty. Yet, despite this effort, many of the conclusions presented below remain somewhat tentative and a few will undoubtedly be found erroneous in years to come.

Brand loyalty is clearly a product-specific phenomenon. That is, consumers are likely to be more brand loyal for some product categories than for others. Some researchers have concluded that more brand switching will occur when price differences are significant between brands and that this will have the most effect on consumers in the extreme levels of both income and education, rather than in a linear relationship to these variables.[7] Possibly, brand switching is a function of the value of time to a consumer. This suggests that upper income people have more "natural" loyalty to brands, but when their preferred brand is out of stock or not carried by a convenient store, upper income consumers will switch to another brand rather than spend the time necessary to find their preferred brand.[8]

The following major conclusions summarize the extent to which marketing decision makers have been able to explain brand loyalty.

1. Perceived risk is positively related to brand loyalty.

2. Store loyalty is commonly associated with brand loyalty. Moreover, store loyalty appears to be an intervening variable between certain consumer characteristics and brand loyalty. In other words, certain consumer characteristics are related to store loyalty which, in turn, is related to brand loyalty.

3. The fewer stores a consumer shops at, the greater the likelihood of brand loyalty occurring.

4. Extensiveness of distribution and market share are positively related to brand loyalty.

Understanding Brand Loyalty

Many different mathematical models have been designed in an attempt to understand brand-loyalty behavior over time. The primary emphasis has been on *stochastic* models, which treat the response of consumers in the marketplace as the outcome of some probabilistic process. A stochastic model, with its built-in probability component, is distinguished from or contrasted with *deterministic* models, in which an attempt is made to predict behavior in exact, or nonprobabilistic, terms.

There are two basic philosophies of stochastic models. The first philosophy recognizes that many factors determine the outcome of behavior even though most of these factors are neither measured nor explicitly included in the model of market response. Such factors may include a wide range of individual consumer variables, such as personality, attitudes, and income, as well as a wide range of exogenous variables, such as advertising, price, and competitive activity. Even though these variables are not explicitly considered in the model, their effect is accounted for in the stochastic nature of the response.

A second philosophy of stochastic models is based on the premise that not only the model of market response but also the actual consumer decision process is stochastic. Stated alternatively, consumer choices are random (probabilistic) because there is a *stochastic element in the brain* that influences choice. Thus, it is not any more possible, even in principle, to provide an explanation for the (stochastic) component than it is to provide an explanation for the outcome of the toss of a coin. This is in sharp contrast to the more dominant stream of consumer research in which the underlying premise is that behavior is caused and can therefore be explained, at least in principle, even if adequate data do not exist to account for behavior at any point in time.

Only one type of brand loyalty model will be presented here, the Markov models. These models consider the influence of past purchases on the probability of current purchases. The number of previous purchases that are assumed to affect the current purchase is designated by the *order* of the model. Thus, first order means only the last purchase affects the current purchase; second order means only the last two purchases affect the current purchase; and so on. Consider the following first-order Markov model with a three-

Last Purchase	Next Purchase		
	A	B	C
A	0.7	0.1	0.2
B	0.3	0.6	0.1
C	0.4	0.1	0.5

Table 16.1
**Hypothetical Markov
Transitional
Probabilities**

brand (A, B, C) product category. Based on past purchase data for a sample of consumers, the marketing researcher estimates the conditional (or transitional) probabilities of moving from one state to another in *any two* consecutive time periods. These transitional probabilities are shown in Table 16.1.

Table 16.1 is interpreted as follows. If a consumer purchased brand A during a certain period, then during the next period there is a 70-percent chance that he will buy A again, a 10-percent chance of buying B, and a 20-percent chance of buying C. Similarly, a buyer of brand B during the last period would have a 30-percent probability of buying A during the next period, a 60-percent chance of buying B, and a 10-percent chance of buying C.

Table 16.1 is called a transitional matrix. It is essentially a measure of brand-switching (or, conversely, brand-loyal) behavior. Most Markov models assume that the matrix is stationary, that is, the transition probabilities remain unchanged through time.

To illustrate the mechanics of the Markov process, we shall follow through a hypothetical computation of probabilities. If a consumer purchased brand A during period I, the probability of buying the different brands during periods II, III, IV, and V would be as follows:[9]

Period	Brand		
	A	B	C
II	0.70	0.10	0.20
III	0.60	0.15	0.25
IV	0.57	0.17	0.26
V	0.55	0.19	0.26

On the other hand, if brand B was purchased during period I, the corresponding probabilities for future periods would be as follows:

Period	Brand		
	A	B	C
II	0.30	0.60	0.10
III	0.43	0.40	0.17
IV	0.49	0.30	0.21
V	0.52	0.25	0.23

Similar computations can be made for brand C by following the procedure outlined in footnote 9.

Managerial Implications of Brand Loyalty

Brand loyalty is one way of segmenting a market. For example, some of the ways a manufacturer of brand A could attempt to increase his or her sales are:

1. increase the number of consumers who are loyal to brand A

2. decrease the number of consumers who are loyal to competing brands

3. convince more nonloyal consumers who purchase the product to purchase brand A

4. increase the amount purchased by consumers who are loyal to brand A

5. convince those who do not purchase the product to purchase brand A.

Marketing programming to any of these segments is practical only if the consumers comprising these segments are identifiable. In some instances, brand loyalty is not a useful basis for segmenting markets. For example, in the case of grocery products, brand-loyal customers do not seem to differ from other customers in terms of attitudes, personality and socioeconomic characteristics, amount purchased, or sensitivity to pricing, dealing, retail advertising, or the introduction of new brands. However, this finding may not be applicable to other product categories and may not even hold for individual grocery products.

These types of strategies, however, are less likely to be effective if loyalty is caused by psychological commitment to a brand. In these situations, the probability that selective attention, comprehension, and recall will weaken the effects of marketing strategies is probably much higher.

To illustrate a somewhat different approach, consider a market where a significant segment of consumers is loyal to a particular brand. Assume that research indicated that these consumers consider certain other brands as acceptable and the remaining brands unacceptable.

What is the most effective marketing strategy for these brands? The most preferred ("loyal") brand could emphasize the importance of the product attribute(s) that has led consumers to become loyal to that brand. Marketers of other acceptable brands could emphasize the comparability between themselves and the "loyal" brand on the attribute(s) and minimize any perceived or real differences. Marketers of unacceptable brands, on the other hand, would probably be better advised to focus their efforts on a different product attribute(s) and make that attribute(s) salient.

Importance of Understanding the Diffusion of Innovations

As indicated previously, diffusion of innovations is a second consumer choice pattern that has proven to be of considerable interest and value to marketing decision makers. The marketing manager's interest in this type of choice pattern stems from the foundation it provides for astute product development decisions. Marketing managers are in general agreement that product development decisions, particularly new product decisions, have a tremendous impact on organizational profit. Several studies have indicated that many firms earn as much as 50 percent of their profit from products developed in the last decade.[10] Product decisions are particularly important because they commit the firm's resources to a specific direction that affects every aspect of the marketing function. Product decisions provide the basis for the decisions made regarding price, promotion, and distribution. Consequently, product decisions must be made with a clear understanding of the firm's objectives and with a thorough understanding of consumer behavior, particularly how the product will diffuse through the market. An understanding of the diffusion of innovations is vital to product decisions because marketing strategists now recognize that the sociopsychological dimensions of products are frequently as important as the products' physical characteristics.

Product Life Cycle

The product life cycle concept has been developed by marketing analysts to describe the generalized pattern of sales and profit that products follow over time. This generalized pattern of sales and profit has been described as distinct stages in the life of a product. Each stage provides the marketing strategist with different opportunities and problems. Identifying the stage a product is in enables the marketing strategist to focus marketing efforts on assuring consumer satisfaction and firm profit. Such adjustment of marketing efforts is only possible if the marketing strategist understands the distinctive consumer preferences that emerge in each stage.

The product life cycle is typically characterized as consisting of four stages: introduction, growth, maturity, and decline. The sales and profit patterns for these four stages are presented in Figure 16.1. The exact shape and length of the product life cycle varies substantially, but most products actually go through such a cycle. Examination of the product life cycle, as illustrated in Figure 16.1, suggests that marketing managers would prefer to get a product through the introductory stage as fast as possible and to prolong the growth and maturity stages as long as possible. The efficiency with which a marketing manager can do so depends upon factors such as competition, technology, promotional efforts, and understanding of consumer behavior.

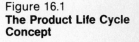

Figure 16.1
**The Product Life Cycle
Concept**

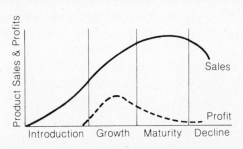

The minicalculator provides an excellent example of a product life cycle characterized by a short introductory stage and prolonged growth and maturity stages. Minicalculators were introduced in the consumer market less than ten years ago. The introductory stage was characterized by high prices, high promotional expenditures, and few competitors. However, well-focused marketing efforts and some technological improvements pushed minicalculators through the introductory stage and into the growth stage in a few short months. The minicalculator's growth stage was characterized by high prices, high promotional expenditures, increases in the number of competitors, major production improvements, and development of other market segments. The maturity stage for minicalculators is now characterized by excess supply capabilities, falling prices, private brands entering the market, declining margins, and some reduction in the number of brands carried by middlemen. The future in producing minicalculators depends on the firm's ability to adjust to the product life cycle by:

1. generating more frequent usage of the minicalculator among present users

2. developing more varied usage among present users of minicalculators

3. identifying and nurturing new users of minicalculators

4. identifying and encouraging new uses for minicalculators.[11]

The effectiveness with which a firm implements any of these strategies is directly dependent on its understanding of consumer decision making. For example, many a household financial officer would willingly spend $10 for a minicalculator to expedite the check-balancing process. Developing this market, however, requires a specially designed calculator and well-focused promotion efforts.

New Product Development

New products have a profound impact on corporate profit and growth and, consequently, are of primary importance to the marketing strategist. A product's profit margin declines early in the product's life cycle (growth stage), meaning that profits can be sustained only by continuously introducing new products. In other words, a company must systematically introduce new products to maintain or increase profits. Furthermore, as the product life cycle continues to shorten, profits can be sustained in the long run only by a continuing flow of successful new products not only to sustain sales volume but also to sustain and increase profits. Continuous innovation of new products, however, is extremely risky because of the high incidence of new product failures. The estimates of new product failures range from 33 percent[12] to 89 percent[13] and can involve millions of dollars. For example, in the late 1960s seventeen new brands of household cleaners were introduced in a nine-month period. Brands like Easy-off, Clean & Kill, Whistle, Power-on, and others produced an estimated loss of approximately $17 million.[14] About this same time, several new brands of mouthwash—including Fact, Vote, Cue, Reef, and others—resulted in a combined loss of over $40 million.

Despite the frequency and magnitude of losses resulting from new product development, marketing strategists continue to espouse the importance of continually developing new products. This view is typically supported by long lists of successful new products that contribute substantially to firm profits. The dilemma that the high failure rate–high profit rate creates has stimulated considerable interest in a research tradition known as diffusion of innovations, the premise being that an understanding of the diffusion of innovations would enable the marketing strategist to enhance the success of new products introduced in the market.

Elements of the Diffusion Process

The diffusion of innovations refers to "the spread of an idea from its source of invention to the ultimate users or adopters."[15] In the marketing context, any product that has recently become available in a market is considered an innovation. The diffusion process is conceptualized as having four basic elements, or analytical units. These elements have been identified as (1) the innovation, (2) the communication of the innovation among individuals, (3) the social system, and (4) time.[16]

The central concept of the diffusion process is that of innovation. *Innovation* has been defined most frequently as any idea or product that is perceived by the potential innovator to be new. Thus, the following would all be considered innovations: (1) the new model cars, (2) a new deodorant, (3) an existing deodorant in a new package or with a different scent, (4) the minicalculator in an untapped market, and (5) cable television in a new geographic area. As is apparent from the preceding examples, the opportunities to innovate new products and services are nearly boundless.

Because these opportunities for innovation are nearly limitless, it is necessary to categorize innovations on the basis of their impact on the social structure accepting them. In the following scheme, innovations are categorized as (1) continuous, (2) dynamically continuous, and (3) discontinuous.

1. A *continuous innovation* has the least disrupting influence on established patterns. Modification of an existing product is characteristic of this type, rather than the establishment of a totally new product. Examples include adding fluoride to toothpaste, new-model automobile changeovers, and adding menthol to cigarettes.

2. A *dynamically continuous innovation* has more disrupting effects than a continuous innovation, although it still does not generally alter established patterns of customer buying and product use. It may involve the creation of a new product or the alteration of an existing product. Examples are electric toothbrushes, the Mustang automobile, and Touch-Tone telephones.

3. A *discontinuous innovation* involves the introduction of an entirely new product that causes buyers to alter their behavior patterns significantly. Examples include television and computers.[17]

The appropriate marketing strategy for any new product depends on the disruption that a product will cause in existing consumer purchase patterns.

The role of communications is a central issue in the study of diffusion and may be of two types, informal and formal. *Informal* communications are nonmarketer dominated, such as reference-group and family influences. There is a temptation to assume that the people who first adopt a product are the ones who influence others to purchase it and that their communications are therefore instrumental in the diffusion process. Interpersonal influence appears to be much more complex, however.[18]

Formal communications are those dominated by marketers. They include advertising, various forms of retailer support, and personal salespeople. When control of communications is possible, questions such as these arise: What types of media are most likely to transmit messages to those persons who are most likely to be the first adopters of an innovation? What media are most likely to be considered authoritative? What messages are most likely to influence new product acceptance?

The diffusion of innovations is a social phenomenon. The word "diffusion" has little meaning except as it relates to a group of people. Acceptance or rejection of a product can apply to an individual person, but diffusion in this sense is a degree of concentration and refers to some group of individuals. Consequently, diffusion research should focus not only on characteristics of a decision-making unit (individual or family) but also on the environment provided by the social system.

Adoption of new products is a temporal phenomenon and needs to be analyzed as such. The decision to adopt a new product, like all other consumption decisions described by the model in this book, is a process rather than an event. People recognize problems, search for alternatives, evaluate new products as potential alternatives, decide to purchase the new product, and perhaps eventually purchase it. The adoption process is not considered complete, however, until postpurchase evaluation and repeat usage or purchase are generated. This is because adoption implies a decision to continue full use of an innovation.[19] To study the rate of diffusion in a social structure, it is necessary to evaluate the exact position of individual consumers in the process that leads to adoption.

Diffusion of Innovations and the Adoption Process

The diffusion of innovations and the consumer adoption process are integrally related. The process that individuals move through in adopting a new product has been conceptualized in a variety of ways. The Adoption Decision-Process Model and the Innovation Decision-Process Model are multistaged conceptualizations that reflect the current level of understanding.

Adoption Decision-Process Model

The Adoption Decision-Process Model, illustrated in Figure 16.2, is based on the information-attitude-behavior conceptualization and re-

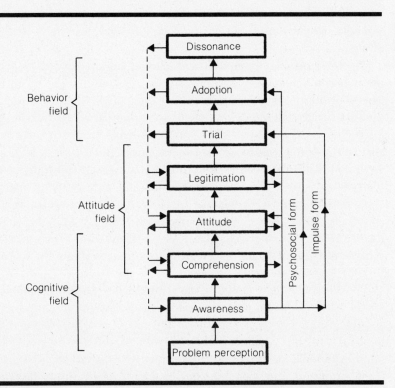

Figure 16.2
Summary Adoption Decision-Process Model

Source: Figure 14.5 (p. 290) from "A Critical Examination of 'Adoption Process' Models of Consumer Behavior" by T. S. Robertson, in *Models of Buyer Behavior* edited by J. N. Sheth. Copyright © 1974 by Harper & Row, Publishers, Inc. By permission of Harper & Row, Publishers, Inc.

flects the most widely accepted view of how promotion functions.[20] The *problem-perception* stage is not the typical beginning of the adoption process but can at times initiate it. For example, a consumer's recognition of a problem with his or her current tennis equipment can produce the search and alternative evaluation that may result in awareness of graphite rackets. The typical beginning of the adoption process—consumer *awareness*—is the point at which a product stimulus penetrates the consumer's filtration system and registers with the consumer. In other words, the consumer recognizes that the product exists. The information processing stages—awareness and comprehension—comprise the cognitive field of the adoption process. *Comprehension* is the consumer's understanding of what a product is and how it performs. The manner in which a consumer processes information is determined by that consumer's abilities. Certain consumers assimilate information more rapidly and thoroughly than do others.

The *attitude* stage refers to the consumer's predisposition to evaluate a product favorably or unfavorably. Although some exceptions can occur, normally a consumer must have a favorable evaluation of a product for the adoption process to continue. However, a favorable attitude toward a product does not assure that product trial will occur. In order for trial to occur, the consumer must have a favorable attitude toward the product *and* must be convinced that purchase of the product is the appropriate course of action. Thus, the *legitimation* stage requires that the consumer be convinced that the new product is socially appropriate and properly priced and, in general, that it meets the basic evaluative criteria. As is evident from Figure 16.2, the comprehension, attitude, and legitimation stages make up the attitude field of the adoption process.

The behavior field includes the legitimation, trial, and adoption stages of the adoption process. *Trial* is the actual use of a product on a rather limited scale. Thus, the initial use of a new product might indicate that the consumer has evaluated a product by means of first-hand experience or an actual commitment to a product. In the final stage, *adoption,* the consumer has evaluated the product favorably and has decided to purchase and/or use the product on a regular basis. In certain instances, the decision to adopt a particular product requires the consumer to choose from several desirable alternatives.

Because the consumer has decided to adopt one alternative in lieu of several others, he or she might experience *cognitive dissonance,* which is psychologically uncomfortable. Normally, consumers attempt to reduce this dissonance by obtaining information that confirms their decision, obtaining social support, or, in some other manner, reestablishing consonance.

This model emphasizes the fact that the adoption process can take many different forms. The rational decision-making form of the adoption process would include all the stages from awareness to adoption. The impulse form refers to the adoption process that goes directly from awareness to trial, thereby omitting the comprehension, attitude, and legitimation stages. The adoption process can also take a third form—psychosocial—in which the consumer skips the comprehension and attitude stages. Numerous factors, such as social characteristics, personality characteristics, and the perceived characteristics of the innovation, determine the form the adoption process will take.

Knowledge of the form the adoption process will take can be of substantial benefit to the marketer of a new product. For example, if the marketing strategist knows that the adoption process that consumers, or a particular segment of consumers, will engage in is the impulse form, marketing efforts can be allocated accordingly. In other words, marketing strategy can exclude any efforts designed to promote comprehension, attitude change, or legitimation. On the other hand, if the rational decision-making form prevails, marketing efforts will have to focus on moving the consumer through all stages of the adoption process.

Using the Adoption Decision-Process Model

An understanding of the consumer adoption process can facilitate the marketing manager's decision making substantially. For example, consider the marketing manager's difficulty in predicting sales: Does a substantial early adoption of a product mean that sales will be great or does it mean that a particular segment, perhaps a small one, is highly interested in the product? Conversely, low sales of a new product might indicate low potential sales or an ineffective promotional program. These difficulties can be overcome by using the adoption process.[21]

Table 16.2
**Classification of
Consumers by Stage of
the Adoption Process**

	Cumulative Percentage of Consumers		
Adoption Stage	January 1979	June 1979	Change (January–June)
Adoption	3	10	7
Trial	10	14	4
Legitimation	16	18	2
Favorable Attitude	25	30	5
Knowledge	45	70	25
Awareness	55	85	30

Source: Adaptation of Table 14.2 (p. 293) from ''A Critical Examination of 'Adoption Process' Models of Consumer Behavior'' by T. S. Robertson in *Models of Buyer Behavior* edited by J. N. Sheth. Copyright © 1974 by Harper & Row, Publishers, Inc. By permission of Harper & Row, Publishers, Inc.

Consider the classification of consumers by stage of the adoption process for an actual product as summarized in Table 16.2. A comparison of the adoption figure from January (3 percent) to June (10 percent) suggests that the new product being considered will be extremely successful. However, if the progress for all stages of the adoption process are examined, the situation does not appear nearly as favorable. During this six-month period, the level of awareness and knowledge has been increased substantially. Unfortunately, the firm's marketing efforts have been relatively unsuccessful in developing favorable attitudes and in advancing legitimation. This indicates that sales will soon level off because the firm's marketing efforts are not moving the consumer toward adoption. This stabilization of sales could be the result of ineffective or poorly focused promotional efforts. An alternative explanation might be that the market for this new product is small but quickly penetrated. Regardless of the actual reason, the marketing manager can correctly anticipate the progress of a new product and make the necessary changes in marketing effort.

Innovation Decision-Process Model

The Innovation Decision-Process Model (Figure 16.3) conceptualizes the process individuals move through in adopting a new product as

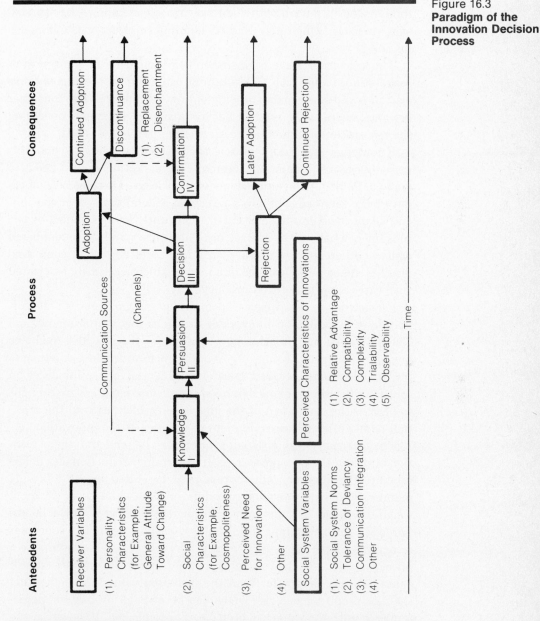

Figure 16.3
**Paradigm of the
Innovation Decision
Process**

Source: Everett M. Rogers and F. Floyd Shoemaker, *Communication of Innovations* (New York: Free Press, 1971), p. 102. Reprinted by permission.

multistaged in nature with the following stages: knowledge, persuasion, decision (which may lead to adoption or rejection), and confirmation.

The knowledge stage begins when a consumer receives physical or social stimuli that give exposure and attention to the innovation's existence and some understanding of how it functions. The consumer becomes aware of the product but has made no judgment concerning the relevance of the product to an existing problem or need.

Knowledge is a result of selective perception, but beyond this many questions remain unanswered. The marketing analyst needs to know more about the antecedents of knowledge. Do some consumers have more knowledge of new products in general than other consumers? Of all the stimulus sets that are constantly being sampled by the consumer, what makes one set have an impact and be remembered while another appears to have no impact and be lost to consciousness? Is increased knowledge of a new product necessarily associated with early adoption of that product?

Persuasion, in the Rogers-Shoemaker paradigm, refers to the formation of favorable or unfavorable attitudes toward the innovation. The individual may imagine how satisfactory the new idea might be in some anticipated future use situation before deciding whether to try it. This might be called "vicarious trial." All of the influences on consumer decision making described in previous chapters are brought to bear in the evaluation of the innovation which leads to the rejection or acceptance (the evaluation) of the idea of the innovation.

The persuasiveness of the innovation may be related to the perception of risk in the new product, with uncertainty reduction as a determinant of evaluation. This notion may be stated in the following manner: When an individual considers a new product, he or she must weigh the potential gains from adopting the product with the potential losses from switching from the product now used. The consumer recognizes that if the new product is adopted, it may be inferior to a present product, or the cost (price of the product plus possible disadvantages) may be greater than the increased value. Thus, adopting the new product has a risk which can be avoided by postponing acceptance until the value has been clearly established. If, however, the product is designed to solve a problem that is of significant concern to the consumer, there is also the risk that value may be lost by delaying adoption of a product that is truly superior to the present product.

The consumer can reduce the risk of adopting the new product and therefore uncertainty about the buying situation by acquiring additional information. A person may seek out news stories, pay particular attention to advertising for the product, subscribe to product-rating services, talk with individuals who have already tried the product, talk with experts on the subject, and, in some instances, even try the product on a limited basis. Each of these information search and evaluation strategies, however, has an economic and/or psychological cost. Moreover, they are unlikely to yield information that will completely reduce uncertainty.

The decision stage involves activities that lead to a choice between adopting or rejecting the innovation. The immediate consideration is whether or not to try the innovation, which is often influenced by the ability to try the innovation on a small scale (including vicarious trial by observing the use of the innovation by others). Innovations that can be purchased in divisible quantities are generally adopted more readily. Trial can sometimes be stimulated by the use of free samples or other small units with low risk.

Figure 16.3 shows that the output of decision can be either rejection or adoption. Rejection can be continuous or it may be reversed by later adoption. Conversely, adoption may be continuous or it may lead to later discontinuance.

Confirmation refers to the process postulated by Rogers and Shoemaker of consumers seeking reinforcement for the innovation decision that has been made. It also refers to the situation in which consumers sometimes reverse previous decisions when exposed to conflicting messages about the innovation.

Discontinuance is, of course, as serious a concern to marketers as the original process of adoption. The rate of discontinuance may be just as important as the rate of adoption, with the corresponding need for marketing strategists to devote attention to preventing discontinuance of innovations. Rogers and Shoemaker report that later adopters are more likely to discontinue innovations than earlier adopters and are generally likely to have the opposite characteristics (in education, social status, change-agency contact, and the like) to those of the innovators. Discontinuance is most likely to occur when the innovation is not integrated into the practices and way of life of

Figure 16.4
The Diffusion Process

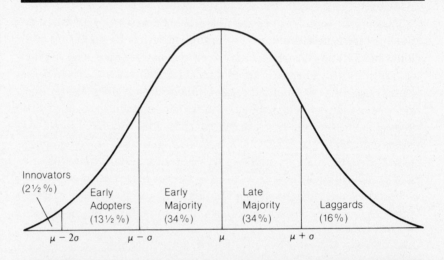

Innovators
(2½%)

Early
Adopters
(13½%)

Early
Majority
(34%)

Late
Majority
(34%)

Laggards
(16%)

$\mu - 2\sigma$ $\mu - \sigma$ μ $\mu + \sigma$

purchasers, suggesting the need for after-the-sale reinforcement activity by marketing strategists designed to ensure continued acceptance and use.

Identifying Innovativeness

Consumer analysts have for some time attempted to identify consumers who adopt new products and services early. Interest in identifying innovators is based on the premise that such information would permit the development of new products that are compatible with the preferences of innovators. In other words, even though all consumers pass through the stages of the adoption process, some consumers adopt the product much sooner than do others.

The diffusion is typically depicted as a cumulative normal distribution such as that shown in Figure 16.4. Initially a product is adopted by a few consumers, and then the number of adopters increases rapidly. Finally, the number of adopters reaches a peak and then diminishes as fewer individuals remain in the nonadopter category. Typically, the first 2.5 percent of consumers to adopt a product are called innovators, the next 13.5 percent are called early adopters, and so on.

Considerable effort has been expended to identify variables that are associated with these consumers. The groups of variables that have been identified as having a particularly pronounced effect on the adoption rate are consumer characteristics and product characteristics. The efforts of consumer analysts to associate innovativeness with consumer characteristics have produced several useful results. In particular, innovativeness has been found to be positively associated with education, income, level of living, aspirations for children, attitude toward change, knowledge of the world and events in general, social status, mobility, and venturesomeness.[22] For example, a study of the diffusion of a new automobile service found that the earliest adopters, compared to the population as a whole, were:

1. much more willing to experiment with new ideas

2. more likely to buy new products (in general) earlier

3. less likely to switch brands because of a small price change

4. less interested in low prices per se

5. less likely to try new convenience items if the innovation represented only minor changes.[23]

Furthermore, innovators were the best-informed segment of the population and engaged in considerable planning before purchasing new products. An understanding of the characteristics of innovators enables the marketing manager to direct the firm's communications to those consumers who are likely to adopt the innovation, thus increasing the effectiveness of promotional efforts.

Consumer analysts have also determined that the acceptance of a new product by innovators is determined to a large degree by the characteristics of the product itself. The product characteristics that seem to have the greatest effect on the adoption rate of a new product are the following.

1. *Relative advantage.* The greater the relative advantage of a new product (the more superior it is to the product it replaces), the more quickly it will be adopted.

2. *Compatibility.* The compatibility of a new product is the degree to which the product is consistent with the existing values and experiences of consumers. The more compatible products encompass favor-

ably held values, the more quickly they will be adopted. A new product's color, design, packaging, and related promotional materials act as a symbol to consumers, communicating to them the compatibility of the new product with their existing values.

3. *Complexity.* The complexity of a product is the degree to which a new product is difficult to understand and use. New products that require detailed personal explanation, for example, are likely to diffuse slowly. Marketing managers introducing complex new products must develop a means of stimulating product trial in order to increase the rate of consumer acceptance.

4. *Communicability.* Communicability is the degree to which the benefits of product use can be communicated to others. Products that are visible in social situations or that lend themselves better to demonstration or description are likely to have a faster rate of adoption.[24]

The preceding generalizations suggest that the marketing manager can affect the rate of new product adoption. For example, the marketer can design a new product specifically to enhance its relative advantage over existing products, maximize compatibility with consumer values and experiences, and maximize the communicability of product benefits while minimizing product complexity. Typically the marketing manager must be willing to make certain concessions with respect to product design. For example, transacting banking business by means of consumer-computer interaction (e.g., automatic teller machines, point-of-sale terminals) provides communicable advantages over existing products but is somewhat inconsistent with consumers' values and experiences. Consequently, the adoption of computer-based consumer banking transactions is likely to be slow.

The generalizations regarding the effects of product characteristics on the adoption rate of new products can also provide considerable direction for the innovating firm's promotional efforts. Promotional efforts must be designed to effectively communicate the product's relative benefits. These benefits must be communicated in a manner that reflects the target market's values and that de-emphasizes the product's complexity.

Summary

The focus of this chapter has been on two consumer choice patterns that are especially important to the marketer. The first topic, brand loyalty, refers to the tendency of consumers to consistently purchase a particular brand over time. Researchers initially considered it to be the sequence of purchasing a specific brand. This led to the classification of consumers into four categories, namely, undivided loyalty, divided loyalty, unstable loyalty, and no loyalty. According to this interpretation, brand loyalty varies substantially among different types of products. The proportion-of-purchases definition considers brand loyalty to be the ratio of purchases of the most frequently purchased brand or set of brands to total purchases within a given product category. The use of this definition facilitated the development of the concept of multibrand loyalty. The preference purchase definition of brand loyalty distinguishes repeat purchase behavior, which focuses only on behavior, from loyalty, which encompasses the antecedents of behavior.

Marketing decision makers have studied brand loyalty extensively and have reached some tentative conclusions. Among them are that brand loyalty is (1) positively related to perceived risk, (2) related to store loyalty, (3) negatively related to the number of stores a consumer shops at, and (4) positively related to extensiveness of distribution and market share. Most of the models developed in an attempt to understand brand loyalty behavior over time have been stochastic models, which treat the response of consumers in the marketplace as the outcome of some probabilistic process. A Markov model of brand loyalty is presented. Such a model assumes that the probability of a purchase of a particular brand in one time period is influenced by the purchases made in one or more previous time periods, and that these probabilities remain unchanged over time.

Brand loyalty can be useful in segmenting markets if the segments are identifiable; the marketer would be wise to consider this when formulating strategy. Some possible strategies based on brand loyalty are listed, but these types of strategies may be ineffective if loyalty is caused by psychological commitment to a brand.

The second topic given attention in this chapter is the diffusion of innovations, which is a choice pattern that provides a foundation for astute product development decisions. Of relevance to this topic is the concept of product life cycle, which describes the generalized pattern of sales and profit that products follow over time as consisting of four distinct stages: introduction, growth, maturity, and decline. A product's profit margin begins to decline in the growth stage of its life cycle. Consequently, continual new product development, although risky, is of primary concern to any firm that wishes to maintain or increase profits. Understanding the diffusion of innovation process can enhance the success of new products introduced in the market.

According to Rogers, the diffusion of innovations refers to "the spread of an idea from its source of invention to its ultimate users or adopters." An innovation is any product that has recently become available in the marketplace. The other elements of the diffusion process are the communication of the innovation among individuals, the social system, and time. The appropriate marketing strategy for any new product depends on the disruption that it will have on existing consumer purchase patterns. The consumer adoption process is integrally related to the diffusion of innovations. The Adoption Decision-Process Model and the Innovation Decision-Process Model are described in detail. They reflect the current level of understanding of the adoption process and can greatly facilitate the marketing manager's decision making.

An understanding of the characteristics of innovators, those consumers who adopt new products and services early, enables the marketing manager to direct the firm's communications to these consumers, thus increasing the effectiveness of promotional efforts. The product characteristics that seem to have the greatest effect on the adoption rate of a new product are: (1) relative advantage, (2) compatibility, (3) complexity, and (4) communicability. The marketing manager can affect the rate of the adoption process by designing products that, in general, rate favorably on these characteristics, but he or she must be willing to make some concessions with respect to product design.

Questions and Issues for Discussion

1. Explain what is meant by the concept of "multibrand loyalty." What are the implications of this concept for marketers?

2. What factors have an effect on consumer brand loyalty? How can a knowledge of these factors help a marketer increase consumer loyalty to his or her brand?

3. What applications can you think of for the Markov models of brand loyalty? Referring to Table 16.1, what should the probabilities suggest to the management of the firm that markets brand C? Recommend some ideas for research that this firm might undertake to better evaluate its position and plan strategy.

4. Name four types of products whose consumers are likely to be brand loyal and explain why. What types of people are probably loyal to brands in these categories?

5. Distinguish between the alternative definitions of brand loyalty. What are the strengths and weaknesses of each? Explain the ways in which each could be useful to the marketer.

6. Describe the four stages of the product life cycle. Which stage of the PLC are the following products currently in? Identify the implications the stage of PLC has for the marketing manager for each of these products.

(a) electric car

(b) cable television

(c) window home air-conditioning units

(d) digital watches

(e) wire eyeglass frames.

7. Quadraphonic sound equipment was introduced in the market in 1971. It was expected to dislodge stereophonic, or two-channel, sound from its dominance in the world of high fidelity. However, it was not very successful in the market. This is partially attributed to consumer confusion about different types of equipment, records, and tapes. Additionally, many experts on sound think buyers were not convinced that the improvement was noticeable enough to warrant the extra $600 on upgrading a stereo system. Describe how an understanding of the diffusion process might have helped marketers augment the success of quadraphonic sound in the market.

8. "New products which are modest failures can often cost millions of dollars. In addition to cash costs, product failures tie up time and talent that might have gone into profitable operations. And consider what damage a failure does to the morale of the sales force." Comment on this statement. What can and should marketers do to minimize the incidence and expense of product failures?

9. Describe the Adoption Decision-Process Model and the Innovation Decision-Process Model. What are the strengths and weaknesses of each?

10. The Solar Company has recently developed a home heating system that stores energy for home heating. Describe the diffusion process for this product. Develop a marketing strategy that will enable the company to accomplish the diffusion.

Case 1. General Mills, Incorporated

General Mills, Incorporated, is the fifth largest diversified food company in the world. In 1968, it produced mainly flour, cake mixes, and breakfast cereals, and had turned many of its brand names into household words (Betty Crocker, Wheaties, Bisquick, and Gold Medal are familiar names to almost anyone). But in the early 1970s, the food processing industry began to have some difficulties. The steady expansion in food consumption, which characterized the two previous decades, was no longer to be found, and in 1975, such consumption actually declined by almost one percent. This was the first drop since the 1930s, and many industry leaders attribute this leveling off in growth to a single cause: inflation.

From 1973 to 1976, food prices increased almost 40 percent, far ahead of housing as the largest item in the average family's budget. "Because most of us stock up on food once or twice a week, food prices are our most visible and most sensitive indicator of inflation, and every little increase is both noticed and resisted," says a marketing analyst. "This is bound to have staggering consequences for basic consumption patterns." He says that likely possibilities are less impulse buying, less inclination to try new products, and less interest in expensive convenience and snack foods. "In turn, you might see greater interest in more basic and economical commodity products that carry lower margins."

The response of many food processors to these developments has

Sources: Some of the information used in Case 1 is from "The Hard Road of the Food Processors," *Business Week*, March 8, 1976, pp. 50–54; and "Marketing Observer," *Business Week*, March 6, 1978, p. 92.

been diversification. General Mills' excellent management has enabled it to do so more effectively than most other firms. By 1976, only 60 percent of the company's business came from food products. The other 40 percent represented travel, clothing, furniture, and what has become one of the nation's biggest game and toy businesses. In that year, General Mills was the proud holder of 60 percent of the cakemix market, 45 percent of the ready-to-eat cereal market, and 40 percent of the game business.

General Mills has responded well to many of the changes taking place in consumption patterns in its product development. It is placing more emphasis on the development of basic products that can withstand a slack economy. "We have to assume that there will be more instability in the economy in the next few years, and this poses a major dilemma for us," remarks one high-ranking executive. "We must not lose sight of the fact that we are selling to the homemaker and the family." An example of the philosophy being adopted at General Mills is the decline in emphasis on whether the market will accept, say, banana-almond cake mixes and the increase in emphasis on whether the market really needs banana-almond cake mixes.

General Mills and other food processors are devoting more and more funds to market research and consumer surveys to get a tighter grip on their markets. During the 1950s and 1960s, consumers were enthusiastic about trying new products and variations on old ones, "and once they latched on to one, their brand loyalty was nearly unshakeable until something newer and better came along." Now, from research, they find that "consumers are angry, suspicious, and skeptical." Says one consumer, "I think there are too many new products on the market. Consumers would be better off if manufacturers would just concentrate on doing a good job with the items they already make and improving them." This attitude may be reflected in the fact that fewer than 25 percent of all new products tested each year ever reach supermarket shelves. Even so, new products in grocery and drug lines were introduced at a rate of 3.3 per day in 1977, according to a publication called *New Product News*.

The inflationary environment and certain other changes in our society are, indeed, having a sharp impact on the attitudes and purchase patterns of consumers. General Mills hired market researchers Yankelovich, Skelly, and White for an extensive study of the American family which they hoped would allow them to pinpoint some of the more significant changes in these attitudes and patterns. Among almost 2200 persons interviewed, 65 percent responded that inflation is having a "fairly serious" or "very serious" impact on their lives, and 56 percent are "insecure about their own financial future." This clearly indicates that consumers are exhibiting and will continue to exhibit an increasing concern for value in their purchases. They have less money to experiment with as their real purchasing power declines. This may increase the perceived risk associated with buying an untried brand. It was also found in this study that fully 20 percent of the families interviewed have given up meat at some meals and 25 percent are cutting back on frozen and prepared foods. In addition, the study found that with 42 percent of wives in the 1976 work force, the homemaker has a greatly increased need for foods that are nutritious, inexpensive, and easy to prepare.

Unfortunately, many food processors have not had the success in coping with the changes that have occurred in the marketplace that General Mills has had. Their capital has been devoured by new product failures and by the development of products with market lives of only 12 to 14 months. Spiraling costs of materials and labor, and stiffer regulatory requirements have crippled some firms. The scramble to diversify hurt many firms who did it unwisely. An executive from one firm says, "We were buying up companies at a hectic clip, but we weren't buying management know-how." The chairman and chief executive of General Mills, James P. McFarland, sums up what he thinks is the key to successful performance in the food business in one short sentence, "You just have to learn to make decisions, based on a shifting mosaic."

Case 1 Questions

1. Explain the implications of the changes that are taking place in the economy in general, and in the market for food items in particular, for brand loyalty patterns.

2. What factors might lead you to believe that General Mills' customers are brand loyal?

3. In detail, explain the nature of the relationship that may exist between the diffusion of innovations and brand loyalty.

4. How could a knowledge of these two concepts (and their possible relationship) benefit firms in the food processing industry?

Case 2. Imaginetics International, Inc.

Imaginetics International, Inc. is ecstatic about its recent product development—a toy Volkswagen van, named George, that "hears" and responds to voice commands. The toy's overwhelming success at trade shows across the nation has delighted company officials, and one marketer loftily refers to it as "a magnificent toy, a super toy." The company predicts that everyone who sees the toy will want one, despite its $30 price tag.

A recent development in the economics of voice control has made such an invention feasible. The toy obeys a predetermined sequence of commands, such as "turn left, go straight, turn right, and stop." However, since George is programmed to respond only to this fixed sequence of motions, the user must say commands in the proper order to obtain a correct response. One way of overcoming this is for the user to extend the sounds in the command, which will cause George to skip a step or two in the sequence. For example, if George is stopped and the user wants it to turn right, he can say, "Ple-e-ease go right" and the left and straight sequences will be passed over. One advantage in the company's favor is that the toy does not actually respond to specific words, but rather to sounds. This will enable Imaginetics to market George in foreign countries as effectively as in the U.S. This, company officials surmise, could make George the "biggest toy in history."

George is activated by a small crystal microphone in its roof. A loud sound triggers an integrated circuit that actuates a relay switch. This sends battery power to the motor that drives a fifth rudder behind and between the front wheels. The rudder controls George's direction. Subsequent sounds cause the rudder wheel to rotate for a

Source: Some of the information used in Case 2 is from "A Toy That Could Change the Toy Business," *Business Week*, June 20, 1977, pp. 60–64.

prescribed number of degrees, which initiates a movement to the left or straight or right, in that sequence.

Imaginetics is predicting sales of 10 million units by 1980. Since the price of George is somewhat dear for a toy, the company is relying on international sales to supplement the attainment of this goal. However, company officials are confident that demand for George will not be heavily stifled by its price because (1) George is a quality product; (2) the toy vans can be produced in quantity; and (3), most important, George is a novelty.

Voice control and man-machine voice communications are the latest developments in other areas such as computer-aided manufacturing, learning aids, security, and aids for the handicapped. One new learning aid is a talking machine that helps children spell. It is equipped with 200 often misspelled words that are stored in a memory analogous to the way a computer stores numbers. The machine speaks words at random, and the children spell out the words using alphabetic keys. The machine then announces whether or not the spelling is correct. Other vocal machines include talking calculators for the blind and voice recognition systems that permit people to talk to computers in order to program them or enter data.

Costs for products such as these are relatively prohibitive for the average consumer; consequently, Imaginetics sees vast potential for inexpensive technology like George. Doors are opening to a totally new class of consumer products, and Imaginetics has the advantage of being one of the market leaders. One marketing analyst recently predicted that voice-response circuits will become a routine component in toys within two years. To instigate this trend, and to establish itself in this potential market, Imaginetics also plans to introduce similar products—such as a plush dog, a cat, and possibly a doll. After that, the company envisions adaptations for a voice-controlled electric wheelchair. The possibilities are endless.

Case 2 Questions

1. Is George a continuous, dynamically continuous, or discontinuous innovation? Explain.

2. Does George have the product characteristics that facilitate early acceptance by innovators? What problems, if any, do you foresee that would impede the diffusion of this product?

3. Using the Adoption Decision-Process Model, develop a detailed promotional strategy for this product.

4. What form would the adoption process take?

Notes

1. "Marketing Observer," *Business Week* (August 4, 1975), p. 66.

2. Ibid.

3. "Marketing Observer," *Business Week* (June 16, 1975), p. 84.

4. "Marketing Observer," *Business Week* (August 4, 1975), p. 66.

5. George Brown, "Brand Loyalty—Fact or Fiction?" *Advertising Age,* Vol. 23 (June 19, 1952), pp. 53-55; (June 30, 1952), pp. 45-47; (July 14, 1952), pp. 54-56; (July 28, 1952), pp. 46-48; (August 11, 1952), pp. 56-58; (September 1, 1952), pp. 80-82; (October 6, 1952), pp. 82-86; (December 1, 1952), pp. 76-79; (January 25, 1953), pp. 75-76.

6. Jacob Jacoby and David B. Kyner, "Brand Loyalty vs. Repeat Purchase Behavior," *Journal of Marketing Research,* Vol. 10 (February 1973), pp. 1-9.

7. William A. Chance and Norman D. French, "An Exploratory Investigation of Brand Switching," *Journal of Marketing Research,* Vol. 9 (May 1972), pp. 226-229.

8. Shmuel Sharir, "Brand Loyalty and the Household's Cost of Time," *Journal of Business,* Vol. 47 (January 1974), pp. 53-55.

9. These probabilities can be computed by methods of matrix algebra or by simply tracing behavior by means of a tree diagram. Only sample computations are shown.

For a consumer buying A during period I, the probabilities during period II are obvious. The probability of his buying A during period III would be $0.7 \times 0.7 + 0.1 \times 0.3 + 0.2 \times 0.4 = 0.60$; for B it would be $0.7 \times 0.1 + 0.1 \times 0.6 + 0.2 \times 0.1 = 0.15$; and for C it would be $0.7 \times 0.2 + 0.1 \times 0.1 + 0.2 \times 0.5 = 0.25$. For the student familiar with matrix algebra, all nine probabilities for period III (three each for different purchases during period I) can be obtained by multiplying the transition matrix by itself. The new matrix can be postmultiplied by the original transition matrix to obtain probabilities for period IV.

10. R. W. Van Camp, "Essential Elements for New Product Success," J. O. Eastlack, Jr., ed., *New Product Development* (Chicago: American Marketing Association, 1968), p. 3.

11. T. Levitt, "Exploit the Product Life Cycle," *Harvard Business Review* (November-December 1965), p. 93.

12. *Management of New Products* (New York: Booz, Allen & Hamilton, Inc., 1965).

13. B. Schorr, "Many New Products Fizzle, Despite Careful Planning, Publicity," *Wall Street Journal* (April 5, 1961), p. 1.

14. T. L. Angeleus, "Why Do Most New Products Fail?" *Advertising Age* (March 24, 1969), pp. 85-86.

15. Everett Rogers, *Diffusion of Innovations* (Glencoe, Ill.: The Free Press, 1965 and 1971).

16. Ibid.

17. Thomas S. Robertson, "The Process of Innovation and the Diffusion of Innovation," *Journal of Marketing,* Vol. 31 (January 1967), pp. 14-19, at p. 15.

18. Thomas S. Robertson, "A Critical Examination of 'Adoption Process' Models of Consumer Behavior," Jagdish Sheth, ed., *Models of Buyer Behavior* (New York: Harper & Row, Publishers, 1974).

19. Rogers, *Diffusion of Innovations,* 1965, p. 17.

20. Robertson, "A Critical Examination of 'Adoption Process' Models of Consumer Behavior," pp. 271-95.

21. Ibid., p. 293.

22. T. S. Robertson, *Innovative Behavior and Communication* (New York: Holt, Rinehart and Winston, Inc., 1974), Chapter 5.

23. R. J. Kegerris, J. F. Engel, and R. D. Blackwell, "Innovativeness and Diffusiveness: A Marketing View of the Characteristics of Earliest Adopters," D. T. Kollat, R. D. Blackwell, and J. F. Engel, eds., *Research in Consumer Behavior* (New York: Holt, Rinehart and Winston, Inc., 1970), pp. 671-89.

24. E. M. Rogers and F. F. Shoemaker, *Communication of Innovations* (New York: Free Press, 1971), pp. 137-57.

Part 5 Consumer Behavior in Perspective

The final section of this book includes two chapters, each differing considerably from the other. Both chapters, however, serve as appropriate ways of concluding this formal study of consumer behavior.

Chapter 17 focuses on some of the ways in which limits have been imposed on marketing strategies developed to influence consumers. The notion is also suggested that any information about consumer behavior must be used with good judgment to avoid exploitation.

Chapter 18 provides a means of taking account of the progress that has been made in the formal study of consumer behavior. It shows the importance of theory development in helping to illuminate reality and that continued progress in consumer behavior study can contribute to improved efficiency in the use of scarce resources.

Chapter **17** Evaluating the Use
of Consumer
Behavior
Knowledge

Outline

Approaches to Regulation
Legal Regulations
Self-interest and Voluntary Codes
Personal Convictions and Ethics

Consumer Protection at the Federal Level

Consumer Protection at the State Level
Selected Fraudulent Practices
Specific Protection from Door-to-Door Sales Representatives
Holder-in-Due-Course
Auto Odometer Readings
A Restitution Option

Evaluating Consumer Protection Laws and Agency Actions

Voluntary Self-regulation

Personal Conviction and Ethics in the Marketplace

An Evaluation of Business Practices

Summary

Questions and Issues for Discussion

Cases

Key Terms

legal regulation

self-interest and voluntary codes

personal convictions

consumer protection

deceptive advertising

ad substantiation

proposed complaint

assurance of discontinuance

bait and switch selling

deceptive pricing

disparagement

door-to-door sales cancellation

holder-in-due-course

mileage statement

small claims court

benefit assuring laws

information disclosure laws

voluntary self-regulation

consumerism management system

social accountability

social responsibility

The text thus far has been devoted almost exclusively to the study of consumer behavior with the purpose of assisting marketing managers to develop strategies. The objective of most of these managers is to be able to more profitably carry out their responsibilities in the competitive market environment. This typically means influencing consumers to buy specific goods and services. At this point, it is reasonable to raise a question about what limits, if any, should be placed on business practices arising out of the use of consumer behavior information.

Approaches to Regulation

Essentially three separate, yet related, approaches are used in the regulation of buinesses' efforts to influence consumers: (1) legal regulations, (2) self-interest and voluntary codes, and (3) personal convictions or ethics. Each approach will be introduced briefly and then treated in greater detail in subsequent sections.

Legal Regulations

Legal regulations are requirements established by law with which business must comply in order to avoid penalty. Legal regulations are enacted to force business conformance to some specific pattern of behavior that is generally considered acceptable to society. A local sign ordinance is an example of a community's effort to regulate such factors as size, color, and placement of signs in the area. The Fair Credit Reporting Act is an example of federal legislation specifying how credit information must be handled.

Self-interest and Voluntary Codes

Self-interest and voluntary codes operate on the premise that particular practices by business not only serve the consumer well, but also are in the best long-run interest of the firms involved. One of the benefits of voluntary codes is to avoid excessive government intervention in business affairs. This is consistent with a laissez-faire economic system which embraces the idea that competition is the best protector against business misconduct and that government intervention should be minimal. That is, any company that abuses the consumer will ultimately lose its market position to its upright competitors. Certainly the establishment of the Advertising Review Board was a belief in the concept of self-regulation. Furthermore, it is one cooperative undertaking that has made some very positive contributions to improving promotional practices.

Personal Convictions and Ethics

The human character traits of personal convictions, or beliefs, stem from an individual's personal values as mediated through the social environment. Ethics is concerned with differentiating between what is fundamentally right and what is wrong. Everyone has some standards by which he or she judges experiences and observed or proposed actions. Because these are personal, it is not really possible for a business firm to have ethics. However, business actions in the marketplace reflect the ethics of its key management personnel. Consequently, the practices of firms can be judged as right or wrong by the general ethical standards or convictions of the majority of people in society. It is not uncommon to think of this process as reviewing business ethics.

Consumer Protection at the Federal Level

The federal laws that are the historical basis for modern consumer protection legislation were established to protect and nurture competition in the marketplace. As mentioned earlier, this was considered the most appropriate route under a laissez-faire economic system. However, as time passed, it was realized that this "indirect" approach was inadequate in a complex marketplace where the competitive system could not respond quickly enough to minimize consumer injury or loss. As a result, various specific pieces of federal legislation have become law which are aimed at specific aspects of doing business. Several selected federal consumer protection laws and their purposes are shown in Table 17.1 to illustrate the vastness of federal involve-

Act	Purposes
Pure Food and Drug Act (1906)	Prohibits adulteration and misbranding of foods and drugs sold in interstate commerce
Food, Drug, and Cosmetic Act (1938)	Prohibits the adulteration and sale of foods, drugs, cosmetics, or therapeutic devices that may endanger public health; allows the Food and Drug Administration to set minimum standards and to establish guides for food products

Table 17.1
Selected Federal Consumer Protection Laws

Table 17.1
(continued)

Act	Purposes
Wool Products Labeling Act (1940)	Protects producers, manufacturers, distributors, and consumers from undisclosed substitutes and mixtures in all types of manufactured wool products
Fur Products Labeling Act (1951)	Protects consumers and others against misbranding, false advertising, and false invoicing of furs and fur products
Flammable Fabrics Act (1953)	Prohibits interstate transportation of dangerously flammable wearing apparel and fabrics
Automobile Information Disclosure Act (1958)	Requires automobile manufacturers to post suggested retail prices on all new passenger vehicles
Textile Fiber Products Identification Act (1958)	Guards producers and consumers against misbranding and false advertising of fiber content of textile fiber products
Cigarette Labeling Act (1965)	Requires cigarette manufacturers to label cigarettes as hazardous to health
Fair Packaging and Labeling Act (1966)	Declares unfair or deceptive packaging or labeling of certain consumer commodities illegal
Child Protection Act (1966)	Excludes from sale potentially harmful toys; allows the FDA to remove dangerous products from the market

Act	Purposes	Table 17.1 (continued)
Truth-in-Lending Act (1968)	Requires full disclosure of all finance charges on consumer credit agreements and in advertisements of credit plans to allow consumers to be better informed regarding their credit purchases	
Child Protection and Toy Safety Act (1969)	Protects children from toys and other products that contain thermal, electrical, or mechanical hazards	
Fair Credit Reporting Act (1970)	Ensures that a consumer's credit report will contain only accurate, relevant, and recent information and will be confidential unless requested for an appropriate reason by a proper party	
Consumer Products Safety Act (1972)	Created an independent agency to protect consumers from unreasonable risk of injury arising from consumer products; agency is empowered to set safety standards	
Magnuson-Moss Warranty-Federal Trade Commission Improvement Act (1975)	Provides for minimum disclosure standards for written consumer product warranties; defines minimum content standards for written warranties; allows the FTC to prescribe interpretive rules and policy statements regarding unfair or deceptive practices	

Source: From William M. Pride and O. C. Ferrell, *Marketing: Basic Concepts and Decisions*, p. 423. Copyright © 1977 by Houghton Mifflin Co. Reprinted by permission.

Table 17.2
**Federal Agencies
Monitoring Consumer
Information**

Agency	Activity
USDA-Agricultural Marketing Service	Approves all labels for meat, poultry, and related products in advance of their use
Federal Trade Commission	Prevents deceptive packaging and advertising; monitors TV, radio, and printed advertising for possible deception and fraud
	Assures truthful labels on wool, fur, and textile products
HEW-Food and Drug Administration	Assures that foods, drugs, devices, and cosmetics are honestly and informatively labeled and packaged
Department of Justice	Enforces federal laws pertaining to consumer fraud through cases referred to it by other government agencies
U.S. Postal Service	Polices mail for possible fraudulent schemes
Securities and Exchange Commission	Sets up regulations to prevent fraud in the securities markets
Department of the Treasury	Prevents consumer deception in the labeling and advertising of alcoholic beverages, tobacco products, and firearms (the FDA and FTC also have authority in this field but refer cases here)

Source: R. N. Katz, ed., *Protecting Consumer Interests: Private Initiative and Public Response* (Cambridge, Mass.: Ballinger Publishing Company, 1976), p. 50. Reprinted with permission from *Protecting Consumer Interests*, Copyright 1976, Ballinger Publishing Company.

ment. The agencies listed in Table 17.2 are responsible for monitoring the information that is provided consumers under the various laws.

No single federal agency is more active in monitoring and attempting to affect the use of consumer behavior information than is the Federal Trade Commission. Established in 1914 by the Federal Trade

Commission Act, the commission itself is composed of five members, with no more than three from one political party, who serve seven-year terms. These members are appointed by the president and confirmed by the Senate. However, the commission employs several thousand staff members—mostly attorneys, economists, and other support personnel.

With its broad policing powers, the FTC becomes involved in a host of business practices. To illustrate the nature of its involvement, attention will be focused on deceptive advertising.

First, there is some confusion over the terms "false" and "deceptive." One view is that a "false" claim is demonstrably false on the basis of objective evidence. For instance, EPA auto mileage tests can be checked to verify a claim made by General Motors. A "deceptive" ad is an implicit or explicit claim that may create an incorrect impression or perception on the part of the consumer. Deception will be singled out here.

Many definitions of deception have been proposed. However, most fall into one of two categories: the *legal,* represented by most FTC rulings, and the *behavioral,* the view upheld in the current marketing literature. The legal definition as found in the *FTC Reporter* is:

An act or practice or representation is a "deceptive" act or practice, which Section 5 of the Federal Trade Commission Act prohibits, if it has the "capacity" or "tendency" to deceive. Actual deception need not be proved or found.

In determining whether a representation is deceptive, its effect upon the "ordinary" purchaser, the "public" or the "average" man is considered. This may include "the ignorant, the unthinking and the credulous"; it does not include a "very stupid person" or "an insignificant and unrepresentative" segment of the public.

In determining whether a representation is deceptive, the entire representation is taken into consideration—the entire advertisement, the entire label or the entire transaction. If a word or term is ambiguous, and one meaning is false, the word or term is held to be deceptive.

Not only what is said, but what is not may constitute a deceptive act. Representations which are too broad to be true in all circumstances must be qualified; qualifications which have been held to be necessary are discussed in connection with specific representations throughout this division. Material facts must be disclosed; disclosures which have been required are set out at ¶ 7545. Inconspicuousness of qualifications and disclosures may be a factor in causing a representation to be held deceptive.

A higher degree of veracity may be required in labeling than in advertising, it has been suggested. The fact that a statement is literally true is no defense for a deceptive statement, however, as discussed at ¶ 7533.

The fact that a challenged word or term is in widespread use in the same manner and under the same circumstances may be a factor in determining that it is not deceptive. Normally, however, the fact that competitors or others are engaged in the same deceptive act is not a defense; see ¶ 9641.

Deception in securing the first contract with a prospective customer is unlawful, even though the initial deception is subsequently clarified. An act which may be deceptive to ultimate consumers or the general public is unlawful even though the immediate customer is not deceived.[1]

The behavioral approach to deception was defined by Gardner.

If an advertisement (or advertising campaign) leaves the average consumer within some reasonable market segment with an impression(s) and/or belief(s) different from what would normally be expected if the average consumer within that market segment had reasonable knowledge and that impression(s) and/or belief(s) is factually untrue or potentially misleading, then deception is said to exist.[2]

The behavioral definition concentrates on what the consumer perceives, rather than on what the advertisement either intended to say or says literally. Furthermore, the definition focuses on the average consumer. Using this perspective, it was suggested that a 67-year-old retired person who has never ridden a motorcycle, is unlikely to do so, and has no interest in motorcycles should not be of concern in determining deception in motorcycle advertising.[3]

What follows is a brief description of the procedures used by the FTC in policing advertising claims.

The FTC may become aware of a possible case of false, misleading or deceptive advertising from a variety of sources, including (1) individual consumer complaints, (2) consumer groups, (3) the courts, (4) competitive businesses, and (5) direct observation by FTC staff members.

After considering the advertising brought to their attention, the commission decides whether or not to pursue the case. This decision is affected by factors such as the seriousness of the issues involved, other evidence that the commission has relating to the case, some estimate of the likelihood of successfully dealing with the central issue, the extent of the benefits that would result from resolving the case, as well as the commission's work load at the time.

If the commission decides to pursue the case, the formal process begins. This effort can be separated into three phases: (1) the exploratory phase, (2) the negotiation phase, and (3) the litigation phase.

The exploratory phase ordinarily starts with a letter being sent to the firm whose advertising, for example, is being questioned. This letter usually contains a copy of the ad involved and a statement of the claim that the commission wants substantiated.

The material submitted in response to this request is then reviewed by the FTC, and the decision is made as to whether to pursue the case further. If the decision is made to continue, the next action would be to subpoena the advertiser, requesting a witness and a large volume of information from the firm and/or its ad agency.

Another review takes place after the responses to the subpoena requests are received by the commission. And again, a decision must be made whether to pursue the case. If the case is dropped, no further action would be taken by either party. However, if the FTC decides to continue, the advertiser typically receives a copy of a complaint or "proposed complaint" which the commission plans to submit for adjudication.

At this point, the process enters the negotiation phase. This involves an informal give and take between the advertiser's management and the commission's staff. The objective of this exchange is to reach a mutually acceptable solution to the case. These negotiations are informal and, consequently, provide considerable flexibility. The central issue may be settled here by a voluntary "assurance of discontinuance" on the part of the advertiser or the signing of a formal consent order. If an advertiser enters into either of these, there is no admission that the ad or ads in question were false, misleading, or deceptive. There is simply an expression of willingness to stop a specified practice. Once signed, such agreements are binding on the advertiser. It has been estimated that 50 percent of all deceptive practice investigations are concluded at this stage on the basis of an informal "assurance of discontinuance" agreement.

If no agreement can be reached between the FTC and the advertiser, then the litigation phase is entered and initiated by the issuance of a formal complaint in the name of the FTC. This is followed by a formal hearing before an administrative law judge. These hearings make use of typical courtroom procedures and are followed by a recommendation from the judge to the commission. This recommendation is reviewed by the five commission members who may affirm, modify, or dismiss the complaint.

If the complaint is upheld by the commissioners, the advertiser has the right to appeal the FTC's decision to the circuit courts. The courts provide a check on the commission which, until this point, was acting as judge, jury, and prosecuting attorney.

Consumer Protection at the State Level

To make sure that their citizens are protected against the exploitive practices of some business persons, state legislatures have enacted laws which are based on the recommendations of the state attorney general's office. Some of these are rather broad, such as Chapter 407 of Missouri's Revised Statutes, while others single out specific practices that are illegal or require particular actions on the part of businesses to protect the consumer.[4] All of these deal with intrastate business practices; however, because of the nature of their business, some firms may be under the jurisdiction of both federal and state regulations.

Selected Fraudulent Practices

What follows are several examples of the kinds of practices to which states have given attention. In some of these situations, the consumer may personally initiate a lawsuit or the attorney general of a state may step in and sue to stop the fraud or deception under his or her power to enforce the law.

"Bait and Switch" Selling

The "bait and switch" tactic typically involves the advertising of an item, such as a vacuum cleaner or bedroom suite, for a very low price to draw prospective customers into the store. Upon arriving, the customer finds the product in disrepair or is told that the goods are out of stock. The salesperson then quickly offers a "better" alternative at a more expensive price. Often the salesperson is not permitted to sell the advertised item; that is, the prospective customer must be switched to a higher priced good. Although one might expect that this practice has been used exclusively by "fly-by-night" businesses, this is not so. State regulatory agencies have brought charges against some of the nation's most successful retailers for the use of bait and switch tactics.

Deceptive Pricing ("Phony Sales")

Deceptive pricing occurs when a retailer runs an ad that promises reduced prices or discounts when, in fact, the advertised items are being sold at regular prices. To be advertised as a sale, it generally must be a bona fide "lower-than-normal" price.

It is not uncommon for some stores to consistently use selected items as phony sales leaders. This practice is most likely to be successful with goods that the consumer buys infrequently and where the prepurchase search period is relatively short. Auto tires and batteries as well as refrigerators are known examples.

Disparagement

When a salesperson disparages, or downgrades, a competitor's product by making false comparisons, this is a form of deception. In Missouri, for example, it would be an issue covered by Chapter 407 of Missouri's Revised Statutes.

Specific Protection from Door-to-Door Sales Representatives

If a consumer enters into a credit contract for the purchase of goods or services from a door-to-door salesperson, in some states he or she is entitled to a three-day "cooling off" period. That is, the contract must state in bold type that the buyer has the right to cancel the agreement without further obligation. Of course, the buyer must be in a position to return the goods to the seller in essentially the same condition as when they were received.

Holder-in-Due-Course

Historically, the law required that when a purchase transaction involved a payment of debt over any period of time, the consumer was obligated to pay the designated amount in full to any creditor holding that account. Rather than tie up their revenues in time payment plans, many retailers sold these accounts to financial institutions that became the "holder-in-due-course" of the debt and the consumer was still obligated to repay the contracted amount. If problems with the good arose and the original seller was the creditor, servicing or other adjustments were likely to occur with the consumer using nonpayment as a defensive move when necessary to assure that the merchandise would be repaired or replaced. However, the secondary creditor did not have the responsibility of handling defective merchandise. Therefore, when problems arose, the consumer had no defense and was prosecuted if he or she had refused to pay.

Under recent legislation in several states, the consumer may use the same defense against a finance company or a bank that is the creditor that he or she could use against the seller of the defective merchandise. In such a situation, consumers will often claim that they were defrauded.

Auto Odometer Readings

In some states, all new and used cars must now have a mileage statement presented to the buyer at the time of sale. The seller has a choice in that he or she can either certify the actual miles or indicate that the true mileage is unknown. Any repairs to the odometer must be noted on the door frame.

A Restitution Option

A number of states have established small claims courts where it is possible for a consumer to file suit to recover damages of less than

$500 without hiring an attorney. These suits are often filed in the magistrate courts, and the hearing is conducted in an informal manner. Typically, a person may only bring a limited number of small claims suits each year.

Evaluating Consumer Protection Laws and Agency Actions

Although all of the legislation directed toward improving consumers' well-being may have been formulated in what was perceived as the consumers' best interests, much of it has been less than completely successful. Several important limitations have plagued most of the nation's legislatures and regulatory agencies, making them ineffective in solving problems facing consumers in the market. The most bothersome of these problems are:

1. lack of technical know-how
2. the starvation budgets of the regulatory agencies
3. lack of uniformity in enforcement
4. enforcement limited to trivia
5. antiquated organizational structures
6. lack of realistic theories of buyer behavior
7. the economic might of the industry.[5]

The most critical problem in both legislation and enforcement is the lack of realistic theories of buyer behavior. It has been contended that "many of the laws enacted to protect the consumer are based on value judgments, on partial knowledge of the realities of consumer behavior, or worse yet, on classic economic concepts of utility that no longer hold true in the marketplace."[6]

The only problem identified above that students of consumer behavior can deal with is the issue of "lack of realistic theories of buyer behavior." The relevance of this issue was first mentioned in Chapter 1. Whether or not we are consciously aware of it, each of us has a theory of consumer behavior. That is, we often feel that we know how people will act under given circumstances. Of course, if these "theories" are accurate in a given situation, they can facilitate decision making. But, if they are not correct, they will probably be dysfunctional, or hinder our efforts. Those same factors apply to legislators and regulatory agencies concerned with consumer protection.

All consumer protection legislation and accompanying action require making some assumptions about consumer behavior. However, some of these assumptions operate at different levels. Consider, for example, so-called "benefit assuring laws." Once passed, this kind of regulation requires no action on the consumer's part to realize the benefits provided through the law. One such bill, which has been introduced into the Missouri Senate, is the Proprietary School Act.[7] The bill would have created a state licensing board for private schools. Several assumptions about consumer behavior were underlying this proposed bill. These included the following:

1. Consumers generally are not able to make appropriate choices among proprietary schools without uniform standards of operations being imposed.

2. A third party, that is, the state licensing board, is a better judge of what is good for the consumer than he is himself.

3. Restricting market entry is a better way of providing consumer protection than contributing to the development of a more well-informed consumer.

These assumptions deal essentially with the consumers' abilities to exercise judgment and to care for themselves. Once the bill is passed, it will deliver its benefits no matter what consumers do.

The suppositions made about consumer behavior can also operate at another level. This occurs when the consumer must take personal initiative in the marketplace to realize the benefits provided under the law. For example, information disclosure laws require packers and manufacturers to include information on the labels so that consumers can become more knowledgeable about the product. Nevertheless, to affect consumers, this information must be read and considered by individuals in their search process. The small claims court system mentioned earlier has been designed to simplify the procedure of handling the grievance settlement of consumer complaints where the dollar value of the claim is small and the victim personally can present the allegations. The intended improvement in gaining access to the judicial system assumes that the potential litigant will have been aware of this avenue of restitution in the first place and will have perceived his or her case as one that qualifies. Concern has been expressed for low-income consumers who fear they will not be listened to even if they have a valid complaint.[8] The litigant will also have to have some understanding of what evidence to present as well as the fundamental procedures to follow to initiate such a case.[9]

What is really being illustrated in the above paragraphs is, first, any assumptions made about consumer behavior must be identified. Second, these assumptions should then be reviewed to determine whether they are consistent with the best information available about consumers, that is, whether they are consistent with contemporary thought on consumer behavior. Finally, in focusing on the involvement of government in protecting the consumer, it is appropriate to set some bounds for this effort. In a very basic sense, because we as a nation are firmly committed to the view that a capitalistic, free enterprise system is the best means of organizing economic activities, it is reasonable to begin here. That is, for a state or federal agency, consumer protection should include any governmental activity designed to assure that consumers realize the benefits they should when interacting in the marketplace.

The consumers' role in the marketplace can be fostered when these agencies assume one of the following goals:[10]

1. Assuring that consumers are not misinformed or uninformed about product features or their legal rights regarding the purchase decision.

2. Enhancing the ability of consumers to protect themselves by breaking down unnatural imbalances between merchants and consumers in the market environment, that is, to eliminate superior bargaining power enjoyed by one party because of biases in the system.

3. Seeing that the marketplace exacts a fair cost of production, distribution, and consumption for the goods and services made available. This includes the control of certain products that may entail long-run social costs not reflected in the selling price of the goods. For example, the social costs of air pollution created in the production of certain products may far exceed their present prices. Furthermore, it may be reasonable for one consumer to be willing to take a 1 in 10,000 chance that his child's sleepwear will catch fire, given a particular fabric coating, but it is equally appropriate for society, through its regulatory agencies, to prevent 100 million consumers from engaging in this risk individually and thereby collectively exposing 10,000 children to possible burns.[11]

Voluntary Self-regulation

It has been suggested that self-regulation is like asking the fox to guard the henhouse. Certainly there are risks in encouraging self-regulation in a given industry. For instance, (1) cooperative groups lack power to enforce compliance to established standards among nonmembers of the group; (2) entry to an industry can actually be restricted by some codes; (3) industry giants can dominate in formulating a plan for regulation; and (4) the public interest can eventually become less crucial.[12]

On the other hand, one of the major advantages of self-regulation can be the savings in cost. Enacting and enforcing legislation is a costly process. Also, other things being equal, voluntary cooperation can be more responsive to changing conditions than laws can.

The most viable plan for individual firms may be to initiate their own internal program for being more socially responsible. Historically, this has not been the pattern. A study conducted a few years ago of 156 companies in the *Fortune* 500 revealed that "planned, coordinated programs of response to consumerism are the exception, not the rule. More common are defensive, isolated responses to specific problems."[13]

However, exceptions to the above findings lead to the conclusion that it is practical for businesses to take a different, more socially responsive posture. Although, historically, Eastman Kodak has been customer oriented, the emergence of modern consumerism has brought about their development of new programs and upgrading of others. Several examples of their responses follow:[14]

1. A product design philosophy that tries to anticipate the customer's difficulties and to design them out

2. A consumer information service supported by a staff of 23 people who answer over 150,000 letters per year

3. Thirty-nine customer service centers throughout the country that offer free advice and minor equipment adjustments and repairs

4. A wide variety of pamphlets and books on photography made available through a nonprofit publication program

5. The establishment of a high level position—Assistant Vice President and General Manager, Customer Equipment Services Division—with the responsibility for providing customer service for all product divisions.

It is essential that management become familiar with the implications of contemporary consumerism and respond accordingly. Constructive positive action, such as that undertaken by Kodak, will be needed.

Progress is being made toward fulfillment of the rights that John F. Kennedy proclaimed for the consumer in 1962: (1) the right to safety; (2) the right to be informed; (3) the right to choose; and (4) the right to be heard.[15] But must this progress come so slowly? As E. B. Weiss said in commenting on a speech made by a former president of a large publishing firm, "Who could disagree that 'some degree of responsibility must rest on and with the consumer'? Who could disagree that it is foolish to regard the consumer as a 'pitiable imbecile'? Yet we (as businesspersons) err in going on to insist not only that the consumer has a right to be wrong, but that marketing must make sure he exercises that right!"[16]

One useful approach to responding to this challenge was developed by Hensel. He called this a consumerism management system and suggested an audit to determine where a company stood from the perspective of the consumer. His consumerism management system consisted of six major components: (1) understanding the consumer's world; (2) redressing grievances and responding to inquiries; (3) creating credibility; (4) improving customer contact; (5) providing consumer information; and (6) organizing for responsive action.[17]

Understanding the consumer's world refers to programs designed to ensure that top management is acquainted with the reality of the consumer's shopping and consumption world—including the inflationary consumption pressures, negative attitudes to business, and inferior retail outlets—which may *not* be a part of the highly paid manager's world.

Redressing grievances and responding to inquiries requires responsive approaches to processing and responding to consumer complaints and inquiries and recognizes the opportunity for an enhanced information feedback system and creation of long-term customers through more effective management of postpurchase communications.

Activities to create credibility include programs to satisfy the consumer's need for a trusted, expert, and personal buying agent. They might include merchandising activities designed to provide a soft-sell, institutional advertising, and meaningful involvement in societal or community problems.

Improving customer contact may include programs that affect the entire distribution channel in an attempt to improve the quality of the consumer/retail store contact. This necessitates management's concern about the importance of a quality consumer experience in retail stores, educational programs to ensure that retail personnel are competent and motivated to assist consumers, manufacturer- or distributor-sponsored educational programs for consumers, improved point-of-sale materials, and so forth.

Providing consumer information is a commitment to provide and join with other responsible parties (members of the distribution channel, consumer advocacy groups, educational institutions, government agencies) to increase the buying intelligence of the consumer through relevant information and educational programs to increase use of the information. This may include nutritional labeling, care labeling, greater clarity in instructions that accompany the product, honest and relevant advertising, and so forth.

Organizing for responsive action requires a firm to make the organizational and management system changes necessary to undertake and encourage all elements of the organization to involve themselves with appropriate consumer programs. To be successful, consumerism response must be made "legitimate" by top management and might include a written "consumer rights" policy, establishing an advisory committee of consumers who have a real voice in company decisions, adequate funding of testing of product claims and safety, and the creation of a high-level consumer affairs executive with sufficient authority to represent effectively the consumer's interest in company decisions.[18]

It is fair to say that advertising, more than any other aspect of marketing, has borne the brunt of criticism directed at business practices aimed at influencing consumer behavior. In an attempt to improve advertising and reduce the negative attitude that is often expressed toward it, Laric and Tucker suggested a means of broadening the traditional approaches to copy research through the inclusion of social accountability considerations. Specifically, they have developed an administrative procedural pattern called the Concept Testing Panel.

The Concept Testing Panel provides for a systematic interface with lawyers, consumer experts, and the consumers that make up the

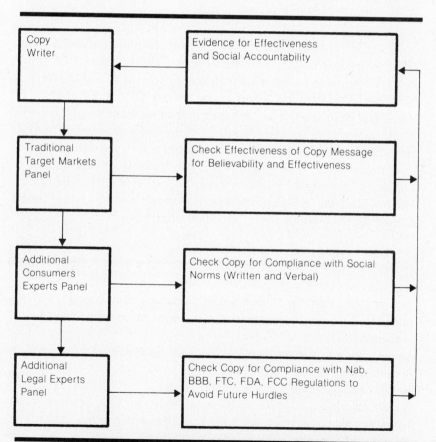

Figure 17.1
**A Flow Chart of
Concept Testing Panels**

Source: M. Laric and L. Tucker, Jr., "Social Accountability and Copy Research: The Concept Testing Panel Approach," C. D. Schick, ed., *Challenge of Change to Advertising Education* (Austin, Texas: American Academy of Advertising, 1976), p. 135. Reprinted by permission.

target market. The key components of the concept and the exchange process are shown in Figure 17.1 as a flow chart of Concept Testing Panels.[19]

Personal Conviction and Ethics in the Marketplace

In speaking of business ethics, Kenneth Boulding said, "There is nothing in a profit system which requires a narrow selfishness and a lack of identification with mankind on the part of the profit maker."[20] The inability of many to differentiate between the profit system, as an organizer of economic life, and the "profit motive," in the bad sense of unadulterated lust for selfish gain, is responsible for a great deal of confusion.

Much has been said about the social responsibility of firms and the ethics of people in business. Social responsibility refers to a firm's being accountable for its actions in the environment within which it functions. This includes being a good citizen (paying a fair share of taxes, not polluting the air or water, providing employment for area residents, keeping business buildings clean and attractive) as well as providing consumers with sound goods and services at fair prices.

Consumers are increasingly willing to express their expectations of business in the marketplace. In Table 17.3, there are two lists of consumption-related expectations which consumers often express about United States manufacturers and their products.

Table 17.3
Consumption-Related Expectations

Manufacturers should . . .	Manufacturers & products should be . . .
provide prompt service on complaints	durable, long lasting
guarantee products to work as advertised	fairly, reasonably priced
be responsive to true needs of consumers	non-polluting
supply clear, accurate information on products	safe
help eliminate environmental pollution	inexpensive to use
care about the needs of individual consumers	exciting, stylish

Table 17.3
(continued)

repair defective products free of charge	easy to use
locate stores for convenience to consumers	dependable, trustworthy
not lie or be deceptive in advertisements	beautiful, attractive
make products available nights and weekends	in a wide variety
use courteous, helpful sales personnel	health-promoting
maintain the lowest prices possible	easy to repair
compete for the business of consumers	resistant to environmental damage
help solve urban decay and unemployment	quiet
work for legislation to protect consumers	comfortable, secure
not misrepresent a product	

Source: D. Vinson, J. Scott, and L. Lamont, "The Role of Personal Values in Marketing and Consumer Behavior," *Journal of Marketing*, Vol. 41 (April 1977), p. 47. Reprinted from the *Journal of Marketing* published by the American Marketing Association.

An Evaluation of Business Practices

Each of us has a somewhat different set of evaluative criteria which we use to judge businesses' successes in serving our needs and desires. Furthermore, most people are likely to think in terms of the performance of specific businesses that they have dealt with rather than some overall index of performance.

In an attempt to measure the quality of business performance as well as the relative image of various institutions, *U.S. News & World Report* conducted a nationwide survey of approximately 11,350 people who were heads of households selected at random from all areas in the United States. Two of the basic findings are presented in Tables 17.4 and 17.5.

In Table 17.4, it is demonstrated that 70 percent of the consumers had had some personal experience with unsatisfactory products or services during the previous year. Furthermore, most of the respondents who had this experience were satisfied with the manner in

Table 17.4
Consumer Activity

Experience with Unsatisfactory Products or Services	Percent of Total Heads of Households
Retail Outlets	
Returned product	70
Complaint handled satisfactorily	81
Manufacturer	
Complained to manufacturer	37
Complaint handled satisfactorily	56
Government	
Complained to local, state, or federal government agency about errors, service, etc.	27
Complaint handled satisfactorily	38

Source: "1978 Study of American Opinion," *Summary Report* (Washington, D.C.: Marketing Department, *U.S. News & World Report*, 1978), p. 9. Copyright 1978 U.S. News & World Report, Inc.

Table 17.5
Trend in Overall Rating of Job Industries

	Good Ratings	
	1978	1976
Airlines	52%	43%
Banks	39	42
Electric Utilities	32	27
Retail Food Chains	32	28
Large Department Stores	31	26
Tire Manufacturers	28	27
Food Manufacturers	28	20
Appliance Manufacturers	27	23
Life Insurance Companies	25	25
Gas Utilities	24	23
Steel Manufacturers	22	23
Gasoline Service Stations	19	18

| | Good Ratings | | Table 17.5 |
	1978	1976	(continued)
Oil and Gasoline Companies	17	16	
Automobile Manufacturers	14	15	
Railroads	13	11	
Automobile Dealers	11	14	
Appliance Repair Service	9	12	

Source: "1978 Study of American Opinion," *Summary Report* (Washington, D.C.: Marketing Department, *U.S. News & World Report*, 1978), p. 17. Copyright 1978 U.S News & World Report, Inc.

which their complaints were handled by retailers. Although fewer had complained to a manufacturer, the majority of their complaints were also handled satisfactorily. The fewest complained to a government agency, but most of these were not resolved satisfactorily.

Taking a somewhat different point of view, Table 17.5 presents a comparative rating of overall performance of seventeen industries in 1976 and 1978. The results concerning business are mixed. Airlines received the greatest favorable reaction in both years, while appliance repair services slipped to the lowest position. It is discouraging to find that such a small proportion of the respondents gave any of the businesses a "good" rating.

Another example of research that examines consumer satisfaction with business is shown in Table 17.6, which graphically demonstrates the level of consumer acceptance of a variety of goods. These data were obtained from a sample of 10,000 households conducted by the Conference Board. The greatest satisfaction was associated with poultry, eggs, small appliances, health insurance, and television sets. The most dissatisfaction was expressed toward gasoline and appliance, home, and auto repairs. Some of these low levels of satisfaction reflect higher-than-normal prices, while others no doubt indicate a widespread shortage of dependable service people.

Summary

Consumer behavior information can be useful to business managers as they develop marketing efforts and attempt to influence consumers toward the selection of their goods and services. It is reasonable to

Table 17.6
**The Degree of
Consumer Acceptance
of Selected Products:
Composite Rating, 1974**

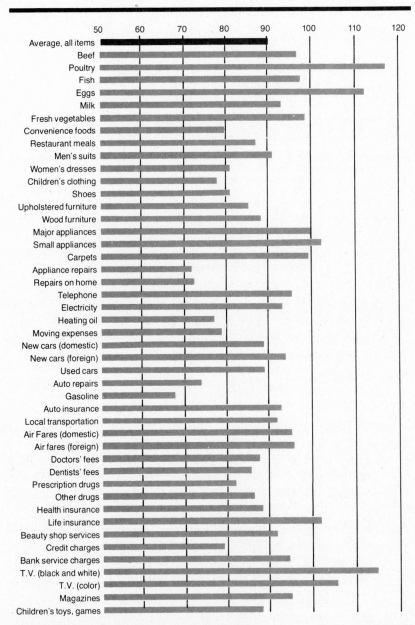

Sources: The Conference Board; National Family Opinion, Inc.

Source: Fabian Linden, "The Consumer's View of Value Received—1974," *The Conference
Board Record* (November 1974), p. 50. Reprinted by permission.

consider what limits, if any, should be placed on the resulting strategies.

Essentially there are three approaches used in the regulation of businesses' efforts to influence consumers: (1) legal regulations, (2) self-interest and voluntary codes, and (3) personal conviction or ethics.

Legal regulations are requirements established by law with which business must comply to avoid penalty; these regulations occur at all levels of government. On a federal level, the Federal Trade Commission has been most active in monitoring and attempting to affect the use of consumer information. One area of FTC supervision is deceptive packaging and advertising in which an implicit or explicit claim could create an incorrect impression or perception on the part of the consumer.

The procedures used in policing advertising claims include becoming aware of possible cases and then deciding whether or not to pursue the investigation. If legal action is undertaken, the effort involves three phases: (1) the exploratory stage, (2) the negotiation stage, and (3) the litigation stage.

State legislatures have also enacted laws to protect the consumer against unfair intrastate market practices. Examples of these practices include: (1) bait and switch selling, (2) deceptive pricing, and (3) disparagement. Other laws deal with (1) door-to-door sales cancellation period, (2) holder-in-due-course, and (3) auto odometer readings. One restitution option available to consumers who are involved in such malpractices is the small claims court.

Several limitations have plagued legislatures and regulatory agencies, making them ineffective in solving problems that face the consumer; however, the lack of realistic theories of buyer behavior appears to be the most critical problem. To avoid the dysfunctional results that often occur, agencies and legislatures could: (1) identify any assumptions made about consumer behavior; (2) review these assumptions to determine whether they are consistent with the best information available about consumers; and (3) set some limitations for the involvement of government in protecting the consumer.

Although some risks are involved, self-regulation has been encouraged due to its major advantages of savings in costs and the fact that voluntary cooperation can be more responsive to changing conditions than can laws. One useful approach to responding to this challenge is

Hensel's consumerism management system, which consists of six major components: (1) understanding the consumer's world; (2) redressing grievances and responding to inquiries; (3) creating credibility; (4) improving customer contact; (5) providing consumer information; and (6) organizing for responsive action. In regard to specific problems involving advertising, Laric and Tucker suggested the Concept Testing Panel as one means of broadening the traditional approaches to copy research through the inclusion of social accountability considerations.

Social responsibility refers to a firm's being accountable for its actions in the environment within which it functions; this is an area in which consumers are increasingly willing to express their expectations. The results of several studies were included to show how consumers rate the efforts of business in serving the needs of households.

Questions and Issues for Discussion

1. "There is no sound way to protect consumers from exploitive practices except by way of business ethics." Why might someone say this?

2. It has been suggested that things would be simpler for all concerned if consumer protection were eliminated at the state level and placed totally under federal control. Evaluate this suggestion.

3. How would you illustrate the FTC's definition of deception in advertising to a men's clothing store proprietor?

4. In reality, there isn't anything that could be said that might not mislead someone. Therefore, shouldn't the intentions of the company be considered in determining whether its ads are illegally deceptive? Defend your answer.

5. Why would modern firms engage in bait and switch tactics when what they are doing is so obvious? Consumers can easily detect this practice; consequently, the laws to deal with it are of little real value. Is this true?

6. Because of the complicated nature of the holder-in-due-course issue, most consumers cannot be expected to understand their rights.

As a result, won't it be possible for businesses to continue their earlier practices? Explain.

7. Discuss the concept of "benefit assuring laws." Should all consumer protection laws be of this type? Give reasons for your answer.

8. Give an example of an unnatural imbalance between merchants and consumers in the buying process. How could this be resolved?

9. Explain what Kenneth Boulding was trying to convey when he said, "There is nothing in a profit system which requires a narrow selfishness and a lack of identification with mankind on the part of the profit maker."

10. Is it possible for a firm to be socially responsible and yet extremely profitable in its sales efforts? Explain.

Case 1. Darcolor Paints

The Darselle Chemical Company produces a line of paints that are available to the consumer in a unique form. These are water-base interior latex paints which are essentially mixed by the consumer. That is, the product is sold in capsule form. To prepare a gallon of paint, the individual simply places two capsules in a mixing container, adds water as instructed, and stirs for about three minutes. The result is a high-quality latex interior paint ready to use. Most Darselle dealers stock inexpensive mixing containers with storage lids.

The Darselle paint line is branded as Darcolor and is sold through department, hardware, and paint stores in the southeastern United States. Most of the advertising for Darcolor is through cooperative arrangements with its dealers. Generally, Darselle prepares newspaper and radio ads as well as in-store material for dealer use on a shared cost basis.

Recently, the company's Customer Relations Department received several letters from local consumer groups and one from a state attorney general's office suggesting that several of their advertisements were deceptive. Darselle's ad agency indicated complete surprise at the letters.

Most of the complaints centered on the issue of a price promotion. Historically, the Darselle paints have been available in fifteen colors and all have sold at a suggested retail price of $9.95 for sufficient capsules to prepare two gallons of paint. Within the last two months, the company has initiated a cooperative promotion to gain trial usage which offers the consumer a "Get-Acquainted Painting Kit." This kit, which sells for $4.95, includes capsules to make one gallon of paint, a pamphlet on painting tips, and a coupon to purchase capsules for another gallon of Darcolor paint at $4.95. The typical ad reads as follows:

SPECIAL GET-ACQUAINTED OFFER FROM DARSELLE
TRIAL PAINTING KIT FOR $4.95

At most paint stores you would have
to spend at least $12.95 to get such
a paint value!

Sales have been encouraging and management's response to the letters has been that what was said in this promotion is conservative in terms of the value of the offer being made. The marketing director made two specific points in defense of the message:

1. Darselle has never sold capsules packaged just to prepare one gallon; they have always been sold in at least two-gallon quantities.

2. The value of Darcolor latex interior paint is comparable to paints sold at prices of $12.95 to $15.95 per gallon. Therefore, the $12.95 mentioned in the advertising is a conservative figure.

The Legal Department of Darselle has just been sent the file of correspondence including the complaint letters. The director of marketing has asked for their opinion on this matter. The initial response was that this will take two weeks to review. The anticipated delay has begun to worry management. Furthermore, a telephone call was received from one Darcolor dealer saying that the local Better Business Bureau has singled out their promotion for some attention, but they do not know what it is.

Case 1 Questions

1. What could possibly be deceptive in the promotional message used by Darselle?

2. What existing knowledge about general consumer behavior should be used to support management's position?

3. What existing knowledge about consumer behavior generally could be used to support the contention that the message is deceptive?

Case 2. Consumers' Need for Information

The following is a quotation from a recent issue of the *FTC News Summary* of the Federal Trade Commission.

> In spite of recent attempts to shed light on the complicated question of buying life insurance, consumers are still in the dark when it comes to figuring out the best protection for their families.
>
> This was the message communicated today by Albert H. Kramer, Director of the FTC's Bureau of Consumer Protection, in testimony on the life insurance industry's responsibility for providing adequate cost information to consumers.
>
> The life insurance industry has enormous impact on American consumers, Kramer told the Subcommittee on Oversight and Investigations of the House Interstate and Foreign Commerce Committee. Eighty percent of the entire adult population of the United States, and over 90 percent of all husband and wife families own some form of life insurance. Citing figures gathered during an FTC study of the industry, he said that by the end of 1976, the total value of life insurance held by Americans amounted to $2.3 trillion.
>
> Preliminary results of an FTC study of life insurance, Kramer said, indicate that consumers may be losing billions of dollars because of uninformed purchase decisions. The major cause of this heavy loss, he stressed, is lack of adequate and meaningful information.
>
> "Clearly the most important information a person must have is the rate of return on the savings element of a cash value insurance policy," he said. "The consumer does not now have that information."
>
> The most appropriate role for the FTC in insurance regulation is to serve as a voice for the consumer and to offer whatever technical assistance it can to federal and state regulators, Kramer said. He indicated that during the next fiscal year, the Commission will work closely with states that are considering insurance cost disclosure regulation.[21]

The next few lines are similar to what was included in a direct mail piece from a major insurance company used to solicit new insurance buyers:

SUBSTANTIALLY INCREASE THE VALUE OF YOUR
INSURANCE ESTATE BY AS MUCH AS $100,000 WITH TERM
LIFE INSURANCE

This is a plan for working people with many demands on their monthly earnings and yet who have a need for protecting their family during its growing years. This kind of insurance gives you maximum coverage during those times of greatest need at the lowest possible cost.

The dollar cost of varying amounts of coverage was then shown by age of the person seeking the insurance. This information was stated in terms of quarterly premiums.

Case 2 Questions

1. What kind of information should follow this company's claim to be consistent with what Albert Kramer suggested in the quotation from the *FTC News Summary?*

2. Describe a means that could be used to further explore what information consumers need to assist them in the search and evaluation process preceding the buying of life insurance. Give the reasons for your suggestions.

Notes

1. *Federal Trade Commission Reporter,* Vol. 2, CCH, ¶ 7530.

2. D. Gardner, "Deception in Advertising: A Conceptual Approach," *Journal of Marketing,* Vol. 39 (January 1975), p. 43.

3. D. Gardner, "Deception in Advertising: A Receiver-Oriented Approach to Understanding," *Journal of Advertising,* Vol. 5 (Winter 1976), pp. 5-11.

4. The Bar Association of Metropolitan St. Louis, Young Lawyers' Section, Consumer Affairs Committee, *Buyer Beware: Consumer Rights Handbook* (St. Louis, Mo.: The Bar Association of Metropolitan St. Louis, 1976), pp. 3-7.

5. J. Sheth and N. Mammana, "Recent Failures in Consumer Protection," *California Management Review* (Spring 1974), pp. 66-68.

6. Ibid., p. 167.

7. C. Block and J. Block, "Behavioral Assumptions Underlying Recent Consumer Protection Legislation in Missouri: Identification and Analysis," H. Nash and D. Robin, eds., *Proceedings: Southern Marketing Association, 1975* (Southern Marketing Association, 1976), pp. 235-36.

8. "Buyer vs. Seller in Small Claims Court," *Consumer Reports,* Vol. 36 (October 1971), p. 627.

9. M. G. Jones and B. B. Boyer, "Improving the Quality of Justice in the Marketplace: The Need for Better Consumer Remedies," *The George Washington Law Review,* Vol. 40 (March 1972), pp. 357–415.

10. T. G. Krattenmaker, "The Federal Trade Commission and Consumer Protection: An Institutional Overview," R. N. Katz, ed., *Protecting Consumer Interests* (Cambridge, Mass.: Ballinger Publishing Company, 1976), pp. 107–10.

11. Ibid., p. 109.

12. R. N. Katz, "Industry Self-Regulation: A Viable Alternative to Government Regulation," R. N. Katz, ed., *Protecting Consumer Interests,* (Cambridge, Mass.: Ballinger Publishing Company, 1976), p. 161.

13. F. Webster, Jr., "Does Business Misunderstand Consumerism?" *Harvard Business Review,* Vol. 51 (September–October 1973), p. 89.

14. Ibid., p. 93.

15. Consumer Advisory Council, *First Report Executive Office of the President* (Washington, D.C.: United States Government Printing Office, October 1963).

16. E. B. Weiss, "Marketers Fiddle While Consumers Burn," *Harvard Business Review,* Vol. 46 (July–August 1968), p. 47.

17. James S. Hensel, *Strategies for Adapting to the Consumerism Movement* (Columbus, Ohio: Management Horizons, Inc., 1974). This section is summarized from Hensel.

18. Milton L. Blum, J. B. Stewart, and E. W. Wheatley, "Consumer Affairs: Viability of the Corporate Response," *Journal of Marketing,* Vol. 38 (April 1974), pp. 13–19.

19. M. Laric and L. Tucker, Jr., "Social Accountability and Copy Research: The Concept Testing Panel Approach," C. D. Schick, ed., *Challenge of Change to Advertising Education* (Austin, Texas: American Academy of Advertising, 1976), pp. 134, 135.

20. Kenneth Boulding, "Ethics and Business: An Economist's View," J. Wish and S. Gamble, eds., *Marketing and Social Issues: An Action Reader* (New York: John Wiley and Sons, Inc., 1971), p. 95.

21. "Consumers Need Better Life Insurance Cost Information, Says FTC Staff," *FTC News Summary,* No. 34 (August 25, 1978), p. 3.

Chapter **18**   Future Directions
of Consumer
Behavior

Outline

Consumer Behavior as a Field of Study
Consumer Behavior as a Science
The Marketer's Interest in Consumer Behavior
Further Applications

Examples of Emerging Applications
Issues of Special Interest: Three Examples
Markets Offering Unique Opportunities

Sources of New Insight into Consumer Behavior

Summary

Questions and Issues for Discussion

Cases

Key Terms

objective of consumer behavior

consumer behavior as a science

public policy development and implementation

social and environmental problems

cross-cultural interests

service marketing

problem-solving approach

problem-oriented research

After having covered a considerable number of topics and issues, we will take the opportunity in this last chapter to bring into perspective the total thrust of consumer behavior as an area of study and to identify the new directions in which the discipline is moving. With these two objectives in mind, we have divided the chapter into three major parts. The first pays specific attention to consumer behavior as a field of study—the directions it has taken and the prospects for the future. The second part of the chapter presents a number of examples of emerging applications of consumer behavior analysis. These include three issues of special interest—the emergence of a new market entity, service marketing, and shopping as a behavioral pattern—and two markets that offer unique opportunities—the youth market and the black middle class. The third and last part of the chapter discusses what appears to be the most promising approach to furthering the understanding of consumer behavior.

Consumer Behavior as a Field of Study

The objective of studying consumer behavior is to understand, explain, and predict actions taken by individuals or small groups, such as the family, in their consumption of goods and services. A great deal of progress has been made in realizing this basic objective. Admittedly, no general or grand theory of consumer behavior exists; consequently, individual buyer behavior is not fully understood. Therefore, much work remains to be done, and many talented analysts will be needed. It is likely that a major share of this further study of consumers will be done by business.

Consumer Behavior as a Science

Despite existing shortcomings, consumer behavior has gained considerable respectability and has even been called a science by some. In relation to this latter point, note that the field has centered around empirical research that for the most part has been carried out using the scientific method. The field of consumer behavior also meets the requirements that differentiate a science from other kinds of investigations. These include the following:[1]

1. A science is general and conceptual. Many consumer analysts have sought to study fundamental behavioral issues that have wide applications. These have included topics such as information search, decision making, and postpurchase evaluation.

2. A science is founded on controlled observation. By using carefully designed studies, the consumer researcher can identify and analyze individual behavioral patterns. These are illustrated by ad readership studies and the analysis of specific product purchase patterns, such as seasonal buying, multiple purchases, and the study of brand switching.

3. A science is oriented toward prediction. Any field of inquiry that has been closely related to business practices would quite naturally be oriented toward prediction. Because of their interest in generating profitable sales, business managers are concerned with forecasting the consequences of particular actions. For example, they are likely to want to know the consequences of increasing their sales force by 10 percent, changing a package design, increasing a product's price, or shortening a warranty period. As a result of these interests, consumer analysts have often attempted to predict consumer reaction to changes in certain business tactics.

4. A science seeks causal connections. Throughout this text, the concern for determining interrelationships among key variables has been stressed. This has included knowing how learning influences consumer behavior and how cultural differences shape one's evaluative criteria.

5. A science strives for explicit explanations of events as well as closure. In consumer behavior, explanations are sought for various behavioral patterns with specific emphasis on the completeness of these. The use of models such as those developed by Engel, Blackwell, and Kollat, and Howard and Sheth is an example of the interest in obtaining a comprehensive view of the purchasing process.

In explaining how scientific inquiry has been used to study the behavioral patterns of consumers, a number of examples have been given that focus on the experiences or behavior of individual consumers in a given market setting. Nevertheless, consumer behavior must deal with aggregates; that is, it is important to keep in mind that any individual consumer is only relevant as a unit of analysis insofar as that person is representative of the individuals who make up a larger market.[2] In day-to-day transactions, business, government, and nonprofit organizations should be interested in the welfare of each individual consumer with whom they deal; but, in their strategy development, these organizations must focus on behavioral patterns that are common to members of various groups. For example, the purchase pattern followed by a particular family in buying a new home is only of interest to the consumer analyst and marketing manager if this pattern is reasonably similar to those of a sizable number of other families making a comparable purchase.

The dominance of marketing interests in the systematic analysis of consumer behavior is evident throughout the book. The following section explores the circumstances that have nurtured this interest.

The Marketer's Interest in Consumer Behavior

As early as Chapter 1, it was noted that even though the study of consumer behavior has much to offer other fields, the greatest interest in it has come from people involved in marketing. It is appropriate at this time to give some further indication as to why this has been true and what the prospects are for the future. There appear to be three primary reasons why marketing practitioners take an active interest in consumer behavior.[3] These are summarized below.

First, some view marketing itself as a relatively advanced art and see the study of consumer behavior as a means of "fine tuning" marketing practices. If, for example, added information about consumer behavior is useful in marketing strategy decisions that result in only a one- or two-percentage-point shift in market share, such study could be a meaningful contribution to profit. To illustrate this, think of the $2.6 billion soft drink market in the United States. Coca-Cola and Pepsi account for 55 percent of the market, followed by 7-Up (7 percent), Royal Crown (6 percent), and Dr Pepper (5 percent). Coke and Pepsi together spend over $130 million annually for advertising in an effort to maintain their dominant positions. Both of these firms have taken seriously Dr Pepper's objective of being number one by the year 2000 and appear to be intent on preventing even small inroads into their respective market shares.[4]

Second, increasingly often, firms are being called on by various critics and regulatory bodies to explain the bases and implications of their actions. Information gained through an analysis of consumer behavior can be used to meet these demands. For example, some critics may challenge Kraft Foods' claims for their new Golden Image imitation colby cheese. Reportedly, retail shelf pamphlets say that "Golden Image . . . looks, cooks and tastes just like natural colby cheese. . . ."[5] The proof of claims such as this one comes only through consumer analysis.

Finally, in a dynamic environment, business firms are finding traditional descriptive marketing research less and less useful. What is being sought more often is an understanding of changing market circumstances and the opportunities they provide. For instance, it was found that women had a difficult time manicuring toenails. Furthermore, these consumers considered their hands and feet as needing more attention because of their increased use of jewelry, such as bracelets and rings, and because of the growing appeal of sandals. In addition, the exercise trends of both men and women in the United States are including more "foot-oriented" sports. Alan Fink, director of new products for Clairol, said that "in essence, we have found that a big segment of America has developed a foot fetish because of changing lifestyles."[6]

Clairol has responded to this identified need by developing Foot Fixer and Nail Works. The latter product is an automatic appliance that can shape fingernails, file toenails, buff nails, and smooth calluses. But Fink was quick to point out that "Clairol doesn't sell appliance hardware. It sells solutions to beauty care problems."[7]

The consumer usage tests with Nail Works conducted among women 15 to 44 years old produced the following findings.

● All the women involved thought that the Nail Works was a good idea.

● Eighty percent indicated that the fingernail head was more effective than the device they had been using.

● Seventy percent considered the toenail head superior to what they had been using.

● Eighty-three percent found the Nail Works to be easy to handle.

In addition to consumer research, Clairol consulted with medical professionals—including podiatrists, orthopedic surgeons, hospitals, and foot clinics—before introducing Nail Works. With these kinds of data, Clairol has been able to successfully introduce a variety of new beauty care appliances.

Although marketing practitioners have shown the greatest interest in consumer behavior, there appears to be a trend toward wider usage. The next section identifies three areas of application that support the observation that a broadening of the horizons of consumer behavior is taking place.

Further Applications

There appears to be a growing realization of the need for undertaking the study of consumer behavior as it relates to public policy development and implementation, social and environmental problems, and cross-cultural interests.[8] Each of these applications holds considerable promise and is described in the next few paragraphs with an explanation of why it is a likely prospect for consumer analysis.

Public Policy Development and Implementation

One of the most pressing reasons for studying consumer behavior in the context of public policy development and implementation is the growing dissatisfaction with the use of microeconomic concepts to guide regulatory processes. These traditional economic concepts and their accompanying models do not offer much insight into consumer actions; consequently, without further assistance, considerable regulation will be founded on little more than intuitive judgment as to how it will affect consumers.

As some agencies attempt to move away from a case-by-case procedure in carrying out their duties, operational guidelines are being developed and imposed on businesses. The market consequences of these actions must be evaluated in terms of their effect on the consumer. Former FTC Commissioner Mayo Thompson made some specific comments with respect to his displeasure concerning one such situation.

The case in point was an industry-wide investigation of growers, wholesalers, and retailers of indoor and outdoor plants in which Thompson called upon the commission to think in terms of the economic costs and benefits that could be expected from issuing guidelines for product information. Recognition of this need for guidelines arose as the commission sought to determine if the distributors involved were in violation of the FTC Act because of their failure to provide toxicity and care information concerning the plants they sell. In a dissenting statement, Commissioner Thompson said:

> This is not a case of deceptive advertising or one involving any of the various other varieties of economic rustling that our law and public policy so rightly condemn. . . . In substance, this agency has decided that the level of agricultural education among home gardeners is not sufficiently

high to permit successful gardening. . . . We are going to tell the country's greenthumbers how often their plants need watering, how much and what kind of fertilizer they need, the kind of soil they require, the amount of sunshine they thrive best on, and—one trembles to say it—perhaps the kind and amount of personal "talking to" they would find most pleasant and gratifying.[9]

Social and Environmental Problems

Some believe that the area of social and environmental problems is one of the most promising for application of consumer behavior because of the possible contribution to societal welfare. For example, consumer decision making for health services has received relatively little attention. Consequently, the social-psychological variables affecting those decisions and the manner in which they can be used in developing marketing strategies for such units as health maintenance organizations, community hospitals, and outpatient surgical centers have not been fully explored.

However, as health services costs continue to rise rapidly, there is growing interest in and support for research into consumer behavior related to the seeking of health care. One early effort to identify key variables that come to bear upon such individual decision making is shown in Figure 18.1.

Another pressing world problem is malnutrition, and contributions to its resolution can be made by consumer behavior. For instance, some revolutionary new foods have been developed specifically for use in underdeveloped countries. However, their impressive nutritional qualities and simple availability do not assure acceptance. The consumption patterns of the people living in underdeveloped countries must be studied to determine their food preferences in such terms as the texture or consistency of the food, its color and aroma. Information on the food's availability, quality, and use also must be distributed. Therefore, it is critical to gain insight into consumer information processing and decision making in these environments. Population control and the reduction of malnutrition are only two examples of possible applications; other areas of interest include environmental pollution and the delivery of public services such as education and health care.

Figure 18.1
**Factors Relating to
Health Behavior**

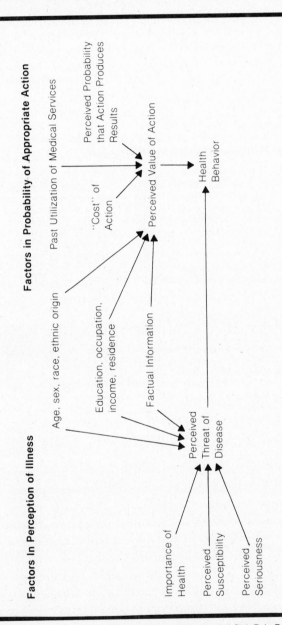

Source: S.V. Kasl and S. Cobb, "Health Behavior, Illness Behavior and Sick Role Behavior."
This article first appeared in *Archives of Environmental Health*, Vol. 12 (February 1966), pp.
246-66, published by HELDREF Publications, Washington, D.C. Reprinted by permission.

Cross-cultural Interests

Historically, cross-cultural research has focused on the differences that exist in behavioral patterns from one country to another. At times this has even resulted in the fostering of certain stereotypes, such as the two proposed by Dichter: "Only one Frenchman out of three brushes his teeth, four out of five Germans change their shirts but once a week."[10]

With the increased multinational character of many large corporations, marketing managers have shown a growing interest in identifying similarities between countries. They are understandably eager to use marketing expertise that has been developed in one country on an international basis. In other words, wherever possible, firms would like to market their products to similar markets in other parts of the world using their domestic strategy. So far, there has been little encouragement that such direct transplanting of marketing efforts will succeed.

For example, one recent exploratory study was specifically designed to determine the extent to which such similarities exist. It investigated the behavioral patterns and attitudes of working and nonworking wives in the United States and France. Attention was given to four areas: (1) grocery purchase behavior, (2) women's clothing purchases, (3) life-style and attitudinal characteristics, and (4) background characteristics.[11] The intent was to identify similarities within each of the two groups of women across these two national boundaries, that is, to determine the extent to which the behavior and attitudes of United States working wives are similar to those of French working wives and to make the same comparison between the nonworking wives' groups. The results of this limited study were not encouraging to those interested in developing universal marketing strategies. The results appear to further uphold the significant impact of cultural factors. Two of the findings are identified below.[12]

1. Differences between the two countries overwhelmingly dominate differences between working and nonworking women. Thus, the specific national environment appears to play a major role in shaping the behavior patterns of consumers, and any attempt to develop a cross-national marketing strategy will require a two-tier design, involving a country-by-country approach.

2. The significance of the differences observed between countries and between demographic groups varies with the product class. The variation was greater in relation to grocery products than clothing. This suggests that the relative importance of cross-national differences and subcultural factors varies from one product to another and should be investigated before developing multinational strategies.

These and similar findings from other studies suggest that substantial investigation of behavioral patterns is necessary if firms are considering entering foreign markets.

Examples of Emerging Applications

This section contains a potpourri of topics that illustrate the variety of issues of special interest to the consumer analyst and presents examples of markets that deserve attention because they offer unique opportunities.

Issues of Special Interest: Three Examples

Any number of topics could have been singled out here for use as examples of the challenges that confront the consumer analyst. The three selected give some indication of the diversity. First, the emergence of a new market entity—the disco—is described. Attention is then given to service marketing and finally to an examination of shopping as an activity other than the purchase of particular goods or services.

The Emergence of a New Market Entity

A relatively new market entity has become a key participant in the flow of information on consumer receptiveness to recordings. The disco, born in the early 1970s, is approaching 15,000 in number and has become a multibillion-dollar business.

The network of discos in the United States has offered the recording industry many opportunities. Undoubtedly, the management of the recording firms feel that this system serves consumer interests as well as their own. The industry is particularly attracted to the following benefits:

1. *Generation of local sales.* Considerable exposure to new records is possible through the disco, and the results show up in local record sales.

2. *Immediate nationwide coverage.* It is not unusual for a record to reach national distribution within a few weeks.

3. *A new test market.* Receptiveness to new releases can be determined through discos. This includes the identification of regional variation in interest.

4. *Introduction of new talent.* The disco can provide exposure for the new recording artist. A number of contemporary music stars have had their beginning in this setting.

5. *Inexpensive promotion.* Costs associated with promoting a recording through a disco are very small; frequently just the cost of the record is involved. In contrast, the more customary promotional strategy used to introduce a contemporary album can cost in excess of $50,000.

Figure 18.2 shows the key components of the marketing system of the recording industry and how the discos fit into this scheme. The disco consumers are typically "between 21 and 30 years old, urban and semiprofessional, with an income of $10,000–$15,000 a year." They are also large purchasers of records. Although most disco DJs do not have an ongoing dialogue with their audiences, the DJs who receive promotional records must complete a rating sheet for each record received. They record audience responses on this rating sheet by using a 1-to-5 scale. This information is then used by record companies to make decisions such as whether to intensify sales promotion efforts in a given region, whether to release another single from the same LP, or whether to switch album emphasis from disco to another market segment.

Ultimately, record companies want to reach the vast contemporary music audience beyond the disco. This is only possible through radio stations with a Top-40 format. Inclusion on the "playlist" of such a station may mean the record is aired as many as 15 times a day.

Figure 18.2
Data Flow: From Disco
to Top-40

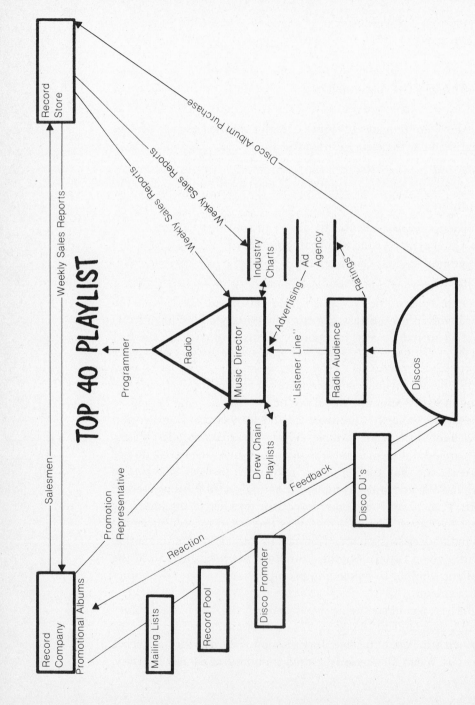

TOP 40 PLAYLIST

Source: M. E. Stibal, "Disco—Birth of a New Marketing System," *Journal of Marketing*, Vol. 41 (October 1977), p. 84. Reprinted from the *Journal of Marketing* published by the American Marketing Association.

Furthermore, getting this treatment on such a station typically means the record's sales increase by 200 to 300 percent.[13]

Attention to Service Marketing

A new emphasis on service marketing is beginning to emerge. In 1976, 45 percent of personal consumption expenditures were for consumer services.[14] Yet, as noted in a recent *Marketing Science Institute Newsletter,* "there have been relatively few studies published on strategic marketing considerations and the service/customer interaction which differentiate service marketing from product marketing."[15] Others have gone further and contended that "marketing seems to be overwhelmingly product oriented."[16]

Increasingly, it is being recognized that what has been learned about the mass marketing of consumer goods cannot necessarily be employed in the service area without modification. A service cannot be stored, touched, tasted, or tried on for its fit. A service is experienced. To illustrate some of the fundamental differences between products and services, consider airline travel versus automobiles. A car is a physical object that is purchased to provide various services, such as basic transportation, prestige, and hauling. Conversely, airline travel is a service that cannot be possessed in a physical manner; it can only be experienced.[17]

It has been suggested by one researcher that to identify the market-held "realities" of a service will require considerable tolerance for subjective, "soft" data. To understand what a service entity is to a market segment, the marketer will need to undertake more initial research than is common in product marketing. Furthermore, it will be research of a kind different from that in product marketing. The service marketer will need to rely heavily on the tools and skills of psychology, sociology, and other behavioral sciences—tools that are more commonly used in product marketing when focusing on image dimensions.

Shopping—There Is More to It than Buying

It has been suggested that consumer behavior be divided into three broad areas including shopping, buying, and consuming.[18] It is also the opinion of some that the analysis of consumer behavior has essentially focused on buyer behavior and virtually has neglected shopping and consumption. In this context, shopping refers to going to a store or shopping center and is an action performed for a number of reasons in addition to that of making a purchase. Exploratory research has identified several reasons for shopping.[19] Discussed here are three that pose attractive opportunities for retailers.

Role Playing. Shopping is sometimes engaged in because it is part of a specific role pattern; that is, it is expected behavior on the part of individuals who assume a given role. For instance, grocery shopping has been a customary activity of the homemaker. It apparently has some appeal beyond the purchase of food and related items because a number of attempts to eliminate the need to physically engage in shopping in the typical way have met with failure. Illustrating this result are the modern computerized services that permit filling grocery needs through telephone ordering and home delivery that have generally been unsuccessful.

Diversion. The act of shopping offers an opportunity for varying the daily routine and represents a form of recreation. To some it can provide nearly free family entertainment without the necessity of formal dress or advanced planning. The common use of the term "browsing" and the readily observable strolling of people through shopping centers substantiates the suggestion that shopping is a national pastime. Innovative shopping center managements have encouraged this form of shopping through the use of atmospherics and the use of the center as a flexible display area for such products as boats, campers, and automobiles and for community-oriented exhibits such as local art fairs, holiday presentations by local school children, and public service displays.

Sensory Stimulation. Retail establishments offer many sensory benefits to their shoppers. People browse through a store looking at merchandise and at each other. They also enjoy handling the goods on display and either trying an item on or trying it out. Sound and scent are being used increasingly in a creative way to develop ambience for shoppers.

Each of the foregoing reasons for shopping offers an opportunity to the marketer. For example, stores or whole centers can be differentiated by the moods they create and offer to the public. It might be possible to group consumers in a particular geographic market on the basis of what shopping atmospheres appeal to them. Some evidence already exists to support the proposition that background music can affect the way consumers shop in a given store. If this is further substantiated, it might be possible to change the tempo of the background music during the business day and to be able to control the efficiency of space usage by leveling out traffic flows. For instance, supermarkets might attempt to move people through the store somewhat more quickly during peak periods by increasing the tempo of the background music and then encourage a more leisurely pace at other times by slowing the tempo.

Markets Offering Unique Opportunities

Several markets are of such size and dynamism that they require special attention. Two are the focus of this section. The first is called the "kaleidoscopic" youth market because of its many contrasts. The second is the black middle class, which illustrates that the black market, like the white, is not homogeneous and that some segments offer considerable sales potential.

The Kaleidoscopic Youth Market

The youth of this country make up a sizable portion of the population and, consequently, are of considerable interest as a target market. Today, 15- to 19-year-olds number over 20 million. They are certainly not a homogeneous group, but members share some common interests and behavioral patterns that deserve special attention from any firm or other organization interested in reaching the youth segment.

Various analysts attribute different dollar values to the expenditures of youth, ranging from a conservative $21 billion to a more generous $43 billion annually.[20] What makes this segment particularly attractive is its discretionary nature; that is, most youths have considerable flexibility over what they buy and where they buy it. Furthermore, mounting evidence shows that some modes of behavior and life-styles are passed from the more youthful segments of the population to the less youthful. In addition, teenagers can have a substantial influence in some family purchase decisions. For example, one study found that of the families studied, the influence of their children was present in 79 percent of the car purchases, 37 percent of their food product purchases, and 24 percent of their vacation plans.[21]

There are indications that what contemporary youths value is at some variance with what older adults value. Such differences have been reflected in varied life-styles and consumption patterns. One study conducted in 1971 compared the value orientations of college seniors toward business and society with those of individuals who had been out of school ten years. A few of the differences are identified in Table 18.1.

If the orientations of the seniors prevail, behavioral patterns significantly different from those of their predecessors are likely to emerge.

Table 18.1
Comparison of Value Orientations

Ten Years Out Of School	College Seniors
1. The System works, with reservations.	The System does not work, but it used to.
2. Material success is desirable and attainable.	Material success is questionable and no longer attainable for everyone.
3. Material success and status go together.	Material success and conventionally defined success are questionable values.
4. Personal self-fulfillment comes with material success.	Personal self-fulfillment might have no relation to material success.
5. Whatever cuts the incentive to work hard is dangerous for the System and its values.	Working too hard and devoting too much attention to work is dangerous for the individual.

Source: Adapted from S. Ward, T. S. Robertson, and W. Capitman, "What Will Be Different about Tomorrow's Consumer?" F. C. Allivine, ed., *Combined Proceedings 1974 Spring and Fall Conferences* (Chicago: American Marketing Association, 1972), pp. 372–73. Reprinted by permission.

There is reason to believe that some such changes will occur. A number of firms are already taking advantage of market opportunities that have arisen among the youth of the early 1970s. For instance, the wine industry found a willing market for sweet wines among a generation weaned on soft drinks. The fashion industry took note of the attractiveness of the army-navy surplus look and capitalized on the interest in casual dress to reintroduce denim.[22]

More recently there appears to be evidence of a move back to an acceptance of the value orientations of the 1950s—a time when materialism was in full bloom. The extent of this movement is unconfirmed, but there are some indications of its strength. One is the renewed interest in the songs of the post-World War II years. A more vivid illustration of the return to conspicuous consumption is evident in the attention given the van as a status symbol.

Just a few years ago, vans were considered unglamorous, utilitarian vehicles driven by plumbers and delivery men. Today some analysts contend that vans have become the centerpiece of a rapidly growing subculture, complete with its own set of values, magazines, and clubs. For many youths aged 16 to 21, the van is a status symbol and an expression of personality. The custom interiors tend to have the character of a well-planned swinging single's apartment—expensive sound system, crushed velvet walls, subdued lighting, and beds with fake fur bedspreads and even satin sheets. The conversion process has reached such a stage of complexity and stylization that, at its most lavish, a van is no less than an art form.[23]

It appears that in addition to the initial price of $4,000 to $15,000 asked for such a vehicle, those involved must have enormous amounts of time to invest. Owners of true show vans often wash them daily and wax them by hand at least three times a week to protect their expensive paint jobs. Such a purchase and such devotion are hardly representative of a lessening interest in material goods or hard work.

To managers who plan to focus on the youth market, it is essential that it be viewed as a dynamic entity. Furthermore, just as it is frequently appropriate to segment the older market to realize its full potential, such an approach might be necessary in marketing to the youths of this country. The consumer analyst can be of great assistance in identifying various behavioral differences that have major implications for segmentation. For instance, there might be significant identifiable differences in groups of youths in terms of the media to which they are exposed or their behavioral patterns might vary noticeably from one major geographic area to another.

The Black Middle Class: A New Market

To many American businesses, blacks as a segment of the total consumer market have not represented sufficient potential to make pursuit of them with a unique marketing strategy worthwhile, or they have been assumed to have behavioral patterns similar to those of the white majority.[24] However, recently increased interest has been shown in what is being called the black middle class. Although this group can be defined in a number of ways, several characteristics have proven most helpful. These include family income, family composition, number of wage earners, occupations, and the attitudes that characterize its members.

In terms of income, the black middle class earns from $8,000 to $15,000 and includes somewhat less than 25 percent of all black households. Nevertheless, it accounts for over 40 percent of the blacks' $54 billion annual spending power. The family composition of this middle-class segment is summarized in Table 18.2.

There is an employed woman in over 60 percent of the black families that include a husband and wife. This compares to only about 40 percent among white families with the same composition. The black middle-class family distinguishes itself from its white counterpart on the basis of several other dimensions as well.[25]

● Only 24 percent of middle-class black family heads have white-collar occupations as compared to 47 percent of the whites.

Table 18.2
Family Composition: All Blacks and the Black Middle Class

Family Composition	All Black Families	Black Middle-Class Families
Husband-wife	61.4%	80.8%
Female head	34.6	14.4
Other male head	4.0	4.6

Source: Adapted from T. C. Taylor, "Black Middle Class: Earn, Baby, Earn," *Sales Management: 1974 Survey of Buying Power,* 113 (July 8, 1974), p. A-6. Reprinted by permission from *Sales Management,* The Marketing Magazine, copyright 1974.

● Sixty percent of the black middle class work at blue-collar jobs versus 51 percent of the whites.

● Many of these black family heads work at jobs that are not ordinarily associated with middle-class status: bus drivers, social workers, postal workers, police officers, and city sanitation workers. However, the money contributed by the second family wage earner often accounts for the middle-class income level.

In terms of personal interests and orientations, there has been a noticeable movement away from the characteristics often used to represent poorer blacks. For instance, among these families there is increasing concern for self-improvement and a strong desire for gaining higher self-esteem. Family cohesiveness is also highly valued. Aspirations often include a better place to live, college for the children, and a home of their own. These changing interest patterns are likely to have considerably more influence on black purchasing patterns than will the upward movement of their incomes.[26]

Some emerging purchasing patterns deserve particular recognition. Firms marketing big-ticket items should pay special attention to the black middle class. Historically, blacks as a group have been said to spend proportionately more on food, alcoholic beverages, soft drinks, and clothing than do whites. However, as the figures in Table 18.3 indicate, blacks are an increasingly attractive market for many more expensive items—those that are often considered symbols of the "good life."

Using 1968–1972 census data, *Sales Management* has constructed what it calls the "black buying index." This index adjusts comparative black and white spending to allow for income differences. When the index is over 100, it shows that the typical black family is outspending the white family when its lower income is taken into account. It shows rather dramatically that the growing discretionary buying power of the emerging black middle class is being used to purchase products such as television sets, stereos, and furniture. Of course, one explanation for these differences lies in the fact that many white families already have these products, whereas numerous blacks do not. As household ownership of such items grows among black families, the differences reflected in this buying index can be expected to be reduced. However, this may take considerable time.[27]

Table 18.3
Black Buying Index

Product Type	Index Value
Automobiles	
New	77
Used	107
Washing machine	125
Kitchen range	160
Refrigerator, freezer	133
Black and white television	243
Color television	103
Radio, phonograph, hi-fi equipment	155
Furniture	153

Source: T. C. Taylor, "Black Middle Class: Earn, Baby, Earn," *Sales Management: 1974 Survey of Buying Power*, 113 (July 8, 1974), p. A-11. Reprinted by permission from *Sales Management*, The Marketing Magazine, copyright 1974.

The importance of the black middle class to marketing managers can be summarized as follows:[28]

1. This group may have a long-term catalytic effect on the black consumer market generally similar to that which the white middle class had following World War II. Some contend that the consumption patterns that emerged in the postwar years had a considerable impact on what has come to be known as the affluent society.

2. Viewing blacks as a homogeneous market of 23 million people with essentially uniform behavioral patterns is no longer appropriate. The black population may have to be segmented when attempting to market certain products, such as travel. The black travel market has grown from $541 million to $1 billion in about five years.[29] It is reasonable to assume that the better educated black professional has more time and money to spend on travel. However, blacks generally are traveling more and often spend considerably more on accommodations and food than does a comparable white family.

3. Because the black middle class is a relatively new phenomenon, it is still not well understood, and it will require substantial research to identify its full dimensions. For example, a variety of black-oriented media are available in some major markets; however, the question still remains as to whether or not it is more economical to use the mass-market media to reach the black middle-class consumer. The appearance of some new black magazines, such as *Essence* for black women, *Encore,* a news magazine, and *Black Creation* for the arts lover, suggests a growing interest in the special media.

4. The black middle class is considerably more susceptible to the impact of economic hard times. A great deal of the potential growth of this emerging market depends on the economic health of the United States. If, for example, there were extended periods of high unemployment, the consequences would likely be substantial for this group of black families.

Sources of New Insight into Consumer Behavior

New insights and theories that are offered as a means of furthering the understanding of consumer behavior have come from a number of sources using varied approaches. Despite this fact, it appears that the problem-solving approach is likely to contribute the most to furthering the understanding of consumer behavior in the foreseeable future.[30] This is based on the assumption that those interested in marketing issues will continue to give substantial attention to consumer analysis. The problem-solving approach is outlined in the diagram shown in Figure 18.3. It is explained briefly in the following paragraphs.

The problem-solving approach has several major phases.[31] These include recognition of a situational marketing problem, identification of the consumer behavior dimensions, development of a behavioral analysis plan, review of existing knowledge from the behavioral sciences generally and from consumer behavior specifically, development of testable propositions and a method of investigation, and finally, carrying out of the research. It should be noted from the diagram that feedback serves two major purposes. First, it provides management with information to assist in making decisions with respect to specific problems at hand, and second, it serves to facilitate understanding of consumer behavior, leading to the development of more complete theories.

A short example will be presented here to illustrate how the prob-

Figure 18.3
**Problem-Solving
Approach to the
Analysis of Consumer
Behavior**

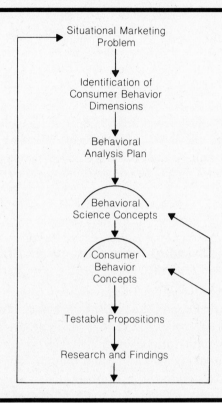

lem-solving approach can evolve. Assume that the T. R. Value Company is in the final planning stage before the introduction of a new nail polish remover called Nail-Renew. The new product is said to work faster, easier, and more neatly and completely than existing brands.

A decision will need to be made soon as to how to introduce Nail-Renew so that the consumer will try it. Two alternatives are under serious consideration. One is that the product be heavily advertised using magazine ads that include a coupon good for a free bottle. The other proposed tactic is that free samples of the product be mass-mailed to all prospective users in several major market areas.

One issue of vital concern to the Value Company management is the extent to which these two alternative marketing tactics can induce consumer innovators to use and adopt this product. To investigate this issue, a plan is developed to use two cities in the Midwest as test locations for determining the relative value of each tactic. These cities are representative of the total market and are reasonably similar in terms of those factors that appear to be important in marketing nail polish remover: number of women, age distribution, education, and life-style characteristics.

After a two-month period, the extent of success of market penetration in each area will be measured. This setting provides the consumer analyst studying the problem with the opportunity to assist management with a specific problem and also to further the knowledge of consumer behavior in general. Under the circumstances surrounding this problem, all the information that can be obtained about the adoption of innovations must be reviewed. Once this has been done, testable propositions should be formulated that focus on the major issue of interest to the firm's management.

One such proposition might be stated: "The probability of new product trial increases as the amount of initiative necessary on the consumer's part is reduced." This proposition can be tested by comparing the number of consumers who have tried the new nail polish remover in each of the two test markets. If the rate of trial is significantly greater in the city where the free sample was mailed to the home, the proposition would be accepted, that is, found to be consistent with the behavior observed. In this situation, the firm's management is supplied with critical information concerning the introduction of its new product.

In identifying the behavioral dimensions of new product opportunities in a mature market, some firms use what can be called problem-oriented research. This focuses on asking people about their problems with existing products, rather than on what they want or need. Tom Dillon, chairman of Batton, Barton, Durstine and Osborn, recently made the following observation to support this approach. "If there is anything that is a universal talent among human beings, it's the ability to complain. They have complained vigorously since they were first plopped into their cribs."[32] In such probing, BBDO has found few product categories in which the consumer has no problems with existing products. Furthermore, they have often found it helpful to define a market in terms of persons who share common problems.

The success in using this approach can be illustrated in the dog food market. When consumers were asked what they wanted in a dog food, the reply was essentially "something that is good for the dog."

However, considerably more has been discovered by asking them to state their problems with dog food. For instance, one key finding was that people felt that dog food had a bad odor when it was put into the refrigerator. It was possible to overcome this.

BBDO has often used focus group discussions to expose problems that consumers have had with a product category. Once this exploratory effort is complete, these problems are placed on a deck of cards. The cards are then exposed to a projectable sample of prime prospective buyers of the product being studied. Following this analysis, which results in an identification of key product-related problems, those found most bothersome are reviewed to see if any may be solvable. If so, possible solutions are then developed and tested in a manner similar to that used to sort out the major problems among prime prospects.

The extent to which the field of consumer behavior is nurtured and grows depends on the dedication of its analysts and the willingness of business, government, and those organizations that make up the nonprofit sector to share their findings. As the field is advanced, it will facilitate more efficient use of our natural resources and assist in raising the level of living for everyone. Furthermore, there is no evidence to show that people can be manipulated through this added knowledge, but there is evidence to show that consumer needs and wants can be better served with it.

Summary

The final chapter attempts to bring into perspective the total thrust of consumer behavior as an area of study and to identify new directions in which the discipline is moving. The objective of consumer behavior is to understand, explain, and predict actions taken by individuals or small groups, such as the family, in their consumption of goods and services. Consumer behavior today is actually a science in that it is general and conceptual, founded on controlled observations, oriented toward prediction, seeks causal connections, and strives for explicit explanations of events as well as closure. Marketing practitioners are taking an active interest in consumer behavior to "fine tune" their actions and to gain an increased understanding of market events through a full explanation of such events. Further consumer analysis applications are likely to occur in the significant areas of: (1) public policy development and implementation—primarily because of growing dissatisfaction with the use of microeconomic concepts to guide regulatory processes, (2) social and environmental problems—population control and the reduction of malnutrition, for example, and (3) cross-cultural interests such as the identification of consumer similarities between countries.

Three issues of special interest are considered: first, the emergence of a new market entity, the disco; second, a look at service marketing; and third, an examination of shopping as something other than a purchase activity.

The recent emergence of the disco has offered the following benefits to the recording industry: (1) generation of local sales, (2) immediate nationwide coverage, (3) a new test market, (4) introduction of new talent, and (5) inexpensive promotion. Feedback from disco DJs is utilized in making numerous kinds of decisions regarding the marketing of a recording.

Increasingly, it is being recognized that what has been learned about the mass marketing of consumer goods cannot necessarily be employed in the service area without modification. Service marketers will need to rely heavily on tools and skills from the behavioral sciences to understand the service entity and to successfully deliver these services to a market segment.

Shopping is frequently engaged in for nonpurchase reasons, such as playing an expected role (homemaker), diverting from a daily routine, or attaining stimulating sensory benefits from the shopping experience.

The youth and the black middle-class markets are viewed as those offering unique opportunities. The youth market is a substantial one made up of relatively independent consumers who are having a significant influence on older markets as well as on family purchase decisions. The marketer must be aware that the black middle-class market (1) might have a long-term catalytic effect on the entire black consumer market, (2) is not a homogeneous composition of 23 million people, (3) is still not well understood and will require substantial research to identify its full dimension, and (4) is considerably more susceptible to the impact of economic hard times than is its white counterpart.

The problem-solving approach appears to be the most likely to contribute new insights in consumer behavior in the near future. The advancement of consumer analysis must complement any relevant findings. The willingness of all sectors to share important results will further the discipline of consumer behavior and benefit the consumer through better need fulfillment.

Questions and Issues for Discussion

1. If consumer behavior is a science, shouldn't it have universal application? Consequently, should it not be possible to use the same appeals to consumers no matter what part of the world they live in?

2. A wealth of information on consumer behavior is generated every year by business firms doing research for their own use. However, most of this is maintained as proprietary information. What practical means could be suggested for sharing this information without giving away competitive secrets?

3. How is a general increase in the level of education likely to affect the following?

(a) the purchase of national brands versus private store brands

(b) the buying of convenience foods

(c) the selection of homes

(d) the amount of time spent searching for purchase-related information

4. Is it reasonable to assume that the youth market as an entity remains rather stable and that different groups just pass through it? Explain your answer.

5. To what extent is it possible to characterize the youth market as a state of mind or set of attitudes rather than as a particular age group? If this is true, it is then possible to have youthful 50-year-olds and nonyouthful 22-year-olds. Comment.

6. Some have contended that consumer behavior as it exists today deals with product purchases and has little or nothing to say about how or why people buy services. Is this an accurate statement?

7. As people in business become more knowledgeable in their understanding of consumer behavior, by what means can consumers improve their skills in buymanship in order to maintain some balance in the marketplace?

8. Is it fair to say that consumerism exists because business generally has been too concerned with short-run profit and has not given enough attention to long-term social responsibility? Discuss.

9. If you were a marketing manager, how would you go about keeping yourself informed of the changes that are taking place in the consumer behavior field? Be specific.

10. Who should study consumer behavior? Is it appropriate to expect all marketing students to take a course in consumer behavior? Is this also true for all business students generally? What specific groups of people should keep well informed about consumer behavior?

Case 1. The Changing Nature of Shopping Center Management

The days of rapid, regional shopping center growth appear to be gone, at least for now, and we are moving into a period of professionalism in center management with a special emphasis on marketing know-how and strategy development. Some experts feel that the industry is in the mature stage of its life cycle and that the fierce competition among centers in some parts of the country exemplifies this.

Noting the above circumstance, it was reported that James McClune, past president of the International Council of Shopping Centers, said that, in today's shopping center industry, "if you fail to plan your marketing approach, you're planning to fail."[33] This recognized need for strategy development is causing some to look to marketing research. Center managements increasingly recognize that their decisions are best made when they have data related to a variety of issues, such as:

1. Definition of the centers' primary trade area in geographical, demographical, and psychographical terms.

2. How a given center compares with its competition from the customers' perspectives, that is, a market position analysis.

3. An analysis of customer patronage patterns with respect to centers accessible to them in fulfilling their needs and desires.

4. Determining the expected effects of alternative center marketing penetration efforts.

The progressive center of today strives to make shopping pleasant and the center a place that consumers want to come back to. To do this, often it is necessary to rely on special events coordinators to plan out-of-the-ordinary activities. Recently, activities at some centers have included disco dancing, summer theatre, boat shows, and art exhibits. In one major midwestern center, professional dancers have been employed. On one occasion, they dressed as mimes wearing sleepwear and strolled throughout one department store with stops at various locations to perform pantomime. A narrator followed the dancers and described their outfits. At another facility, actors were also used to attract crowds, but in this setting, attention was gained by their unusual mannequinlike performance.

In some ways, one might say that the centers that have held band concerts and art exhibits are attempting to capture some of the drawing power of the old town square—an enjoyable place for entertainment and socializing. For older people, the shopping centers have offered people-watching opportunities and a sense of personal contact. Even if the elderly can't be as active personally as they once were, they can participate vicariously by watching other people.

What has just been described is the orientation of the major shopping center of today. However, this is not necessarily what will be successful in the next ten years. A number of observations have been made by concerned professionals of possible factors that may influence future center operations.

1. Aggressive efforts are being made to renovate the downtown areas of many major cities. To some extent, this includes creating a shopping-center-like atmosphere.

2. The demand increases for longer store hours to accommodate varied work schedules of the population. For example, with more women working during the day and early evening, late weekday hours may be necessary.

3. Costs of maintaining nonrentable space are increasing. Mall settings are particularly popular in centers and really useful for holding events that attract crowds. However, these mall areas are extremely costly to keep attractive. For example, heating and air-conditioning costs have skyrocketed.

4. Freestanding, noncenter discounters have continued to attract large numbers of price-conscious shoppers. Furthermore, some of the discounters have begun to upgrade their interiors and product line offerings.

Case 1 Questions

1. What fundamental macro aspects of consumer behavior will likely have the greatest impact on the future of regional shopping centers? Give the rationale for your answer.

2. If you were the marketing director for a chain of six regional shopping centers, how would you begin a research program that would help you understand consumer attitudes and preferences for centers? Develop a four- or five-step plan for such an investigation.

Case 2. The New Product Adventure

As virtually everyone knows, the vast majority of new products fail. That is, after being introduced and on the market for a reasonable period of time, most products do not generate sufficient sales volume to make it profitable to sustain production given alternative uses of company resources. Nevertheless, a continuous flow of new products into the market is supported by companies willing to take the necessary risk of failure for the possible payoff of success. This is also nurtured by the realization that firms generally must be innovative in their offerings just to survive.

What follows is a list of several new products that were described briefly in a recent issue of *Advertising Age*.[34] No doubt, some of these will be successful, but if the past is an indication of the future, most will fail.

● Colgate-Palmolive: *Fluorigard* dental rinse, a mouthwash with fluoride

● Cosco International: *Apple Sidra,* an apple-flavored soda

● General Foods: *Increda Bubble* bubble gum, a gum with "granular particles" in it that melt and pop in the mouth leaving a soft gum

● Union Underwear Company: *Underoos,* children's underwear where the T-shirts and panties resemble uniforms worn by such characters as Superman, Wonder Woman, and Spiderman

● Keebler Company: *Coconut Crisp* crackers, a coconut-flavored graham cracker

● Norton Simon, Inc.: *Wallaby Squash,* a lightly carbonated lemon-flavored soft drink offered as part of the Canada Dry line

● Pet, Inc.: *Quelle Quiche,* a frozen quiche pie that comes in two varieties—Quiche Lorraine and Spinach Quiche

Most of the firms that have created these new products have made at least a preliminary analysis of several fundamental issues that are likely to affect their product's success. Typically, the five questions that follow will have been explored:

1. What group of consumers is likely to make up the market of greatest demand?

2. What kind of retail stores would be the best to seek as outlets to carry the new brand?

3. What price range would likely be the most acceptable given consumer expectations?

4. Which brands will probably constitute its major competition?

5. What promotional appeals are worth serious consideration in attempting to attract consumers?

Case 2 Questions

1. Prepare a statement indicating your professional view as to the likelihood of success of each brand listed above. This should be an educated judgment based on your current knowledge of consumer behavior. Give the reasons for your evaluation of each brand.

2. Select one brand listed above, and:

    (a) propose research into the product's life cycle

    (b) plan a marketing strategy for the youth market

    (c) plan a strategy for the black middle-class market.

Notes

1. T. S. Robertson and S. Ward, "Consumer Behavior Research: Promise and Prospects," S. Ward and T. S. Robertson, eds., *Consumer Behavior: Theoretical Sources* (Englewood Cliffs, N.J.: Prentice-Hall, Inc., 1973), p. 7.

2. F. Hansen, *Consumer Choice Behavior* (New York: The Free Press, 1972), p. 6.

3. Robertson and Ward, "Consumer Behavior Research," p. 8.

4. "Dr Pepper: Pitted against the Soft-Drink Giants," *Business Week* (October 6, 1975), p. 70.

5. L. Edwards, "Kraft Testing First Imitation Colby Cheese," *Advertising Age,* Vol. 46 (September 15, 1975), p. 1.

6. "Clairol Does Its Marketing by Solving Beauty Problems: Fink," *Marketing News,* Vol. XI (June 2, 1978), p. 7.

7. Ibid.

8. J. N. Sheth, *Models of Buyer Behavior: Conceptual, Quantitative, and Empirical* (New York: Harper & Row, Publishers, 1974), pp. 400-02.

9. "FTC's Deficiencies as Seen by a Commission, or Ham on Wry with Mayo," *The 4A Newsletter,* Vol. 15 (July 24, 1975), pp. 7-8.

10. E. Dichter, "The World Customer," *Harvard Business Review,* Vol. 40 (July-August 1962), p. 113.

11. S. P. Douglas, *Cross-cultural Comparisons: The Myth of the Stereotype* (Cambridge, Mass.: Marketing Science Institute, May, 1975), p. 3.

12. Ibid., p. 20.

13. M. E. Stibal, "Disco—Birth of a New Marketing System," *Journal of Marketing,* Vol. 41 (October 1977), pp. 82-87.

14. U. S. Department of Commerce, *Survey of Current Business,* Vol. 57 (July 1977), p. 28.

15. Marketing Science Institute, *Newsletter* (March 1977), p. 1.

16. G. L. Shostack, "Breaking Free from Product Marketing," *Journal of Marketing,* Vol. 41 (April 1977), p. 73.

17. Ibid., p. 74.

18. E. M. Tauber, "Why Do People Shop?" *Journal of Marketing,* Vol. 36 (October 1972), p. 47.

19. Ibid., pp. 46-49.

20. H. N. Windeshausen and P. A. Williams, *Sacramento Metropolitan Teenage Market Study,* Occasional Paper No. 2 (Sacramento, Calif.: Center for Research, School of Business and Public Administration, California State University, 1975), p. 4.

21. C. B. Axford, "How Banks Can Relate Their 'Thing' to Youth," *Burroughs Clearing House* (June 1970), p. 81.

22. S. Ward, T. S. Robertson, and W. Capitman, "What Will Be Different about Tomorrow's Consumer?" F. C. Allivine, ed., *Combined Proceedings 1974 Spring and Fall Conferences* (Chicago: American Marketing Association, 1975), p. 374.

23. "The Van: Latest Status Symbol for Youth," *The Columbia (Missouri) Daily Tribune* (September 26, 1975), p. 16.

24. D. P. Gibson, *The $30 Billion Negro* (New York: The Macmillan Company, 1969), pp. 11-13.

25. T. C. Taylor, "Black Middle Class: Earn, Baby, Earn," *Sales Management: 1974 Survey of Buying Power,* Vol. 113 (July 8, 1974), p. A-11.

26. Ibid., p. A-6.

27. Ibid., p. A-11.

28. Ibid., p. A-5.

29. Gibson, *The $30 Billion Negro,* p. 214.

30. Robertson and Ward, "Consumer Behavior Research," pp. 17-18.

31. Ibid., p. 18.

32. "Forget Wants, Needs, Listen to Consumers' Problems: Dillon," *Marketing News,* Vol. XI (June 2, 1978), p. 6.

33. "Management, Marketing Mean More Now at Malls," *The Kansas City Star* (April 9, 1978), p. 1E.

34. "Colgate's Fluorigard Adds New Slant to Mouthwash Market," *Advertising Age* (August 7, 1978), pp. 53, 54.

Glossary

Acculturation The learning of culture or subculture different from the one in which the person was raised.

Active memory Temporary storage location where incoming information and information stored in long-term memory are brought together. It is here that new input is categorized and interpreted.

Adoption A stage in the consumer's acceptance process where the consumer adopts the new product and commits himself or herself to using it regularly.

Affective component The consumer's overall feeling of like or dislike for an attitude object.

Aha experience A problem-solving situation where there is perceived to be one correct or acceptable response. This solution may be recognized after some trial and error.

Analogue model A model that portrays various properties of something by a different set of properties—for example, road map.

Analysis for pertinence After the initial response, further processing to determine a stimulus's pertinence to a consumer.

Atmospherics The conscious designing of space and its various dimensions to create certain environmental effects in the buying situation.

Attention A phase of consumer information processing that takes special note of something among a number of possibilities.

Autonomic decision making Specific family purchasing decisions made most often by either the wife or husband.

Awareness A stage in the consumer's acceptance process in which a product stimulus penetrates the consumer's filtration system and registers with him or her.

Bachelor state—family life cycle A category of the family life cycle—a household including one young, single person not living at home.

Behavioral component The consumer's action tendency or expected behavior.

Belief Information linking a given alternative to a particular evaluative criterion and specifying the extent to which the alternative possesses the desired attribute.

Black buying index An index that adjusts comparative black and white spending to allow for income differences. It was developed by *Sales and Marketing Management*.

Brand loyalty (1) The tendency of consumers to consistently purchase a particular brand over time; (2) the proportion of total purchases within a given product category devoted to the most frequently purchased brand or set of brands.

CAD A scaling technique developed for the measurement of personal orientation and behavioral tendencies.

Centrality of attitudes The close relationship of attitudes to the consumer's self-concept and basic values.

Classical conditioning A learning process in which the relevant action follows some triggering event.

Classical psychological model A model which maintains that attitudes are made up of three components: cognitive, affective, and behavioral.

Closure The process of bringing consumers to the point where the evidence before them conclusively suggests that the product or service being offered should be bought—that is, showing that the product fully meets all their needs and wants.

Cognitive component Element of the classical psychological model referring to the manner in which a consumer perceives information about a product, service, advertisement, or retail outlet.

Cognitive development theory Theory that assumes a child is an active participant in his or her own development toward becoming a mature adult consumer. This means that through natural maturation and interactions with the environment, the child moves through a series of stages in the ability to organize market information and experiences and thoughts about them.

Concentrated marketing Marketing that satisfies the distinctive needs of a single segment in the market by designing a product and marketing program that focuses on those needs.

Conflict models of man Models that describe human behavior as the result of the struggle between good and evil or at least between opposing forces; among the earliest models of human behavior.

Consumerism An orientation to the study of consumer behavior which includes a high level of concern for issues related to consumer welfare.

Covert involvement The internal responses to stimuli, such as mental or emotional feeling. A consumer may experience some of the benefits of a product or service by simply thinking about it.

Cross-cultural analysis The comparison of similarities and differences among countries in the behavioral and material aspects of their cultures.

Cues Stimuli which are external to the individual and can emanate to the person from any environmental source.

Culture The complex set of values, ideas, attitudes, and other meaningful symbols which are created by people to shape human behavior and which are transmitted from one generation to the next.

Daily life routine The pattern of behavior each family develops to cope with the day-to-day demands placed upon it.

Decision-process approach (1) An approach which views a purchase as simply one stage in a particular course of action undertaken by a consumer; (2) a way to study consumer behavior empirically by describing how consumers actually make decisions and including the impact of various influences on the purchase process.

Demarketing The effort directed toward the orderly reduction of demand among consumers for selected goods and services.

Demographic factors Variables such as age, education, sex, ethnic origin, income, and geographic area of residence which may be used as descriptive characteristics to delineate market segments.

Differentiated marketing Strategy for dealing with specific markets by satisfying the unique needs of the various segments through distinctive products and specific programs.

Diffusion of innovation The spread of an idea from its source of invention or creation to its ultimate users or adopters.

Direct marketing A marketing system which offers products and services to present and potential customers or prospects through the use of various promotional media, singly or in combination, in order to effect a direct action response by mail, telephone, or personal visit.

Distributive approach A way to study consumer behavior empirically by focusing on behavioral outcomes—that is, on the purchase act rather than the purchase process. This approach attempts to determine the relationship between the outcome of consumer decision making and a variety of independent variables such as income, social class, race, and marital status.

Drive A strong internal stimulus that impels action; a force that arouses an individual and keeps him or her ready to respond—thus, the basis of motivation.

Ego The part of the personality that functions to control and direct the id's impulses so that gratification can be achieved in a socially acceptable manner.

Ego-defensive function The human tendency to avoid situations or forces inconsistent with the ego or self-image.

Empty nest I—family life cycle A category of the family life cycle that includes older married couples who have no children living with them but whose household head is employed.

Empty nest II—family life cycle A category of the family life cycle including older married couples with no children living at home and with the household head retired.

Enculturation The process of absorbing or learning the culture in which one is raised. Also referred to as socialization.

Evoked set The range of brands of some product group assembled by the consumer that can feasibly be looked upon as a true alternative. For example, if only three brands of ballpoint pens are considered before the purchase, these three brands are the evoked set. Also called consideration group.

Exposure A phase of information processing in which the person comes in contact with external stimuli from various physical and social sources.

Extended decision-process behavior Most comprehensive type of consumer decision making represented by the complete Engel, Blackwell, and Kollat model.

Extended family The nuclear family plus other relatives such as grandparents, uncles, aunts, cousins, and in-laws.

External search The act of seeking information from any source outside the individual who is engaged in the search process.

Family A group of two or more persons who are related by blood, marriage, or legal adoption.

Family life cycle Changes in family composition over time which may substantially alter the family needs, decision-making process, and market behavior.

Family of orientation The family into which one is born or adopted.

Family of procreation A new family unit capable of existence as a separate entity.

Fear appeals Organization of message content so as to arouse the anxieties or fears of the consumer.

Formal groups Groups characterized by an explicit structure, specified membership requirements, and, typically, a specified goal.

Full nest I—family life cycle A category of the family life cycle including young married couples with the youngest child under six.

Full nest II—family life cycle A category of the family life cycle including young married couples with the youngest child six years or older.

Full nest III—family life cycle A category of the family life cycle, including older married couples with dependent children.

Functional utility The performance characteristics of a product, such as tire traction and riding comfort.

Gatekeeper concept A concept in which an individual acts as a valve or filter affecting the flow of information coming into the family or other decision-making unit.

Generalization The process that enables the individual to respond to a new stimulus as he or she has learned to respond to a similar but somewhat different one in the past.

Hierarchy-of-effects model A model that provides a concise and lucid, although not completely valid, explanation of how attitudes can be changed through advertising. The model suggests not only that attitudes are made up of several components but that those components are arranged in a particular order. One form of the model is AIDA—Attention, Interest, Desire, Action.

Household A living unit or entity for consumption purposes, consisting of one or more persons. All families are households; however, not all households are families.

Id Based on Freud's conceptualization of personality, the genetically implanted component containing basic cravings or instincts.

Inculcate To transmit or transfer between generations the attitudes, values, and beliefs (culture) of the older generation by shared experiences and expression by influential members. This process occurs mainly in the family but may occur in other reference groups also.

Informal group A group which usually develops on the basis of proximity, interests, or similar circumstances and has explicit structure or membership requirements.

Information processing The means by which a sensory input is transformed, reduced, elaborated, stored, recovered, and used by a consumer in decision-making situations.

Instrumental conditioning A process of learning in which the response or action sought precedes the conditioning stimulus; referred to as trial and error learning.

Intention A planned action within a specified time frame which may or may not be thwarted by intervening variables such as inhibitors.

Internal search The conscious recall and consideration of specific information and experiences that appear to be relevant to the recognized problem that the consumer faces.

Learning Changes in responses and response tendencies due to the effects of experience.

Lewin's formula A conceptual view of human behavior, which is portrayed as the result of the interaction among components of what is viewed as one's life space:

$$B = f(P,E)$$

where:

B = behavior
f = function
P = person
E = environment

Life space The total "facts" that exist psychologically for an individual at a given moment in time; the totality of the individual's world as he or she perceives it. In this context, a thing exists only if it has demonstrable effects upon behavior.

Life-style concept The patterns in which people live and spend money and time.

Logic trap The fallacy of relying upon intuitive reasoning and simple logic as a substitute for empirical investigation as a means of understanding consumer behavior.

Machine models of man Models which view a person as simply a physiological machine responding to genetically implanted drives and environmental stimulation; often refered to as the S-R model.

Marketing concept Concept of organizing resources toward the fulfillment of unmet needs; often described as a consumer orientation.

Market segmentation The subdividing of a market into homogeneous subsets of prospective consumers where any subset may conceivably be selected as a market target to be reached with a distinct marketing mix.

Markov models Brand loyalty models which consider the influence of past purchases on the probability of current purchases.

Medium image The perception of the source, or medium, which can influence its impact. For example, what consumers in a given target market think of television as a mode of communication is the image of television as a medium.

Mental completing The human tendency to remember incomplete patterns better than those that are complete.

Middle majority The lower-middle and upper-lower social classes which comprise the largest group of consumers in America.

Model Any simplified representation of some occurrence or phenomenon.

Motive An early marketing term used to explain consumer behavior as an internal urge which often assumed the entire burden of explanation for a consumer's actions.

Multiattribute model A model in which attitudes consist of two components: beliefs about the attributes of an object and evaluation of the beliefs.

Myopic view of behavior The tendency to define the behavior of others in terms of one's own personal experiences.

Normative function A function performed by a reference group—a group having a consensus of opinion with which the individual agrees and in which the person seeks to gain or maintain acceptance.

Norms Statements or beliefs expressed by the majority of group members and defining what the activities of the members should be.

Nuclear family The immediate kin group of father and/or mother and their offspring or adopted children who ordinarily live together.

Open-system model A model of human behavior which views people as being essentially purposive, interdependent with the physical and social environment, and actively involved in transactions with that environment as goals are pursued.

Other directed A term used by Reisman to indicate that some people rely more on immediate social stimuli than on other sources of stimulation as behavioral cues.

Oversimplification The tendency toward isolating one particular characteristic to explain the purchasing behavior of a consumer.

Permanent memory A component of the information handling process—the source of effects upon consumer behavior; also called long-term memory.

Personality Individual uniqueness which is observable in the form of rather consistent modes of behavior.

Postpurchase evaluation The consumer's evaluation or assessment of the purchase decision that was made.

Preattentive processing The triggering of an initial response when a consumer is presented with a new stimulus.

Primary drives Drives essentially based upon innate physiological needs such as thirst, hunger, pain avoidance, and sex.

Primary group An aggregate of individuals which is small enough and intimate enough that all members can communicate regularly with each other on a face-to-face basis.

Problem recognition A stage of the consumer decision process occurring when an individual perceives a difference between an ideal or desired state and an actual state.

Problem-solving approach Recognition of a situational marketing problem, identification of the consumer behavior dimensions, development of a behavioral analysis plan, formulation of testable propositions and of a method of investigation, and, finally, carrying out of research.

Product life cycle Generalized pattern of sales and profit that products follow over time, including distinct stages in the lives of products.

Psychoanalytic theory Theory indicating that personality is composed of three interdependent forces—the id, the ego, and the superego; also known as Freudian theory.

Psychographics The study of the interrelationships among consumer activities, interests, and opinions.

Purchasing processes The purchase act itself and those encounters which are part of the circumstances making up the immediate surroundings of the act of buying.

Reference group A group to which one aspires to belong and to conform to its perceived norms.

Reinforcement The matching of consequences or outcomes of a response with the anticipated benefits.

Retention (1) The final information processing stage which refers to those impressions from consumption related stimuli that are stored in the consumer's conscious memory; (2) the remembering of learned material and experiences over time.

Role dominance The extent to which one member of the family has greater influence in the family decision-making process than other members.

Role specialization The tendency for the husband or the wife to assume greater responsibility in making certain decisions because one is more knowledgeable in particular decision areas.

Search The purposeful attention given to the gathering and assembling of information related to the satisfaction of some perceived need, want, or desire.

Secondary drives Learned drives—those that are acquired over time through experience.

Secondary group A group to which people belong but have relatively little face-to-face exchange with other members. Examples of secondary groups are professional associations, university classes, and many community service organizations.

Selective exposure Part of information processing in which the consumer restricts his or her exposure to various sources.

Semantic generation The process of establishing meaning for words that essentially have no meaning.

Semantic satiation The condition that occurs when a particular word or phrase has been overused to the extent that it becomes less meaningful. Examples are *cut-rate* and *discount.*

Short-term memory A component of the information handling process that retains content somewhat longer than sensory memory.

Simplifiers Consumers characterized by a behavioral pattern used to reduce perceived risk. When confronted with some confusion, individuals who follow this pattern selectively screen out information that is not consistent with their predisposition, thus simplifying the context within which a decision can be made.

Social aggregates A collection of persons occupying the same approximate space. Members of aggregates may have common attitudes and behavioral patterns even though they do not purposefully meet and exchange information.

Social class A relatively permanent and homogeneous division in a society within which individuals or families share similar values, life-styles, interests, and behavior.

Social responsibility The accountability of a firm to society for its actions in the environment within which it functions; includes paying a fair share of taxes, not polluting the air or water, providing employment for area residents, keeping business buildings clean and attractive, and providing consumers with sound goods and services at fair prices.

Society A collection of individuals who share a particular set of symbols and conduct their interpersonal and collective behavior according to the prescriptions of that group of people.

Solitary survivor—family life cycle Actually two different categories of the family life cycle—one including a single surviving spouse still in the labor force, and the other including a single surviving spouse who is retired.

Store image A composite of the impressions which consumers have with respect to a particular store or service establishment.

Subculture A group of people within a larger culture who have modified the way they deal with their environment and with persons enough to be at variance with the general living patterns.

Superego The personality's representation of society's norms and values acting to inhibit the impulses emanating from the id that would be contrary to social norms.

Syncratic decision making Family decision making where both husband and wife exert equal influence.

Target markets Specific groups of consumers (segments) within the broader consumer market who hold the greatest interest for management in marketing its products or services.

Theory An explanation of a set of phenomena, including the identification of important variables and an indication of their interrelationships.

Trait-factor theory Theory that considers an individual's personality to be composed of a set of traits or factors that are relatively enduring and distinctive and that affect behavior.

Trial A stage in the consumer's adoption process where the consumer purchases the new product to determine whether it provides the anticipated benefits.

Triple appeal A concept developed by Lasswell under which, in advertising, an effective message arouses id impulses toward basic drives while appeasing the superego by suggesting that the impulses are justified. The ego is reached by emphasizing the logic of a proposed action.

Undifferentiated marketing A strategy of segmenting markets by satisfying the needs of the mass market with a single product and single marketing program.

Values Deeply internalized personal feelings that may affect one's behavior and judgment.

Vicarious practice Observational learning in which the object of attention is seen in use. This concept is closely related to the concept of covert involvement.

Author Index

Asch, S. E., 159

Bales, R. F., 181
Bayton, J. A., 280
Bird, C. E., 30
Blackwell, Roger D., 17, 24, 28, 29, 45, 183, 230, 247, 250, 271, 296, 303, 327, 337, 369, 403, 404, 439, 442, 475, 476, 505, 511, 603
Boulding, Kenneth, 588
Bourne, F. S., 163
Boyd, H. W., 182, 308
Britt, S. H., 284
Bronfenbrenner, U., 275
Burr, P. L., 477

Capitman, W., 616
Chamberlain, John, 5
Cobb, S., 608
Cohen, J. B., 26, 220

Davis, 198, 199
Dichter, E., 609
Dillon, Tom, 623
Dunn, 115

Ehrenberg, 115
Engel, James F., 17, 24, 28, 29, 45, 183, 230, 251, 296, 303, 327, 333, 337, 369, 403, 404, 439, 442, 475, 476, 505, 511, 603

Ferber, R., 188, 189, 192, 201, 203
Ferrell, O. C., 573
Festinger, L., 19, 159
Fink, A., 605
Fishbein, M., 327, 329, 330, 331, 336, 337
Freud, S., 25

Gardner, 576
Goodhardt, 115

Hawes, Douglass K., 250
Hensel, 585, 594
Hollander, E. P., 101
Homans, 158
Horney, K., 25
Howard, John A., 24, 29, 42, 43, 603
Hull, C. L., 26

Jung, C., 25

Kasl, S. V., 608
Katona, G., 270
Kelly, George, 231
Kennedy, John F., 585
Kollat, David T., 17, 24, 28, 29, 45, 183, 230, 247, 271, 296, 303, 327, 337, 369, 403, 404, 439, 442, 475, 476, 505, 511, 603
Kotler, P., 491

Lamont, L., 589
Laric, M., 587
Lasswell, H. D., 25
Lavidge, R. J., 326
Lee, J. A., 201
Levy, S. J., 182, 186
Lewin, K., 16, 28
Linden, Fabian, 592
Listman, R. J., 447
Lorimor, 116

McClure, James, 627
McPeck, Phil, 305

Maslow, A., 19, 380-381
May, E. G., 478
Menninger, 25
Mundell, R. A., 21
Munson, 233
Murphy, Thomas A., 516
Myers, J. H., 25

Nicholas, 482, 483
Nicosia, F., 24, 29

Painter, 482, 483
Parsons, T., 181
Pavlov, 26
Plummer, 252, 254
Pride, William M., 573

Ray, M. L., 308
Reisman, D., 17, 183
Reynolds, F. D., 25
Rigaux, B. P., 198, 199
Riggsby, Arthur, 92
Robertson, T. S., 547, 550, 616
Rogers, Everett M., 551, 552, 553, 558
Roseborough, H., 183

Scott, J., 589
Sethi, 116
Sexton, 128
Sheth, J. N., 24, 29, 43, 190, 191, 192,
        203, 484, 485, 496, 547, 603
Shoemaker, F. F., 551, 552, 553
Skinner, B. F., 26

Sorenson, 114
Spence, 26
Steiner, G. A., 326
Stibal, M. E., 612
Strong, E. C., 308

Taylor, T. C., 618, 620
Thompson, J., 25, 27, 29, 606-607
Trendex, 193
Tucker, L., Jr., 11, 587

Van Houten, 25, 27, 29
Veblen, T., 146
Venkatesan, M., 159
Villani, K. E., 221
Vinson, D., 233, 589

Ward, S., 616
Warner, W. L., 165
Wattenberg, B. J., 193
Weiss, F. B., 585
Wells, W. D., 252
Weichmann, 114
Williams, 482, 483
Wims, Earl, 301, 302, 306, 307
Wind, Y., 221

Subject Index

Abercrombie and Fitch, 481-482
Acceptance, 415-416
Acculturation, 101, 122
Accumulated information, 302, 314
Active memory, 50, 51, 53, 404, 422
Activity, 231, 248
Actual state, 369, 370, 376, 383
Adaptive characteristics, 102, 105
Adidas, 171
Adjustment function, 341, 353
Adoption, 546-556
Adoption-decision process model,
    547-550, 558
Ad substantiation, 577
Advertising, 88-91, 93-95, 108, 112, 116,
    126, 234, 278, 345, 346, 409, 418
Advertising review board, 570
Affective component, 324, 325, 342-343,
    352
Affective term, 330
Aggregate demand, 21, 22
Aggregate factors, 76, 77, 90
Aggressive, 216
Aggressiveness, 26
Aha experience, 282, 284, 287
Albany Inc., 391
Alternative evaluation, 40, 45, 52, 56,
    61-63, 65, 127-128
American Association of Advertising
    Agencies, 88, 89, 93
Amish, 120
Analysis for pertinence, 408-410, 423
Analytical approaches, 106-107
Anheuser-Busch, 68-69
Anticipated circumstances, 55, 334
Arousal, 413
Assurance of discontinuance, 577
Atmosphere, 489, 491-492, 496
Atmospherics, 491-493, 496
Attention, 50-51, 406, 418, 420, 421
    measurement of, 413

Attention-attracting devices, 411
Attitude change strategies, 338-340, 353
Attitudes, 23, 29, 43, 53-55, 56-57,
    88-90, 100, 129, 157, 324, 325, 327,
    328, 334, 340-341, 342, 343-344, 345,
    352-353
    consistency of, 343-344, 353
    functions of, 341-342
    organization of, 342-343
Attribute adequacy models, 328, 352
Authority, rejection of, 111
Automatic response behavior, 42
Automobile industry, 79, 134-136
Awareness, 375, 548

Bachelor stage, 87-88, 192, 193
Back-translation, 117
Bait and switch selling tactics, 578-579
Behavioral component, 326, 342, 352
Behavioral cues, 17
Behavioral implications, 79-80, 85, 87, 90
Behavioral patterns, 100, 103, 104
Behavioral propositions, 9
Behavioral science concepts, 22
Behavioral scientists, 20
Beliefs, 52-54, 56-57, 327, 328, 330,
    334-336
Benefit assuring laws, 582
Benefit research, 522, 523
Black buying index, 619
Black consumption patterns, 126
Black market, 619-620, 625
Black middle class, 618-621, 625
Black subcultures, 119-126, 130
Brand choice, 222
Brand comprehension, 445
Brand confidence, 445
Brand, connotative meaning of, 445
Brand loyalty, 58, 127, 165, 268, 535-541,
    556-557
Brand names, 116, 409, 456

Brand preferences, 416–417
Brand substitution, 506–508, 522
Brand switching, 537
Budson Yogurt, 355
Bureau of Labor Statistics, 178
Burger King, 462–463
Buyer/seller relationship, 483–486, 496
Buying behavior, 16, 20, 21, 22–24
Buying decision, 20

Cable TV, 257, 258
CAD scaling, 26, 216, 217
Cal Design Construction, 92
California Personality Inventory, 221
Case method of comparison, 115–116
Centrality, 343–344
Central processing unit, 403
Cereal, 112, 202
Children, 95, 156, 178, 183, 201, 204, 286
Choice, 20, 45–46, 55–57, 63–64, 65, 128,
    504, 508–510, 520–523
Choice patterns, 21
Christian faith, 108, 120
Christian Scientists, 120
Church membership, 106
Citicar, 71
Clarifiers, 448
Classical conditioning, 267
Classical economist, 19, 20
Classical psychological model, 324, 325,
    352
Classical view, 20
Cleveland's Electric Vehicle Associates
    Inc., 71
Clinical psychology, 25
Closure, 285, 489, 494, 496
Clutter, 457
Coca-Cola, 114
Cognition crib, 275
Cognitive abilities, 160
Cognitive component, 324, 342, 343, 352
Cognitive consistency, 409–410, 416, 418
Cognitive development theory, 274, 275,
    286
Cognitive dissonance theory, 19, 549
Cognitive inconsistency, 417, 421
Cognitive processes, 27
Cognitive skills, 275
Cohesiveness, 159
Colgate-Palmolive, 112
Color, 412–413
Communicability, 556
Communication, 457
Communications, formal and informal,
    546

Comparative function, 162
Compatibility, 555
Compensatory models, 328, 352–353
Competition, 4
Complete knowledge, 20
Complexity, 556
Compliance, 26
Compliant, 216
Comprehension, 413, 415–416, 420, 541,
    548
Comprehensive interaction models, 29
Concept testing panel, 587–588
Conditioning stimulus, 267
Confirmation, 553
Conflict models, 25–26, 29
Conformity, 159
Conjoint analysis, 148
Conjunctive models, 328, 353
Consideration group, 452
Conspicuous consumption theory,
    146–147
Consumer analyst, 8, 21, 24, 110, 158,
    406
Consumer behavior, 6–7, 16, 22–24, 102,
    103, 109, 152, 213, 216, 221, 253, 286,
    369, 581, 602–604, 624
  theory of, 114
Consumer characteristics, 540
Consumer decision-process model, 45
Consumer management system, 585, 594
Consumer needs, 13
Consumer-oriented, 13
Consumer protection, 571
Consumership, 273, 274, 286
Consumers Union, 456
Consumption-related personality inven-
    tories, 224, 253
Constructs, 231
Continuous innovation, 544, 545
Convenience, 311
Convenience products, 223
Corrective advertising, 349
Cosmetics, 113
Covert involvement, 283, 284, 287
Creative eroticism, 108–109, 130
Credibility, 347, 351–352, 353
Crime prevention, 79
Cross-cultural analysis, 111–118, 130
Cross-cultural interests, 609–610
Cross-cultural marketing research,
    115–118
Cross-cultural marketing strategies,
    113–115
Cues, 278, 287
Cultural empathy, 113

Cultural influences, 98
Cultural norms, 15
Culturalogical orientation, 100
Cultural shock, 113
Cultural values, 101, 102, 103, 104
Culture, 100-111, 119, 129-130

Daily life routine, 187
Daniel Yankelovich, Inc., 109
Deceptive advertising, 575-576
Deceptive pricing, 579
Decision maker, 21
Decision-making process, 56-57, 65
Decision-process approach, 39-41, 65
Decision-process model, 188
Deductive approach, 20
Demand analysis, 21-22
Demand forecast, 195
Demographics, 23, 29, 77-80, 83
Demographic variables, 223
Depletion, 383
Detached, 216, 217
Deterministic models, 538
Differentiation, 313
Diffusion of innovations, 535, 541,
    544-546, 557-558
Direct mail, 436
Direct marketing, 446
Direct questioning, 310, 315
Disco, 610-613, 625
Discontinuous innovation, 545
Discretionary fund, 87
Disjunctive model, 328, 329, 353
Disparagement, 579
Dissatisfaction, 512, 516-517, 523
Dissonance, 56-57, 65
Distortion, 414
Distraction, 348, 353
Distributive approach, 38-39, 65
Divided loyalty, 535
Divorce rate, 106
Door-to-door sales, 579
Drives, 26, 276, 277, 287
Dual-brand loyalty, 536

Economy car, 105
Education, 79, 83, 106-107, 110, 120
Edwards Personal Preference Schedule,
    221
Effective exposure, 13
Ego, 25, 214, 253
Ego-defensive function, 341, 353
Elcar, 71
Eldercare Corp., 207, 208

Electric car, 70
Emotional utility, 485
Empirical investigation, 11
Empty nest I, 192
Empty nest II, 192, 194
Enculturation, 101
Engel, Blackwell, and Kollat model, 28,
    45-58, 65
Entertainment, 87, 275
Environment, 17, 20, 26, 28, 274, 275,
    299
Environmental influences, 97, 367
Environmental problems, 607
Estée Lauder, 113
Ethnic subcultures, 119-120, 121-122
Ethnocentric orientation, 115
Evaluation of new markets, 14
Evaluative criteria, 7, 52-54, 61-63, 153,
    295-304, 309, 310-314, 315, 316, 318,
    327, 329, 477
    variability of, 298, 299, 313
Evoked set, 452
Exogenous variables, 44
Expectancy-value models, 328, 329-333,
    334-336, 337, 352
Exposure, 50-52, 405, 406, 417-418, 420,
    435-437
Extended family, 180
Extensive problem solving, 42, 58, 65
External stimuli, 46-48
Exxon, 282
Eyeglasses, 5
Eye make-up users, 460

Factor analysis, 248
Family, 102, 103, 105-106, 122, 125, 153,
    156, 177, 179-184, 187-195, 203
    characteristics of, 376, 377
    circumstances of, 384
    life cycle of, 192, 203
Family of orientation, 180
Family of procreation, 180
Fear appeals, 346, 353
Federal Trade Commission, 95, 574
Female careerism, 111
Filter, 50-52
Financial considerations, 377
Fishbein model, 327, 329, 330-332,
    352-353
Food preparation, 316
Foreign markets, 111-113, 130
Formal groups, 155, 166
Frame of reference, 274
Freudian theory, 214, 253
Full nest I, 192

Full nest II, 192, 194
Full nest III, 192
Functional utility, 485
Fundamental values, 103
Future shock, 411

Galvanic skin response (GSR), 413
Gatekeeper concept, 200, 203
Generalization, 278
General Mills, Inc., 4, 112, 560
General Motors, 119–120
Geocentric orientation, 115
Geographic mobility, 14
Geographic shifts, 79
Geographic subcultures, 119–121
Golf, 126
Goodyear Tire and Rubber, 112
Gordon Personal Profile, 221
Grand theory, 19
Gratification, 102, 104
Great Midwestern Trade Bank, 357
Group characteristics, 164, 166

Hierarchy-of-effects, 325, 326, 352
Hierarchy of needs theory, 381
Highly complex problem recognition, 373, 389
Historical consumption patterns, 80
Hold, 370, 371
Holder-in-due-course, 580
Household, 181
Housewives, 84
Howard-Sheth model, 42–44
Human behavior, 22–29
Humor, 347–348, 353
Hunt-Wesson, 116
Hypotheses, 18–19
Hypothetical constructs, 42

Id, 25, 214, 253
Ideal state, 368–370, 371, 376, 377–389
Ideation, 267
Impulse purchasing, 508
Income, 120, 122, 124, 127, 307
Income-consumption relationship, 20
Income versus social class dispute, 152
Inculcated, 103
Independent variables, 38–39
Indifference curve analysis, 21
Indirect questioning, 311, 312, 315
Industry demand, 21
Influencing function, 183
Informal groups, 156, 166
Information, 368, 369, 388, 389
Information disclosure laws, 582

Information processing, 49–52, 402–405, 417, 420–421, 422
Information search, 463
Innovation, 545–546
Innovation decision-process model, 550–553, 558
Innovativeness, 304, 555
Input variables, 42
Instrumental conditioning, 267
Integrative-comprehensive models, 41–42
Integrative-comprehensive theory, 24–25, 29
Intensive distribution strategy, 385
Intentions, 43, 52–53, 55, 56, 327, 334, 335, 336, 504, 522
Interest rate information, 449
Interests, 231, 254, 375
International markets, 112
Interpersonal attitudes, 185, 186
Intervening variable, 224, 226, 229
Investigation, FTC, 576–578

Japan, 6, 112–113
Jewish faith, 108, 120
Johnson Stores Incorporated, 168

Kentucky Fried Chicken, 112
Kibbutz, 182
Kitchen appliances, 225
Knowledge, 552
Knowledge function, 341, 342, 353
Kodak, 281

Language problems, 116
Learning, 17, 101, 102–103, 265, 267–286
Learning concepts, 282–286
Learning constructs, 44
Learning process, 275–287
Learning theory, 42, 282, 350
Legal regulations, 570, 593
Legitimization, 548
Leisure time, 109–110, 130, 153
Lenox, 5
Lewinian formula, 16–17
Lewin's model, 16
Lexiographic model, 328, 329, 353
Life cycle stages, 87–88
Life space, 16–17
Life-style, 55, 81–82, 91, 109, 160, 229–254, 304
    measurement of, 232
Life-style concept, 229, 248, 254
Life-style research, 253
Likert scale, 248
Limited problem solving, 42, 58

Living Bible, The, 382
Logic Trap, 11
Long-term memory, 403-404, 416
Low-income market, 130

Machine models, 25, 26
Macromarketing, 12-13
Magazines, 460-461
Market awareness, 338
Market composition, 85
Market forces, 307
Marketing analysis, 387
Marketing concept, 4, 13
Marketing effort, 379, 384, 387
Marketing manager, 13, 384
Marketing practitioners, 22, 29
Marketing research, 380
Marketing strategy, 103, 104, 108,
    113-115, 223-229, 315, 337, 384, 389
Marketing thought, 22
Market opportunities, 14, 28, 76
Market segment, 14
Markov model, 538-539, 557
Massification theory, 152
Mass media, 418
Mass retailing, 494
Media selection, 38, 459-460
Mediating function, 183, 184
Medical care, 80
Medium image, 453
Memory, 403-404, 416, 417
Mental completing, 285, 287
Mental content, 27
Mental processing, 27
Mental rehearsal, 283
Message content, 346, 353
Message discrepancy, 345-346, 353
Message formulation, 461
Message structure, 349, 353
Micromarketing, 13
Middle range theory, 19
Mileage statement, 580
Miller Brewing Company, 67
Minicalculators, 543-544
Mobile homes, 429
Model, 18
Modeling, 284
Models of man, 18-19, 25, 273
Moderator variable, 224, 226
Monitor, 109
Mormons, 120
Motivational determinants, 17, 29
Motivational research, 215
Motivations, 159, 375
Motive activation, 380

Motives, 43, 46-47, 368, 369, 380-382,
    389
Multiattribute models, 327, 328, 352
Multibrand loyalty, 536
Multinationals, 114, 115
Multi-phasic screening, 319
Myopic view of behavior, 9-10
Mysticism, 110

National Academy of Sciences, 70
Nationality subcultures, 119-120
National Opinion Research Center, 182
Natural light beer, 67
Needs, 26
Need states, 408-409
Nestlé, 114
Newly married stage, 87-88, 192, 193
Newsweek magazine, 460
Noncompensatory models, 328-329, 353
Normative function, 157, 161-162
Normative perspective, 20
Norms, 55, 103, 120, 157-159
Novelty, 110, 379-380, 411
Noxema, 109
Nuclear family, 179, 180, 181, 203
Nutritional labeling, 449

Objective methods, 148
Observational learning, 284
Occupation, 145, 148, 153
Open-system models, 25, 27, 29, 48, 275
Opinion, 231, 232, 254
Order of presentation, 350, 353
Organizational chart, 16
Organizational image, 455
Other directed, 17
Outcomes, 40, 45-46, 55-56, 64, 65
Outcomes of choice, 504, 510, 520, 522
Outdoor advertising, 436
Output variables, 42
Oversimplification, 10-11

Passive dictation, 202
Patronage patterns, 14
Patronage routine, 477, 496
Perceived instrumentality, 329-330
Permanent memory, 444
Personal convictions and ethics, 570-571,
    588
Personal grooming products, 217
Personal interactions, 146
Personality, 25, 49, 55-56, 119, 214, 216,
    217, 222, 224-226, 232, 253, 254, 304
Personality inventories, 221, 224-226
Personality research, 222

Personality theory, 253
Personality variables, 222
Personalization, 110
Personal motives, 300, 314
Personal performance, 145
Personal preferences, 20
Personal selling, 461
Persuasion, 552
Pertinence, 416
Pessimism, 20
Physical self-enhancement, 110
Physiological, 381
Pizazz, 282
Playboy magazine, 116, 460
Point-of-purchase advertising, 490, 496
Polaroid, 281
Political propaganda, 25
Pontiac, 282
Possessions, 146-147
Post-choice dissonance, 517-519, 522-523
Postdecision information search, 519
Postpurchase activities, 8, 28, 57
Postpurchase evaluation, 521, 523
Poverty level, 122, 123
Preference polls, 94
Preference purchase, 536-537
Preferences, 20
Preliminary classification, 406, 407-408, 410
Prepotency, 381
Prepurchase activities, 7
Preschools, 106
Present product line effect, 76, 91
Price, 234, 313
Primacy, 350
Primary groups, 155, 166
Problem-oriented research, 623
Problem recognition, 39, 45-48, 53, 56, 60, 65, 368, 370, 372-376, 383-389
    determinants of, 376
Problem research, 522, 523
Problem solving, 273
Problem-solving approach, 621-622, 626
Procter and Gamble, 4, 114
Product, 234
Product categories, 163
Product choice, 222
Product development, 544
Product image, 414
Product life cycle, 542-544, 557-558
    maturity stage of, 308
Professional growth, 77, 91
Promotion, 379, 388, 519
Promotional tactics, 118
Propensity to save, 21, 127

Propensity to spend, 21
Proposed complaint, 577
Proximity, 405, 407
Psychoanalytic theory, 25, 214-216, 229, 253
Psychographics, 230, 251, 460
Psychographic variables, 254
Psychological orientation, 100
Psychology, 8, 24-26, 270
Public opinion, 88-90
Public policy,
    development of, 606
    formation of, 14-16
    implementation of, 606
Pupil dilation response (PDR), 413
Purchase act, 8, 39, 57
Purchase intentions, 385
Purchase probability scale, 386
Purchasing processes, 473-474, 495-496
Puritan ethic, 108
Purposive behavior, 27

QUBE, 257, 258
Quebec, 112

Racial discrimination, 125-126
Radio, 127
Reader's Digest, 460
Recall, 415-416, 421, 422, 541
Reception, 51, 405, 413-416
Receptiveness, 458, 464
Recreation, 109
Red Cross, 285
Reevaluation of alternatives, 519
Reference groups, 27, 102, 161-165, 378, 506
Reference-group theory, 162
Regiocentric orientation, 115
Reinforcement, 279, 280, 287
Relative advantage, 555
Religion, 106, 108
Religious subcultures, 120
Reminder factors, 489-490
Repetition, 350-351, 353, 411, 423
Representativeness, 10
Reputational method, 148
Resource allocation, 12, 20
Response, 278, 287, 405, 416-417
Retention, 280, 281, 287
Revlon, 114
Reward, 26
R. H. Bruskin Associates, 94
Risk, 58, 304, 441, 448, 537
R. J. Reynolds, 31
Role accumulation, 201
Role dominance, 197

Role specialization, 197, 199, 203
Role transition, 201
Romanticism, 110
Rosenberg model, 329–330, 352–353
Routinized purchase behavior, 44, 48, 58, 270

Safety, 381
Salem cigarettes, 285
Satisfaction, 510–516, 523
Savings and loan associations, 4, 14
Schlitz, 68
Schools, 106
Science, 602–603
Search, 41, 45–46, 48–49, 56, 60–61, 65, 126–127, 370–372, 389, 437, 438, 463
    constraints on, 450
    external, 438, 446–452, 464
    internal, 438, 442–445, 463
    preliminary, 449–452, 464
Sears, Roebuck and Company, 70, 168
Sebring-Vanguard Inc., 71
Secondary groups, 155, 166
Segmentation, 121, 223, 225, 253, 254, 418
Selective attention, 418, 420, 541
Selective exposure, 406, 417–418
Selective information, 417
    processing of, 417
Selective perception, 27
Selective reception, 420–421
Selective screening, 52
Selectivity, 402
Self-actualization, 381
Self-concept, 159, 160
Self-improvement, 111
Self-interest and voluntary codes, 570
Self-perception, 186
Seller, 485
Semantic differential, 116
Semantic generation, 282, 287
Semantic satiation, 283, 287
Sensory memory, 444
Sensory overload, 411, 423
Sensuousness, 110
Serta mattress, 109
Service marketing, 613, 625
Seventh Day Adventists, 120
Sexual attitudes, 111, 178
Sheth model, 203
Shopping, 128–129, 613–615, 625
Short-term memory, 444
Simple problem recognition, 372, 389
Simplified decision-making framework, 188

Simplifiers, 448
Size and position, 412
Small claims courts, 580–581
Smoke alarms, 426
Social accountability, 587
Social aggregates, 154
Social class, 144–153, 184, 203
    determinants of, 144–145
    distribution of in U.S., 149–150
    lower lower class as, 152
    lower middle class as, 230, 251
    lower upper class as, 150
    measurement of, 147–149
    upper lower class as, 151
    upper middle class as, 150
    upper upper class as, 150
Social exchange theory, 158
Social forces, 305
Social groups, 103, 154, 155, 166
Social inhibitors, 437
Socialization, 101, 103, 156, 181, 232
    orientation of to learning, 275
    research in, 275
Social mores, 4, 15
Social norms, 159, 334–335
Social patterns, 81–83
Social phenomenon, 104
Social problems, 607
Social psychological theory, 216, 253
Social psychology, 8
Social responsibility, 588, 594
Social roles, 159–160
Social scientists, 23, 29
Social settings, 17
Social values, 109
Social variables, 216
Society, 101, 104, 107, 130
Solitary survivor, 192
Somewhat complicated problem recognition, 373, 389
S-O-R relationship, 273
Standardization-localization controversy, 114
Standard Rate and Data Service, 460
Stimulus-response theory, 26
Stochastic models, 538, 557
Stoko Company, 395
Store image, 478–483, 495
Store loyalty, 537
Store selection, 474, 495
Strategy development, 23, 29
Subcultures, 119–122, 125–126, 130
Subjective methods, 148
Subliminal communication, 290
Subliminal perception, 410, 423

Superego, 25, 214, 253
Symbolic learning, 267
Syncratic decision, 198
Systematic cross-border analysis, 114

Target audience, 405-406
Target markets, 195
Television, 275, 453-454
Tennis shoe market, 170
Tension reduction, 447
Testimonials, 455
Theology of pleasure, 108
Theories of human behavior, 9,
   16-18
Thinking, 267, 273
Time magazine, 460
Time-series studies, 22
Timing, 458-459
Tokyo, 112
Toothpaste, 112
Trait-factor theory, 217, 222, 229,
   253
Traits, 222, 225
Transactional view of human behavior,
   27, 29
Transitional martrix, 539
Travel services, 84
Trends in U.S. values, 110-111
Trial, 548, 553
Trial-and-error learning, 267, 284
Tripartite interpersonal model, 26
Triple appeal, 25
Triple-brand loyalty, 536
True to Life magazine, 461
Two-dollar bills, 289
Two-sided messages, 349-350, 353

Unanticipated changes, 336
Unanticipated circumstances, 504, 507,
   522
Undivided loyalty, 535
Unilever, 114
Unionism, 107

United States, 105-111, 149
   culture in, 105-111
   values in, 105-111
Unit pricing, 448
Universities, 106
University of Michigan Survey Research
   Center, 20
Unplanned consumer choice, 508-509,
   522
Unstable loyalty, 535
Unstructured message, 347, 353
U.S. Department of Commerce, 122
Utility maximization, 20

Vacuum cleaners, 394, 395
Value expressive function, 341, 353
Value orientations, 147
Values, 100-101, 103, 104, 105-111, 119,
   122, 129, 130, 184, 230, 232, 233, 254,
   329-330, 409
Value source, 233, 254
Vantage Machines, Inc., 205, 206
Vehicle image, 455
Vicarious practice, 282, 284, 287
Vicarious trial, 552
Vick's Nyquil, 415
Vlasic Foods, 5
Volkswagen Dasher, 58-65
Voluntary self-regulation, 584

Warner Communications, Inc., 257, 258
Warner's Index of Status Characteristics,
   148
Wilson T2000, 304
Women, 14, 81-84, 86, 91, 110, 111, 222,
   468
Women's movement, 81, 178
Workaholic, 109
Work ethic, 111

Young single adult, 85-88, 91
Youthfulness, 107-108
Youth market, 615-618, 625